Fundamentals
of Human Ecology

Fundamentals of Human Ecology

Edward J. Kormondy

Chancellor (retired), University of Hawaii-Hilo/West Oahu

Daniel E. Brown

Professor of Anthropology, University of Hawaii-Hilo

PRENTICE HALL, Upper Saddle River, New Jersey 07458

Library of Congress Cataloging-in-Publication Data

KORMONDY, EDWARD JOHN
  Fundamentals of human ecology / Edward J. Kormondy and Daniel E.
Brown.
      p.   cm.
  Includes bibliographical references and index.
  ISBN 0-13-315177-8
  1. Human ecology.   I. Brown, Daniel E.   II. Title.
  GF43.K67 1998
  304.2—dc21   97–29105
                                                            CIP

Editorial director: Charlyce Jones Owen
Acquisitions editor: Nancy Roberts
Project manager: Joan Stone
Prepress and manufacturing buyer: Mary Ann Gloriande
Line art coordinator: Michele Giusti
Marketing manager: Christopher DeJohn
Cover director: Jayne Conte
Cover photograph: Ralph M. Garruto
Editorial assistant: Maureen Diana

This book was set 10/12 Baskerville by Clarinda
and was printed and bound by Hamilton Printing Company.
The cover was printed by Phoenix Color Corp.

Printed in the United States of America

10 9 8 7 6 5 4 3 2 1

ISBN 0-13-315177-8

Prentice-Hall International (UK) Limited,London
Prentice-Hall of Australia Pty. Limited, Sydney
Prentice-Hall Canada Inc., Toronto
Prentice-Hall Hispanoamericana, S.A., Mexico
Prentice-Hall of India Private Limited, New Delhi
Prentice-Hall of Japan, Inc., Tokyo
Pearson Education Asia Pte. Ltd., Singapore
Editora Prentice-Hall do Brasil, Ltda., Rio de Janeiro

dedicated to
Dorothy and Jack Brown
and to the memory of
Frances and Anthony Kormondy

our parents

Contents

Chapter 2
Basic Concepts of Ecology, *28*

Chapter 3
Approaches to Human Ecology, *41*

Chapter 13
Ecological Energetics,   *309*

Chapter 14
Human Adaptation and Energy Flow,   *331*

Chapter 15
Nutrient Cycling in Ecosystems,   *359*

PART V   CONCLUSION

Chapter 18
Human Ecology and the Ecology of Humans,   *428*

Preface

Our goal for this text is to present the fundamentals of ecology and their application to humans through an integrated approach to human ecology, blending biological ecology with social science approaches. Although previous exposure to basic courses in biology and anthropology would provide for the added depth this text intends, students who lack that background will be able to enlarge their intellectual horizons in this exciting interdisciplinary field.

We have used a problem-based approach by dealing with both environmentally based problems and those of anthropogenic origin. In doing so, we have taken as objective an approach as possible so as to allow students to arrive at their own conclusions. Among the major issues with which we deal are the processes involved with human population growth and their relationship to general principles of population ecology, the kinds of environmental stressors humans confront and the major kinds of coping strategies for dealing with them, the major resources humans need and the ones that are difficult to obtain for human populations residing in specific habitats, and both the effect of diverse cultural backgrounds on how humans cope with environmental problems and the effect of environmental problems on how culture changes.

In addressing these issues, we have attempted to minimize technical jargon while recognizing that certain basic terms are fundamental to full understanding. The frequent examples from the anthropological literature deal mostly with small-sized groups in fairly homogeneous environments, allowing for simplification of human ecology without undue distortion of the larger picture.

To facilitate understanding and learning, each chapter has a list of key terms that conveys basic terminology, facilitating a solid understanding of the subject matter. Each chapter also contains a list of key points to sharpen the focus of the learner. A glossary serves as reinforcement of terms and as a reference tool, and a comprehensive list of references allows for further, more in-depth study. For the most part, the titles are those found in most college libraries, since they are the major publications in the fields of ecology and anthropology (e.g., *Science, Scientific American, Ecology*, and *Journal of Anthropology*).

ACKNOWLEDGMENTS

In the collaborative development of an integrated treatment of human ecology from the biological and anthropological perspective, we are indebted to many people. First and foremost are the scientists whose publications form the basis of the concepts, principles, and provocative issues that underlie the fields of ecology and anthropology. We have consciously recognized this underpinning by citing their work. Second are our colleagues, past and present, with whom it has been an intellectual joy to discuss, challenge, be challenged by, and learn various dimensions of the subject matter at hand. While it is often dangerous to list such colleagues for fear of inadvertently omitting someone whose help is deeply appreciated, here is a short list of those who gave special help during the preparation of this text: Paul and Thelma Baker, Norris Durham, Ralph Garruto, Joel M. Hanna, Gary James, Michael Little, Craig and Carol Severance, and R. Brooke Thomas. Third are those who provided specific technical assistance: here we specifically identify Helen Rogers and Susan Maesato, University of Hawaii-Hilo librarians; Susan Yugawa, University of Hawaii-Hilo media specialist; Eric Flower, Director of Library, University of Hawaii-West Oahu; and the staff at Ernie's Camera Shop, Glendale, CA. Next are the reviewers of the manuscript, David L. Carlson, Texas A&M University; Robert A. Halberstein, University of Miami; Jane H. Underwood, University of Arizona; and William G. Davis, University of California, Davis, whose critical reading and suggestions served to improve the presentation. Not to be forgotten is the strong guidance and assistance of our editor, Nancy Roberts, and the excellent publication support of Joan Stone and others. Finally, we acknowledge the unwavering and patient support of family and close friends during the many hours taken from them to think and write. For all this assistance, we express our sincere gratitude and humble thanks.

As Cassius says in Shakespeare's *Tragedy of Julius Caesar,* "The fault, dear Brutus, is not in our stars, But in ourselves." And so it is with this treatise. The faults or failings of our text lie in us alone, not with any who have assisted in various ways. Thus, we will be grateful for your suggestions, comments, and corrections.

Edward J. Kormondy   Daniel E. Brown
Los Angeles, California   *Hilo, Hawaii*

Credits

Figure 1-1 adapted from Biological Science: An Inquiry into Life by John A. Moore, Bentley Glass, and William V. Mayer, copyright © 1963 by the American Institute of Biological Sciences, Washington, DC and renewed 1991 by John A. Moore, reprinted by permission of Harcourt Brace & Company. Figures 1-2, 2-1, 2-2, 5-1, 5-3, 5-4, 5-5, 5-6, 8-4, 11-5, 11-9, 11-10, 12-2, 12-4, 12-6, 12-7, 12-8, 12-9, 12-10, 13-1, 13-2, 15-2, 15-5, 15-6, 18-2 from *Concepts of ecology* 4/E by Kormondy, © 1996. Reprinted by permission of Prentice-Hall, Inc., Upper Saddle River, NJ. Figures 11-13 and 11-14 reproduced by permission from M. A. Little and G. E. Morren, Jr. 1976. *Ecology, energetics, and human variability*. Dubuque, IA: Wm. C. Brown Company. Based on data from R. Dyson-Hudson. 1972. Pastoralism: Self image and behavioral reality. In *Perspectives on nomadism*, ed. W. Irons and N. Dyson-Hudson. Leiden: E. J. Brill. Figure 12-1 from Basic Ecology by Eugene P. Odum, copyright © 1983 by Saunders College Publishing, reproduced by permission of the publisher. Figure 13-8 from Fundamentals of Ecology, Second Edition by Eugene P. Odum, copyright © 1959 by Saunders College Publishing and renewed 1987 by Eugene P. Odum and Howard T. Odum, reproduced by permission of the publisher.

Fundamentals
of Human Ecology

1

Evolution: Then and Now

INTRODUCTION

It may seem strange to begin a textbook on human ecology with a discussion of evolution. However, to gain some understanding of the ways in which different human populations have adapted to their different environments, it is important to know how adaptation takes place. But we also need to know how human populations as different as the Inuit of the polar north and the Tuareg of the Sahara Desert have come to be. Thus, we need to have some knowledge of the variation within species and of the origin and evolution of species as well. We will first briefly discuss two major theories of evolution and the mechanisms by which species originate; this will be followed by a discussion of the nature of adaptation and then an overview of the origin and evolution of the human species.

THE CONTEXT
OF EVOLUTIONARY THOUGHT

During the eighteenth and nineteenth centuries, knowledge of the past expanded with the discovery of fossils and into the then present through worldwide explorations by the likes of James Cook, Alexander Humboldt, and George Vancouver, all of whom built on the earlier pioneering explorations of Christopher Columbus, Ferdinand Magellan, and Marco Polo. Both of these forces, fossil discoveries and worldwide explorations, increased awareness not only of the tremendous diversity of past and present life but also of the oftentimes striking similarities and distributional patterns of plants and animals. Tangible evidence from the fossil record demonstrated an immensity of time as well as the phenomenon of change as characteristics of living things. The fossil record also constituted a mounting body of evidence, often referred to as "the facts of evolution" by those who did not believe that each organism had been specially created by a supreme being. The confrontation with morphological similarities too striking to be dismissed as capricious suggested to both philosophers and scientists that organisms undergo an orderly, fathomable process of change—evolution—and that there has been a progression of organic forms over eons of time.

MAJOR THEORIES OF EVOLUTION

To explain this phenomenon of organic change over time, a number of scientists proposed various rational, although largely speculative, schemes and mechanisms. Because of their influence then and now, only two major ideas are singled out here for brief elaboration: the inheritance of acquired characteristics and evolution by natural selection.

Inheritance of Acquired Characteristics

The first biologist of stature to devise a scheme rationalizing the evolutionary development of life and maintaining that species were not fixed but rather changed and developed (evolved) was the French naturalist Jean Baptiste de Lamarck (1744–1829). Lamarck proposed what has become called the theory of **inheritance of acquired characteristics.** Incidentally, he was also the first person to use the terms *vertebrate* and *invertebrate* and to popularize the term *biology*.

It was Lamarck's basic contention, first presented in 1801 and then enlarged in his 1809 book *Philosophie Zoologique,* that *"the environment affects the shape and organization of animals,* that is to say that when the environment becomes very different, it produces in course of time corresponding modifications in the shape and organisation of animals."* It was his belief that organisms gradually changed into more complex levels of organization because of a built-in drive for perfection up the "Chain of Being," that is, a progression toward higher forms. He held that this drive was centered in nerve fibers that, by means of a vaguely defined fluid, directed changes in body parts. Further, he noted in his two "laws": (1) "In every animal . . . a more frequent and continuous use of any organ gradually strengthens, develops and enlarges that organ . . . while the permanent disuse of any organ imperceptibly weakens and deteriorates it . . . until it finally disappears" and (2) "All the acquisitions or losses . . . are preserved by reproduction."

Among the examples Lamarck cited in defense of his theory were those of moles, in which the eyes have withered away from disuse in their lightless environment. For the case of organisms developing new characteristics because of use, Lamarck cited water birds that separate the digits of their feet in trying to strike the water and move about on its surface; he proposed that this led to the development of webs. Yet another example involved the then recently discovered giraffe. According to Lamarck, tree-browsing ancestral antelopes stretched their necks, tongues, and legs to get at all the leaves possible, thereby lengthening them. These acquired, longer body parts were then passed successively to subsequent generations, each of which continued the stretching process until the long-necked, long-tongued, and long-legged giraffe resulted (Figure 1–1a).

Given his wide-ranging insights, it is not surprising that the idea of inheritance of acquired characteristics was seminal in Aristotle's thinking more than 2,000 years earlier than Lamarck's time.

Figure 1–1   (a) Evolution of the giraffe according to the theory of inheritance of acquired characteristics; (b) evolution of the giraffe according to the theory of natural selection. (Figure adapted from *Biological science: An inquiry into life* by John A. Moore, Bentley Glass, and William V. Mayer; copyright © 1963 by the American Institute of Biological Sciences, Washington, DC and renewed 1991 by John A. Moore, reprinted by permission of Harcourt Brace & Company.)

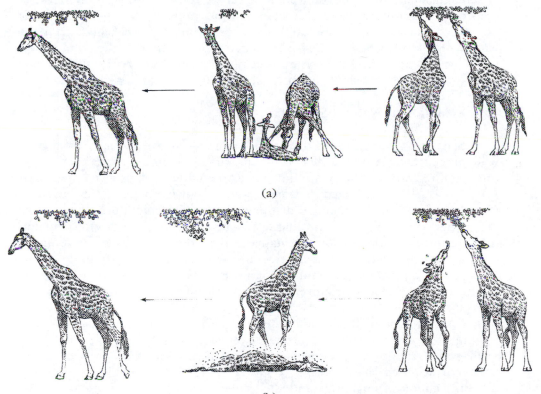

(a)

(b)

As logically attractive as the theory of inheritance of acquired characteristics was, it nonetheless foundered on two substantive bases: first, that organisms could purposefully will change in a given direction (and specifically that the end products could determine and direct the nature of the change, a teleological point of view); and second, that acquired characteristics could in fact be inherited. Regarding the latter, German biologist August Weismann (1834–1914) conducted an experiment in which he cut off the tails of 1,592 mice over 22 generations, but each generation continued to be born with tails.

These results notwithstanding, Lamarckian inheritance of acquired characteristics may have some explanatory value in understanding the evolution or, more properly, development of human culture. There is some purposiveness in cultural evolution, and acquired characteristics in culture can be passed down to younger generations by what some anthropologists have termed *selective retention* (Staski and Marks 1992). Later on we will examine briefly some ideas about trends of culture change that relate to notions of human adaptation and ecology.

Although eventually discredited, Lamarck did create an intellectual climate in which people were able to accept organic evolution as fact. His explanation of adaptation was accepted by many nineteenth-century naturalists, including Charles Darwin, and has occasionally resurfaced, often for sociopolitical reasons, as in the instance of Soviet biologist Trofim Lysenko in the 1930s and 1940s. Lysenko maintained that he could alter the genetic constitution of strains of wheat by properly controlling the environment. This viewpoint was highly supportive of Soviet economic and philosophical theories of the time and especially during the leadership of Joseph Stalin, who gave Lysenko strong support to the point of suppressing dissenters. Lysenko was eventually discredited, but Soviet biology had been done almost irreparable harm in the interim (Broad and Wade 1982).

Evolution by Natural Selection

Scientists are products of their time, "standing on the shoulders of giants" who preceded them or are their contemporaries. In the early decades of the nineteenth century, many naturalists, Lamarck aside, still believed that each species was perfectly adapted to its environment. Further, many held that there was little individual variation and that any selection that might occur took place only when geological forces produced a change in the physical environment, thus stimulating variation. Representative of the most conservative viewpoint of the day was the founder of taxonomy, the Swedish botanist Carolus Linnaeus who lived in the eighteenth century. In Linnaeus's view, each species was seen as an immutable product of a supreme being, a part of an overall divine plan.

Charles Darwin. Given the intellectual climate of his time, it is not surprising that Charles Darwin's (1809–1882) original selection theory (in an 1844 essay) retained a strong element of this teleological philosophy of inheritance of acquired characteristics (Ospovat 1981). However, his exposure to the distribution of organisms and the geological relations of present to past inhabitants of South America that came to him during his now-famous voyage on H. M. S. 'Beagle' (1831–1836) resulted in a radical rethinking of his original ideas. In his own words in his 1859 *The Origin of Species of Means of Natural Selection:*

> When on board H. M. S. 'Beagle,' as naturalist, I was much struck with certain facts in the distribution of the organic beings inhabiting South America, and in the geological relations of the present to the past inhabitants of that continent. . . . In considering the Origin of Species, it is quite conceivable that a naturalist, reflecting on the mutual affinities of organic beings, on their embryological relations, their geographical distribution, geological succession, and other such facts, might come to the conclusion that species had not been independently created, but had descended, like varieties, from other species.

Charles Darwin and Alfred Russel Wallace. It is beyond the scope and purpose of this text to explore in detail the fascinating development of Darwin's thinking or to discuss the consequences on scientific and religious thought that developed from his theory, especially when it was applied to humans. However, what must be noted is that independent of Darwin, another naturalist of stature, Alfred Russel Wallace (1823–1913), had simultaneously conceptualized identical ideas on the origin and evolution of species. This came to him as a result of his extensive studies in the Amazon basin, the Malay peninsula, and the East Indian islands (Wallace 1859). Of further coincidence in the development of Wallace's and Darwin's independent speculations on evolution by natural selection was the fact that both had read and were stimulated by another of the seminal essays in science. This was economist Thomas Robert Malthus's (1766–1828) *Essay on Population,* published in 1798 (Mayer 1987).

It was Malthus's contention that populations increased geometrically whereas food supplies increased arithmetically. Thus populations would always outrun food supplies, but human numbers would be held down by famine, disease, and war. Because of bitter reaction to his essay, Malthus acknowledged, in the second edition (1803), moral restraint in the form of delayed marriage and sexual continence as added constraints on population growth.

The impact of Malthus on Darwin is conveyed directly in the latter's *The Origin of Species by Means of Natural Selection:*

> As many more individuals of each species are born than can possibly survive; and as, consequently, there is a frequently recurring struggle for existence, it follows that any being, if it vary however slightly in any manner profitable to itself, under the complex and sometimes varying conditions of life, will have a better chance of surviving, and thus be *naturally selected*. From the strong principle of inheritance, any selected variety will tend to propagate its new and modified form.

Darwin's Theory of Natural Selection. In contemporary language, Darwin's **theory of natural selection** can be restated as follows:

1. More offspring tend to be produced in any population than can survive to reproductive age;

2. Individuals in a population vary in form and behavior, with much of the variation being inheritable;
3. Some of the variation improves chances of survival and reproduction in the "struggle for existence" under existing conditions; and
4. The preservation of favorable inheritable individual differences and variations (differential reproduction) and the loss of harmful ones is "natural selection or the Survival of the Fittest."

In the form of a more rigorously constructed syllogism, the latter three steps might be constructed as:

If two populations diverge from a common ancestor and

If those two populations become better adapted to the environment than their ancestors

Then they would be expected to supplant the ancestor and drive it to extinction (Allen 1995).

By comparison with Lamarck's interpretation, the origin of giraffes according to Darwinian natural selection would be as follows: (1) ancestral giraffes had necks that varied in length, the variations being hereditary; (2) competition and natural selection led to survival of longer-necked offspring at the expense of shorter-necked ones because the former could reach leaves higher on trees; (3) eventually only long-necked giraffes survived the competition (Figure 1–1b).

Neo-Darwinism

As creative and influential as Darwin's theory was, and is, it was advanced without a causal explanation of the physical basis of inheritance and variation. However, as of 1859, the physical basis of heredity was yet to be discovered. In fact, it was not promulgated until 1900 even though it was initially discovered by Gregor Mendel in 1866. Nonetheless, it was not until the 1930s that Darwin's theory of natural selection and Mendel's concepts of genetics were co-mingled into what has become known as **Neo-Darwinism.**

The inheritable variations described by Darwin are the result of changes, or mutations, in the genetic material. These changes may involve a gene through an alteration of its sequence of the purines and pyrimidines that constitute DNA (deoxyribonucleic acid). A mutation may also occur by an alteration in a chromosome caused by a "mistake" in its replication that results in losses or duplications of chromosomal segments, among other possible errors.

Another source of variation, besides gene or chromosomal mutation, results from the recombination of genes that occurs at the time of mating. This comes about through the independent assortment of chromosomes during the formation of sex cells (meiosis) and fertilization between genetically varied sperm and eggs. Particularly in plants, a doubling of chromosome number (ploidy) can also result in new species.

A number of species have arisen by hybridization, a process in which genetic recombination allows two distinct species to form a third distinct species. Many of our modern grains, for example, are the result of both natural and laboratory-induced hybridization. However, not all hybrids are distinct species capable of reproducing their kind, a prime example being the mule, which is a hybrid of a horse and a donkey.

The details of these processes can be pursued in a general biology textbook and are not really germane to our central purpose, which is to explain how these inheritable variations lead to the origin of new species.

THE ORIGIN OF SPECIES

Reproductive Isolation

To pursue the origin of species, we must first establish what a species is. For sexually reproducing organisms, a **species** is a population in which the individuals interbreed, produce fertile offspring, and do not breed successfully with other populations.

The failure of one population to breed with other populations is referred to as **reproductive isolation** and can come about in a variety of ways. There may be differences in the structure or function of reproductive organs (e.g., differences in arrangement of floral parts that allow pollination by a given insect species in one case and not in another), the sex cells may be incompatible (e.g., the eggs release a biochemical substance that attracts the sperm of one population and repels those of another), there may be a difference in the time when reproduction occurs (e.g., spring for one population and summer for another), or there may be differences in behavior (e.g., male courtship attracting females of the same population but not of others).

Most scientists agree that the most important reproductive isolating mechanism, at least initially, is geographic. A barrier that sets apart a population into two or more subpopulations can set the stage for separating the species into two. These barriers might be of quick occurrence, as in the case of a flood or flow of lava, or require a long period of time, as in the case of mountain building or continental drift.

Although most scientists believe that geographic isolation is the predominant mechanism in speciation, there are a growing number of findings in which a new species forms right in the midst of its parent population (Gibbons 1996a).

Once one or more isolating mechanisms operate, then the process of speciation can begin. The inheritable variations caused by mutation may differ within the two reproductively isolated subpopulations and, in different environments, be favorable to one population and not the other. Initial differences may also exist due to the **founder effect** in which the founding population's genetic composition is different in degree if not kind from the original population. Also, owing to chance, there may be random changes in the genetic composition of one or both of the separated populations, a phenomenon referred to as **genetic drift**.

Selection

Once separated chemically, behaviorally, mechanically, geographically, or however, natural selection can act on the genetic composition of the isolated populations differently. In the case of **stabilizing selection** (also called *maintenance selection*), a balance develops in a particular characteristic such as size or weight, avoiding the extremes at either end of the spectrum. Stabilizing selection tends to occur in an environment that changes little in space or time. Human birth weight is an example of this kind of stabilizing selection: on the average, newborns weigh between 3.2 and 3.6 kilograms, survival being increasingly reduced at the extremes of very light and very heavy weights except sometimes by Herculean efforts.

Directional selection (sometimes called **diversifying selection**) results in a more or less steady shift in response to an environmental change or even a new environment. The increasing resistance of animal or plant pest populations to a given insecticide is a classic instance of this kind of selection, as is the increasing resistance of disease-causing organisms to antibiotic exposure. Individual inheritable variation to the pesticide results in the survival of those individuals having such resistance. The continuing application of the pesticide in increased dosages brings about selection in favor of those most resistant individuals, be they few or many. Thus, over time, the population as a whole moves in the direction of resistance.

Sexual selection occurs where there are differences in the appearance and/or behavior between the two sexes, a phenomenon especially dramatic in many birds and mammals. The brighter plumage of some male birds and the courtship behavior of others serves as an attraction to females to select mates and thus results in preserving those characteristics in the population. The establishment of territories and harems are other instances in which sexual selection acts as a mechanism of natural selection.

GRADUALISM AND PUNCTUATION IN EVOLUTION

The processes we have described suggest, in general, that both the origin and subsequent evolution of species occur slowly. **Gradualism** is the term best applied to these changes that result from the various isolating and selection mechanisms we have discussed. Fossil sequences of some groups support this phenomenon of gradual change over time.

Gradualism, however, fails to explain the substantial number of cases in the fossil record in which new species are morphologically distinct when they first appear as well as the absence of intermediate forms in many plant and animal groups. To accommodate these much more common paleontological findings, a start-and-stop pattern known as **punctuated equilibrium** was proposed by Stephen Jay Gould, of Harvard University, and Niles Eldredge, of the American Museum of Natural History (Eldredge and Gould 1972; Gould and Eldredge 1977).

According to the theory of punctuated equilibrium, most morphological changes occur during speciation by processes such as the founder effect and directional selection. This is then followed by a period of stabilizing selection. For example, once it appeared, the horseshoe crab has shown virtually no variation in morphology for 500 million years, the ginkgo tree for 200 million years, and the opossum for 75 million years. These organisms are examples of groups in evolutionary stasis, or equilibrium.

By contrast, the sudden appearance or burst (i.e., punctuation) of new groups morphologically distinct from one another can be seen in the fossil record of freshwater mollusks in northern Kenya (Williamson 1981), among other examples. The 400 meter thick deposits in the Turkana Basin cover a period of several million years and contain 13 mollusk lineages. In these sequences, new species appeared relatively quickly followed by long intervals in which there was little morphological change and then by the sudden (in a geological time frame) appearance of a new species.

Although he set out to demonstrate gradualism in fossil bryozoa (marine, corallike animals), Alan Cheetham instead found punctuation in species that persisted for 2 million to 6 million years and then, in less than 160,000 years, split off new species that coexisted with their ancestor species (Kerr 1995). Punctuation has also been determined in sea urchins, frogs, and ascidians, situations in which long periods of evolutionary stasis in developmental mechanisms and larvae have been interrupted by rapid, extensive, and mechanistically significant changes that coincided with changes in life history strategy (Wray 1995).

As is the case for virtually all theories, especially relatively new ones, punctuated equilibrium has not been as fully accepted as the longer-established concept of gradualism inherent in Darwinian natural selection has, but it is rapidly gaining many proponents (Kerr 1995). The fossil record is increasingly yielding evidence much more supportive of punctuated equilibrium than of gradualism. For example, although the first evidence of life dates to 3.6 billion to 3.4 billion years BP (before present), the only life forms prior to the beginning of the Cambrian period (543 million to 510 million years BP) were algae, bacteria, and plankton. Then within a period of the first 10 million years of the Cambrian appeared the ancestors of nearly all the animals that now swim, fly, or crawl (Nash 1995). Another major "explosion" occurred in the evolution of birds, with all the modern lineages appearing within a 10 million year period beginning 65 million years BP (Feduccia 1995).

It would appear that accumulating evidence increasingly supports the concept of punctualism as a major evolutionary mode. This, however, does not displace the concept of gradualism but rather provides an alternative explanation of some evolutionary events. Evolutionary gradualism does take place and has been well documented in some species; in others, major leaps appear to have occurred in brief periods of time. The possibility of punctualism having occurred in the human lineage will be discussed later in the chapter.

In any event, natural selection is operative in both models—quickly or gradually.

ADAPTATION

Adaptation may be defined, from an evolutionary perspective, as the process of developing or enhancing structural, physiological, and/or behavioral characteristics that improve chances for survival and reproduction in a given environment. It is this concept that is inherent in natural selection. However, adaptations may also be considered to be the structural, physiological, and/or behavioral characteristics themselves—the shape of a bird's beak, the inborn resistance or proclivity to a particular disease, or a particular mating behavior.

Virtually everything about any given species can be regarded as an adaptation assuring its survival and reproductive success in the particular environment at that particular time. Thus, the fur of the Arctic fox which thickens in winter not only provides insulation, its change from summer brown to winter white aids the animal's concealment from predators as well as prey. The acute eyesight of birds of prey, the use of sonar by a number of marine mammals, the water storage capacity of desert plants, all are among the innumerable examples that might be cited. For our immediate needs, we will consider only one major example to convey the nature and importance of adaptation.

Darwin's Finches

In 1835 during the voyage of the *Beagle*, Darwin visited the Galápagos Islands, which lie some 1,000 km west of Ecuador. Here he was struck by, among other findings, the presence of different species of finches, each on a different island (and still another different one on the more isolated Cocos Island) and each adapted to a particular feeding situation (Figure 1–2). In his own words from *The Origin of Species by Means of Natural Selection:*

> The most curious fact is the perfect gradation in size of the beaks in the different species of *Geospiza*, from one as large as that of a haw-finch to that of chaffinch, and even to that of a warbler. The beak of *Catocornis* is somewhat like that of a starling; and that of the fourth subgroup, *Camarhyncus*, is slightly parrot-shaped. Seeing this gradation and diversity of structure in one small, intimately related group of birds, one might really fancy that from an original paucity of birds in the archipelago, one species had been taken and modified for different ends.

Although Darwin's original observations on the Galápagos finches were profound, as the foregoing quotation indicates, his collecting methodology was not as precise as many contemporary biology textbooks suggest. It has been determined that he did not consistently record the island location of the different species (Quammen 1996); this probably accounts for the fact that the role geographic isolation plays in speciation was almost unrecognized in his publications.

Our present understanding of the role geographic isolation played in the evolution of the fourteen finch species is the result of studies by the British ornithologist David Lack (1961), who detailed the adaptations and behavior of the finches. As Lack determined, of the six species of *Geospiza*, three are ground

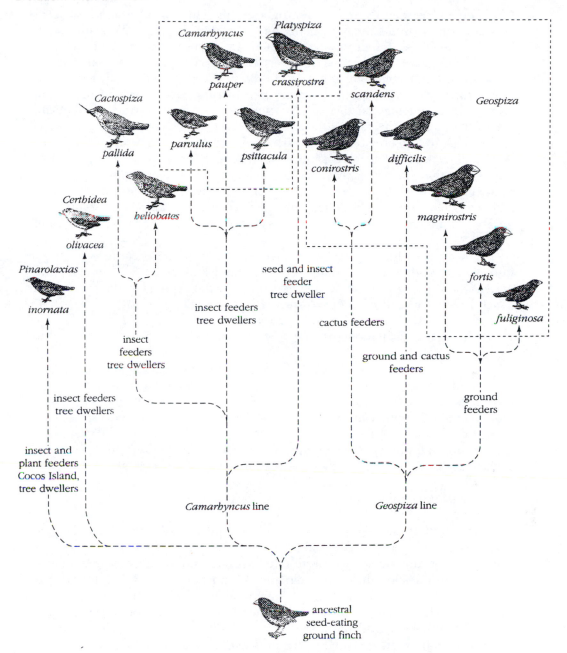

Figure 1–2 Adaptive radiation in Darwin's finches. (Redrawn by permission from E. J. Kormondy et al. 1977. *Biology: The integrity of organisms.* Copyright © Wadsworth Publishing Co., Belmont, CA.)

feeders; two feed mainly on nectar, fruit, and soft tissues of cactus (and eat seeds as well); the sixth feeding on both the ground and cactus. All crush seeds between the bases of their powerful bills but also have a strong bite at the tip of the bill. The other eight species are tree dwellers with a less powerful crush at the base and a stronger bite at the tip of their beaks; they feed mostly on insects. Some (the *Camarhyncus* group) excavate insects from wood with their beaks and also feed on soft insects; two species (the *Cactospiza*) are capable of powerful probing and tip biting and also have developed the behavior of using cactus spines to poke into crevices in tree bark to extricate insects. Feeding on hard or soft seeds as well as on insects and plant tissues is facilitated by the parrotlike beak of another species (*Platyspiza*), and the strong probing and grasping feature of the needle-nosed bill of yet another species (*Certhidea*) is a different adaptation to feeding on insects. The fourteenth species, occurring on Cocos Island and feeding on insects and plant tissues, has a weak, probing, grasping type of bill (Figure 1–2).

Among the different feeding behaviors, that of *Geospiza difficilis* is the most unusual. In addition to feeding on the ground and cactus, it seeks out the masked booby, a large seabird, and gets through the feathers to the soft tissues which it then punctures and proceeds to drink the oozing blood!

Character Displacement

Darwin's finches are one of the original examples of a fascinating pattern observed in the distribution of animals and plants, a situation known as **character displacement.** This pattern is characterized by closely related species living together being recognizably different while being virtually indistinguishable when each occurs alone (Grant 1994). Some recent experimental evidence supports the concept that interspecific competition (which we will discuss in detail later) is the driving force in evolving these adaptational differences (Schluter 1994).

Adaptive Radiation

Interpreting this array of finches from the perspective of evolution by natural selection, the base or parental stock were likely ground dwellers feeding on insects. As the population spread to different islands, becoming geographically isolated, natural selection favored different beak types in the different environments, resulting in a branching out, or **adaptive radiation,** from the original population. Had Darwin visited the Hawaiian Islands, also of volcanic origin like the Galápagos, he would have been struck by the adaptive radiation that has occurred in birds known as honeycreepers and among two different groups of tree snails (Figure 1–3).

Adaptive radiation, as in the case of the evolution of major plant and animal groups, Darwin's finches, and Hawaii's honeycreepers, is a major evolutionary pattern, repeated over and over again in the fossil and contemporary record. It is a pattern that is also fundamental to the evolution of primates, and

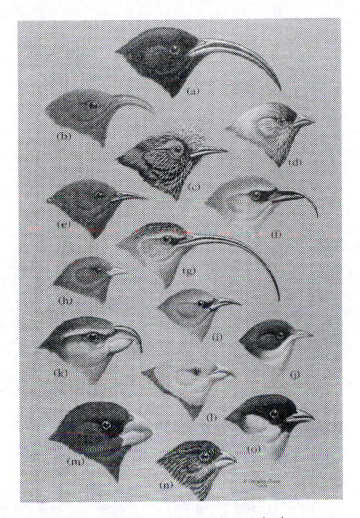

Figure 1–3 Variation in bill morphology and color patterns of selected Hawaiian honeycreepers: (a) mamo *(Drepanis pacifica);* (b) iiwi *(Vestiaria coccinea);* (c) crested honeycreeper *(Palameria dolei);* (d) ula-ai-hawane *(Ciridops anna);* (e) apapane *(Himationes s. sanguinea);* (f) akiapolaau *(Hemignathus monroi);* (g) Kauai akialoa *(Hemignathus procerus);* (h) Hawaii akepa (male, *Loxops c. coccinea);* (i) Hawaii amakihi *(Hemignathus v. virens);* (j) Kauai creeper *(Oreomystis bairdi);* (k) Maui parrotbill *(Pseudonestor xanthrophrys);* (l) ou (male, *Psittirostra psittacea);* (m) grosbeak finch *(Chloridops kona);* (n) Nihoa finch (female, *Telespyza ultima);* (o) poouli *(Melamprosops pheosoma).* (Painting by and courtesy of H. Douglas Pratt, Jr.)

thus of humans. It is timely then to review briefly the origin and evolution of humans from an ecological perspective.

THE ORIGIN AND EVOLUTION OF HUMANS

In his 1871 *Descent of Man and Selection in Relation to Sex,* Darwin proposed a theory for the origin of humans that was consistent with his general thesis of evolutionary origins. In his words, "man is descended from some less highly organized form . . . a hairy, tailed quadruped, probably arboreal in its habits and an inhabitant of the Old World." He mustered biological evidence largely from the comparative embryology and anatomy of living forms and some archeological evidence in the form of stones that had been uncovered at the beginning of the 1800s and obviously had been chipped by humans. At the time, there was very little fossil evidence of humans even though fossils of what later became known as the Neandertals had been discovered in 1856. However, these now-recognized cousins of modern humans were regarded at the time as being modern humans with pathological conditions whose skulls had been bashed.

In the more than hundred years since Darwin's theory was published, a considerable body of tangible evidence in the form of fossil skeletal and cultural finds has accumulated. Nonetheless, the broad outline of human origin stated by Darwin still stands: humans are animal in origin, having descended from an Old World, hairy, tailed, quadrupedal, arboreal lineage. From this origin, Neo-Darwinian evolutionary theory would hypothesize a series of genetically variable and reproductively isolated populations operated upon by natural selection that became differentially adapted to different environments.

Of great significance in creating the different environments crucial to human evolution is the fact that while the latter was taking place so was continuing continental drift. The separation of the great land mass known as Pangaea had begun between 180 million and 135 million years BP during the Jurassic Period, and the separated tropical land mass known as Laurasia began further separation during the time primates were developing, some 65 million years BP. The result of these plate tectonic movements, as they are known, was a pronounced shift in climate, particularly beginning about 15 million years BP, with cooling trends and declining rainfall in what is now Africa as well as elsewhere. Marine records of African climate document a shift toward more arid conditions beginning 2.8 million years BP (deMenocal 1995). The shift in climate led to the eventual replacement of tropical and subtropical forests by grasslands, or savannas as they are more generally known in the tropics. The arboreal ancestors of the human stock thus could have become reproductively isolated in the forests that remained scattered during this transition to grassland, thereby setting the stage for the origin and evolution of new groups.

The coincidence of the climatic shift to more arid conditions and the major evolutionary changes of African hominids (and other vertebrates) suggests the significance environmental change plays in evolutionary development (deMenocal 1995; Potts 1996). As we will see, long periods of evolutionary stasis were replaced by recent evolutionary punctuations in human evolution, all perhaps induced by the advent of the Ice Age.

Human Origins

Humans are classified as primates, a group that appeared some 65 million years BP, and more precisely during the Paleocene dating 65 million to 54 million years BP, at the time of a major adaptive radiation of placental mammals. Fossil evidence indicates that the early primates arose from small, ground-dwelling, nocturnal insectivores, some of which were adapted for life in trees. It was this latter group of what became primitive primates that gave rise to what are known today as prosimians, which include lemurs (Figure 1–4) and lorises, and possibly tarsiers. During the Oligocene (38 million to 25 million years BP), the evolving primates underwent further adaptive radiation that led eventually to the three major primate anthropoid branches generally recognized today: New World monkeys (Ceboids), Old World Monkeys (Cercopithecoids), and apes/humans (Hominoids) (Coppens 1994). It is this latter group to which our attention will be addressed.

Figure 1–4 The Eocene prosimian *Notharctus osborni*. (Negative/transparency 324543, Courtesy Department of Library Services, American Museum of Natural History.)

The Earliest Primates.   The earliest fossils that are clearly recognizable as primates are dated about 50 million years BP, during the Lower Eocene. These early fossils appear to represent ancestors of living tarsiers and lemurs, suggesting a very early divergence of these two primate groups, both of which were widespread in Europe and North America (Kennedy 1980). The jury is still out as to whether the oldest anthropoid, or higher primate, is a fossil called *Eosimias* ("dawn monkey"), dating to 40 million years BP or *Catopithecus,* which dates to 37 million years BP (Culotta 1995a). The 1995 discovery in China of the complete lower dentition of a new species of *Eosimias* would appear to tip the balance toward that genus being at the base of the earliest anthropoids (Beard et al. 1996; Kay et al. 1997).

The earliest definitive anthropoids date from about 35 million years BP (the Oligocene), with both New World platyrrhine (flat nosed, with the nostrils pointed sideways) and Old World catarrhine (narrow nosed, with the nostrils pointing downward) forms being found (Simons 1972). *Aegyptopithecus* ("Egyptian ape"), a representative of the Oligocene catarrhines, had the molar cusp pattern of an ape (namely, five cusps instead of four as found in Old World monkeys), the basic quadrupedal body structure and external tail of a monkey, and the relative brain size of a lemur. *Aegyptopithecus* is a candidate for being the earliest of the catarrhines.

"The Age of the Apes," so named because of the number and diversity of Hominoids, was the period from about 25 million to 6 million years BP (the Miocene). During this time, the different kinds of apes ranged from the generalized and arboreal *Proconsul* to the huge, terrestrial *Gigantopithecus*. As noted earlier, during this time period a major climatic change occurred in eastern and northern Africa, resulting in increased aridity that, in turn, led to a replacement of rainforest with tropical savannas by the late Miocene. Adaptations to these new environmental conditions resulted in a secondary return to terrestrial life by several Hominoid species, as well as by many Cercopithecoids (Old World monkeys) (Kennedy 1980). Among these Hominoids were ancestors of *Homo sapiens*, the hominids.

The Earliest Hominids.   The Hominoid line diverged at a point some 5 million to 8 million years BP leading to the **pongids,** which include modern gorillas and chimpanzees and their ancestors, as well as the **hominids,** modern and ancestral humans. Other apes among the Hominoids, such as gibbons and orangutans, diverged earlier. Hominids are characterized by bipedal locomotion, an omnivorous diet, and, later, increased cranial capacity and organization, all three of which are regarded as adaptations to living in open savannas instead of protected forests like their forebears. Not all scientists, however, are convinced that our ancestors became bipedal to survive in the African savannas (Shreeve 1996b). Nonetheless, the savanna habitat is one of the factors that has made the unraveling of human evolution difficult—our ancestors lived and died where their bodies were subject to scavengers and their bones to weathering by the sun and rain or erosion by acid soils. Thus, the human fossil record is less productive than it is for many other groups. The fact that humans, then and now, are not a prolific species and have both a long gestation and generation time are also factors in producing a small fossil record. Nonetheless, the finds to date are both remarkable and provide enough evidence to track the major features and trends in human evolution.

Since 1974, the evolutionary story of human origins has changed with dramatic rapidity, pushing back the time of the first appearance of our ancestors to 4.4 million years BP.

Australopithecus afarensis.   In 1974, the earliest known hominid was *Australopithecus* ("Southern Ape") *afarensis*, based on fossil bones dubbed "Lucy" by her discoverer Donald Johanson, who was listening to a recording of the Beatles' "Lucy in the Sky with Diamonds" when he was examining her remains (Figure 1-5). Lucy, dated to be about 3.1 million years old, was only 1.1 meters tall, weighed about 30 kg, and had a forward-thrust jaw and chimpanzee-sized braincase. The 25-year-old "Lucy" was clearly hominid in walking upright on legs that could be fully straightened. Famed anthropologist Mary Leakey confirmed

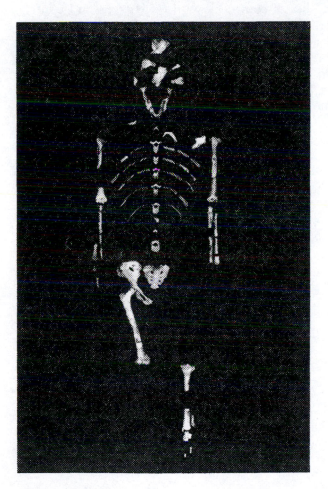

Figure 1–5   The earliest known hominid, "Lucy," properly known as *Australopithecus afarensis*. (© Institute of Human Origins. Courtesy Institute of Human Origins.)

this anatomical conclusion from fossil footprints that clearly demonstrate upright walking on two limbs in contrast to the waddling, four-limbed gait termed "knuckle-walking" that is characteristic of many apes (Figure 1–6).

Other fossil remains belonging to Lucy's species date to 3.9 million years BP, perhaps indicating an evolutionary stasis of 0.8 million years. Among these fossil remains is the first complete skull of a male *A. afarensis* that was found in the early 1990s and dated from 3 million to 3.4 million years BP (Kimbel et al. 1994). Fossil limb bones, particularly those of the forearm (the ulna), indicate that *afarensis* not only walked upright but also retained the ability to climb trees. Hominid footbones recovered from Sterkfontein, South Africa, and dated as 3 million to 3.5 million years old have a forefoot adapted to bipedalism but an apelike great toe adapted for climbing (Clarke and Tobias 1995; Gore 1996). Perhaps even more striking evidence from the fossil finds is the dimorphism (two forms) that existed in this human ancestral species, the males being considerably larger and more robust. There has been speculation, however, that Lucy was actually a male, since her pelvis might not have allowed for giving birth. This perspective, along with studies of cranial blood flow patterns and dental measurements, adds further fuel to the fire that the larger and smaller *A. afarensis* might actually be separate species (Falk et al. 1995; Shreeve 1995).

Ardipithecus ramidus. In 1992–1993, fossil remains of the most remote and possibly the root species of hominids were discovered in Ethiopia and are now named *Ardipithecus ramidus* (root) (White et al. 1994; Fischman 1994).

Figure 1–6 A comparison of the feet of apes, modern humans, and *Australopithecus afarensis;* the latter was made from a cast of the footprints discovered by Mary Leakey at Laetoli, Africa.

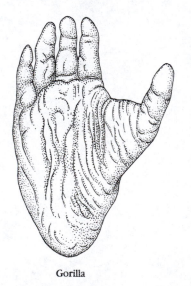

Gorilla   Modern   Australopithecus
                           human beings   afarensis

Because of its age of 4.4 million years, dating almost to the era when hominids and pongids diverged, some paleontologists are bold enough to claim *A. ramidus* may be the long-sought "missing link" (Wood 1994).

Australopithecus anamensis.   Crowding the field of early hominids is *Australopithecus anamensis* ("lake" in the Turkanan language), discovered in 1995 in Kenya by Meave Leakey, daughter-in-law of the famed Mary and Louis Leakey and wife of Richard, also of anthropological fame (Culotta 1995b). Dated as being 3.9 million years old, *A. anamensis* makes an excellent candidate for an intermediate between *A. ramidus* and *A. afarensis.*

Ecotones and Early Hominids.   These early australopithecine hominids may have lived at the junction between forests and savannas. Such a junction between two (or more) different types of environments is known as an **ecotone.** Since an ecotone contains some components of both of its adjacent environments, it is richer in resources than either of them alone. A species living in an ecotone thus has access to a rich set of resources, in this case some of both the forest and the savanna (Campbell 1983). By the same token, a species living in an ecotone must have sufficient behavioral flexibility to be able to adapt to two different kinds of environmental challenges. It is generally believed that life in this forest-savanna ecotone may have contributed to the development of bipedalism, omnivorous eating habits, and encephalization (increase in relative brain size).

Australopithecus africanus.   Before becoming extinct about 3 million years ago, *Australopithecus afarensis* may have given rise to at least three additional flourishing lines: *Australopithecus africanus; Paranthropus robustus;* and *P. boisei.* The latter two species, which are sometimes placed in the genus *Australopithecus*, became extinct between 1 million (*A. boisei*) and 1.5 million years BP (*A. robustus*), apparently playing no role in the further evolution of humans. The *africanus* line, however, is significant in that some, but not all, scientists believe that it gave rise to the next major step in human evolution, *Homo habilis*, between 2 million and 2.5 million years BP and perhaps to other lineages, including *Homo rudolfensis* and even *Homo erectus.*

Fifty years prior to the finding of the ancestral species represented by Lucy, Raymond Dart had extricated the fossil skull and jaw of a small child, about six years old, and named it the Taung baby for the location in which it was found in South Africa. Dart christened his find *Australopithecus africanus* and concluded that the Taung baby had stood erect based solely on the position of the foramen magnum, the hole in the base of the skull through which the spinal cord passes. In the Taung baby, this hole is underneath the skull, as it is in humans with erect posture, rather than toward the back of the skull, as it is in apes and monkeys. Some ten years later, as well as subsequently, additional fossil skeletons confirmed Dart's interpretation of the upright posture as well as the presence of more than one australopithecine species.

The position of *Australopithecus africanus* in the human lineage has been brought into question by examination of hundreds of specimens that had been unavailable during a prolonged boycott of the Union of South Africa's long-standing apartheid government. Study of this fossil bonanza indicates that the body proportions of *A. africanus* were actually more primitive and apelike, and perhaps thereby more suited to a life in trees, than those of *A. afarensis*, its presumed ancestor (Shreeve 1996a). If this proves to be the case, perhaps *A. afarensis* was an early separate experiment in terrestrial bipedalism that shared a common ancestor with *A. africanus* but then became extinct. In this scenario, *A. africanus* subsequently and gradually shed its apelike proportions and eventually evolved into *Homo habilis,* the only two known partial skeletons of which do have more apelike body proportions.

The oldest *Homo* fossil so far found, an upper jaw from Hadar, Ethiopia, has been dated to 2.33 million years BP. Whether the jaw represents *Homo habilis* or its more or less immediate ancestor is not yet resolved (Kimbel et al. 1996).

Homo habilis.   It is generally agreed that *Homo habilis,* or its possible ancestor, arose from *Australopithecus* stock about 2.5 million years BP and became extinct about 1 million years later. *Homo habilis* (handy man) was a contemporary of and may have competed with *Paranthropus (Australopithecus) robustus* and *P. (A.) boisei.* Except for being taller and having a larger cranium, *H. habilis* probably looked like its earlier more or less apelike kin. But significantly, and perhaps unlike its predecessors who used existing materials as tools, *H. habilis* appears to have made tools by hammering on rocks to shape them. Although there is not complete agreement, it is likely they were scavengers rather than hunters, intelligent enough to anticipate the behavior of predators, like lions and leopards, and scavengers, like hyenas and jackals, and thus move quickly to get their food before or after the others did.

Some anthropologists, but by no means all (see Winterhalder 1980), believe that differences between hominid species at this time, particularly between *Homo habilis* and the robust species sometimes placed in the genus *Paranthropus,* may have been accentuated by a process known as **niche divergence.** This phenomenon is often seen in instances where similar species diverge from one another in their ecological role, an adaptation that reduces competition for commonly sought resources. We shall have more to say about niche divergence in Chapter 2.

Although it lasted only about a half million years, *H. habilis* may have spawned a new species, *Homo erectus,* the first skeletons of which date to about 1.8 million years BP. Until more recent discoveries, *H. erectus* was thought to have existed to about 300,000 years BP and hence be an ancestor of, but not contemporary with, *H. sapiens.* Fossil finds in central Java described in 1996 appear to indicate that *H. erectus* was still around 27,000 years BP and thus would have coexisted with *H. sapiens* in Southeast Asia (Swisher et al. 1996).

Homo erectus. Standing an average of 1.7 meters tall, *H. erectus* retained the apelike skull (flattened forehead, prominent brow ridges) and jaw (no chin) of its forebears, but its cranium was enlarged in relation to overall increased size, thereby allowing for increased brain development that provided the plasticity to adapt to different environments and to disperse widely.

In addition to the fossils of *H. erectus* that were discovered in Java in 1891 and Peking, China, in 1929, its presence throughout Indonesia, Asia, Europe as well as Africa indicates a tremendous capacity to disperse and adapt to diverse environments. If the predecessors of *H. erectus* originated in East Africa as evidence implies, they would have had to travel on foot some 12,000 kilometers (km) to get to Java and Peking, 4,800 km to Algeria, and 8,000 km to central Europe. These locations ranged environmentally from the humidity of the tropics and the aridity of northern Africa to the frigidity of northern China and Europe! The discovery and use of fire to cook and for warmth along with more effective tools doubtless were major factors in their survival. It is also likely that hunting of larger animals required planning and coordination, suggesting some mechanism of communication, perhaps a primitive form of speech. And, important for our story, it is this species that many, but not all, anthropologists believe gave rise to contemporary humans, *Homo sapiens*.

Homo sapiens. Perhaps between 500,000 and 100,000 years BP, early versions of *Homo sapiens* appeared on the scene. Fossils of *H. sapiens* are divided into two groups: archaic and modern. Both the archaic and modern forms had large brains, averaging at or even above the present average of 1,350 cubic centimeters. Archaic forms, including the subspecies *H. sapiens neanderthalensis* (Neandertal), are characterized by long, low skulls and robust facial skeletons including moderate-sized brow ridges and large jaws. Modern *H. sapiens* is characterized by a more rounded, vaulted skull, a chin, smaller teeth and jaws, and a more gracile (i.e., less robust) face than the archaic forms.

It is the modern forms of *H. sapiens* that have had such an extraordinary impact on their environment. To them has been attributed an important role in the extinction of many mammalian species at the close of the Pleistocene, as well as the major changes in the landscape that have come with the development and intensification of agricultural and other activities.

Although there is still not common agreement about many aspects of the Neandertals, the "cave men" of Europe, they did persist while their modern brethren were evolving elsewhere than in Europe (Gore 1996). However, once *H. sapiens sapiens* arrived in Europe, the Neandertals were outcompeted or perhaps decimated by plague. Whatever, they disappeared from the fossil record about 35,000 years BP.

Adding to but perhaps helping to solve the evolutionary puzzle, both Neandertals and early modern humans inhabited the caves of Mount Carmel in what is now central Israel some 40,000 to 100,000 years BP. That is, they were in the same place at about the same time, hunted the same prey, used similar tools, and buried their dead in the same manner. Studies of Mount Carmel fossils show that in comparison with *H. sapiens sapiens,* Neandertal upper-arm bones were stronger, the result of more vigorous use as is the case in tennis players, and their hip bones were so shaped as to indicate they were more active as children (Gibbons 1996a). The behavioral speculations derived from these anatomical observations are that the stronger upper-arm bones may mean that Neandertals depended on food that was not as easy to process; the hip anatomy suggests that children followed along with the adults as the group hunted and foraged. In contrast, more efficient food processing by early modern humans and a social organization wherein youngsters could stay safely in camp could have given this group the evolutionary edge.

Whether Neandertals contributed any genes to modern humans continues to be debated. There is no question, however, about what they left—a rich legacy of their culture in their caves, rock shelters, and camps, including evidence of ceremonial burial of their dead (Stringer and Gamble 1993; Gore 1996).

Complexity in the Evolution of Humans

While it is comforting to have a story line that is more or less straight lined, it is often the case in science that bumps created by new finds, such as the finding of the more apelike features of *Australopithecus afarensis,* result in a squiggled tale that is not easily unraveled. The story line of human evolution presented above suggests a fairly straight line with some major branching from *Ardipithecus ramidus* to *Australopithecus anamensis, A. afarensis* (or perhaps, as suggested above, this may have been a dead end), *A. africanus, Homo habilis, H. erectus,* and finally *H. sapiens sapiens* (Figure 1–7). It also suggests that there was a single originating location, East Africa, with geographic dispersal and adaptive radiation accommodating to the new environments and environmental shifts that accompanied continental drift and the onset of the Ice Age.

Some findings in the early 1990s, however, have raised bumps in this East Africa birthplace story line. For one, based on dating of fossils known as the Mojokerto child skullcap and Sangiran face and cranium, it may be that *Homo erectus* left Africa for Indonesia 1.7 million to 1.8 million years BP rather than 1 million years BP (Swisher et al. 1994). This would have been barely 100,000 years after the species first appeared, making its plasticity for dispersal and adaptability the more remarkable. One of the implications of this finding is that *H. erectus* would have had time to evolve into two different groups, one African and one Asian. But if it was the African branch that evolved into *H. sapiens,* what happened to the Asian group?

Evidence of another ancient wanderer preceding *H. erectus,* and perhaps even its ancestor, reached central China about 1.7 million to 1.9 million years ago, nearly 800,000 years earlier than had been thought (Culotta 1995b; Larrick and Ciochon 1996). If these early wanderers can be shown to be ancestors of *H. erectus,* an Asian rather than African origin might be on the table. This would cast *H. erectus* as an Asian sideline in hominid evolution (Gibbons 1994).

At this juncture, we need to consider another perturbation in our story line. This is of a modern-looking fossil skull found in 1984 in an ancient cave

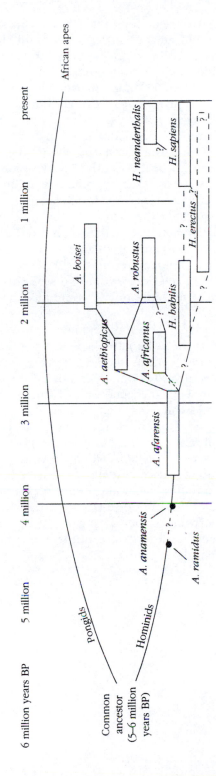

Figure 1–7 Evolutionary line of humans from *Ardipithecus ramidus* to *Homo sapiens* as it is understood today.

locality in Liaoning Province in northeast China. This skull has been dated as at least 200,000 years old (Tiemal et al. 1994). Not only is this nearly twice as old as any of the other remains of *H. sapiens* found in China, but also the skull has features that resemble those of contemporary Asians. Among several implications of this discovery, should its dating prove to be correct, is that *H. sapiens* may not have evolved just in Africa but in China and perhaps elsewhere as well as being a contemporary of *H. erectus*.

Based on fossil and DNA evidence (Fischman 1996), most scientists believe that *H. sapiens* evolved in Africa about 100,000 to 200,000 years BP and spread from there throughout Europe, Asia, the Pacific islands, and North and then South America (Figure 1–8a). This hypothesis is often termed "out of Africa." They also believe that its predecessor, *H. erectus*, was a contemporary that also spread throughout much of the same territory except for North and South America and the more remote Pacific islands, but did so a million or more years earlier. For example, the earliest European fossil hominids date to 780,000 years BP in southern Spain (Carbonelli et al. 1995). The "out-of-Africa" theory has been bolstered by the discovery, previously discussed, that *H. erectus* may have survived to 27,000 years BP, indicating it would have been a contemporary of *H. sapiens*.

A quite different idea, the "multiregional hypothesis," is held by other scientists who believe that the regionally dispersed populations of *H. erectus* could have continued to interbreed, as modern humans actually or potentially do today. This would have provided opportunities for the evolution of *H. sapiens* in a number of places at about the same time (Figure 1–8b). Although the oldest modern European and Asian fossils known to date are less than 40,000 years old and thus support the idea of an African origin, the discovery of the 200,000-year-old Chinese skull raises another bump in the story line of human evolution. Future finds in China and elsewhere will eventually provide the answers. The story of human evolution is decidedly not yet finished.

For those wishing more detail and depth on human evolution, two popular accounts of the story that are up-to-date to the early 1990s are those by Neal Boaz (1993) and Piero and Alberto Angela (1993). But caution! The story changes rapidly as new fossil finds are unearthed, refined dating occurs, and new genetic evidence is discovered.

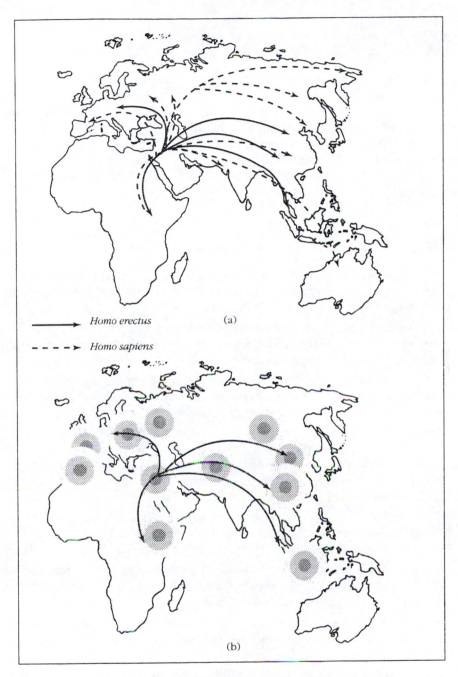

Figure 1–8 (a) The "out-of-Africa" hypothesis of dispersal of *Homo sapiens* and *Homo erectus*. According to this hypothesis there were two great migrations out of Africa, with *H. erectus* beginning its spread about 1.8 million to 2 million years BP and *H. sapiens* about 100,000 years BP. (b) The "multiregional hypothesis" of dispersal of *H. sapiens* and *H. erectus*. According to this hypothesis, following its initial spread, regional populations of *H. erectus* may have evolved into *H. sapiens* in many places while intermingling with one another.

KEY TERMS

adaptation	genetic drift	niche divergence
adaptive radiation	gradualism	pongids
BP	hominids	punctuated equilibrium
character displacement	inheritance of acquired	reproductive isolation
directional selection	characteristics	sexual selection
diversifying selection	natural selection	species
ecotone	Neo-Darwinism	stabilizing selection
founder effect		

KEY POINTS

☐ Fossil discoveries and worldwide explorations during the eighteenth and nineteenth centuries increased awareness of the tremendous diversity of life and the immensity of time in which life has been on Earth.

☐ French naturalist Jean Baptiste de Lamarck proposed that evolution occurred through the inheritance of acquired characteristics, the acquisitions and losses being preserved by reproduction.

☐ English naturalist Charles Darwin proposed a theory of evolution based on natural selection in which characteristics conducive to survival in the "struggle for existence" are favored, resulting in "survival of the fittest."

☐ Independently of but contemporaneously with Darwin, Alfred Russel Wallace conceptualized evolution by natural selection. Both Darwin and Wallace had been influenced by the essay on population by Thomas Malthus that contended population growth exceeded the growth in food supplies, the latter thus controlling the former along with other factors such as war and disease.

☐ The explanation of the variation on which Darwinian natural selection acted came through Gregor Mendel's studies on the physical basis of heredity and led eventually to a merging of Darwinism and Mendelism as Neo-Darwinism.

☐ Variations in the genetic composition of a population are the result of mutations of genes or chromosomes, recombination of genes at the time of mating, doubling of chromosomes, and hybridization.

☐ Speciation is dependent on the occurrence of reproductive isolation, which sets the stage for subpopulations to diverge; geographic isolation is the most important kind of reproductive isolation.

☐ Natural selection can be stabilizing, in which extremes are avoided; directional, in which a steady shift occurs; or sexual, in which differences in the sexes develop.

☐ The theory of punctuated equilibrium explains the relatively sudden appearance of new species and is in contrast to the theory of natural selection being a gradual process.

☐ The structural, physiological, and/or behavioral adaptations that improve chances for survival in a given environment are the result of natural selection.

☐ Adaptive radiation from a parental stock occurs as subpopulations are modified to the particularities of their environment.

☐ Contemporary humans are descended from an Old World, hairy, tailed, quadrupedal, arboreal, primate ancestor. Primates originated some 65 million to 54 million years BP at the time of a major adaptive radiation of placental mammals.

☐ The three major primate anthropoid branches (New World monkeys, Old World monkeys, and apes/humans, or Hominoids) were present by the early Oligocene, 35 million years BP.

☐ Climate change during the "Age of the Apes," about 25 million to 6 million years BP, led to increased aridity that resulted in replacement of rainforest by tropical savanna in East Africa and a return to terrestrial life by several Hominoid species, including ancestors of Homo sapiens.

☐ The Hominoid line diverged some 5 million to 8 million years BP leading to the pongids, represented today by gorillas and chimpanzees, and hominids, modern and ancestral humans.

☐ The earliest known hominid, Ardipithecus ramidus, appeared some 4.4 million years BP.

☐ Based on contemporary and rapidly changing understanding of early human evolution as new fossils are discovered, the lineage from Ardipithecus ramidus to Homo sapiens does not appear to be linear and involves some deadend branching and some directional selection.

☐ It is generally agreed that the Homo lineage developed from the Australopithecus lineage and that within the former, the lineage appears to be more or less direct from H. habilis to H. erectus to H. sapiens.

☐ Considerable debate centers on whether the birthplace of Homo sapiens from H. erectus was only in East Africa, the "out-of-Africa hypothesis," or in many places, the "multiregional hypothesis."

2

Basic Concepts of Ecology

INTRODUCTION

From its Greek derivation, **ecology** literally means "study of the house." But, more broadly, it refers to the scientific study of the environment, including its living and nonliving components. Insofar as its practitioners describe, classify, hypothesize, and test, ecology fits the classical mold of a science. However, because of its involvement with geology, physics, chemistry, and mathematics, its disciplinary boundaries are porous. This porosity is increased even further as ecology extends its interfaces to human interactions, including aesthetics, ethics, politics, societies, law, and economics. At once this makes ecology subject to different channels of scientific inquiry, from the reductionist approach in the study of individual species to the holistic in investigating the totality of environments on planet Earth. All this notwithstanding, a central core of ecological science has been developed, and it is this central core that we will explore in this chapter.

HISTORY OF THE FIELD

As with so many fields of inquiry, the roots of ecology can be traced to the days of the greatest of Greek philosophers, Aristotle. Among the many epithets applied to him, Aristotle was a true natural historian, interested in just about everything. It was his successor at the Lyceum, Theophrastus, however, who began more formal and systematic study of the environment. Aristotle and Theophrastus notwithstanding, the first ecologists were doubtless our hominid forebears. Had they not figured out how to use the resources of their environment, we wouldn't be here today. While their "study" of the environment would not qualify as science as defined today, they must have eventually noted associations of weather and plants, resulting in early forms of both agriculture and aquaculture.

Although the tradition of the natural historian extended more or less uninterruptedly from the time of our remote ancestors through to the likes of Aristotle and Theophrastus, its greatest flowering occurred in the eighteenth and nineteenth centuries. Names like Buffon, Linnaeus, Reaumur, Darwin, Wallace, Humboldt, Audubon, Thoreau, Muir, and many, many others amply qualify as among the greatest students of natural history. These natural historians gave careful attention to detail, precisely measured and recorded information, recognized and interpreted variables, hypothesized and theorized, and developed new tools of analysis. With few exceptions, however, natural history studies lacked the unifying focus essential to the development of concepts and theories. This focus comes through the delimiting of a field by defining it, thereby setting the boundaries of its scope of inquiry.

Defining Ecology

The term *ecology* was coined by one Hanns Reiter, but it was the German biologist Ernst Haeckel who, in 1866, provided its definition in noting: "By ecology we mean the body of knowledge concerning the economy of nature—the investigation of the total relations of the animal both to its inorganic and to its organic environment" (Haeckel 1870). However, it was the end of the nineteenth century before the term came into wider use and recognition; it finally became institutionalized with the formation of the British Ecological Society in 1913 and the Ecological Society of America in 1915.

Over the years, in spite of Haeckel's dictum, ecology has had different interpretations. Charles Elton (1927), a British ecologist, defined it as "scientific natural history," concerned with the "sociology and economics of animals." American plant ecologist Frederick Clements (1905) regarded it as "the science of the community," and German ecologist Karl Friederichs (1958) as "the science of the environment" *(Umweltlehre)*. These somewhat different points of focus have largely been subsumed in the more pervasive concept advanced by American ecologist Eugene Odum, who defined it as "the study of the structure and function of nature" (Odum 1959) and later as "the study of the structure and function of ecosystems" (Odum 1962). This being the current operative definition, we need now to define the term *ecosystem*. For an indepth discussion of the formulation and later development of the ecosystem concept, see Golley (1993).

ECOSYSTEMS

The term **ecosystem,** a shortened version of **ecological system,** was coined by British ecologist Arthur Tansley (1935), who defined it as: "the whole system . . . including not only the organism-complex, but also the whole complex of physical factors forming what we call the environment." In other words, an ecosystem is an organizational unit consisting of both living and nonliving things that occur in a particular place.

Ecosystems can be very large, like a forest or desert, or much more cir-cumscribed, as in an aquarium or test tube. Setting the boundaries of an ecosys-tem is somewhat arbitrary, but not capricious. For example, the boundary of an ocean may seem to be more or less distinct at first consideration; however, since the tide moves in and out and at different distances daily and over a lunar month, is the boundary at the lowest low tide, the highest low tide, the lowest high tide, or the highest high tide? Likewise with a forest bordered by a grass-land: between these two ecosystems is a region that contains varying degrees of mixtures of grasses and trees. Such a boundary, as you learned in Chapter 1, is called an *ecotone*. Where in the ecotone the forest, or grassland, ecosystem begins or ends becomes a somewhat arbitrary demarcation by the person studying the situation. Given the variability in overall biological and nonbiological resources that exist in ecotones, setting the boundaries of an ecosystem for study can be critical. In actual practice, however, this is seldom an unresolvable problem. In other fields of learning, boundary setting is again often somewhat arbitrary: where does sociology leave off and anthropology begin, or physics and chem-istry, and so on? In point of fact, in fields of study as well as in ecotones, one finds challenges and opportunities within the defined constraints of the subject matter or the ecosystem.

With whatever limitation the concept of an ecosystem bears, its acceptance marked the rise of modern ecology, enabling it to reach sophisticated levels of abstraction and develop increasingly powerful theoretical constructs and methodologies (Kormondy and McCormick 1981). To a major degree, the pre-dominance of the ecosystem concept globally reflects the powerful influence of American ecology and ecologists in graduate and postgraduate study, textbooks, and professional journals.

Systems

Although we often use the term indiscriminately, **system** does carry a pre-cise meaning. It consists of two or more components that interact and that are surrounded by an environment with which they may or may not interact (O'Neill et al. 1986). Among the characteristics of a system is organization, the stem *organic* suggesting association with living things. Among the properties of organization, several are significant for ecosystems: an organization exists inde-pendently of specific components (e.g., an individual tree may die, but the for-est's organization remains); the components are interdependent (e.g., when removed from its colony, a social insect does not often survive); the system has a function (e.g., the component parts each have functions that, together, produce a function of the whole); the system is presently or was at one time dynamic (e.g., change occurs or has occurred); and a sliding scale of organization exists (e.g., two populations may independently coexist in an area or they may be intertwined in a complex relationship).

Components of Ecosystems

To some extent, a system is a somewhat arbitrary unit of the universe selected for study; in this sense it is a construct of the human mind. In the case of ecological systems, the two major components are the **biotic** (living) and **abiotic** (nonliving). As we shall see, these components carry with them an organizational structure that is imposed on the ecosystem.

The biotic component is the particular assembly of plants, animals, and microbes existing in an abiotic setting. The latter consists of chemical substances, including inorganic elements and compounds such as calcium and oxygen, water and carbon dioxide, carbonates and phosphates, and an array of organic compounds that are, for the most part, byproducts of the activities of organisms. The abiotic component also includes such physical factors and gradients as moisture, wind, currents, tides, and solar radiation.

Ecosystems are real—like a pond, a field, a forest, an ocean, or even an aquarium. They are also abstract in the sense of being conceptual schemes developed from a knowledge of real systems. In any case, each ecosystem is a unique combination of particular abiotic and biotic components. Even with this uniqueness, ecosystems have in common certain general structural and functional attributes that are recognizable, analyzable, and predictable. We will now explore these attributes in greater detail.

THE ORGANIZATION OF ECOSYSTEMS

Producers, Consumers, and Decomposers

The structural biotic components of an ecosystem are involved in different roles in two fundamental functions—the moving of energy and the moving of nutrients through the system. **Energy,** the capacity to do work, is needed to drive the many interactions that take place within and among the biotic components and between the biotic and abiotic components of an ecosystem. **Nutrients** are the very stuff of life, elements such as calcium and iron and compounds such as carbon dioxide and water or carbohydrates and proteins. Without energy, a system expires; without appropriate nutrients, a system malfunctions. Producers, consumers, and decomposers constitute the structural architecture of ecosystems and simultaneously perform the vital functions.

Producers.   **Producers** are the first link in the movement of energy through an ecosystem. It is this group of organisms, typically green, chlorophyll-bearing plants, such as the algae of a pond, the grass of a field, and the trees of a forest, that capture the radiant energy of the sun. The capturing process is called **photosynthesis,** whereby carbon dioxide is combined with water to form energy-rich, simple carbohydrates that are subsequently converted into more complex carbohydrates, proteins, and lipids. Playing a generally less prolific role in this primary energy capture are purple bacteria, which get their carbon dioxide from inorganic compounds, and certain chemosynthetic bacteria that have the capacity to combine oxygen with simple inorganic compounds.

Producers really don't produce energy; they convert or transduce it from one form, radiant, to another, chemical. But the term *producer* is so firmly entrenched in the ecological literature that more aptly descriptive terminology is out of the question.

Another term that is frequently used to describe producers is *autotroph.* An **autotroph** (literally, "self-feeding") is an organism that captures energy and subsequently uses it to synthesize molecules that serve the nutritional requirements of its own growth and metabolism. By contrast, a **heterotroph** (literally, "other feeding") is an organism whose nutritional needs are met by feeding on other organisms; heterotrophs are also termed *consumers.*

Consumers.   **Consumers** are organisms that derive their nutrition from producers; that is, they are heterotrophs. A **primary consumer** obtains its food directly from producers; common domesticated examples include cattle, sheep, chickens, and horses. Primary consumers are also referred to as **herbivores** (literally, "plant eaters"). A **secondary consumer** obtains its food by eating primary consumers; since the latter are animals (a few exceptions exist in the plant world), secondary consumers are also called **carnivores** (literally, "meat eaters"). Tigers, hyenas, and coyotes are among the many kinds of carnivores. Bears and humans, among others, are referred to as **omnivores** (literally, "all eaters"), since they derive their nutrition from producers directly as well as from primary consumers.

The autotroph-heterotroph or producer–primary consumer–secondary consumer linkage results in a chain of energy movement that is known as a **food chain.** In very simple ecosystems, a food chain may have only three links; in more complex systems, five or six links is the typical maximum. For example, among Laplanders, the food chain is reindeer moss (which is actually a lichen, an association of an alga and a fungus) to reindeer to human (Figure 2–1). In more complex ecosystems, a given food chain is usually interlinked with other food chains, resulting in a **food web** (Figure 2–2).

Implicit in the preceding discussion and more or less explicit in Figures 2–1 and 2–2 is that the direction of energy is one way, from autotroph to heterotroph, from producer to herbivore to carnivore. This is one of the most fundamental of ecological concepts, namely, the unidirectional, noncyclic flow of energy. Although we will pursue this phenomenon in greater detail in a subsequent chap-

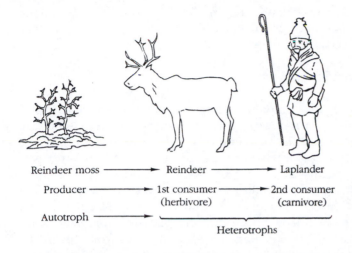

Reindeer moss ⎯⎯⎯⎯⎯→ Reindeer ⎯⎯⎯⎯⎯→ Laplander

Producer ⎯⎯⎯⎯⎯→ 1st consumer ⎯⎯⎯⎯⎯→ 2nd consumer
                        (herbivore)   (carnivore)

Autotroph ⎯⎯⎯⎯⎯→ ⎧⎯⎯⎯⎯⎯⎯⎯⎯⎯⎯⎯⎯⎯⎯⎯⎯⎯⎫
                              Heterotrophs

Figure 2–1 A simple food chain among Laplanders. The reindeer moss is the producer, an autotroph; the reindeer and the Laplander are heterotrophs, the former a primary consumer of herbivore and the latter a secondary consumer or carnivore.

ter, suffice it for now to say that the explanation of this one-way flow is to be found in the energy losses that occur at each transfer along the chain and in the efficiency of energy utilization that occurs within each link of the chain.

Decomposers. **Decomposers,** consisting chiefly of bacteria and fungi, are heterotrophs that derive their nutrition from both producers (mostly fungi) and consumers (mostly bacteria). Instead of ingesting their food as is the case for other heterotrophs, decomposers release from their bodies enzymes that do much of the digestion of plant and animal tissues, the products of which are then absorbed. In addition to moving energy along its unidirectional pathway, the decomposers perform a most critical ecosystem function. They mineralize the organic matter of plants and animals; that is, their enzymatic activity releases

Figure 2–2 A simplified food web involving heterotrophic humans as both herbivore and carnivore.

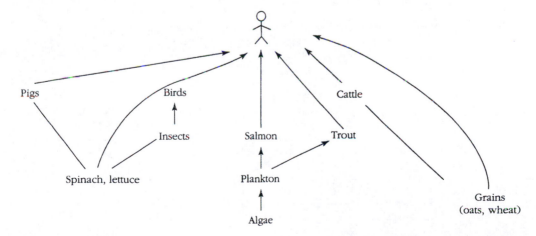

to the environment the elements bound up in those tissues, thereby making them available for reuse, primarily by producers but also by other organisms. Thus, the nutrients in an ecosystem recycle.

Energy Flow and Nutrient Cycling

As we have just noted, two fundamental properties of ecosystems result from the relationships among producers, consumers, and decomposers—the unidirectional flow of energy and the recycling of nutrients (Figure 2–3).

As producers convert radiant energy into chemical energy in the process of photosynthesis, they incorporate a number of elements and compounds into their protoplasm, incorporation that results in growth, development, and reproduction. In addition to the carbon dioxide and water that are paramount in this conversion, elements such as nitrogen, sulfur, phosphorus, and magnesium along with some 15 or more other nutrients are also taken up from the abiotic environment, mostly from the soil. When herbivores consume producers, chemical energy in the form of carbohydrates, proteins, and lipids, along with a host of other nutrients, is transferred. This transfer occurs as well from herbivore to carnivore and from producer and consumer to decomposer. In these transfers, for reasons to be made explicit in a later chapter, the energy at each step is diminished, but not so the nutrients. Through decomposition, the nutrients are released to the environment, from which they can be taken up by producers, thus beginning a new cycle of utilization.

As you may have already surmised, if energy moves in only one direction, then there must be a continual supply of it at the front end to sustain an ecosystem. Because energy is lost irretrievably as it moves through an ecosystem, it must be replaced on a continuing basis. Some of the loss occurs as heat, a by-product of metabolic activity; some can be lost from a given ecosystem and

Figure 2–3   The unidirectional movement of energy and the recycling of nutrients in an ecosystem.

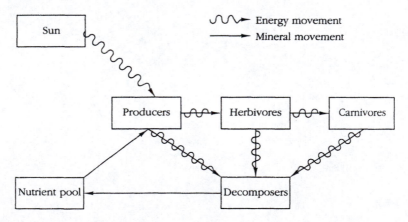

imported by another through agencies such as wind, flood, and animal movement. And although nutrients are recycled, they too can be lost from one ecosystem to another by those same winds, floods, and animal movements. They can also get lost from circulation by being bound up in sediments or other long-term storage, for example as coal and oil.

Energy flow and nutrient cycling have considerable implications for humans, past and present. Meeting today's demands for food for a burgeoning world population necessitates an intimate knowledge of the efficiency and output of producers and the degree of dependence on the availability and abundance of essential nutrients. Because of cycling, toxic substances such as pesticides and radioactive forms of nutrients can become incorporated in human food chains and webs, creating major health problems.

NICHES AND HABITATS

Niche

Energy flow and nutrient cycling do not take place in an abstract set of producers, consumers, and decomposers. These generic terms apply to real organisms—real plants, animals, and microbes—each species of which plays a particular if not unique role in a given ecosystem. From the viewpoint of systematic biology, each species is a unique combination of morphology, physiology, and behavior; from the viewpoint of ecology, each species also has unique ecological attributes as well. The sum total of these ecological attributes is the organism's **niche,** its role in ecological processes—what it does, where it is, and what is done to it. Some species are an energy source only for certain other species, whereas others serve a wider range of consumers. Some play a specific role in one phase of nutrient cycling and not in other phases. Some plants are more efficient in capturing energy at a particular altitude or in a particular climate, whereas others function well over a broad spectrum of altitudes or climates. The ecological role, or niche, of a species contributes to the uniqueness of any given ecosystem. Since no two ecosystems are likely to have precisely the same biological composition, different species may perform the same ecological role in those different ecosystems; such species are regarded as equivalents with respect to their niche.

Habitat

Whatever its niche, a species lives and plays out its role somewhere. That somewhere, a place, is the species' **habitat.** The habitat of a kangaroo rat is desert, that of a polar bear Arctic ice; one dimension of the niche of the kangaroo rat is that of an herbivore, while that of the polar bear is a carnivore.

We can refer to the desert as the **macrohabitat,** or **macroenvironment,** of a desert rat, that is, the generalized type of environment in which it is found. This use conveys that the desert rat is adapted to life in an arid and hot environment.

To survive in such an environment, the desert rat is not found all over the desert but in quite specific subunits of it, that is, under rocks during the day and ranging over a limited area at night. This more circumscribed part of the habitat is known as the **microhabitat, or microenvironment.**

For humans, the habitat is broad, encompassing polar to tropic environments; on a microlevel, their habitat can be considered the city or town in which they live or even the place in which they sleep. It can even be extended to the layer of air between the body and its overlying layer of clothing. It is all a matter of defining the limits, an often forgotten necessity when talking in general terms. As we will see throughout this discourse on human ecology, people do live in the macroenvironment of tundra and tropic, but their microenvironment is sometimes highly restricted, often designed and constructed to offset the stresses of the macroenvironment. An igloo and an air-conditioned living room come to mind.

SPECIES, POPULATIONS, AND COMMUNITIES

As noted in the previous chapter, a species is a population of individuals that are and remain distinct because they do not normally interbreed with other individuals, that is, other species. The species population may be widely distributed, as in the case of humans and the pesky housefly, or be quite restricted to a particular macro- or even microhabitat, as in the case of the desert rat.

As ecosystems have structure and organization, so do species populations. Not only do they have morphological, physiological, and behavioral attributes, but species populations are also dynamic—they increase and decrease in numbers because of differences in the number of births and deaths, they mature, they reproduce, they disperse. In the previous chapter, we learned that humans in the form of *Homo erectus* dispersed quite widely. Was this in part because a local population got too large to be sustained, thereby forcing some individuals to move out and on? Maybe. We know that happens to other populations. In a later chapter we will consider in some detail not only some general patterns of population growth but, importantly, factors that regulate population size and affect dispersal.

Likewise, in a later chapter, we will consider ecosystems in a more concrete fashion as communities, assemblages of individuals interacting and thereby affecting the structure, function, and dynamics of those communities. Briefly, an **ecological community** is the biotic components (plants, animals, and microbes) that are found in an ecosystem, or a subunit of a major ecosystem. For example, one may study the soil community in a grassland (worms, insects, microbes, algae, etc.) or the arboreal community of a forest (birds, mammals, fungi, insects, etc.). Not unlike the populations of species that compose it, an ecological community occupying a given physicochemical environment, such as desert or a pond, undergoes change—it develops, ages, and either maintains itself or dies out. In a later chapter, we will also consider the very broad ecological communities known as biomes—tundra, coniferous forest, deciduous forest, grassland, desert, and tropical rainforest.

SPACE, TIME, AND ECOSYSTEMS

In addition to the structural and functional aspects that we have briefly explored, ecosystems have other attributes. They occur in space and exist in time—they have width, depth, and height as well as a past, present, and future (Figure 2–4). Spatial dimensions pose many a problem in studying the dynamics of an ecosystem; the time factor likewise. If we study a desert only during the day, we would miss the myriad organisms that are nocturnal; if we study a pond only in summer, we would miss the dynamics of what occurs under ice in winter. If we study an open field today and come back 10 or 20 years later, we would likely find a very different set of conditions and organisms. It is this series of changes, the spatial and temporal dimension, that makes ecology a moving target and thus a continual challenge.

One additional factor needs to be noted—the interrelatedness of ecosystems. As no organism is sufficient unto itself, neither is an ecosystem. They are

Figure 2–4   Model of an ecosystem showing its spatial and temporal dimensions, its relationship to other ecosystems, the unidirectional flow of energy, and the cyclic movement of nutrients. (Modified from E. J. Kormondy. 1974. In *Human ecology,* F. Sargent II, ed. Amsterdam: North Holland Publishing Co.)

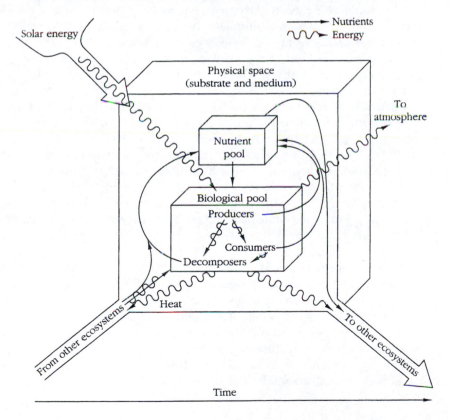

not discrete entities isolated sharply from other ecosystems. No pond exists that is not surrounded by another ecosystem, a field or woods perhaps, or that is not connected by a stream to another pond to which it contributes its organic and nutrient matter. Many species move from one ecosystem to another in the course of their activities—the golden plover moves from the Arctic to the equator and beyond annually. These movements result in the transfer of energy and nutrients from one ecosystem to another.

On the broadest scale, in one way or another, all ecosystems on Earth are interconnected and interrelated. This gigantic network of ecosystems constitutes the thin layer of our planet known as the **ecosphere,** or **biosphere.** It is, in part, because of this vast network that an insult to a given ecosystem in a given locale often has an impact on other ecosystems far removed. The instance of a volcanic eruption in the Philippines having fallout thousands of miles away is an example of a natural event, that of sulfur spewed into the atmosphere from midwestern American factories resulting in acid rain in the northeastern part of the country is an anthropogenic one.

CYBERNETICS AND ECOSYSTEMS

To a considerable extent, ecosystems, particularly mature ones, are self-regulating entities. Self-regulation maintains a homeostatic state, one in which major and minor perturbations are responded to in such a way that there is no significant net change. This kind of response, or feedback, must be opposite to the imposing change; that is, the feedback must be negative. Negative feedback is feedback that regulates a process or set of events by turning it off or slowing it down. Negative feedback is the basic principle of the home thermostat that "turns off" the heating unit when the temperature exceeds a preset level but allows it to operate when the temperature is below the set level. Similar feedback occurs at sublevels in ecosystems: when nutrient release exceeds a certain level, feedback, largely through chemical equilibria, inhibits further release; when a population exceeds a certain size, various events are triggered that curtail further reproduction. We shall be exploring some of these feedback mechanisms and their role as we gain some undersanding of the **cybernetics,** or science of control, of ecosystems.

It does need to be pointed out that the emphasis in a cybernetic system is stability and negative feedback as described briefly in the previous paragraph. As O'Neill et al. (1986) note, however, not everything about ecosystem behavior is well regulated, and many phenomena are more easily conceptualized as unstable, positive-feedback systems. The building of automobile freeways seems to be an apt example of a positive-feedback system: as more freeways are built, more cars use them; greater use of the freeways increases the demand for more of them; and on and on. The widespread presence of positive-feedback processes in ecosysems is discussed by DeAngelis et al. (1986).

KEY TERMS

abiotic
autotroph
biosphere
biotic
carnivore
consumers
cybernetics
decomposers
ecological community
ecological system
ecology

ecosphere
ecosystem
energy
food chain
food web
habitat
herbivore
heterotroph
macroenvironment
macrohabitat

microenvironment
microhabitat
niche
nutrients
omnivore
photosynthesis
primary consumer
producers
secondary consumer
system

KEY POINTS

☐ Natural historians from the Greeks on, and especially during the eighteenth and nineteenth centuries, contributed significantly to an understanding of the geographic distribution of organisms but lacked a unifying focus essential to the development of concepts and theories of biogeography.

☐ *Ecology,* a term coined by Hanns Reiter in the nineteenth century, refers to the scientific study of the environment, including its living (biotic) and nonliving (abiotic) components.

☐ An ecosystem is an organizational unit consisting of both living and nonliving things occurring in a particular place.

☐ A system consists of two or more components that interact and is surrounded by an environment with which it may or may not interact; among the chief characteristics of a system is organization.

☐ Energy, the capacity to do work, in an ecosystem is ultimately derived from the sun and flows through ecosystems from producers to consumers and from both to decomposers in unidirectional fashion; that is, it does not recycle. It must be continuously supplied to keep an ecosystem functioning.

☐ The flow of energy from producers to consumers and from both to decomposers in a simple ecosystem results in a chain of movement known as a food chain. In complex ecosystems food chains are interlinked as a food web.

☐ Nutrients, including elements and compounds, are cycled as energy flows through ecosystems and then is available for recycling.

☐ An organism's niche is its role in ecological processes—what it does, where it is, and what is done to it—whereas its habitat is the physical place in which the organism exists.

☐   Species populations have morphological, physiological, and behavioral attributes as do assemblages of species populations that are known as ecological communities.

☐   Ecosystems occur in space and exist in time—they have width, depth, and height as well as a past, present, and future.

☐   All ecosystems are interconnected and interrelated in a gigantic network constituting the thin layer of Earth known as the ecosphere, or biosphere.

☐   Ecosystems, in some large measure, are cybernetic, that is, self-regulating entities that maintain a homeostatic state through negative feedback.

3

Approaches
to Human Ecology

ANTHROPOLOGICAL BACKGROUND

Anthropology can be defined as the study of human behavioral and biological diversity, both geographical and temporal. Diversity, or variation, in populations is an important aspect of evolution, as stated in Chapter 1, and thus evolution is a major theoretical underpinning of anthropology. Anthropologists study all normal (as well as pathological) human variability throughout the world, both in the present and the past. In this latter sense, anthropology may reasonably be defined as the study of the natural history of the human species.

CULTURE

A major concept for understanding human behavior at the population level is **culture,** the set of understandings and learned behavior patterns that are shared by the people in a society. Culture, in a sense, is a set of rules for living that includes a group's behavior, values, language, and technology. Culture is what is learned as opposed to what is inherited through genetics, and it is passed down from generation to generation through socialization processes. Some anthropologists view culture as a unique human adaptation, different in kind as well as degree from the social behavior of other species. This notion of the unique nature of human culture is controversial, being disputed by many scholars, including some primatologists. Also under dispute is the notion that culture is necessarily adaptive; some of the understandings shared by individuals within a society can be maladaptive. We may wonder if, for example, the Judeo–Christian notion to "be fruitful and multiply" may, within Western culture, have maladaptive long-term consequences for ourselves and other species in our environment.

Many of the specific rules of a culture are simply conventions, such as customs and traditions. There appears to be no natural advantage to the convention of whether one drives on the right or left side of the road, but once the convention is set, it may well matter very much that individuals adhere to it! People tend to believe that their culture's shared understandings are more than pure convention, that these understandings are somehow the "natural" or "right" way to do things. This can carry over into fairly mundane ideas, such as the Western idea that one should never slurp one's soup, while in traditional Chinese culture it is considered important to eat noisily to demonstrate enjoyment of the food. People from either culture may feel uncomfortable in the presence of one who slurps—or doesn't slurp—and, beyond that, believe that the person with the other convention is not acting properly. The notion that one's own cultural conventions are superior to or more natural than those of other cultures is universally found among people and is termed **ethnocentrism** by anthropologists. Ethnocentrism is usually viewed as an adaptive attribute, as it tends to act as a unifying force among people who share a given culture, although it can also lead to xenophobia (fear or hatred of what is foreign) and provincialism, which in a shrinking world can result in conflict.

Ecological Anthropology

Ecological anthropology studies the ecology of human populations throughout the world, in the past as well as the present. The focus is on how human groups have managed to function and persist in diverse environments and how the population's ecology has influenced, directly or indirectly, characteristics of the culture associated with the group. Early theoretical approaches in ecological anthropology emphasized the effect a population's environment had on its culture. The fundamental aim of this work was to explain human cultural diversity in terms of the environments to which populations were exposed. Specific cultural traits were seen as resulting from specific environmental conditions.

ENVIRONMENTAL DETERMINISM

Early Approaches

In works attributed to the Greek physician Hippocrates, especially *Airs, Waters, and Places,* a clear case was made for specific environmental attributes being the cause of specific human attributes. Hippocrates' works lay out the humor theory, in which people were believed to be composed of four "humors":

blood, phlegm, yellow bile, and black bile. The balance of these four humors in a person determined his or her personality, health, and appearance (including racial differences). Furthermore, specific features of the environment shifted the humoral balance, thus affecting public health, regional differences in biology ("race"), and specific cultural traits. For instance:

> Inhabitants of mountainous, rocky, well-watered country at high altitude, where the margin of seasonal climatic variation is wide, will tend to have large-built bodies constitutionally adapted for courage and endurance, and in such natures there will be a considerable element of ferocity and brutality. (*Airs, Waters, and Places*, cited in Dubos 1965)

The idea that specific features of the environment have a causal effect on the presence of specific cultural features is termed **environmental determinism.** This is arguably the oldest major theoretical approach to human ecology, as it clearly encompasses Hippocrates' vision of human-environment relationships. For most of Western history, when human ecology was considered at all, this approach predominated. In the eighteenth century, for instance, Montesquieu ascribed a cause-and-effect relationship between environment and social phenomena, maintaining that climate had a direct influence on behavior and personality (Honigmann 1976).

Environmental determinism became particularly well developed around the turn of the twentieth century, when geographers and anthropologists (the so-called anthropogeographers) attempted to explain the increasingly numerous and detailed descriptions of non-Western cultures by reference to the environments in which these groups were located.

Culture Areas

A finding that was used by environmental determinists as evidence supporting their theoretical approach was the existence of what anthropologists term **culture areas.** Culture areas refer to regions of the world within which both the basic environmental conditions and the cultures of human populations are similar. Examples of culture areas are Polynesia and, traditionally, the Great Plains region of America.

The environmental determinists viewed the similarities in cultures found within culture areas as resulting from the common environmental features of the region. For instance, the native Americans residing in the Great Basin, including the Western Shoshoni, Ute, and Northern Paiute, were all foraging people before Western contact. They were nomadic, moving in small family groups to track wild plant and animal food sources through the seasonal and other less predictable changes of the environment (Steward 1955). These groups also shared related languages (Shoshonean), simple technologies, and an ideology of individualism and self-reliance, among many other cultural features. The similar cultural patterns shared by the groups in the Great Basin were attributed to cause-and-effect processes of adaptation to a similar environment.

Limitations of Determinism

If one views past historic eras through the eyes—ideas, beliefs, and knowledge—of contemporary society, some of the writing of the determinists can seem fairly bizarre. For instance, Montesquieu noted that the heat of southern lands, by acting through the nerves and blood, would cause indolence and strong sexuality (Honigmann 1976), and Huntington (1945) stated that cycles of weather can have important effects on the psychological status of people residing in a region. One of Huntington's points was that cool temperatures and stormy weather foster mental alertness, implying that because of their regions' climate, Europeans and Americans are bound to have highly developed civilizations. Inherent in much of this writing is the scholar's own ethnocentrism: environments in other parts of the world are seen as leading to cultural or psychological attributes that have a negative connotation, while the environment from which the writer hails is seen as causing the ultimate in human efficiency, nobility, and intelligence.

This connection of ethnocentrism with determinism is mostly a function of determinism's long history. Scholarly concerns with ethnocentrism and an attempt to view human cultures objectively (often referred to as "cultural relativism") began only in the twentieth century with Franz Boas's work in American anthropology. In objectively assessing the environmental determinism approach to human ecology, it is important to look beyond biased instances of ethnocentrism and judge the approach on its own merits.

A major drawback to environmental determinism is the simplistic way it connects environmental features with cultural traits. The environment, in a sense, is seen as "preceding" culture and thus able to determine it (see Figure 3–1a for a simple illustration). Many determinists were more sophisticated in approaching some of the complexity in environment-culture relationships; for instance, Ratzel's recognition of the importance of migration and diffusion of cultural traits across a region (Moran 1982). Nevertheless, the main notion of a one-way causation from environment to human culture is a hallmark of determinism (Bennett 1976). It is this aspect of environmental determinism that led to scholarly critiques from anthropologists and geographers early in the twentieth century and to the formation of a major new approach to human ecology: environmental possibilism.

ENVIRONMENTAL POSSIBILISM

Criticism of simplistic ideas of environmental causation and the overly generalized theories of the development of culture associated with them came from Franz Boas and his students, beginning in the late 1890s, but becoming more popular in the 1920s and 1930s. Often considered the founder of modern studies of anthropology in the United States, Boas was struck by the complexity of culture and believed that simple causal explanations were unlikely to be useful

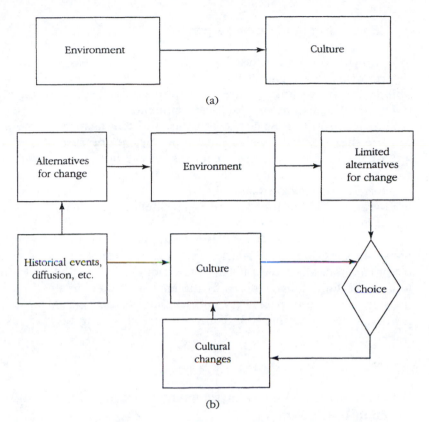

Figure 3–1 Flowchart of human ecology theories. (a) Environmental determinism; (b) Environmental possibilism.

in understanding human diversity (Boas 1896). Furthermore, he had little patience for armchair theorizing. He instilled an empirical approach to anthropology that has been a hallmark of the discipline since. Boas's students Robert H. Lowie and Alfred L. Kroeber, along with geographers such as Carl Sauer, elaborated on Boas's ideas to formulate a new approach to human ecology: **environmental possibilism.** This approach emphasized the primacy of specific historical events in the creation of cultures through continuous change over time. To Kroeber, the immediate cause of specific cultural features was *other* cultural features. Environment was important only in limiting the possibilities in a culture—hence the term *environmental possibilism*. For example, a human group in a region with too short a growing season could never develop certain kinds of agriculture. A region that did have a long enough growing season might or might not contain human cultures with a specific type of agriculture; that would depend on historical events (including, for instance, contact with a different society that possessed that type of agriculture).

Possibilism and Culture Areas

Lowie and Kroeber used the idea of culture areas, previously utilized by determinists, as evidence for their own views about human ecology. To the possibilists, cultures within culture areas were similar because of historical connections, not because of simplistic environmental influences. For example, such Polynesian groups as Samoans, Tongans, and Hawaiians were viewed as similar because they derived from a common people, not because of their shared tropical island environment. This explains why other tropical islanders, such as native Americans from the Caribbean region, were quite different from the Polynesians. It also helps explain why Maoris (Polynesians who reside in the more temperate New Zealand) are still very similar in their culture to the tropical island Polynesian groups.

To return to the Great Basin example, similarities between the various Shoshoni-speaking native Americans could be explained by the combination of historical, including diffusional, connections between the cultural groups as well as the limitations imposed by the environment. The environmental limitations included the inability to cultivate maize, despite its presence relatively nearby in the (present) U.S. Southwest region among the various pueblo cultures.

Similarities Between Environmental Determinism and Possibilism

While environmental possibilism was developed as a counter to the earlier environmental determinism approach to human ecology, there are many similarities between the two approaches. In general, in both approaches environment precedes culture (Bennett 1976). In possibilism, cultures choose from among alternatives, with the environment determining the range of alternatives. Thus, in a harsh environment like the Great Basin region, there may be few alternatives for a culture. If the alternatives are reduced to one choice, possibilism is reduced to determinism.

According to possibilists, culture takes on the major role in determining later cultural change in most environments, but the causation of cultural diversity begins with the environment and is essentially a one-way process. This is illustrated in Figure 3–1b, where it can be seen that arrows representing causation come from the environment to culture, although in a complex manner, but no arrows point from culture to the environment. However, Kroeber understood that the environment and cultures may interact with each other in a complex way (Kroeber 1939). He did not pursue this notion of environment-culture interaction (Moran 1982), but the idea was taken up by the anthropologist Julian Steward in his approach, termed *cultural ecology*.

CULTURAL ECOLOGY

Julian Steward instilled a strong empirical tradition in his followers beginning in the 1930s. The essence of his notion of **cultural ecology** is that a group's means of **subsistence** (the major means of obtaining food) is strongly related to other parts of the group's culture. He referred to a group's subsistence, including its basic economy and technology, as the **culture core.** The culture core influences a group's social organization and social structure. Social organization in turn influences a group's ideology and religion. The environment is viewed by cultural ecologists as having a direct effect only on the culture core, its effect on other aspects of culture such as social organization and ideology being only indirect. Moreover, the culture core is viewed as also influencing the environment. That is, the connection between environment and culture is two-way, allowing for cybernetic approaches to the understanding of environment-culture interaction. This is illustrated in Figure 3–2.

Figure 3–2 Flowchart of cultural ecology theory. Note the two-way relationship between the environment and the culture core, but one-way relationships between the culture core and other aspects of culture.

Problem and Method in Cultural Ecology

Steward's original method of cultural ecology consists of three procedures: (1) to analyze the two-way relationship between the culture core and the environment; (2) to study the cultural anthropology of a given subsistence system, that is, the patterns of behavior associated with a group's culture core; and (3) to study the (generally one-way) relationship between the behaviors associated with the culture core and other parts of culture such as social organization and ideology (Hardesty 1977).

Relation Between the Environment and the Culture Core. Steward's emphasis on the two-way relationship between the environment and the culture core allowed study of the modification of the external environment by human culture. As the complexity of technology increases humans can modify their environment more and therefore have more latitude for a certain range of possible behavior patterns. Thus, technology becomes an important area of study for the cultural ecologist.

Behavior Patterns Associated with the Culture Core. The types of behaviors associated with the culture core are the main area of study within cultural ecology. These include how people go about making their living, what choices they have in behaviors, and how their subsistence constrains their behavior. Other concerns include whether the behaviors are performed individually or in groups and whether the subsistence activities require transporting people to resources or resources to people.

Effects of Culture Core Behavior Patterns on Other Aspects of Culture. In analyzing the relationship between behaviors associated with the culture core and other aspects of culture, one must again be concerned with the degree of latitude in behavior permitted. In some cases, subsistence behaviors greatly constrain other cultural activities, while in other cases there is much room for choice. In the latter case, historical influences are of the most importance in determining other parts of culture. Steward cautions that study of this third procedure within the method of cultural ecology requires a broad view, as many forces such as "demography, settlement pattern, kinship structures, land tenure, land use, and other key cultural features" (Steward 1955: 42) must be considered, along with their interrelationships. Steward goes further, suggesting that improvements in subsistence lead to general changes in culture, a form of cultural evolution. This evolution consists largely of what he called new "levels of sociocultural integration." For instance, the change from foraging for wild-food resources to subsistence based upon agriculture led to a change from a society based primarily on the nuclear family to a multifamily "folk society" (Honigmann 1976).

Major Types of Human Subsistence Patterns

A major contribution of Steward's approach was to stimulate a large number of field studies with an emphasis on the subsistence system of various human groups. Anthropologists have found that subsistence systems can be divided into major types: foraging, pastoralism, horticulture, and intensive agriculture. Of course, each of these major types subsumes a diversity of subsistence activities. Nevertheless, there are some commonalities within the major subsistence types. These commonalities make the classification of human societies by subsistence type useful in ecological studies. The major types of subsistence will be discussed in more detail in Chapter 11.

The Practice of Cultural Ecology

To exemplify how cultural ecology is carried out in practice, we return to our example of the Great Basin Shoshoni. Cultural ecologists would analyze their ecology by at first noting that the resource-poor environment with dispersed food and both sparse and temporally unpredictable rainfall places great constraints on subsistence. The foragers in this environment necessarily distributed themselves in small, flexible groups across the landscape so that they did not overtax their resources, then aggregated into larger groups during the winter, when information exchange occurred. The small group-size of the foragers led to a social organization based largely on the nuclear family, although larger kinship groups were recognized based on descent from ancestral males (termed *patrilineal kinship*). This type of social organization in turn led to values on independence and self-sufficiency, with religious affairs considered an individual concern (Steward 1955).

In carrying out their investigations, cultural ecologists have placed a great deal of emphasis on cultural phenomena and relatively little on environmental concerns. This is in large part because cultural ecologists are cultural anthropologists, often with little formal training in ecology. Some anthropologists, notably Vayda and Rappaport (1968), have identified weaknesses in the cultural ecology approach. For instance, cultural ecology has focused almost entirely on resource acquisition (especially food) to the exclusion of other ecological concerns. On the positive side, the approach has yielded a great deal of information about subsistence activities and how these behavior patterns influence other cultural phenomena. However, the approach has paid little attention to how humans adjust to environmental stresses and has not considered biological adaptations made by humans to the environment. For instance, in the Great Basin example above, cultural ecologists would not focus on biological adaptations to hot-dry conditions with significant ultraviolet radiation. Nor would they emphasize the natural energy flow and nutrient cycling among organisms in the Great Basin ecosystem, although these processes may have significance for understanding of human ecology in the region. Vayda and Rappaport suggest that a better understanding of human ecology requires the incorporation of ideas from the field of biological ecology. These ideas, as we shall see, become more important in later approaches to human ecology.

It is apparent that human ecology is incredibly complex, requiring consideration of many aspects of human experience. Accordingly, human ecology has had input from many other fields. It is time now to turn to some of these other fields that have provided insights into this multidisciplinary field of study.

OTHER APPROACHES TO HUMAN ECOLOGY

Human ecology has been approached from many perspectives, reflecting differences in academic disciplines as well as the complexity of the subject. These have included sociological, psychological, architectural, and even linguistic approaches, among many others.

Sociological Ecology

Sociological ecology is based in part upon the use of an analogy between the natural environments and those made by humans. For instance, beginning with the work of Park (Park et al. 1925; Park 1936), urban society has been analyzed based on an analogy with the ecosystem, and competition, cooperation, symbiosis, dominance, succession, and so on are seen as processes that occur among elements of urban society (Darling and Dasmann 1969; Moran 1982). Competition is usually singled out as the most important of these forces (Young 1974). These "biotic" forces are important in establishing human relationships and thus are important in providing a foundation for cultural forces.

Sociologists have tended to focus on correlations between spatial and either sociocultural or psychological variables. For instance, sociological ecologists have suggested that populations in an urban setting are distributed spatially based on income, education, and other socioeconomic distinctions. This spatial arrangement leads to the formation of neighborhoods with differential attributes. Individuals move into and out of neighborhoods as their personal socioeconomic attributes change, while the neighborhoods themselves are fairly stable in attributes (Bennett 1976). The main biotic force that is thought to produce these spatial arrangements is competition. According to many sociological ecologists, the competition is economic.

The analogies used in traditional sociological ecology are useful but only if not overinterpreted. Societies, even urban ones, are *not* ecosystems. In particular, natural ecosystems are composed of numerous species, and interspecific relationships are fundamentally different from intraspecific ones, as discussed in Chapter 4. In fact, some sociologists maintain that this approach to ecology is intrinsically anthropocentric and argue for a change to an environmental sociology that goes beyond analogy to study the interaction between the environment and human society (Catton and Dunlap 1978). They view the interaction between the environment and society as being two-way in a similar manner as cultural ecologists such as Steward conceive of the relationship between environment and culture. Environmental sociology differs from the anthropological approach described earlier by focusing on social processes and structures, such as the effect of environmental problems on stratification and resulting differential economic effects based on social class, or how patterns of social stratification influence a group's response to an environmental problem.

Psychological Approaches

Two major approaches are used within the discipline of psychology for the study of human ecology: ecological psychology and environmental psychology. **Ecological psychology** attempts to predict behavior based on careful, often quantitative, observation of the environment in which the behavior occurs. In other words, the goal is to understand correlations between types of environmental units and common behaviors, with the notion that at least some of these environmental units have "great coercive power over the behavior that occurs within them" (Barker 1968).

Environmental psychology focuses on the perception individuals have of their environment, in particular how people perceive environmental resources, threats, and problems (Bennett 1976). For example, environmental psychologists have studied perceived requirements in wilderness areas for users of national park and other wilderness facilities (Heimstra and McFarling 1974).

A topic that has been carefully studied by environmental psychologists is overcrowding. Studies done with animals such as rats have suggested that there is a close association between population density and such ill effects as stress and pathological behavior at high population levels (Calhoun 1962). Studies on human populations at very high densities have shown that overcrowding leads to such ill effects as high rates of psychosomatic disorders, increased arousal, anxiety, and high rates of violent behavior (Coleman 1972). Work with humans both in the laboratory and in natural settings suggests, however, that the relationship between population density and these effects is not so simple. There is a distinction between population density and overcrowding: the latter is a psychological condition in which people are distressed by *perceptions* of high population density (Dubos 1965). Moreover, human perceptions of overcrowding are influenced by such factors as compartmentalization of space (for instance, whether there are walls or other barriers dividing the population into smaller groups or, contrariwise, if the space is relatively open), cultural conceptions of privacy and group affiliation, perceived friendliness of neighbors, and changes from previous conditions (Carey 1972; Stokols 1972). Thus, understanding the effects of an "ecological" variable, population density, requires consideration of a psychological concept, the perception of overcrowding.

Architectural and Urban-Planning Approaches

Architectural and planning approaches apply some of the ideas generated by psychological and sociological approaches to human ecology, particularly the notion that artificial physical environments can be very influential in determining social processes and individual behaviors within them (Moos 1974). Investigators have variously studied the behavioral effects of furniture arrangement, absence of windows, room size, room shape, and so forth on social and psychological variables (Griffin et al. 1969). Whyte (1988) conducted research on the use of urban space, including sidewalks and parks, discovering that simple physical variables are not enough to predict how people use urban spaces. People congregated in areas where sitting space was available, but usually only in places where they could then watch other people. These applications of ideas about human reactions to the environment are difficult to carry out in practice, as the number of possible variables to consider is immense. The difficulty increases many times over when cultural differences are introduced into the equation.

Ethnoecology

Emic Versus Etic Perspectives.   Decisions related to subsistence or other aspects of human ecology are not always based on complete information. Also, throughout history most human populations have not had scientifically trained ecologists on retainer to provide advice. Ecologically based decisions are based on people's *perceptions* of the environment and their relationship to it. Cultural anthropologists have attempted to take an emic approach in studying how people from different cultures perceive the world. An **emic** perspective is one in which the investigator attempts subjectively to see an individual's world view through the eyes of that individual. This is distinct from taking an objective, outsider's viewpoint, an **etic** approach, which is more commonly found in studies of human ecology. An emic perspective is used in the approach termed **ethnoecology,** or *ethnosystematics* (Vayda and Rappaport 1968). This approach is derived from linguistics and attempts to derive people's viewpoint from their language.

The Methodology of Ethnoecology.   Ethnoecologists focus on the way in which people classify things in their language. People are asked what language terms are lumped with other terms, what terms are considered subsets of other terms (i.e., constructing a hierarchy of terms), and what terms are oppositions to other terms. That is, ethnoecologists construct folk taxonomies (Fowler 1977), with particular emphasis on taxonomies of environmental elements, subsistence activities, and the like. **Componential analysis** is used to derive meaningful components, or characteristics, that make up terms (Fowler 1977). For instance, the English term *filly* has components of gender and age as well as a component that identifies a species of domesticated animal. Terms are also analyzed using **keys.** Here, terms are evaluated based on a number of yes/no attributes that divide the world into a series of alternative categories.

In practice, ethnoecology involves exhaustive work on the language uses of people in a given culture. Some interesting differences are found, for instance, in differentiating the terms (using English interpretations) *plants* and *useful*. Among Tzeltal Mayans, plants are classified based on morphology, with their classification similar to that of a Western botanist (Berlin et al. 1974), while for Northern Paiute "plants" are a secondary category, with some of what we (and the Tzeltal Mayans) would classify as plants found in the category "things that are used" and others in the category "things that are not used" (Fowler and Leland 1967).

The Ethnoecology of the Kanam.   Bulmer (1967) has examined the ethnoecology of the Kanam horticulturalists of New Guinea. He notes that the Kanam taxonomy of living forms agrees in the majority of cases with Western taxonomy at the species level but also notes that the higher levels of Kanam taxonomy are much different from Western ones. The basis for distinctions made at higher levels is complex, with many aspects of Kanam culture involved. For instance, the Kanam classify a bird called a cassowary in a category of its own, distinct from the category into which bats, which are mammals, and all other birds are classified. The reasons for the separation of the cassowary from other birds (in the sense Western scientists use the term) involve distinctions about the environment that the Kanam believe are important. For instance, the Kanam distinguish vertical layers in their environment, which includes highly stratified tropical rainforest. The flightless cassowary lives in a different layer than other birds. The Kanam also distinguish horizontal partitions in the environment, namely, homestead, garden, open country, and forest. Birds and bats are found in all horizontal areas, but cassowaries are confined to the forest, with its connotations of danger.

The Value of Ethnoecology.   Studies in ethnoecology, such as that of Bulmer (1967) among the Kanam, point beyond how people conceptualize natural objects in their environment. The manner in which people categorize objects affects the way they utilize them. For instance, virtually all people differentiate between nutrients and food. Cockroaches, beetles, slugs, and so forth are potential nutrients for people, at least if they are prepared properly; for Americans these nutrients are definitely not accepted as food, in part because of their classification as "bugs," "vermin," or "creepy-crawlies"—categories that clearly do not match those in Western biological science. Hence, an understanding of the choices people make in their relationship with their environment requires an understanding of how people conceive of and categorize that environment.

Ethnoecological studies are very hard to carry out. They require extensive knowledge of a population's language and how the language relates to other aspects of culture. Moreover, there may well be variability within a population on how the natural world is classified. Variation may be based on educational and/or socioeconomic differences within the population, on occupational specialization, or on regional or other differences. Thus, the ethnoecologist is often confronted with a multitude of native classifications.

BIOLOGICAL AND EVOLUTIONARY APPROACHES TO HUMAN ECOLOGY

The evolutionary theory of Darwin ushered in a new perspective on the relationships of humans with their environment. The notion of adaptation to the environment became an important concept in the study of human evolution, drawing ecological and evolutionary approaches together. By the late 1940s, human ecologists had begun to integrate evolutionary and ecological approaches into the study of human cultures.

Leslie White

Leslie White influenced many anthropologists with his ecological approach to cultural evolution. He reasoned that culture primarily serves as a device to gather and use energy on behalf of human populations, energy being a critical factor in the maintenance and development of societies. Energy is required for organization, and the more energy available to a society, the more organized it could be. This organization is evidenced in high population density and in greater complexity of political and social structure. To White, cultural evolution occurs as cultures become more effective, or more efficient, at gathering energy. In a given region, a culture that obtains more energy per capita per year than other cultures tends to dominate, or the other groups take on the energy-rich culture's ideas, so that in the long term the groups in the region tend to become more and more effective (or efficient) at energy capture.

White's approach to environment-culture interaction was quite different from that of the cultural ecologists in that it did not address the specific cultural features that had been the focus of most anthropologists. He stated: "History is concerned with particular events, unique in time and place. Evolution is concerned with classes of things and events, regardless of particular time and place" (White 1959: 30). He believed that, in the long term, the general process of evolution was more significant than the particular circumstances in which it took place. While White's ideas had a great impact on human ecological studies, many anthropologists were dissatisfied with them because the anthropologists' main interest was in the very "particular events" that White did not address.

Steward's Multilinear Evolution

Julian Steward, who introduced the cultural ecology approach, also theorized about cultural evolution. His approach was different from White's but was also based upon an ecological foundation. Unlike White, Steward was interested in "particular events" but did not assign equal weight to each one. He believed that "significant regularities in cultural change occur" but that "the cultural traditions of different areas may be wholly or partly distinctive" (Steward 1955: 18–19). Steward argues that what drives culture change is "adaptive processes through which a historically derived culture is modified in a particular environment" (p. 21). As noted earlier in this chapter, Steward believed that a general change that seems to characterize culture change throughout the world is a tendency to adopt more complex levels of cultural integration. This general trend occurs simultaneously with more particularistic, historically based changes, leading to many lines of evolution. Thus, cultural diversity is maintained although general features of culture change may exist. This notion of general change superimposed upon unique historical developments was elaborated by Sahlins (1960) among others.

Some theories of cultural evolution were based on analogies with the theory of biological evolution. The theories utilize what have been termed "generating" and "selective" forces in evolution. As we saw in Chapter 1, the generating force in biological evolution consists of genetic variability, ultimately due to mutation, while natural selection serves as the selective force. In cultural evolution, the generating force is sociocultural variation, ultimately due to innovations (whether *de novo* or through diffusion from other cultures), while "selective retention" acts as a selecting force. The latter is quite complex, involving various forms of selection, including selective survival of complete societies, selective borrowing from other groups, selective transmittal to later generations, selective spread of alternatives within a society, and selection based upon rational planning (Campbell 1965). People have the ability to transmit acquired characteristics of their culture to their offspring, whereas they cannot transmit acquired characteristics of their biology. This makes the two evolutionary processes distinct and places limits on the applicability of the analogy between the two processes.

Human Biology and Evolutionary Ecology

An integrated approach bringing ecological ideas into notions of human evolution and human biology was clearly stated by the 1950s (Coon et al. 1950). Human biologists posed questions about races and human genetics in terms of evolutionary, and thus adaptive, processes. Human biology quickly branched out into subdisciplines that focused on population genetics, demography, environmental physiology, and epidemiology, as well as the more traditional studies of body form and composition (Little and Haas 1989). These studies included approaches similar to environmental determinism (here of population biological traits rather than of specific cultural features) such as a hypothesized simple relationship between climate and body form. The studies also included more sophisticated approaches involving genetics, isolation, marriage patterns, and climatic variables, among others, in understanding the spatial pattern of biological differences among, for instance, aboriginal Australian populations (Birdsell 1953).

This evolutionary ecology approach was also used in studies of human paleoecology. Here the biological features noted in hominid fossils are related to the remains of plants and animals from the same time period and in proximity to the human fossil site. The paleontologist also attempts to reconstruct the ancient climate and the general type of ecosystem in which the hominids lived. Some researchers, for example, have suggested that the two (or more) hominid species coexisting on the African savanna two million years ago may have competed for resources, thus causing selection for individuals with niches different from those used by members of the other species (Boaz 1977; Swedlund 1974). This would lead to what ecologists call "niche divergence," and a rapid change in both species that would reduce their competition for resources. This overly simplistic view of competition in early hominids led to its association with the hypothesis that only one hominid could have existed at a given time in East Africa, although more recently the possible contribution of competitive relationships to early hominid diversity has been described (Winterhalder 1980 and 1981b). In fact, these hominids may not have had competitive relationships at all (Blumenberg and Todd 1974).

Underlying these evolutionary ecological approaches in biological anthropology, and in biology as a whole, is the basic idea that biological (and, for that matter, behavioral) attributes are adaptive. That is, due to evolutionary selection, humans (or any biological population) will have become adapted to their environment, and characteristics that are present *must* be adaptive (Gould and Lewontin 1979). In practice, one can therefore take any characteristic of a given human population and invent an "adaptive story" to explain its presence. Critics have suggested that this "adaptationist" approach cannot be falsified and thus is not proper science. It may be that characteristics of human populations are not related to adaptation; some characteristics may even be maladaptive. Thus, an understanding of human behavior must at least sometimes acknowledge nonadaptive explanations (Amundson 1990). A spatial analysis of the distribution of biological traits among native Australians, for example, suggests that much of that distribution is based upon genetic drift or other nonadaptive factors (Birdsell 1993).

In a sense, this restates some of the arguments between the earlier deterministic and possibilistic approaches, although at a greater level of ecological sophistication. Also, these approaches were originally applied predominately to biological traits and did not address questions of behavioral or cultural attributes of human populations. One critic has stated that the cultural ecological approaches have not developed any general theories of human ecology, while evolutionary approaches are "bloated" with theory but lack empirical tests for the theories (Smith 1991).

More recent theoretical work that has followed these evolutionary approaches to human ecology has attempted to integrate biological and cultural aspects of human populations. It has also attempted to address concerns about the adaptationist approach and a need for empirical testing of theory.

INTEGRATION OF SOCIOCULTURAL AND BIOLOGICAL APPROACHES

Several approaches currently used within human ecology attempt to integrate some of the various perspectives that have been noted, many based more firmly in the paradigm of biological ecology than earlier approaches. Two of these approaches are briefly described here: the "new-ecology" paradigm and human population biology, including evolutionary ecological approaches.

The "New-Ecology" Paradigm

The "new-ecology" **paradigm** represents an attempt by cultural anthropologists at "a reintegration of the analysis of cultural adaptations with general ecological analysis" (Brush 1975: 803). A major change from previous approaches by cultural anthropologists is in the very unit of study: from cultures to populations (Vayda and McCay 1975). This is more than a change in names; a shift to the study of populations allows human ecologists to utilize the concepts and methods of biological ecology in evaluating human ecology. The paradigm utilizes a systems approach with cybernetic relationships among environmental conditions and characteristics of the human population.

Environmental Problems.   A central theme of the new-ecology paradigm is a focus on environmental problems, their effects on human populations, and the response of people to them (Vayda and McCay 1975; Vayda and Rappaport 1968). These problems can be related to subsistence, as cultural ecologists have emphasized, to other resource problems (such as water or soil), or to environmental stressors (such as extremes of temperature or pathogens). The problems may exist as part of the "natural" ecosystem or stem from human-generated causes, including degradation of the environment by human activities.

Ecosystem Approach.   The ecosystem approach in ecological anthropology is based on a simple premise: human populations should be viewed in the context of the total ecosystem in which they live. This is a different perspective than treating human society as analogous to a biological ecosystem. In the ecosystem approach human populations are one part of a larger whole and must be understood in relation to this encompassing milieu.

In practice, the ecosystem approach has divided ecosystems into major types or biomes, and attempted to make generalizations about human populations that are in the same biome. Clearly, human populations that are in the same biome must deal with similar environmental problems. There are limitations to the generalizations that can be made, however. For instance, studies of human populations in different regions of the Amazon rainforest have shown that localized differences in ecosystems have marked repercussions on the ecology of the humans who live there (Moran 1991; Sponsel 1986). This approach is discussed in greater detail in Chapter 12.

Further Integration.   Anthropology has a tradition of taking a broad view of human concerns, often crossing disciplinary boundaries and integrating concepts. The new-ecology paradigm has fostered such multidisciplinary approaches to human ecology problems. In particular, the paradigm has led cultural anthropologists to consider biological as well as sociocultural approaches to their discipline.

Human Population Biology

Human population biology builds on the human evolutionary biology approach of the 1950s by expanding its perspective to include all human adaptive processes, behavioral and biological. The field grew out of the International Biological Program (IBP) of the 1960s, in which ecosystem studies of general ecology were expanded to include intensive studies of single human populations (Golley 1993). The field has been characterized by its multidisciplinary approach to research, in which researchers from many fields collaborate on common investigatory goals (Baker 1982, 1988b; Baker and Weiner 1966). The major goal is to understand human adaptability both at the population and the individual level, entailing integration of research in genetics, demography, growth and development, epidemiology, environmental physiology, resource acquisition, and nutrition, as well as cultural and behavioral processes that relate to environmental concerns (Little and Haas 1989). Thus, human population biology, like the new-ecology paradigm, integrates sociocultural and biological approaches to human ecology.

Use of Models. A **model** is a simplification of something in the world. The model can represent an object (such as a plastic replica of a fighter jet), an organization (such as a flowchart of the positions within a corporation), or a process, whether known or hypothesized (such as energy flow in an ecosystem). Because human population biology encompasses numerous and complex processes, practitioners often utilize models as **heuristic** (used to help understanding without necessarily being "true") devices to reduce complexity and facilitate understanding.

The use of simple models has led to fears of **reductionism,** in which the reduction in the details of circumstances leads to a loss of important information for understanding (Winterhalder and Smith 1992). However, the reductionism found in human population biology models is usually of the type described by Mayr (1988) as "constitutive reductionism," in which phenomena are broken down into constituent parts for closer examination, as opposed to "explanatory reductionism," in which phenomena at high hierarchical levels are explained in terms of processes at lower levels—for instance, reducing explanation of the behavior of living organisms to physical and chemical processes (Winterhalder and Smith 1992). Models must be understood as heuristic instruments as opposed to theories of reality.

Middle-Level Theory. Human population biology has also addressed concerns about the adaptationist approach that appears to be central to its perspective on human ecology. These concerns are met by testing hypotheses about specific human populations by using models of their ecology. As noted by Winterhalder and Smith (1992), evolutionary ecology analyses typically take the form of the following question: "In what environmental circumstances are the costs and benefits of behavior X such that selection would favor its evolution?" (p. 23). This type of analysis allows generalizations to be made while also dealing with specific circumstances that permit testing of hypotheses.

Evolutionary ecology represents an approach that takes a "middle level" of analysis between very general, ultimate questions about natural selection and very specific questions that lead to purely descriptive research (Smith 1991). In the study of human ecology it is sometimes difficult to frame questions in such a way that they permit hypothesis testing, but this is the onus taken on by human ecologists today. There is currently a widespread understanding of the complexity of human ecological problems and the need for modeling, hypothesis generation, and rigorous hypothesis testing. Succeeding chapters in this text address some of the understanding that has come from integrative approaches to human ecology that are framed within the broader perspectives of biological ecology.

Integrated Approaches to Human Ecology

The two integrated approaches to human ecology discussed here form the major perspectives used in this textbook. Our notion is that human ecology becomes more comprehensible when the perspectives of biological ecology are applied. On the other hand, we also recognize that humans are a unique species that requires a special approach. By integrating the approaches taken to human ecology, we attempt to illustrate the connections between biology and behavior in human adaptation. We also attempt to evaluate human ecology based upon empirical work that addresses the question of when human activities are adaptive at all.

The study of human ecology must surely rate as one of the most complex tasks for a student, since it incorporates perspectives from both the natural and the social sciences. This broad scope also makes human ecology one of the most fascinating of endeavors. What follows is an introduction to the subject's complexity, highlighting what makes it so interesting.

KEY TERMS

anthropology	emic	keys
componential analysis	environmental determinism	model
cultural ecology	environmental possibilism	paradigm
culture	environmental psychology	reductionism
culture areas	ethnocentrism	sociological ecology
culture core	ethnoecology	subsistence
ecological anthropology	etic	
ecological psychology	heuristic	

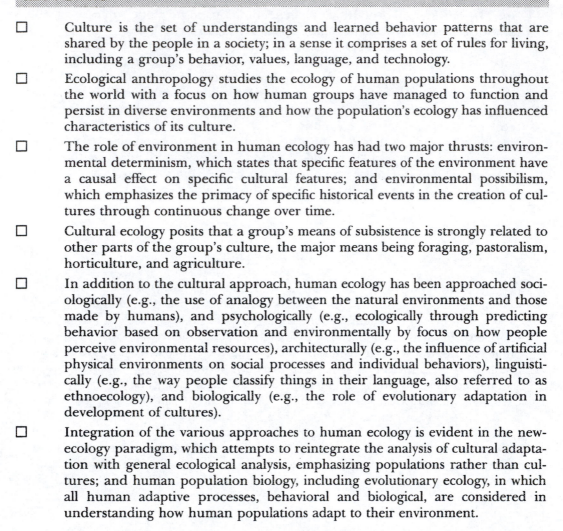

KEY POINTS

☐   Culture is the set of understandings and learned behavior patterns that are shared by the people in a society; in a sense it comprises a set of rules for living, including a group's behavior, values, language, and technology.

☐   Ecological anthropology studies the ecology of human populations throughout the world with a focus on how human groups have managed to function and persist in diverse environments and how the population's ecology has influenced characteristics of its culture.

☐   The role of environment in human ecology has had two major thrusts: environmental determinism, which states that specific features of the environment have a causal effect on specific cultural features; and environmental possibilism, which emphasizes the primacy of specific historical events in the creation of cultures through continuous change over time.

☐   Cultural ecology posits that a group's means of subsistence is strongly related to other parts of the group's culture, the major means being foraging, pastoralism, horticulture, and agriculture.

☐   In addition to the cultural approach, human ecology has been approached sociologically (e.g., the use of analogy between the natural environments and those made by humans), and psychologically (e.g., ecologically through predicting behavior based on observation and environmentally by focus on how people perceive environmental resources), architecturally (e.g., the influence of artificial physical environments on social processes and individual behaviors), linguistically (e.g., the way people classify things in their language, also referred to as ethnoecology), and biologically (e.g., the role of evolutionary adaptation in development of cultures).

☐   Integration of the various approaches to human ecology is evident in the new-ecology paradigm, which attempts to reintegrate the analysis of cultural adaptation with general ecological analysis, emphasizing populations rather than cultures; and human population biology, including evolutionary ecology, in which all human adaptive processes, behavioral and biological, are considered in understanding how human populations adapt to their environment.

4

Population Ecology

INTRODUCTION

From even your most casual observations you are probably aware that there are changes in various plant and animal populations in your environment. Certain kinds of plants bloom only in the spring, others in the fall; deciduous trees lose their leaves in the fall and leaf out in the spring; houseflies are around pretty much all year long, but pesky ants and bees bother you largely during the summer months. You may also have noticed that in some years insect pests such as mosquitos are more abundant, or that flowers don't do so well, or that there are fewer songbirds, or that there aren't as many trout in the streams. In a very general sense, all these changes are manifestations of the dynamics of population growth and regulation. In this chapter, we will consider the general characteristics of population growth, of birth and death rates, the age structure of populations and how that affects growth, and finally the role of abiotic and biotic factors in regulating populations. In the following chapter, we will look at these basic ecological principles in the context of human populations.

POPULATION GROWTH

Biotic Potential and Environmental Resistance

There is a well-ensconced population dictum that notes that populations tend to increase geometrically. For example, assume that 1 female housefly produces 120 offspring, half of which are female, and each of which then produces 120 offspring. From that first generation of 1 fertilized female, the population expands to 120 in the second generation (assuming that the first female dies after reproducing) and to 7,200 in the third (again assuming that all the second-generation females die after reproducing). By the end of seven generations, which is the normal for one year, there would be 5,598,720,000 houseflies! The redoubtable natural historian Charles Darwin estimated that, given their normal reproductive patterns, a single pair of elephants would have over 19 million descendants alive after 750 years.

Such geometric increases to astronomical numbers don't usually occur due to forces that work in the opposing direction. For example, shortly before the turn of the nineteenth century, when the English sparrow was introduced into the United States, it was estimated that there would be about 14 sparrows per hectare by about 1920. In fact there was less than one. During that 20-year period a number of environmental changes that worked against this potential increase took place, among them the development of sparrow-eating behavior by hawks and owls and a marked decrease in the horse population of cities and thereby of the droppings on which sparrows fed.

Inherent in and characteristic of species populations, whether houseflies, elephants, sparrows—or humans—is the capacity to reproduce at a given rate. This is often referred to as the **biotic potential** of a species. Opposing the biotic potential is the totality of environmental forces, abiotic and biotic, that prevent that potential from being realized. These collective forces are called **environmental resistance** and are responsible for keeping a population in check. These two terms were introduced by American ecologist Royal Chapman (1928). On occasion, these checks fail to operate effectively, resulting in exploding populations such as occurred in the great desert locust plagues of biblical and more recent times. We will first consider the biotic potential of populations, a result of the interaction of birth rate, or **natality,** and death rate, or **mortality.** Subsequently, we will explore the environmental resistance that abiotic and biotic factors impose on population growth.

Population Growth Curves

With some variations, there are two basic shapes of population growth curves, an **S-shape** (usually called the **sigmoid growth curve**) and a **J-shape.** As their names imply, the former is smoothly curvilinear, while the latter is abrupt.

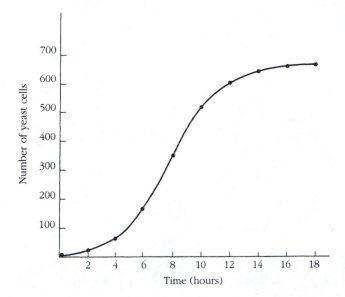

Figure 4-1 The sigmoid growth curve of yeast cells in the laboratory.

Sigmoid Growth Curve. Figure 4–1 is derived from one of the classic studies on population ecology, one conducted in the 1920s on the growth of yeast cells in culture (Pearl 1928). As you can see, the resulting graph of numbers of individuals at different times is in the shape of an S that looks a bit lazy. Sometimes the laziness is stretched out even more, and other times it is much more erect; whichever, the characteristic S- or sigmoidal shape is obvious. What the curve relates is that from an initial population of one to few individuals there is a progressive geometric increase that eventually slows down and then levels off to an equilibrium level in which births equal deaths.

If we superimpose a graph of the change in number of individuals over a given time period, or **growth rate** (Figure 4–2), we find that the rate increases to its maximum at the point of 8 hours, after which it drops off markedly, reaching zero when the population is stable. This must be so, for if the growth rate continued high, the growth curve would continue to go up—but it doesn't. It levels off as the growth rate comes to zero. It is pertinent to point out on the growth curve that the inflection point (where the curve begins leveling off) is where the growth rate begins to drop.

Carrying Capacity. During the rapid-growth phase (up to 8 hours), the yeast cells divide rapidly (technically in a process called budding) such that in spite of some cells dying off, the total number of survivors increases markedly. Subsequently, the cells divide less rapidly but still in excess of the numbers that die off. Finally, the rate of new additions (natality) is equal to the rate at which individuals die off (mortality). This equilibrium phase indicates that the population has reached the maximum that the environment can support, a limit referred to as the **carrying capacity.**

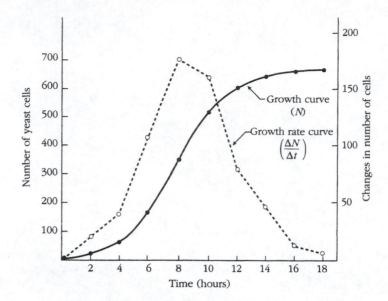

Figure 4–2   The sigmoid growth curve and growth rate curve of yeast cells in the laboratory.

Can carrying capacity be increased or decreased? Definitely. For example, if a means is used to remove the toxic wastes produced by the yeast cells, the population will grow larger; if the toxic wastes are allowed to remain, the population will shrink and may even die off completely. Likewise, a shift in temperature, a change in the amount of nutrients, or transfer of the population to a larger or smaller container will alter the carrying capacity. Thus, carrying capacity, like so many other ecological attributes, is subject to change by altering the factors involved in environmental resistance.

J-Shaped Curve.   Although the sigmoid growth curve applies very widely to species populations, there are numerous instances in which this is not the case. For example, many algal populations undergo extremely rapid growth on a seasonal basis (usually referred to as a bloom) and then die off rapidly; likewise for many insect species that survive but one season and for most annual plants that bloom, produce seeds, and die off (Figure 4–3). In all these instances, the shape of the growth curve is that of a J—a rapid exponential growth up to the limits imposed by the environment (e.g., nutrients, temperature, moisture, toxic wastes) at which point the population undergoes a rapid dieoff.

Fluctuations and Equilibrium.   The general picture conveyed by the S-shaped growth curve is that of equilibrium at the end of the road. However, equilibrium is not a static but rather a dynamic state with fluctuations around the mean. In some populations, the fluctuations are minimal and may be fairly regular; in others, the fluctuations may be quite dramatic as well as erratic. We will dis-

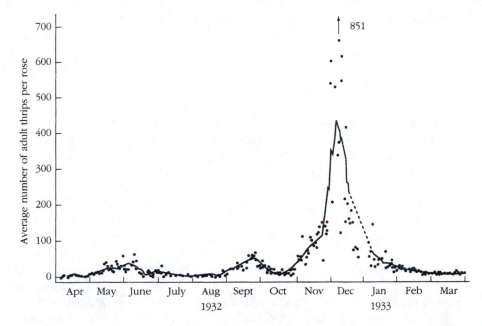

Figure 4–3   The J-shaped growth curve of an insect feeding on roses in southern Australia. Each point represents a daily record; the curve is a 15-day moving average computed for a given date by averaging the data of that day with the previous 15 days. (Redrawn by permission from J. Davidson and H. G. Andrewartha. 1948. *Journal of Animal Ecology* 17:193-99.)

cuss examples of these fluctuations and very regularized oscillations as they are found in the relationship of predators and prey, parasite and host, and other interspecific interactions as well as intraspecific factors later in this chapter.

In the case of the J-shaped curve, there is no equilibrium unless one considers near or actual extinction to be that.

More on Biotic Potential

Although not made explicit in the foregoing discussion, it should be intuitively evident that the potential for a species population at any given time and place to increase is dependent on the **reproductive potential** of each individual, that is, the number of offspring that can be produced and the number of individuals present. If there is one individual that produces two, a population doubling to two occurs; however, if there are one hundred individuals each of which produces four, the increase is quadrupled to four hundred. In the case of the housefly cited at the beginning of the chapter, the reproductive potential of each female is 120 and the size of subsequent generations is geometrically conditioned by the number of females present in the producing generation.

The reproductive potential of a species is not, however, a constant. Its value is different under different environmental conditions, abiotic and biotic.

Abiotic factors influencing reproductive potential include temperature, moisture, and the availability of nutrients; biotic factors include the number of individuals of the population present in the given area, that is, the density of the population, the individuals' ages, age at the onset and end of reproduction stage, and length of life.

Intrinsic Rate of Natural Increase.   Measured under optimal conditions, the biotic potential of a species population is called its **intrinsic rate of natural increase.** These optimal conditions include the ideal among all the forces identified in the previous paragraph—physical and chemical factors, age, physiological well-being, population density, and so on.

To obtain the value of the intrinsic rate of natural increase, many variables need to be manipulated until there is a high degree of stabilization of the results. For this reason, precious few incontrovertible data on the topic exist, but there are reasonable speculations based on the best approximations. For example, there appears to be an inverse relationship between the intrinsic rate of natural increase and the length of a generation, or **generation time**—the longer the latter, the smaller the former. For example, in insects and rodents for which data obtain, the former's intrinsic rate of natural increase is about ten times that of the latter, but the insects' generation time is three to seven times longer. Also, generally, the larger the animal, the smaller the value of the intrinsic rate of natural increase. Finally, the larger the value of the intrinsic rate of natural increase, the more likely it is that the environment is more harsh; more individuals need to be produced to sustain the population.

Net Reproductive Rate.   An additional dimension of reproductive potential is the **net reproductive rate,** that is, the number of female offspring that replace each female of the previous generation. In the case of the housefly, the net reproductive rate was 60: $1 \times 60 = 60$ females in the second generation, and $60 \times 60 = 3,600$ females in the third, and $3,600 \times 60 = 218,000$ females in the fourth, and so on.

In a stabilized population, not only is the intrinsic rate of natural increase reduced to zero, the net reproductive rate is maintained at 1, that is, each female is replaced by one female. Were this not the case and if each female were replaced by two or more, the population would not be stable but would increase. What this means is that in a stable population of houseflies, if 60, or 3,600, or 218,000 new individuals are produced, as many must die.

A final point on biotic potential: The relationship between net reproductive rate and generation time can give some indication of environmental resistance. For example, although the intrinsic rate of natural increase is about the same, the net reproduction rate in the Norway rat is five times that of the English vole, a mouselike animal. This suggests that five times as many rats fail to come to maturity. When generation time is considered, this being 50 percent greater in rats, it means that three times as many rats are produced each year as voles. In other words, environmental resistance is greater for rats than for voles or, alternatively, it is much less for voles.

Although a great deal more can be discussed about biotic potential, the central ideas of reproductive potential, intrinsic rate of natural increase, and net reproduction rate are the keys to understanding the forces that push the population growth curve upward in either a sigmoid- or J-shape. We now need to look at the forces of environmental resistance that tend to push a growth curve downward. At the bottom line, these are the forces that are involved in the mortality, or survivorship, of a population.

MORTALITY AND SURVIVORSHIP

You may be aware that the cost of buying life insurance increases with age because the likelihood of dying increases with age. To determine the probable life expectancy of a prospective insurance buyer and thereby the cost of an insurance policy, the agent consults what is known as an actuarial table. This statistically derived table indicates the probability of survival to a certain age based on factors like age, sex, and, at one time, race.

Since data on human survival are relatively easy to obtain, historically from church records and today from government agencies, an actuarial table is quite accurate. Nonetheless, it is a table of probability as it applies to a whole population, not to a given individual. Basically, it is a table of betting odds, since any given individual could be an "exception to the rule" and may live longer or die earlier than the age cohort used in the table.

For populations "in the wild," such tables are not easily constructed. However, through extensive field studies (e.g., banding or tagging of birds, turtles, or salmon) and controlled laboratory studies, comparable actuarial or life tables on a number of animals have been constructed beginning with the pioneering work of American ecologist Edward S. Deevey, Jr. (1947).

With life history data in hand, the construction of a life table is not overly difficult but requires more explication than is warranted for our purposes. For those interested, consult the Deevey article and also the survivorship tables found in a contemporary almanac or a government document. For our purposes, only one column of a life table is significant, that which gives the expected or probable number of survivors in a population at various age intervals. These data can be graphed to produce a **survivorship curve.**

Survivorship Curves

With the wide variety of organisms, we would expect—and, indeed, we observe—a considerable variety of survivorship patterns. They extend from those with low mortality (high survivorship) throughout most of the life span to those with high initial mortality (low survivorship). Pearl (1928) identified three major types of survivorship curves (Figure 4–4).

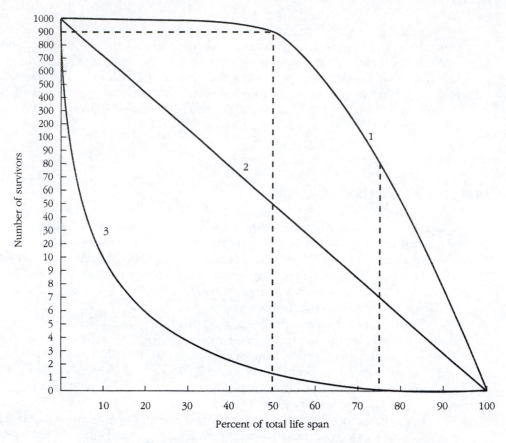

Figure 4–4   The three major types of survivorship curves. The vertical coordinate is loga-rithmic, a straight line indicating a constant rate with respect to age; the horizontal is the percent of maximum life span, which differs in actual time for each organism. The number of survivors at any given time can be read directly from the graph; for example, in Type 1 about 920 individuals are still alive at the midpoint (50 percent) of the life span.

Type I Survivorship.   Type I survivorship is represented by a convex curve in which mortality is low initially and throughout more than half the life span, after which it increases markedly, sometimes precipitously. Species having this pattern have a relatively long life expectancy at birth, and, even at about one-third of the life span, an individual has a high probability of living to a ripe old age. Type I survivorship is characteristic of a wide spectrum of species, including evergreen trees, monarch butterflies, mountain sheep—and modern humans in developed countries. Among plants, some desert dwellers as well as some orchids show this survivorship pattern.

Organisms characterized by Type I survivorship have a **mean life expectancy** that is closer to the maximum life expectancy than in the other types. Mean life expectancy is the point at which one-half of the population is still alive;

technically, this should be the *median* rather than *mean* life expectancy, but the latter usage is too deeply embedded in the population literature to be replaced. In the case of humans, the mean life expectancy has moved progressively closer to the maximum. In the United States, life expectancy at birth was as follows:

	White Males	White Females	Nonwhite Males	Nonwhite Females
1850	38.3	40.5	n/a	n/a
1900	48.3	51.1	32.5	35.0
1950	66.3	72.0	58.9	62.7
1990	72.7	79.4	67.0	75.2

These marked changes are the results of improved sanitation with a consequent reduction of disease, vastly improved nutrition, and significant advances in preventive and corrective medicine. How much closer to the physiological limit of some 100 to 110 years the mean can be pushed is an intriguing question. How society will meet the challenges of housing, feeding, and attending to a substantially larger contingent of older persons is more than intriguing.

Type II Survivorship.   Type II survivorship is represented by a straight line in which mortality is more or less constant (the straight line on a logarithmic coordinate) throughout the life span until near its end. For individuals whose species are characterized by this type of survivorship, there is less chance for survival to old age than for those of Type I, and the mean duration of life is about one-third or less than the total life span. The classic laboratory invertebrate *Hydra* shows this type of survivorship, as do gulls, American robins, grizzly bears, grey squirrels, and Mediterranean fruit flies, as well as a number of herbaceous annual plants.

Type III Survivorship.   Type III survivorship is characterized by a concave curve in which mortality is extremely high initially but decreases markedly for much of the remainder of the life span. As much as three-fourths of a population may die off within the first 10 percent of the life span without much change in the death rate thereafter until the latter part, when it again accelerates. Individuals whose species show this type of survivorship have a low life expectancy at birth, the mean duration of life being about one-fifteenth of the life span. Among species exhibiting this type of survivorship are blacktail deer, British robins, the Columbian ground squirrel, and, showing even more extreme deflection toward the lower-left quadrant, profligate egg-laying groups like teleost fish, amphibians, and many mollusks. Most annual as well as long-lived plants fall in this pattern, with an even more extreme early mortality.

Variations in Survivorship

One of the implications of the mortality patterns just described is that they are as characteristic of a species as is its biotic potential, intrinsic rate of natural increase, and net reproductive rate as well as its morphology, physiology, and behavior. Yet within each species there are differences.

In the tabulation of human life expectancy differences were noted due to sex as well as to race. There is in humans an inherent biological difference that favors a higher mortality in men than women in general. This is the case throughout the life span, the ratio never being less than 1:1 in modern American whites (Table 4–1). In 1960, this ratio peaked in the age group 55–64, but in 1991 in age group 45–54. These differences are the biological basis of there being many more girls than boys, more widows than widowers, and many more older women than older men. It's a fact of life—or death! More or less comparable differences in survival based on sex are common in other human societies as well as in many other species on which studies have been conducted. These inherent differences are compounded by exposure to risks. For example, although there is a greater percentage of male smokers and hence a greater death rate among males due to lung cancer, emphysema, and various heart diseases, the difference is getting smaller because of the increase in smoking, and consequently death rates, among females.

Biological differences other than sex also result in intraspecific differences in survival. For example, among different mutants of the fruit fly *Drosophila*, some show a Type I survivorship, others a Type II, and yet others a survivorship pattern between the two.

As might well be expected, environmental factors can modify a survivorship pattern as it does birth rate. Population density is one of many critical factors affecting the pattern; higher and even lower densities than the optimum can adversely affect survivorship.

TABLE 4–1 The Ratio of Female to Male Deaths Among American Whites, 1960 and 1991.

Age Group	1960	1991
Under 1 year	1:1.34	1:1.31
1–4	1:1.17	1:1.10
5–14	1:1.67	1:1.50
15–24	1:1.28	1:1.28
25–34	1:1.78	1:1.33
35–44	1:1.74	1:1.25
45–54	1:2.03	1:1.80
55–64	1:2.07	1:1.77
65–74	1:1.75	1:1.70
75–84	1:1.34	1:1.59
over 85	1:1.12	1:1.30

Source: Data from U.S. Census Bureau and other sources.

AGE STRUCTURE

Implicit as an outcome of the different types of survivorship is a difference in **age structure** of a population, the relative proportions of young, middle-aged, and older individuals in the population depending on the type of survivorship pattern characteristic of its kind. If one were to assume a continuous input at the left side of the graph in Figure 4–4, characteristic age distributions of different age classes should result. For example, in those groups having Type I survivorship, a greater portion of the population would be in the older age group than would be the case of a Type II population. However, since populations are affected by shifts in input (natality and immigration) and output (mortality and emigration), shifts in the age structure would be expected.

Major Age Groups

As proposed by Bodenheimer (1958), three major age groups are recognized in populations: prereproductive, or expanding; reproductive, or stable; and postreproductive, or diminishing (Figure 4–5).

Expanding Population.   In an expanding population (Figure 4–5a), the birth rate is high, and population growth may be exponential. The proportion of reproductive-age individuals is higher than the other two groups, constituting 40 or more percent of the total; prereproductives are also considerable and may more or less equal the proportion of reproductives; the postreproductive group is the smallest of the three. In such a situation, each successive generation will have more individuals than the preceding one if birth rates remain constant. This produces a pyramid-shaped age structure. If you mentally or actually construct the age structure of the housefly after seven generations there would be nearly 5.6 trillion very young individuals at the base, 7,200 three steps from the top, 120 at two steps, and 1 at the very top.

Figure 4–5   The age structure of different types of populations: (a) prereproductive or expanding; (b) reproductive or stable; (c) postreproductive or diminishing. (Reproduced with kind permission from Kluwer Academic Publishers, based on F. S. Bodenheimer. 1958. *Monographiae Biologicae* 6:1–276.)

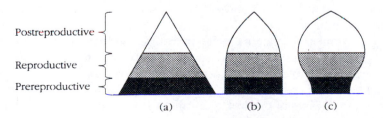

Postreproductive
Reproductive
Prereproductive

(a)   (b)   (c)

Stable Population.   As the instrinsic rate of natural increase nears zero and the net reproductive rate approaches one, the rate of growth slows and then stabilizes. At this point, the prereproductive and postreproductive age groups become more or less equal in percentage, and the reproductive group is the largest, producing a bell-shaped structure (Figure 4–5b).

Diminishing Population.   Population diminishes when the birth rate is drastically reduced. In this case, the prereproductive group dwindles markedly in proportion to the reproductive and postreproductive groups, the latter two being more or less equal in percentage. The result is an urn-shaped age structure (Figure 4–5c). Since few individuals are at the input end, the population will diminish in size and eventually may be eliminated altogether.

Species Differences in Age Structure

Because they differ in many other ways, it is not surprising that different species have characteristic age structures based on their "ecological ages." In some human groups, the prereproductive period (birth to about age 13 to 15) occupies about 21 percent of mean life expectancy, the reproductive (13–15 to about 45 for women) about 42 percent, and the postreproductive period about 37 percent. In rats these proportions are about 25, 20, and 55 percent, respectively. By contrast, many insects spend well over half their life cycle in the prereproductive stage. The human louse spends 68 percent of its life cycle in the egg stage and 26 percent in the larval stage, for a total of 94 percent in the prereproductive stage (Evans and Smith 1952).

Among plants, some annuals have very long prereproductive stages (as seeds) extending from the spring of one year to that of the next. In biennial plants, those that bloom in the second year, nearly 2 years are spent in the prereproductive stage. Among woody plants, conifers have a shorter prereproductive number of years than deciduous trees, about 10 in the former and 20 in the latter for trees surviving over 200 years. In general, plants with short prereproductive periods have shorter longevity, and those with long prereproductive periods have greater longevity and hence a long reproductive period.

As might be expected, geography can affect age distribution. For example, a certain species of dragonfly's life history is so regulated by temperature that it takes 2 years for it to develop to sexual maturity in southern Michigan but only 1 year in Florida (Kormondy 1959). As a result, the age structure in each population is different.

Within the human species there are differences in age structure that are the result of inherent differences in natality and mortality rates coupled with a bedeviling complex of social, cultural, and economic factors. We will explore a number of aspects of human populations, including the different age structures in different parts of the world, in the next chapter. For now, we turn to the general matter of population regulation.

POPULATION REGULATION

In spite of the differences in growth patterns typified by the "equilibrium level" of S-shaped growth curves of sheep, water fleas, blowflies, and other species, populations seem to have an inherent ability to maintain themselves or to be so regulated as to be maintained. We have already briefly shown that two major factors of a population's growth pattern, namely, natality and mortality, are subject to both abiotic and biotic environmental influences. A more systematic consideration of the role played by these components in determining population size and distribution is the focus of the following sections.

The Role of Abiotic Factors

In our earlier discussion of limiting factors, it was shown that the supply or availability of particular nutrients can be a major player in the functioning of a species or even an ecosystem. We saw that temperature and moisture also affect species and ecosystems. However, can a nutrient or physical factor regulate a population's size, density, or distribution?

Nutrients. Although not universally the case, studies of a number of species have demonstrated that the amount and availability of particular nutrients can play a critical role in regulating population growth and distribution. For example, Aumann and Emlen (1965) showed that the level of sodium in the soil is the critical factor limiting the population of meadow voles (*Microtus pennsylvanicus*). Low sodium levels tend to restrict population growth through physiological (adrenocortical) responses associated with crowding; high sodium levels tend to unleash population growth to the limits imposed by some other factor.

Except in deep shade, low levels of phosphorus in the soil regulate the distribution of the nettle (*Urtica dioica*), while the amount of this nutrient regulates its growth (Piggott and Taylor, 1964). Lightfoot and Whitford (1987) found that the number of arthropods on the foliage of creosote bush (*Larrea tridentata*) increased significantly in late spring on plants treated with nitrogen fertilization. It is presumed that these plant-eating arthropods are capable of finding variable amounts of nitrogen in the foliage; where they succeed in doing so, their densities increase.

Physical Factors. Physical factors characterized by gradations also play a significant role in population regulation of different species. The incidence and quality of light quite obviously play a substantial role for autotrophs, which are dependent on sunlight for photosynthesis. Seasonal changes in sunlight, temperature, and moisture also affect a number of plant and animal species.

Drought. In 1973, a severe drought in the Caribbean lowlands of Costa Rica caused a correspondingly severe shortage of the flowers fed upon by the long-tailed hermit hummingbird (*Phaethornis superciliosus*) (Stiles 1992). This

drought occurred during the birds' breeding season; as a consequence, breeding behavior of the males was reduced, successful breeding by females was drastically reduced, and the body weights of both sexes dropped below the levels of
a normal lean season. Furthermore, survivorship of the breeding males dropped
from the normal 90 percent to 60 percent, and the total breeding population of
the following year was one-third lower than before the drought. It took 3 or 4
years for the population of breeding males to recover the numbers and age
structure of the predrought period. It is conjectural but reasonable to presume
that periodic drought would serve to regulate the hummingbird population.

Flooding.   In contrast to drought, flash floods and floods of exceedingly
high levels often have catastrophic consequences on populations. The midwestern United States is often subject to flooding of the Missouri and Mississippi
Rivers and their tributaries and the southeastern part of the country to large
and smaller rivers in that region.

Although generally nondiscriminating in its impact on plant and animal
populations, a curious case of adaptation to flash flooding obtains in the instance
of the live-bearing Sonoran topminnow *(Poeciliopsis occidentalis)*, a native of the
arid American Southwest (Meffe 1984). Behavioral adaptations, including a
quick response and proper orientation to the high discharges characteristic of
flash floods, enable the species to sustain only modest losses. By contrast, the
morphologically similar mosquitofish *(Gambusia affinis)*, a native of the more
moist central and eastern United States but introduced into the Southwest in
1926, experiences considerable population depletion in flash floods. Of further
interest, the mosquitofish preys on the topminnow, typically replacing it within
1 to 3 years after being introduced, the replacement being most rapid in localities that rarely or never flood. In areas subject to flash flooding, however, the
mosquitofish population is periodically reduced before that of the topminnow
because of the latter's behavioral adaptation to flooding. As a result, the predator and prey coexist in such situations with fluctuations occurring in both populations.

Food.   Intuitively there would appear to be a relationship of population
growth and regulation to availability of food. That famine affects population size
as well as distribution in humans is evident both historically and in contemporary times. However, whether famine is more catastrophic, that is, unpredictable
and severely damaging, than regulatory is debatable. Nonetheless, after famine
has depleted a population, growth resurges in the presence of ample food, setting the stage for another death wave during the next famine.

The effect of the amount and availability of food is more easily determined
among nonhuman populations. For example, Stemberger and Gilbert (1985)
studied the effects of five to seven algal food concentrations on population
growth in eight species of planktonic rotifers of different body sizes. The food
concentration required to maintain a population growth rate at zero was found
to vary by a factor of 17. The smallest species sustain their populations at the
lowest food concentrations, suggesting that they are well adapted to living in

food-poor environments; by contrast, the larger species, requiring large food concentrations, appear to be adapted to food-rich environments.

Weather.   Aperiodic weather changes such as hurricanes, tornadoes, blizzards, and heat waves can decimate a population, but they generally do not regulate it. Periodic weather changes such as those associated with seasonal progression and involving changes in temperature and moisture may, however, play a substantial role in regulating some populations, particularly annual and deciduous plants and animals directly dependent for their survival on such plants. Whether weather is a direct regulator or has its impact indirectly by affecting other factors is yet another warmly debated topic among ecologists.

The Role of Biotic Factors

Interactions between species involve a number of different relationships, all of which can be subsumed under the term **symbiosis,** which, from its Greek origins, means simply "living together." In some cases, the two symbiotic populations have no effect on each other **(neutralism);** in most cases there is greater or lesser impact. **Competition** may involve a mutual inhibition or an indirect effect in situations in which a common resource (e.g., food) is in short supply. In instances of **parasitism** and **predation,** one population adversely affects the other by direct attack, parasites generally being smaller than their host and predators larger. Well-adapted parasites generally do not destroy their hosts, whereas predators do; in this sense, as British ecologist Charles Elton put it, predators destroy their capital while parasites live on the interest earned by the capital. In **commensalism,** which literally means "feeding at the table," one population is benefited while the other is not affected (a good example is the relationship between cockroaches and humans). **Protocooperation** is a situation in which both populations benefit but the relationship is not obligatory; by contrast, **mutualism** is a situation in which both benefit and neither can survive without the other (the relationship between nitrogen-fixing bacteria and leguminous plants, which we will discuss in Chapter 15, is a case in point).

At face value, these different kinds of symbiotic relationships suggest that some may well play a regulatory role in population growth and development. An exploration of that possible role is in order.

Parasitism.   Parasites include a broad range of organisms including viruses, protozoans, fungi, helminths, and numerous arthropods. American ecologist Robert May (1983) has made a useful distinction of parasites based on their population biology rather than their taxonomy: **microparasites** (viruses, bacteria, fungi) have direct reproduction, usually at high rates, within the host; **macroparasites** (helminths, arthropods) have no direct reproduction within the host. Furthermore, most viral, bacterial, and fungal microparasites tend to be small in size, have short generation times, and the duration of their infection tends to be short relative to the average life span of the host. Hosts that recover usually possess immunity against reinfection, and thus the infection is of a transient nature. By contrast, macroparasites are typically larger and have much longer generation times than microparasites; their infections tend to be chronic or persistent, with hosts being continually reinfected.

That parasites are a major contributor to many ecological interactions (Price et al. 1986) and especially to mortality in numerous species is well recognized; in humans, for example, it is generally agreed that parasitic infections are a major factor in infant mortality in developing countries, the human survival curve being Type III instead of the typical Type I. However, the extent to which parasitic diseases have a regulatory effect on natural populations is more problematic to assess.

A classic instance of parasitism involves the American chestnut tree *(Castanea dentata)* and the Chinese sac fungus *(Cryphonectria parasitica)*, the latter having been accidentally introduced into the United States in 1904. In China, the fungus, a parasite on the bark of the oriental chestnut, is kept in check by a number of abiotic and biotic factors. But the majestic, towering American chestnut, once the predominant hardwood in Appalachian forests, proved no match for the minuscule fungus. By 1950, about 3.6 million ha (hectares) of American chestnuts were dead or dying; except for adventitious shoots from the roots, it was virtually extinct (Anagnostakis 1982). Further studies have determined that the parasitic fungus is itself a victim of yet another parasite (technically referred to as hyperparasitism) that alters its ability to kill susceptible chestnut tree hosts. Underway are experiments to get the parasitized parasite to disperse naturally and replace the more virulent, as yet nonparasitized, form. It is possible that release of the less virulent strains, some now genetically engineered, could lead to restoration of the magnificent chestnut (Choi and Nuss 1992).

Another classic instance of adaptation to a parasite involves the sickle-cell trait and malaria in humans (discussed in greater detail in Chapter 9). The genetically inherited abnormal hemoglobin and the resultant sickle shape of red blood cells (instead of the usual doughnutlike appearance) is less efficient and has a smaller capacity for oxygen—both inimical to survival of host and parasite. This sickling of the red blood cells, adaptive in some human populations living in malarial areas, and particularly West Africa, confers a higher degree of resistance to malaria, a disease caused by a protozoan parasite. The resistance is due to a lower rate of parasitic infection because of the low oxygen level in the sickled red blood cells. Outside malarial areas, the sickle condition is less advantageous and tends to be selected against. Hence, it is not so frequent in later generations of African American populations in the United States and elsewhere.

Generally speaking, parasitic infections appear to be more effective as regulatory agents among newly introduced species of plants and animals or when parasites are introduced into new regions (May 1983). Well-adapted parasites are relatively harmless to their hosts, an advantage to both symbionts. The development of an avirulent status can follow a number of coevolutionary pathways that depend on the interplay of virulence and the ability of the parasite to be transmitted.

Predation.   In many ways, host-parasite and predator-prey relationships are quite similar: the parasite and predator are benefited while the host and prey, respectively, are adversely affected to greater or lesser degrees. As already noted, however, predators live on capital whereas parasites live on interest. A few examples of the numerous studies on predator-prey interactions should substantiate the accuracy of this capital-interest analogy and also provide insight into the role of predation in population regulation.

One of the classic studies on predation was conducted by Russian biologist G. F. Gause (1934) involving two ciliated protozoans, *Paramecium caudatum,* which thrives on yeast and bacteria, and *Didinium nasutum,* which thrives on paramecia. In one set of studies, the introduction of paramecia into test tubes with a given supply of bacteria was followed in varying periods of time by the introduction of didinium. The general pattern in each case was the same—the increase and decrease of prey was a phase ahead of the successive increase and decrease of the predator (Figure 4–6a). Gause produced an out-of-phase oscillating pattern in both populations by repeated introductions of first the prey and then the predator (Figure 4–6b). In these two situations, the regulation of each population depends on the other. If the prey is completely eliminated, the predator dies out; but if some prey survive to reproduce (by finding hiding places perhaps) or other individuals immigrate (here accomplished by artificial introduction), not only does its population survive, but so does that of the predator.

Such stabilization was demonstrated in studies by R. A. Pastorak (1981) on a fly *(Chaoborus)* whose larvae prey upon both a cladoceran *(Daphnia)* and a copepod *(Diaptomus),* doing so indiscriminately when the larvae's guts are empty. Behaviorally, the fly larvae are adapted to encounter and capture the faster-swimming daphnia more frequently; however, when their guts become filled, the larvae avoid the daphnia and feed on the copepod. In this way, the populations of prey tend to oscillate while that of the predator tends to remain at an equilibrium level.

Other studies on predator-prey relationships have demonstrated the effect of size in their interactions. Among numerous studies is one by O'Brien (1979), who showed that large fish feed on large-sized animal plankton (generally small plants and animals living in the upper part of a body of water and drifting with the current) because the latter are more easily located. However, the density of the fish predators waxes and wanes as the density of their prey fluctuates because of predation.

Other factors affecting predator-prey interactions include spatial distribution, allowing more opportunity for prey to avoid predators; latitude, since predation is more intense in lower latitudes where physical factors are more constant, and, hence, biotic factors tend to be more influential; and anthropogenic activities, the near extinction of western North America's bison being but one of numerous examples.

The investigation of predator-prey relationships has been preeminent among ecologists, leading to more publications on the topic than any other (Kuno 1987). Not surprisingly, the occasional oversimplification that laboratory-

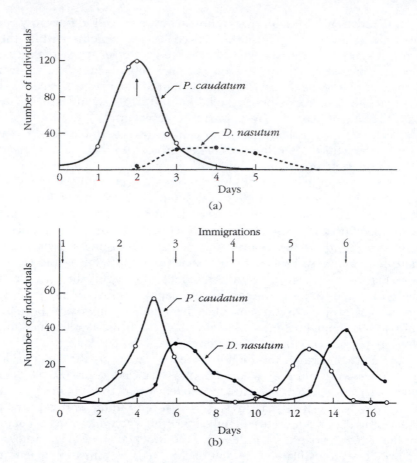

Figure 4–6 Prey-predator relationships in two ciliated protozoans, *Paramecium caudatum* and *Didinium nasutum*: (a) in a homogenous environment in which the prey (paramecia) is introduced first and only once followed in two days by the introduction of the predator (didinia); (b) in a homogenous environment in which there are repeated out-of-phase introductions of prey and predator. (Redrawn from G. F. Gause. 1934. *The struggle for existence.* Baltimore, MD: Williams & Wilkins.)

induced models and theory led to is not always supported by field studies or more intensive mathematical analysis (Berryman 1992). Nonetheless, it can be stated that in some instances, predator-prey relationships do result in varying degrees of regulation in both populations.

Interspecific Competition. If two different species populations require a common resource, such as a nutrient, space, light, or moisture, that is potentially limited and actually becomes so, they are said to be in competition for it. Under such conditions, can they exist together or will one displace the other? If they do exist together, how is this achieved, and can or do they maintain the same population size as when separate? Does competition play a comparable role to predator–prey relations in population regulation?

Most ecologists hold that interspecific competition plays a significant role in population regulation and in setting distributional limits, thus directly affecting the structure of biological communities and perhaps adaptive radiation as well. Debate continues, however, over the relative importance of predation and competition in regulating populations.

Although competition is a widespread phenomenon exhibited by microbes to mammals, empirical evidence is elusive: controlled laboratory experiments usually involve simplified competitive systems whose results cannot be applied to the complexity that obtains in natural ecosystems. Furthermore, the complexity of variables operating in natural ecosystems confounds the interpretation of results, making alternative plausible explanations possible.

The most studied of competitive interactions are those in which a common environmental requirement is in short supply, resulting in either passive or active contesting for that resource. Independent of each other, Lotka (1925) and Volterra (1928) developed mathematical formulations relating to competing populations, formulations that indicated that only one species will survive. Because of his empirical studies on competing populations that showed this effect, this principle is referred to as **Gause's principle.** It is also known as the **competitive exclusion principle,** so named by American ecologist Garrett Hardin (1960).

Among the many studies on competition, the classic one by Gause (1934), from which the competitive exclusion principle was initially derived, is particularly instructive. As shown in Figure 4–7, each of two species of *Paramecium* grown separately shows a quite typical sigmoid growth pattern. They also show that pattern during the first 6 to 8 days when grown together, after which *Paramecium aurelia* shows a gradual increase and *P. caudatum* declines markedly. This result demonstrates quite clearly the competitive exclusion principle and is comparable to results obtained on a wide spectrum of plants and animals competing for a common resource. The evolution of Darwin's finches, discussed in Chapter 1, is an instance of adaptation by shifting of a niche to avoid competitive exclusion.

The interaction of Gause's paramecia can be considered passive competition, a quite ubiquitous kind of interspecific relationship. However, there are also numerous examples of both aggressive competition in which overt fighting occurs (e.g., for mates or food) as well as subtle competition (e.g., one barnacle species prying another loose or simply growing over it).

Size is usually of advantage in competitive interactions; for example, Dickman (1986) showed that the larger and more territorial Australian dasyurid marsupial *Antechinus swainsonii* outcompeted its smaller counterpart, *A. stuartii*, for food. The greater success of the former was evidenced by increased numbers, enhanced survival of the newly weaned young, decreased arboreal activity, and increased movement within and expansion of its territorial area.

Most students are surprised to learn that competition occurs among microbes (Fredrickson and Stephanopoulos 1981) and plants as well as animals.

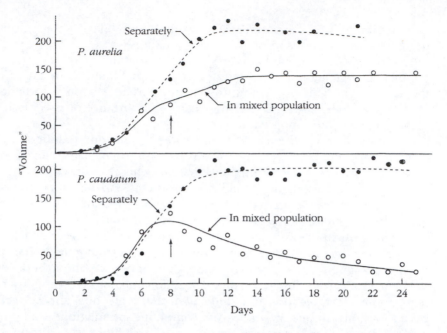

Figure 4–7 The growth of two closely related ciliated protozoans, *Paramecium aurelia* and *P. caudatum*, when grown separately and in mixed culture demonstrating competitive exclusion of *P. caudatum*. (Redrawn from G. F. Gause. 1934. *The struggle for existence*. Baltimore: Williams & Wilkins.)

Competition in plants is usually subtle, involving differential responses to factors such as moisture and light or by differential biological/physiological capabilities (e.g., greater seed production, more rapid seed germination, release of inhibiting chemicals). As but one example among many, Harrington (1991) showed a differential response to moisture stress with a perennial grass known as woolybutt *(Eragrostis eriopoda)*, which survived without summer irrigation in the semiarid grazing lands of eastern Australia while all seedlings of a shrub, hopbush *(Dodonaea attenuata)*, died off. Under ordinary circumstances, the hopbush invades and outcompetes woolybutt, thereby taking over the grazing lands.

Intraspecific Competition. Since each species occupies a usually specific niche in an ecosystem, as described in Chapter 2, competitive exclusion would be expected to be most intense among individuals of the same species, since their requirements, although varying with age and sex, are fundamentally the same. In fact, numerous studies on plants and animals have shown that the adverse impact of increased crowding and resulting interference in competition for food, space, or other vital factors appears to contribute to the regulation of populations. This phenomenon has led to a school of thought, dating to Thomas Malthus (1798), that maintains that populations of plants and animals are regulated by **density-dependent** factors, that is, processes that either increase mortality or decrease natality as the density of the population increases. Density-dependent feedback would, under such a thesis, hold a population within certain limits.

The alternative school of population regulation, namely, that of **density-independent** factors, holds that abiotic interactions and a number of interspecific situations such as predation; competition; and parasitism are more important in population regulation. A full assessment of the density-dependent and density-independent viewpoints is beyond the scope of this book, but a brief look is warranted.

Some investigations like those on water fleas and flour beetles have been conducted in laboratory settings; others were under natural conditions and sometimes supplemented by laboratory experiments; yet others, and increasingly so, are based on computer modeling (Levin et al. 1997). Studies that extend from microbes to mammals and flowering plants generally substantiate the commonalities of the negative effects of crowding on natality, mortality, and size. For example, Weiner (1985) demonstrates that, in monoculture, the annual plants *Trifolium incarnatum* and *Lolium multiflorum* both showed an increase in size inequality with increasing density, suggesting interference by the larger plants usurping resources and suppressing the growth of smaller individuals.

These studies notwithstanding, they do not necessarily prove a causal basis for population regulation, nor do they preclude alternative explanations. As a case in point, spruce budworm *(Choristoneura fumiferana)* populations have been oscillating for the past two centuries at an average of 35 years in the province of New Brunswick, Canada (Royama 1984). This phenomenon suggests the operation of intraspecific competition or perhaps predation. However, Royama concluded that the oscillations are not caused by predation, food shortage, weather, or dispersal of young larvae but by a combination of parasitoids and infections (and possibly other factors) that may be affected by density.

Density-Dependent Population Self-Regulation. Although various factors may be involved as direct causal agents, it is nonetheless the general case that increased density tends to lead to decreased natality and increased mortality. This results in regular or irregular fluctuations in population size by what Australian ecologist A. J. Nicholson (1957) referred to as self-adjustment to change of the population constituting a self-governing system.

Nicholson's study on blowflies is a classic case in point (Figure 4–8). Here the adjustment of population size is tied directly to egg production. At high densities, competition among adults for food is so severe that no individuals are able to develop eggs. Mortality reduces the population of adults to the point at which some individuals are able to obtain enough food to permit the development and laying of eggs. From that point until new adults hatch requires 16 days—2 for development of the eggs in the female and 14 for development from the egg-larva-pupa stages to the adult. During this time the initial adult population continues to decline and is replaced by a new generation that increases in size, with

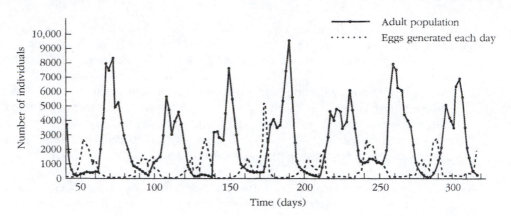

Figure 4–8 The growth curve of the blowfly *(Phoenicia cuprina)* in the laboratory, show-ing an initial J-shaped curve followed by rather regular fluctuations. (Redrawn by permis-sion from A. J. Nicholson. 1955. *Australian Journal of Zoology* 2:9-65.)

the built-in time lag involved in growing up, until competition again precludes egg production.

In different species, other density-dependent factors appear to serve in population self-governing. Among factors proposed by different investigators are sociopsychological stress-inducing changes in hormonal output, particularly from the adrenal cortex, changes that adversely affect reproduction; periodic changes in the quantity and quality of food; natural selection that favors certain hereditary characteristics and thereby alters the population's gene pool; and social behavior such as cannibalism and territoriality.

It is not of surprise that given the multiplicity of factors differentially affect-ing species populations at different stages of their life history there is little con-sensus and much debate in ecological circles about what the controlling factors are in population dynamics. What is generally conceded is that interactions affecting population dynamics may be "top down" (e.g., predators, competitors, behavior) and/or "bottom up" (e.g., resources and other abiotic factors) (Matson and Berryman 1992) and that combinations of both types may act simultane-ously, independently, sequentially, circularly, or otherwise. No pat answers appear to apply universally in this intriguing field of population ecology.

KEY TERMS

age structure
biotic potential
carrying capacity
commensalism
competition

competitive exclusion
  principle
density-dependent
density-independent
environmental resistance

Gause's principle
generation time
growth rate
intrinsic rate of natural
  increase

J-shaped growth curve   natality   reproductive potential
macroparasites   net reproductive rate sigmoid growth curve
mean life expectancy   neutralism   S-shaped growth curve
microparasites   parasitism   survivorship curve
mortality   predation   symbiosis
mutualism   protocooperation

KEY POINTS

☐   Populations tend to increase geometrically at a given rate, referred to as the biotic potential; this potential is kept in check by the totality of environmental forces, biotic and abiotic, referred to as environmental resistance.

☐   There are two basic shapes of population growth curves, an S-shape, also known as the sigmoid growth curve, and a J-shape; in the former, there is a progressive geometric increase that eventually slows down and then levels off at an equilibrium level at which births equal deaths. In a J-shaped growth curve no equilibrium is attained, and the geometric increase is often followed by a precipitous drop as deaths far exceed births.

☐   The equilibrium phase of population growth indicates that the population has reached the maximum that the environment can support, a limit referred to as the carrying capacity. Equilibrium is a dynamic state with fluctuations around the mean.

☐   The reproductive potential of each individual in a population varies under different abiotic and biotic environmental conditions.

☐   The intrinsic rate of natural increase of a population is its biotic potential measured under optimal conditions; in general, the higher the intrinsic rate of natural increase the shorter the length of a generation, the smaller the size of the animal, and the harsher the environment.

☐   There are three major types of survivorship curves: Type I, represented by a convex curve, in which mortality is low initially and throughout more than half the life span, after which it increases markedly, and in which the mean life expectancy is close to the maximum life expectancy; Type II, represented by a straight line, in which mortality is more or less constant throughout the life span; and Type III, represented by a concave curve, in which mortality is extremely high initially but decreases markedly for much of the remainder of the life span.

☐   Variations in survivorship based on sex and other inherent biological differences are compounded by interaction with various environmental factors such as population density.

☐   An expanding population has a pyramid-shaped age structure with larger prereproductive and typically smaller reproductive and postreproductive groups; a stable population has a bell-shaped age structure with pre- and postreproductive groups being about equal and the reproductive group being the largest; a diminishing population has an urn-shaped age structure, in which the prereproductive group is much smaller than the reproductive and postreproductive groups, which are more or less equal in percentage.

☐ Species have characteristic age structures based on their prereproductive, reproductive, and postreproductive periods, all of which are subject to alteration due to environmental factors.

☐ Population size and distribution are regulated by a variety of abiotic factors such as nutrients, physical factors, drought, flooding, food, and weather, as well as by biotic factors such as parasitism, predation, and interspecific and intraspecific competition.

☐ Host-parasite and predator-prey relationships are similar: the parasite and predator benefit while the host and prey are adversely affected to greater or lesser degrees. They differ in that predators live on capital whereas parasites live on interest.

☐ In general, parasitic infections are more effective as population regulatory agents among newly introduced hosts or when the parasites are introduced into new regions. Well-adapted parasites are often relatively harmless to their hosts.

☐ Predator-prey interactions result in varying degrees of regulation of both populations and are affected by a variety of factors including avoidance by prey; presence of alternative prey; size, availability, and spatial distribution of prey; latitude; and anthropogenic activities.

☐ Gause's principle, also referred to as the competitive exclusion principle, posits that when two species compete actively or passively for a common environmental resource that is in short supply, only one species will survive unless one species switches resources to survive.

☐ Populations may be regulated by density-dependent factors, that is, processes that increase mortality or decrease natality as the density of the population increases, or by density-independent factors that do not depend on the size of the population.

☐ Interactions affecting population dynamics may be "top down" (e.g., by predators, competitors, behavior) or "bottom up" (e.g., resources and other abiotic factors); combinations of both types may act simultaneously, independently, sequentially, circularly, or otherwise.

5

The Human Population

INTRODUCTION

Perhaps the first warning of the disparity between human population growth and its means of subsistence was voiced by Tertullian, a Latin ecclesiastical writer in Carthage, who noted around A.D. 200:

> We are burdensome to the world, the resources are scarcely adequate to us; and our needs straiten us and complaints are everywhere while already nature does not sustain us.

In more modern times, it was English economist Thomas Robert Malthus (1766–1834) who articulated this disparity in a quite direct message. In his 1798 treatise *An Essay on the Principle of Population, as It Affects the Future Improvement of Society,* Malthus stated boldly and unequivocally:

> I said that population, when unchecked, increased in a geometrical ratio, and subsistence for man in an arithmetical ratio.

Malthus's concern was prompted by the rapid increase in population that began with the onset of the Industrial Revolution, an increase seen as being counterproductive to progressing toward an ideal society, a major goal of the Age of Reason.

Malthus maintained that, because of their differential growth characteristics, human populations would always outrun their food supply, and therefore human numbers would have to be kept down by famine, disease, or war. In response to the storm of abuse the first edition of his *Essay* engendered, he admitted, in a second edition published in 1803, that moral restraint (delayed marriage and sexual continence) might also counter the increase in population.

In more recent times, Malthusian doom has been characterized in such expressions as "the population bomb" and the "population explosion," both allusions to the rapid increase in the size of the human population. Some years ago, a historian colleague coined the metaphor "the mushroom crowd," an analogue to the symmetry of an above-ground atomic blast. The phrase is apt in some respects: the rapidity of mushroom, and population, growth; the collective characteristic implied—many hyphae forming the fruiting body, many people forming the population body; and so on. But to a biologist, the mushroom metaphor has an alternative meaning—that of a largely temporary and purely reproductive structure and of organisms that are exclusively decompositional in activity. Human populations, in contrast, are more permanent, perform a large amount of nonreproductive activity, and are capable of creative output.

The preceding chapter on population ecology explained that for many populations the growth curve is sigmoidal. If this is the case for the human population, where is it on its growth curve? What about its growth rate? Is it still accelerating, or is it in the deceleration phase? Is it attaining some degree of equilibrium? Or, quite alternatively, is it in an exponential growth pattern that will terminate in a J-shaped curve? If self-regulation is the pattern in some populations, does it operate in the human population? From both archaeological and recorded history, we know that human populations have been subject to famine, disease, and pestilence and have engaged in warfare, infanticide, contraception, and celibacy (Langer 1972; Dickeman 1975). These factors have adversely affected population growth, but to what extent are they regulatory? All these questions and more serve as the focus of this chapter.

GLOBAL POPULATION GROWTH

Growth Pattern

The overall growth of the human population to date (Figure 5–1) has been exponential; in fact, it looks frighteningly similar to a J-shaped curve. If, however, we were to assume it will come to an equilibrium where natality and mortality cancel each other out, when might this occur? If current trends continue, equilibrium could occur by 2110, at which point the world population would be about 10.5 billion, or twice its 1990 size. If natality were to decrease at a faster pace, stabilization could occur by 2040, with a population of about 8 billion. But if deceleration were to occur at a slower pace than at present, stabilization would not occur until about 2130, with a population of about 14 billion—nearly three times the 1990 size.

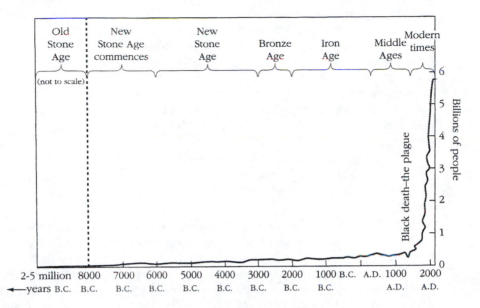

Figure 5–1 Growth of world population throughout human history. Data prior to 1800 are estimates; data from 1800 from various sources.

Increases by Billions. The time it has taken for the human population to increase by increments of one billion has shortened dramatically over the course of recent history:

> From 0 to 1 billion—1800, or 2 million to 5 million years (estimated)
> From 1 billion to 2 billion—1930, or 130 years
> From 2 billion to 3 billion—1960, or 30 years
> From 3 billion to 4 billion—1975, or 15 years
> From 4 billion to 5 billion—1987, or 12 years
> From 5 billion to 6 billion—1999, or 12 years (based on present trends)

Doubling Time. **Doubling time** indicates the number of years in which a population would double in size if the then present growth rates were to continue. For example, a population of 1 million with a constant rate of growth and a 10-year doubling time would reach 2 million in 10 years, 4 million in 20 years, 8 million in 30 years, and so on.

The method of determining doubling time is derived directly from the exponential formula for continuous compounding used, for example, in computing money left on deposit in a savings bank. Doubling time for a population is calculated by dividing 69.3 (or 70 in round numbers) by the population's growth rate expressed as a percent. Thus, if the growth rate is 2 percent a year, the doubling time would be approximately 35 years (70/2 = 35, or more precisely, 69.3/2 = 34.7). Likewise, if the interest rate on your deposit were 10 percent a year, the initial deposit would double in 6.9 years.

It is important to note that projections of doubling time in the future are just that—projections. Whether such estimates are realized will depend on a host of factors such as birth and death rates, age structure, and migration. Nonetheless, the use of doubling time gives a quick approximation of the future or a retrospective on the past. For example, applying this concept to the human population, we can see the dramatic reduction in the time it has taken to double the human population in the past (actual numbers and years) and the projected doubling time based on trends since 1965:

> From 0.75 billion to 1.6 billion—1750–1900, or 150 years (actual)
> From 1.6 billion to 3.3 billion—1900–1965, or 65 years (actual)
> From 3.3 billion to 7.0 billion—1965–2005, or 40 years (projection)

In 1982, when the population was 4.5 billion and the growth rate 1.7 percent a year, the world's population was projected to double in 41 years; in 1990, when the world's population stood at 5.3 billion and the growth rate 1.8, the doubling time was projected to be 39 years (or approximately in the year 2030). At that rate, and given no other demographic changes, the world's population would be 10.6 billion in 2029, 21.2 billion in 2068, and about 30 billion in 2107!

However, the United Nations Population Division's assessment is that the world's population is stabilizing sooner than previously thought. New information on fertility rates (the number of children women bear), for example, indicates that these rates are now lower in many areas; for example, in South Central Asia, the fertility rate dropped from a projection of 4.12 in 1994 to 3.74 in 1996. As a result, in only two years, the United Nations estimated world population in 2050 dropped in 1996 to between 7.7 and 11.2 billion from between 7.9 and 11.9 in 1994 (Haub 1997).

The growth rate of the human population peaked in 1965 at almost 2 percent, the doubling time then being 35 years (Table 5–1). It has been dropping since that time, and by 1996, it had dropped to 1.5 percent, for a doubling time of 47 years. The United Nations has projected a drop to 0.93 percent in the period 2020–2025, for a doubling time of 75 years. Given those projections, the world's population would be about 12 billion in 2047 and 16 billion in 2100. It is pertinent to note, however, that the decline in growth rate stagnated in the 1980s (Horiuchi 1992).

TABLE 5–1 Annual Rates of Population Growth (in percent)

Region	1950–1955	1960–1965	1975–1980	1990	1996
World	1.77	1.99	1.81	1.80	1.50
More developed countries	1.28	1.19	0.67	0.50	0.10
Less developed countries	2.00	2.35	2.21	2.10	2.20

Source: Data from various publications of the Population Reference Bureau, Inc.

Regional Population Growth. While the global picture of human population growth conveys certain characteristics, that of regional and even local populations is quite different. Shanghai, for example, had a population of 5.8 million in 1950, 14.3 million in 1980, and is projected to have nearly 24 million in 2000; by contrast, London's population of 10.4 million in 1950 shrank to 10 million in 1980 and is expected to be less than 10 million in 2000.

The most striking difference in the projected growth of the human population is that which exists between the developing regions of the world (Africa, South Asia, Latin America) and the developed regions (Europe, North America, the former USSR) (Figure 5–2 and Table 5–2).

Based on United Nations data, by 2025 the world's population is projected to increase by 2.5 billion from its 5.7 billion level of 1995. Of this projected increase, less than 200 million (6 percent) is expected to be in the developed countries, and 2.3 billion (94 percent) in developing countries. More pointedly, 70 percent of this increase is projected to take place in 20 less developed countries (increases in millions in parentheses): India (592), China (357), Nigeria (188), Pakistan (144), Bangladesh (119), Brazil (95), Indonesia (83), Ethiopia (66), Iran (66), Zaire (64), Mexico (62), Tanzania (58), Kenya (53), Viet Nam (51), Philippines (49), Egypt (40), Uganda (37), Sudan (34), Turkey (34), and South Africa (28).

India's 1995 population of 931 million, with an annual rate of increase of 1.9, is projected to double to 1.86 billion in 36 years, the year 2031. By contrast, China, which now has the largest population of any nation (1.2 billion), is projected to have 1.7 billion people by that date because its annual rate of increase is considerably less, namely 1.1.

Figure 5–2 Human population growth in developing and developed countries, 1750–2100. Data beyond 1985 are projections. (Redrawn by permission from T. W. Merrick. 1986. *Population Bulletin* 41(2) World population in transition. Population Reference Bureau, Washington, DC.)

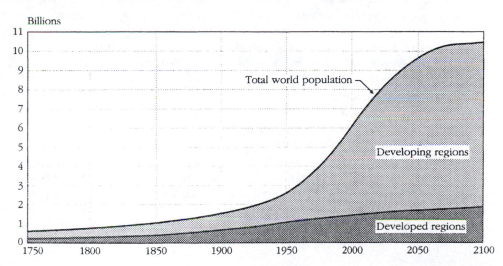

TABLE 5–2   Population Estimates from 1980 to 2025 from Major Areas and Regions of the World

Area	*Population (millions)*							
	1980	*1985*	*1990*	*1995*	*2000*	*2010*	*2020*	*2025*
World	4,453	4,842	5,248	5,677 (5,702)	6,123	6,987	7,793	8,162
Africa	476	553	645	753 (720)	877	1,170	1,488	1,642
Latin America	362	406	453	501 (481)	550	647	742	787
North America	252	263	275	287 (293)	298	319	339	348
East Asia	1,182	1,252	1,317	1,390 (1,442)	1,470	1,589	1,662	1,696
South Asia	1,408	1,572	1,740	1,909 (2,008)	2,074	2,379	2,654	2,771
Europe	484	492	499	505 (729)	510	515	518	518
Oceania	23	25	27	29 (28)	30	34	38	40
USSR	265	279	291	303	314	334	352	361

Source: Based on medium estimates and projections of the United Nations as assessed in 1982. Figures in parentheses for 1995 are estimates by the Population Reference Bureau, Inc.

In addition to the projections of number of people in different regions of the world, it is important to consider the factor of density (Table 5–3), especially given its role in regulating populations in general. Certainly, one should anticipate different sets of problems in regions with low density but high growth rates (Africa, Latin America) compared with those having low density and low growth rates (North America, the former USSR).

Regional Age Structure.   These strikingly different growth patterns are reflected, as you would expect, in their age structures (Figure 5–3). Characteristically, as you can see, about 40 percent of the population is under 15 years of age in the developing countries.

Comparison of the age structure in these six major regions of the world between 1965 and 1990 allows for several significant observations: (1) the age structures of Europe and North America have become discernably urn-shaped (i.e., a progressively more stabilized population edging toward diminishing size). These changes, more marked in North America's age structure than in Europe's, are the result of a considerable drop in birth rate with the result that the prereproductive proportion of the populations has dropped from 25 to 20 percent in Europe and, more dramatically, from 32 to 21 percent in North America. (2) Age structure in the USSR (data were projected just prior to the dissolution of that nation into its several nation states) has moved to a more definite bell shape, symbolic of a stabilized or stabilizing population with a marked increase in postreproductives and decrease in prereproductives. The trend suggests that some of the nations formerly making up the USSR are moving toward an urn-shaped age structure. (3) Virtually no change has occurred in the heavily prereproductive age structure of South Asian and African populations in spite of increased efforts at birth control that, in some large measure, have been countered by increased survival of children because of improved nutrition, sanitation, and health care. (4) In Latin America, there has been a marked drop in

TABLE 5–3 Basic Demographic Measures of the Major Areas and Regions of the World, 1995

	Birth Rate	Death Rate	Average Annual Rate of Growth	Doubling Time (years)	Total Population (millions)[a]	Total Area (10^6 km^2)	Density per km^2	Per Capita Gross National Product ($US)
Total World	24	9	1.5	46	5,771 (32/6)	135	42.4	4,740
Africa	41	13	2.8	25	7,732 (44/3)	30	24.4	660
North America	15	9	0.6	114	295 (22/13)	22	13.4	25,220
Europe	11	11	-0.1	0	728 (1.5/19)	5	145.6	12,310
Asia	24	8	1.6	43	3,501 (32/5)	27	129.7	2,150
Latin America	26	7	1.9	36	486 (35/5)	21	23.1	3,290
Oceania	19	7	1.1	60	29 (26/10)	9	3.2	13,770

[a]Figures in parentheses indicate percentage under age 15/over age 65.

Source: Based in part on 1995 *World Population Data Sheet,* Population Reference Bureau, Inc.

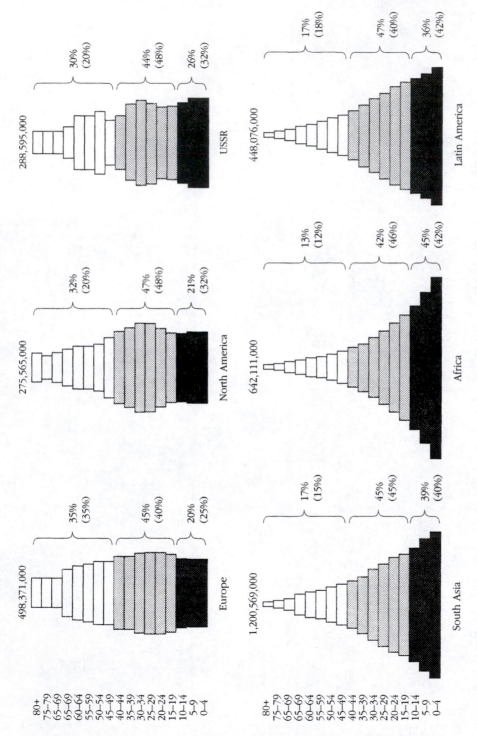

Figure 5-3 Age structure in human populations in the major areas of the world based on a medium projection by the United Nations from the estimated 1988 population. Each segment in the horizontal scale represents 1 percent of the total population; black bars are the prereproductive groups, gray bars the reproductive groups, and clear bars the postreproductive groups. The numbers at the top of each age structure are the projected population for 1990, and the percentages within the parentheses are the proportions of the population as of 1965. (Adapted from United Nations Population Studies no. 122. 1991. *The sex and age distributions of population. The 1990 revision of the United Nations global population estimates and projections.*)

prereproductives, suggesting a progressive move toward a bell-shaped age structure indicative of a stabilizing population.

Median Age. While population pyramids show the general shape of age structure, they do not provide rates or measures that can be compared over time with other populations. However, **median age,** the age at which exactly half the population is younger and half is older, does provide such a measure. In general, developing societies have rapidly growing populations with low median ages, while developed societies have slow-growing or near-stationary populations with high median ages. For example, in 1990, Jordan had a median age of 16, compared with 37 for Denmark (McFalls 1991).

Between 1967 and 1990, the median age of the U.S. population rose from 28 to 32.9 and is projected to reach 39.3 by 2020 and 41.8 by 2030. Several factors are causal: the large baby boom population (those born between 1945 and 1965) is in or approaching middle age; the proportion of children is declining because of low fertility; and the increased longevity brought about by better nutrition, sanitation, and health care is resulting in an increase in the population of the elderly (also see the later section on the graying of the world's population).

NATALITY AND MORTALITY

With this background of past and projected human population growth, we can address the two forces that are behind these changes, natality, or birth rate, and mortality, or death rate. Both natality and mortality are calculated on number per 1,000 individuals per year; thus, natality is the number of births per 1,000 people per year and mortality the number of deaths per 1,000 people per year.

As you may have already surmised, the more important of these two opposing forces in the growth of human populations to date has been the reduction in mortality (Figure 5–4). Birth rates have dropped from about 40 to 15 since the middle of the nineteenth century in developed countries while remaining at a level of about 40 until the middle of the twentieth century in developing countries. Birth rates in developing countries, while dropping, generally stand twice as high as those in developed countries. The death rate in developing countries, however, has dropped dramatically since the middle of the twentieth century and is now close to that of developed countries on a worldwide scale. With a continuing high birth rate but a dramatically reduced death rate, the gap between the two, which reflects the increase in population, has been increasing. This is the explanation behind the projected growth in developing countries, as seen in Figure 5–2.

Changes in Life Expectancy

As explained in the previous chapter, **life expectancy** is the estimated life span at the time of birth. Life expectancy worldwide, for example, increased from age 61 in 1980 (72 for developed countries and 57 for developing countries) to age 64 in 1990 (74 for developed countries and 61 for developing countries).

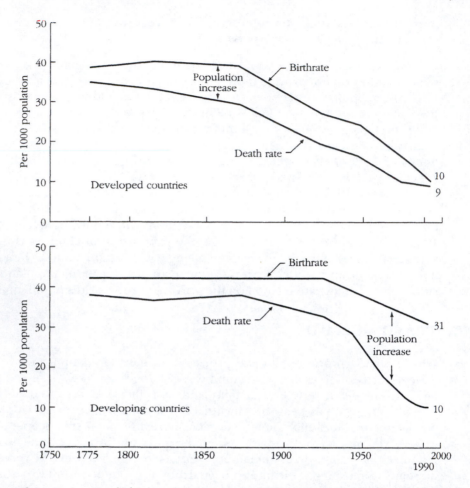

Figure 5–4 Crude birth and death rates in developed and developing countries from 1775 to 1990. (Based on United Nations and Population Reference Bureau, Inc. estimates)

For insurance purposes, life expectancy, based on survivorship curves converted to actuarial tables, is estimated at any given age, typically the age at which a policy is issued. Thus, at birth, life expectancy in the United States was age 76 in 1995 but at age 35 it drops to 41 (meaning that at age 35, one would be expected on average to live an additional 41 years) whereas at age 85 it drops to 6.

In the short span since the Pilgrims landed on Plymouth Rock, life expectancy at birth in the United States advanced from

33 to 47 by 1900
47 to 60 by 1930
60 to 71 by 1971
71 to 76 by 1995

There have been and continue to be significant differences in life expectancy by gender and ethnicity (Figure 5–5). For example, based on 1988 death certificates, life expectancy for Caucasians in the United States stood at 75.6 (up from 75.3 in 1984) but at 69.2 for African Americans, the latter figure being down from 69.7 in 1984. The reversal for African Americans seems to be related at least in part to the large increase in the number of early deaths caused by homicides, car accidents, drug abuse, and AIDS. This group has higher death rates from many ailments, including cancer, heart disease, stroke, diabetes, liver trouble, and kidney failure, suggesting that a combination of genetics, diet, and social factors contribute to the lower life expectancy.

Olshansky et al. (1990) suggest that for life expectancy at birth to increase from present levels to what has been referred to as the average biological limit to life (age 85), mortality rates from all causes of death would need to decline at all ages by 55 percent, and at ages 50 and over by 60 percent. Inasmuch as such rates of decline are not considered likely, it is improbable that life expectancy at birth will exceed the age of 85.

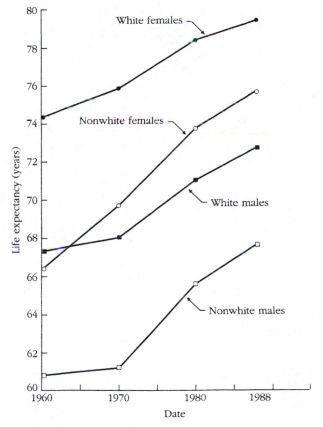

Figure 5–5   Life expectancy at birth in the United States, 1960–1988. (Data from *Statistical Abstracts of the United States 1990.)*

Mortality in the United States

In the period 1910 to 1975, the total death rate in the United States, all ages included, dropped from 14.7 to 9.0 and has been sustained at that level (Figure 5–6). (The dramatic rise in death rates in 1918 seen in Figure 5–6 is attributed to a devastating flu pandemic that affected virtually the entire world.) During the 1910–1975 period, a differential in mortality by gender and ethnicity nonetheless existed, as in the case of life expectancy. For example, in the period 1900 to 1988, the total death rate dropped from 17.2 to 8.8, but for nonwhite males the drop was to 9.9, for white males 9.6, for white females 8.6, and for nonwhite females 7.3.

The mortality or survivorship curve for humans in developed countries, as noted in the previous chapter, is Type I, which is characterized by a relatively high infant mortality, a low death rate until about 50, and then an increasing rate. **Infant mortality** is defined as the number of deaths per 1,000 individuals between birth and 1 year of age. Again, as expected from the foregoing discussion of life expectancy and mortality in general, infant mortality also differs by gender and ethnicity; in general, the drop from 1900 to 1971 was by 90 percent, and from 1971 to 1987 by 50 percent:

	1900	*1971*	*1987*
White females	142.6	14.6	7.6
White males	175.9	19.1	9.6
Nonwhite females	299.5	26.2	13.6
Nonwhite males	369.3	32.3	16.9

Figure 5–6 Birth and death rates in the United States, 1910–1996. (Based on data of the Population Reference Bureau, Inc.)

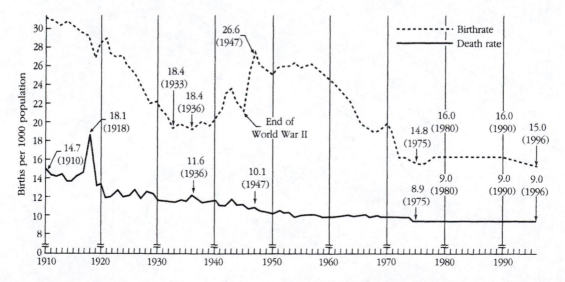

Mortality on a Global Level

These data again underscore the significant drop in mortality, in this case at the infant level in the United States and, as seen in Table 5–4, throughout the world. Nonetheless, infant mortality in the United States in 1996 (7.5) was in twenty-seventh place and more than twice that of Iceland (3.4). It varied from seven in affluent suburbs up to 60 for migrant farm workers. In 1980, the United States ranked sixteenth with a rate of 13, the same as what was then East Germany. Given the leadership the United States has shown in so many areas, its infant mortality rate is not laudable.

The 1980 infant mortality rates varied widely between developed and developing countries: in Africa, from a low of 35 in Mauritius to a high of 198 in Gambia; in Asia, from a low of 8 in Japan to a high of 206 in Afghanistan; in Latin America, from a low of 15 in Jamaica to a high of 168 in Bolivia.

TABLE 5–4   The 30 Countries with the Lowest and Highest Infant Mortality Rates in 1996, Compared with Their 1980 Rates

	Lowest			*Highest*	
	1996	*1980*		*1996*	*1980*
Iceland	3.4	11	Afghanistan	163	205
Singapore	4.0	12	Mozambique	148	148
Japan	4.2	8	Sierra Leone	143	208
Norway	4.4	9	Guinea-Bisseau	140	208
Sweden	4.4	8	Guinea	139	165
Finland	4.7	9	Angola	137	154
Hong Kong	5.0	12	Malawi	134	149
Switzerland	5.1	10	Niger	123	200
Taiwan	5.1	25	Mauritania	123	187
Luxembourg	5.3	11	Chad	122	165
Denmark	5.4	9	Somalia	122	177
Austria	5.5	15	Bhutan	121	150
Netherlands	5.5	10	Ethiopia	120	162
Germany	5.5	14	Uganda	115	120
Liechtenstein	5.6	?	Liberia	113	148
Australia	5.8	12	Burundi	112	140
Ireland	5.9	16	Cambodia	111	212
Macao	6.0	78	Rwanda	110	127
Martinique	6.0	32	Congo	109	180
Canada	6.2	12	Zaire	108	160
United Kingdom	6.2	14	Zambia	107	144
Netherlands Antilles	6.3	25	Mali	106	190
Slovenia	6.5	?	Djibouti	105	?
Israel	6.9	15	Eritrea	105	?
Spain	7.2	16	Equatorial Guinea	103	165
Brunei	7.4	20	Laos	102	175
United States	7.5	13	Central African Republic	97	190
Belgium	7.6	12	Gabon	95	?
Italy	8.3	18	Burkina Faso	94	?
Malta	9.1	16	Gambia	90	190

Source: Data from the 1980 and 1990 World Population Data Sheets, Population Reference Bureau, Inc.

Comparison of the 1996 and 1980 rates demonstrates some dramatic drops in infant mortality; others now "off the chart" include Bangladesh (88 to 153), Cameroon (65 to 157), Senegal (68 to 160), and Nigeria (68 to 157).

Natality in the United States

As the population of the United States surged between the mid-1940s and late 1970s (the so-called baby boom), natality actually declined from a peak of 26.6 in 1947 to a low of 14.8 in 1979 (Figure 5–6). During this period, mortality moved downward slowly from 10 to 9. Had the peak birth rate continued and been accompanied by low mortality, the population of the United States would have reached over 370 million by the year 2000 instead of the present estimate of about 325 million.

A rather popular notion is that birth rate is tied to economic conditions. In point of fact, in the United States, the lowest birth rates prior to World War II occurred during the Great Depression of the 1930s. However, natality began and continued a quite dramatic drop in the late 1950s and into the mid-1960s, a period of unprecedented prosperity. Contrariwise, in Sweden during a period of economic depression (1930–1936), the net reproduction rate dropped to 0.81, below the replacement level of 1 (Davis 1967).

With any given rate of natality, the total number of births in general is a reflection of the total population size. That is, the more units of 1,000 individuals in a population, the greater the number of births. For example, in 1920, when the population of the United States was 92 million, there were 2.8 million live births; in 1957, when the population was about 170 million, the highest number of live births was recorded, namely, 4.3 million. Although the total population continued to grow after that date, natality continued a more or less steady decline until 1980, when it reached its lowest point, with 3.6 million live births (the population then being 227 million). Although the total population continued a slow rate of growth after 1980, reaching 249 million in 1990, the number of live births continued to climb, peaking in that year at 4.2 million. A considerable component of this latter rise is a dramatic surge in births to unmarried women, particularly striking among unmarried teenagers, where the rate has tripled (Figure 5–7).

Fertility Rate.   These changes are, in large measure, a function of the **fertility rate,** the number of live births per 1,000 women between the ages of 15 and 49. In 1933, the fertility rate was 76, increased to 123 in 1957, and dropped steadily to 97 in 1965 and to a low of 65.4 in 1984, where it has hovered since.

Inasmuch as the women born between the late 1940s and early 1960s, the some 50 million so-called baby boomers, were or will be in their fertile period in the 1970s to 2000, their impact on fertility rate, natality, and population growth is regarded as unknown if not problematic (Bouvier and DeVita 1991).

Factors Affecting Natality.   During the preindustrial/technological period, when agriculture was the economic mainstay, large families were an advan-

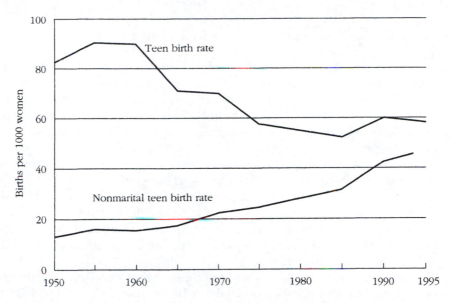

Figure 5–7   Birth rates for all U.S. teens and all unmarried teens (ages 15–19), 1950–1995. (Redrawn by permission from Population Reference Bureau, *Population Today,* Washington, DC.)

tage in tending to the many needs of farming. As the manufacturing economy emerged, this being capital-intensive rather than labor-intensive, increasing urbanization in more limited space occurred, a disadvantage for large families. The downward trends in both natality and fertility rates indicate the operation of self-imposed control, trends that were well underway before such contemporary family-planning agents as the contraceptive pill/injection, the intrauterine device (IUD), and abortion were widely employed (Westoff 1986).

Abortion, an intensely divisive and emotional public issue in the United States (and elsewhere), has not always been so. In the early decades of the republic, abortion was legal under colonial common law and remained so under American common law provided that the pregnancy was terminated before the perception of fetal movement, about the midpoint of gestation. It was primarily the recourse for women "wronged by duplicitous suitors" or whose pregnancies were the result of illicit relationships. In the 1830s and 1840s, abortionists openly advertised in the daily press, as did pharmaceutical firms promoting their abortifacients. Physicians of the time estimated abortion rates at about one of every four live births, a number strikingly close to that of the 1960s and 1970s!

During the mid-1800s, a number of forces joined to restrict access to abortion: fear for the safety of women, negative reaction to overt advertising, concern about falling birth rates, and the aspiration of medical practitioners to upgrade their profession. Actually it was the American Medical Association, founded in 1847, that brought the greatest pressure for legal change. Curiously,

120 years later, 87 percent of American physicians favored liberalization of antiabortion laws!

The period from the mid-1880s to nearly a century later was marked by abortion being driven underground, where it continued to be widespread, but decidedly with more potentially deleterious consequences under often less than optimal circumstances. The 1950s and 1960s was a period of increasing effectiveness for American women, who called for control over their own reproductive processes. This was coupled with an increased recognition of the inequality of access to abortion: the wealthy and well connected could arrange for safe abortions discretely; the poor and uninformed couldn't. The key legal change came in the historic 1973 U.S. Supreme Court ruling in *Roe* v. *Wade,* which conveyed to women, as part of their constitutional right to privacy, the option to terminate a pregnancy prior to the point at which a fetus could survive outside the womb. In effect, this ruling returned the nation to the status of abortion in the days of the early republic.

Prior to *Roe* v. *Wade,* as a result of a number of state-level legalizations, it is estimated that the number of legal abortions rose from 200,000 in 1970 to 500,000 in 1971 (Sklar and Berkov 1975). After *Roe* v. *Wade,* the number increased to over 1.5 million by 1980, about where it has remained since (Cates 1982) (e.g., the number in 1988 was 1.6 million). As readers know, the abortion issue remains socially, religiously, and politically charged, especially in the United States. It was paramount during the debates of the 1994 United Nations World Conference on Population and Development, with some Catholic and Islamic nations offering the greatest antiabortion protests. This conference reached consensus that gender equity is a major key in curbing population growth (Linden 1994).

Demographic Transition

The preceding discussion of the decline in both mortality and natality in the United States would find its parallel in other industrialized countries, especially during the nineteenth century. This pattern has led to the characterization **demographic transition:** as countries become industrialized there is a decline in mortality followed by a decline in natality. Such countries move from fast to slow to zero growth and eventually decline in population size (an urn-shaped age structure). The transition typically occurs over several decades.

In the preindustrial stage, high natality compensates for high mortality; the population as a whole grows very slowly or not at all. Shortly after industrialization begins, mortality drops because of better nutrition, sanitation, and health care, while natality remains high; the result is rapid population growth. As industrialization proceeds and the need for extra hands becomes not only unnecessary but disadvantageous and even dysfunctional, especially in cities, natality decreases, approaching the mortality rate. Population growth continues but at a slower rate. This period is characteristic of countries like the United States, Japan, the former Soviet Union, Canada, Australia, and most of industrialized Western Europe. In much later stages of industrialization, the birth rate declines further and equals or falls below the death rate; zero population growth or even a decline in size characterizes the population as is seen today in countries such as Austria, Germany, Sweden, Hungary, and Denmark.

Classical demographic transition, a consequence of industrialization, is thus characterized by a decline in birth rate after economic growth brings improvements in living conditions, including education. As we will see in the next section, birth rates in developing countries have fallen and are falling in spite of the absence of the economic improvement that brings improved living conditions. Furthermore, the decline in birth rates has moved over the course of years rather than decades. The growing influence and scope of family-planning programs, new contraceptive technologies, increasing gender equity, and the educational power of mass media appear to have played a major role in this non-classical demographic transition (Livi-Bacci 1992; Robey et al. 1993).

Natality on a Global Level

At several points throughout this chapter, the discrepancy between the decline in natality and mortality between developed and developing countries and regions has been noted. While mortality is about the same for developing and developed areas, namely, about 10, natality remains twice as high, about 30 for developing regions and 15 for the developed ones. From another perspective, the number of births to women between 15 and 49 years of age tends to be well below 2 in developed countries and much above 2, in some countries greater than 7, in developing regions (Table 5–5). These differences in reproduction translate to the startling estimate that while the world's population is expected to double to some 11 billion by 2037, 96 percent of the increase will occur in the developing parts of the world!

These apocalyptic doomsday projections hold even though there have been changes in the reproductive behavior of women in developing nations wherein the birth rate has declined by one-third since the mid-1960s, women having an average of four instead of six children. In some nations, the decline has been dramatic: in Thailand, from 4.6 children in 1975 to 2.3 in 1987, in Colombia, from 4.7 children in 1975 to 2.3 in 1987; a decline of 46 percent between 1971 and 1991 in Indonesia and of 31 percent in Morocco from 1980 to 1992 (Robey et al. 1993).

The major factors that have brought about these changes are the effective use of contraception, including sterilization; an increase in the age at which women first marry; the length of time after childbirth that a woman cannot conceive; increased career opportunities and possibly the improved status of women; and abortion. In other words, family planning, though that term is too often used in the more restrictive sense of contraception. Abortions, for example, are estimated to number 25 million annually, most performed under illegal or unsafe conditions, or both (Henshaw and van Vort 1992). Contraception includes both traditional (e.g., abstinence using the rhythm method and

TABLE 5–5 Countries with the Lowest and Highest Number of Children Born to Women Between the Ages of 15 and 49

Lowest			
1.5 or Below	*1.6 to 1.8*	*1.9 to 2.1*	*2.2 to 2.5*
1.3 Italy	1.6 Belgium	1.9 Cuba	2.2 Guadaloupe
1.4 Austria	Denmark	2.0 Bulgaria	Ireland
Hong Kong	Japan	Malta	Puerto Rico
Luxembourg	Portugal	Mauritius	2.3 Bahamas
West Germany	Switzerland	Netherlands	China
1.5 Greece	South Korea	Antilles	Iceland
Netherlands	1.7 Antigua and Barbuda	New Zealand	Romania
Spain	Canada	Singapore	Sri Lanka
	East Germany	Sweden	2.4 Cyprus
	Finland	United States	Jamaica
	1.8 Australia	Yugoslavia	Reunion
	Barbados	2.1 Czechoslovakia	Uruguay
	France	Martinique	2.5 Chile
	Hungary	Poland	North Korea
	Norway		
	Taiwan		

Highest			
6.0 to 6.3	*6.4 to 6.7*	*6.8 to 7.1*	*7.2 and Above*
6.0 Congo	6.4 Angola	6.8 Syria	7.2 Burkina Faso
6.1 Algeria	Gambia	7.0 Benin	Oman
Namibia	Liberia	Burundi	Saudi Arabia
Nepal	Mozambique	Gaza	Togo
6.2 Ethiopia	Senegal	Iraq	Zambia
Guinea	Sudan	South Yemen	7.4 Cote D'Ivoire
Swaziland	6.5 Mauritania	7.1 Afghanistan	Uganda
Zaire	Nigeria	Comoros	7.6 North Yemen
6.3 Iran	Sierra Leone	Niger	7.7 Malawi
Ghana	6.6 Djibouti	Tanzania	8.3 Rwanda
Solomon Islands	Madagascar		
	Maldives		
	Somalia		
	6.7 Kenya		
	Pakistan		

Source: Data from *1990 World Population Data Report,* Population Reference Bureau, Inc.

withdrawal of the penis before ejaculation) and modern (e.g., IUDs, condoms, sterilization) methods. Modern contraception is practiced by 54 percent of women in Asia (39 percent if China is excluded), 53 percent in Latin America, 30 to 40 percent in the Muslim countries of the Middle East and North Africa, 48 percent in countries in the southern tip of Africa, and less than 10 percent in mid-Africa. These numbers compare with 65 to 75 percent in North America and Western Europe, but only 20 percent in the former Soviet Union (Doyle 1996). Sterilization is the most common method of family planning except in Africa and the Middle East (Robey et al. 1993).

The expected addition of some 6 billion people over the next century in Africa, Asia, and Latin America compounds the task of reducing poverty, avoiding malnutrition and starvation, and bringing about sustainable development. John Bongaarts (1994b) of the Population Council explores in depth three broad policy options to slow this population explosion. These include: (1) reducing unwanted pregnancies by strengthening family-planning programs (the unmet need for contraception is nearly 25 percent in sub-Saharan Africa) through knowledge of and access to family-planning services; (2) reducing the demand for large families through investments in human development, including raising educational levels, improving the economic, social, and legal status of women, and decreasing infant and child mortality; and (3) interrupting population momentum, that is, the tendency of population size to increase for some time after fertility reaches a level consistent with long-range population stability. This can be achieved by additional declines in lifetime fertility to below the replacement level and raising the average age of women at childbearing.

These are formidable objectives fraught with political, economic, social, and often religious overtones. As we will see in the final section of this chapter, they do warrant careful consideration in view of the likely untoward consequences of the current burgeoning rate of population growth, particularly in developing regions of the world.

Natality at the Local Level

There are great differences in natality among populations; to understand why these differences occur requires study at the local level. Many of the differences are due to cultural practices, although some are due to differences in **fecundity,** an individual's biological capacity to reproduce.

Biological Factors and Fecundity.   Biological factors that may decrease fecundity in a population include poor nutrition and health, shortened length of the reproductive period, and prolonged periods of lactation. Women who have very low levels of body fat often stop menstruating and thus temporarily lose their ability to reproduce. This has been noted in female athletes in wealthy societies as well as in women suffering from malnutrition (Ellison et al. 1986; Frisch 1987). A classic study of the effect of malnutrition on natality centered on the impact of the Dutch famine of 1944–1945 on birth rate in that population (Stein and Susser 1975). There have also been reports of seasonal differences in births among some human populations, differences that have been linked to seasonal differences in food supply (Leslie and Fry 1989).

A more important effect of malnutrition on a population's natality may be in delaying the age of menarche, that is, the onset of menstruation or the beginning of a female's reproductive years. Poor health may contribute to delayed menarche (Gage et al. 1989). While less is known about the effects of nutrition and health on the age of menopause, that is, when women end their reproductive years (Bongaarts 1980), there is some evidence for a younger average age of menopause among malnourished groups (Gage et al. 1989). Interruptions to a woman's reproductive span can also affect her total reproductive span. Lactation has been observed to lengthen the period after pregnancy before the return of menstrual cycles (McElroy and Townsend 1989), thus increasing the time reproductive life is interrupted.

Cultural Factors and Natality.   Cultural factors appear to have a much greater effect on natality than biological ones. Most directly, abortion and infanticide limit reported natality (for example, rarely are infanticides officially reported as births). Other cultural factors that affect natality include notions about extramarital sex, customary age of marriage, remarriage during widowhood or after divorce, commonality of divorce, coital frequency, postpartum (or other) sex taboos (that is, prescribed periods when people are not to engage in sex), customary length for breast-feeding, as well as contraception (Moore et al. 1980).

Contemporary Japan, among other places, demonstrates the interplay of cultural factors in regulating natality (Jitsukawa and Djerassi 1994). In spite of its own medical advisory committee's recommendation in 1986, the Ministry of Health and Welfare by 1994 had not legalized the use of a low-dose steroid oral contraceptive. The ban has been attributed to concern that legalization would degrade sexual mores and to the medical community's fear of losing several hundred million dollars derived from performing abortions, the income from which is frequently undisclosed to tax authorities. Some critics of the ban see it as one more example of the government's policy toward favoring procreation rather than contraception because of the worry regarding the aging of the Japanese population (see the later section, "Graying of the World's Population"). Not unlike their counterparts in the United States, a nationalistic religious organization, *Seicho no Ie,* opposes the relatively easy access to abortion permitted under Japanese law, while abortion and the use of condoms and the *Ogino* calendar rhythm method are supported by feminists over more effective female methods such as oral contraceptives. Many feminists in Japan see the "Pill" as requiring women, rather than men, to take full responsibility for birth control and view the artificial regulation of the natural hormonal cycle with synthetic steroids as a violation of body ecology by a technology developed by males. The stalemate results in an almost total dependence in Japan on condoms, the rhythm method, and abortion (about a half million a year).

People's perceptions about reproductive biology can also affect natality. People from cultural groups in several countries, including Afghanistan, India, Pakistan, and Peru (Nichter and Nichter 1987), believe that a woman is most fertile during or soon after her menses. This belief is related to the notion that the womb is usually closed but opens to allow menstrual blood to escape and sperm to enter. A possible consequence of this belief is the failure of rhythm methods because of individual variability or, alternatively, to reduced fertility if people try

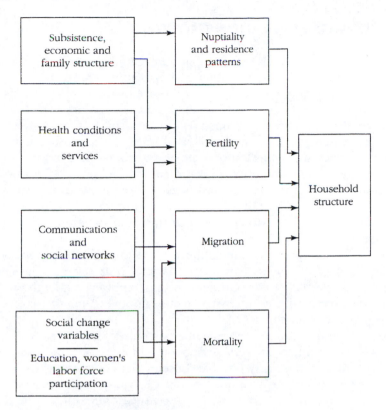

Figure 5–8   Sociocultural factors in demographic decisions related to household structure. (Redrawn by permission from The demography of Samoan populations by S. F. Harbison. In *The changing Samoans: Behavior and health in transition*, edited by Paul T. Baker, Joel Hanna, et al., 63–92. Copyright © 1986 by Oxford University Press, Inc. Used by permission of Oxford University Press, Inc.)

to maximize chances of fertility by confining sexual activity to within a few days of a woman's menses.

Demographic events such as fertility, marriage, and migration may be viewed as the result of decisions by individuals (Hull 1983). These decisions are not simply determined by cultural factors but rather by an individual's attempts to maximize goals in the context of his or her cultural traditions (Harbison 1986). Figure 5–8 shows the types of factors that help determine household structure for people in a given cultural group.

It is evident that an understanding of the influence of the human population increase on a global level requires a deeper understanding of the types of biological and cultural influences at the level of individual populations.

IMPLICATIONS OF POPULATION GROWTH

It should be intuitively evident that a burgeoning world population carries with it both cultural and environmental implications. More people create the need for more housing, more schools, and more health care as well as more food and better distribution of it, more water, more wastes, more fuel—more, more, more. Some of these additional demands create secondary ones such as the potential for increased pollution of air, soil, and water. On the other hand, more of some of the foregoing means less of some other things—less space for each individual, fewer forests or woodlots as they are cut for fuel or to accommodate more agriculture, and so on. More can mean less. More people in a given amount of space can lead to social and political unrest and emigration. In the state of global interconnectedness that exists today, such unrest anywhere carries implications elsewhere.

All this notwithstanding, there are those who see population growth as beneficial to economic growth, the latter being regarded a sine qua non for "progress" (Simon 1990). Other economists, however, take the position that such growth carries with it an environmental impoverishment that is too often taken for progress (Repetto 1990).

Without assuming the role of a pessimistic Cassandra (recall it was she who was given prophetic powers by Apollo in an attempt to win her love), let us look at but three of the many possible consequences of current world growth—aging, nutrition, and desertification, the first carrying significant cultural implications and the latter two environmental ones. At least one other issue has already been touched upon—controlling population growth through family planning. All these issues, and the many not discussed, are substantial topics in themselves and about which an abundance of literature exists. Here we will but highlight some aspects of the impact of population growth on the three selected topics.

GRAYING OF THE WORLD'S POPULATION

With the inroads being made on fertility and mortality, a consequence of major magnitude is beginning to be felt worldwide, namely, the aging of the human population (Holden 1996). Life expectancy has been increasing in all the developed countries, with Japan leading the pack since 1980, Japanese men now having a life expectancy of about 76 years and women about 82 (Oshima 1996). The number of elderly (those over 65 years of age) is growing at the rate of 2.4 percent a year, for a doubling time of 29 years. In 1985, there were 290 million elderly in the world, with a projection of 410 million by the year 2000 (Bureau of the Census 1987). In 1995, the estimate grew to 342 million.

By international standards, a population is "aged" when persons aged 65 or older account for more than 7 percent of the total population. Accordingly, Sweden is the "oldest country" in the sense of having the highest percentage of elderly (17 percent). Fifty-four percent of the elderly live in developing countries, a proportion that is projected to reach 69 percent by 2025. Based on estimates by the United Nations in 1988 (Martin 1991), current and projected percentages of the elderly in selected locations are

	1995	2025
Japan	16	23.7
United States	16	19.6
Singapore	7	19.1
China	6	13.0
South Korea	5	13.9
Malaysia	4	9.3

China's rapid transition to low fertility (i.e., the one-child family policy) and low mortality result in a potential 4-2-1 population pyramid of four grandparents, two parents, and one child. With mortality at an already low level, natality will have a greater influence on population aging in China (Tien et al. 1992). This can be seen in the present figures and projected increase in the percentage of elderly: 1982—4.9 percent; 1990—5.9 percent; 2000—7.0 percent; and 2025—13 percent. Numerically, these increases translate to 1980—50 million elderly; 1990—66 million (the combined populations of California, New York, Texas, and Florida—the four largest U.S. states); 2020—167 million, about one-quarter of the world's elderly (Tempest 1996). This increase has already placed a strain on the retirement pension system in China, which currently affects a relatively small portion of the population, largely those in urban areas.

Public policies dealing with aging range from attempts in Singapore to reverse it by encouraging more births, to efforts in Japan to accommodate it by increasing employment opportunities for older workers, thereby decreasing the impact on economic growth and public expenditures (Martin 1991). As noted in the section on cultural factors and natality, there is some reason to believe the Japanese government is encouraging procreation to offset this aging phenomenon (Jitsukawa and Djerassi 1994).

To date, the United States, whose elderly population is increasing more slowly than that in East Asia because of its longer postwar baby boom, has not developed any substantial policies for this inevitability. During the latter part of this century, the large U.S. baby boom population (those born between 1945 and 1965) will have contributed mightily to the economy, but this same population in but a few subsequent years will put a major strain on health care and most notably the Social Security System, the major burden passing on to the post–baby boom (sometimes called "baby bust") generation, which, because of a sharp drop in fertility rates, is much smaller. Perhaps there will be time to learn from our East Asian neighbors?

Cultures respond differently to their aging members. In the United States, there has been in general a negative connotation to aging and to the elderly. This view is markedly different from that common in many nonindustrialized cultures (Simmons 1970) and in Japan, where the elderly usually are respected (Palmore 1975). Generally speaking, there appears to be much diversity in the status of and attitudes toward the elderly within many cultural groups (Moore et al. 1980), status being related to many variables, including economics, family structure, dependency, health, and so on. Another factor that may weigh more heavily in the future is the sheer number of elderly in the society and of the very elderly (over age 75), a relatively new phenomenon to which cultures will have to adapt. It remains to be seen how different cultures will in fact adapt to the quite likely substantial increases of the elderly in their midst.

FEEDING THE HUMAN POPULATION

Whatever projections of human population growth are used, it is unquestionable that the world population will increase. Whether this increase will be to twice the world's 1990 size of 5.5 billion by 2040 or to 14 billion by 2080 depends on when the replacement level (i.e., one female being replaced by one offspring) is reached. However, even without this increase, the world has been subject to episodic starvation as well as both episodic and chronic malnutrition.

Extent of Starvation and Malnutrition

The World Bank (1986) has estimated that more than 700 million people, or about 13 percent of the world's population, lack enough food for an active and healthy life, with the largest concentrations in Asia and sub-Saharan Africa. More recent estimates place the number at 950 million people (i.e., about one in five people) chronically malnourished, that is, too hungry to lead active productive lives (McAfee 1990). Other estimates suggest that the number of hungry people increased five times faster in the 1980s than in the previous decade (World Food Council 1989). Still others have estimated that perhaps a quarter of the world's population goes hungry during at least some season of each year (Clark 1989). UNICEF (1990) estimated that over 150 million children under age 5 suffer from malnutrition; again, most of these children live in Asia and sub-Saharan Africa. Malnutrition and its related diseases are responsible for the death of as many as 15 million children a year (McAfee 1990).

In 1986, the World Bank estimated that between 340 million and 730 million people in developing countries lacked the income to ensure an adequate intake of dietary energy (Hendry 1988). Another way of stating this is that in 1980, 34 percent of the people in 87 developing countries did not obtain enough calories for an active working life, and 16 percent did not obtain enough calories to prevent stunted growth and serious health risks. About 80 percent of those who are undernourished live in countries with very low average incomes, two-thirds of the total residing in Asia and one-fifth in sub-Saharan Africa.

Malnutrition results from not enough food, a deficiency of one or more essential nutrients (e.g., protein, calcium, vitamin C), or genetic or environmental illness that interferes with digestion, absorption, or metabolism. (This topic will be covered in more detail in Chapter 9.) Too much food or too much of one type of nutrient is also regarded as a form of malnutrition and occurs primarily in the affluent parts of Western cultures in which obesity is all too common. The extent and demography of starvation and malnutrition suggest that the answer lies in both expanded production of food, particularly highly nutritious kinds, and more equitable distribution of that food.

Earth's Carrying Capacity

One of the more contentious debates in environmental circles revolves around carrying capacity of the planet, that is, the maximum number of people that can be supported on Earth (see Pulliam and Haddad 1994 for an extended discussion of carrying capacity). One finds a range of optimists and pessimists and a number between the two extremes (Bongaarts 1994a). Given the range of opinion based on different assumptions and sometimes conflicting data, it is not easy to develop a dispassionate position. We hope the following comes close.

Realistic Considerations.   Although a theoretical basis for estimating carrying capacity can be derived from a knowledge of energy flow in different ecosystems (see Chapter 13), a more realistic consideration of the Earth's carrying capacity is necessary. In 1984, the United Nations Food and Agriculture Organization analyzed soil and climate data from 117 developing countries to estimate the food production potential for 15 major crops at three different levels of farming practice: (1) low-input, or subsistence agriculture; (2) intermediate, with some modern technology, conservation measures, and improved cropping patterns; and (3), high-level, equivalent of farming practices in industrialized countries (Hendry 1988). Even though there are many limitations to the FAO study, it did show that from a global perspective, subsistence-level agriculture would have been capable of supporting more than double the 1975 population of 2 billion in the 117 countries. However, by the end of the century, the margin would have narrowed significantly. By contrast, intermediate levels of agriculture could theoretically support four times the population projected for the year 2000, and high-level inputs and practices nine times that population size.

At the national level, however, the FAO study found that of the 117 countries, 54 would have been unable to feed their 1975 population (more than 1 billion people) from subsistence-level agriculture. Intermediate-level agriculture would have reduced the number of countries at risk to 24 (these countries have 4 percent of the total population); high-technology agriculture would have led to only 13 countries being in critical condition (these have but 1 percent of the total population). The situation becomes exacerbated, according to this FAO study, for the projected population in the year 2000, when the number of critical countries would be increased to 64 at low-level agriculture, 28 at the intermediate level, and 17 at high levels.

Capacity of the Land.   The amount of arable and grazing land in the world amounts to about half the total land surface, exclusive of the ice-covered portions of Antarctica and Greenland (Table 5–6). Less than half of all arable

TABLE 5–6 Total Land Surface of the World Including Arable and Grazing Land

Land Surface	Hectares
Total land surface (exclusive of ice-covered portions of Antarctica and Greenland)	13.0×10^9
Unusable (deserts, mountains, tundra, sandy or lateritic soils)	6.6×10^9
Arable	
Currently in use	1.4×10^9
Currently not used	1.8×10^9
Grazing	
Currently in use	1.8×10^9
Currently not used	1.4×10^9

Source: Data from United Nations Food and Agriculture Organization (FAO), 1992, *FAO Production Yearbook* and other encyclopedic sources.

land and more than half of all grazing land are currently in use. Of the soil that is suitable for agriculture, only 11 percent has no limitations, that is, it is sufficiently rich in nutrients not to need fertilizers and has sufficient moisture so as not to require irrigation (Hendry 1988). Twenty-eight percent of potentially arable land would require irrigation, and 23 percent would require fertilization; the remaining 38 percent includes soils that are too shallow (22 percent), too wet (10 percent), or are permafrost (6 percent).

These limitations notwithstanding, there was a 179 percent increase in croplands between 1950 and 1990 (from 538×10^6 to $1,501 \times 10^6$ ha) and a 1 percent reduction in grasslands and pastureland over the same period (Repetto 1987). On a regional basis, the increase in cropland ranged from a low of −4 percent in Europe to a high of 841 percent in Asian developed countries. In Latin American and African nations, the substantial increase in cropland and pastureland was largely at the expense of forests, a topic treated later in this chapter.

On a worldwide basis, 1 ha of land currently supports about three people, compared with highly productive farmland, as in the U.S. Midwest, which can support 24 persons. Complicating the problem is the fact that much arable land is devoted to inedible or nonnutritive crops, such as cotton, tobacco, rubber, and coffee, or the production of food for poultry and livestock. This latter component increases in societies with improving economies. The rapidly expanding economy of China, for example, is leading to increased demand for foods that require a great deal of land to produce. About half to two-thirds of all currently used arable land, barring fertilization and irrigation, must lie fallow or is used for pasturage.

World Food Production

Food Production Needs. The current rate of increase of agricultural output in many developed countries is about 2 percent a year; to meet the needs of populations with moderate growth rates of about 2 percent a year, agricultural output must increase 3 to 4.5 percent (Wortman 1980). It is obvious that agricultural output must increase considerably more for those populations with higher growth rates. According to Crosson and Rosenberg (1989), world production of food is growing faster than the world's population, a finding that would cause Malthus to turn in his grave. In the 1960s, production of cereals increased annually by 3.7 percent, whereas population increased by 2 percent; in the 1970s, the respective increases were 2.5 and 1.8 percent; and in the 1980s, 2.1 and 1.6 percent. If the food supply were to increase at the latter pace, there would be enough food for a stable world population of 10 billion in 100 years.

Prospects for Future Food Production.   Non-Malthusians look to the increased use of irrigation, fertilizers, and Western agricultural technology to increase food production, a set of conditions sometimes referred to as the Green Revolution, especially when coupled with genetic manipulation of the three major grain crops—wheat, rice, and corn. Particularly in the 1960s and 1970s, such practices did in fact lead to increased productivity. Grain yields per ha have continued to increase over the past 10 years in spite of increasing use of poor land, according to a study by the Consultative Group on International Agricultural Research (Holmes 1993). Nonetheless, the well-intentioned move toward the capital-intensive, highly mechanized Western model of agriculture may not suit every developing region, for which systems of intensive polyculture (the growing of different crops on a rotational basis), as in rice cultivation, may be more appropriate (Bray 1994).

Although much of the increase can be attributed to intensified agriculture, that is, irrigation and use of fertilizers and pesticides (Reganold et al. 1990; Brady 1982), a considerable component of the increase is the result of genetic manipulation such as combining high-yield but fragile strains with low-yield but sturdy ones and by replacing less efficient photosynthetic strategies of some plants with more efficient ones.

Genetic manipulation, however, runs the risk of eroding the genetic diversity of crop plants that forms the genetic basis for evolutionary adaptation to changing environments. This concern has led to the establishment of "gene banks," repositories for the gene pool of crop plants (Plucknett et al. 1987). Efforts to conserve this invaluable genetic heritage are especially important when one considers that the tropics contain the richest reservoirs of plant resources while the bulk of the capital and technology to develop these resources exists in the major industrial countries.

As noted, arid lands constitute 28 percent of those that are potentially suitable for agriculture. In the United States alone there are over 200,000 ha of arid and semiarid range land, and there are even larger areas in Africa, Australia, and South America (Hinman 1984). Significantly, 90 percent of our food comes from a dozen crops, none of which is capable of being grown in arid conditions. There are xerophytic plants (i.e., those that grow in arid conditions), however, and some of them have already shown economic, if not food, value. Among their products are rubber from guayule; seed oil from jojoba, buffalo gourd, and bladderpod; and resin from gumweed. Of real economic value is the fact that after these products have been removed from the plants, the remaining material can be used for fuel, a valuable commodity in arid lands. Achieving sustainable use of renewable resources such as food will involve increasing yields while simultaneously protecting the environment (Plucknett and Winkelmann 1995; Rosenberg et al. 1993)

It is probably self-evident that these changes in agricultural practices involve cultural adaptation away from often longstanding patterns, not necessarily an easy accommodation. No less difficult a transition would be a change in food habits, such as a greater exploitation of marine resources like algae and seaweeds, that could also sustain a larger world population. It has been estimated, for example, that the amount of food that feeds America's population would feed seven times that number of Chinese on the average Chinese diet! However, as China's population grows and per capita income increases, the diet diversifies from a monotonous fare, in which a starchy staple such as rice supplies 70 percent or more of calories, to more meat, milk, and eggs, creating a surge in grain demand. These cultural changes coupled with a massive conversion of cropland to nonfarm use raises the specter that China will soon no longer be able to feed itself, its demand for food then overwhelming the export capacity of the United States and other producers (Brown 1994).

A Word on Rice

The first "green revolution" affecting rice probably began with Neolithic people who began the domestication of grasses belonging to the genus *Oryza*, the ancestor of today's rice. Rice is important, if not unique, among grain crops for two major reasons: it produces more calories per unit of cultivated area, corn being next; and it, unlike other grains, is grown almost entirely for direct human consumption. In the 1980s, 40 percent of the world's population depended on rice for at least half their diet, yet rice is grown on only 11 percent of the world's arable land (Van Slyke 1988).

Over 95 percent of the world's rice is grown in East, Southeast, and South Asia, China being the largest producer of all, with some 36 percent of the total (Figure 5–9). Within China, the Yangtze Valley accounts for 75 percent of the nation's output or about 25 percent of the world's total (Van Slyke 1988). Historically, although some was shipped on the Yangtze River system, about 90 percent was consumed in the producing area.

Although the pattern and technology of rice production has apparently changed little over several thousand years—the rice paddy, intensive cultivation, enormous amounts of hand labor—the acreage involved has been pushed to the limit, aided and abetted by irrigation and terracing. This permits much greater yields per ha than less-intensive methods of agriculture. About A.D. 1000, improved strains of rice were introduced, probably from Cambodia; the most significant of these new strains were early ripeners, which made two crops a year

Figure 5-9   Rice paddy agriculture along the shores of Lake Dian, near Kunming, Yunnan Province, China, as viewed from the Western Hills. (Photo by E. Kormondy)

on the same land possible. Today, improved strains—the "green revolution" of rice more resistant to disease, wilting, and early dropping of grains—continue to be developed through the International Rice Institute in the Philippines. It is largely the work of this organization that has helped make much of Asia self-sufficient in rice.

DESERTIFICATION

The Extent of Desertification

In a geological context, **desertification,** the process of desert formation and expansion, has been the result of climatic changes; in a contemporary context, desertification is largely of anthropogenic origin. Geological history accounts for the presence of the great deserts of the world: the hyperarid (e.g., the Sahara in Africa and the Mojave in North America), the arid (e.g., the Sahel in Africa and Gobi in China), and the semiarid (e.g., the Great Plains of North America and the Kalahari in Africa). Anthropogenic agricultural activity accounts for the salt desert that now exists where once the fertile Tigris-Euphrates Valley flourished. It also accounts for the current annual rate of global desertification that consumes some 80,000 km^2 (about the size of the state of Maine) and for the total area threatened by future desertification, namely 39,000,000 km^2 (an area equal to that of the United States, the former USSR, and Australia combined).

Gupta (1988) has estimated that desertification of the world has affected an area larger than Brazil, whose land area is larger than the contiguous 48 United States. Desertification is ongoing in some 22 African countries, including the several countries in the Sahel zone (the arid region bordering the southern edge of the Sahara), where the rate of deforestation is rampant at seven times the Third World average (Brown and Flavin 1988). And, according to The World Bank (1986), desertification in Mali alone has expanded the Sahara southward by 350 km in 20 years.

Causal Factors of Desertification.   Among herding peoples, overgrazing is the predominant cause of desertification, particularly in situations where drought exacerbates the need for grazing opportunities. The cutting of forests for fuel, thereby removing the natural protection of windbreaks and the source of humus for the soil, is another factor, one that is extenuated as a larger population has the need for more fuel. Cultivation and irrigation, overgrazing, deforestation, mining, recreation, and urbanization are all factors involved in desertification. Cultivation and irrigation contribute to wind erosion of improperly cultivated soil, consumptive use of water, salinization of soil, and even abandonment of agricultural lands, which subsequently become barren.

Overgrazing, however, is often the common denominator of desertification in arid and semiarid regions. In the southwestern United States, land that could support 16,000 sheep is subject to grazing by over 140,000; and in western India, the area available for grazing dropped from 13 million to 11 million ha as the population of goats, sheep, and cattle increased from 9 million to 14 million.

Semiarid grasslands are frequently homogenous ecosystems with respect to water, nitrogen, and other soil resources; that is, these resources are distributed with considerable regularity. Long-term grazing, however, leads to an increase of heterogeneity of these resources, allowing invasion by desert shrubs that are not dependent as are grasses on uniform distribution of resources (Schlesinger et al. 1990). In turn, this invasion leads to further localization of soil resources under shrub canopies and loss of soil fertility by erosion and gaseous emission in the barren areas between shrubs. Such a situation is an example of positive feedback and has led to desertification of formerly productive land in southern New Mexico and in other regions, such as the Sahel.

The Impact of Desertification

Those most adversely affected by desertification are pastoral nomads, who account for about 6 percent of the world's population living in arid environments. Prior to 1968, 65 percent of Mauritania's population were nomadic pastoralists (Erbsen 1979). Then a severe drought struck the Sahel (Beshir and Mubarek 1989); as many as 250,000 people and millions of animals died over a 6-year period. The nomads who survived migrated in large numbers to the capital city of Nouakchott, whose population grew from 12,300 in 1964 to about 200,000 in 1980. Nouakchott, which means "windy city," is itself threatened by desert takeover, the Sahel's sands drifting relentlessly and unceasingly through the city's streets. Mauritania's desertification has been exacerbated by recurrent droughts (Glantz 1987), but even when and if sufficient rains fall, the Sahel area in general will continue to feel the pressure of increasing population and increasing rural-to-urban migration (Walsh 1988; Beshir and Mubarek 1989).

The situation in China is no less severe. Deserts make up more than 13 percent of the land area (Walker 1982), and although various methods are being used to convert them to farmland, the rate of desertification continues to accelerate. From 1949 to the mid-1980s, desertified areas increased by 65,000 km^2, with degenerated grasslands covering one-fifth of that total (Jin and Cheng 1989). Coupled with forest destruction, expansion of agricultural areas, overgrazing, and water loss, soil erosion is estimated to be 5 billion tons annually, equivalent to the country's annual fertilizer output.

CONCLUDING COMMENT

The topics that have just been surveyed—graying, nutrition, and desertification, along with the many that haven't, including housing and health care; pollution of air, water, and soil; waste disposal; deforestation; global warming; acid precipitation; epidemic and endemic diseases; and migration—provide a basis for due concern about potential if not real impacts of human population growth. Whether some or all of these impacts are viewed pessimistically or optimistically, they are matters of paramount importance to the quality of life of Earth's inhabitants. Given the interrelatedness of nations and peoples, an adverse impact in one place ultimately has some effect elsewhere. Because of differences in cultural practices and expectations, the side effects will be different in different regions. From a holistic perspective, however, we are one piece of the whole, the whole is the sum of its parts, and each part warrants its proper share of the whole. One can but wish for the wisdom of Solomon in addressing these complex interrelated situations.

KEY TERMS

demographic transition	**fecundity**	**life expectancy**
desertification	**fertility rate**	**malnutrition**
doubling time	**infant mortality**	**median age**

KEY POINTS

☐ The overall growth of the human population to date has been exponential, approximating that of a J-shaped growth curve, the current doubling time being approximately 45 years.

☐ It is projected that 94 percent of the increase in the human population by 2025 will occur in developing countries, 70 percent of it in 20 of the less developed countries.

☐ About 40 percent of the population is under 15 years of age in developing countries, producing the pyramid-shaped age structure of an expanding population; by contrast, developed countries exhibit either a bell- or an urn-shaped age structure.

☐ Developing societies have low median ages while developed societies have high median ages.

☐ Birth rates (natality) have dropped from 40 to 15 births per 1,000 people per year since the middle of the nineteenth century in developed countries while remaining at the level of 40 in developing countries until the middle of the twentieth century.

☐ Life expectancy has increased significantly throughout the world as a result of better nutrition, sanitation, and health care; nonetheless, there are substantial differences between developed and developing countries as well as between the sexes and some ethnic groups.

☐ Infant mortality is generally higher in developing countries and lower in developed countries.

☐ Abortion, legal under common law in the early days of the United States, was driven underground from the mid-1800s and reversed in 1973 by the U.S. Supreme Court in *Roe* v. *Wade*.

☐ As countries become industrialized, a demographic transition occurs in which a decline in mortality is followed by a decline in natality as economic growth brings improvements in living conditions, including education.

☐ The major factors in reduction of global natality are subsumed under the term *family planning*, including contraception, increase in age at which women marry, length of time after childbirth that a woman cannot conceive, increased career opportunities for and improved status of women, and abortion.

☐ Policy options to slow human population growth include reducing unwanted pregnancies, reducing the demand for large families, and interrupting population momentum.

☐ Biological factors that may affect fecundity include nutrition and health, length of the reproductive period, and the period of lactation.

☐ Cultural factors affecting fecundity include abortion and infanticide, notions about extramarital sex, customary age of marriage, remarriage during widowhood or after divorce, commonality of divorce and coital frequency, postpartum or other sex taboos, customary length for breast-feeding, and contraception.

☐ Among the possible consequences of current world growth are aging, starvation and malnutrition, and desertification.

☐ The number of elderly (those over age 65) is increasing at a rate of 2.4 percent a year, for a doubling time of 29 years. More than half of the world's elderly live in developing countries, a proportion projected to reach 69 percent by 2025.

☐ About one-fifth of the world's population is chronically malnourished, and malnutrition is responsible for the deaths of 15 million children a year. Feeding the world's population is conditioned by the Earth's carrying capacity, on which there is little agreement. Feeding the population will doubtless require greater use of irrigation, fertilization, and technology.

☐ Desertification is largely of anthropogenic origin from overgrazing, improper cultivation of soil, deforestation, mining, recreation, and urbanization. The current annual rate of desertification is equivalent to the size of the state of Maine and, in the future, may equal the size of the United States, the former USSR, and Australia combined.

6

Stress and Environmental Physiology

INTRODUCTION

All organisms, including humans, must adjust to environmental problems to survive and reproduce. The study of these adjustments constitutes an important part of evolutionary biology and ecology.

J. B. S. Haldane (1932) has described three species of sponges that live in intertidal zones. They have the ability to eject water forcefully over large distances, an ability that appears to have no utility for an intertidal dweller. However, an unusual catastrophe, for instance, a violent storm or extremely low tide combined with hot temperatures, could result in the death of most individuals in a population. In this case the only survivors would be the few individuals who live in sheltered spots such as caves, where their water ejection mechanism would be an important adaptation to water stagnation.

In studying the way in which organisms are adapted to the environment, ecologists have been impressed by the presence of "hidden" adaptations: organisms are adaptable to conditions beyond what they are ordinarily exposed to, often being able to withstand highly stressful conditions. An **environmental stress** is an external (to an organism) condition that causes a potentially injurious change in biological systems (Hoffmann and Parsons 1991). The stress may be quite rare, such as severe droughts that occur no more than once a century. It appears that if selection is intense enough, individuals with the genetic potential to survive and, eventually, reproduce despite the stress will pass on this genetic potential to future generations. Thus, the population will evolve through these fits and starts of selection to adapt to these rare stresses. Ecologists have therefore given special consideration to how living organisms deal with conditions that represent special challenges to the individuals that make up biological populations.

Adaptation is the process of adjustment and change in an organism that enables it to survive, reproduce, and function (Baker 1966b; Lasker 1969; Mazess 1975). These adaptive changes ultimately result from the action of natural selection.

Much evidence for the importance of rare or acyclic environmental stress on biological populations exists. Observations of extreme temperatures causing high mortality rates in marine invertebrates are frequent, and large fish kills have been noted after such unusual events as volcanic eruptions (Hoffmann and Parsons 1991). Unusual environmental stresses have also been implicated in extinctions, as occurred to several populations of the checkerspot butterfly (*Euphydryas*) during a major drought in California in 1975–1977 (Ehrlich et al. 1980).

In a sense, we can view natural selection as working mostly under extreme conditions. Populations are adapted less specifically to "average" conditions in a given environment than they are to the range of conditions present over a period of time.

TOLERANCE RANGES AND LIMITING FACTORS

Law of the Minimum

Organisms face numerous environmental stresses at any time. One can imagine that there is a "least common denominator" among the stresses: an individual must be able to deal with *all* stresses in the environment. An organism that deals with all stresses except one may well become a late, unlamented individual with no offspring to grieve for its passing. This idea of a least common denominator was embodied in the so-called **Law of the Minimum,** attributed to Justus Liebig in 1840. This "law" implies that an organism (and a population) is no stronger than the weakest link in its ecological chain of requirements. While this usually refers to having enough of all needed resources, it can also refer to such conditions as temperature, alkalinity, salinity, and so forth, where conditions below some minimum value constitute insuperable stress. Under steady-state conditions, the condition or material present in amounts or degree most closely approaching the critical minimum needed will tend to be the limiting one. This is referred to as a **limiting factor** for a population and again can represent a resource or a stress. This law is not necessarily true during "transient-state" conditions (that is, when environmental conditions are in a state of rapid flux).

Law of Tolerance

The notion employed in the Law of the Minimum has been expanded to account for the possibility that there can be a *maximum* tolerable amount or degree of some environmental condition. This is included in the so-called **Law of Tolerance** developed by V. E. Shelford in 1913. It states that either a deficiency or an excess of some factor may limit an organism or a population. Thus, organisms have both an ecological minimum and a maximum for their tolerance of environmental conditions. The range of tolerance is also referred to as the **ecological amplitude** for each of the factors in the environment (Bolen and Robinson 1995).

Organisms may have a wide range of tolerance for one environmental factor but a narrow range for another. Organisms with wide ranges of tolerance for all or most factors are likely to be broadly distributed geographically, while organisms with narrow ranges of tolerance for one or more factors usually have a confined range. Some organisms with narrow ranges of tolerance can be used as markers for certain factors found in the environment. For example, some foraminifera (a type of plankton) are so sensitive to water temperature, that water temperature can be inferred within a degree or two simply by observing which foraminifera are present.

When conditions are not optimal for an organism with respect to one factor, limits of tolerance for other factors may be reduced. For example, if house plants are poorly fertilized, they may be more vulnerable to their keeper's memory lapses concerning watering.

Limiting factors allow some predictions regarding where populations are likely to be found geographically, but often organisms are not found in those environments where conditions are seemingly at the optimum for that particular species. This may be due to competition, parasites, or other negative biological interactions with different species in areas where optimal conditions are otherwise met.

The period of reproduction is critical—environmental factors are most likely to be limiting at this time. In a sense, reproductive periods sometimes lead to a narrowing of a population's ranges of tolerance.

Optimal conditions are often found near the center of a range of tolerance (but not always), as seen in Figure 6–1. Usually the farther from the center, the more "difficulty" encountered by the organism. Adaptation becomes increasingly costly as extreme conditions are approached, and this cost is taken from the organism's ability to grow and reproduce. As can be seen in Figure 6–1, environmental stress occurs when conditions approach the tolerance limits for a population.

Density-Dependent Versus Density-Independent Limiting Factors

Ecologists often separate density-dependent from density-independent limiting factors on the basis of whether the limiting factors are affected by the number of individuals present, that is, the density of the population. Density-

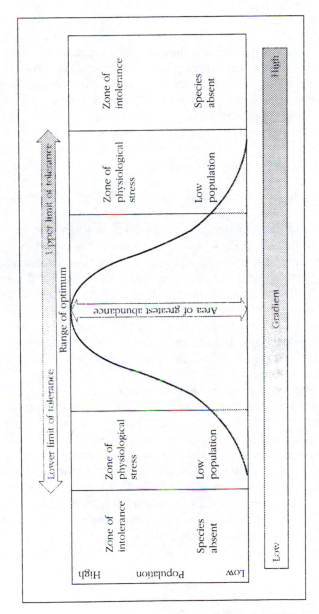

Figure 6–1 Tolerance to a gradient of environmental conditions.

dependent limiting factors have more or less severe impact on an organism depending on the density (size per unit area) of the organism's population. For instance, if the limiting factor is severe cold, population size has little to do with the problem. Thus, cold may in most cases be considered a density-independent limiting factor. If the limiting factor is protein in the food supply, however, population density may be very important in determining how much protein is available to individual organisms. Density-dependent limiting factors like protein resources are important in limiting the population size and composition of a given species in a given environment, whereas density-independent limiting factors may be more of a determinant of whether a given species will be present at all in a given environment. In other words, both density-dependent and density-independent limiting factors limit the range of a species, while density-dependent factors also limit the size of populations within a species' range.

Sources of Environmental Stress

Environmental stresses can be heuristically divided into those stemming from physical or biological sources; some organisms, particularly humans, must also deal with social sources of stress. Confining our considerations to land vertebrates, the major kinds of physical stresses encountered include extremes of heat, barometric pressure, humidity, light, other radiation, and dust or other pollutants. Biological stresses may include predators, parasites (pathogens in general), and a deficiency or excess of specific nutrients. Social stresses are less easily characterized but include concerns about mating and reproduction, and competition within families, within groups, and between groups for resources that are perceived to be important.

While the word *stress* has been used here to refer to environmental conditions, the word is sometimes used to refer to the condition of an organism. Physicists tend to separate the term *stress* (the load, or environmental condition) from *strain* (the condition of the material—or organism). In biology, the stressful nature of an environmental condition is based upon the organism's range of tolerance (one organism's stress may be another's optimum), so it is much more difficult to separate stress from strain. In this text, *stress* refers to both environmental and organismal conditions when tolerance ranges are approached or exceeded. The term *stressor* or *environmental stress* refers to environmental conditions, while *response* or *biological response* refers to the biological condition of the organism related to the stressor. Chapter 10 contains a more detailed discussion of stress definitions.

ENVIRONMENTAL PHYSIOLOGY

Environmental physiology is the study of the adaptation of individuals to environmental change and stress. The field is very quantitative in orientation as a result of its physiological roots. While the history of the field can be traced as far back as Hippocrates and his notions of the environment's influence on humor balance, the modern field may well trace its origins to Boyle's (1674) study of the effects of low oxygen levels at high altitude on individual organisms (cited in Hall 1969).

Walter B. Cannon ([1915], 1959, 1932) introduced the concept of **homeostasis,** or the relative constancy of internal bodily conditions, in his seminal books *Bodily Changes in Pain, Hunger, Fear and Rage* and *The Wisdom of the Body.* This notion deals with an individual's tolerance ranges for internal conditions within its body. Cannon noted the relatively narrow ranges of tolerance for many conditions and observed that physiological processes actively function to maintain conditions within those narrow ranges. Homeostasis is thus seen as a dynamic process that underlies all physiological adaptations. Organisms use physiological processes to maintain narrow ranges of internal conditions despite their existence in environments where conditions may either periodically or constantly exceed those ranges. Examples of homeostatic mechanisms include those involved in maintaining internal body temperature within a narrow range (particularly in homeotherms) but also include mechanisms for maintaining a balance of pH, body water, tissue oxygen, sugar levels, blood pressure, and a host of other internal conditions. In fact, the notion of homeostasis is central to the understanding of body functioning in general. Environmental physiology can be seen as the study of physiological adjustment to extreme environmental conditions where homeostasis is difficult to maintain (Folk 1974).

Types of Biological Adaptation to Environmental Stress

Organisms have many ways of adjusting to environmental variability. These can be divided into responses that are strictly genetically determined versus those that exhibit **phenotypic plasticity** (observable biological changes that are induced by the environment). Observable changes in organisms that vary as a function of environmental variation are referred to as **reaction norms** (Stearns 1989).

Acclimatization. **Acclimatization** is a form of phenotypic plasticity that enables an individual to compensate over a period of days or weeks to a complex of environmental factors, including, for instance, seasonal changes (Folk 1974). An example among humans occurs when newcomers to high altitude adjust over several days to lowered oxygen pressure (see Chapter 8). Acclimatization is a form of phenotypic plasticity that is reversible: people lose their acclimatization to high-mountain environments after they return to sea level.

Developmental Adaptations. Some phenotypic adjustments are not reversible. They are attained during growth and development, when the organism is exposed to constant or frequent environmental stresses of an intense nature. Many ecologists classify this as a form of acclimatization. Another type of developmental adaptation, referred to as "developmental conversion," occurs when exposure in early life determines which genetic programs are activated in an organism (Hoffmann and Parsons 1991). The ability of people native to the Andes to engage in high activity levels in the low-oxygen-pressure environment of high altitudes (see Chapter 8 for a more detailed discussion) may represent a developmental acclimatization, as the children of native Andeans who have migrated to sea level do not possess as good a work capacity upon returning to high altitude as those people who grew up in the highlands (Frisancho et al. 1994).

Demographic Adjustments.   When environmental stress is very intense or prolonged, it may lead to changes in the size or composition of a population. This includes density-dependent factors but also includes any environmental stress that particularly affects a given age or sex group in the population. For instance, we will see that young children are more susceptible to certain forms of protein malnutrition than infants, older children, or adults are (Chapter 9). Hence, population structure may be changed due to an environmental stress. A population's distribution in the environment may also be affected by stress conditions: individuals may avoid hazardous areas or either spread out or congregate as strategies of dealing with, for instance, potential predation. Organisms relying on stealth to avoid predation may spread out, while others congregate, relying on numbers for protection.

Genetic Adaptations.   In the long run, all biological adaptations are based upon the genetic background of organisms. Many adaptations are "hardwired" into the organism: there is little or no flexibility in response. However, even for responses that show great plasticity, organisms still require the genetic basis that permits such flexibility. When we observe an extreme case of flexibility in human behavioral responses to stress, it is clearly the result of the central nervous system that develops from the human genome.

Which Type of Adaptation Is Best?

Ecologists have attempted to sort through the costs and benefits of the different types of adaptation. Are there special costs to having plasticity? The observation that many organisms are specialized in their adaptations and confined in their distribution suggests that such costs may exist (Hoffmann and Parsons 1991). Stress resistance can be viewed as an additional maintenance cost (Sibly and Calow 1986), leaving less energy or resources available for reproduction, growth, or other important functions. The resistance would more than compensate for its cost, however, when organisms are in stressful conditions, but it might be selected against under optimal environmental conditions. However, stress resistance may not necessarily come at an energy cost; in fact, one type of stress resistance may be selection for very efficient use of a given resource when the environmental stress is the minimal level of that resource. This efficiency, while not needed as much under optimal conditions, would not be selected against (Koehn and Bayne 1989). Clearly, general models are limited by the seemingly limitless possibilities for costs and benefits of stress resistance, particularly in heterogeneous, or changing, environments.

Lively (1986) uses a model in which organisms could have two different phenotypes with different levels of adaptation to two different environmental conditions: stressful and nonstressful. Three genotypes were considered: one always leading to the phenotype resistant to stressful conditions; the second always leading to the phenotype less resistant to stressful conditions; and the third possessing plasticity, so the ultimate phenotype would appear depending on environmental conditions encountered during development (i.e., irreversible developmental adaptation). Lively's model shows that the plastic genotype will persist in the population if the resistant phenotype comes at some cost and if the organisms with the plastic genotype develop the appropriate phenotype (i.e., the resistant form in stressful conditions and the less resistant form in nonstressful conditions) in the majority of cases. Therefore, irreversible developmental adaptations may be selected for in environments where there is predictability of environmental conditions over a sufficiently long time period.

Human ecologists have also considered the relative costs and benefits of reversible acclimatization versus irreversible developmental adaptations (Harrison 1966). Commitment to an irreversible adaptation, whether through developmental or strict genetic processes, may not be favored where great environmental variability is common.

HUMAN ADAPTABILITY

Human adaptability is the term used to describe the study of "the basic biological flexibility of human populations" (Baker 1988b: 439). It is, in a sense, the study of the environmental physiology of humans. While the basics of human adaptability are much like those found in the study of the environmental physiology of any other species, humans present a special challenge: the degree to which they modify the environment through behavioral and cultural means requires a more complex analytical technique for understanding their adaptation. A main point in dealing with humans is in differentiating between the large, "outside" environment (the macroenvironment) and the small, "artificial" environment that we create (the microenvironment).

A clear example of this difference is in the temperatures inside and outside a centrally heated suburban home in New England during the winter. For the most part, New Englanders biologically experience a subtropical environment each winter, whether through their heated houses or their greatly insulated clothing worn when outside. Other organisms create tolerable microenvironments, such as ant colonies or bee hives. Honey bees (*Apis mellifera*) can keep temperature at a fairly even 35°C in the hive's central brood area throughout the year, even in temperate climates with great seasonal temperature variability (Southwick and Heldmaier 1987). Humans are distinguished by the degree to which they manipulate the environment toward their own ends.

The "Single-Stressor" Model

A "single-stressor" model has been developed by human ecologists to allow differentiation of the macroenvironment and microenvironment (Thomas et al. 1979), as shown in Figure 6–2. This model includes both behavioral and biological adaptations, allowing analysis of the complex means used by human populations to adjust to environmental stresses (Thomas et al. 1989).

In the model, the macroenvironment is seen as modified by a "buffer" made up of behavioral and cultural adaptations of human groups. This cultural buffer transforms the macroenvironment to a microenvironment. Human physiological adaptations are in response to the microenvironment and are viewed in the model as constituting a second buffer between the *milieu interieur* and the external macroenvironment. The maintenance of homeostasis is the measure of success for this double-buffer system. Deviation from homeostasis leads to a change in adaptive processes in degree or type of strategy used.

Persistent deviation from homeostasis can lead to an individual's death or the breakdown of the system itself. Certainly, changes in population size, structure, and/or distribution can result. These demographic changes are included in the model. The model permits identification of environmental stresses that have a significant impact on human groups, including possible selective effects.

Figure 6–2   Single-stressor model of human adaptability. (Redrawn by permission from The ecology of work by R. B. Thomas. In *Physiological anthropology*, by Selma T. Damon, 59–79. Copyright ©1975 by Oxford University Press, Inc. Used by permission of Oxford University Press, Inc.)

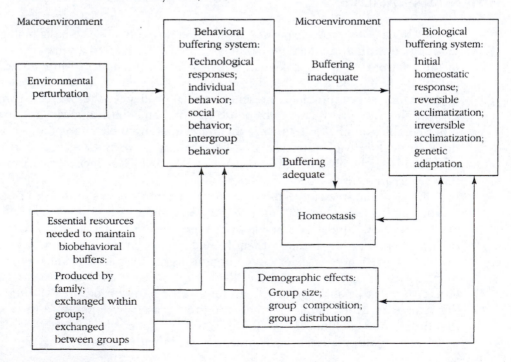

Essential and Key Resources.   The model also notes that adaptations do not always come free. Adaptive activities often must be supported by resources. For instance, in the centrally heated New England house enormous amounts of resources are used including fuel, maintenance costs of complex heating systems, insulation materials, and so forth. Materials that are required to support a group are referred to as **essential resources.** Essential resources are often easily obtained, for instance, the oxygen needed for metabolism is usually freely available.

Some of these necessary resources are expensive, rare, or simply difficult to get hold of: these are referred to as **key resources.** In many ways, identification of key resources is one of the most important tasks of a human ecologist as they are in many ways the limiting factors for human groups in a given ecosystem. An understanding of a group's ability to obtain and distribute key resources truly represents an important key to understanding their ability to adapt in general, including their ability to compete with other human groups that require the same resource.

Properties of Stressors and Responses.   Thomas and coauthors (1979) have added to the single-stressor model (see Figure 6–3). They attempt to make the model generalizable to many types of stress by focusing on properties of environmental stressors, such as intensity, duration, frequency, and predictability, as opposed to type of stressor (such as cold, heat, and hypoxia), as a means of increasing comparability of human adaptive responses to diverse environmental features. A focus on properties of the stressor allows an assessment of the degree of threat, or relative risk, represented by the stressor to human individuals and populations. These researchers further point out that properties of responses can also be identified, including time to engage, strength, duration, frequency, and reversibility. The type of response made by a human group is dependent on the properties of the response as well as the type and properties of environmental stressor. Accordingly, if the single-stressor model is to provide a framework for hypothesizing about types of adaptive responses, we will need to know about the properties of stressors and responses as well as the type of stressor being dealt with.

Effectiveness, Efficiency, and Risk.   There are further complications to understanding human responses to environmental stressors. For instance, individual responses are usually less complex than responses involving cooperation with others, with potential problems growing as the number of and distance of relationship with other people increase. Beyond this, how should the response be evaluated: by its effectiveness, by its efficiency, or by its relative degree of risk? For instance, while central heating is a very effective means of dealing with a cold macroenvironment and seems appropriate to suburban New Englanders, does this response make sense to residents of Honolulu, who are faced with a night or two of sub-15°C (i.e., sub-60°F) temperatures each year? Providing the Hawaiian residents with greatly insulated houses complete with expensive heating systems to deal with this mild, infrequent cold stress certainly seems like overkill! The efficiency of the response, a measure of its cost-effectiveness (one must balance benefits with costs), must be ranked very low in the Honolulu setting.

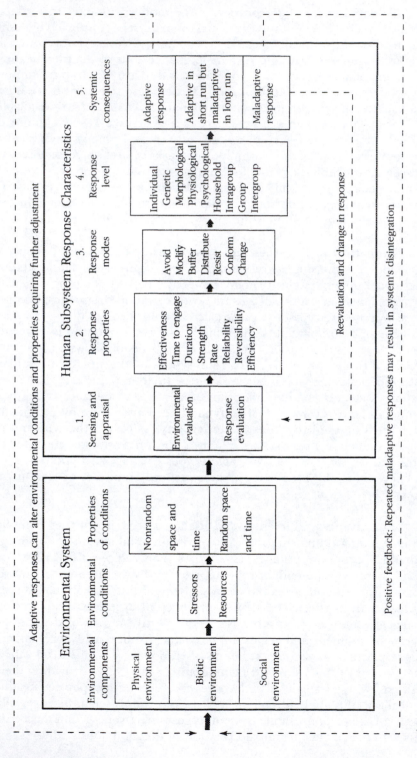

Figure 6–3 Elaborated single-stressor model, showing properties of stressors and responses. (Redrawn by permission from R. B. Thomas, B. Winterhalder, and S. D. McRae. 1979. *Yearbook of Physical Anthropology* 22:1–46.)

In addition to understanding the potential effectiveness of given responses to environmental stressors, the human group must be able to determine the stakes involved in a risky response as well as to evaluate the cost of essential resources to support the possible responses. The field of risk analysis has developed recently, attempting to quantify risk assessment and thereby enable informed choices by risk managers (Morgan 1993). Informal risk analysis has been ongoing in human populations for millennia, however.

Limitations of the Single-Stressor Model.   A limitation of the single-stressor model is its consideration of only one stressor at a time. Human populations are in fact faced with numerous stressors simultaneously, and their responses to a given stressor may be partly determined by their concomitant responses to other stressors. For instance, in the example of providing centrally heated, highly insulated houses for Honolulu residents, we failed to consider the detrimental effect of such houses on the residents' adaptation to the much more common warm, humid conditions they routinely face. Nonhuman populations also face multiple environmental stresses. The relative success of plant populations along environmental gradients, for example, is largely determined by interactions among several major stress factors (Osmond et al. 1987).

Another limitation of the single-stressor model is that it considers only stressors in the macroenvironment. As we shall see, humans are adept at creating their own stressors in their culturally constructed microenvironments. Other models are needed to deal with these problems. Chapter 10 continues this discussion, including a model for "general stress."

CONCLUSION

The human group must be able to perceive and evaluate stressors and responses. They must also balance short-term with long-term costs and benefits. One of the tasks of the human ecologist is to compare some sort of optimal strategy predicted by midrange theoretical models with what the group actually does. In fact, many ecological models have as their purpose the identification of a best, or "optimal," strategy for an individual or population. These predictions have little meaning for the real world if organisms do not in fact behave in an optimal or at least near-optimal manner. Human ecologists have minimized this problem by focusing many of their studies on populations under intensive environmental stresses, where there is less leeway for maladaptive responses. The problem of optimal strategies is reexamined in Chapter 11, where we consider how humans deal with resource problems.

Ecological studies of how organisms adapt to stress have taken on more than academic importance. The high rate of species extinction and ensuing loss of global biodiversity is in part a consequence of the environmental changes caused by humankind. The rate of this loss may accelerate because of increased changes brought on by human activities, some acting on a global scale. Ideas of species conservation must be grounded in sound concepts of biological stress resistance along with other considerations. While the next chapters illustrate the incredible flexibility of humans in the face of environmental stress, we must note that there are limits to any species' flexibility. Knowledge of our own limits seems to be in order.

KEY TERMS

acclimatization   homeostasis   limiting factor
ecological amplitude   key resources   phenotypic plasticity
environmental stress   Law of the Minimum   reaction norms
essential resources   Law of Tolerance

KEY POINTS

☐ Adaptation to environmental stress involves cultural and biological changes to ensure the survival and continuity of a species.

☐ Organisms are limited by the presence of requisite ecological factors in at least minimal amounts and characterized by a range of tolerance to those ecological factors, doing best under optimal conditions.

☐ Some factors are limiting depending on the density of a population whereas others are independent of population density.

☐ Environmental stresses stem from physical (e.g., temperature, moisture), biological (e.g., predators, parasites), and social (e.g., hierarchies) sources.

☐ Homeostasis, or the relative constancy of internal bodily conditions, depends on an individual's tolerance ranges for internal conditions within its body.

☐ Biological adaptation to environmental stress occurs genetically (e.g., changes in physical structure or physiological processes) and phenotypically (e.g., acclimatization, changes in size and composition of a population).

☐ According to the single-stressor model, the macroenvironment is modified by behavioral and cultural adaptations that transform it to a microenvironment; physiological adaptations are a response to the latter.

☐ Essential resources are those materials required to support a group, whereas key resources are those essential resources that are expensive, rare, or difficult to acquire.

☐ Among the properties of environmental stressors are intensity, duration, frequency, and predictability; responses to stressors are evaluated by effectiveness, efficiency, and degree of risk.

7

Human Adaptation to Cold and Heat

INTRODUCTION

Most of us can easily conjure up the image of an Eskimo hunter dealing with subzero temperatures during a blizzard or of Tuareg people in a caravan on the Sahara dealing with the scorching temperatures of midday, even if we have never faced conditions that severe. We have all faced some discomfort from cold and hot temperatures and therefore can identify with people who deal with these problems at such extremes.

Of all the physical stressors with which biological organisms must cope, the most studied are temperature extremes. Each species has a characteristic range of tolerance for environmental temperature, with both cold and hot conditions requiring adaptive processes and presenting limits beyond which individuals within the species cannot function. Studies of the effect of hot and cold macroenvironmental conditions on humans illustrate the similarities and differences between the human species and other animals in processes of adaptability.

THERMOREGULATION

In simple terms, organisms generate heat through metabolism and exchange heat between their body surface and the environment. Organisms vary in ability to store heat in their bodies, but over the long term maintenance of homeostasis requires that a balance be achieved between heat gain and loss. This balancing is referred to as **thermoregulation**.

Heat is generated as a waste product during the metabolic conversion of food into energy in living organisms. Physiologists customarily divide metabolic activity into two types: basal metabolism and active metabolism. **Basal metabolism** (M_b) represents the metabolic activity that is generated by animals during complete rest, but while awake (Guyton 1971). When they become active, animals generate additional heat as a byproduct of the additional energy requirements of muscular work; this is referred to as **active metabolism** (M_a). Among mammals, basal metabolism is in part related to body mass, although smaller mammals tend to have higher basal metabolic rates per mass than larger mammals (Feist and White 1989).

Heat Exchange

Heat exchange through the body surface occurs through four different processes: conduction (K), convection (C), radiation (R), and evaporation (E). For all of these processes, the rate of heat exchange is proportional to the surface area of the body.

Conduction refers to the transfer of heat between two solid objects in physical contact. Here the heat exchange involves molecule-to-molecule energy exchange due to collisions between the molecules at the contact surface. The rate of conduction depends on such factors as the area of the surfaces in contact, the temperature differences between the surfaces, and the thermal conductivity of the materials making up the objects (Gates 1980).

Convection refers to heat exchange between an object and a fluid (gas or liquid), again through energy exchanged in molecular collisions. A major characteristic of convective exchange is that the heat difference between the object and fluid causes the fluid to move. For instance, if the skin is warmer than the surrounding air, the skin will heat the air in contact with it, causing the air to rise. Cooler air will replace the warm, rising air at the skin's surface. This type of convection is termed *natural* or *free convection* (Hanna and Brown 1983). A second form of convection, termed *forced convection,* occurs when the fluid is moving because of an outside force (e.g., wind). When forced convection is present, it frequently is of greater importance than natural convection for heat exchange. The air movement in forced convection leads to a more rapid heat exchange between the skin and the air: if no air movement occurs, a layer of warm air accumulates around the skin and effectively slows heat exchange.

Radiation refers to the exchange of electromagnetic energy between objects in "sight" of each other. The energy is exchanged at a wide range of wavelengths, including the infrared emissions that are used by night scopes to track living organisms. Objects emit energy in all directions to their surroundings and also absorb energy that has been radiated from objects surrounding them. The net gain or loss of heat depends on an object's temperature, the temperature of objects visible to it, the object's reflectance and surface area, and the surface area of the objects visible to it (Kerslake 1972).

Evaporation refers to an object's heat loss because of the conversion of a liquid to gas on its surface. Energy, referred to as the latent heat of vaporization, is required to convert a liquid to a gas. The latent heat of vaporization is different for different substances but also depends upon the temperature and mass of the liquid. The rate of heat loss due to evaporation depends on surface area, vapor pressure of the surroundings, the object's surface temperature, and the amount of liquid present on the surface (Hanna and Brown 1983).

Core Versus Shell

Physiologists typically divide the body into two zones when considering thermoregulation: the core and the shell. The core of the body represents the internal part of the trunk and the braincase. It is usually constrained to a very narrow range of temperature, approximately $35°C$ to $41°C$ (Sawka and Wenger 1988), beyond which body function maintenance may be compromised. The shell is represented by superficial tissues of the body and the appendages. Unlike the core, it has a quite broad range of tolerance for temperature, ranging from slightly below $0°C$ for short periods before frostbite becomes a concern to temperatures where burning of tissues can occur.

The duration of the stress is an important consideration in chances for cold or heat injury to extremities, such as frostbite, chilblain, and trenchfoot (Hamlet 1988). When temperatures go below about $15°C$—well above conditions for which cold injury is a risk—people begin to lose manual dexterity, a problem that can prevent completion of necessary work. Nevertheless, when heat is gained or lost from the body, the shell is typically sacrificed in favor of the core; that is, core temperature tends to be maintained within strict limits while shell temperature changes more widely.

Heat Balance Equation

The effect of all of these factors on an organism's heat content is summarized in the heat balance equation:

$$\Delta S = M_b + M_a \pm K \pm C \pm R - E$$

where ΔS is the change in the amount of heat contained by the body. The equation notes that metabolism always leads to heat gain, evaporation always involves heat loss, and the other methods of heat exchange can result in either a gain or loss of heat depending upon local conditions. Over the long term, $\Delta S = 0$ if homeostasis is to be maintained.

The heat balance equation is a guide to the processes that must be considered in dealing with human adaptation to hot and cold conditions. For instance, humans adapt to hot conditions by minimizing active metabolism if possible and increasing heat loss from convection, conduction, radiation, and particularly evaporation. In cold conditions, humans tend to increase muscular activity, seek to insulate themselves from heat exchange with the environment, and attempt to stay dry. The remainder of this chapter will explore some of the complex adaptations that have been used to combat cold and heat, beginning with cold stress. Initially, consideration must be given to the kinds of macroenvironments that contain temperature extremes, since adaptive processes depend upon the characteristics of the stress being confronted.

COLD MACROENVIRONMENTS

Humans have adapted to many kinds of cold macroenvironments. These include cool nighttime conditions in tropical and semitropical arid habitats, cold nights in high altitudes, and the cold winter seasons found in arctic and many temperate latitudes. These types of cold habitats have been contacted at different times in human prehistory (Hanna et al. 1989). As you are aware from our earlier discussion, humans evolved in tropical savannas, which are characterized by cool evenings with subfreezing temperatures present on some nights (Cole 1986). These conditions present some dangers to unprotected humans but represent more of a discomfort than a life-threatening condition for contemporary people (Hanna et al. 1989). Tropical environments also contain rainy and windy seasons that are cool; however, they are not usually serious threats to modern humans.

Mountainous Areas

People living in mountainous regions at high altitude confront more extreme cold conditions than people in tropical areas do, with clear skies allowing much radiative heat loss to space at night and thin air permitting a rapid drop in ambient temperature. High altitudes are usually characterized by relatively small seasonal temperature changes but marked diurnal temperature changes compared with sea-level areas at the same latitude (Little and Hanna 1978). In general, temperature declines as elevation increases. Ambient temperatures in the Andean town of Nuñoa (about 4000 m altitude) were measured at −6°C at 6 AM and 20°C at 1 PM (Little and Hanna 1978). Similarly, in Tibet, daily temperature ranges of 33°C are common (Ekvall 1968). These conditions are relatively new to human evolution. The earliest evidence for human habitation of such macroenvironments is dated between about 10,000 and 12,000 years ago in the Andes (Lynch 1978) and perhaps to an earlier date in the Himalayas (Zhimin 1982), although the archaeology of the latter region is still in its infancy.

Arctic and Temperate Regions

Much more intense cold is felt during winter seasons in arctic zones and inland temperate regions (Hanna et al. 1989). Arctic areas where contemporary humans reside have temperatures reaching as low as −70°C (Edholm and Lewis

1964) and winter seasons with monthly mean temperatures below freezing lasting up to 8 months.

Human populations first entered temperate regions between 500,000 and one million years ago (Kennedy 1980). For example, the *Homo erectus* site at Zhoukoutien, near the modern city of Beijing, has been dated at about 500,000 years BP. Winters at that time and place would have represented a serious adaptive challenge.

Clearly, adaptive responses differ based on the properties of the cold macroenvironments in which humans reside, with responses based not only on the intensity of the cold but also on the frequency, duration, and predictability of the stress.

Other Factors

Another important consideration is wind speed, as the increased forced convection of windy conditions in cold environments leads to "wind chill," increasing the rate of heat loss from the body. Humidity is also a major concern because of its effect on evaporation rates. Generally, the higher the humidity the lower the evaporation rate and vice versa.

Cold macroenvironments have yet other conditions that affect human ecology. One is blizzards, during which whiteout conditions can impede any attempt at productive activity or lead to individuals getting lost away from permanent shelter. Another problem in some cold environments is a deep snowpack, which may make transportation very difficult (Marchand 1987).

Perhaps the greatest single problem with seasonally cold environments is the reduction in resource availability over long periods of time, requiring either storage or special acquisition techniques. Thus, human adaptive activities must be concerned with these indirect effects of cold as well as with the direct problem of low temperature.

CULTURAL ADAPTATIONS TO COLD

Humans have used multiple strategies for dealing with cold macroenvironments, constructing microenvironments that approach tropical conditions in many instances. These cultural buffers to cold stress require resources and therefore come with a cost. The degree to which a group or individual will allocate resources to cold adaptation depends in part on the characteristics of the cold: mild cold or cold of short duration may lead groups to settle for less effective, but also less costly, techniques for buffering themselves from the macroenvironmental stress. Cultural adaptations include various means of increasing insulation, scheduling high activity for situations in which cold conditions cannot be avoided, sharing body heat, generating warmth through the use of heated foods and water and through fire, and using various means to avoid getting wet.

Clothing

A major means of insulation is the use of clothing. In general, the thicker the clothing, the better the insulative value. The insulative value of clothing is measured in terms of the **"clo"** unit, with one clo equal to the thermal resistance of **$0.155°C/m^2/W$,** where m^2 equals the surface area in square meters and W refers to heat in watts. The clo unit, devised at the beginning of World War II, was designed such that a standard business suit of the time had an insulative value of 1 clo (McIntyre 1981). Clothing insulates in large part by trapping air (Adolph 1949; Gonzalez 1988); this can be accomplished through use of either large weaves or multiple layers. But problems can arise if clothing provides too much insulation, particularly when an active person produces a great deal of metabolic heat and therefore sweats.

A special consideration is the avoidance of getting wet, since water-soaked clothing loses much of its insulative value; also, wet clothing results in a great loss of heat through evaporation. The thermoregulatory concern is for avoiding both external water and perspiration.

Inuit.   The Eskimos, or Inuit as they prefer to be called, traditionally wore clothes in many layers, which served to trap air, thus enhancing insulation (Moran 1982). Their clothing utilized many drawstrings, which permitted controlling the amount of ventilation, thus preventing overheating when physical activity increased. Traditional Inuit clothing had an outer layer that was relatively impermeable to water and also acted as a windbreaker (Figure 7–1). Among the Davis Strait tribes, people typically wore a long stocking made of deerskin that reached above the knee, two pairs of trousers made of deer- or sealskin, birdskin slippers, boots, and a hooded jacket made of sealskin (Boas [1888] 1964). Inuit clothing provided insulation of from 7 to 12 clo units (Frisancho 1993).

Quechuas.   In the Peruvian Andes, natives of high altitude such as the Quechuas studied in Nuñoa also wear several layers of clothing (Hanna 1968). This layering allows for a great deal of insulation but also permits taking off or putting on layers as the temperature changes during the day, an adaptation to the great diurnal changes in temperature. Men often wear several pairs of woolen underwear and pants, a knitted undershirt, cotton long-sleeved shirt, and woolen jacket. Only the cotton shirt is store-bought, the other articles being made by the Quechuas from their own resources. Women's outfits are similar, with several layered woolen skirts and a long-sleeved jacket. The woolen items that are made from unprocessed wool contain lanolin, the latter a water repellant. The outer layer of clothing, a felt hat, and either a poncho for men or a shawl for women, is of a tighter weave, relatively impermeable to water, and of a dark color (Figure 7–2). These attributes of the outer layer reduce the problem of wetness and enhance heat gain from solar radiation (Little and Hanna 1978). The Andeans either go barefoot or wear rubber tire sandals, so their feet are exposed to cold.

Figure 7–1 Inuit traditional clothing. (From *The Netsilik Eskimo* by Asen Balikci. Copyright © 1970 by Asen Balikci. (Used by permission of Doubleday, a division of Bantam Doubleday Dell Publishing Group, Inc.)

In general, clothing of the Quechuas is very effective, as has been demonstrated in laboratory and field experiments (Hanna 1970). Their clothing is estimated to have insulative values of 1.21 clo for men and 1.43 clo for women, not counting hats, shawls, and ponchos (Little and Hanna 1978).

Bedding

Bedding is also used for insulation, and, like clothing, its insulative value depends on thickness and looseness of weave. Bedding is of particular concern, as it is usually used when macroenvironmental temperatures are at their lowest and when metabolic heat generation is also minimized. Since bedding is usually used indoors, there is less concern about its permeability to water. In some

Figure 7–2   Quechua people wearing traditional clothing. (Photo courtesy of M. A. Little)

populations, people sleep in family groups, thus sharing body heat during the night. Tests done on native bedding in the Andes, traditionally made from coarse llama wool, show that it is very effective in insulating people from outside cold (Little and Hanna 1978).

Housing

Housing, or shelter in general, is another major cultural adaptation to cold macroenvironments. As with clothing, the critical factor in housing is insulation, which minimizes heat loss from radiation and convection. Insulation is achieved through materials that are good insulators, thick walls, and minimizing drafts that would increase ventilation (Rapoport 1969). Additionally, flooring (when present) reduces conductive heat loss, particularly for infants who crawl on the ground. In cold macroenvironments, houses that minimize surface area relative to volume are favored, as this reduces heat exchange with the outside. In fact, some people, such as the Aleuts (Laughlin 1980), use semisubterranean shelters to reduce exposed surface area and increase insulation.

The Igloo.   The ideal house form in a cold climate is spherical in shape, thick-walled of insulating materials, windowless with a small entry, and floored with insulative material. The Central Inuit igloo immediately comes to mind, as this hemispherical structure is made of thick snow blocks (snow is an excellent insulator) and has a single, small entryway (Figure 7–3). The entrance is a curved tunnel that reduces drafts and is often protected by a snow wall that acts as a windbreak (Rapoport 1969). The floor in the living area is raised, thereby avoiding wind and also taking advantage of rising warm air. A similar structure adapted for cold, snowy conditions is the Athapaskan Quin-zhee found in sub-arctic Canada. It is a temporary shelter built by making a large pile of snow, letting it set for an hour or two, and then hollowing out a small interior living space. The Quin-zhee can be constructed in a short period of time with little need for tools beyond a small shovel or even a snowshoe (Marchand 1987).

Quechua Houses.   Two forms of houses are common among high-altitude Quechua people. One is rectangular with doorways sometimes hung with a wooden door, is without windows, is constructed of adobe (sun-dried bricks), and has a roof of tile or grass and straw (Hanna 1968) (Figure 7–4). This type of house can maintain an internal temperature 10°C above outdoor ambient temperature (Baker 1966a).

The second house type is more temporary and is small, circular, and constructed of stone walls with occasional use of mud as a sealant and has a straw roof (Hanna 1968) (Figure 7–5). The temporary house form is much less effective as an insulator; tests suggest only a 3.7°C difference between inside and outside (Baker 1966a). The second house type is usually associated with pastoral activities, whereas the first house is located in agricultural settlements. Thus, effectiveness at cold adaptation is sacrificed for ease and economy of construction.

Activity Scheduling

Activity scheduling is another important behavioral adaptation to cold. Humans behave much like other animals exposed to a cold macroenvironment; they bask in the sun when possible to increase radiant heat gain and avoid particularly stressful microenvironments such as shaded areas, regions exposed to wind, and water/dampness. People also often engage in muscular activity when they are exposed to cold conditions, for instance, when they must go outdoors to work. However, possible exhaustion due to long-term exposure limits the amount of such activity.

Northern Algonkian men occasionally engage in work that requires fine coordination while exposed to cold conditions; they remove mittens and work at a very rapid pace to minimize the time their hands are exposed (Steegmann et al. 1983).

Alcohol and Other Agents

Humans have also been known to ingest alcohol or other pharmacological agents to aid in cold adaptation. Alcohol does provide short-term benefit in the cold: it is metabolized quickly, increasing heat generation by the body. In the long term, however, alcohol use is maladaptive because it stimulates dilation of

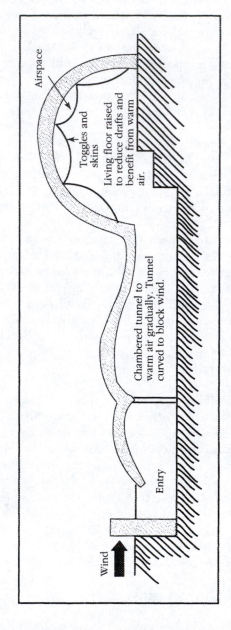

Figure 7–3 Diagram of igloo. (Redrawn from *House form and culture* by Rapoport, Amos, ©1969. (Reprinted by permission of Prentice-Hall, Inc., Upper Saddle River, NJ.)

Figure 7–4   Permanent adobe house of the Quechua from the highlands of Peru can be seen in the background. (Photo courtesy of H. J. Jacobi)

superficial blood vessels. Vasodilation leads to an increased rate of heat loss from the body, effectively reducing biological insulation.

Joel M. Hanna (1971) and Michael A. Little (1970) have explored the effects of coca ingestion among Quechua Indians on their ability to adapt to cold. They noted that the chewing of coca leaves, a traditional custom among Andeans, leads to a mild constriction of blood vessels in the fingers and toes and thus a slight reduction in heat loss. Since it is their hands and feet that are most commonly exposed to cold, this slight advantage may take on significance in some stressful conditions.

Fire

A more direct means for creating a warm microenvironment is through the use of fire. The earliest clear evidence for the controlled use of fire comes from archaeological sites at Zhoukoutien (China), Terra Amata (France), and Vértesszöllös (Hungary) in layers dated at about 400,000 years BP (Kennedy 1980).

The benefits of the use of fire in a cold environment are obvious but they come at a cost: fuel. Some cold environments are located above timberline, necessitating fuel use from nonwood sources such as seal oil lamps by the Inuit and dung fires by the Quechuas. It is most effective to build fires inside insulated

Figure 7–5 Temporary stone-walled house of pastoralists, Peruvian highlands. (Photo courtesy of H. J. Jacobi)

houses to retain heat, although usually some mechanism for getting rid of smoke that minimizes the creation of drafts must be devised.

The optimal use of fire is to heat foods or liquids that can be conveyed directly into the body core. In some groups, the ingestion of hot food or drink is timed to precede or coincide with acute cold exposure. The Algonkians of northern Canada, for example, take frequent tea breaks while hunting in cold conditions, and the fire that heats the tea also warms and dries their clothing (Marano 1983).

Additional Adaptations

People also have other cultural means of dealing with the indirect effects of cold. For instance, the Inuit have developed knowledge of ice and such technological devices as ice probes to avoid hazardous thin-ice conditions (Moran 1982). They also develop hunting partnerships that provide assistance should an individual have an accident such as falling into cold water. Many arctic peoples use snowshoes to get around in snowy conditions. Glare from snow with resulting potential snow blindness is also a problem on sunny days, and the use of goggles, such as the wooden ones with thin slits used by Inuit (Stefánsson 1913), or visors is common.

COLD MICROENVIRONMENTS

The ability of people to buffer themselves from environmental cold through behavioral or cultural buffers is indeed remarkable. Most human microenvironments can be described as tropical or subtropical, despite quite different macroenvironmental conditions. There are situations in which these buffers are ineffective, and humans must rely on biological adaptations to cope with cold microenvironments. A particular problem occurs when people are exposed to water, which removes heat up to 25 times faster than air and can also cause heat loss through evaporative cooling. As noted earlier, clothing loses much of its insulative properties when it becomes wet.

In considering human biological responses to cold, it is helpful to divide cold microenvironments into two types of exposure: whole-body and extremity-only. Additionally, responses differ based on whether the exposure is to cold air or cold water. The intensity of the stress, and therefore the type and degree of response, differs based on these types of exposure.

BIOLOGICAL RESPONSES TO COLD

There are two major forms of biological adaptation to cold stress: insulative and metabolic. **Insulative adaptation** involves body size, form, and composition, as well as regulation of blood flow. **Metabolic adaptation** involves basal metabolism as well as metabolic heat generation by both voluntary and involuntary muscular activity.

Insulative Adaptations

As noted at the beginning of the chapter, metabolic heat generation is proportional to the body's mass, which in turn is closely related to volume. On the other hand, heat exchange (principally heat loss in a cold climate) with the outside environment occurs through the body's surface, measured as surface area. Thus, warm-blooded animals in cold climates generally have minimized body surface area in relation to body volume. This idea has been summarized in two ecological "rules," Bergmann's and Allen's rules.

Bergmann's and Allen's Rules. **Bergmann's rule,** originally proposed in 1847, states that in a widely distributed, homeothermic ("warm-blooded") species, animals in colder environments will tend to be of larger body size than animals in temperate environments (Roberts 1978). Since volume and mass increase in three dimensions (by the cube) and area increases in only two dimensions (by the square) as body size increases, volume increases faster than surface area as general body size increases. Therefore, larger animals of the same shape will have larger ratios of volume to surface area.

Allen's rule, dating to 1877, states that in widely distributed homeotherms, populations in cold climates will tend to have shorter extremities. Again, this physiological difference serves to minimize the surface area to volume ratio (Hanna et al. 1989).

Anthropologists have attempted to discover whether these ecological rules apply to humans. One of the largest studies was done by Derek Roberts (1978), who noted a significant correlation between average weight of human populations and environmental temperature as well as a clear negative relationship between relative arm length and temperature. Roberts's results suggest that both Bergmann's and Allen's rules do apply to humans. These relationships are strongest when the temperature of the coldest month is used in calculations, as opposed to the average temperature for the entire year, suggesting that the observed variability in surface area to volume relationships between animals is in fact due to cold adaptation (Hanna et al. 1989). A possible mechanism for Allen's rule is the effect of cold on limb growth. Animal studies have shown that individuals reared in the cold have smaller limb length than animals with identical genetic backgrounds reared in warmer environments. Evidence that this may also be true for humans was shown in a study by Stinson and Frisancho (1978). They compared Quechua Indian children raised at high altitude with children of highland migrants raised in warmer rainforest environments at sea level. The major difference between the two groups was that the high-altitude children had shorter limb length. This study suggests that the lower surface-area-to-volume ratio found among cold-exposed people may stem from developmental processes as well as adaptively based genetic differences.

Facial Form. Since faces are frequently exposed to cold conditions more than other parts of the body, some anthropologists have postulated that diversity in human facial form is a result of cold adaptation. People in cold climates are more likely to have narrower noses (Steegmann 1975) and flatter faces (Coon et al. 1950). However, results from a study done on facial skin temperature during cold exposure of men of Japanese and Caucasian ancestry in Hawaii suggest that flat faces are not necessarily more adaptive for cold conditions (Steegmann 1972).

Subcutaneous Fat. Another insulative adaptation to cold is a thick layer of subcutaneous fat, an adaptation perhaps too many of us possess, cold or not. The insulative value of subcutaneous fat was demonstrated by Baker and Daniels (1956) when they noted that skin temperature was lower at sites on the body surface that had thicker layers of subcutaneous fat. Other studies have demonstrated lowered heat loss in people with more subcutaneous fat during exposure to both cold air and water (Keatinge 1960; Smith and Hanna 1975). Subcutaneous fat that is distributed evenly on the body may be even more effective as an insulator.

Vascular Adaptations. Diverting blood from the surface of the body to deeper levels is another way of insulating the core from a cold environment. **Vasoconstriction,** the narrowing of superficial blood vessels, is a principal means of insulation. Shifting blood flow to deeper vessels slows heat exchange between the body core and shell, thus reducing the rate of heat loss from the body to the air. In fact, due to vasoconstriction the heat conductivity of the blood is reduced by about 40 percent at a microenvironmental temperature of 15°C compared with its level at 35°C (Frisancho 1993). Deep arteries are located immediately adjacent to veins, allowing heat exchange between the blood in the arteries and veins (Kerslake 1972). This **countercurrent heat exchange** warms venous blood that has cooled in peripheral areas (i.e., arms and legs) before it returns to the core, thus reducing heat loss from the core.

Changes in blood flow during cold exposure sometimes become more complex than simple superficial vasoconstriction. In peripheries—particularly fingers—exposed to cold water, initial vasoconstriction is frequently followed by **vasodilation,** followed in a rhythmic pattern by successive constrictions and dilations. This has been called the "hunting response," or more formally **cold-induced vasodilation** (CIVD). The CIVD response seems to be accentuated in people who frequently have peripheries exposed to cold conditions, from natives in arctic regions to fish filleters (Nelms and Soper 1962) and North Sea fishermen (Krog et al. 1960), and may reflect a compromise adaptation for keeping peripheries warm (through vasodilation) while still slowing heat loss from the body core (through vasoconstriction).

Metabolic Adaptations

Metabolic adjustments to increase heat generation involve muscular activity such as the voluntary activities just discussed. Involuntary muscular activity involves **shivering,** which is induced by skin receptors that are activated by the lowering of skin temperature (Frisancho 1993). There is also a central nervous system component to shivering, as animal studies have shown that transection of the spinal cord in animals leads to the cessation of shivering in the area below the surgery (LeBlanc 1975). Apparently, the skin's thermal receptors are linked to the hypothalamus in the brain where the central temperature regulating center is located. Shivering can lead to a doubling or tripling of the basal metabolic rate. It also leads to an increase in heat loss because peripheral blood vessels dilate.

Another metabolic adaptation to cold, termed **nonshivering thermogenesis,** occurs in some mammals. This adaptation is thought to involve brown adipose tissue, which releases norepinephrine, a hormone that causes a general increase in the basal metabolic rate particularly due to changes in lipid metabolism (LeBlanc 1975). There is no reliable evidence for this in humans, but some intriguing results suggesting its presence in a special group of humans have been found (Hong 1973). Humans do increase their use of such energy sources as glucose during cold exposure (Vallerand et al. 1995), although this may be due to muscular activity.

ACCLIMATIZATION TO WHOLE-BODY EXPOSURE TO COLD

With mild cold exposure, humans rely on insulation through vasoconstriction of superficial blood vessels to buffer their cores. Continued or increased stress leads to initiation of metabolic responses, with muscle tensing followed by outright shivering if voluntary activity is not undertaken (Hanna et al. 1989). Shivering increases blood flow to the shell and thus increases the rate of heat loss. Also, during shivering, the individual may lose much of his or her work capacity due to loss of control over muscle function. Results of experimental studies done on people exposed over several days to cold suggest that people **habituate** to the cold; that is, they become generally less reactive to it. Cold habituation is manifested in a lowering of the shivering threshold (Young 1988) as well as by a reduction in the sympathetic nervous system (SNS) response to cold (LeBlanc 1978). The benefits of this adaptation are to allow sleep and also to increase insulation.

Australian Aborigines

Early studies on aboriginal peoples from central Australia noted that they were exposed to cold air at night, the clear skies of the deserts causing considerable radiative heat loss. In winter, night temperatures around freezing were common, but the aborigines wore no clothing and used minimal shelter. These people differed from unacclimatized Europeans who were exposed to comparable nighttime conditions: the Australians slept through the night and did not shiver, while the Europeans stayed awake all night shivering (Scholander et al. 1958). Also, the Europeans had higher skin temperatures, suggesting that the shivering had increased their rate of heat loss (Figure 7–6).

The San of the Kalahari Desert (formerly known as bushmen to Westerners) who live in traditional ways are also exposed seasonally to cool nights; they show responses similar to those of the aboriginal Australian people, although some shivering does occur (Wyndham and Morrison 1958).

Arctic Dwellers

Studies of arctic dwellers such as the Inuit, Lapps, and native Americans from subarctic regions have shown very different responses to whole-body cold exposure: like unacclimatized Europeans they shiver and thereby increase their metabolic rate, although studies suggest that their rate of shivering may be less than that of unacclimatized people (Young 1988). There is some evidence that people who are native to arctic or subarctic regions maintain a higher basal metabolic rate (Hanna et al. 1989), perhaps because of increased heat generation from a high-protein diet (Young 1988). The higher basal metabolism allows an equivalent metabolic heat gain during acute exposure to cold with less shivering. In fact, responses of Inuit to cold do not indicate physiological adapta-

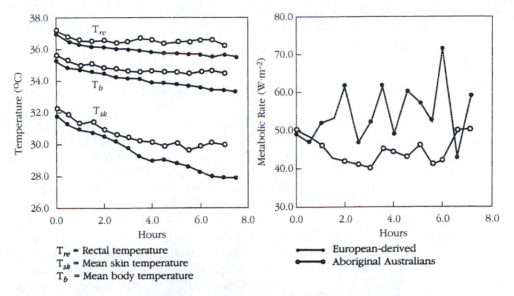

T_{re} = Rectal temperature
T_{sk} = Mean skin temperature
T_b = Mean body temperature

European-derived
Aboriginal Australians

Figure 7–6   Body temperature and metabolic rate of aboriginal Australian and European-derived people. (Redrawn by permission from H. T. Hammel et al. 1959. Thermal and metabolic responses of the Australian aborigine exposed to moderate cold in summer. *Journal of Applied Physiology* 14:605–15.)

tion: their cultural/behavioral buffer appears to be so effective that they are rarely exposed to a cold microenvironment.

Ama Divers

Perhaps the most extreme example known of whole-body cold exposure occurs among the Ama women divers of Korea. These women, who dive for abalone and other marine food resources throughout the year, are exposed to water temperatures as low as 10°C. Until recently, they wore only light cotton bathing suits, which did not provide effective insulation against the cold water.

Physiological studies on the Ama divers showed a consistent pattern of seasonal changes in basal metabolic rate: the women had a higher M_b in the winter, while nondiving women in the same villages did not show a seasonal change (Kang et al. 1963). These results suggest that nonshivering thermogenesis occurred in the divers.

The Ama divers also differed from nondiving people in having lower shivering thresholds, perhaps due to habituation. Ama divers appeared to be better insulated from cold than nondivers for a given amount of fat. This is probably related to vascular changes: the divers either had greater vasoconstriction responses or possessed more efficient countercurrent heat exchange mechanisms than nondivers.

Since 1977, the Ama divers have worn wet suits, which are effective insulators in the water. Physiological studies in the following years have documented a steady decline in the special biological adaptations that the women had shown, and by 1981 there was no seasonal difference between divers and nondivers in basal metabolism (Young 1988).

ACCLIMATIZATION TO PERIPHERAL COLD EXPOSURE

For many people who reside in cold macroenvironments, it is more common for only the peripheries—primarily hands and feet—to be exposed to cold, rather than entire bodies, thanks to clothing, bedding, and other cultural adaptations. The biological impact of this is much greater when the exposure is to cold water.

Populations differ in their biological response to peripheral exposure. For instance, when Inuit hands are exposed to cold water, the rate at which their hand temperatures drop is slower than in nonacclimatized people. Similarly, high-altitude Andean natives show higher skin temperatures in their feet and hands when exposed to cold than nonacclimatized people do. The higher skin temperatures suggest that these groups maintain greater blood flow to their extremities during cold exposure (Frisancho 1993), due at least in part to cold-induced vasodilation (CIVD).

Similar responses to peripheral cold exposure are found in European people who have become acclimatized to peripheral cold exposure. For instance, fish filleters (Nelms and Soper 1962) and North Sea fishermen (Krog et al. 1960) also show enhanced hand temperatures under cold exposure. The population differences in biological responses to peripheral cold exposure are therefore likely to be due to individual acclimatization as opposed to genetic adaptations specific only to certain human groups.

ADAPTIVE CONSEQUENCES OF COLD STRESS

One cannot help being unimpressed with human biological adaptability to cold, at least in comparison with many other mammals. What is quite impressive on the other hand is how humans have utilized cultural means to deal with cold macroenvironments, creating survivable, and often comfortable, microenvironments in extremely cold climates. A telling observation was made by Steegmann and colleagues (1983) in summarizing a large multidisciplinary study of northern Algonkians who live in subarctic conditions: "both as a threat to survival and health and as a matter of concern in everyday life, low temperature matters little." Of course, there are prices to be paid, principally in terms of resources that are essential for constructing the microenvironments, including clothing and building materials, associated tools, fuel, and perhaps extra food to accommodate the increased metabolic costs of heat generation. What is harder to calculate are the costs, such as possible resources that are not obtained, incurred from avoiding cold.

In a demographic sense, some individuals are at greater risk than others of suffering injury or death from cold, notably young children (Little and Hochner

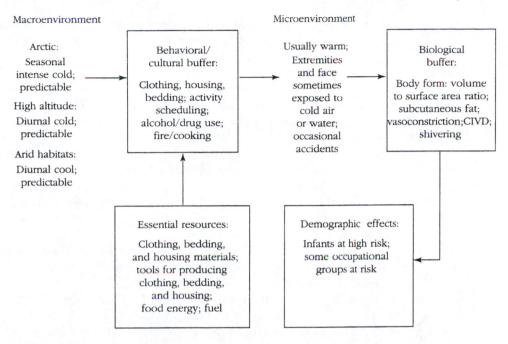

Figure 7–7   Single-stressor model of human adaptation to cold.

1973). Children are small, accordingly have a large surface-area-to-volume ratio, and, until they learn to walk, are exposed to conductive heat loss from crawling on cold surfaces. Although evidence is only indirect, infants may have a special defense in their pads of brown adipose tissue, tissue that has been linked with nonshivering thermogenesis in other animals. Evenki reindeer herders of Siberia show slow growth rates during late childhood and adolescence despite adequate food intake; their slowed growth may be due to allocation of food energy to increased metabolic requirements associated with adaptation to cold and away from support of growth (Leonard et al. 1994).

Human adaptability to cold stress is summarized in Figure 7–7. The single-stressor model is used, showing both the behavioral/cultural and biological buffers, as well as potential demographic effects and resources essential for the buffers.

HOT-DRY MACROENVIRONMENTS

There are two major types of hot macroenvironments: hot-dry and warm-humid. The adaptive problems and responses are so different in these types of conditions that we consider the two types separately.

Hot-dry environments include hot deserts and savannas, both of which are hot and dry year-round; and also more temperate deserts and grasslands, which are seasonally hot-dry. The aridity of these environments permits high rates of solar radiative heat gain because of the clear, dry air (Fitzpatrick 1979), with midday temperatures in deserts of about 57°C. The high heat also leads to rapid air movement, increasing convective heat gain.

The aridity of these environments often exceeds the tolerance limits of trees and most other plants, and therefore there is little natural shade. Beyond the direct problem of heat, people must cope with other problems of these environments, such as limited availability of food and water in hot deserts (Hanna and Brown 1983). Seasonally hot-dry environments usually do not present such formidable adaptive challenges, as cooler weather leads to less evaporation and thus greater retention of the rain that does fall. If there is a seasonal wet season, water may be retained below the ground or in storage tissues of living organisms well into the dry season.

Another characteristic of hot-dry macroenvironments is that they are usually cool during the night because the clear, dry air permits rapid reradiation of heat to space. Temperatures at night may drop below freezing despite reaching very high levels in the daytime.

Ancestral hominids lived in hot-dry conditions (Clark 1980). Over hundreds of thousands of years it is likely that our ancestors evolved special adaptations to these types of environments, particularly since cultural adaptations were probably rudimentary for much of this time. Cultural adaptations to these conditions in contemporary humans are diverse, often complex, and usually quite effective.

Cultural Adaptations to Hot-Dry Conditions

Adaptations to hot-dry conditions involve activity scheduling, insulation, shading, and use of evaporative cooling (Hanna and Brown 1979). These behavioral/cultural adaptations are usually quite effective in creating comfortable microenvironments.

Activity Scheduling. Activity scheduling simply entails avoiding hot places or times and especially avoiding the generation of metabolic heat through activity at the hottest times of the day. Aside from mad dogs and certain European colonists, virtually all people in hot-dry climates utilize such activity scheduling strategies as siestas.

Housing. Surprisingly, technological adaptations utilize strategies similar to those used in dealing with cold stress. Housing in hot-dry environments tends to utilize insulation to delay heat entry during the daytime and also to delay heat loss at night. Houses tend to be made of high-heat-capacity materials such as stone or adobe, have shapes that minimize surface area to volume, have small windows and doors, and are also often built close together, such as the traditional houses of the Pueblo Indians (see Figure 7–8). Houses are sometimes built underground in whole or part, such as the pit houses found in the southwestern United States. Fires for cooking purposes are often located away from

Figure 7–8   Pueblo housing illustrating the emphasis on insulation from low surface area, small windows, and thick walls. (Photo courtesy of J. Stone)

other housing areas or outside residential houses altogether (Hanna and Brown 1983).

Clothing.   Clothing is utilized to reduce solar radiative heat gain (Adolph 1949) and to inhibit convective heating from hot winds. It also serves to deter sunburn. Insulation through the use of trapped air is critical for effectiveness, although clothing must also be permeable to water to allow for evaporative cooling by sweat. For both houses and clothing, use of light, reflective colors reduces radiative heat gain, although dark-colored clothing protects better against sunburn (Hanna and Brown 1979). For instance, among the Sahara-dwelling Tuareg, traditional clothing is dark blue or black (Nicolaisen 1963).

Shading.   Any type of shading can aid in heat stress reduction. Umbrellas, which take their name from the Latin *umbra*, meaning "shade," are used widely by people in hot-dry climates. Buildings in these climates often have awnings or other means of providing shade. Where water resources permit, strategic planting of trees can also increase shade in places where people must be outside at hot times of the day.

Evaporative Cooling.   The primary means of dealing with heat in hot-dry climates is evaporative cooling, if water resources are sufficient to permit it. These adaptations can take the form of simply wetting down areas near residences or work areas, wetting millet screens in windows as in North India (Planalp 1971), or more complex methods. One of these complex methods is used in Arabia, where people have two courtyards immediately outside their residences. One courtyard is built of stone, while the other, on the other side of the house, consists of a garden with trees, shrubs, and, where resources permit, water. The stone courtyard heats up, creating a great deal of convection as the hot air rises from the stone. Cool air from the garden is drawn through the house to replace the air above the stone courtyard, and the residence is effectively air conditioned (Rapoport 1969). Many structures in Iran use wind towers to generate air movement used in passive cooling (Bahadori 1978).

HOT-DRY MICROENVIRONMENTS

Cultural adaptations to dry heat are effective in providing more comfortable microenvironments most of the time. People are nonetheless exposed to hot-dry microenvironments in some circumstances, particularly when they must travel or work in hot conditions or when water resources are too scarce to be available for evaporative cooling of the surroundings. The latter is the case for the G/wi San people of the central Kalahari Desert (Silberbauer 1981). In these cases people must fall back on their biological responses, which, as we will see, are formidable.

The greatest concern in hot-dry environments is high activity in hot surroundings, as internal heat is generated at a time when it is difficult to lose heat to the environment. Those who have watched the Kona Ironman Triathlon on television, where athletes voluntarily submit to consecutive long-distance swims, bicycle races, and marathon runs, with the latter two occurring at midday in a hot-dry macroenvironment, probably have the sense that all our cultural adaptations may not be needed if our bodies can withstand that intensity of heat stress. Indeed, humans are biologically very well adapted to hot-dry heat, unlike our adaptation to cold, suggesting that many of the cultural responses to heat are for comfort rather than survival.

Biological Responses

Heat Transfer. The major means of dealing with dry heat is to enhance heat transfer from the core to the shell and from the shell to the environment as well as to lose heat at the body surface through evaporation. Thermoregulatory centers in the brain are stimulated when body heat increases beyond a threshold, and these centers activate physiological adjustments to increase heat transfer to the shell and to initiate water evaporation at the body surface (Hanna and Brown 1983).

In many respects, the rapid transfer of heat from the core to the body surface during heat stress involves mechanisms that are the opposite of those used to adapt to cold, where the goal is to slow heat loss from the core. Bergmann's and Allen's rules still apply, with smaller, longer-limbed individuals favored in hot climates; the very linear body form of the Tuareg people of the Sahara is an example (Briggs 1975). Decreased insulation from reduced fat stores is also favorable in adapting to heat. Uneven distribution of fat may even be favored in hot climates (Baker 1958).

Vascular Responses. Superficial blood flow is increased upon stimulation by the sympathetic nervous system through vasodilation of superficial veins, with other vessels constricted to permit a fairly constant maintenance of blood pressure (Wyndham et al. 1968). High skin temperature also directly stimulates blood vessel dilation without the necessity of nervous stimulation (Sawka and Wenger 1988). Blood flow is particularly directed into hands and feet, which, because of their great surface areas, act as radiators in rapidly exchanging heat with the environment through convection and radiation. Also, blood flow shifts primarily to arteries that are not immediately adjacent to veins; therefore blood is not significantly rewarmed after cooling in the peripheries.

Peripheral dilation leads to greater pooling of blood in the circulation, which in turn stimulates the heart to beat faster and harder. This increased cardiovascular strain can lead to fatalities in extreme circumstances, particularly in people with preexisting heart conditions (Sawka and Wenger 1988).

Sweating. The main adaptation of humans to dry-heat stress is the ability to sweat copiously. Perspiration begins at skin temperatures of about 35°C, but people are quite variable in the skin temperature threshold for sweating. Perspiration usually begins on the trunk and spreads to the limbs in unacclimatized people, but this pattern is reversed, with initial sweating onset in the limbs, in acclimatized individuals (Hofler 1968). Since limbs have greater surface-area-to-volume ratios, the effectiveness of evaporative heat loss may be maximized in the limbs.

Humans have a very effective sweating mechanism. Our response is based primarily on our specialized **eccrine sweat glands.** These glands produce liquid that consists of water with a salt (electrolyte) concentration about equal to that of body water in general (Hanna and Brown 1983). Many other mammals rely principally on **apocrine sweat glands,** which are associated with hair follicles and secrete a fluid rich in lipids and proteins. Humans have a higher density of eccrine sweat glands than other mammals, with over a million active glands (Baker 1988a). The phrase "sweating like a horse" does not fit the facts: the maximal sweat rate of 100 gm/m^2/hr for horses pales before the maximal sweat rate of 500 gm/m^2/hr for humans (Folk 1974). Eccrine gland activity is controlled by the sympathetic nervous system, with both local skin temperature and core temperature involved in stimulating the onset of sweating (Kerslake 1972).

Our sweat production capability exceeds the evaporation rate except in extremely dry conditions, leading to what Newman (1975) refers to as "dripping sweat." Fortunately, the metabolic cost of eccrine sweat gland activity is low, although it is costly in terms of water resources (Newman 1970). The body does not contain reserve stores of water, so a high sweat rate can lead to dehydration. Humans undergo "voluntary dehydration" during high heat loads, as thirst does not equal water loss under extreme conditions. This voluntary dehydration can amount to 3 to 5 percent of body weight, which can lead to serious consequences in a decline in blood volume (Weiner 1980).

Acclimatization.   Humans who have acclimatized to heat increase their maximal sweat rate and also begin sweating at lower skin and core temperatures (Wenger 1988). The earlier onset of sweating permits cooling to begin earlier and can reduce the overall heat stress on the individual. Acclimatized people also produce less salty sweat because of improved sodium reabsorption by eccrine sweat glands, resulting in less salt loss during a given heat load. All healthy people can acclimatize to heat stress, even those from populations with long histories in cold climates (Edholm and Weiner 1981).

A question remains regarding whether some human populations are better biologically adapted to heat than others because of genetic adaptations that have arisen as part of evolutionary selection. This is a difficult question to answer, since all humans have an extremely effective biological heat response after acclimatization. Studies have been carried out on individuals from many different groups who are naturally exposed to hot-dry conditions, such as the San from the Kalahari Desert, the Bantu from South Africa, and Arabs from the Sahara desert region in comparison with people from groups that are not located in hot-dry climates. Results suggest that acclimatization is much more important in accounting for individual variability in heat adaptation than is population affiliation (Hanna et al. 1989).

Figure 7–9 summarizes human adaptive responses to hot-dry conditions. It is based on the single-stressor model that has served to organize the discussion in this chapter.

WARM-HUMID MACROENVIRONMENTS

Warm-humid macroenvironments, represented in the extreme by tropical rainforests, differ significantly from hot-dry macroenvironments in the characteristics of heat stress. Because of moisture in the air and frequent cloudiness, solar radiative heat gain is less during the day. Radiative heat loss at night is also reduced, resulting in much less diurnal variation in temperature. Humid areas never get as hot, nor do they get as cool, as arid regions.

Air temperature in humid areas is usually cooler than body core temperature, allowing efficient convective cooling. Warm-humid environments usually contain extensive vegetation that is also cooler than core temperature, permitting radiative heat loss. Vegetation also provides abundant shade. Water resources are plentiful, allowing replacement of liquids lost by perspiration. The humidity greatly slows evaporation, however, and therefore limits its cooling effects.

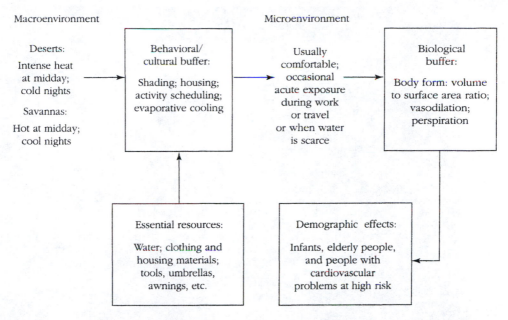

Figure 7–9 Single-stressor model of human adaptation to dry heat.

Cultural Adaptations

Behavioral and cultural adaptations to warm-humid environments are limited compared with those for hot-dry environments. Since there is little diurnal variation in temperature, activity scheduling has little value as a means of avoiding heat stress. Also, cultural practices that enhance evaporative cooling are not as effective in humid conditions because of the slow evaporation rate. The major cultural adaptations to humid heat involve ventilation to facilitate convective cooling. Short of the use of dehumidifiers, little else can be done.

Clothing. Optimal clothing in warm-humid climates can be described succinctly: as little as possible. Many traditional peoples in warm-humid climates have worn minimal clothing. Some people have worn no clothing at all, or loincloths. Where contact with Western culture or other industrialized societies occurs, it is common for men to wear shorts or loincloths, sometimes with shirts, while women wear sarongs or similar light clothing (Dentan 1979). For example, among the Djuka of French Guiana, the descendants of African slaves who gained their freedom in the South American rainforest, males wear little more than shorts (Figure 7–10).

Housing. In housing, the optimal design is to have a roof for shade and shelter from rain, but to have little else. Walls are minimal, floors are raised and open to air circulation from below, and vents are present in or near the roof to

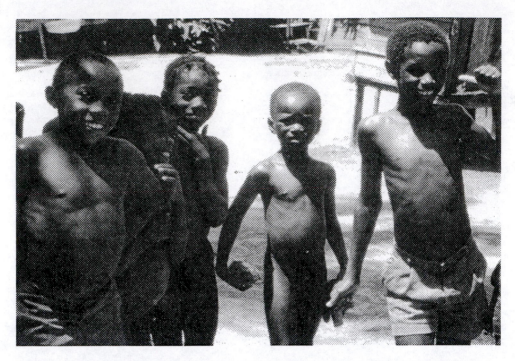

Figure 7–10   Photograph of Djuka boys, illustrating the minimal clothing worn in warm, humid conditions. (Photo courtesy of Norris Durham)

allow warm air to escape (Hanna and Brown 1979). An example of this kind of housing is found in Papua New Guinea (Figure 7–11). Houses are raised on stilts several feet above the ground, flooring boards usually have gaps between them, walls have openings for ventilation below the roof, and pitched thatch roofs have extended gables for enhanced shading. This type of house maximizes ventilation, although the thatched roof traps some air that insulates the house from solar radiation.

WARM-HUMID MICROENVIRONMENTS

While ambient air in warm-humid macroenvironments is rarely hotter than the body core, cultural adaptations to modify the environment are relatively ineffective. Thus, people are often exposed to heat stress in humid climates, particularly when they must engage in muscular activity. Therefore, the problem is shedding metabolically generated heat, not blocking environmental heat. The good news is that there is usually sufficient water available to replace that lost in perspiration; the bad news is that because of the lowered rate of evaporation, perspiration is not very useful in cooling. Human microenvironments in warm-humid climates are not very different from shady, airy, natural conditions in the region.

Figure 7–11   Photograph of a house in the warm, humid conditions found in Papua New Guinea. Notice the stilts, extended eaves, and fairly open-walled design. (Photo courtesy of Ralph Garruto)

Biological Responses

The physiological response to heat in humid conditions is the same as it is in dry conditions: vasodilation of peripheral blood vessels and perspiration. Also, an increased surface-area-to-volume ratio is beneficial. The major difference from dry conditions is the slowed evaporation of sweat and thus a reduced rate of cooling. It may be that body form takes on more importance in humid than in arid climates because of the ineffectiveness of sweating in heat adaptation. It is clearly the case that in warm-humid climates populations with the smallest average body size tend to be found, such as the pygmy groups in Africa and many aboriginal groups of Southeast Asia who have small average body size. Perhaps Bergmann's rule has more applicability to humans when their main biological adaptation to heat, perspiration, is rendered ineffective.

ADAPTIVE CONSEQUENCES OF HEAT STRESS

Humans have a very effective biological adaptation to hot-dry conditions in contrast to their generally poor biological adaptability to cold. People from many cultural traditions have made good use of cultural responses to create comfortable microenvironments in hot-dry climates, chiefly through utilization of activity scheduling, shading, insulation to take advantage of diurnal temperature changes, and evaporative-cooling techniques. Humans for the most part do not really require these cultural buffers except in extreme conditions, given their superior biological ability to cope with dry heat.

There are, however, problems associated with heat exposure, especially when people are working under hot conditions. Difficulties cover a spectrum of symptoms (Hubbard and Armstrong 1988) including

> Heat cramps, primarily due to salt depletion
>
> Heat exhaustion, when decreased fluid volume leads to collapse
>
> Heat syncope, when blood supply to the brain decreases, causing loss of consciousness
>
> Heat stroke, characterized by marked behavioral changes including confusion, vertigo, disorientation, and coma, often leading to cellular damage

Some individuals in a population are at greater risk from illness or death from heat exposure, particularly the very young, the elderly, and people who have preexisting heart disease. Newborns have a limited sweating capability, as many of their eccrine sweat glands are inactive (Hey and Katz 1969). The elderly are at great risk primarily because of lowered physical fitness and a lack of acclimatization; however, people of advanced age deal quite effectively with moderate heat stress when they are physically fit (Robinson et al. 1965). People with heart ailments are at risk under heat stress because of the increase in heart rate and concomitant strain that occurs with acute exposure to heat. These severe negative consequences of heat stress occur more commonly under humid conditions, when evaporative cooling is rendered ineffective.

Figure 7–12 summarizes human adaptive responses to humid heat. Both biological and behavioral/cultural buffers are noted, as well as essential resources and possible demographic effects.

CONCLUSION

Human cultural adaptations to cold and hot-dry environments are very effective. Humans are able to create microenvironments that are nearly thermoneutral in a wide variety of climatic regimes. This ability has been of major importance in permitting the species to expand its range to include most terrestrial environments. While their ability to deal with warm-humid climates is not as impressive as for cold environments, these conditions are rarely dangerous, unless they must engage in prolonged high activity levels.

In dealing with temperature extremes, as with other environmental stressors, people must balance effectiveness with efficiency in their responses. The most effective way of dealing with cold is to build expensive housing and burn a great deal of fuel for central heating. For high-altitude and arctic peoples, who live where trees are scarce or absent, the most effective means of dealing with

Macroenvironment   Microenvironment

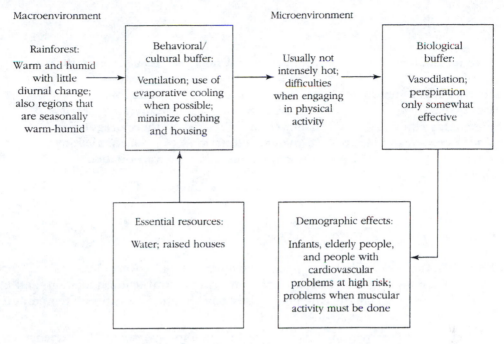

Figure 7–12   Single-stressor model of human adaptation to humid heat.

cold are simply too costly. The environmental stress of cold can be so severe, however, that these people cannot be too penurious with their response. Thus, people make compromises between effectiveness and efficiency. The strategies used must also avoid increasing risk of injury or death. They must be dependable and capable of implementation without putting people in harm's way.

Human biological responses to cold and humid heat are not extraordinarily effective, but their biological adaptability to dry heat may deserve a rating of extraordinary compared with other mammals. It is no coincidence that fossil evidence suggests that hominids evolved in a hot-dry region. Humans have, however, evolved a different kind of adaptation than that found among other mammals. They have been called "naked apes" because of their relative lack of hair (Morris 1967); they have also been called a "sweaty and thirsty naked animal" (Newman 1970) because of their prodigious sweating ability, resulting in a great need to drink water to replace perspiration. The lack of hair leads to a greater heat gain from solar radiation, but it also permits more rapid heat loss from evaporation. Thus, human biology appears to be an adaptation for rapid unloading of heat, such as when doing vigorous activity in hot conditions (Hanna and Brown 1983). This type of adaptation requires ready access to a dependable water supply. Voluntary dehydration may permit humans to "take care of business" with intensive muscular activity and, upon completion of work, to begin replacing body water. Whatever the details of human evolutionary adaptations to extremes of heat, there is ample evidence to suggest that, clothing or not, humans are tropical animals.

KEY TERMS

active metalloism
Allen's rule
apocrine sweat glands
basal metabolism
Bergmann's rule
cold-induced vasodilation
conduction
convection

countercurrent heat
  exchange
eccrine sweat glands
evaporation
habituation
insulative adaptation
metabolic adaptation

nonshivering thermo-
  genesis
radiation
shivering
thermoregulation
vasoconstriction
vasodilation

KEY POINTS

☐ Thermoregulation, the homeostatic balancing between heat gained through metabolism and its loss through conduction, convection, radiation, and evaporation, results in the core of the body having a narrow range of temperature tolerance, the shell having a broad range.

☐ Cold macroenvironments include mountainous areas that experience marked diurnal temperature changes, arctic areas, and winter seasons in temperate regions, all of which can reduce resource availability over long periods of time.

☐ Cultural adaptations to cold macroenvironments occur by constructing warm microenvironments through the use of insulative clothing, bedding, and housing; activity scheduling; ingestion of alcohol and other pharmacological agents; and the use of fire.

☐ Biological responses to cold are of two forms: insulative through the reduction of body surface area, presence of subcutaneous fat, vasoconstriction of superficial blood vessels, and countercurrent heat exchange; and metabolic through shivering and nonshivering thermogenesis.

☐ Habituation to whole-body exposure to cold involves a lowering of the shivering threshold as well as a reduction in the sympathetic nervous system response to cold and has been observed in Australian aborigines and the Kalahari San.

☐ Acclimatization to peripheral cold exposure includes a slower rate of hand temperature drop and resulting higher foot and hand skin temperature in Inuit, high-altitude Andean natives, and northern European fish filleters.

☐ Cultural adaptations to the hot-dry environments of hot deserts and savannas include activity scheduling, insulated housing, lightweight and light-colored clothing, shading, and evaporative cooling.

☐ Biological responses to hot-dry environments include enhanced heat transfer from the body core to the shell and from the shell to the environment by evaporation, vasodilation of superficial blood vessels, and sweating. Acclimatization involves an increase in maximal sweat rates that begin at lower skin and core temperatures.

☐ Cultural adaptations to the warm-humid environments typical of tropical rain-forests include as little use of clothing as possible and housing that includes a roof and little else.

☐ Biological responses to warm-humid environments include vasodilation of peripheral blood vessels and sweating, albeit with reduced rate of evaporation, across an increased body surface area.

☐ Among the consequences of heat stress are cramps, heat exhaustion, heat syncope, and heat stroke, with the young, the elderly, and those with preexisting heart disease being the most vulnerable.

8

Adaptation to Altitude, High Activity, and Other Physical Stressors

INTRODUCTION

Human populations have been confronted with several other physical stressors besides temperature extremes. This chapter will briefly explore how people have coped with some of them, including high-altitude **hypoxia** (low oxygen levels), the self-induced stress of intense activity levels, and such natural hazards as storms, earthquakes, tsunamis (seismic sea waves), and volcanic eruptions.

HIGH-ALTITUDE HYPOXIA

As noted in the previous chapter, humans are relatively new to high-altitude environments in an evolutionary sense. Archaeologists have little confidence in dating the precise time when people first established permanent habitations in the high mountains, but it is clear that people have lived in such environments in the Himalayas and Andes for millennia (Lynch 1978; Zhimin 1982). Converting this time duration to a figure of over 400 generations, as suggested by Reader (1988), implies that sufficient time has passed to permit significant genetic adaptations in native highland populations.

High mountains are stimulating, starkly beautiful, but also dangerous—particularly upon initial arrival (Figure 8–1). High mountain regions pose many adaptive problems for human populations, including

Figure 8–1   Astronomical observatory at the summit of Mauna Kea, Hawaii. (Photo by D. E. Brown)

diurnal cold, aridity, high levels of ultraviolet radiation, dustiness, poor soils, an impoverished biota, rugged terrain, and isolation from other human groups (Baker 1984) (see Figure 8–2). There is one stressor found naturally only at high altitude: hypoxia. The discussion here will focus on this unique stress at high altitude.

Hypoxia at high altitude is a result of lower **barometric pressure.** Air pressure at any location is based largely on the amount of air above that location; the weight of the air above pushes down on lower air, creating an increased density of air molecules, and thus increased pressure. Since the amount, or height, of air decreases with altitude, barometric pressure decreases as well. Figure 8–2a illustrates the general relationship between altitude and barometric pressure. As barometric pressure decreases, so does the molecular density of oxygen in the air. The percentage of oxygen in the air (about 21 percent) is no different at high altitude than at sea level—there are simply fewer air molecules of any kind in a given volume of air. So each breath one takes at high altitude has fewer molecules of oxygen in it for a given depth of breath; it is this which creates hypoxic conditions for living organisms.

Given the nature of hypoxic stress, what can people in high mountain environments do to create more comfortable microenvironments? If one excludes the impractical possibilities of living in pressurized chambers or carrying oxygen tanks on one's back, there is very little that can be done. In fact, this inability to deal with hypoxia through our behavior has attracted human biologists to the problem, since people are essentially thrown back on their biological buffers to see them through. There is one behavioral adaptation short of heading for sea level that is possible: to minimize physical activity, since this decreases metabolic demands for oxygen.

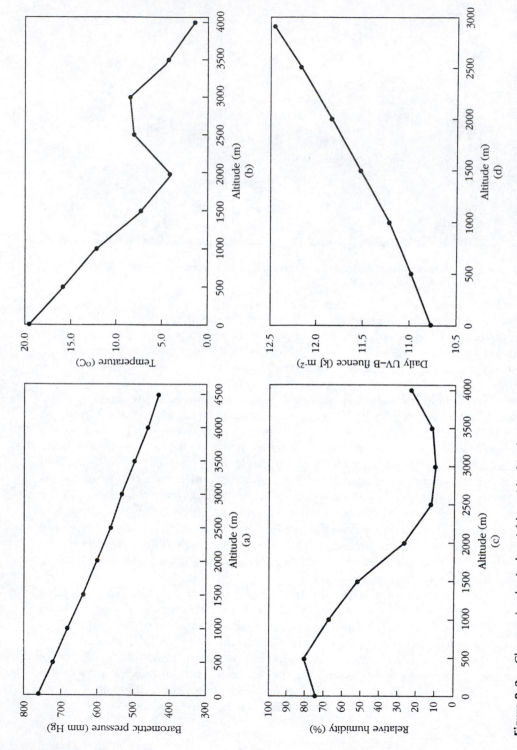

Figure 8–2 Changes in physical variables with altitude. (a) Barometric pressure changes with altitude. (b) Temperature changes with altitude. (c) Relative humidity changes with altitude. (d) Ultraviolet-B fluence changes with altitude. (Data in b and c from a "typical" day on slopes of Mauna Kea, Hawaii [from Juvik, unpublished]. Data in d from Haleakala, Hawaii [from J. H. Sullivan et al. 1992. *American Journal of Botany* 79:737–43.])

Biological Adaptations to Hypoxia

Our biological adaptations to hypoxia involve increasing the efficiency and effectiveness of oxygen transport into our bodies and to our tissues, where it is used in metabolism, while adjusting to body changes that are side effects of the adaptations. Major differences in our coping ability have been found that are related to acclimatization, with changes occurring within a day or two and continuing over weeks of exposure. There are additional differences in coping ability between highland natives and native lowlanders who have acclimatized to altitude as adults.

The biological response to hypoxia can be broken up into the following stages for the purpose of analysis: oxygen transport from the air to lungs, oxygen transport from lungs to blood, blood transport to body tissues, oxygen transport from blood into the tissues, and cellular changes in oxygen utilization. We'll discuss these stages separately. In all cases we will use an elevation of about 4,000 m for high altitude, allowing a clear contrast with sea level.

Oxygen Transfer to Lungs. Immediately upon exposure to hypoxic conditions, there is an increase in **ventilation rate,** the total amount of air moving into and out of the lungs in a given amount of time. This is accomplished by an increase in both the rate and depth of breathing. The increased ventilation rate is stimulated by chemical receptors (chemoreceptors) in the carotid and aortic bodies that are located in peripheral blood vessels (Fulco and Cymerman 1988). The chemoreceptors detect the lowered blood oxygen concentration providing a cybernetic, negative-feedback, response (Heath and Williams 1977).

The increased ventilation serves to bring more oxygen into the lungs, but also leads to an increase in the expiration rate of carbon dioxide. The loss of carbon dioxide affects the general acid-base balance of the body, due to carbon dioxide's critical role in the following chemical equilibrium:

$$CO_2 + H_2O \rightleftarrows H_2CO_3 \rightleftarrows HCO_3^- + H^+$$

H_2CO_3, or carbonic acid, is a major acid in body fluids. Loss of CO_2 through exhalation leads to a leftward shift in this formula to restore equilibrium. This, in turn, leads to a relative loss of acidity in body fluids, resulting in respiratory alkalosis (a physiological condition of high alkalinity caused by high ventilation). In particular, the alkalinity of cerebrospinal fluid is increased (Lenfant and Sullivan 1971), which in turn causes receptors in the medullary region of the brain to inhibit the ventilation rate, hence reducing the CO_2 loss that created the respiratory alkalosis (Heath and Williams 1977). Thus, the enhanced ventilation necessary to increase oxygen input in a hypoxic environment is countered by brain mechanisms to inhibit respiratory alkalosis, resulting in limits to ventilation rate.

Within a few days of exposure, there is an increase in excretion rates of bicarbonate ions from the body by the kidney. The removal of these alkaline materials

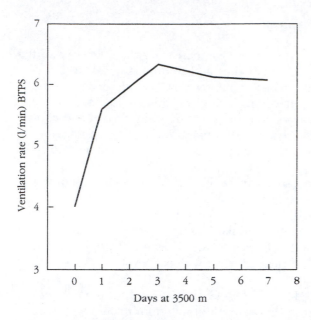

Figure 8–3 Changes in ventilation rate as a function of time during acute exposure to high altitude (3,500 m). (Based on data from S. S. Purkayastha et al. 1995. *Journal of Applied Physiology* 79:487–92.)

helps restore the acid-base balance of body fluids, and in turn this removes the inhibition of ventilation, allowing a faster ventilation rate (Figure 8–3). At this point, people have developed some acclimatization and can usually handle the hypoxic stress of altitude unless they engage in strenuous physical labor.

Natives of high altitude generally do not hyperventilate as much as people newly exposed to hypoxic conditions at any given exercise level. Both Himalayan sherpas and Andean peoples show a lowered hypoxic **ventilatory drive,** that is, a lowered sensitivity of ventilation rate to hypoxic exposure. Apparently the chemoreceptors are not as sensitive to lowered oxygen levels in the natives, and thus they do not stimulate as great an increase in ventilation rate upon exposure to hypoxic conditions as is found in newcomers to altitude (Santolaya et al. 1989). This blunted hypoxic drive appears to occur only in individuals who grow up in hypoxic environments; it is virtually irreversible once developed in an individual (Mazess 1970). There is evidence that the cerebrospinal fluid in natives is more acidic than in newcomers to high altitude and that this acidity may be the main stimulus to ventilation rate in the natives (Lahiri 1977). Thus, the physiological basis of increased ventilation may be quite different between people who are acclimatizing to high-altitude environments and people who are natives to such environments. Native Tibetans differ from other high-altitude natives in that they do not develop a blunted hypoxic drive (Zhang et al. 1993; Beall et al. 1997).

Oxygen Transfer from Lungs to Blood.   Oxygen exchange with the blood occurs in tiny air sacs **(alveoli)** in the lungs. The movement of oxygen from an alveolus to the adjacent blood capillaries occurs through the passive process of diffusion. The rate of diffusion is based on many factors, including the surface area of alveoli and blood capillaries, the thickness of tissues separating the alveolar air from blood, and the difference in oxygen concentration between the alveolar air and blood. Another major factor is the blood's oxygen carrying ability; most of this ability is due to the protein **hemoglobin.** Each molecule of hemoglobin combines chemically with up to four oxygen molecules. Under high oxygen concentrations, oxygen tends to attach to hemoglobin, while in conditions of low oxygen concentration hemoglobin tends to release oxygen molecules. This permits hemoglobin to "load up" with oxygen in the high concentration areas of the lungs' alveoli, while unloading it in the low concentration areas of body tissues where oxygen is needed.

Only a portion of the lungs' alveoli are used under normal sea-level conditions. Similarly, under these conditions many capillaries in the lung are constricted, with blood supply directed toward actively used capillaries. Low oxygen concentrations stimulate the vasoconstriction, ensuring that the blood is directed toward healthy, active regions of the lungs. When ventilation increases, as occurs upon exposure to high-altitude hypoxia or during intense muscular activity, more alveoli become active, and more capillaries in the lungs dilate, increasing perfusion of the lungs with blood. This increases the surface area of alveolus-blood connections in the lung, speeding diffusion of oxygen into the blood (West 1979).

Under the general hypoxic conditions at high altitude, the lung's mechanism of vasoconstricting blood vessels in areas of low oxygen concentration leads to a generalized vasoconstriction of all pulmonary blood vessels. Blood is distributed throughout the lung with no loss of volume and therefore the vasoconstriction raises blood pressure in the lungs. This is enhanced by the buildup of smooth muscle in the walls of pulmonary arterioles (Bouverot 1985). In long-term residents of high altitude, the right ventricle of the heart, which pumps blood to the lungs, becomes enlarged as a result of its increased muscular effort. Again, native Tibetans may differ from other peoples at high altitude in that they do not develop high blood pressure in their lungs (Groves et al. 1993). The differences between Tibetans and other high-altitude peoples suggests that Tibetans have a special genetically based adaptation to high-altitude hypoxia (Zhang et al. 1993).

In some native populations of high mountain regions, such as the Quechua of the Andes, people have higher average lung sizes relative to their total body size than do individuals from sea-level regions. Much study has gone into whether these large lung sizes are genetically determined, and thus evolutionary adaptations, or if they are due to developmental processes that occur in any person raised at high altitude. The answer appears to be: both. Quechua raised at sea level average somewhat higher lung volumes than non-Quechua lowlanders; this suggests a genetic trait. Conversely, Quechua raised at sea level have lower average lung volumes than highland-raised Quechua (Greksa 1988), suggesting that development plays a significant role. Lung volume in migrants of European ancestry to high altitude appears to be related to the age at which they migrated (Greksa 1988); however, it does not reach levels found in Andean natives even if the European-derived people have been born and raised at high altitude (Greksa and Beall 1989). Tibetan people, however, do not show the enlarged lungs that are common in Andean populations (Beall 1984). Hence, the enlarged lungs found among some native high-altitude populations are due both to developmental forces common to all people and to genetically based population differences.

Exposure to high altitude also stimulates the secretion of erythropoietin, a hormone that in turn stimulates production of red blood cells (Albrecht and Littell 1972; Siri et al. 1966). Over several weeks, the percentage of blood occupied by red blood cells increases from about 43–47 percent to well over 50 percent on average (Ballew et al. 1989), a condition termed **polycythemia.** Since red blood cells contain hemoglobin, this increases the oxygen-carrying capacity of the blood. Polycythemia also makes blood more viscous—thicker—and thus places an increased strain on the cardiovascular system (Ballew et al. 1989). In addition to polycythemia, the concentration of hemoglobin in blood also increases in people who reside for several weeks at high altitude, from an average of about 15 g/100 ml to 18-20 g/100 ml (Quilici and Vergnes 1978; Ballew et al. 1989).

Natives of high altitude also have high hemoglobin concentrations and are somewhat polycythemic, although Himalayan populations tend to show lower values than Andean groups do. The difference between these two major high-altitude populations may be partly due to the fact that many of the studied Andean groups were in mining communities, and the mining activities increased hypoxic stress (Frisancho 1988). When only nonmining communities are compared, little difference in hemoglobin concentration is found between the populations (Frisancho and Greksa 1989). However, results from other investigations suggest that even when carefully controlled comparisons are made, Andeans tend to have higher rates of polycythemia than Himalayan groups do (Winslow et al. 1989). Tibetan newborn infants have lower hemoglobin concentrations than non-Tibetan infants also born at high altitude (Niermeyer et al. 1995), and ethnic differences in hemoglobin concentrations between native and nonnative infants born at high altitude in the Andes have also been reported (Ballew and Haas 1986). These differences may reflect lower in utero levels of hypoxia in the native infants.

Circulation of Blood to Tissues.   Circulatory responses to high-altitude hypoxia are primarily based upon distributional changes. There is a transitory increase in heart rate and cardiac output upon acute exposure, but this rapidly declines to preexposure values. While an increased cardiac output speeds the rate at which blood delivers oxygen to tissues, this is offset by the increased oxygen needs of the heart muscle as well as increased strain on the cardiovascular system. The initial increase in heart rate is due to a sympathetic nervous system response (Heath and Williams 1977) that is found upon initial exposure to virtually any stress and thus may not be directly related to hypoxia.

The distribution of blood circulation is changed under hypoxic conditions, with blood flow largely directed from less critical areas such as the skin to essential organs such as the brain (Lenfant and Sullivan 1971). This accounts for the pallor characteristic of people in high mountain environments. There is also evidence for an increase in the number of active capillaries during acclimatization (Kayser et al. 1991; Frisancho 1993). This shortens the average distance any given tissue cell is from a capillary and its oxygen-rich blood. The increased number of blood vessels is clearly apparent in the heart; Andean natives have a greater average number of secondary branches in their coronary heart blood vessels than sea-level residents (Heath and Williams 1977).

Oxygen Transfer from Blood to Tissue.   Oxygen is transferred from capillary blood to tissue cells by both active and passive means. Passive diffusion is influenced by similar factors as discussed for oxygen loading of blood in the lungs. An increase in the number of active capillaries increases diffusion rates both by increasing the surface area over which transport occurs and by decreasing the average distance between the capillary and a given tissue cell.

Oxygen transfer is actively assisted by a tissue protein, myoglobin, the levels of which are increased in muscles of people acclimatized to high altitude (Hurtado 1964; Reynafarje 1962). Myoglobin levels also are raised in muscles that are habitually used in work (Frisancho 1993), these increased levels serving as a general adaptation for a faster rate of oxygen transfer to cells.

Early studies suggested that at high altitude there is a tendency for hemoglobin to be less "sticky" to oxygen molecules (Lenfant and Sullivan 1971). This is apparently related to the greater alkalinity of blood that, in turn, causes an increase in a particular protein (2,3-diphosphoglycerate or 2,3-DPG) in red blood cells. While this change enhances the unloading of oxygen from hemoglobin at the tissue level, it also slows the uptake of oxygen by hemoglobin in the lungs (Quilici and Vergnes 1978). Later research has called the earlier results into question, and now there is dispute as to whether any change in hemoglobin's affinity for oxygen occurs at high altitude (Ballew et al. 1989).

Cellular Changes in Oxygen Utilization.   The activity of enzymes involved in oxidative metabolism (i.e., metabolism requiring the presence of oxygen) in cells is increased in natives of high altitude. There is also a shift in metabolic pathways used in the cells (specifically from the Embden-Meyerhof pathway to the pentose-phosphate pathway) to a more efficient means of providing energy for a given amount of oxygen (Frisancho 1993). It is unclear if sea-level natives develop similar adaptations upon acclimatization to high altitude.

Adaptive Consequences of Hypoxic Stress

There are special problems for people due to the hypoxic conditions of high mountain environments, especially upon initial exposure. The risk and severity of problems increases with the altitude attained and the rate of ascent. These problems include acute mountain sickness, pulmonary edema, cerebral edema, subacute infantile mountain sickness, and chronic mountain sickness.

Acute Mountain Sickness.   **Acute mountain sickness** is a very common ailment of people when they first arrive at high altitude. Common symptoms include headaches, dizziness, light-headedness, and feeling faint, all due to low-ered oxygen intake. Other symptoms, including nausea and vomiting, are due to respiratory alkalosis. Acute mountain sickness usually lasts only a day or two and is completely reversible upon acclimatization to high altitude or return to sea level (Carson et al. 1969). It, however, can be fatal if the body fails to respond quickly enough and particularly if edema ensues.

Edema.   Edema is an abnormal accumulation of fluid resulting in swelling. **Pulmonary edema** is not as common as acute mountain sickness but is a much more serious problem. When edema occurs in the lung, oxygen trans-port into the blood can be blocked. People can literally drown in their own body fluid (Houston 1992). Pulmonary edema is very rare in people acclimatized to high altitude but is a risk for people who are recently arrived at altitude, partic-ularly if they engage in heavy work (Hultgren 1979). Even more rare is **cerebral edema,** where fluid enters brain tissue. This ailment can lead to severe behav-ioral disorders, convulsions, and death (Malconian and Rock 1988; Severing-haus 1995). For either of these two forms of edema, immediate evacuation from high altitude is necessary.

Subacute Infantile Mountain Sickness.   While the problems just noted are rarely found in high-altitude natives or in people who have acclimatized to hypoxic environments, some problems remain. A particularly deadly disease, **subacute infantile mountain sickness,** is found in some infants born or brought to high altitude. These infants have low oxygen levels in their blood and tend to have highly elevated levels of polycythemia. They have a high risk of mortality if not brought to sea level. A recent study undertaken in Tibet compared infants born to sea-level–born Chinese (ethnic Han) mothers with infants born to native Tibetan mothers. The Han infants show a high incidence of infantile mountain sickness, evidenced by fairly low levels of oxygen in their arterial blood, but no cases were found among the native Tibetan infants (Nier-meyer et al. 1994, 1995).

Chronic Mountain Sickness.   Another problem that sometimes strikes natives or long-term residents of high altitude is **chronic mountain sickness.** This ailment is characterized by a loss of acclimatization, a lowered ventilation rate, and a great increase in polycythemia. Again, victims must leave high-altitude regions or risk severe, even fatal, consequences. The frequency of chronic moun-tain sickness is reported to be higher in Andean natives than in Himalayans, but this may be partly due to a lack of adequate data from the Himalayan region (Winslow 1984).

Adaptation to Mountain Environments

People who live permanently at high altitude, including Andeans, Ethiopians (Harrison et al. 1969), and Himalayans, have, in general, adapted well to the problems of high-altitude environments. This successful adaptation is shown both at the individual level, in terms of work capacity, and at the population level, for instance in the complexity of social systems that have developed in the high mountains.

Work Capacity at High Altitude. People who live at high altitudes must engage in work to gain subsistence, and this occasionally requires doing intense muscular activity. A clear example involves preparing fields for the planting and harvesting of potatoes in the Andes (see Figure 8–4). This task, accomplished with a digging stick or foot plow, termed a *taclla*, on soil that is often partially frozen, puts individuals in need of a rapid supply of oxygen in a hypoxic environment. Remarkably, high-altitude natives have a **work capacity,** that is, the ability to use oxygen at a fast rate, at high elevations that is equivalent to that of other peoples under sea-level conditions (Weitz 1984; Favier et al. 1995). This may be partly due to enhanced metabolism of glucose, and thus more energy availability, in the hearts of high-altitude natives (Holden et al. 1995).

Figure 8–4 Harvesting white potatoes in the high Andes village of Pueblo Llano, Venezuela. (Photo by E. J. Kormondy)

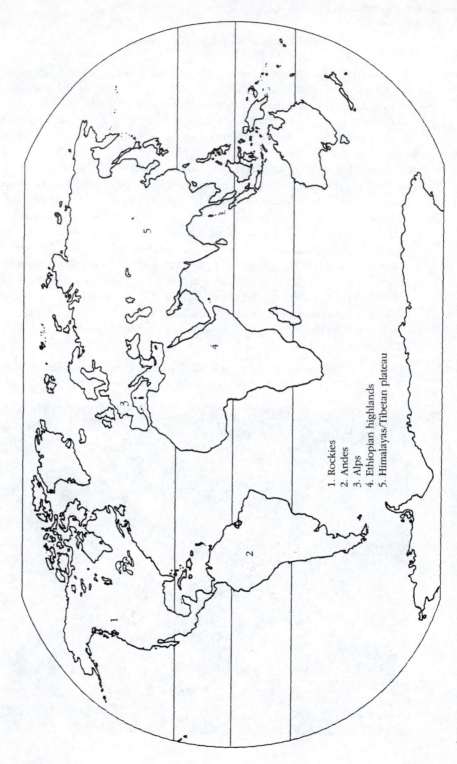

1. Rockies
2. Andes
3. Alps
4. Ethiopian highlands
5. Himalayas/Tibetan plateau

Figure 8–5 Map of high-altitude regions of the world.

Research by Frisancho et al. (1994) suggests that the great success that high-land natives have in adapting to high-altitude hypoxia as manifested in their high work capacities is primarily the result of developmental processes. People from lowland populations do not develop such high work capacities, even if resident for many years at high altitude, if they moved to high altitude after adulthood (Frisancho and Greksa 1989). People descended from high-altitude natives who grow up at sea level also do not show high work capacities under hypoxic conditions. Among the individuals who grow up at high altitudes, those who had high habitual physical activity during development have higher work capacities as adults (Frisancho et al. 1994). Adolescence appears to be a critical time for developing higher work capacity at high altitudes (Greksa et al. 1985). In sum, the combination of high activity and residence at high altitude during the developmental period appears to be necessary to yield an adult whose body can handle high work loads at high altitude.

Population Level Adaptations.   People have adapted to high mountain environments independently in several places on Earth, including the highlands of Ethiopia and Tibet, the Andes, and the Himalayas. Figure 8–5 shows where high-altitude regions are found globally. Given the wide distribution of these regions it should not be surprising that studies have shown some biological differences at the population level in the way humans have adjusted. Many adaptations are common to all regions, however, and these are summarized in Figure 8–6.

Figure 8–6   Single-stressor model of human adaptation to high-altitude hypoxia.

Macroenvironment

Low barometric pressure; aridity; diurnal cold

Behavioral/ cultural buffer:

Low activity levels; avoidance of high altitude

Microenvironment

Hypoxic conditions, especially when exercising

Biological buffer:

Fast ventilation; polycythemia; for natives: increased vascularization; large lungs; high work capacity

Essential resources:

None

Demographic effects:

Infants and people with respiratory ailments at high risk

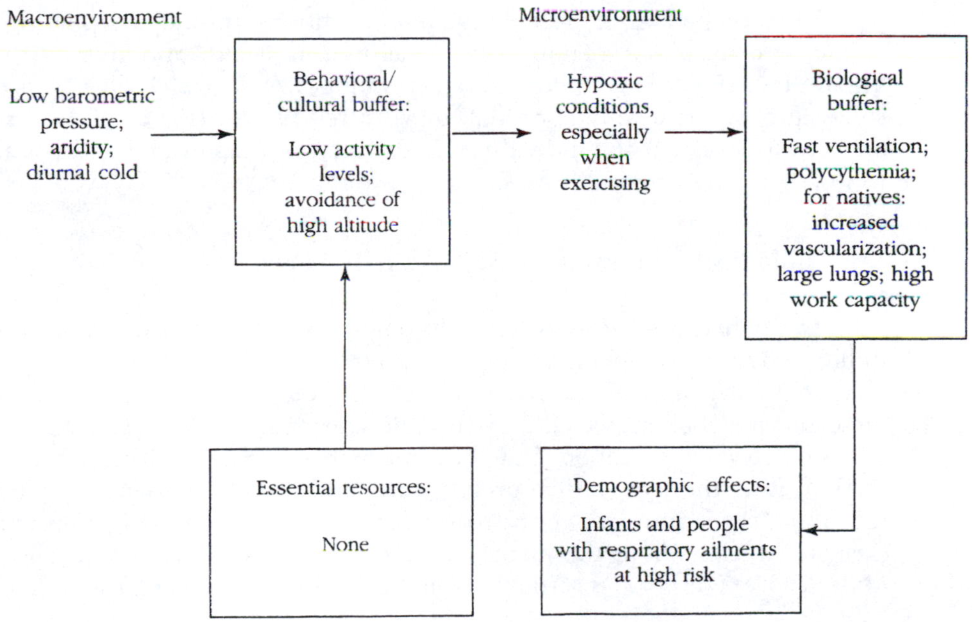

HIGH ACTIVITY LEVELS

Since activity is self-administered as opposed to being an outside force from the macroenvironment, we must consider human adaptability to high activity levels slightly differently than we have approached the stressors noted in the previous chapter and earlier in this one. Still, high activity is often due to ecological considerations. It is engaged in as part of one's work in obtaining resources and buffering oneself from stress, whether this be running after prey or building shelter or transplanting rice or the host of other tasks, pleasant or unpleasant, that people must do in order to survive. People may also perversely engage in strenuous activity for fun or sport, such as the Kona triathletes mentioned in the last chapter.

Human Work Requirements

There is incredible diversity in the types of work people must engage in throughout the world. The kinds of work depend on the stressors and resources of the macroenvironment, subsistence type of the population, and the technology available to the people to assist with their tasks. People generally attempt to minimize the amount of effort they must give to work, while maximizing what is gained by the work. That is, people are thought to optimize for efficiency when doing work. Research in ecological anthropology since the late 1970s has focused on this efficiency in foraging techniques, under the general term **optimal foraging strategies.**

We can abstract some important, general characteristics of physical activity used in work: strength, power, speed, and endurance. These in turn may be dependent on body size, muscularity, physical fitness, training, experience, motivation, and technique (Thomas 1975) as well as health and nutritional status (Weitz et al. 1989). Much of this is shown in Figure 8–7, which illustrates the way some of these factors influence human work requirements at both the individual and group levels. At the individual level, much of human biological adaptation to work involves physical fitness.

Biological Responses to High Activity Levels

Individual Response to Acute Exposure.   When people begin to engage in high physical activity levels they are faced with a need for an increase in both heat tolerance and efficiency in use of oxygen. High activity levels involve increased metabolism, which in turn generates heat (Edholm 1967) and a need for faster oxygen utilization. Initial response to exercise involves increasing ventilation rate through faster breath rate and depth, enhancing circulation through a faster and stronger heartbeat, and a routing of blood preferentially to skeletal muscles where the increased metabolism is occurring (Morehouse and Miller 1967). The blood is rerouted from less critical areas, such as skin. As exercise

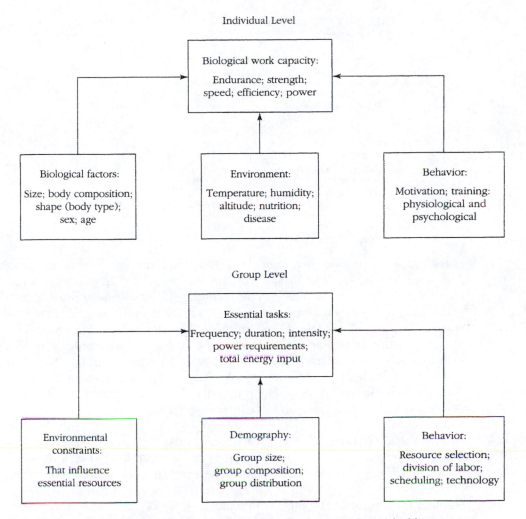

Figure 8–7   Model of human work requirements. (Redrawn and modified by permission from P. O. Åstrand and K. Rodahl, 1970. *Textbook of work physiology.* New York: McGraw-Hill Inc.)

continues and body heat increases, skin blood vessels dilate to allow more efficient unloading of heat to the environment from the body surface. Sweating commences when skin temperature rises to a critical temperature.

   Physical Fitness.   Physical fitness, defined as the ability to maintain homeostatic conditions during strenuous activity or to rapidly restore those conditions after the exercise (Åstrand 1956), involves two general biological adaptive processes already discussed: heat tolerance and efficient use of oxygen. Individuals who are physically fit are acclimatized to heat, showing the same adaptations noted in the previous chapter including a higher sweat capacity,

TABLE 8-1   Differences Between a Fit and an Unfit Person

	Fit	Unfit
Easy Work		
Oxygen consumption	Lower	Higher
Pulse rate	Lower	Higher
Blood pressure	Lower	Higher
Lactic acid	Lower	Higher
Time for recovery	Faster	Slower
Exhausting Work		
Maximal oxygen consumption	Higher	Lower
Maximal pulse rate	Usually lower	Usually higher
Duration before exhaustion	Longer	Shorter
Recovery of blood pressure	Faster	Slower
Recovery of pulse rate	Faster	Slower

faster initiation of sweating, and a reduced salt concentration in perspiration. Also, individuals who are physically fit show some of the adaptations noted for high-altitude hypoxia acclimatization, including faster diffusion of oxygen from lungs to blood and an increase in vascularization—numbers of active blood vessels—particularly in the skeletal muscles (Morehouse and Miller 1967).

Physically fit people are more efficient at doing work at any given work-load than people who are not fit, and fit people also have a greater work capac-ity, having the ability to accomplish tasks that would be impossible for a person who is not fit. Table 8-1 shows the differences between a physically fit and unfit person both at submaximal and maximal workloads.

Aerobic Capacity.   Doing work requires energy, and the major way in which we get energy is through oxidizing, or burning, food stored in the form of carbohydrates, proteins, and lipids. The level of work we can accomplish is based upon the rate at which we can produce energy through oxidizing, or **aerobic,** metabolism. The highest rate at which we can consume oxygen for use in our metabolism is referred to as our **aerobic capacity;** this is an important component of physical fitness. If we should attempt to do work requiring greater energy levels than we can produce through aerobic metabolism, we must fall back on much less efficient anaerobic (not requiring oxygen) forms of metabolism. When this occurs, our stored food is not completely broken down by oxygen into carbon dioxide and water, the usual major end products of metabolism. Instead, it is broken down into intermediate organic chemicals such as lactic acid, which build up in the body until work levels decrease enough to permit oxidation of these intermediate forms. The buildup of lactic acid causes the muscle soreness and fatigue common when we "overdo it." The need to break down these chemicals after we reduce our workload constitutes our "oxygen debt," a debt we see repaid when a sprinter in a track meet pants while at rest after a race. A major component of physical fitness is an increase in aerobic capacity.

Speed and Strength.   Physical activity is based on the movement of levers: bones act as the levers and muscles pull on them. Levers can be built to maximize speed or power, or as a compromise between the two, based upon the relative lengths of the power and load arms of the lever and the angle at which the muscle attaches to the lever. The human body is generally built for speed rather than power, as power arms tend to be shorter than load arms (Morehouse and Miller 1967). **Muscle strength,** which is defined as the amount of force a muscle can provide, is based upon the cross-sectional area of muscle, with thicker muscle providing more strength (Bar-Or 1983). An additional consideration is the muscle fiber type: physiologists generally differentiate between fast- and slow-twitch muscle fibers, although this may be an oversimplification. Slow-twitch fibers appear to be specially adapted for efficient aerobic metabolism; for example, they have large numbers of mitochondria, a type of cellular organelle that acts as the aerobic powerhouse of the body's cells. Fast-twitch fibers, on the other hand, appear better suited to anaerobic metabolism (Bouchard et al. 1981). While both types of fiber are found in each muscle, people vary in the proportion of muscle fibers that are of each type, and there is even a difference in the proportions of the fibers between muscles in the same individual. Thus, people differ in their abilities to do certain types of work based upon proportions of muscle fiber type. The degree to which these differences are genetically based is still unknown. Since the fiber type differentiation takes place by one year of age (Bar-Or 1983), individual differences in activity during development have little effect.

Age and Sex Differences.   During growth and development, many physical changes occur that affect an individual's ability to do work. Children have a lower aerobic capacity than adults do. However, since children are smaller and lighter, tasks involving movement of their bodies require less work, and thus a measure of *relative* aerobic capacity, for instance aerobic capacity per body weight, sometimes termed **aerobic power,** may be more appropriate. Boys on average have an aerobic power about equal to that of adult men, while girls actually average an aerobic power greater than adult women (Bar-Or 1983). For females, the decline in average aerobic power is due to increased adiposity (fatness) that occurs during adolescence. Adolescence appears to be a key time in the establishment of sex differences in work capacity. Before adolescence there is little difference between girls and boys in aerobic capacity and power. During adolescence males average a greater relative increase in muscularity, and thus increased strength and aerobic power. By the end of adolescence, females have an aerobic power about 80 percent of the male average (Bouchard et al. 1981). However, if adipose tissue is discounted and aerobic power is computed in terms of lean body mass, virtually no sex difference is present. The sex differences in aerobic capacity may be partly due to differential activity levels between male and female youths that are a consequence of cultural expectations (Weitz et al. 1989).

Aerobic capacity, aerobic power, and other measures of physical fitness tend to decline with age in adults. Much of the decline is not due to physiological aging per se, but rather in part to decreased activity levels in the elderly. After age 50, there is a general decline in lean body mass, which includes muscle, and with this decline there is a corresponding decrease in strength (Shephard 1987). This decrease in lean tissue is also seen in aging athletes, suggesting that it is not based solely on a decreased activity level.

Adaptive Consequences of Differential Work Capacity

The ecological import of variability in work capacity is in the differential capacity of individuals to do essential tasks. Human cultures differ in their expectations of work for people in general and also in the way tasks are apportioned by age-sex groups within the society. Where ecological needs demand strenuous work, only some people in the population may be capable of the work, based on age, sex, fitness, or other individual differences. Less strenuous tasks that are long-lasting may also be possible just for some members of a group since people can only keep up a workload of about 40 percent of their maximal aerobic power for a full day's work over the long term (Shephard 1987).

The Economic Unit.   The primary economic unit differs in different human cultural groups, ranging from essentially individual self-sufficiency to units involving large extended families (Haviland 1990). The economic unit, or work unit, may also vary depending upon the task. Where self-reliant groups are small, work loads heavy, and age-sex differences important, these self-reliant groups may be vulnerable to the loss of one of its workers to disease, death, or temporary absence. A recent study in the Andes shows that families suffer productive deficits when an adult becomes ill, and therefore sick people may opt to continue working during critical periods despite potential long-term harm to their health (Leatherman and Thomas 1987). Similar disruptions occur in populations where young people, frequently males, leave for varying lengths of time to engage in wage labor, leaving difficult subsistence work to people in other demographic groups. Hence, any society's traditional division of labor can be construed as only an ideal, with disruptions due to health, mortality, and temporary absence sometimes forcing people to attempt work at or beyond the limits of their capacity.

Impact of Modernization.   Work capacity, being based on habitual physical activity levels, has been greatly affected by the process of modernization in many populations. This process often involves a decrease in physical activity levels and consequently a decrease in aerobic power. Among Inuits studied in the village of Igloolik, for instance, villagers with sedentary, Western lifestyles had a measured aerobic power about 81 percent of that measured in traditional hunters from the same village (Rode and Shephard 1971). Besides increasing vulnerability to the development of many chronic illnesses, the lowered physical fitness that frequently comes with modernization may lead people to lose their ability to engage in traditional subsistence activities without physiological strain.

NATURAL HAZARDS

Human populations must also cope with physical stressors that are difficult to predict in terms of time, place, and intensity. These stressors, usually referred to as **natural hazards,** include storms, earthquakes, tsunamis, and volcanic eruptions. Because of their relative unpredictability, these hazards can cause a great many injuries and deaths, as well as much property destruction, when they occur. While technological advances have helped make these hazards more predictable, population expansion and growth in high risk areas have made more people vulnerable to possible catastrophe.

Storms

Storms can be represented by many forms of extreme weather conditions, from thunderstorms to blizzards and any of the various kinds of cyclones (hurricanes, typhoons, and tornadoes). Thunderstorms are usually limited in their destructive effects, although lightning, rain-induced mud slides, and other such hazards are associated with them. This is a particular problem in areas with steep slopes such as mountainsides, especially where deforestation or agricultural terracing is common. In the latter case, floods induced by monsoons or other heavy rains can not only cause dangerous landslides but also devastate the population's resource base through the erosion of topsoil. This has become readily apparent throughout the Himalayan region but is also common in many other tropical mountain regions (Wijkman and Timberlake 1988).

Blizzards. Blizzards are of great potential import for human groups in arctic, subarctic, temperate, and mountain ecosystems, as they can limit productive activities and cause people to get lost away from shelter. In the United States, people have frozen to death when stranded in automobiles during winter storms, although greater numbers of injuries result from indirect effects of the storms such as traffic accidents. Wind-blown snow in nonblizzard conditions can have ecological effects on people. The Inujjuamiut of Arctic Canada studied by Smith (1991) experienced about ten days per month of blowing snow conditions between November and April, limiting visibility and thus hindering their foraging.

Tropical Cyclones. The greatest destruction from storms comes from tropical cyclones, termed variously cyclones, hurricanes, or typhoons. They all involve high winds of 80 miles per hour or higher, but typically with maximum wind speeds of 105 miles per hour (Palm 1990). While destruction caused by the wind, and deaths and injuries due to flying debris or collapsing shelters are a considerable hazard, the greatest danger from these storms comes from storm surge in coastal areas, where huge waves can be generated. One of the worst recent natural disasters was caused by the cyclone that affected Bangladesh in 1970. The storm hit around the time of high tide, contributing to the destruction by wave action. It is estimated that 225,000 deaths and millions of dollars in crop damage occurred within a few hours (Burton et al. 1978).

One reason for the high toll of tropical cyclones in recent times, often despite increased predictability that comes with modern meteorological technology, is the increased human population in shoreline areas susceptible to cyclone damage. Of particular concern is the frequent location of shantytowns or other poor neighborhoods in vulnerable areas, as available shelters are not usually constructed well and thus are susceptible to severe damage (Wijkman and Timberlake 1988).

The people who are arguably the most vulnerable to tropical cyclones (typhoons, in this case) are the inhabitants of Micronesian coral atolls in the central Pacific. Most atolls have islands with average elevations just a few meters above sea level and maximal elevations of only a few meters above the average. When a large typhoon sweeps over an atoll islet, it can destroy most vegetation, cause serious erosion of what little land was present to begin with on the islet, and displace the small amount of fresh water underground with salt water (Alkire 1978). Many people have drowned or been otherwise killed during great typhoons in Micronesia, but a greater source of mortality has been the famines that ensue after the storm has wiped out a population's resources. One can wonder how a population can cope with such a horrendous stress, but Alkire (1978) suggests that Micronesians have found a means to do this. In a sense their strategy is to spread the risk by maintaining cooperative trade relations with inhabitants of other islands, including high islands—volcanic islands that are usually much higher in elevation than coral atoll islets—when they are within a reasonable distance. After a typhoon has struck, people seek help from their neighbors who may have been outside the main track of the storm. People also often migrate to other islands, at least until resources such as breadfruit trees, taro, and coconuts on their original islands have rebounded (Alkire 1978).

Tornadoes. Tornadoes are also very hazardous cyclonic storms, although their destructive path tends to be much narrower than is the case for tropical cyclones. They are also more difficult to predict in advance, making behavioral adaptations difficult. In many areas of the U.S. Midwest and Southeast, people have relied upon storm cellars to provide shelter from wind damage. Because of their relatively narrow path, the resource loss in their aftermath is much less than typically found after a tropical cyclone. However, due to their great wind speed, rapid storm movement, and pressure, tornadoes account for the highest number of deaths and economic loss in the United States of all natural hazards (Palm 1990).

Earthquakes

Earthquakes are very difficult to predict, although certain regions, particularly the Pacific Rim, are known to be at greater risk. The Tangshan, China, quake in 1977 was estimated to have killed 242,000 people, despite the nation's extensive efforts to predict and prepare for earthquakes (Wijkman and Timberlake 1988). Since most injuries and deaths are caused by structural collapse or fires, it would make sense to deal with earthquake hazards by banning combustible materials or the construction of large structures in high risk areas. A quick tour through California will dissuade the human ecologist that people will always behave in an adaptive fashion in such environments.

Perhaps the large city with the highest risk of a catastrophic earthquake is not Los Angeles but Tokyo. The great earthquake of 1923 resulted in a fire that burned for three days, a death toll of 59,000, and a loss of about 370,000 buildings (Burton et al. 1978). The population of Tokyo is now many times that of 1923, and much of the city is still vulnerable to fire. An earthquake of equal magnitude to that of 1923 would likely lead to a catastrophe far greater than occurred at that time. The repercussions of such an earthquake would shake financial markets throughout the world.

Tsunamis

An indirect hazard caused by earthquakes is the generation of **tsunamis,** or seismic sea waves. The energy of the earthquake generates sea waves that spread out in all directions across the ocean. The speed of the tsunami is proportional to the depth of the water across which it moves; the deeper the water, the faster the wave. When a tsunami approaches a coast, the shallower water slows the wave, allowing water behind it to pile up and the height of the wave to increase (Myles 1985). In areas where the wave is constricted, such as in bays, the height increases still more. Thus, a tsunami may be barely discernible in midocean but become a towering wave when it reaches a coastline.

A visitor to the city of Hilo, Hawaii, is impressed by the beautiful parkland that surrounds the coastline of the city, filled with soccer fields, volleyball courts, and other recreation facilities (Figure 8–8). While one would like to credit the city's planning department with a wonderful sense of values, the reality is quite different. Hilo was hit by two very large tsunamis in the past half-century (1946 and 1960), both leading to numerous deaths and much destruction (Dudley and Lee 1988). The parks of Hilo are located where much of the downtown portion of the city once was (Severance 1979). Figure 8–9 shows some of the devastation caused by the 1960 tsunami.

One of the largest tsunamis recorded resulted from an earthquake coincident with the eruption of Krakatoa in Indonesia; the wave at Marak was estimated as taller than 40 m. Nearly 37,000 people were killed by this tsunami, chiefly along the coasts of Java and Sumatra (Myles 1985). Other catastrophic

Figure 8–8   The waterfront of Hilo, Hawaii, in 1997. (Photo by D. E. Brown)

tsunamis have hit the Pacific coast of South America and Japan, among other coastal regions. Technological advances, including a Pacific tsunami warning system, have allowed better predictability of oceanwide tsunamis, and this has permitted early warning and evacuations of high risk areas. There is still a danger from locally generated tsunamis. People living in coastal areas are often taught that if they feel a major earthquake they should seek high ground immediately. As with tropical cyclones, the population increase in coastal areas has led to the possibility of greater catastrophe.

Volcanic Eruptions

Some of the greatest damage caused by volcanic eruptions is caused by earthquakes and earthquake-generated tsunamis associated with them. Volcanoes have directly caused a great deal of misery, however. Volcanic soils on the slopes of active volcanoes are often quite rich for agricultural purposes, and this may lead to high population densities on these slopes. Violent eruptions can lead to damage from quick moving lava flows, ash fall, and mudflows. Even slow-moving lava can inexorably wipe out permanent structures.

Compared to the natural hazards considered previously, volcanic eruptions do not directly kill as many people. The eruption of Mt. Pelee killed about 29,000 people on the island of Martinique in 1902, but that represents over half the deaths caused by all volcanoes this century (Wijkman and Timberlake 1988). The catastrophes caused by the eruptions of Mt. Etna and Mt. Vesuvius throughout history may have exaggerated the overall effects of eruptions on

Figure 8–9   Hilo, Hawaii, immediately after the 1960 tsunami. (Photo courtesy of Pacific Tsunami Museum, Hawaii Tribune-Herald Collection)

human ecology. Certainly these eruptions have had a historical impact, from the destruction of Herculaneum and Pompeii in A.D. 79 (Bullard 1979) to the deaths of many soldiers in Keōua's army on the Island of Hawaii by Kilauea's eruption in 1790 that contributed to Kamehameha's campaign to take over all of Hawaii (Swanson and Christiansen 1973).

The ecological effects of eruptions go well beyond initial destructive effects. Land may be rendered unproductive for agriculture for long periods after an eruption, and native forests or other vegetation may be extensively damaged (Rees 1979). People may be forced to migrate permanently to different areas. Extensive regional effects can come from great eruptions, and, as evidenced by the eruptions of Mt. St. Helens, in the state of Washington, and Mt. Pinatubo, in the Philippines, eruptions can also have climatic effects on a global scale (Zielinski et al. 1994). This is probably best seen as a result of the eruption of Tambora in Indonesia in 1815, where the sulfuric acid droplets blasted into the stratosphere led to a decreased global temperature; the following year has been called "the year without a summer," with snow in June and widespread crop failures in high temperate regions (Simkin 1994; Stommel and Stommel 1979).

Adaptive Consequences of Natural Hazards

As already noted, natural hazards can have devastating consequences for human populations. Today improved technology allows better warning of such hazards as cyclones or other storms, incipient volcanic eruptions, and long-range tsunamis. Prediction of earthquakes and locally generated tsunamis is still problematical at best. Ironically, despite improved ability to anticipate some hazards, the amount of destruction appears to be rising. This may be due to population pressure that pushes people into residing in hazardous areas.

Compared to the other physical stressors discussed thus far, natural hazards appear to present greater problems for human populations. This is due to the greater predictability of the other stressors. Thus, given a chance to prepare for such problems as cold, heat, and high-altitude hypoxia, people can cope. When a major environmental stress is not predictable, it presents a much greater challenge to human adaptive capabilities. In fact, people consistently overestimate the frequency of relatively unpredictable or rare hazards, while underestimating the importance of better understood risks (Morgan 1993). This may be a means of factoring in the importance of predictability in preparing for stressful circumstances.

KEY TERMS

acute mountain sickness	edema	polycythemia
aerobic	hemoglobin	pulmonary edema
aerobic capacity	hypoxia	subacute infantile
aerobic power	muscle strength	mountain sickness
alveoli	natural hazards	tsunamis
barometric pressure	optimal foraging	ventilation rate
cerebral edema	strategies	ventilatory drive
chronic mountain sickness	physical fitness	work capacity

KEY POINTS

☐ Biological adaptations to hypoxia include an increase in ventilation rate upon initial exposure followed by acclimatization, a lowered ventilatory drive in individuals who grow up in such environments, increased perfusion of the lungs with blood as a result of more alveoli becoming active and more lung capillaries dilating, enlargement of the right ventricle, higher average lung size, increase in the percentage of blood occupied by red cells, higher hemoglobin concentration, increased distribution of blood to vital organs, increase in diffusion rates assisted by the tissue protein myoglobin, and increased activity of enzymes in metabolism.

☐   Hypoxic conditions of high mountains may lead to acute mountain sickness, pulmonary edema, cerebral edema, subacute infantile mountain sickness, and chronic mountain sickness.

☐   Developmental adaptations to mountain environments include a high work capacity, that is, the capacity to use oxygen at a fast rate.

☐   High activity levels in obtaining resources and buffering against stress are conditioned by physical fitness, which is characterized by heat tolerance and efficient use of oxygen via aerobic metabolism, both of which tend to decline with age in adults and differ according to gender.

☐   Work capacity has been greatly affected by modernization and involves a decrease in physical activity levels and a consequent decrease in aerobic power and physical fitness that increases vulnerability to the development of chronic illnesses.

☐   Natural hazards, such as storms, earthquakes, tsunamis, and volcanic eruptions, are difficult to predict in terms of time, place, and intensity and, compounded by population growth in high risk areas, increase vulnerability to possible catastrophe.

9

Adaptation to Biotic Stressors: Malnutrition and Infectious Disease

In addition to physical stressors in their environment, humans must also deal with biologically based problems. This chapter deals with problems of the human food chain, namely, how people adapt to circumstances in which either they cannot obtain enough food resources, or organisms (pathogens) attempt to use *them* as a food resource. These two problems are, in fact, interrelated.

MALNUTRITION: THE PRICE OF FAILURE

Malnutrition may be defined as any type of poor nutrition, including having too much or too little food, or having an improper balance of nutrients (Relethford 1994). In this chapter the focus will be primarily on **undernutrition,** in which the amount of either food in general or specific nutrients required from the diet are inadequate. If we were to use the single-stressor model for undernutrition, the "behavioral/ cultural buffer" would consist of all human activities related to subsistence, which constitutes a large part of the study of cultural ecology. A review of basic ideas about these activities is included in Part IV of this book. Here, we will focus on what happens when these activities fail to one degree or another.

In the modern world, malnutrition stems from economic and sociopolitical causes. Although there are presently enough food resources in the world to feed all people a diet with necessary nutrients, malnutrition is all too common. In a sense, malnutrition is a problem of distribution, not production. This global view is, however, oversimplistic, as variability in ability to produce food at the local level is an important factor in creating pockets of malnutrition. As already noted in Part II, the rapid increase in human population size may lead to global shortfalls in food production in the future.

Human ecologists view malnutrition as a measure of ecological failure: it is a sign that a population has not successfully adapted to its environment. In fact, a human ecologist beginning research on a given population would not go far wrong to start by looking for nutritional problems. If nutritional problems exist, they can affect how people deal with all other aspects of their ecology.

There are many forms of malnutrition based upon which of the numerous different nutrients essential for the human diet are deficient. By contrast, modernized societies are faced with a different kind of malnutrition: overnutrition, a dietary problem that will be explored in the next chapter.

PROTEIN-CALORIE MALNUTRITION

One of the major forms of malnutrition is caused by a deficiency in the energy content of food, measured in kcal (kilocalories), and/or a deficiency in protein. This form of malnutrition ranges from total starvation, where no food is eaten, to moderate forms of undernutrition, to diets that are sufficient in caloric content but lack sufficient protein. We will discuss diets that are deficient in protein separately from diets deficient in calories, although some nutritionists have suggested that it may be difficult to differentiate between the effects of these deficiencies (Stinnett 1983; Gopalan 1992).

Protein Deficiency

Protein is an essential component of all living organisms. It is the organic compound that makes up, wholly or in part, most of the enzymes, chemical messengers, cell membrane receptors, and structural constituents of organisms. Proteins are necessary for growth, reproduction, and daily survival; no organism can survive for long without the ability to produce necessary proteins.

Protein Composition.   Proteins are composed of building blocks called amino acids that are connected to each other in long chains. There are 20 different amino acids; their number and particularly the order in which they are linked in a protein chain determine both the structure and function of any particular protein molecule. When a protein is eaten, it is broken down into its constituent amino acids that are then used in the synthesis of human proteins.

Proteins must have a precise order of amino acids to maintain their function. If one type of amino acid is missing, humans and other organisms cannot properly make their necessary proteins; this makes for a "least common denominator" in the synthesis of protein from constituent amino acids. Twelve of the amino acids can be chemically produced in the human body by transformation from other dietary elements, so if one type is in short supply it can be produced as needed. The other eight amino acids are called "essential" amino acids because they cannot be transformed from other dietary elements by humans (National Academy of Sciences 1974). These essential amino acids must be present in the diet.

Protein malnutrition should therefore be considered as a general form of amino acid deficiency, with different specific types of malnutrition depending on which amino acids are in short supply. Because the end result of all forms of amino acid deficiency is the inability to produce proteins, the biological effects of the different types of amino acid deficiency are the same.

Protein Quality of Foods.   Eating protein is not sufficient to prevent protein malnutrition: one must eat protein that has the proper ratio of essential amino acids for human needs. Since humans are evolutionary related to other living organisms, they share protein requirements. The specific make-up of proteins has changed with time during evolution, and thus the amino acid make-up of the proteins of different organisms is not precisely the same. In general, however, the closer the evolutionary relationship between two species of organisms, the closer the ratio of amino acids in their proteins. Thus, when humans eat meat, the animal-derived protein is more likely to match their amino acid needs than plant-derived proteins are. Populations with a predominately vegetarian diet are more likely to be exposed to protein malnutrition unless the diet is sufficiently broad that it includes plants with different amino acid proportions and thus approximates the ratio of essential amino acids required by humans. **Protein quality** refers to the degree to which a given type of dietary protein matches the ratio of essential amino acids required by humans.

A classic example of this matching of vegetable foods to obtain high quality protein is found in Mesoamerica (today's Mexico and much of Central America), an area with a long history of major urban cultures that developed from an agricultural base consisting chiefly of maize (corn) and beans. Maize is deficient in the essential amino acids isoleucine and lysine, while beans have a relatively high proportion of these amino acids; conversely, maize has a high proportion of the sulfur-containing amino acids methionine and cystine, while beans are relatively deficient in them (see Figure 9–1). By eating two foods that individually have only poor to moderate protein quality, the Mesoamerican peoples have a high quality protein diet. When the two foods are not in the diet, protein malnutrition may occur.

The Background of Protein Deficiency.   Protein deficiency is one of the leading forms of malnutrition. It is particularly common in developing countries, especially in tropical regions where common foods tend to be high in carbohydrates but low in protein. This is frequently seen in agricultural populations that depend on a single plant food for the majority of their diet (Stini 1975). Also, people with parasitic infections may lose protein either directly to

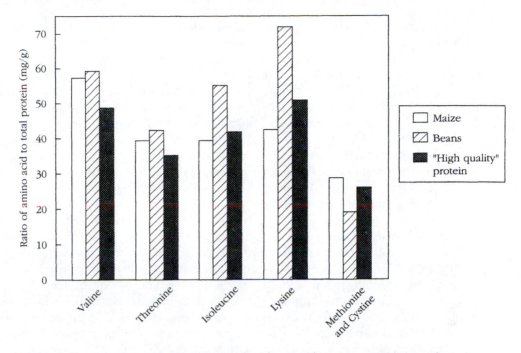

Figure 9–1   Proportions of essential amino acids to total protein content in maize and beans in comparison with established proportions in "high quality" protein. (Based on data from National Academy of Sciences. 1974. *Recommended daily allowances.* 8th Ed. Washington, DC: National Academy of Sciences.)

the parasite or through continuous leakage of blood due to the parasite's activities. Diets that are borderline in protein quality and quantity can lead to malnutrition when combined with parasitic infection.

Protein malnutrition is often a disease associated with weaning. Young children who previously received sufficient protein from breast milk may be switched to a poor-protein diet upon weaning. The child's rapid growth rate increases daily protein needs, exacerbating the problem. By the age of five growth rates decline, reducing the severity of protein malnutrition problems (Farb and Armelagos 1980). Also, as the child grows, more biological protein reserves develop and can be utilized during short-term protein shortages.

Biological Effects of Protein Malnutrition.   Most cases of protein malnutrition occur when protein intake is somewhat below required values over long periods. A major means of adjusting to periods of mild to moderate protein deficiency is secretion of serum proteins such as albumin into the intestine, where they are digested into amino acids and used in the production of required proteins. The secretion of albumin into the intestine also increases the efficiency of uptake of amino acids from food (Stini 1975). If the malnutrition is more severe, or prolonged, skeletal muscle is broken down as a protein source. If the protein malnutrition is chronic, the effects may be very severe.

Effects of Chronic Protein Malnutrition in Children.   Protein malnutrition during pregnancy leads to lowered birth weight and therefore to greater risk of infant mortality. Infants, and more commonly weanlings, are adversely affected by protein malnutrition. Growth slows or ceases during the period of malnutrition, evidenced by large numbers of short-for-age children in a population. Also, skeletal and reproductive development slows, resulting in retarded skeletal maturity and, in girls, delayed menarche (first menstrual period) (Frisancho 1993). After the period of malnutrition ends, there is often a compensatory fast rate of growth, termed *catch-up growth,* if the malnutrition ends before the growth period is over. In many cases, children will attain "normal" stature-for-age after the catch-up period. Girls tend to recover better from protein deficiency than boys do (Stini 1972).

Severe protein malnutrition in childhood leads to the deficiency disease termed **kwashiorkor,** a word derived from the Ga language of Africa and meaning "disease that occurs when displaced from the breast by another child" (Jelliffe 1968). The symptoms of the disease include muscle atrophy, growth failure, skin rash, edema, and in some cases depigmentation of skin or hair. Ironically, children with kwashiorkor have distended abdomens, but this denotes loss of abdominal muscle tone, not a full stomach (see Figure 9–2). The major cause of death associated with kwashiorkor is infection. Deficient protein reduces immune system activity, leaving victims vulnerable to myriad infectious agents (Stinnett 1983), as will be discussed in more detail later.

Total Undernutrition: Protein-Calorie Deficiency

While a diet with sufficient calories but insufficient protein is possible, the reverse is not. Amino acids have caloric value, hence a diet with insufficient calories is also deficient in amino acids. Individuals confronted with protein-calorie malnutrition must adapt to the problems of protein deficiency noted earlier, as well as the problems of what ecologists term "a negative energy balance," meaning that a person's dietary energy consumption is less than his or her energy expenditure (both basal and active metabolism). The energy that is expended must come from somewhere; in humans, various biological energy reserves are present.

Human Biological Energy Reserves.   As a short-term energy resource, people rely on glycogen, a starch stored in the liver and muscles. When blood sugar levels are high, a hormone termed *insulin* is secreted that stimulates **glycogenesis** (the synthesis of glycogen from the simple sugar glucose). When blood sugar levels are low, as occurs with undernutrition, the hormone glucagon is secreted that stimulates **glycogenolysis** (the breakdown of glycogen into glucose). Glycogen is used to maintain fairly constant sugar levels in the blood despite variable food intake. Sugar is a major short-term source of energy for the human body, ensuring a constant supply of energy. The glycogen supply is not useful for long-term energy needs, as it represents a relatively small amount

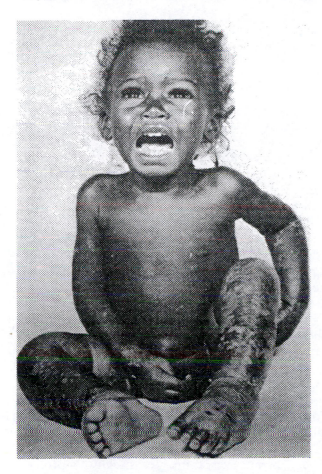

Figure 9–2   A child with kwashiorkor.
(Photo reprinted by permission from D. B.
Jelliffe. 1969. *Child nutrition in develop-
ing countries: A handbook for
fieldworkers.* Washington, DC: U.S.
Agency for International Development.)

of energy. During severe workloads, such as in a marathon race, the glycogen
supply can be completely depleted within 2 hours (when this occurs, the
marathoner, in runners' parlance, "hits the wall"). Even under more normal
workloads, the glycogen stores are depleted within 16 hours if there is no
dietary caloric input (Frisancho 1993; Solomon and Davis 1983).

Another form of energy storage is represented by protein, since amino
acids can be metabolized, including being used as a source of glycogen synthesis
(Guyton 1971). As noted, amino acids can be utilized from plasma proteins and
from skeletal muscle tissue. Insulin is the major controller of skeletal muscle
breakdown. It actually stimulates **anabolism** (tissue buildup), so low levels—as
occurs during undernutrition—lead to breakdown of skeletal muscle tissue. In
long-term protein-calorie malnutrition, physiological processes occur that serve
to conserve the body's protein stores in favor of the use of the major form of
energy storage: body fat.

It is clear that body fat is the major long-term storage depot for energy. In
the United States, adults average about 15 kg of adipose tissue. This amounts to

about 135,000 kcal of energy, approximately the total amount of energy used in 70 days by a fairly inactive person. Most populations average much less body fat than those of the United States and accordingly have lower reserves of energy.

The Cori Cycle.   While fat is the major source of energy reserves, there are problems with its use, as human skeletal muscle and brain cannot directly use fat as an energy source, relying instead on glucose. The **Cori cycle,** an adaptive process for conserving glucose, involves a switch to anaerobic metabolism in muscle tissue, with glucose broken down into lactose instead of into the smaller molecules of carbon dioxide and water. The breakdown of glucose releases energy in the muscle. Lactose, in turn, can be used as a building block for the resynthesis of glucose in the liver, a process requiring energy (Young and Scrimshaw 1971). In fact, the breakdown of glucose in muscle to lactose and then glucose synthesis from lactose results in a net *loss* of energy. While it may seem maladaptive to lose energy during dietary caloric deficiency, the positive effect of the cycle is that the energy that is used in glucose synthesis comes from lipid (fat) metabolism. Thus, the Cori cycle employs energy from the body's fat deposits to be used to recycle glucose for use in muscle and brain metabolism (Figure 9–3). A similar biochemical cycle involving the conversion of alanine into glucose has also been identified (Young and Scrimshaw 1971).

Responses During Prolonged Starvation.   In the early stages of severe undernutrition, a marked decrease in body weight becomes evident, with most of the decrease due to loss of fat. For a 70 kg male during severe undernutrition, the basal requirement of calories (about 1,800 kcal/day) is met by the breakdown of approximately 200 g of body fat (Stini 1981); in almost all cases, however, calorie requirements are actually above the "basal" level. If the diet is relatively protein

Figure 9–3   The Cori cycle.

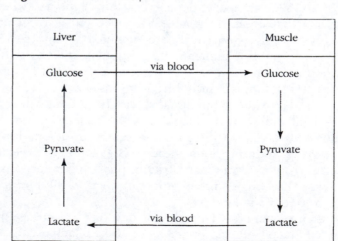

deficient along with being generally reduced in amount, protein loss from the body will also occur (McCance and Widdowson 1965). The basal metabolic rate and body temperature also are reduced (Keys et al. 1950), which may be adaptive by reducing daily calorie requirements; however, in a cold environment such reductions may actually be maladaptive. Another major change that occurs during starvation is the production of chemicals termed *ketones* as a byproduct of fat metabolism. Ketones are not produced during fat metabolism in well-fed animals. Ketones can accumulate, creating the condition known as ketosis, which can be a serious health risk. However, ketones, especially B-hydroxybutyrate and acetoacetate, can be utilized by brain cells as an energy source instead of glucose (Cahill 1970; Stryer 1988). This permits a great degree of protein conservation; for example, starving people only burn about 20 g of protein a day from muscle after this process kicks in, as compared with the 75 g/day burned in early stages of starvation. Hormones appear to play an important role in the physiological changes that occur during protein-calorie malnutrition, particularly insulin, glucagon, the steroid hormones produced in the cortex of the adrenal gland, and possibly growth hormone.

Effects of Protein-Calorie Malnutrition. In adults, protein-calorie malnutrition has many negative effects, including all those noted earlier in the discussion of protein deficiency. The most obvious effect is a great loss of body weight. While most of the weight loss is from body fat stores, there is also a considerable loss of body protein, particularly from skeletal muscle mass. Physical work capacity also declines, but only during prolonged periods of protein-calorie deficiency (Frisancho 1993). For women about to give birth, this form of malnutrition can extend the labor period by nearly five hours on average (Newman 1962), a potentially serious risk to both mother and infant. Also, prolonged protein-calorie malnutrition can cause problems with lactation and thus can lead to increased infant mortality. There are also important psychological and behavioral effects of prolonged deficiency, including apathy and inactivity (Keys et al. 1950), which do, however, serve to reduce energy requirements.

As with protein deficiency, the effects of protein-calorie malnutrition are much greater in children, in cases of severe malnutrition leading to a disease termed **marasmus.** Children suffering from this syndrome combine the muscle depletion of kwashiorkor with a loss of most body fat. There is also a considerable slowing, or cessation, of growth, and a characteristic "wizened" appearance of the head (see Figure 9–4). Vomiting and diarrhea are common in marasmus, causing dehydration. While marasmus has traditionally been seen as a consequence of protein-calorie malnutrition and kwashiorkor a consequence of protein deficiency alone, these syndromes are now seen possibly to be different manifestations of the same disease, a disease caused by protein-calorie malnutrition. For instance, in villages studied in India, some children will be found suffering from one of the syndromes and some from the other even though they all are apparently reacting to the same general type of nutritional deficiency (Gopalan 1992).

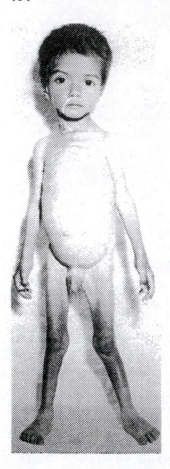

Figure 9–4 A child with marasmus. (Photo reprinted by permission from UNICEF, as published in D. B. Jelliffe. 1969. *Child nutrition in developing countries: A handbook for fieldworkers.* Washington, DC: U.S. Agency for International Development.)

As with protein deficiency, a major problem for victims of protein-calorie malnutrition is an increase in susceptibility to disease. This is apparently due primarily to a decline in cell-mediated immune response but also due to effects on other portions of the immune system (Haas and Harrison 1977; Scrimshaw et al. 1968). Few people die of starvation; instead, they die of an infectious disease that their weakened immune system cannot overcome. For example, among populations in rural Senegal, mortality rates, particularly due to diarrheal diseases, are higher in the rainy season, a time when protein-calorie malnutrition is common (Simondon et al. 1993).

The biological responses to protein-calorie malnutrition are best viewed as temporary measures, buying time until proper nutrition can be obtained. Seasonal caloric deficits may have been common in traditional societies in the past; they have been found in many contemporary populations. Problems often arise when people must expend a great deal of energy in preparing fields and planting crops at a time when the previous year's harvest is depleted (de Garine and Koppert 1990; Ferro-Luzzi and Branca 1993). When caloric intake is too low, one's body consumes itself to meet energy needs. An individual can lose up to about 40 percent of body weight (and 20 percent of body protein) before death. Individuals who have been through a period of starvation once may deal with a second period of famine more efficiently than a "novice," suggesting adaptation to periodic famine. The adaptive nature of the process is further revealed by the priority in which the body feeds on itself: from least critical materials such as body fat to more vital materials such as muscle. It is likely no coincidence that the two biological systems most spared during starvation are the central nervous system and the reproductive system, as these represent the two major adaptive concerns for any biological organism: survival and reproduction.

VITAMIN DEFICIENCIES

Besides the major nutritional components of food—carbohydrates, fat, and protein—food contains many *micronutrients* (food components needed only in small amounts) necessary for human health and function. Among micronutrients are minerals such as iodine and zinc and those accessory food factors, vitamins. We will briefly discuss some of the more common forms of vitamin deficiency, the effects of such forms of malnutrition, and mineral deficiencies.

Vitamin A Deficiency

Vitamin A (retinol) is found in green and yellow vegetables, milk, butter, and cheese; it can also be synthesized in the body from beta-carotene, which is found in many plant foods. It is stored in the liver, but impaired liver function can hamper storage, contributing to deficiency. Vitamin A is required for normal functioning of certain epithelial cells of the body. Deficiency can cause "night blindness," dry skin, and cloudiness of the cornea. If the deficiency is prolonged, permanent blindness can result (Wood 1979).

Vitamin A deficiency is all too common in South Asia but is also found in other regions of the world, particularly in West Asia and Latin America. The deficiency is common among poor farmers who do not have enough land to grow vegetables other than cereal staples. It is often associated with protein-calorie malnutrition, but not necessarily: in parts of Africa where protein-calorie malnutrition is common, the availability of red palm oil as a food prevents vitamin A deficiency (World Health Organization 1963).

Thiamine Deficiency

Thiamine, also known as vitamin B_1, functions in the metabolism of carbohydrates, and therefore thiamine deficiency is particularly problematical where diets are low in the vitamin but high in carbohydrates. Although thiamine is found in most foods, including pork, liver, whole grains, and legumes, deficiencies are found in populations that rely on rice as a major part of the diet. Interestingly, thiamine deficiency was found more commonly in relatively well-off peasants in rice-growing areas, and less commonly in very poor people or in the rich. This is because of the way thiamine is distributed in rice—it is found predominately in the pericarp portion of rice surrounding the grain. Many rice-eating peoples prefer highly milled rice, a process that removes most of the thiamine, as does excessive soaking of the rice in its preparation. Well-off peasants could afford to mill their rice while the poor peasants could not, thus the former were more likely to develop thiamine deficiency. Rich people, who could afford a more varied diet, were also protected from the disease.

Thiamine deficiency is also more prevalent in areas that have initiated modernization or development, as this often leads quickly to the start-up of small rice mills (World Health Organization 1963). Much rice today is "fortified" with thiamine, and this has led to a great reduction in the prevalence of thiamine deficiency. In developed countries, thiamine deficiency is primarily a disease of alcoholism, as alcoholics often fail to eat properly and thus have a diet with insufficient vitamins and other important nutrients (Pyke 1970).

Severe thiamine deficiency causes the deficiency disease termed **beriberi.** It is a deadly disease, having led to thousands of deaths in poor, rice-growing regions such as Southeast Asia. Because of the importance of carbohydrate metabolism in making vital glucose available for muscle and brain tissue, beriberi results in cardiovascular and neurological problems (Dreyfus 1979).

Niacin Deficiency

Niacin, also known as vitamin B_3, is in low supply in corn, and deficiencies of this vitamin are pretty much confined to predominately maize-eating populations; it is, however, found in liver, lean meat, grains, and legumes. The amino acid tryptophan can be converted into niacin in the body, but it is also relatively deficient in maize (Pyke 1970).

The deficiency disease associated with low niacin intake is **pellagra.** Clinical signs begin with skin problems that resemble sunburn, including the distinctive "Casal's collar," a skin condition resembling a necklace (Wood 1979), but later more severe dermatitis, diarrhea, and neurological symptoms appear. The condition can be fatal (Newman 1962), but even when less severe it causes impaired work capacity and psychiatric disorders (K. V. Bailey 1975). Pellagra has been found in poor people living in the southern United States as well as in other areas highly reliant on maize as a dietary staple.

Vitamin C Deficiency

Hominoids, one type of bat, and guinea pigs are among the only mammals that cannot synthesize ascorbic acid, or vitamin C, in their bodies. Ascorbic acid functions in the biochemical pathway in which the amino acid proline is converted into collagen. Collagen in turn functions as a chemical that binds together cells in body tissues, notably cartilage, bone, and teeth. Thus, vitamin

C deficiency is associated with poor wound healing and the breakdown of old scars from past healing. The result is widespread hemorrhaging (bleeding), often internal, which leads to sore joints and gums, among other symptoms. The deficiency disease associated with vitamin C is termed **scurvy** and has been found primarily in late winter or early spring in populations with no access to fresh fruits, especially citrus varieties, or vegetables such as tomatoes and green peppers, or, earlier in history, among sailors on long voyages during which similar dietary deficiencies occurred. In fact, this led to the practice of rationing lime juice to British sailors, who became nicknamed "Limeys" because of the practice. In developed countries, vitamin C deficiency is primarily a disease of elderly people who are unable to get out to purchase fresh fruits on a regular basis or alcoholics who fail to maintain a proper diet (Wood 1979).

Vitamin D Deficiency

Vitamin D can be obtained in the diet (e.g., eggs and dairy products), but it also can be synthesized from steroids contained in food. The synthesis, which involves ultraviolet radiation from sunlight to drive the reaction, takes place in superficial skin layers (Cavalli-Sforza 1981). Light skin facilitates the reaction, while clothing blocks sunlight from the skin and thus inhibits the reaction. In regions with intense sunlight, the reaction produces sufficient vitamin D even when skin color is quite dark. In fact, some anthropologists have suggested that light-colored skin evolved partly as an adaptation to synthesize adequate amounts of vitamin D in peoples living in northern latitudes with relatively low levels of solar radiation, while dark skin is seen as an adaptation to filter out ultraviolet radiation and prevent hypervitaminosis D (too much vitamin D) (Loomis 1967). In passing, it might be noted that light-skinned people are more prone to skin cancer from prolonged exposure to ultraviolet rays of the sun. It seems the human body cannot have it both ways—light skin to generate vitamin D and dark skin to protect against skin cancer. This provides an explanation for **Gloger's Rule,** the general tendency for skin color in species with broad geographic ranges to vary from dark to light as latitude increases.

Vitamin D is needed for absorption of calcium from the intestine and calcium's subsequent use in the formation of bone and teeth. The childhood deficiency disease associated with vitamin D is **rickets** (see Figure 9–5). It is characterized by the bowing of bones, delayed tooth eruption (in children), and defective development of tooth enamel (Adair 1987). **Osteomalacia** is the term for the same disease when manifested in adults, among whom it is found most commonly in pregnant and lactating women. Rickets and osteomalacia are found mostly in populations living in cloudy temperate areas or in crowded tropical towns where little light gets in. In some populations rickets and osteomalacia are more common among females independent of pregnancy and lactation status, particularly where cultural practices restrict females primarily to indoors or where they are expected to heavily clothe themselves when they are outside. This is the situation in India, where wealthy Moslems, who stay indoors

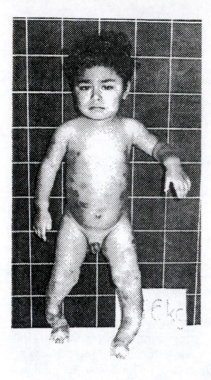

Figure 9–5 Young child with rickets. (Photo by Dr. J. D. L. Hansen reprinted by permission from S. Davidson, R. Passmore, J. F. Brock, and A. S. Truswell. 1975. *Human nutrition and dietetics.* 6th ed. Edinburgh: Churchill Livingston.)

more than other Indian groups, have a higher frequency of rickets and osteomalacia than the other groups (Weiss and Mann 1990).

MINERAL DEFICIENCIES

Iron Deficiencies

Although iron occurs naturally in eggs, lean meats, legumes, whole grains, and green, leafy vegetables, iron deficiency has been termed "the most prevalent nutritional problem in the world today" (Scrimshaw 1991, p. 46). Estimates for developing countries run as high as 67 percent of children and 33 percent of women in childbearing years having some form of iron deficiency. But iron deficiency is also found in developed countries, particularly among women. Most of the body's iron is used in the protein hemoglobin, which carries oxygen and carbon dioxide in the blood. A severe iron deficiency can lead to **anemia** as red blood cell production becomes defective due to lack of hemoglobin. Anemia has many ill effects on people, from lowered work capacity to poor intellectual performance. There apparently is biological variability among people in the degree of capacity to function under conditions of iron deficiency (Haas and Pelletier 1989), but under severe iron shortages all people will show symptoms. When people become anemic, they respond physiologically much as people do under high-altitude hypoxia, for instance by increasing ventilation rate and the concentration of biochemicals used for oxygen transport in tissues (Haas and Pelletier 1989). On a population level, iron deficiency and the resultant anemia can lead to a loss of productivity, and this in turn can lead to additional problems with malnutrition.

Like so many other nutritional disorders, young children are at highest risk. With iron deficiency, it is infants who are particularly vulnerable, in part because their growth requires a high intake of iron and in part because milk, including human breast milk, is a poor source of iron (Jelliffe 1968). Women are also at risk because of the monthly loss of blood and its contained iron in the menses. Treatment of anemic children, and even those with subclinical iron deficiency, with additional dietary iron has increased performance on various behavioral and intellectual tests (Scrimshaw 1991). Similarly, iron treatments in adults can raise work capacity (Spurr 1983).

Iodine Deficiency

Iodine is an important chemical component of thyroid hormones and a deficiency of the mineral can lead to reduced thyroid function. The thyroid gland often swells in an attempt to increase hormone production. This condition is termed **goiter** (see Figure 9–6). In extreme cases, goiters are disfiguring, and they can even cause pressure on the trachea (windpipe) if they get very large.

The symptoms of iodine deficiency are those of reduced thyroid gland function: somnolence (victims often sleep up to 14 to 16 hours a day), muscular sluggishness, lowered pulse, increased body weight, constipation, decreased growth of hair, scaliness of skin, and an increase in blood lipids that can lead to an increase in arteriosclerosis. **Myxedema,** the term for severe loss of thyroid function, is characterized by widespread edema in the body. If thyroid function is severely depressed during infancy or early childhood, **cretinism** can develop. This extreme form of thyroid disfunction can lead to permanent neurological damage and resultant retardation if it is not treated within a few months. The common addition of iodine to table salt in the United States has virtually eliminated iodine deficiency in the country. Natural sources of iodine include seafood, vegetables, and dairy products.

Prevalence of cretinism is highest in mountain populations, including those in the Alps (prior to preventative measures being undertaken), the Andes, and New Guinea, where iodine levels are generally low in the environment (Wood 1979). In a study of poor people in Ecuador, Greene (1977) found that 10 percent of the population were cretins, and nearly 20 percent of the "normal" people in that population appeared subnormal by U.S. standards on tests of motor and mental skills. Not only does this high level of neurological problems affect the population as a whole in its ability to get resources, but, Greene asserts, it also helps maintain a highly stratified social system in which poor peasants of native American ancestry are exploited by a richer, European-derived segment of the population.

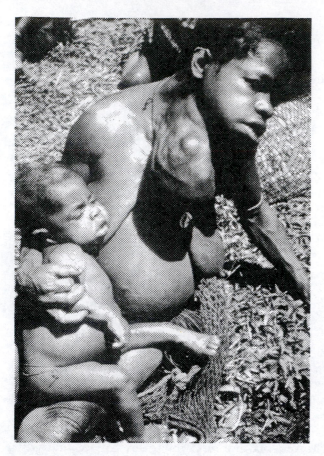

Figure 9–6   A woman exhibiting a large goiter. These signs of iodine deficiency are common in the highlands of Papua New Guinea. (Photo reprinted by permission of the author from D. C. Gajdusek and R. M. Garruto. 1975. The focus of hyperendemic goiter, cretinism, and associated deaf-mutism in western New Guinea. In *Biosocial interrelations in population adaptation,* E. Watts, F. E. Johnston, and G. W. Lasker, eds., 267–85. The Hague: Mouton Publishers.)

Calcium Deficiency

Calcium deficiency syndromes are closely linked to problems caused by vitamin D deficiency, since the latter is important in the body's utilization of calcium. The mineral is important for formation of bones and teeth during development and for their maintenance. Calcium is also important for the normal functioning of the nervous system. This mineral is at high concentrations in such dietary items as dairy products and dark green, leafy vegetables such as broccoli.

Calcium deficiencies can lead to slow bone growth and to **osteoporosis** (decreased bone mass), with the latter particularly prevalent in postmenopausal women. Osteoporosis makes bone very susceptible to fracture. Severe deficiencies can also lead to neuromuscular problems such as tetany, with such symptoms as muscle spasms, confusion, and convulsions (McElroy and Townsend 1989). Low calcium levels may be in part responsible for the arctic hysterias (*pibloktok*) seen in some Inuit populations (Foulks 1972). Pibloktok is characterized by muscle spasms, confusion, and depression, followed by unresponsiveness to other people that is often accompanied by abnormal behaviors such as running from people, jumping in snow or water, ripping off clothing, and throwing objects (McElroy and Townsend 1989). The condition has variously been considered a psychosis, a "culture-bound reactive syndrome" (a neurotic condition specific to a certain culture), a neurological disorder related to epilepsy, food poisoning, a viral infection, and a reaction to heat stress in addition to the calcium deficiency hypothesis.

ADAPTATION AND MALNUTRITION

Much of the human response to malnutrition may not be adaptive at all. Behavioral responses may be inappropriate and can even increase the severity of malnutrition. Biological changes associated with malnutrition may simply be physiological responses to the absence or shortage of required resources. However, there do appear to be mechanisms in place for some nutritional deficiencies that serve to delay the worst consequences.

Food Versus Nutrients

In all human populations, a difference may be found between *food* and *nutrients*. Food is a culturally defined concept, including all substances considered edible. Nutrients are chemicals needed by the body and include carbohydrates, lipids, protein, vitamins, and minerals. Foods that are considered gourmet items in one culture may be considered repulsive in another (Bryant et al. 1985). A clear case of this is found in variation in attitudes toward the eating of insects. Westerners tend to be repulsed by the notion of insects as a food source, although these invertebrates have been an important, and favored, food resource in a majority of human societies. On the other hand, Western preferences for ham and eggs are viewed as repulsive by many people from other cultures (Farb and Armelagos 1980).

There are many factors influencing people's choices in food, including environmental ones: people tend to eat foods produced from locally available organisms and distrust foreign products. Alternatively, during rapid culture change foreign goods may attain prestige, with local foods perceived as inferior. Many decisions about what is edible are based on cultural conventions—that is, cultural definitions of what constitutes food may not always be based on objective criteria about what is the best nutrition. Cultural conventions also are involved in decisions of how much of given foods should be eaten and who should be eating them. There are many age-sex distinctions in what are appropriate foods. There may also be special diets for pregnant or lactating women.

Not all of the cultural conventions about what constitutes food are adaptive in a nutritional sense. Important sources of nutrients may be defined as inedible and thus not utilized. Also, important nutrient sources may be reserved for infrequent times or denied to people who particularly need them. Clearly, cultural or behavioral responses to the food supply are not necessarily adaptive.

Biological Adaptation to Malnutrition

As noted earlier, biological defenses to undernutrition are best viewed as buying time until proper nutritional intake can be restored. Since children are usually more severely affected by malnutrition than other people are, it is likely that strong selection takes place for attributes that allow getting through the hard times, so that reproduction and passing on of these attributes, where genetically determined, can occur.

Nutritional problems cannot be viewed alone. They affect a population's ability to deal with many other stressors, as well as its ability to obtain resources, for instance by limiting work capacity. Malnutrition therefore affects all other areas of a population's ecology. In no domain is this impact more deeply felt than in people's ability to withstand infectious disease. We therefore will consider infectious disease as an environmental stressor and then focus on the interaction of malnutrition and disease in human populations.

INFECTIOUS DISEASE AS A BIOTIC STRESSOR

Scientists in the nineteenth century, including Louis Pasteur, formulated the germ theory of disease, which postulated that communicable diseases are caused by small, usually microscopic, organisms that act as infectious disease agents (germs). This view, however, is an oversimplification. Many infectious agents are nearly ubiquitous in the environment, causing disease only in some instances and to some individuals (Dubos 1965). It is clear that these diseases are actually caused by some combination of parasite and host condition, along with environmental circumstances that inhibit or accentuate the infectious nature of the parasite.

An example of the interaction of parasite, host condition, and environmental circumstances for a human infectious disease is found in the tuberculosis epidemic in Western industrialized countries. According to Dubos (1987), the terrible toll from tuberculosis in the nineteenth century was in part due to the stresses of long working hours, poor nutrition, and generally poor living standards. As living standards improved, tuberculosis rates immediately declined. The decline in tuberculosis rates was very noticeable before the turn of the century, *preceding* the introduction of any specific therapy or prophylaxis. Moreover, tuberculosis mortality showed a sharp rise in parts of Europe during World Wars I and II, but resumed a general downward course as soon as the wars ended. Also, tuberculosis increased in Germany during the 1920s during a period of great economic turmoil (including hyperinflation). These data are *not* explainable by changed infection rates but rather appear to be due to changes in the host (humans) that allow an infection to become virulent during stressful conditions.

A key to understanding infectious diseases and their historic development in human populations is consideration of the general concepts of parasitism discussed earlier. Host-parasite relationships are particularly of interest, especially in human populations.

A Note on Disease "Rates"

Disease "rates" may mean many things to an epidemiologist. Two major ways of determining how common disease is in a population is from measuring the number of fatalities due to the disease per population size, termed the **mortality rate** from the disease, or from measuring the number of people suffering from the disease in relation to population size, termed the **morbidity rate.** The benefit of using mortality rates—as opposed to morbidity rates—as a quantitative measure of disease rates is that deaths are commonly well reported, so information can be obtained, while many instances of sickness may go unreported. The disadvantage of using mortality rates is obviously that not all illnesses result in death.

There are two common means of measuring morbidity rates: through a disease's prevalence and through its incidence. The **prevalence rate** of a disease is the number of cases of the disease at any given point in time. The **incidence rate** of a disease is defined as the number of new cases that appear during a given period of time. For acute, short-term diseases that patients either recover from or die from quickly, prevalence and incidence rates are of similar value, but for diseases that linger for a long time, such as diabetes or malaria, there is a great deal of difference between the two rates. For instance, a population may have a high prevalence of a chronic disease even though new cases are rare.

Host-Parasite Relationships

As noted in Chapter 4, parasites and their hosts tend to coevolve a "peaceful coexistence" in many cases. That is, there appears to be evolutionary selection both in favor of hosts that do not die or become so ill that reproductive success is lowered and in favor of parasites that do not kill their host (the "golden goose"). There is some evidence for this coevolution of host and parasite to result in less virulence.

A classic experimental study demonstrating the diminution of virulence in host-parasite systems was carried out with the housefly and a parasitic wasp (Pimentel and Stone 1968). The wasp paralyzes the fly and lays its eggs in the fly's body. When the eggs hatch, the larvae feed on the hapless fly. Flies and wasps were placed in a large, multicell cage with features designed to slow dispersal of the wasps. When first introduced to the cage, the population density of both host and parasite fluctuated wildly, with population "crashes" of both species, due to high virulence of the parasite. After the flies and wasps had been cultured together for two years, an equilibrium developed, with lower virulence and therefore more stable population densities of both species over time.

Host-parasite coevolution has also been observed in nature. Rabbits became a serious pest in Australia after their introduction from Europe in 1859.

In an attempt to control the rabbit population, the myxomatosis virus, a parasite specific to a rabbit host, was introduced and began to spread through the continent's rabbit population in 1950. The virus was quite virulent, virtually exterminating rabbits in some regions. By 1957, however, epidemiologists noted lower virulence of myxomatosis and greater resistance among the rabbits. This trend continued until an equilibrium was established, with the rabbit population at about 20 percent of its size before the virus was introduced (Burnet and White 1972).

Genetic variability in the host population, particularly in genes related to the immune system itself, may be very important in permitting a host population to rapidly adapt to a new disease agent (Black 1992). This is particularly important in viral diseases, as viruses are rapidly selected to deal with their host's specific immune system. If passed on to a human with a similar or identical genetically based immune system, the virus is preadapted to its new host's immune response and thus causes a more severe disease.

Natural selection against parasite virulence will occur only if there is an advantage to the parasite to keeping its host alive and well. For parasites that can easily change hosts, there may be no change in virulence over time (Ewald 1993, 1994). An important consideration for understanding human infectious disease and its change in virulence over time is the manner in which the parasite is transmitted from host to host. The next sections of this chapter will discuss major ways that parasites are transmitted to humans, using the mode of transmission as an organizing principle. Four major modes of transmission of infectious agents may be considered: vectors, direct human-to-human contact, sanitation routes, and intimate human contact. We will discuss these in turn.

VECTOR-BORNE DISEASE

Vectors are the vehicles by which parasites are transferred from an infected to a susceptible host. They most commonly are arthropods, a large biological grouping that includes insects, spiders, and shrimp among others. Vectors can be considered in two groups: mechanical and biological agents. As a mechanical agent, the vector simply transfers parasites by external contact (e.g., a fly gets germs on its feet from landing on excrement, then lands on food, where the parasites are deposited). As a biological agent, the vector itself becomes infected (with or without symptoms of its own). In some cases the parasite is obligated to go through part of its life cycle in a specific vector. In general, vector-borne diseases can be easily transmitted even when the host is ill, and therefore these diseases tend to remain virulent even after long association with humans (Ewald 1993).

Disease transmission can be heavily involved with characteristics of vectors such as ecological requirements, age-sex distribution, their number in the region, life-cycle stages (these may have separate requirements—e.g., the larval stage may require different conditions than the adult), contacts with host(s), and susceptibility to pick up the parasite (and, later, to pass it on to the host) (World Health Organization 1972).

Another important consideration is **disease reservoirs** (sources of a disease). Reservoirs are usually thought of as all of the hosts of a given pathogen in a given area, or as the organism(s) from which the vector derives its infection. If, for example, a rabbit harbors a microorganism that may be pathogenic (causing disease) to humans, the rabbit is part of the disease's reservoir. Humans infected with that pathogen are also part of the reservoir. An organism does not have to get disease symptoms to be part of the reservoir mechanism. In attempting to limit or eradicate a disease, the characteristics of the reservoir(s) become very important.

In vector-borne diseases of humans, behaviors that involve interaction between individual people and vectors are very significant in decreasing or enhancing the spread of the disease. Also of concern are human activities that enhance the reproduction and spread of vectors, or activities that affect vector contact with reservoirs.

Vector-borne diseases have doubtless afflicted humanity throughout hominid evolution, and some of them have had major impacts on human ecology and biology. Two examples of vector-borne diseases will be discussed briefly here: malaria and onchocerciasis. The examples are chosen to give an idea of how vector-borne diseases can affect human ecology.

Malaria

Malaria has probably been the greatest killer of humans over the past several millennia. There are between 300 million and 500 million cases of malaria at any given time, and nearly 2.7 million people die from the disease each year (Nussenzweig and Long 1994). It is caused by several species of protozoa in the genus *Plasmodium*, particularly *P. vivax*, *P. malariae*, and *P. falciparum*. The latter is the most deadly form of the disease and will be the focus in this section.

Transmission of Malaria.　The pathogenic protozoa are passed by means of mosquitoes of the genus *Anopheles*. The mosquitoes are biological vectors, with an important portion of the protozoan's life cycle taking place in the mosquito (Burnet and White 1972). When a mosquito "bites" (actually injects its needle-like probosis into) an infected person, it may obtain sexually differentiated forms of *Plasmodium* in its blood meal. These forms unite in the mosquito's intestine, producing "sporozoite" forms of the protozoa that eventually are carried to its salivary glands. It takes about 20 days from initial infection of the mosquito until the sporozoites arrive in the salivary gland. When the mosquito now bites another human, the sporozoites are transferred to that person.

In humans, the sporozoites are carried in the blood to the liver, where they multiply as "merozoites" and are released into the bloodstream where they infect red blood cells. They derive nutrition from the cells and multiply inside them, eventually killing the cells and reentering the bloodstream, where new red blood cell hosts are infected.

Infected humans go through a characteristic pattern of recurrent bouts of severe fever that correspond to the cycle of infection and multiplication in red blood cells. The infection can often be fatal, particularly in children, but many people develop some immunity to the parasite. After a time, a new, sexually differentiated form of *Plasmodium* ("gametocytes") appears in the bloodstream that is able to infect a mosquito that bites its host.

Behavioral and Cultural Buffers to Malaria. We can use the single-stressor model that was introduced in the previous chapters to organize our discussion of malaria. *Plasmodium* parasites can be viewed as environmental stressors present in many mosquitoes. Humans can create a microenvironment with fewer or less severe *Plasmodium* infections in a number of ways. An obvious way to deal with the disease is through simple behavioral avoidance of places where and times when mosquitoes are common. This is actually far from easy, as *Anopheles* mosquitoes have adapted to human microenvironments quite well.

Other behavioral responses that may be helpful include the use of screening and mosquito nets, application of insecticides, and the destruction of mosquito breeding sites. In fact, the introduction of human agricultural activities in the past may have greatly increased mosquito breeding sites by providing stagnant pools of water (McElroy and Townsend 1989) and thus increased the prevalence of malaria.

Malaria can also be reduced by taking special precautions in shielding those who are infected from further contact with the mosquito vector. Treatment with quinine and related substances, as well as other pharmaceutical agents, including non-Western medications (Etkin and Ross 1991), may reduce the time an individual harbors *Plasmodium* capable of infecting mosquitoes as well as helping victims recover from the disease. Other behavioral measures, such as the development of vaccines (Godson 1985; Nussenzweig and Long 1994; Stoute et al. 1997) and the creation of genetic variants of mosquitoes that cannot pass on the disease (Aldhous 1993) are still only in the planning or testing stage.

Biological Buffers to Malaria. Humans have evolved immune systems that are quite effective in fighting infectious diseases. *Plasmodium* parasites have also evolved a very effective means of defeating the human immune response. Still, people do build up at least partial immunity to malaria, but only after several years of infection and illness. Thus children are the most common victims of the disease.

Humans have evolved some special biological adaptations to malaria that involve genetic variants of hemoglobin. The most well-known case of genetically based resistance to malaria is the **sickle-cell trait.** Sickle cell represents a small mutation in the gene that determines the hemoglobin molecule. This mutation leads to a hemoglobin molecule that tends to "stick" to other hemoglobin molecules, particularly when the molecule is in its unoxygenated form (that is, after the hemoglobin has delivered its oxygen load to body tissues) (Edelstein 1986). The hemoglobin molecule complex can form large fibrous structures inside red blood cells, with these structures sometimes distending the cells into a characteristic sickle shape. For individuals who have received sickle-cell genes from both parents and thus can make only this form of hemoglobin, a severe form of anemia results that leads to early death unless heroic medical procedures available only recently in developed countries can be employed.

Given the fatal consequences of this mutation, human biologists have long puzzled why some populations have high frequencies of the trait. Populations with high frequencies of sickle cell usually also have (or have recently had) high prevalences of malaria. This observation led to studies that showed that people heterozygous for sickle cell (that is, people with a gene from one parent for the mutated hemoglobin and a gene from the other parent for "normal" hemoglobin) were somewhat resistant to malaria. In particular, people with the heterozygous condition were less likely to die from childhood malaria than people with only "normal" hemoglobin genes. When sickling of blood cells occurs in heterozygous individuals, the affected red blood cells lose potassium, and this causes *Plasmodium* that have infected the cells to die (Friedman and Trager 1981).

Sickle cell thus represents a **balanced polymorphism.** That is, it represents a genetic trait that exists in multiple forms because heterozygotes are selected over either homozygote (only one form of a gene in an individual). In this case, individuals homozygous for sickle cell usually die in childhood due to severe anemia, while individuals homozygous for normal hemoglobin are more likely to die of malaria. The heterozygote does not suffer from severe anemia and is somewhat resistant to malaria.

Other hemoglobin mutations are thought to be related to malaria resistance in a similar manner to sickle cell. Thalassemia is an inherited class of hemoglobin mutations that is found in high frequencies in populations exposed to malaria. Hemoglobin C is another type of hemoglobin mutation found in conjunction with high rates of malaria. There are also mutations in red blood cell enzymes, particularly glucose-6-phosphate dehydrogenase, that seem to be associated with the distribution of malaria (Greene 1993). Although these other genetic polymorphisms are not as well understood as sickle cell in its association with malaria, it does appear that malaria has served as an important selective factor in human evolution. During the time when widespread use of DDT as an insecticide against mosquitoes was effective (before mosquitoes became resistant and the disruptive side effects of DDT use were discovered), human population growth in malarial regions frequently skyrocketed (Burnet and White 1972), suggesting that malaria has been and is yet an important regulator of human population size in many parts of the world. Figure 9–7 illustrates the single-stressor model applied to human adaptation to malaria.

Onchocerciasis

Onchocerciasis is a filarial (a type of parasitic worm) disease passed by a black fly vector. The parasite of the disease is *Onchocerca volvulus* and the vector is *Simulium damnosum*. While this disease is not usually fatal, the parasites move

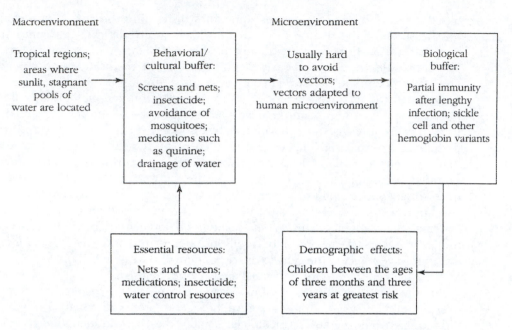

Figure 9-7   Single-stressor model of human adaptation to malaria.

by way of the bloodstream into the eye, where they frequently cause blindness. Since each female worm can produce about 2,000 microfillariae per day and can stay resident in the human body for decades (Desowitz 1981), victims can suffer a huge parasite burden. The black flies typically breed in highly oxygenated water, with rocks in swift-flowing streams often being preferred sites. Because of this, onchocerciasis is often termed "river blindness."

Because onchocerciasis is rarely fatal, it is unlikely that it has exerted significant selective pressure on humans (Kliks 1983). That does not mean that the disease has no ecological effects. On the contrary, there is evidence that the disease has regulated human population density in portions of Africa. For instance, human population density in some river valleys in northern Ghana was quite low compared with neighboring regions (Patterson 1978) even though these valleys had the potential to be high in food production. Villages near swiftly flowing rivers had blindness rates as high as 30 percent in adults. This incredibly high rate of disability had effects on human productivity even though the blind often participated in agricultural activities. In fact, children were often assigned oversight of several blind adults in their work activities.

There is evidence of a pattern of settlement of these river valleys followed by abandonment of villages throughout recent history (Patterson 1978). Colonial policies in several areas of Africa led to resettlement of some of these valleys. The introduction of ferries and other development projects at or near the rivers increased disease rates.

It was not until the 1940s that Western medical personnel began to understand the importance of the disease and its mode of transmission. It was not until 30 years later, beginning in 1974, that a major river blindness control program (the Onchocerciasis Control Program) began throughout many areas in Africa. This program has allowed resettlement of the fertile river valleys previously affected in western Africa (McMillan 1993). In the 1980s effective treatments were devised (involving dispensing of the drug ivermectin) that allowed settlement of these river valleys without the huge toll of disability that was commonplace previously (Taylor et al. 1990; Malatt and Taylor 1992).

Onchocerciasis is an example of a disease that has had major ecological effects on human populations despite the rarity of mortality it caused. As of 1987, the World Health Organization reported that about 18 million people were infected with onchocerciasis, with one to two million of those infected becoming blind. In hyperendemic regions, nearly 50 percent of the population became blind during their lifetimes (Taylor et al. 1990). As onchocerciasis demonstrates, disease has other effects on human ecology besides being the direct cause of death.

DISEASES PASSED THROUGH DIRECT CONTACT

Direct contact diseases are commonly spread by the droplet route, where coughs, sneezes, or simple close contact with respiring victims can serve to pass the disease-causing agents. Many of the diseases passed by this route are specific to humans, although this is not necessarily always the case.

Because the mode of transmission is from person to person, human population characteristics are very important factors in the presence and persistence of such diseases. There appears to be a minimum population size for the persistence of these diseases, particularly ones for which people develop immunity after exposure. Other factors of importance include the time period that individuals are infectious, the number and types of contacts with other people (for instance, whether the community is "partitioned" into subgroups with little contact between individuals outside these small groups or whether contact is more random throughout the community), the proportion of people who have immunity to the disease, and contacts between people in the community and outsiders. Because direct contact diseases are the simplest to model, although even these diseases can lead to complex analyses, mathematical models have been constructed to predict disease patterns in societies (N. T. J. Bailey 1975; Sattenspiel 1990).

Many of the direct contact diseases have arisen in association with the rise of intensified agriculture and its resulting high human population density in separate regions of the world (McKeown 1988). These diseases are spread to other human populations when contact is made, and they can prove to be devastating to the new host populations (McNeill 1976). We'll now examine two of these direct contact diseases, measles and influenza, in slightly more detail, and then discuss the impact of "new" diseases on "virgin" populations.

Measles

Until the development of safe and effective vaccines against **measles,** it was one of those annoying, but not greatly feared, childhood diseases that seemed to act as an initiation rite into adulthood in developed countries. In fact, however, measles can have very negative repercussions, including postmeasles encephalitis, which has a high mortality rate and often leaves survivors with permanent neurological disabilities (Katz and Enders 1965). Widespread vaccination has made the disease and its negative effects rare in developed countries.

Mode of Transmission.   Measles is caused by infection with the measles virus that is transmitted through contact with fluid discharged from the nose, mouth, or eyes of an infected person (the "droplet route"). Although monkeys are susceptible to infection, they are not a reservoir. In fact, no animal reservoir is known. Humans who have survived infection with measles virus attain lifelong immunity to the disease, and no long-term carriers are known to exist. This makes measles a relatively simple disease to model, but note the "relatively" qualification: there are suggestions that some of the patterns in measles outbreaks are irregular and explainable only when highly complex models are employed (Pool 1989b).

Island Populations and Measles Epidemics.   Studies of the relationship between population size and measles epidemics have been carried out on island populations. Graphs of the number of measles cases over time in a population are divided into three basic types, unimaginatively termed Type I, II, and III waves, respectively (Figure 9–8). Type I waves are found in island communities with large populations and consist of curves that are continuous (there is never a time when no cases are found) and usually regular. Type II waves are associated with medium-sized populations; these curves are usually regular, but there are times when no measles cases are present. Type III waves are associated with small island communities and consist of irregular curves with times of no measles cases (Cliff and Haggett 1984).

Adaptations to Measles.   The human immune system adapts well to measles, as most people develop a lifelong immunity after a single bout of the disease. Vaccination serves the same purpose, effectively immunizing people against the virus. The disease is often much more severe when it strikes adults than when it occurs in children. For this reason, it may actually be adaptive for a population, in the absence of vaccine, to allow children to be exposed to the disease. As we shall see, it is populations that have never been exposed to the virus that are most vulnerable to this potentially deadly disease.

Influenza

Like measles, **influenza** is caused by a virus that is transmitted directly between humans by the droplet route. Influenza is quite different from measles in other respects, however. Humans do not develop lifelong immunity to

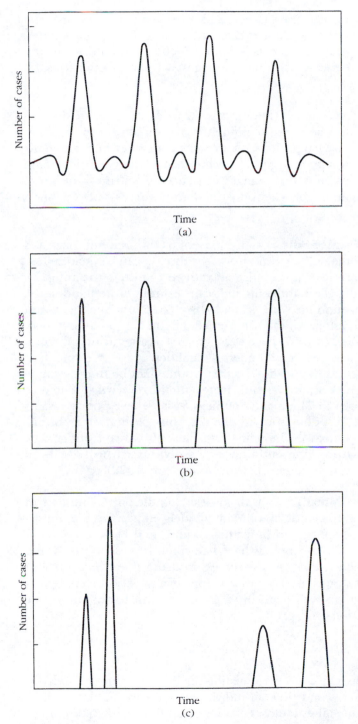

Figure 9–8 Incidence rates over time for measles in island populations. (a) Type I, found in large populations. (b) Type II, found in medium-sized populations. (c) Type III, found in small populations.

influenza after a single bout with the disease, and there is an animal reservoir for the disease, particularly among domesticated animals such as pigs. Another difference from measles is that there is no single, effective vaccine against influenza. Accordingly, this disease probably is the most significant infectious disease in developed countries.

Antigenic Drift in Influenza.   Influenza is, in a sense, a set of diseases instead of a single one. This is because the influenza virus mutates rapidly, causing its outer protein coat to change its structure (a process termed **antigenic drift**). The human immune system targets a specific viral coat structure when it acts against the disease, and thus the changes in structure foil the buildup of immunity. This also accounts for the only moderate success of flu shots (influenza vaccines).

Pandemics and Antigenic Shifts.   While most of us think of influenza as a mild annoyance or a welcome holiday from work, the disease can be deadly. This is particularly true when a large change, called an **antigenic shift,** in the antigenic structure of the virus occurs. This antigenic shift can result in large **pandemics,** where influenza spreads around the world. The 1918–1920 pandemic was one of the deadliest epidemics in history, killing between 25 million and 50 million people (Burnet and White 1972). In 1957 there was a greater pandemic of influenza, although this one did not lead to large numbers of fatalities.

The large antigenic shifts that lead to pandemics may not be due to simple mutations but rather to new strains arising from animal reservoirs. Some of these new strains have arisen in China and Southeast Asia, where poor peasants often live in close contact with domesticated animals, thus facilitating transmission from the reservoir to humans. The new strains may also arise from genetic recombination of viruses from different strains in individuals who have been infected with multiple types of influenza (Burnet and White 1972).

Models of Influenza Spread.   As with measles, mathematical models of the spread of influenza have been devised. Many models emphasize the importance of the patterns of movements of individuals within and between populations (Sattenspiel 1990). While the models have had some success in predicting general patterns of epidemics, there is less success in using them in control of the disease. Because new strains are continually appearing, periodic epidemics appear inevitable unless improved forms of vaccines that can handle antigenic drift, and even antigenic shifts, are produced.

Virgin Soil Epidemics

When a disease is introduced to a population for the first time, no individuals have previous immunity, and thus all individuals are susceptible to infection. These so-called **virgin soil epidemics** can be calamitous, with estimates of up to 90 percent mortality in populations exposed to several new diseases after contact with people from cosmopolitan, urban cultures where many direct contact diseases have become endemic. High estimates for mortality after contact because of these types of epidemics have been made for native Americans (Dobyns 1983; Romenofsky 1987; Verano and Ubelaker 1992) and for Pacific Islanders (Kirkendall 1994), with such viral diseases as smallpox and measles often cited as major killers.

There have been many suggested reasons for the high mortality associated with virgin soil epidemics. There may be a difference in genetic susceptibility of the host populations (Baker 1988a), although this has not been definitively demonstrated (Burnet and White 1972). These populations may have possessed less genetic diversity, particularly in genes related to the immune system, than other populations, making them slower to adapt to the new diseases (Black 1992). A major cause of the increased mortality in virgin soil epidemics is that *everyone* is susceptible. Thus, adults who were never exposed to the disease as children will become infected, usually with much worse symptomology than normally occurs in children. Also, entire communities may become ill at the same time, with no one to take on nursing duties or to carry out essential tasks for resource gathering or maintenance against stressors. Added to this is the psychological stress of an entire society being affected by a strange and terrifying new disease.

Part of the horror of the devastations after Western contact for native Americans and Pacific Islanders was that a succession of deadly diseases usually struck. Hence, a population struggling for normalcy after the ravages of one epidemic would often face another severe epidemic. The result would often be social disruption and even the collapse of the culture, particularly if the diseases occurred in conjunction with colonial or other invasive activity by the cosmopolitan culture. There is no way to precisely account for the degree of mortality suffered by these virgin populations due to imprecise historic accounts, difficulties in reconstructing precontact population size, and the tendency for the effects of the disease to be spread to different populations or subpopulations in advance of direct contact with people from the cosmopolitan populations. What is clear is that these epidemics changed history (McNeill 1976). For instance, it is unlikely that the Spanish conquistadors would have had such success against the huge armies of the Inca and Aztec empires without the disruptive effect on these people by devastating virgin soil epidemics.

DISEASES PASSED THROUGH SANITATION ROUTES

Diseases passed through sanitation routes have been and remain diseases of the poor since they are usually spread through unsanitary drinking water and food. A major mode of transmission of such diseases is the "fecal-oral route" in which parasites are passed from one person to another through contamination of water and food. Such contamination can occur by mechanical vectors such as flies that land on food or through the mixing of sewage and drinking water, as occurs when a population relies on a single water source for all purposes (Figure 9–9).

Figure 9–9   Cleaning clothes in river water, French Guiana. (Photograph courtesy of Norris Durham)

Diseases of poor sanitation may have become common when sedentary life became the norm, which occurred, by and large, after the development of agriculture. Nomadic foragers may have been able to move away from their sanitation problems before they became severe. Unfortunately, evidence for disease rates is missing for foragers until contemporary times, and even then the epidemiological picture is blurred by the effects of contact with agricultural and industrial-based populations (McKeown 1988). However, the absence of helminth (a kind of worm) eggs and other signs of parasitic infection in fossils of early humans suggests that these diseases may have had less significance in earlier times (Dunn 1968).

Diseases passed through sanitation routes are principally affected by human behaviors related to defecation, water use, and food preparation and storage. These behaviors may be indirectly affected by people's belief systems (Paul 1958). For instance, use of latrines or other sanitation methods may be affected by people's beliefs about witchcraft and sorcery, where body parts and wastes may be used to magically induce illness or death.

In some instances, development projects in the developing world may have inadvertently led to increased transmission of these types of diseases. For example, Micronesian atoll dwellers traditionally defecated on ocean-facing beaches, relying on tides and waves to wash the wastes away. Well-meaning foreigners, perhaps due to their ideas of aesthetically clean South Seas beaches as an ideal, built latrines on stilts over the inner lagoons of the atolls. Since people are often in lagoon waters for fishing and other productive activities, the latrines created an opportunity for disease transmission among the atoll residents, a concern accentuated by the importation of parasites by travelers.

Two diseases will be used to illustrate how people's behavior influences diseases passed through sanitation routes: hookworm and cholera. The former is usually viewed more as an annoyance than as a life-threatening disease, while the latter is a major cause of mortality for some human populations. Both have significance for human ecology.

Hookworm

Hookworm infections of humans with the parasitic worms *Necator americanus* and *Ancyclostoma duodenale* occur in well-watered tropical and subtropical regions throughout the world since the eggs and larvae of the parasite require warm, moist conditions to survive (Schad et al. 1983). Humans have sometimes created these conditions in macroenvironments that would not otherwise be suitable to the parasites. Approximately one billion people are infected with hookworm at any given time (Hotez and Pritchard 1995).

Humans are normally the only hosts of these parasites, with transmission by fecal contamination of soil and entry through pores or hair follicles in the skin (Belding 1965). The worms live in the human intestine for up to five years, where they feed on blood and tissue liquids. Each worm produces about 10,000 eggs per day. Larvae hatch within a day or two of elimination, and develop in feces or fecal-contaminated soil.

Feces are usually avoided by people, but after extensive breakdown in the soil, people can no longer perceive contaminated places (Schad et al. 1983). Hence, use of latrines or the wearing of covered footwear would greatly reduce the chances for hookworm transmission. People who work with soil, such as farmers and miners, may be at high risk for infection, the risk being extremely high for farmers who use human excrement as fertilizer, as occurs in China. Also at high risk are people transiently exposed to unsanitary conditions, for instance on the infamous slave ships that brought Africans to the New World (Wood 1979).

Hookworm infection involves a continual loss of blood, which can cause or exacerbate prior conditions of anemia or iron deficiency. In fact, parasitic infections such as hookworm can be important factors in growth retardation among children in poor agricultural societies. Chronic infection also causes a loss in work capacity. On the other hand, mild iron-deficiency anemia may give people some resistance to bacterial infections (Desowitz 1981), suggesting how complex human disease interactions can be. Also, when there is a heavy parasitic hookworm load, biological effects can include exhaustion and cardiac failure (Belding 1965). Hookworm may sometimes be fatal, particularly when infants are infected (Hotez and Pritchard 1995).

Cholera

Cholera is a ancient affliction, a description matching its symptomology being found in writings of Thucydides in ancient Athens. It has been suggested that cholera developed when village life, and community water systems for the villages, developed (Fenner 1970). While various acute diarrheal diseases have been termed *cholera,* formal identification of the disease is now confined to conditions caused by the bacteria genus *Vibrio,* and particularly by the species *Vibrio cholerae.* This disease has also been termed *Asiatic cholera,* solely a human disease under normal conditions. In 1992 there were 461,783 cases reported in 68 countries, with 8,072 deaths (World Health Organization 1993).

Cholera is characterized by a sudden onset of cramps, diarrhea, and vomiting. The major negative effects are caused by dehydration, which occurs quickly, with several liters of fluid lost in the first five hours after symptoms commence (Goodner 1965). This can rapidly result in shock and subsequent death from a combination of acidosis and dehydration (Spink 1978).

Cholera is a waterborne disease and often appears in epidemic form when a large group of people has been exposed to drinking water containing the bacteria. Since humans are the only host for the disease, transmission requires contamination of drinking water by human fecal material. Contaminated food, if uncooked, can also serve as a mode of transmission. People do not remain carriers of the pathogen for long, and therefore these epidemics tend to be short-term and episodic in nature. However, there are regions with endemic cholera, particularly large areas of India, but it is unclear how the disease is maintained in endemic form.

Behavioral measures to control cholera outbreaks involve cleaning water supplies and the use of quarantine. Water boiling is a major means of cholera prevention but is costly in resources (fuel) and time. Medical anthropologists working with public health officials faced great problems in attempting to increase the use of boiled water in a poor, rural Peruvian community, in part because of the people's belief that boiling changed the nature of water, making it dangerous for people to drink (Wellin 1955). Quarantine of people and of food helps prevent the spread of the disease, although the speed of modern transportation makes this difficult. People also resist quarantine, making enforcement an onerous task.

Attempts at producing an effective vaccine have not yet had great success. During a cholera epidemic, vaccines can be given to help stem the incidence rate, but a large proportion of the population must be inoculated for it to have much effect (Goodner 1965). Further, vaccines do not provide long-term protection against cholera at this time. For those who have become infected with cholera, antibiotic treatment is usually effective but requires the presence or rapid importation of antibiotics during an epidemic, which is an expense that some communities can ill afford. The most important form of treatment is replacement of fluids, a therapy that is relatively inexpensive and poses no difficulty with storage since refrigeration is not needed.

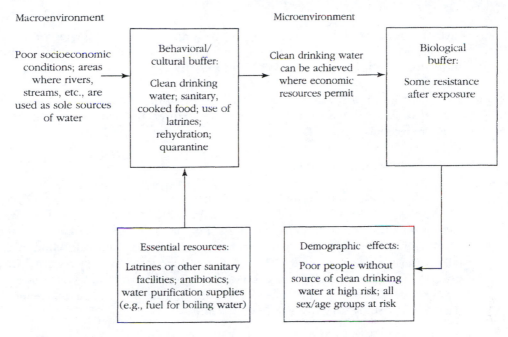

Figure 9–10   Single-stressor model of human adaptation to cholera.

Humans may possess a genetic adaptation to cholera that, like sickle cell and malaria, functions through a balanced polymorphism. In the case of cholera, research using mice as a model biological system suggests that humans who have a single copy of a genetic mutation in the cystic fibrosis gene, which codes for a protein used in the conductance of chloride ions through the membranes of cells in many epithelial tissues, may be somewhat resistant to cholera (Gabriel et al. 1994). People with two copies of the mutation, and thus are homozygous, develop cystic fibrosis, a fatal disorder. People homozygous for the "normal," nonmutated gene are more vulnerable to cholera than heterozygotes are, and thus the heterozygote condition is selected. This hypothesis of a balanced polymorphism helps explain the high frequency of cystic fibrosis in Caucasian populations.

In sum, cholera can be viewed as an economic disease. It is fully preventable if people are provided with clean drinking water and adequate sanitation facilities. Unfortunately, the cost of these resources is too dear for many populations. Figure 9–10 illustrates a single-stressor model for cholera.

DISEASES PASSED THROUGH INTIMATE CONTACT

Diseases passed through intimate contact consist chiefly of sexually transmitted diseases but also of diseases passed through body fluids in general, whether blood, saliva, or semen, or by direct skin contact. Thus, these diseases are greatly influenced by sexual mores as well as by other types of behaviors related to exchange of body fluids, such as shared needles from illicit drug use, improper sterilization of medical equipment, or even transplantation of body organs.

Two examples will be used for this type of disease transmission: the treponemal diseases that may actually represent different forms of a single disease, **treponematosis,** and **AIDS.**

Treponemal Diseases

The treponemal diseases consist of several conditions caused by spirochetes (a type of bacteria) in the genus *Treponema*. Different species of *Treponema* are stated to cause the different conditions, but there is some debate over whether these are actually different species and in fact whether these conditions are actually different diseases at all (Wood 1979). In general, the treponemal diseases are skin diseases, although they can also involve other tissues. Four major forms of treponemal disease are venereal syphilis, yaws, pinta, and nonvenereal (or endemic) syphilis, some of which are deadly.

Venereal Syphilis. **Venereal syphilis** is the treponemal disease best known in most of the developed world. As its name implies, venereal syphilis is a sexually transmitted disease (over 90 percent of infections are transmitted by genital contact) caused by the infectious agent *Treponema pallidum*, but the disease can also be passed from mother to fetus in utero. Humans are the only natural host, although nonhuman primates and rabbits have been infected experimentally (Turner 1965).

Within 10 to 60 days after infection lesions, termed *chancres*, develop, along with enlargement of the lymph nodes in the genital area. Within a few weeks a skin rash typically appears over much of the body. At this stage of the disease, lesions may also appear in the joints, eyes, mucous membranes, and the central nervous system. Usually the host develops antibodies to the spirochetes, and the disease enters a latent stage. With no treatment, about half of those infected will eventually enter a further stage of the disease, sometimes years later (Turner 1965). This later stage can involve serious damage to the central nervous or cardiovascular system and can be fatal.

Venereal syphilis was one of the first diseases for which a specific antibacterial treatment was devised. At the turn of the twentieth century, German bacteriologist Paul Ehrlich, in his search for a "magic bullet" to kill pathogens (but not hurt the host), developed salvarsan, an arsenic derivative that proved eventually, however, to be a very flawed magic bullet (Dubos 1987). Nevertheless, it was somewhat successful in treating advanced cases of syphilis. After their development, antibiotics, particularly penicillin, took over from the arsenic-derived drugs. Currently there is concern about the development of drug-resistant forms of syphilis, although this is a greater problem for gonorrhea among sexually transmitted diseases than it is for syphilis (Cohen 1992).

Yaws.   **Yaws** is a disease of great antiquity caused by *Treponema pertenue*. This species is very similar to *T. pallidum* in most characteristics. The lesions caused by the disease are somewhat different, however, having a yellow to red ("raspberry") color surrounded by a region of inflammation. An initial lesion appears in individuals about 3 to 4 weeks after infection, and from 6 to 12 weeks later secondary lesions develop that are similar in appearance to the original one. Lesions may reappear in further stages of the disease for months to years after initial infection, and these outbreaks are usually debilitating and painful (Wood 1979). Late stages of the disease can involve serious damage to bone and skin tissue.

Yaws is found in tropical regions throughout the world, usually among poor children. It is transmitted by direct contact with an open lesion that contains spirochetes, although flies may sometimes act as mechanical vectors (Turner 1965). The point of entry is usually through cuts or other minor wounds.

Penicillin has proved to be very effective in the treatment of yaws, bringing rapid cures to victims (Brown et al. 1970). Public health campaigns have virtually eliminated yaws from many areas where it had been endemic for millennia.

Pinta.   **Pinta** is caused by *Treponema carateum* and manifests itself as a mild skin disease. It is found primarily in hilly areas of Mexico, Central America, and parts of South America. The disease symptoms begin with scaly skin lesions that eventually get a blue coloration. In later stages of the disease, depigmentation of affected areas of skin leads to a patchy appearance. Sweat glands in these areas no longer function. Otherwise, there are no negative physical effects from the disease, although social stigma is sometimes an important consequence (Wood 1979).

Nonvenereal (Endemic) Syphilis.   The causal agent for **nonvenereal syphilis** (also termed *bejel*) is the same as that for venereal syphilis: *Treponema pallidum*. Spread by skin contact, but also through contaminated drinking water or food, it is found typically in semiarid regions of the Old World and once was particularly prevalent among nomads of Central Asia. Lesions often appear around the mouth (Brown et al. 1970), and thus an important mode of transmission is through oral routes, from kissing to sharing drinking vessels. As with yaws, bone and skin destruction can occur in late stages of the disease which is treatable with antibiotics such as penicillin.

Treponemal Disease.   There are great similarities in the biology of the *Treponema* species and in their response to treatment. People who have had one of the treponemal diseases are resistant to the others. For instance, people infected with yaws almost never contract venereal syphilis. Consequently, public health measures that have greatly reduced the prevalence of yaws have ironically led to great increases in the prevalence of syphilis.

Because of the great similarity of the diseases, debate has occurred as to whether they are actually slightly different manifestations of a single disease. Hudson (1965) has suggested that treponemal disease began as a yawslike condition that adapted to human microenvironments in diverse ways to produce the illnesses found today. Similarly, Cockburn (1963) believes that treponemes have evolved along with their human hosts and adapted to various environmental conditions. On the other hand, some scholars maintain that venereal syphilis is a separate disease that developed in the New World and was brought to Europe by Columbus's sailors upon their return in 1493 (Baker and Armelagos 1988). Whether treponemal infections are one disease or many, clear understanding of each demands knowledge of the others.

Treponemal disease is still common throughout the world despite easily available treatment through antibiotics. Preventative measures involve "safe sex," control of prostitution, and decreasing sexual promiscuity, behavioral and attitudinal changes that are very difficult to achieve. The stigma associated with this disease makes for underreporting of cases, increasing the difficulty of controlling it. Since the majority of treponemal cases are transmitted nonsexually (Hudson 1965), far more difficult measures involving improved economic conditions in developing nations are required. Although the disease is passed through intimate contact, better sanitation and improved health care delivery can do much to control it.

AIDS

The attitude among many people in the developed world that infectious diseases were to a great extent a problem of the past was forcibly changed in the 1980s as a new, terrifying epidemic of a fatal disease spread throughout the world. The disease came to be termed AIDS, short for Acquired Immune Deficiency Syndrome. The disease is unusual both in its mode of transmission, to be discussed, and in its target within the body: the immune system itself.

The agent of AIDS is a virus referred to as the human immunodeficiency virus (HIV). HIV is a **retrovirus,** meaning that its genetic information is carried in an RNA molecule instead of DNA. The information in the RNA is copied onto a DNA molecule using a special enzyme termed reverse transcriptase, and the resulting DNA may become attached to the host cell's own DNA. This DNA may at some later time replicate itself into RNA molecules that either become part of new viruses or may code for proteins necessary for HIV replication (Stine 1993).

One of the characteristic features of HIV is its extremely fast mutation rate, even faster than that of influenza viruses. This leads to establishment of several strains of the virus in a single host's body, as the initial infecting virus mutates during replication. In fact, there are two major forms of HIV known to exist today, HIV-1 and HIV-2, each of which has many mutant strains. These mutations may help the virus evade the host's immune system, as antigens that stimulate immune response change in the mutated strains.

The Effects of AIDS.   HIV infects human cells that contain certain types of proteins, called CD4 or T4 receptor antigens, on their surface. The major cells with this type of surface receptors are T4, or T helper, cells. These cells are an important element of the immune system, helping to recognize invasions by viruses, fungi, and other parasites. Long-term HIV infection leads to a depletion of the T helper cells, and the victim becomes susceptible to infections from many of the pathogens that these cells help combat. Thus, the individual suffers from a deficiency of his or her own immune system, eventually succumbing to one of numerous opportunistic infections.

Transmission.   The first cases of AIDS recognized in the developed world were found among gay men, particularly in major urban centers in the United States and Europe. Soon thereafter cases were found among women who were the sexual partners of men who were bisexual, and cases were also found in many infants born to women who harbored the virus. The disease was seen as being transmitted by sexual activities, but particularly through homosexual sexual activities (Grmek 1990). Any sexual activity that involves bleeding by one of the partners facilitates transmission. Within a few years this was understood to be too simplistic, as evidence for the importance of heterosexual activities in the spread of AIDS became clear. The disease is also spread by contact with blood products—originally through infected blood donated to blood banks, but more commonly by contaminated needles after the blood supply was screened for HIV. In the West, the people most at risk for AIDS are intravenous drug users and homosexual men who do not practice safe sex.

Early efforts at coping with the spread of AIDS were inhibited by discomfort with frank discussions of sexual practices and the stigma associated with both homosexual practices and drug use among many people (Des Jarlais and Friedman 1994). These problems persist in interfering with understanding precisely the means by which AIDS spreads and estimates of future incidence, since research on the sexual practices of people in developed countries remains highly controversial.

Africa.   One of the regions that has been affected the most by the AIDS pandemic is Africa, but on this continent the disease is mostly spread by heterosexual activity. The high frequency of AIDS in large areas of Africa may be due to a longer history of the disease there. Specific sexual practices common to given cultural groups in Africa have a great effect on the rate of transmission, with these practices being quite diverse among the many groups throughout the continent. There is a general association between the highest rates of AIDS in Africa, the so-called AIDS belt, and groups where nearly all men are uncircumcised (Caldwell and Caldwell 1996).

Thailand.   Another region that has faced a particular challenge from the AIDS pandemic is Thailand. Here also the disease is mainly a heterosexual one. Studies have shown a specific route for infection. Males in Thailand are required to spend one year as conscripts in the military. During their military service, sexual relations with prostitutes are common. It has also been considered "unmanly" to use condoms. Thus, the prostitutes have high prevalences of HIV infection, and many men are infected during their year of military service. The men then spread the disease to their home villages once their terms are over (Dickman 1991). Much prevention work in Thailand has focused on blocking this route of infection, mainly through education about safe sex practices.

The Long-Term Effects of AIDS.   Besides the misery and death directly caused by AIDS, the disease has other, more indirect effects. One effect has been a marked change in sexual practices among homosexual men in developed countries that has led to a sharp decrease in AIDS incidence among people in this group. Attitudes toward sex and sexual practices have changed more slowly among heterosexuals, but some change has occurred. Unfortunately, the group most at risk among heterosexuals, teenagers and young adults, has not shown as much change in sexual practices as seems warranted by the AIDS epidemic (Kegeles et al. 1988).

Another indirect effect of AIDS has been an increase in the frequency of other infectious diseases that had become rare in developed countries. One such example is the rise in tuberculosis. This bacterial disease was once a major killer, but the combination of sanitation and antibiotics led to sharp declines in the disease's prevalence. Tuberculosis cases have increased, beginning in the mid-1980s, with many new strains of multidrug-resistant bacteria appearing in tuberculosis cases among AIDS patients (Purvis 1991). These strains may spread to the population at large, leading to fears that tuberculosis may reemerge as a major threat to populations throughout the world.

AIDS has certainly made clear to the populations of the developed world that people are not invincible to infectious diseases. Vaccines and antibiotics have changed the competition between people and pathogens, but they have not eliminated it.

INTERACTION OF INFECTIOUS DISEASE, MALNUTRITION, AND OTHER STRESSORS

Malnutrition is not only a major stressor for humans in its own right but also modifies the impact of other stressors (Haas and Pelletier 1989). Disease may be viewed in the same manner.

Malnutrition and Disease

As noted earlier, one of the major biological effects of protein-calorie malnutrition is a reduction in immune system function, with consequent vulnerability to infection. There are numerous examples of populations facing nutritional scarcity that then suffered increased illness and mortality from infectious diseases. Famines caused by warfare have often led to high levels of disease. Dysentery, smallpox, typhus, and typhoid (the latter two referred to as "camp fever") were frequent causes of mortality during the American Revolutionary War (Stinnett 1983), while the Dutch, as noted earlier in the chapter, were faced with high death rates from tuberculosis during famines caused by World War II.

There are also many examples of peacetime famines that led to increased infection rates. For instance, there is evidence that crop failures in the Middle Ages led to high mortality from respiratory infections (Cartwright 1972). In contemporary times, there is often an association between seasonal variability in food intake and infectious disease incidence, for instance among East African pastoralists (Little 1989) and poor Andean farmers (Leonard and Thomas 1988). Brown et al. (1981) documented very high rates (90 percent) of systemic infection in Bangladeshi children with severe protein-calorie malnutrition.

The association between disease and malnutrition also goes in the other direction: infections can lead to nutritional problems. This is in part a physiological process whereby digestion is inhibited by pathogens, or injuries due to the pathogen cause a loss of blood or other material from the body that requires dietary replacement.

Disease causes nutritional deficiencies in a more indirect manner by reducing work capacity of people and thus limiting their productive capacity. This may occur through loss of work time, a reduction in muscle mass by the illness, or reduction in capacity of the cardiovascular or pulmonary systems due to the disease (Weitz et al. 1989).

Among Quechua living in the Peruvian Andes, measurable economic deficits are incurred during illnesses experienced by farmers, particularly those from the poorest families (Leatherman et al. 1987; Thomas et al. 1988). This is in part due to the fact that the poorer families are also deficient in "social resources," people who can pitch in and help during a difficult time such as during sickness. For many people, however, social resources are adequate to allow help in productive activities until their illness has run its course. For chronic infections where a large proportion of the population is affected, as occurs in several regions from schistosomiasis, a general loss of work capacity of a majority of people may reduce overall productivity of the human population. Also, long-term malnutrition and chronic parasitic infections during childhood can stunt growth, and the reduced muscle mass of adults in such populations may inhibit their ability to do essential tasks (Weitz et al. 1989).

Relation of Effect of Disease and Malnutrition on Other Stressors

Both disease and malnutrition have important interactions with human adaptability to other stressors. For instance, anemia due to either iron deficiency or heavy parasite loads is a devastating problem at high altitude, where hypoxic conditions demand an effective oxygen-carrying capacity by the blood (Haas et al. 1988). Similarly, the loss of subcutaneous fat during severe undernutrition reduces an individual's ability to cope with cold stress.

The complex interrelationship between these macroenvironmental stressors indicates a weakness in the single-stressor model that has been employed frequently in the past few chapters. The model's name suggests its limitation: it deals with only a single stressor at a time, while in the real world populations are simultaneously confronted with multiple stressors. Further limitations of the model will be seen when we confront the complex stressors created by human cultures in modernized society that will be discussed in the next chapter.

CONCLUSION

The two stressors discussed in this chapter have been, and remain, major selective forces on human populations. Medical personnel joyfully proclaimed the coming of an end to infectious diseases, buoyed by the success of antibiotics and vaccines. The evolution of antibiotic resistance in human pathogens and the antigenic shifts that foil our attempts at effective vaccines have caused infectious disease to reemerge as an adversary in the developed world. In reality, it had never ceased being one in the developing world.

The mid-1990s "green revolution" in agriculture offered promise of an end to starvation; it didn't for a host of reasons. Unfortunately, malnutrition remains a serious threat in much of the world, particularly where armed conflict between human populations, or—worse—within a single society, leads to disruption of productive activity and shipments of food aid. More than 500 million children are currently affected by protein-calorie deficiency, night blindness due to vitamin A deficiency is found in approximately six million Asians, and iron and iodine deficiencies each afflict millions worldwide, causing anemia and cretinism, respectively (Mascie-Taylor 1991).

The effects of malnutrition and parasitic diseases that exacerbate the effects of undernutrition can be especially pernicious to children. There is abundant evidence that chronic malnutrition in young children can have serious effects on mental development, with intellectual abilities inhibited throughout life (Brown and Pollitt 1996). It is possible that such mental impairment can lead to difficulty in obtaining resources as an adult, setting the stage for the next generation's malnutrition.

Famine and pestilence remain two of the horsemen of the apocalypse, riding all too closely with their fellow horsemen, war and death. Humans have adapted to these two mounted stressors both behaviorally and biologically, but they are confronted with living adversaries who have also adapted to humans. It is an evolutionary "arms race" in which adaptation must be viewed as a *process* rather than as some perfect state.

KEY TERMS

AIDS	hookworm	pellagra
anabolism	kwashiorkor	pinta
anemia	incidence rate	prevalence rate
antigenic drift	influenza	protein quality
antigenic shift	malaria	retrovirus
balanced polymorphism	marasmus	rickets
beriberi	measles	scurvy
cholera	morbidity rate	sickle-cell trait
Cori cycle	mortality rate	treponematosis
cretinism	myxedema	undernutrition
disease reservoirs	nonvenereal syphilis	vector
Gloger's Rule	onchocerciasis	venereal syphilis
glycogenesis	osteomalacia	virgin soil epidemics
glycogenolysis	osteoporosis	yaws
goiter	pandemic	

KEY POINTS

☐ Malnutrition, any type of poor nutrition, is largely a problem of distribution and is a measure of ecological failure to adapt.

☐ Protein malnutrition, one of the leading forms of malnutrition particularly in developing countries, is a general form of amino acid deficiency, with different specific types of malnutrition depending on which amino acids are in short supply; it leads to lowered birth weight, subsequently to slowing or cessation of growth, and in severe situations in children to the disease kwashiorkor.

☐ Physiological adaptation to protein malnutrition includes secretion of serum proteins into the intestine, where they are digested into amino acids, and in more severe instances the breaking down of skeletal muscle.

☐ Protein-calorie malnutrition results in the effects of protein malnutrition compounded by a lack of energy that is manifested in decline in physical work capacity, extension of the period of birth labor, problems with lactation, increased susceptibility to disease, and, in severe cases in children, to the disease marasmus.

☐ Protein-calorie malnutrition necessitates physiological adaptation not only to protein deficiency but also by utilizing such energy reserves as glycogen stored in liver and muscles, plasma proteins and skeletal muscle tissue, and body fat, the latter used both directly and indirectly via the Cori cycle.

☐ Vitamins, accessory food factors found in various food sources, and micronutrients such as iron and iodine are vital and typically specific to the normal functioning of a wide variety of body processes (e.g., vitamin A and epithelial cells, vitamin D and calcium absorption, iron and hemoglobin production, and iodine and thyroid metabolism).

☐ Measurements of how common a disease is in a population are determined by mortality rate (fatalities per population size) and morbidity rate (the number suffering from a disease per population size), the latter measured by prevalence rate (the number of cases at a given time) and incidence rate (the number of new cases over a given time period).

☐ Diseases involving a vector that transmits parasites from an infected to a susceptible host include malaria and onchocerciasis to which there are both behavioral and cultural buffers involved with vector avoidance and biological responses, although both diseases have had severe impacts on human populations.

☐ Diseases passed by direct contact by way of the droplet route include measles and influenza, immunity to which can be developed in the former either naturally or by vaccination but not the latter because of the high rate of mutation of the causative viruses.

☐ Recorded history notes a number of virgin soil epidemics following contact with populations carrying a disease who have prior immunity; the contacted population lacks such immunity, and thus all individuals are susceptible to infection.

☐ Hookworm and cholera are diseases passed through sanitation routes that are affected by defecation, water use, and food preparation and storage.

☐ Diseases passed through intimate contact include various treponemal diseases such as venereal and nonvenereal syphilis, yaws, and pinta and acquired immune deficiency syndrome (AIDS).

☐ In the interaction between malnutrition and infectious disease, the former can lead to a reduction in immune system function thereby increasing vulnerability to infection, and infection can lead to nutritional problems through inhibition of digestion or loss of blood or other material that requires dietary replacement.

☐ Although malnutrition and disease are major selective forces on human populations, there is a complex interrelationship among disease, malnutrition, and other stressors (e.g., heat, cold, aridity).

10

Modernization, Stress, and Chronic Disease

Human adaptation has been presented so far as involving the creation of a more congenial microenvironment and reliance on biological responses only when the macroenvironmental stress is not fully handled by behavioral means. For the modern, urban environment with which most of us cope on a daily basis, this approach to human adaptability is inadequate. In fact, many of the stressors with which we must deal are of our own making. The urban microenvironment has many stressors in it, from air pollution to crime to traffic jams to final examinations for college students, that have little to do with the macroenvironment in which our city or suburb happens to be located. While these stressors may differ from those considered in the previous chapters, they are stressors nevertheless, and persistence of modern human populations for the long term depends on the ability to cope with these self-induced environmental challenges.

This chapter will focus on the stressors of the urban/suburban environment found in developed countries throughout the world and on the effects of these stressors. Further, our focus will be primarily on how these problems affect individuals as opposed to government agencies or other major organizations. Three major topics are covered: pollution, general stress, and adiposity. The first two topics represent stressors that are encountered by all individuals in the urban microenvironment, while the third is a common outcome of the tendency for overnutrition and infrequent physical activity that all too often characterize modern lifestyles.

The study of human adaptation to the urban microenvironment is more than an academic exercise. Serious health problems arise from inadequate coping with these stressors, represented particularly by such chronic diseases as cancer, hypertension, heart disease, and diabetes mellitus.

MAJOR CHRONIC DISEASES IN MODERNIZED POPULATIONS

The prevalence of major chronic diseases increases in populations that shift from a traditional to a modernized mode of life. This increase has sometimes been brushed off with the statement, "That's because people now live long enough to get these diseases." The statement has some merit because life expectancy does tend to increase considerably in populations that have modernized. That is not the entire answer though, as precursors to chronic disease states are found in higher frequency even among young adults living in modernized societies compared with those in traditional ones. The following will briefly outline features of major chronic diseases and evidence for their increase in modernized settings, using the Pacific Basin as a regional case study. Among the inhabitants of the Pacific island countries of Polynesia, Micronesia, and Melanesia, modernization is associated with lowered mortality from infectious diseases but increased mortality from some major chronic diseases (Taylor et al. 1991).

Cancer

Cancer is a term used for a condition in which there is uncontrolled growth of the cells of one's own body. There are many forms of cancer, with many different causes. In general, however, cells become cancerous because of mutations that alter genes that control cellular growth and reproduction. These mutations can "turn on" certain genes (so-called oncogenes) or "turn off" others (cancer suppressor genes).

Causes of Cancer.   While the proximate cause of cancer may be genetic mutation, ultimate causal factors may include a number of hereditary and environmental factors that affect the rate of mutation. In essence, any environmental **mutagen** (a physical or chemical agent that increases the rate of mutation) can be considered a potential contributing cause of cancer. Known mutagens include many chemicals in air pollution (including cigarette smoke), viruses, and both natural and artificial sources of radiation (Kupchella 1987).

Specific forms of cancer, such as lung, breast, prostate, and colon cancer, appear to have differing major risk factors that may be related to differential environmental exposure of the different tissues. For instance, risk for lung cancer is strongly related to cigarette smoke and other forms of air pollution, while risk for stomach and colon cancer appears to be strongly influenced by dietary elements (Spitz and Newell 1992). There are also differences in cancer risk based on occupation (Williams et al. 1977).

Population Differences in Cancer Incidence.   There are great differences in cancer incidence between countries, as well as differences within countries based on regional or ethnic differences (Muir 1976; Mervis 1995). Studies of migrants have demonstrated that environmental differences account for much of the variability in cancer incidence, as migrant populations tend to develop the cancer profiles of their new environment and lose those of their native region. A clear example is seen among the Japanese American population in Hawaii. Stomach cancer rates, which are very high in Japan, are lower in the Japanese Americans, with these rates even lower in second-generation Japanese Americans than in their immigrant parents (Haenszel et al. 1972). Conversely, incidence of cancer of the large intestine is much higher among Japanese Americans than in Japanese who reside in Japan, with rates in the immigrants approaching that of the U.S. population as a whole.

Cancer in Pacific Populations.   Rates of cancer prevalence, and of cancer mortality, are higher in modernized than in traditional societies. This is clearly the case among Pacific Islanders. Significant associations have been found between many indicators of modernization, such as rate of urbanization, level of formal education, per capita GDP (Gross Domestic Product, a measure of average income), and amount of imports per capita, on one hand, and proportion of mortality from cancer on the other hand (Taylor et al. 1991). Discouragingly, there is even a strong positive relation between the number of doctors per capita and proportional mortality from cancer among these Polynesian, Micronesian, and Melanesian populations. This does not necessarily mean that doctors are causing cancer; in this instance, the number of doctors per capita can be viewed simply as another measure of modernization.

Cancer in China.   The huge, diverse population of China permits epidemiological study of the varying cancer prevalence within different regions of the country. Populations in some regions of China suffer from very high prevalence of stomach and esophageal cancer, and these high rates have been linked to a combination of environmental, genetic, and dietary factors (Mervis 1995). For instance, people living in Linxian County have a mortality rate from esophageal cancer that is over ten times China's national mortality rate, and 100 times the U.S. rate for Caucasians. When nutritional supplementation allowed addition of vitamins and minerals to the normal diet of some of the people in the county, their risk for this cancer dropped significantly (Blot et al. 1993). On the other hand, in the more modernized urban center of Shanghai, diets high in animal sources of food, although rich in nutrients, are associated with higher risk for the development of endometrial cancer in women (Shu et al. 1993). As China's economy leads to greater wealth and the spread of modernized conditions through many regions of the country, the epidemiology of cancer in China is likely to change significantly.

Modernized Environments and Cancer Risk.   We can state with confidence that the rise in disease and death from cancer found in our modernized society is not simply a byproduct of longer life. There are elements of our environment that foster increased risk of cancer. Given the complex nature of modernized society and also the complex nature of cancer causation, it is not easy to pinpoint a single feature of modern environments that is "the cause" of the increased cancer rates. Some possible risk-increasing features will be considered later in this chapter.

Hypertension

Causes of Hypertension.   Hypertension is more a symptom than a disease, being defined as persistently high arterial blood pressure. Hypertension may be caused by diseases, such as various kidney problems. However, for the vast majority of cases of hypertension, usually labeled primary, or "essential," hypertension, no specific cause is known. In general, any factor that increases the volume of the blood or that reduces (constricts) the internal volume of blood vessels, or both, will increase blood pressure. This represents an enormous number of possible factors, from fluid and electrolyte intake to perspiration, environmental temperature, physical activity, and sympathetic nervous system activation, among many others. Hypertension is related to all of the following: age, sex (males are at greater risk), socioeconomic status (poor people are at greater risk), heredity, diet, weight and amount of body fat, stress, and rapid social change.

Effects of Hypertension.   While the causes of hypertension are numerous and in many cases poorly understood, its effects are much clearer. Hypertension is associated with greatly increased risk for stroke, heart disease, blindness, and kidney failure. In fact, elevated blood pressure is an omen of a shortened life expectancy for people in developed countries.

Modernization and Hypertension.   As with cancer, hypertension is more common among people living in modernized societies than in more traditional settings. One indicator of this is the characteristic rise in blood pressure with age seen in all developed countries. This was originally thought to be a part of the normal physiological process of aging. When medical and anthropological researchers began to report blood pressure measurements from traditional societies where there was little or no rise with age, the traditional populations were seen as abnormal, due to disease or malnutrition. After many reports of populations with little or no increase in blood pressure with age, including groups from many different macroenvironments and with greatly differing cultural backgrounds, subsistence types, and diets (James and Baker 1990), it became clear that the abnormal populations are those residing in modernized environments.

Populations that change from a traditional to a modernized setting, whether through migration to a modernized area or *in situ* modernization, usually show increased rates of hypertension. Again, Pacific Islanders present clear examples of this. Several populations have shown increased blood pressure and clinically defined hypertension in amounts approximately proportional to their degree of modernization, with evidence from Samoan (Baker 1986; McGarvey and Schendel 1986), Tokelauan (Wessen et al. 1992), Maori (Prior 1974), Solomon Islander (Page et al. 1974), and some New Guinea populations (Schall 1991).

In some Pacific Islander populations there is a sex difference in blood pressure responses to modernization, with men generally showing greater blood pressure increases than women. Variability in blood pressure response among population subgroups, as defined by sex or a given age group or in some other manner, may depend on the specific nature of changes in lifestyle that occur with modernization for a specific group. For instance, circumstances for a given group may be such that young adult men are exposed more to new, "foreign" ideas during rapid modernization, and hence this subgroup is more likely to exhibit increased blood pressure. Other circumstances may lead to increased risk for other subgroups in given populations.

The increase in rates of hypertension in modernized societies suggests that conditions within the modernized microenvironment somehow increase risk for this disease. Like cancer, hypertension is a complex condition with multiple causes, so no simple answer exists for precisely what specific feature of the modernized environment may be its cause. Later in the chapter we will briefly discuss some of the general features of modernized microenvironments that may contribute to the hypertension problem.

Heart Disease

Heart disease in its many forms is the leading cause of death in the United States and in the developed world as a whole. Here we limit discussion to diseases of the heart proper as opposed to the entire cardiovascular system. The major form of heart disease is that of the coronary arteries, the vessels that supply the heart muscle with blood. Coronary artery disease involves atherosclerotic lesions in these vessels. **Atherosclerosis** refers to the existence of hard, lipid-containing deposits called **plaques** on the interior wall of arteries. These plaques can enlarge and may cause a blood clot, or thrombus, to form on its surface, leading to partial or complete occlusion of the blood vessel. When an occlusion occurs in coronary arteries, blood supply to a portion of the heart can be blocked, leading to a heart attack.

Another form of coronary artery disease is due to **arteriosclerosis,** or hardening of the arteries, in which the blood vessel wall becomes fragile and thus susceptible to aneurysm (a ballooning out of the blood vessel wall because of a weakened structure) or rupture.

The mortality rate from coronary heart disease varies almost tenfold among developed countries, with Japan among the lowest and English-speaking countries such as the United Kingdom, Australia, New Zealand, and the United States among the highest (National Research Council 1989). Data from 1990–1991 suggest that several countries in Eastern Europe have now surpassed the English-speaking countries in heart disease mortality (World Health Organization 1993b). Less developed countries, such as Guatemala and Thailand, have even lower mortality rates than Japan.

Modernization is therefore related to increased coronary heart disease mortality. Given the great differences in incidence of, and mortality from, coronary heart disease among populations of developed countries, however, modernization per se is not a simple cause of coronary heart disease. Nevertheless, some aspects of modernization that are found unequally in these countries must contribute significantly to the disease burden of people. This notion is buttressed by migration studies that have shown that Japanese adopt the mortality pattern of the country they move to within a generation or two. Japanese Americans on the U.S. West Coast tripled their coronary heart disease incidence within a generation of migration, while in Hawaii the incidence rate doubled in a single generation (Marmot et al. 1975).

Diabetes Mellitus

Diabetes mellitus is a disorder involving the incapacity of the body to metabolize carbohydrates in a normal manner. This incapacity is due to an inability to produce or utilize the hormone insulin. **Insulin** is produced by beta cells in the pancreas, with production stimulated by a rise in blood sugar levels. Insulin is released into the bloodstream where it is carried throughout the body and attaches to chemical receptors located on the outer membranes of cells in all body tissues. Attachment of insulin to the receptor causes many changes in the cell, including an increase in the uptake of sugar, which is then metabolized within the cell. The uptake of sugar by cells leads to a decrease in blood sugar levels, and thence a discontinuation of the stimulus to produce insulin. Finally, circulating insulin is cleared from the blood in large part by the liver.

Causes of Diabetes.   When insulin is not produced or does not function properly, blood sugar levels remain elevated, as body cells cannot take in the sugar. This persistent elevation of blood sugar levels is a defining characteristic of diabetes, of which there are two major forms. **Insulin-dependent diabetes mellitus** (IDDM) often appears first in young people and is thus sometimes referred to as juvenile diabetes. It is apparently caused by an autoimmune response; the individual's own immune system recognizes the insulin-producing beta cells as a foreign antigen and attacks them. The result of the attack is an inability to produce insulin.

Noninsulin-dependent diabetes mellitus (NIDDM) is a much more common form of the disease, usually with a late onset. In this form of diabetes, insulin is still produced, but body cells have fewer insulin receptors in their membranes and therefore do not respond well to it. NIDDM is closely associated with obesity; high levels of body fat greatly increase the risk of developing the disease. People who are obese have high levels of circulating lipids in their blood, and these lipids slow liver clearance of insulin. This causes chronically high levels of insulin in the blood, which leads to cellular adaptation to the constant stimulation by reducing the number of insulin receptors in their membranes. The resulting insensitivity to insulin slows glucose uptake, causing insulin production to be increased, which in turn leads to further reduction in insulin receptors in cells. This cycle of decreased insulin sensitivity of cells and increased insulin production continues until the beta cells are exhausted. NIDDM is the final result of this process.

Effects of Diabetes.   Although the two forms of diabetes have different causes, their effects are similar. Without treatment, the cells of a victim starve in the midst of plenty, as sugar cannot get inside the cells. There is a shift to reliance on fat metabolism for energy, but this can lead to both ketosis and acidosis (conditions in which the body has too many of the metabolic products of lipid breakdown—termed ketone bodies—or too much acidity, respectively), potentially fatal problems. Also, the glucose-rich body fluids constitute a hazard because of their attraction for pathogens such as bacteria as well as the chemical changes that glucose can cause to proteins in the body. Glucose combines with proteins in a process termed **glycosylation,** and it is believed that this process accelerates cellular aging. Glycosylation may contribute to the thickening of blood vessel walls seen in many diabetics, leading to impaired blood circulation (Notkins 1979). Side effects of diabetes due to glycosylation and poor circulation include renal disease, blindness, poor wound healing, and gangrene in extremities (Kerson 1985; Palumbo and Melton 1985).

Diabetes and Modernization.   NIDDM, the most common form of diabetes, is associated with modernization in populations throughout the world (Hutt and Burkitt 1986) but is particularly prevalent in modernized populations of Native Americans (Szathmáry 1994) and Pacific Islanders (Baker 1984b), suggesting an interaction between genetics and modernization in the causation of the disease. For instance, NIDDM has low prevalences in traditional Micronesian and Polynesian populations, such as residents of Pukapuka and rural areas of Western Samoa (Zimmet et al. 1982), but very high prevalences in these populations when they become modernized, such as Nauruans (Zimmet et al. 1982), urban Maoris (Prior and Davidson 1966), and native Hawaiians (Look 1982).

The Thrifty Genotype Hypothesis.   The **thrifty genotype hypothesis** posits a relationship among increased fatness, genetics, and NIDDM (Neel 1982). The hypothesis suggests that certain human populations have a history of feast-and-famine cycles in their food supply, where time periods of plenty are interspersed with periods of scarcity. Humans adapt to this cycle by becoming very efficient at laying down fat during feast times, and living off the fat to get through the famine periods. People with a genetic background that permits this

metabolic efficiency are more successful at surviving and reproducing, thus leading to natural selection of a "thrifty" genotype. However, if the environment
should change such that feast times are continuous, these people would have a
tendency to lay down fat efficiently leading to high rates of obesity and, eventually, NIDDM. The high rates of obesity and NIDDM among Pacific Islanders
and Native Americans have been explained by this hypothesis.

Modernization and Chronic Diseases

The evidence just presented shows that rates of chronic disease are
increased in populations living in modernized settings, but this fact alone does
not identify the actual factors involved in disease causation. We will now turn to
some of the factors in modernized environments thought to play a causal role in
the development of chronic diseases. Specifically, we will briefly consider three
factors: pollution, general stress, and adiposity.

POLLUTION

Pollution will be considered in some detail in Chapter 15; here, we will focus more
specifically on the presumed connection between pollution and chronic diseases.
A preliminary definition of **pollution** is a resource that is "out of place" in the
environment, leading to either too much or too little of a substance from the perspective of specific ecological communities. A major connection between pollution
and disease appears to be between exposure to high concentrations of certain
chemicals produced in industrial processes and high rates of certain forms of cancer. Three major forms of pollution will be discussed: air, water, and solid waste.

Air Pollution

Air pollution is not limited to modernized environments. Both natural and
anthropogenic (generated by human activities) air pollution predate the emergence of our species. We will focus here on anthropogenic sources of pollution.

Smoke.   Smoke is one of the most common forms of air pollution.
Humans have been producing high concentrations of smoke in their living areas
since our ancestors learned to control fire approximately a half million years
ago. While there is little agreement on the magnitude of health risks from wood
fire smoke, there has been some discussion of its contribution to respiratory
problems. Data from some traditional societies including groups in New Guinea
(Anderson 1978), Nepal (Pandey et al. 1989), Gambia (Armstrong and Campbell
1991), Zimbabwe (Collings et al. 1990), and among Native Americans in the
United States (Morris et al. 1990) suggest that smoke from wood fires contributes to respiratory disease in children. Also, lung cancer incidence has been

shown to be related to use of coal-burning stoves in Shenyang, China (Xu et al. 1989). We must be aware that a causal connection between air pollution and disease may have a long history in human populations and hence be associated not only with recent modernized conditions.

Much more is understood about the health risks of inhaling tobacco smoke, particularly from cigarettes. In fact, cigarette smoking is considered to be the greatest single preventable cause of morbidity and mortality in the United States as well as much of the developed world (Bloom 1988). About 30 percent of cancer deaths in the United States are attributed to smoking, and this behavior is also a major contributor to other major illnesses including heart disease and chronic respiratory diseases such as emphysema (USDHEW 1971). Cigarette smoking is estimated to have four times the risk for lung cancer than the presence of residential coal smoke in Shenyang (Xu et al. 1989). Air pollution caused by cigarette smoking is also a cause of serious illness in healthy nonsmokers, particularly in the children of parents who smoke (USDHHS 1986).

Smog.   A more recent form of air pollution in human history results from the combination of smoke—particularly from the burning of fossil fuels such as coal—with fog to create **smog.** A newer version is photochemical smog caused by the action of sunlight on some of the chemicals found in air pollution; these are commonly associated with automobile exhaust. London and Los Angeles are most notorious for these types of pollution, but smog has become a common urban problem in modernized societies. The infamous smog disaster in England in December 1952 resulted in approximately 5,000 deaths, many attributed to high sulfur dioxide levels during this time period (Greenwood and Edwards 1973). The worst air pollution disaster in the United States occurred over a two-day period in Donora, Pennsylvania, in 1948, resulting in twenty deaths (Owen and Chiras 1995).

Major Chemicals in Air Pollution.   The major chemicals in air pollution that cause health problems are carbon monoxide, nitrogen oxides, sulfur oxides, and hydrocarbons. In addition, air pollution includes particles of ash and various metals that can damage health. Carbon monoxide is highly poisonous, combining with hemoglobin and in so doing causing the protein to lose its ability to carry oxygen. While carbon monoxide poisoning can often be fatal by itself, it can also indirectly cause sickness or death by placing a strain on the respiratory and cardiovascular systems. Nitrogen oxides can have similar effects (Ehrlich et al. 1973). Sulfur oxides such as sulfur dioxide have been implicated as contributing to severe respiratory diseases such as asthma and emphysema due to the irritation they cause to the air passages in the lungs. Hydrocarbons come in many forms, making clear connections with disease difficult, but there is reasonable evidence that at least some forms of hydrocarbons contribute to the burden of cancer in populations living in highly polluted regions (Ehrlich et al. 1973). Particulate air pollution can cause damage to the respiratory tract after settling on the surfaces of the bronchial tubes (Franke and Franke 1975).

The Pollution Standards Index. A pollution standards index has been devised for urban areas, with values over 100 being considered unhealthy and those over 300 being hazardous. On the basis of these ratings, Los Angeles has the most polluted air of all cities in the United States, with 156 days during 1991 listed in the unhealthful or hazardous ranges (Owen and Chiras 1995). Use of this index has allowed observation of changes in a given area's pollution problem and has provided information used in the passing of standards for clean air at national and local levels (Figure 10–1).

Water Pollution

Water pollution also is a cause of human health problems, due both to infectious diseases such as those transmitted because of poor sanitation, as discussed in the previous chapter, and illnesses caused by the ingestion of toxic chemicals. We will focus on the latter in this section.

Figure 10–1 Air pollution in Los Angeles. A view of downtown from Griffith Observatory. (Photo by Ken Lubas used by permission of Los Angeles Times Syndicate.)

Industrial Sources of Water Pollution.   Many industrial wastes get into both freshwater and marine environments, with the resultant major human health problems stemming primarily from their leakage into ground water. Sources of these industrial wastes include landfills or other hazardous waste disposal sites and gasoline storage tanks, many of which are now corroded and leaky (Owen and Chiras 1995).

Agricultural Sources of Water Pollution.   Another major source of toxic chemical pollutants is the agricultural sector in industrialized nations. The heavy use of chemical fertilizers, herbicides, and pesticides on croplands leads to runoff of these chemicals into streams, lakes, and rivers, as well as their seepage into underground aquifers. All of these water sources have been used to provide drinking water for human populations.

Health Effects of Water Pollution.   The magnitude of the health effects of chemical pollutants is largely unknown, but general statements can be made. Heavy-metal poisoning, which is discussed in Chapter 15, has led to neurological and other major disabilities as well as fatalities. Toxic organic pollutants are also believed to cause severe illnesses, such as childhood leukemia and severe kidney and liver disease. The difficulty in determining the precise ill effects of specific pollutants on humans is due to the complex chemical concoction that is ingested by human victims of water pollution. It is very difficult to isolate specific chemicals that cause harm, let alone sort through the possibilities for harmful interaction among them. For instance, polychlorinated biphenyls (PCBs) and the industrial solvent TCE are believed to cause health problems to humans when they are ingested in high concentrations. When both PCBs and TCE are present together, they have a synergistic effect, causing much greater problems than either does alone (Owen and Chiras 1995).

Also, many contaminants are transformed in the body, and while most of these changes result in detoxification, some biological transformations can actually *create* harmful chemicals (Lippman and Schlesinger 1979). These biological transformations are sometimes made by nonpathogenic bacteria in our gastrointestinal tracts, for example in the transformation of relatively harmless nitrates in our drinking water, originating from fertilizers, to toxic nitrites (Ehrlich et al. 1973).

The contribution of water pollution to cancer rates has been exaggerated in the popular press, leading to what Elizabeth Whelan terms "toxic terror" (Whelan 1993), with figures as high as 90 percent of all cancers attributed to various forms of pollution. Excluding smoking, the percentage of cancers attributable to pollution is more likely on the order of 1 to 5 percent (Doll and Peto 1981). While this figure is far below the "toxic terror" rates reported in some media, it still represents a vast amount of suffering that is, at least in principle, quite preventable.

Solid Wastes

Solid wastes represent another form of human pollution that is of great antiquity. In fact, the study of ancient wastes, or midden, is a major occupation for archaeologists, who obtain insights into the lifestyles of ancient people from the wastes they have left behind. Future archaeologists will have an embarrassment of riches from today's affluent societies.

The vast amount of solid wastes has become a serious problem in developed countries such as the United States. They are a source of air pollution when burned or simply blown as dust into residential areas. They are also a source of water pollution when rain or other water allows seepage of contaminants into surface or ground water. More directly, contaminants can be brought to residential areas by such animals as rodents, birds, or insects that utilize landfills as feeding grounds. One of the greatest direct hazards comes from ingestion of lead from paint or plaster, particularly by children (Schell 1991). The indirect effects of solid wastes through contamination of air and water are a serious concern and may exceed their direct effects.

Pollution and Health: Conclusions

In brief, pollution appears to be a major source of the disease problems of modernized societies, with the most impact caused by tobacco smoke. Unfortunately, there has been a tendency either to minimize or exaggerate the health effects of pollutants based on economic or political considerations. Scientific studies have helped focus on particularly dangerous substances in our wastes that need to be controlled, such as asbestos and PCBs, while toning down some of the "toxic terror" of the tabloids. Still, there is much that is unknown about the health effects of various contaminants. It would seem prudent to tighten standards for clean air and water and find means of reducing our solid wastes before we are overwhelmed by them.

GENERAL STRESS AND CHRONIC DISEASE

We have reviewed the effects of specific stressors on human populations, but to deal with the problems faced by people in modernized environments we need to consider stress in a more general sense. General stress is a complex and often misunderstood concept, so a brief introduction to the topic is warranted.

A Definition of General Stress

The concept of general stress is usually attributed to Hans Selye, based on his studies in the 1930s (summarized in Selye 1956) but also derives from the work of Walter B. Cannon ([1915] 1959). Selye noted both in human patients and in research on laboratory rats that at least a portion of the physiological response to a wide variety of stressors contained a common element. This led him to postulate that a component of the initial response, which he termed the *alarm reaction,* to any stress is essentially the same in all individuals. This nonspecific response characterizes what has been termed *general stress.* There are also aspects of stress responses that are particular to individuals or to given stressors, with these specific reactions *not* considered a part of the general stress response.

Stimulus or Response?   Stress researchers have debated if general stress is properly considered a stimulus or a response. In other words, is general stress an environmental variable that people must adapt to, or is general stress a bodily reaction to the environment? In fact, a majority of researchers would define general stress as neither. It is considered to be a *mediating variable* in psychological parlance: a factor that is, in a sense, conceived as being *between* a stimulus and response and mediating their interaction. In a biological sense, general stress is the nonspecific demand on the body for adaptive activity (Selye 1973). An environmental stimulus may lead to such a nonspecific demand but is not identical to it.

In this view, general stress is a cognitive variable, where individuals' perceptions of a given stimulus determine whether a biological stress reaction will occur (Pearson et al. 1993). Some believe that the stimulus must be viewed as a threat of some kind that is not easily coped with (Lazarus 1966, 1993), and thus creates a demand for adaptation. A threat in this context is anything that can disrupt homeostasis, the normal functioning of the body. What is perceived as stressful by one individual will not necessarily be considered stressful by another, as people differ in what is viewed as a threat and in what is seen as difficult or easy to cope with.

The Biological Response to General Stress

In practical terms, it is difficult to observe "demands," whether specific or not, and therefore researchers have tended to identify stress in terms of the presence or absence of an organism's response. There are two major forms of biological response to general stress, one involving the pituitary and adrenal glands and the other involving the sympathetic nervous system.

The Pituitary-Adrenal Response to Stress.   Animals exposed to a wide variety of stressors, from cold temperatures to electric shocks to loud noises to caustic chemicals, have reactions that include a stimulation of the pituitary gland leading to release of the hormone ACTH (adrenocorticotropic hormone) (Selye 1956). ACTH in turn stimulates the cortex of the adrenal gland to release a number of steroid hormones including cortisol (Figure 10–2). These corticosteroid hormones have three major effects:

1. They cause an increase of blood glucose levels from metabolic activities involving, in part, the breakdown of proteins;
2. They increase the frequency and severity of ulcers in the gastrointestinal tract; and
3. They suppress the immune system, both inhibiting inflammatory reactions and causing a decrease in the amount of circulating lymphocytes.

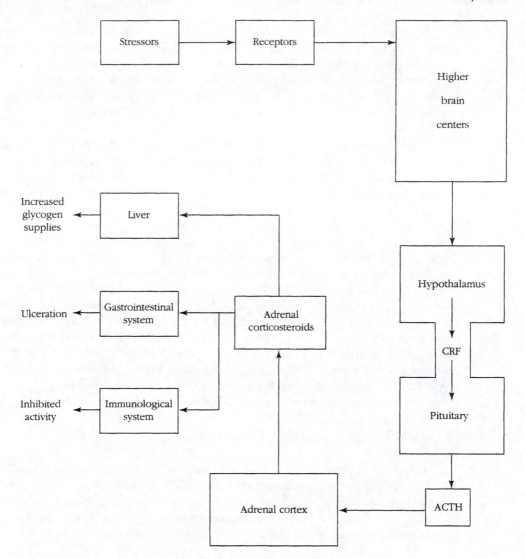

Figure 10–2   Model of the pituitary-adrenal cortical stress response. (Redrawn by permission of the American Anthropological Association from D. E. Brown. 1981. *American Anthropologist* 83 (March):74–92. Not for further reproduction.)

The Sympathetic Nervous System Response to General Stress.   Another aspect of the biological response to general stress is activation of the sympathetic nervous system. This involves stimulation of the autonomic nerves that secrete norepinephrine as well as causing the medulla of the adrenal gland to secrete epinephrine (Elliot and Eisdorfer 1982). These chemicals are also termed *adrenaline* and *noradrenaline*, respectively.

These two chemicals, sometimes characterized as neurotransmitters and sometimes as hormones, have diverse physiological effects as illustrated in Figure 10–3. The effects are sometimes termed the *fight-or-flight reaction*, since they prepare the organism for major physical effort. The reaction includes loading the blood with glucose, a quick energy fuel source, and oxygen to burn this fuel, increasing the rate of blood circulation and routing the blood preferentially to skeletal muscles. The organism is now indeed prepared to fight or flee. There is evidence that this reaction also causes impaired immune system activity independently of similar effects by cortisol (Herbert and Cohen 1993).

Figure 10–3 Model of the sympathetic-adrenal medullary stress response. (Redrawn by permission of the American Anthropological Association from D. E. Brown. 1981. *American Anthropologist* 83 (March):74–92. Not for further reproduction.)

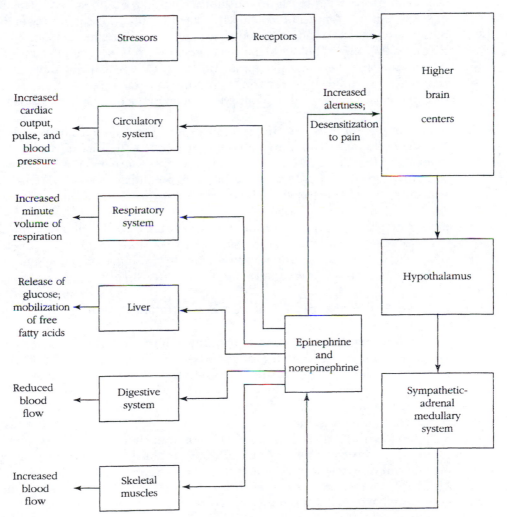

Proposed Causes of General Stress.   Studies on the causes of general stress in people have been carried out in laboratories as well as during people's "normal" activities. These studies have included people's responses to specific stimuli, such as noise or disturbing films, under a broad range of conditions (Frankenhaeuser 1973). People have also been monitored during real-life events that have been selected for their presumed stressfulness, such as soldiers in combat or during training exercises of paratroopers. Other research has focused on occupational differences in stress responses (Frankenhaeuser and Gardell 1976), while others have looked at the potential stressfulness of specific situations that are common to urban settings, such as daily commuting by public transport (Lundberg 1976). These studies suggest that situations characterized by novelty, unpredictability, or perceived lack of control lead to increased stress responses (James et al. 1989).

One major finding of this stress research is the notion that the amount of activation of stress responses is constantly changing in individuals. The amount of stress response is much more closely related to conditions occurring at the time of measurement as opposed to longstanding traits of the individual (James and Brown 1997). In psychological parlance, general stress is a state, not a trait, of the individual. Still, there are factors in individuals' lives that put them at greater chance for encountering conditions that stimulate general stress responses. Much research has been devoted to identifying such risk factors for high stress.

Consequences of the Biological Response to General Stress.   The general stress response as outlined above, which forms the "alarm reaction" to any stress, is generally considered an adaptive response by the organism. The response allows the organism to cope with potentially stressful circumstances. However, problems arise when the response is overly prolonged or too frequent. The sympathetic response causes deep, erratic heartbeats and increases in both pulse rate and blood pressure, the combination of which can strain the cardiovascular system (Friedman and Rosenman 1974). Both the pituitary-adrenal and sympathetic nervous system responses, by decreasing immune system activity, make the organism more vulnerable to infectious disease.

General Stress and the Urban Environment

It has long been assumed that urban life in modernized environments is associated with greater amounts of general stress. Psychologists and physiologists have modeled urban stressors in laboratory research (cf., Frankenhaeuser 1973; Glass and Singer 1972) and have shown that problems associated with modernized environments, from noise to bureaucratic hassles, lead to biological stress responses in human subjects.

Research that directly focuses on people in their normal lives in modernized settings has been less common, in part because of the difficulty in creating meaningful research designs that can control for some of the myriad factors that can lead to stress responses. A few brief examples will illustrate some of the findings as well as some of the difficulty in carrying out such research.

Life in an English Village. Intensive studies on factors related to the excretion of epinephrine and norepinephrine were undertaken in the English village of Oxfordshire (Harrison et al. 1981; Jenner et al. 1979). Occupational stress, life dissatisfaction, cigarette smoking, and copious coffee consumption were all related to high rates of epinephrine excretion. It appears that daily activities are the major factor determining stress levels as defined by the hormone excretion rates and that job-related activities may be most important for ordinary working people.

Epinephrine levels in these English villagers were affected by levels of psychosocial arousal. These levels were just as likely to be labeled as pleasant than unpleasant (Harrison 1995). Thus, levels of stress hormones are a measure of general arousal, not simple measures of negative events ("distress").

Migration of Filipinos to Hawaii. In research carried out in the late 1970s, Brown (1981, 1982) studied a community of Filipino Americans residing in the Honolulu metropolitan area, including immigrants as well as second- and third-generation Filipino Americans stemming from rural areas of the Philippines. These Filipinos lived in a residential community in which houses were all similarly constructed, and people all qualified for residence by means of prior residence in a former plantation camp set up for Filipino laborers and by having fairly low incomes. Thus, some socioeconomic factors were common to all residents of the community.

The study looked at many aspects of their lifestyles and health, and included the collection of urine samples over a 72-hour period. These were assayed for the amount of epinephrine and norepinephrine excreted, with values related to the individual's degree of modernization on a scale constructed based on behavioral and socioeconomic variables (Brown 1982). The results of this part of the study indicated that Filipino Americans with an intermediate level of modernization tend to excrete greater amounts of stress hormones than those with a lower or higher score on the modernization scale (Figure 10–4).

The people with low scores on the modernization scale may insulate themselves from the urban Honolulu environment, maintaining a rural lifestyle, usually speaking in their native Filipino language, and interacting primarily with other Filipinos. The people with high scores on the index represent the immigrants who have successfully accommodated to their new environment, behaving more like typical Honolulu residents ("locals") than other immigrants. It is the immigrants with an intermediate level of modernization who are exposed to modern life but have not developed the behaviors and skills to easily cope with it who show evidence of chronically high general stress levels.

Samoans, Stress, and Modernization. Several studies have examined the effect of modernization on Samoans. By the 1980s, most Samoans living in American Samoa and those who migrated to either the United States or New Zealand were living in quite modernized circumstances. At the same time, many

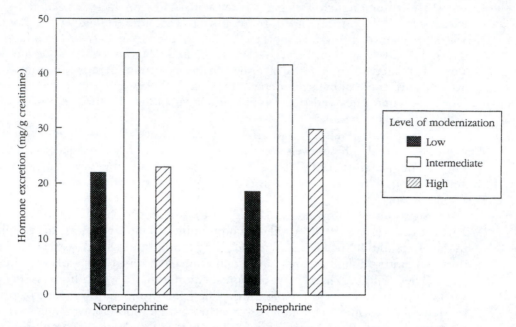

Figure 10–4   Urinary norepinephrine and epinephrine excretion rates (presented as micrograms per gram of creatinine excreted) in Filipino American immigrants based on level of modernization. Epinephrine values × 4. (Based on data from D. E. Brown. 1982. *Annals of Human Biology* 9:553–63 by permission of Taylor & Francis.)

Samoans lived in more traditional settings, particularly rural areas of Western Samoa, where little modernization had occurred. Even these areas had become more modernized in the late 1980s and the 1990s.

A study conducted in Western Samoa in 1981 (James 1984; James et al. 1987) compared four groups of Samoan men: rural agriculturalists, urban manual laborers, urban sedentary workers, and urban college students. Urinary epinephrine levels were higher in the more modernized urban groups, although the urban manual laborers had high excretion levels only during the day; at night their excretion levels more closely matched those of the rural people. The urban laborers may have had nonwork environments that were more traditional than the sedentary workers and students, who were viewed as being more modernized. Thus, stress levels were shown to generally rise with increasing modernization.

Another study conducted among Samoans sampled populations in Western Samoa, American Samoa, and a migrant population in Honolulu, Hawaii (Pearson et al. 1990). This study did not find general differences in epinephrine excretion rates among the samples, perhaps in part because it did not emphasize occupational differences as the earlier study had and thus did not emphasize differences in modernization. Both studies showed that epinephrine excretion is related to psychosocial factors, with these factors taking on greater or lesser significance depending on the population's place of residence.

In fact, the Samoan studies suggest that given behaviors can take on different meanings in different settings (Pearson et al. 1993). For example, the amount of social support an individual has is generally considered a factor that reduces stress (Kirschbaum et al. 1995), and this appears to be the case for many Samoans. However, in modernized settings a great deal of social support can have a negative side: greater social obligations. Indeed, Samoan migrants in California may have higher stress levels when they have larger social networks because increased social obligations more than balance increased social support (Hanna et al. 1986).

General Stress in Riot Victims: Los Angeles.   The Los Angeles riots of 1993 caused a great deal of property damage, as well as injuries and death. A major portion of the property damage occurred to businesses owned by merchants who were of Korean ethnicity. Cortisol secretion rates were measured six weeks after the riots through salivary samples taken from Korean Americans residing in Los Angeles (Byun et al. 1994). The people were divided into groups based on the amount of "life change" they experienced during the riots. Those who experienced the most impact had significantly elevated cortisol levels and lowered immunoglobulin levels, indicative of an inhibited immune system. These physiological changes were maintained for several months after the riots (Byun, personal communication).

Cortisol, Stress, Socioeconomic Conditions, and Childhood Illnesses. Mark Flinn and his colleagues (Flinn et al. 1995; Flinn and England 1997) have carried out a long-term project in a rural Caribbean village on the island of Dominica from 1988 to 1993. Their research has combined standard ethnographic fieldwork methods from cultural anthropology with more formalized questionnaires and interviews and collection of salivary cortisol and immunoglobulin samples in a number of children. One of their findings is an association of infectious disease with high cortisol "bursts" previous to onset of symptoms (Flinn and England 1993).

They also have found that high cortisol levels are associated with employment of the children's mothers outside the village and an unstable marital relationship of their parent(s). Children who live in households with nonrelatives, stepfathers, and half siblings, or with single mothers without kin support have higher average levels of cortisol secretion than children in other households, for instance those in which both parents reside (Flinn and England 1995). Events that cause the greatest increases in cortisol excretion commonly involve conflict or change within the family. Other socioeconomic variables, such as income, property ownership, and education level of parents, have relatively little association with either the child's cortisol levels or his or her health.

Ambulatory Blood Pressure in the Daily Lives of People Working in New York City.   Monitors have been developed that allow the recording of blood pressure in people throughout the day as they go about their normal activities.

These "ambulatory" blood pressure monitors, when used in conjunction with diaries, observation, or other forms of self-reports, allow identification of specific events or activities that cause blood pressure to increase or decrease in an individual. Blood pressure seems to be elevated more by how people feel about activities than by the activities themselves. For example, blood pressure elevations are more closely related to reports of emotions than to specific types of activities among women working in New York City (James 1991). Elevated blood pressure is also associated with being at work or commuting as opposed to being at home. Complexities arise here as well: the impact of a reported emotion on blood pressure depends upon the setting in which it is experienced (James et al. 1986).

Studies on General Stress and Modernization.   The brief examples just noted give an idea of the state of our knowledge of how modern life and the process of urbanization are related to general stress responses. Clearly, this knowledge is limited. There is evidence that stress levels rise during modernization, but they may fall once individuals have adapted to their new circumstances. Hence, we may need to differentiate between the effects of life in a modern environment and the effects of the *process* of modernization. The difficulties in measuring an individual's degree of modernization, as well as his or her stress level, are great, particularly if these measures are to be comparable across cultural boundaries. Certainly individuals who are undergoing the modernization process commonly confront situations that can be characterized as unpredictable, novel, or beyond their perceived control. These, as we have seen, are the characteristics of stimuli that elicit stress responses in people.

A great deal of the complexity seen in people's responses to daily life events can be summarized in the word *perception*. Since general stress is apparently triggered by perceptions of threats, a given stimulus may be considered stressful to one person but merely challenging or even pleasantly stimulating to another. Seen this way, stressful life events can be defined only in a statistical, population level sense. Still, there are many groups of people, defined by ethnicity, gender, socioeconomic level, or other traits, for which given situations are likely to be perceived as stressful, allowing us to unravel the interaction of person and stimulus that leads to general stress and, all too often, to chronic diseases such as those of the cardiovascular system that are associated with high stress.

ADIPOSITY AND CHRONIC DISEASE

Another health risk associated with modernized environments is a tendency for increased **adiposity** (amount of body fat). In fact, in many modernized populations a large percentage of people are obese (excessively fat), although this is not true of all populations (Baker 1984a). We will look briefly at causes and effects of this increase in biological fat stores associated with modernized settings.

Causes of Increased Adiposity

The question of causes of increased adiposity is a no-brainer: there's more going in than coming out. In energetic terms, there are more food calories consumed than metabolic calories burned by the individual, leading to a caloric excess being stored as fat. This can be viewed as the effects of a type of malnutrition termed **overnutrition.**

Things are actually not so simple when one goes a step farther. There is normally an exquisite balance between input and output, with people's body weight, and fat stores, held fairly constant over great daily and longer-term changes in diet and physical activity levels. With obesity, there is an apparent breakdown in maintenance of the balance between diet and activity, and the cause of this breakdown is still little understood. There is some evidence that a mutation for a gene that encodes a hormone excreted by fat cells may be responsible for at least some forms of obesity in mice (Rink 1994; Zhang et al. 1994), but researchers have not found this same type of mutation in humans (Gibbs 1996).

Human fatness levels vary due to genetic background (Stunkard et al. 1986), sex, age, and a host of "environmental" variables such as eating and exercise habits, stress levels, smoking, and socioeconomic status (Garn and Clark 1976; Powers 1980). Modernization very often is another such environmental variable (McGarvey et al. 1989), although modernization-based adiposity appears to be magnified in a few populations. This has been particularly documented in native American (Wendorf 1989; Szathmáry 1994) and Pacific Islander (Baker 1984) populations. For both of these groups individuals with traditional lifestyles rarely became obese, but obesity has become common in modernized settings. This, as noted earlier in the chapter, has been explained by Neel's "thrifty genotype" hypothesis.

Effects of Increased Adiposity

High levels of body fat are associated with greater prevalence of many chronic diseases, including cardiovascular diseases, diabetes, and some forms of cancer (Sjöström 1993). Perhaps the clearest linkage has been with NIDDM, or non-insulin-dependent diabetes mellitus, as noted earlier in this chapter.

Body fat distribution, independent of total fatness, may also be related to risk of morbidity from some chronic diseases. In particular, fat situated in the abdominal area appears to create a risk for development of cardiovascular diseases, diabetes, and some forms of cancer (National Research Council 1989). This increased risk is due to the great mobility of lipids from abdominal fat cells into the blood, compared with the lower turnover rate of lipids from fat cells in some other parts of the body, such as the thigh region. In other words, for a given amount of adiposity, people with fat predominately in their abdominal region will tend to maintain higher levels of lipids in their blood. It is the circulating lipids that provide the elevated risk for many chronic diseases. Body fat distribution appears to be strongly influenced by inheritance (Bouchard et al. 1988; Mueller 1988; Crews and James 1991) but also is influenced by such factors as total adiposity, sex, and age.

Increased adiposity is associated both with populations undergoing modernization and those that have been modernized for some time. We will present two brief case studies: one of the United States population as a whole and the other of Samoan populations that have rapidly modernized over the past two generations.

Adiposity in the United States Population

Several national-level studies on body size have been carried out in the United States, including the National Health and Nutrition Examination Survey (NHANES), using samples of people from many areas in the United States. The NHANES survey has been carried out three times, beginning in the 1960s, with successive surveys showing increased average adiposity in Americans and an increased rate of obesity. This has led to concern about an "epidemic" of obesity in the United States (Stamler 1993). For instance, it is estimated that 34 million American adults were overweight between 1976 and 1980, with 12.4 million of them considered severely overweight (Abraham et al. 1983). Depending upon the way obesity is defined, between 12 percent (National Research Council 1989) and 59 percent (Gibbs 1996) of Americans are classified as obese.

The trends are even worse for children in the United States, with 27.1 percent of children aged 6 to 11 years old and 21.9 percent of adolescents estimated to be obese (Gortmaker et al. 1987). This is problematical for two reasons: childhood obesity is associated with important health risk factors (Berenson 1980) and is an omen of adult obesity (Garn and Lavelle 1985). Therefore, there is a high probability that the rate of adult obesity in the United States will increase still further in the future.

Obesity runs in families, and therefore children of obese parents are more likely to become obese themselves (Garn and Clark 1976). This is not simply due to biological inheritance. Other factors that are related to childhood obesity include socioeconomic status, family size, and such behavioral variables as amount of time spent watching television. It remains to be seen if this increase in childhood obesity continues in the United States. It appears that programs involving increased physical activity offer the best hope for changing this trend, but it is unclear if any of these programs has made a marked improvement in a community's rate of childhood obesity (Epstein 1993).

Adiposity in Samoan Populations

Samoans have reached very high levels of adiposity upon modernization. In fact, the Samoan population in the San Francisco region has been characterized as the fattest human population that has been studied (Pawson and Janes 1981). In research carried out in the late 1970s and early 1980s, five Samoan populations were compared: rural, fairly traditional Western Samoa; rural, somewhat modernized American Samoa; urban American Samoa; migrants to urban Hawaii; and migrants to urban California. Comparisons of body weight and triceps skinfold measurements (a measure of body fat) are shown in Figure 10–5 for the five populations, with males and females shown separately. In general, there is a major difference between the Western Samoan population and the other four, suggesting that the shift from a traditional to a modernized lifestyle causes a rapid increase in adiposity. Further increases in modernization cause smaller changes in adiposity (Pawson 1986), although later studies have suggested that fatness levels of Samoans have continued to increase in the 1980s and 1990s (Zhai et al. 1993).

The high fatness levels of Samoans are found at early ages. American Samoan infants have high birth weights (Bindon and Zansky 1986) and maintain higher weights for a given age throughout childhood relative to averages in the United States (which we have already seen is a fat population). In Western Samoa, birth weights are about average compared with other populations, but within a few months infants weigh significantly more than United States infants of the same age, although relative weight for age declines in later infancy (Bindon and Zansky 1986). In general, Western Samoan children had lower

Figure 10–5   Average body weight (left two columns) and triceps skinfold measurements (right two columns) in five Samoan populations: comparisons of fatness. (Data from The morphological characteristics of Samoan adults by I. G. Pawson. In *The changing Samoans: Behavior and health in transition,* edited by Paul T. Baker, Joel Hanna, et al., 254–74. Copyright © 1986 by Oxford University Press, Inc. Used by permission of Oxford University Press, Inc.)

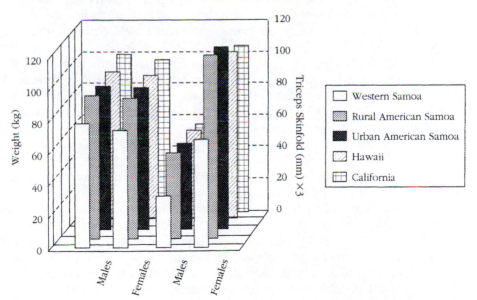

levels of adiposity than American Samoan and Hawaii-based Samoan populations, much as was seen among the adults.

Since the Samoan studies were carried out in the 1970s and early 1980s, modernization has increased. Adiposity has increased among Western Samoans, but it has also continued to increase in other Samoan populations. For example, among young adult women, 25 percent of Western Samoans and 63 percent of American Samoans are characterized as "severely overweight" in the early 1990s (Zhai et al. 1993). Other Pacific Islander populations are going through similar changes, with modernization accompanied by increasing rates of obesity and related chronic diseases.

The great increase in adiposity that accompanies modernization in Samoans may be related to the thrifty genotype hypothesis that was discussed earlier. The high levels of adiposity seen in Samoans is also found among many other Pacific Islander populations, as well as among Native American groups, and these levels are accompanied by rising mortality rates from diabetes and cardiovascular disease. Adiposity is much more than an aesthetic concern. It is becoming a serious health risk factor in many human populations.

CONCLUSION

The evidence is persuasive that modernization leads to increases in serious chronic disease rates, with these increases related to the increased pollution, general stress, and adiposity that comes with modernized life. This increase in illness may reflect a breakdown in human adaptation due to the rapidity of environmental change represented by modernization. We may indeed inhabit bodies adapted to stone age life, whether of foraging or early agricultural communities. Certainly, given the long generation time of humans, the few thousand years of urban life have not provided sufficient time for major genetic changes. When one considers that many changes of modernization can be measured over a period of years instead of centuries or millennia, it is quite possible that some genetically based adaptations are now obsolete. The fight-or-flight reaction helps us run from a lion, but does it help us escape from a traffic jam? The increased cardiovascular effort has no use as we simmer in our automobiles and may lead to increased risk of heart disease.

The rapidity of modernization may also outspeed a population's ability to change its behavioral adaptations. For individuals, the behaviors and values learned in childhood may no longer be meaningful in a changed society by the time adulthood is reached. One can also imagine that biologically based developmental adaptations may become detrimental to individuals whose environment changes rapidly. Rapid change in any environment often leads to difficulties for the resident biological community. It should come as no surprise that humans, too, must cope with environmental changes by changing their basic means of adapting. With modernization, rapid change seems to be the only constant, and therefore human adaptive abilities may face a serious challenge in the future.

KEY TERMS

adiposity
anthropogenic
arteriosclerosis
atherosclerosis
cancer
diabetes mellitus
glycosylation

hypertension
insulin
insulin-dependent
   diabetes mellitus
mutagen
non-insulin-dependent
   diabetes mellitus

overnutrition
plaques
pollution
smog
thrifty genotype
  hypothesis

KEY POINTS

☐   Among the stressors of the urban/suburban environment in developed countries are pollution and general stress, which affect all individuals, and adiposity, which results from overnutrition and infrequent physical activity.

☐   A combination of environmental, genetic, and dietary factors results in major chronic diseases such as cancer, hypertension, heart disease, and non-insulin-dependent diabetes mellitus having a higher incidence in modernized as against traditional societies.

☐   The thrifty genotype hypothesis may explain the ability of humans to adapt to feast-and-famine cycles by laying down fat during the former and living off it during the latter. People with thrifty genes may become more vulnerable to non-insulin-dependent diabetes mellitus in modernized environments.

☐   Forms of pollution that are associated with increased incidence of certain types of cancer are certain chemicals found in smoke and smog and other forms of air pollution, toxic chemicals in water from industrial wastes and agricultural runoff, and contaminants in solid waste, some of which may also pollute air and water.

☐   Stress is regarded as an environmental variable to which people must adapt, a bodily reaction to the environment (the "alarm reaction"), and a variable that mediates between a stimulus and a response, depending on the perceptions of a given stimulus.

☐   There are two major forms of biological response to general stress: the pituitary-adrenal response resulting in increased blood glucose levels, the frequency and severity of gastrointestinal ulcers, and suppression of the immune system; and the sympathetic nervous system response resulting in the secretion of adrenaline and noradrenaline that increase glucose and oxygen blood levels, the rate of blood circulation, and routing of blood to skeletal muscles, all of which can be described as the "fight-or-flight reaction."

☐   Evidence from various populations, including immigrant Filipinos and Samoans, riot victims in Los Angeles, Caribbean children subject to infectious disease, and urban New Yorkers, indicates that stress levels rise during modernization but may fall once individuals have adapted to their new circumstances, in all instances being triggered by perceptions of threat.

☐   Increased adiposity, which is associated with cardiovascular disease, non-insulin-dependent diabetes mellitus, and some forms of cancer, is associated with populations undergoing modernization (e.g., Samoans in urban situations in Samoa and abroad) as well as those that have been modernized for some time (e.g., American children and adults).

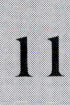

Resources
and Community Ecology

All organisms need to obtain substances, termed *resources*, from the environment in order to survive and reproduce. These resources include food, water, and often some form of shelter from environmental stressors, whether physical, such as extremes of temperature, or biological, such as predators or parasites. Resources may also include sexual partners, materials, or territory needed for reproductive purposes, from wooing a mate to protecting offspring. As noted in Chapter 6, those resources without which an organism cannot function are termed *essential resources*, while those essential resources that are difficult to obtain, are rare, or are costly are termed *key resources*. In this and the chapters immediately following, we will see that understanding how organisms obtain key resources is indeed a key to understanding their ecology and level of adaptive success.

Resources often serve as limiting factors for populations (Tilman 1982). When resources are limiting factors, they are usually density-dependent, and they therefore place limits on the size of a population that can be supported in a given ecosystem. Key resources may therefore determine the carrying capacity of an ecosystem for a given biological population.

EFFICIENCY AND RISK IN THE USE OF RESOURCES

In Chapter 6, we noted that organisms, including humans, must balance effectiveness, efficiency, and risk in determining their response to environmental stress. This balance is also necessary for determining resource acquisition strategies. Simple economics can be used to illustrate the balancing act for humans. For example, suppose one has the choice of investing $1 million in real estate and selling it for a profit of $5,000 after one year, or investing $20,000 in stocks and selling them for a profit of $3,000 after a year. In the first case there is more total profit, but only 0.5 percent gain after one year, while in the second case there is a 15 percent annual gain. Most investors would opt for the second investment, thus putting efficiency (in this case, annual gain as a percentage of initial investment) ahead of effectiveness (analogous to gross profit). The example becomes more complex if we add a difference in assessment of the risk of the investments. Perhaps the land investment involves little risk for losing money, while the stock investment has a one-third chance of incurring a loss after one year. In this case, the decision on which investment is best becomes more difficult.

Organisms are faced with similar cost-benefit scenarios with regard to accessing resources; those that adopt successful strategies survive. For instance, while a grown wildebeest represents a large gain in resources for a cheetah, the predator may have to expend a great deal of time and energy in pursuing its intended prey and may also incur the risks of getting injured or of having the prey escape. The cheetah may be better off pursuing a young Thompson's gazelle, which is a much smaller animal. There will be smaller total profit (amount of food obtained) but less effort in obtaining it and less risk of losing out entirely or getting hurt.

In dealing with resources in the human context, human ecology merges with **economics,** which is defined as the study of how people allocate scarce resources for various uses (Schneider 1974). Economics includes the study of resource uses that go beyond basic subsistence, including recreation, social status, and values (Jochim 1981). Control of resources is also related to political control over other people, which in turn may affect subsistence strategies that require coordination of the labor of a number of people. Because a broad study of resource acquisition in human populations goes beyond what we can consider here, we will consider only human uses of resources that are directly related to subsistence.

Renewable and Nonrenewable Resources

In dealing with human populations, we must distinguish between **renewable** and **nonrenewable resources.** As the words imply, a renewable resource is replaceable (e.g., oxygen) whereas a nonrenewable resource is not (e.g., fossil fuels). This distinction is somewhat artificial, as virtually all resources are renewable if sufficient time is allowed. Fossil fuels, generally regarded as nonrenewable, are in fact renewable if one is willing to wait the millions of years needed to create new petroleum. Similarly, although phosphates are regarded as nonrenewable, if one allows enough time for the exposure of marine sediments on land followed by erosion, phosphate resources are regenerated. But these time frames go beyond what is reasonable for understanding human ecology, and thus we can confidently consider many resources as nonrenewable in human terms.

Since some resources are essentially nonrenewable and others are only slowly renewed, humans have created ecological problems by overuse of resources in the long term. Environmentalists have deplored the depletion of nonrenewable resources by modern populations and have often alluded to the "good old days" of sustainable resource use by "ecologically noble savages" (Alvard 1993a, 1993b). Unfortunately, evidence suggests that human populations have not necessarily ever been very noble about their environment. For example, in observations made on Piro hunters of the Peruvian rain forest, Alvard (1993a) reported that the hunters did not conserve prey species that were identified as vulnerable to overhunting. The hunters tended to maximize their short-term gains in food rather than optimize long-term conservation of resources. Additional examples of this lack of sustainable resource use by nonmodernized populations will be noted in Chapter 18.

The Role of Technology and Resource Use

Technology is a major consideration in human resource use and abuse. New technology may permit use of resources previously impossible to obtain. For instance, human use of fire for cooking beginning about 500,000 years BP made it possible to use many plant foods that were otherwise inedible. New technology also allows more effective and/or more efficient resource use. For example, the availability of guns has allowed the Ye'kwana of the Amazon region to hunt birds and arboreal monkeys more effectively than other Amazonian groups who do not have guns (Jochim 1981). The availability of fine mesh nets has allowed Cree Indians to obtain small fish species but also allows them to catch immature fish of larger species thereby depleting those species in local waters (Berkes 1977). Here, technology permits abuse of resources in the long term. In fact, the major difference between traditional peoples and modernized groups in resource abuse appears to be the scale of human activities; modernized populations are much larger in size and more complex technologically, and therefore they can do more damage than traditional peoples, both past and present.

MAJOR TYPES OF HUMAN SUBSISTENCE PATTERNS

Food is an essential resource for all human populations and has merited special attention from human ecologists, particularly from cultural ecologists (see Chapter 3). Subsistence systems can be divided into four major types: foraging, pastoralism, horticulture, and intensive agriculture. Within each of these major categories there are diverse subsistence activities, but there are some commonalities in human resource use within the major subsistence types.

Foraging

Foraging refers to subsistence activities that rely on wild food resources for the major portion of the food supply. This usually entails a combination of gathering wild plants and fishing or hunting for wild animals. Until about 12,000 BP, all humans were foragers, but now only a minuscule proportion of humans still can be classified in this subsistence type.

The diversity of foragers even in contemporary times is great: from traditional Inuit of the Canadian Arctic who rely chiefly on fishing and the hunting of marine mammals to traditional San hunter-gatherers of the Kalahari Desert who rely chiefly on plant resources for food. Modern foragers tend to live in environments that are marginal—arctic, desert, and rainforest—where agriculture is impossible, difficult, or too expensive to be worthwhile (Figure 11–1). In other words, contemporary human groups living in environments that will support other subsistence systems have opted for those other systems. It is therefore difficult to equate modern foragers with the prehistoric humans who foraged in

Figure 11–1 Aboriginal Australian family setting out for a day of foraging. (Photo courtesy of Robert Tonkinson. 1974. *The jigalong mob: Aboriginal victors of the desert crusade.* Menlo Park, CA: Benjamin/Cummings Publishing Co.)

virtually all land environments, as the latter usually lived in more congenial environments and also did not either compete with or trade with agriculturalists.

Some generalities can be made about modern foragers. People who rely on wild food resources are more directly influenced by the environment than groups which utilize domesticated organisms and thus may be more constrained in their behaviors than agriculturalists. Most foraging groups are small, as resources are usually relatively scarce, and also mobile, moving to follow resources.

There are consequences of small group size and mobility. People within the small groups, termed **bands,** know everyone else in the group personally; in fact, most people within a band are in the same kinship (family) group. This personal knowledge allows bands to function without a need for many formalized institutions (such as courts, police, and the like), relying instead on friendship, gossip, and rumor to keep people's behavior in line with cultural expectations.

People who frequently "move house" develop a value on traveling lightly—as moving numerous boxes filled with favorite books and one's rock collection becomes quickly unappealing. This is true for foragers as well, who also must literally carry their belongings on their travels due to the absence of domesticated animals to use as beasts of burden. Thus, foragers tend to place little value on material possessions compared with more sedentary people. This enables forager bands to be relatively egalitarian.

A major exception to the foregoing discussion was found among traditional foragers who lived along the northwest coast of North America. Wild food resources, particularly the salmon fishery, were so abundant that many of the foraging groups were able to sustain fairly large populations, a fairly sedentary lifestyle, and a social organization more similar to agricultural groups than to other foragers.

A primary necessity of forager bands is flexibility. Wild resources may fluctuate considerably on a seasonal or year-to-year basis, and people must be able to adjust demographically to adapt to these fluctuations. In many forager cultures, bands are actually fairly fluid social units that can either break apart or join together as need arises (Netting 1986).

Much work on foragers has explored the question of how difficult it is to meet their subsistence needs. Thomas Hobbes, a seventeenth-century philosopher, stated that people's lives in the "State of Nature" were "poor, nasty, brutish, and short." Most early views of foragers followed Hobbes's notion. That perception changed markedly in the 1960s, when early empirical work on foragers suggested that they represented "the original affluent society" (Sahlins 1972) where subsistence needs were easily met, leaving much time for leisure activities. Research in the 1980s and 1990s suggests that there is no simple "easy" versus "hard" answer to the subsistence effort of foragers, let alone to the question of what "affluence" or "leisure" means to a forager (Bird-David 1992). There is great diversity among foragers and also much variation within a foraging group depending on seasonal or other local considerations.

Pastoralism

Pastoralism refers to the reliance on herding of domesticated animals as the major food resource for a society. As with foragers, contemporary pastoralists display a wide cultural diversity and are found in many different types of environments. Like foragers, modern pastoralists tend to be found in somewhat marginal environments where food crops are unreliable or cannot be produced in enough quantity to support the group's resource needs (Figure 11–2). These environments include arid grasslands, high mountain environments, and some subarctic regions.

Other similarities between pastoralists and foragers are the low population densities that pastoralism can support and the frequent need for mobility of pastoralist groups. Animals may be available to help with transport, allowing pastoralists to carry more possessions with them. Also, the better transport capabilities of pastoralists may give them the ability to move their herds while keeping the human population relatively sedentary, moving people back and forth from homestead to herds.

Figure 11–2   A Tibetan pastoralist with his herd of goats on the highway between Lhasa and Shigatse, Tibet. (Photo by E. Kormondy)

Pastoralists often also cultivate some plants for food resources as environmental conditions permit. An alternative to plant cultivation is utilizing trade relationships with people who are better able to grow crops, such as those in better watered or lower-altitude regions.

Pastoralist population sizes are generally well below those found in people with subsistence types other than foraging. Pastoral groups do tend to be larger than foraging groups, thus necessitating more formalized systems of social control but also usually permitting a basically egalitarian society. In many ways pastoralists are intermediate in demography and level of sociocultural integration between foragers and crop agriculturalists.

Horticulture

Subsistence agriculture using simple tools and without the use of complex irrigation and fertilization techniques is referred to as **horticulture.** While cultural ecologists usually refer to horticulture as a major subsistence type different from intensive agriculture, in which sophisticated tools, irrigation, and fertilization are commonly used, the difference between these two subsistence types is based more on degree than on a clear qualitative distinction. There are general differences, however. Horticultural practices take place in smaller land areas than intensive agriculture does—gardens, not fields. A horticultural plot usually must lie fallow for relatively long periods after use, while intensive agricultural techniques permit shorter or no fallow periods. Horticulturalists usually work less hard than intensive agriculturalists, unless the latter can utilize fossil fuels to do some of the work for them, but horticulturalists cannot produce as much food for a given land area. This does not mean that horticulturalists are lazy, ignorant, or inefficient. On the contrary, horticulturalists have sustained agricultural activities in regions where intensive techniques have led to disaster.

Horticulture is found in many environmental regimes, from rainforest to arid grasslands to temperate woodlands. It is not found in highly marginal environments, requiring adequate growing seasons and sufficient soil nutrients and water for plant growth.

A major form of horticulture is **swidden** or **slash-and-burn agriculture.** Commonly practiced in tropical rainforest environments, swidden agriculture involves cutting down natural vegatation in the intended garden area, letting the cut vegetation dry out, and then burning the dried vegetation (Figure 11–3). This serves to clear the garden area, drive off some insect pests, and leave a layer of ash to serve as fertilizer for the domesticated plants that are sown soon after the burning. Gardens are usually only utilized for one or two years before harvests decline markedly, as no additional fertilizers are generally used. Depending on local conditions, swidden gardens are then left fallow for periods of between five and twenty years. At this time, natural vegatation has grown back into secondary rainforest, which is then slashed and burned, with the cycle restarted. Swidden agriculturalists usually prefer to use the secondary regrowth from past gardens rather than primary rainforest as sites for new gardens.

Figure 11–3 Preparation of a swidden garden on the island of Vita Leve, Fiji, by the burning off of natural vegetation. (Photo courtesy of James Juvik)

The success of swiddens may be partly due to the fact that they mimic the natural environment of the rainforest (Geertz 1963). Like the rainforest, for instance, swiddens contain a high level of species diversity (Figure 11–4). Conklin (1954) noted as many as forty different cultigens (domesticated plants) in one garden of the Hanunóo, a people who live in the Philippines. This diversity helps protect against the devastating effects of disease or insects that are usually somewhat specialized in their hosts or prey and thus can wipe out a given crop.

Swiddens are often characterized by vertical zonation like the surrounding rainforest, with tubers, vines, bushy shrubs, and fruit trees all growing in the same garden. The multiple plant layers protect the soil from the hard rainfall that characterizes such environments. Both swiddens and natural rainforests are also characterized by a fairly direct cycle of nutrients from plants to other living plants, either through the ash layer in the gardens or the soil nutrients in the natural rainforest.

While swidden agriculture is the most common kind of horticulture practiced today, many other forms are found. One example involves the traditional agricultural practices of the western Pueblo in North America, who relied on

Figure 11–4   Swidden garden in the Solomon Islands showing diversity in crops, including cassava, yams, and taro. (Photo courtesy of Sonia Juvik)

floodwater farming. They usually planted maize deeply and in clusters in areas that become flooded during the rainy season, as deeper soil stayed wetter longer and the clump of maize allowed some protection for plants in the center of the cluster from the arid winds common to the region. People planted gardens in several places to reduce risk and used several cultigens besides maize, including beans and squash (Bates and Plog 1991).

Horticulturalists can generally support much greater population densities than foragers or pastoralists can. As a consequence, the degree of formalization of social interactions tends to be greater among these agriculturalists than among nonagriculturalists. However, the diversity of horticultural societies precludes simple analysis of the effects of horticulture as a subsistence type on culture as a whole. Local conditions, such as the size of gardens, number of people needed to cultivate the gardens, etc., are important in determining the effects of subsistence behavior on other aspects of the group's culture.

Intensive Agriculture

Intensive agriculture represents a much greater human impact on the natural environment. Technology and labor are used to create artificial ecological systems, with domesticated plants and animals supplanting the native community, and human use of fertilizers and irrigation systems supplanting natural nutrient

Figure 11–5   Rice terraces near Mount Agung, island of Bali, Indonesia. (Photo by E. J. Kormondy)

cycles. Indeed, in some places the entire landscape has been reshaped by people, with terracing, leveling, damming, and other major changes to the natural geography of a region (see Figure 11–5).

Human ecologists tend to divide intensive agriculture into two major types. **Labor-intensive agriculture** derives most of the energy used to transform the natural world into an artificial landscape from human muscular effort. **Subsidized agriculture,** on the other hand, relies on fossil fuels or other external energy sources to power the transformations. Common to both types of intensive agriculture is the effectiveness of food production: an enormous amount of resources can be obtained per unit of land. This high density of resources can support a large human population density, and it is only intensive agriculture that can support urban populations.

The rise of intensive agriculture seems to go against human nature: people have to work longer and harder than they usually must for other major forms of subsistence. The question of why people intensify their agricultural efforts is usually answered in one of two ways. Many scholars argue that population increase is the driving force of intensification, while others suggest that political pressure from rising elites or colonial powers drives the process (Netting 1986). Perhaps both forces are at work (see Figure 11–6).

Boserup (1965) stated that increasing scarcity of land, primarily because of population pressure, forced people to produce more food per land area. Using

Figure 11–6   A taro patch on a Micronesian atoll. Labor-intensive agriculture of this sort has permitted large population densities to be supported on islands with very small land area. (Photo courtesy of Craig Severance)

swidden agriculturalists as an example, increased pressure on land would lead agriculturalists to shorten fallow periods between slash-and-burn activities, eventually to the point where land would be reused before secondary regrowth of forests. This represents a change from forest fallow to bush fallow farming and comes with a cost: humans must now help replenish soil beyond the ash layer from the burning of natural plants regrowing in the gardens. This process may continue if population density increases further, with pressure for even shorter fallow periods, and eventually annual cropping or multicropping (multiple harvests per year on a given piece of land). Each step up this chain of increasing agricultural land use requires more effort and increasing use of fertilization on the part of the farmers to allow continued production.

The classic example of labor-intensive agriculture is the rice paddy systems found in Southeast Asia (see Figure 11–7). Hanks (1972) has provided data that demonstrate that the intensification of rice growing is associated with increased population density in the region. Swidden farmers who are rice growers average about 31 people per square mile, while those with very intensive rice growing techniques including transplantation of rice into prepared paddies average about 988 people per square mile. Associated with these increases in population density is increased labor cost, although production efficiency, defined as production per labor cost, does not decline (Hanks 1972).

Figure 11–7   Rice paddies on the island of Lombok, Indonesia. (Photo by E. J. Kormondy)

It is with the incredible yields of subsidized agriculture that intensification reaches its highest production levels. The use of fossil fuels to run machinery and produce synthetic fertilizers allows enormous amounts of energy to be invested in farm fields. Production efficiency seems very high but only if the energy value of fossil fuels is excluded. For instance, according to Harris (1988), a corn farmer in Iowa produces 81 bushels of corn per acre representing over 8 million kcal (1 kilocalorie = 1,000 calories) of energy with only about nine hours of work, for an energetic efficiency of 5,000 kcal produced for every kcal expended. This phenomenal efficiency figure must be tempered by the fact that three-fourths of U.S. cropland is used for animal feed, and energy costs have gone into the manufacturing of farm machinery, as well as fuel, fertilizer, and pesticides, not to mention transportation, packaging, and processing of the food. It is estimated that nearly 3 million kcal of energy goes directly into each acre of cropland (Pimentel et al. 1976). U.S. agriculture may represent a net loss of energy—that is, the energy value it takes to produce the food may be greater than the energy value of the harvest! In 1970 it was estimated that 8 kcal of fossil fuel energy was expended for each kcal of human food energy produced (Harris 1988). Since fossil fuels are not a renewable resource, it is clear that the American form of subsidized agriculture is not sustainable over the long term.

Limitations of Subsistence Type as a Category of Human Resource Use

Subsistence types provide a good first approximation of the way in which human populations provide for their resource needs. However, resource needs are not confined to food, although food is a major requirement for all people. Also, the specifics by which people of similar subsistence type differ are determined in part by the type of living organisms present in their macroenvironment. These organisms determine what food sources are available as wild forage or as possible cultigens, as well as serving as weeds or pests that detract from people's food production. To fully understand human resource use, we must understand basic ecological principles of resource acquisition for all organisms. An important starting point is the place of organisms as parts of ecological communities, and how characteristics of these communities determine what sorts of resources are available.

COMMUNITY ECOLOGY

Resource requirements are the basis for important connections among populations in ecosystems. Specifically, the need for food links organisms in an ecosystem in a fundamental way: they eat or are eaten by each other. As we saw in Chapter 4, organisms sometimes cooperate with other organisms, either of their own or different species, to obtain food; in other cases organisms compete with each other for resources. These types of interactions also link organisms in biological communities. The structure and form of biological communities is studied in the field termed **community ecology**.

The Nature of an Ecological Community

An **ecological community** can be regarded as an assemblage of species populations that have the potential for interaction. More precisely, a community may be defined as an interactive assemblage of species occurring together within a particular geographic area, a set of species whose ecological functions and dynamics are in some way interdependent (Putman 1994). These interactions include overt competitive interaction and feeding relationships as well as more subtle manifestations such as reliance of plants on animals for pollination and seed dispersal or of animals on plants for meeting habitat (shelter) requirements. As might then be expected, ecological communities come in all sizes, shapes, and degrees of interaction of their constituent populations.

Interactions among species populations constituting an ecological community give rise to properties of the community that may not be inherent, readily recognized, or easily predicted from those of the species populations themselves. In this context, an ecological community is holistic, the totality of its properties being greater than the sum of its individual parts. Begon et al. (1986) have referred to these properties as *emergent,* noting in analogy that a cake has emergent properties of texture and flavor not apparent by consideration of its ingredients. For example, an aggregation of 1,000 trees on a plot of land has a different set of properties than 1,000 trees in dispersed arrangement; the former results in reduced insolation to the forest floor and the accumulation of a layer of rotting leaves, neither of which characterizes the latter.

That properties of a community (or for that matter an ecosystem) are emergent, a derivative of being holistic, is not universally accepted, however. Part of the debate centers around the very nature of a community, namely as to whether it is uniquely individualistic or is a unitary entity like an organism. Another part of the debate focuses on the assignment of the term *emergent* to properties that are regarded by others as merely collective (Salt 1979, among others). For example, in the latter viewpoint, the age structure of a population is regarded as the result of the combined ages of all the individuals making up the population. Likewise, community respiration can be seen as a collective community characteristic since it is an aggregation of the totality of respiration carried on by the individuals in the community.

The Form and Structure of Ecological Communities

The form and structure, or **physiognomy,** of a community can be described in a number of ways, each assessing somewhat different aspects, each having certain advantages and limitations, and, as might be expected, each having its proponents in ecological circles.

Growth Forms.   Perhaps the least technical characterization of a community's structure, particularly as applied to plants, employs commonly recognized **growth forms** such as evergreens and deciduous trees, woody and herbaceous shrubs, herbs, and so on. Within each of these general categories one can distinguish further between needle-leaved, broad-leaved, and sclerophyll (hard, leathery leaf) evergreens or succulents, thorn and rosette among shrubs or ferns, and grasses and forbs among herbs.

Life Forms.   A variation of plant growth form, referred to as **life form,** was developed at the turn of the twentieth century by the Danish botanist Raunkiaer (1934) based on the relation of the ground surface to the plant's embryonic or regenerating (meristematic) tissue. The latter remains inactive during unfavorable climatic regimes and resumes activity when favorable conditions return. The categories Raunkiaer recognized were based on the "amount and kind of protection afforded to the buds and shoot apices" that are composed of meristematic tissue.

Because the ability of a plant to survive in a given environment depends on its being adapted to that environment, and because the life form is a morphological adaptation, it should follow that given life forms would be more prevalent in some environments than in others. Certain grasses, for instance, predominate over herbs and shrubs in heavily grazed areas subject to fire by having their growing tips below the ground level. In contrast, herbs and shrubs have their growing tips above the ground; thus they are susceptible to both fire and grazing.

There is a predominance of herbs and shrubs in moist tropical regions; here the exposed buds are not subjected to such adversities as low temperature or aridity. Desert areas would require, among other drought-resisting adaptations, maximum protection of buds and regenerating parts from high temperature and aridity. Not surprising, a high preponderance of annual plants that produce seeds are found in such environments. Intermediate between these climatic extremes, and their corresponding sharp differences in amount of protection afforded the propagative organ, is the moist-temperate region, which is dominated by plants with their buds situated at the soil surface and protected by the bases of their leaves and stems.

Stratification.   Both the life and growth form of plants emphasize height. Even a casual glance at a plant community conveys differences in the heights, or **vertical stratification,** of the components. Trees are generally taller than shrubs, which are usually taller than herbs, and the latter than mosses and lichens. Tropical forests are characterized typically by a marked vertical stratification, especially in areas where the canopy is broken (Figure 11-8). Vertical stratification results in the upper strata, or canopy, receiving a larger proportion of solar energy, and in instances of particularly dense foliage, little sunlight reaches the ground, reducing photosynthesis and plant growth at that level.

In terrestrial situations, variations in plant structure and stratification within a community lead to stratification of the environment (e.g., light penetration, humidity) and animal components (e.g., ground dwellers, arboreal dwellers), whereas in aquatic systems stratification of the environment (temperature differences, light penetration, etc.) leads to stratification of both the plant and animal assemblages. For example, floating and motile plankton generally occur in the upper portions, whereas free-swimming fish occur in the next lower segment, followed by sedentary (e.g., corals) or bottom dwelling (e.g., crabs, clams) forms, the latter in turn followed by those that burrow below the bottom surface.

Vertical stratification also occurs among land animals. Forest birds tend to be vertically stratified, with some species feeding and nesting only in the canopy, others near or on the ground, and yet others at various levels in between (see Figure 1–2). Similarly, in a forest squirrels nest high above the ground, mice at or near the ground surface, and moles beneath the surface.

Zonation.   Horizontal changes in the physical environment are reflected in **zonation** changes in plant and animal components of ecological communities. For example, as one proceeds from a lake's edge, the first zone is that of vegetation rooted in the bottom but extended above the water level; this is

(a)

(b)

Figure 11–8 Tropical rainforest in Panama showing tiered structure of vegetation. (a) Aerial view near Canal Zone. (b) Clearing for pipeline, Canal Zone. (Photos courtesy of Gerrit Davidse, Missouri Botanical Garden)

followed by a zone of floating vegetation, subsequently by one of submerged vegetation, and finally one which is characterized by phytoplankton, that may be regarded as unrooted vegetation. Similar zonation is to be found in terrestrial situations where soil characteristics change from, for example, more moist to drier conditions.

Horizontal Dispersion.   The horizontal spacing, or **dispersion,** of plants and animals can also be used to describe the structure of an ecological community. There are three basic patterns of dispersal: random, uniform or regular, and clumped or contagious (Figure 11–9); two additional patterns exist in combinations of random and clumped and uniform and clumped.

Although a community may show truly random distribution (verifiable by its fit to a Poisson distribution), more often a number of factors result in various degrees of clumping (or contagion), a regularity in spacing, or a combination of the latter. Most often, a clumping of resources (e.g., water, nutrients) leads to clumping of organisms; reproductive patterns may also account for clumping. The availability of a resource, such as ground water, or the release of biological inhibitors by sedentary plants may inhibit other individuals of the species from developing within the radius of the inhibitor's effect (Rice 1974); both situations can result in a more or less regular dispersal of that species. And, of course, in agricultural situations, regular spacing of orchard trees such as oranges, peaches, and macadamia nuts is quite common.

Trophic Structure.   Yet another productive categorization of community structure is the use of trophic (feeding) levels. Under this schema, the plant or animal community can be described by assignment to the category of producers, consumers (primary, secondary, or tertiary), or decomposers. These trophic levels and their disposition into food webs carry influences and constraints on the organization and dynamics of communities (Pimm et al. 1991; Putman 1994; among others). For example, according to current food web theory, simple communities should be more sensitive to the loss of plant species than complex ones because in the former the consumers are dependent on only a few species and cannot survive their loss.

Figure 11–9   Basic patterns of dispersal: (a) Random; (b) uniform; (c) clumped.

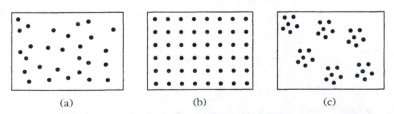

      (a)   (b)   (c)

Phylogenetic Composition. Perhaps one of the more obvious and easily comprehended means of describing a community is by identifying the constituent assemblages of species. Thus a forest community might be described by its **phylogeny** (the relationships of groups of organisms as reflected by their evolutionary history) as spruce-fir, beech-maple, or oak-hickory and an animal community as microarthropods of the soil, benthic fish, airborne insects, and so on.

Classification of Communities

The tendency to bring a semblance of organization to complex entities is commonplace: not content to call a rock a rock, mineralogists have developed hundreds of categories based, in large measure, on chemical composition; not content to call a chemical a chemical, chemists have identified more than one hundred elements based on atomic structure (number of protons in the nucleus) and hundreds of thousands of compounds of such elements; not content to call an animal an animal or a plant a plant, taxonomists have clustered them into kinds of similar nature called species, species into genera, genera into families, and so on. Ecologists are not to be outdone, and thus a number of schema have been employed to bring a degree of order out of not so much disorder as the complexity of ecological communities. As in the case of taxonomists, there are "lumpers" and "splitters" among ecologists, referring respectively to those who tend to aggregate and those who tend to make finer discriminations among the entities being described.

Not surprisingly, classifications of communities, most notably of plants, are, for the most part, based on the structural characteristics described previously. Physiognomy of the dominant growth form is commonly employed as a classification criterion at both local levels and over broad geographic areas (e.g., evergreen or deciduous forests). Dominant species serve as another criterion of classification (e.g., spruce-fir forest, beech-maple forest). Further refinement can be obtained by classifying according to the dominant species at each vertical stratification (e.g., squirrel, mouse, mole).

Classification into discrete categories implies that more or less sharp discontinuities are present among the entities being segregated. While such discrimination is possible in the classification of chemical elements, it becomes less feasible with biological entities and increasingly so as one moves from distinguishing among species to differentiating among ecological communities. Except in some circumstances where a major physical discontinuity exists, as in the instance of a very high, precipitous cliff, community boundaries are more often blurred, one community's constituents extending into another's and vice versa.

FUNCTIONAL ASPECTS OF COMMUNITIES

Because they consist of living organisms, communities are not static entities. Like the species that compose them, ecological communities are dynamic and undergo more or less constant change in physiognomy and composition owing to changes both in the environment and in the characteristics of the life cycles of the organisms themselves. For example, on the cooler and more moist north slopes of mountains in temperate areas, many herbs have bloomed by late spring; however, on the drier and warmer south slopes, the maximum period of herbaceous activity is during early summer. Likewise, insects overwintering as pupae emerge under certain conditions of temperature, moisture, and even the length of the **photoperiod** (day length), one of many examples being the late summer cicadas so common in temperate climates.

Each species has its own characteristic pattern of sequential development that is largely attuned to and regulated by major environmental climatic gradients. It is not surprising, then, that whole communities demonstrate phenomena attuned to naturally recurring events. Thus, in a deciduous forest, spring brings release from dormancy and a resurgence of vegetative activity that culminates in leafing out of the deciduous trees. Fall brings the onset of dormancy and a curtailment of activity manifested in leaf color change and drop. Because natural geophysical phenomena recur at different intervals, and because different species respond differentially to such stimuli, different rhythms would be expected among different communities. Thus the sugar maple community that leafs out in spring and undergoes leaf fall in autumn is responding to an annual rhythm, that of a shift in photoperiod. Similarly, this same group of plants responds during the growing season to the diurnal rhythm of alternative periods of light and darkness by undergoing photosynthesis during the day but not at night.

Seasonal Changes in Various Ecological Parameters

Because of the change in inclination of the Earth's axis with respect to the sun over the course of a year (Figure 11–10), the total solar radiation received at a given geographical latitude varies at different times of the year (Figure 11–11). As might be anticipated, such changes elicit a differential progression of responses by given species to both the quality and quantity of light as well as to the temperature and other climatic differences that recur more or less periodically. In addition to changes in photoperiod, seasonal changes also often occur in moisture and temperature. In general, such periodic phenomena in organisms that are tied to periodic environmental change are referred to as **phenology.**

Phenological responses among animals tend to be most easily observed in reproductive activities. Some of these periodic activities are triggered by hormonal rhythms, the rhythms themselves often being cued by changes in environmental factors such as light, temperature, and moisture. Many insect species respond to recurring temperature and photoperiod changes in their development rates and adult reproductive activity (Wolda 1988).

Amazonian Amphibia. Among the many examples that could be cited of phenological responses in both plants and animals, a study in Manaus, Brazil, on amphibian breeding will suffice. In Manaus, where rainfall is seasonal, being

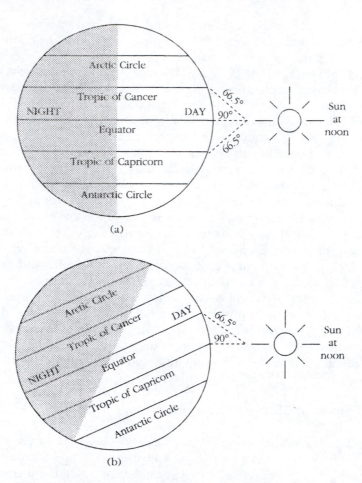

(a)

(b)

Figure 11–10 (a) Inclination of the sun in the northern hemisphere at fall and spring equinoxes. The sun is directly (90°) over the equator and is at 66.5° at the Tropics of Cancer and Capricorn. (b) Inclination of the sun at the winter solstice. The sun is directly (90°) over the Tropic of Capricorn and is at 66.5° over the equator. At this time, the area above the Arctic Circle is in darkness 24 hours a day, while the area below the Antarctic Circle is in light 24 hours a day; the opposite occurs during the summer solstice, when the sun is directly (90°) over the Tropic of Cancer.

wetter in midwinter and late spring, Gascon (1991) observed two distinct phenological patterns in an amphibian community: a group of five frog species bred during the entire rainy season, and another group of some 18 species bred only after heavy rains. Further, most of the latter group adjusted their breeding to the earlier rains that occurred in the second year of the study. Gascon noted that these two patterns of phenology occur in other tropical amphibian communities as well. Interestingly, two species not only bred independently of rainfall but at

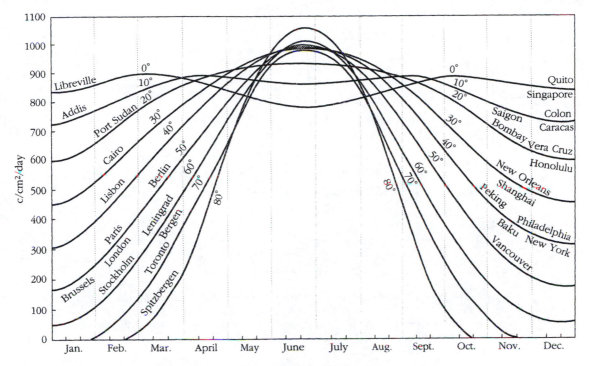

Figure 11–11 Daily totals of solar radiation received on a horizontal surface for different geographic latitudes at different times of the year and based on a solar flux value of 1.94 gcal/cm²/min. (Redrawn by permission from D. M. Gates. 1962. *Energy exchange in the biosphere.* New York: Harper and Row.)

the same time each year suggesting the operation of some other environmental cue or an internal biological rhythm.

Periodism and Temperature

Aquatic Communities. Because of the high specific heat of water (i.e., the amount of heat required to raise the temperature of a given amount of water), daily changes in ambient temperature have only modest effects on freshwater and marine communities, whereas the more prolonged temperature changes associated with the seasons, particularly in temperate zones, have a more marked effect. In temperate freshwater ponds and even large temperate lakes, the water in the lake literally turns over in the fall, the result of colder air temperatures cooling surface waters that become more dense and then sink; this turnover results in a significant diminution of biological activity that resumes after the spring turnover. As should be anticipated, the seasonal changes in boreal forest aquatic communities are much more marked.

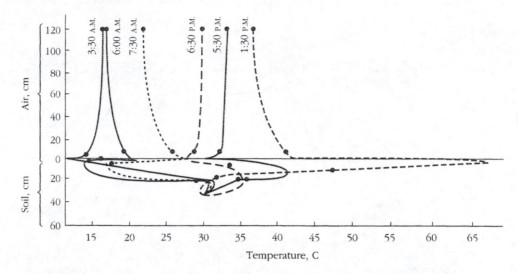

Figure 11–12   The daily cycle of air and soil temperatures from a vegetated sandy area in the Nevada desert on a clear day, July 31, 1953. (Redrawn by permission of the publisher from *Plants and the ecosystem* by W. D. Billings, © 1964. Belmont, CA: Wadsworth Publishing Co.)

Terrestrial Communities.   Unlike aquatic environments, wherein temperature change is mitigated by the specific heat of water, ambient temperature changes can result in significant periodic activity within a community. Most marked of such periodism is found in desert situations, where the difference between the warmest and coolest parts of a day may be in the order of 60°C or more (Figure 11–12). In addition to a number of diurnal periodic physiological changes in plants (e.g., closure of stomata), most animals tend to be inactive during the heat of the day, often burrowing into the ground, and to be active nocturnally.

TEMPORAL VARIABILITY IN RESOURCES

Communities change over time. These changes may be due to rare cataclysms such as volcanic eruptions to less rare but difficult to predict stressors such as forest fires, hurricanes, or anthropogenic stressors; or to periodic changes in the environment, such as seasonal changes, as well as to changes induced by the community itself. In particular, communities tend to follow a fairly predictable pattern of changes, termed **succession.** For example, in a series of studies, among which is a classic, American ecologist Henry C. Cowles (1899) showed that the different communities initially present in Indiana in such diverse habitats as flood plains, sand ridges, shallow and deep ponds, and clay banks all demonstrated a quite predictable sequential series of structural changes, each culminating in a more or less stable community of beech-maple forest. Although the degree of such regularity and predictability was disputed by a number of later ecologists (including Jackson et al. 1988), it is the case that structural and compositional changes in a community over time, both in the present and in the geological past, are recognizable. One specific example in some detail should be instructive.

Succession on New Islands

The opportunity to study succession in newly created environments is relatively limited to situations like beach ponds (Kormondy 1969), recent lava flows, and newly emerged islands. An opportunity for the latter was provided between 1882 and 1886, when the water level of Lake Hjalmaren in Sweden was lowered about 130 cm, resulting in the emergence of a large number of new islands. Beginning in 1886 and extending through 1985, a series of five plant surveys was conducted on the islands at several time intervals (1886, 1892, 1903–1904, 1927–1928, and 1984–1985) by various investigators; these were analyzed by Rydin and Borgegard (1991), who conducted the last survey. Their report focuses on the 30 islands for which a complete 100-year set of data obtained.

Successional Stages. Of the 112 plant species that occurred on at least 10 islands or were abundant on at least 3 islands in any one of the surveys, six major categories or stages of species composition were recognized based on frequency or abundance: (1) pioneers (13 species) reached their maximum at the first survey, decreasing drastically after the first or second survey; (2) pioneer stayers (6 species) reached many islands by the first survey and remained at similar levels until the fourth or fifth survey; (3) early successionals (16 species) showed a distinct increase between surveys 1 and 2, a maximum in the second or third, and a decline thereafter; (4) early successional stayers (10 species) had a distinct increase between surveys 1 and 2 but no subsequent decline; (5) midsuccessionals (20 species) had a maximum at survey 3 and/or 4 and declined after the latter; (6) midsuccessional stayers and late species (47 species) reached their maximum between survey 3 and/or 4 but maintained their importance in the fifth survey or increased between survey 4 and 5, reaching a maximum in the latter.

PERTURBATIONS AND SUCCESSION

The series of changes in communities observed in newly created environments such as new islands are referred to as **primary succession. Secondary succession** refers to those sequential changes that occur when an established ecological community is disturbed and subsequently undergoes changes in its structure and function. Whether the secondary sequence follows the pattern of the primary sequence depends on a host of abiotic and biotic factors both as agents of the disturbance and as components of the redeveloping community. Among the former are fires, ice storms, floods, drought, high winds, landslides, and large waves. Among the biotic factors are such direct interactions as grazing, predation, competition, infection (disease), and the indirect effects of habitat modification caused by activities such as the digging of burrows by earthworms and rodents or the damming of streams by beavers. Of considerable consequence are numerous human actions such as bulldozing, construction, and pollution.

The extent of the impact of a disturbance on an established community depends, among other things, on the severity of the disturbance, the time of its occurrence in the successional process, the multiple interactions that occur among the members of the surviving community, and the proximity to other communities of like or dissimilar nature. The role of disturbance in ecological communities has been an arena of increased ecological interest and has led to the phrase **patch dynamics** (Thompson 1978) to describe the common focus of such efforts on the conditions created by disturbance (frequency, severity, intensity, and predictability) and the responses of organisms to the disturbances. Excellent reviews of the role of disturbance on ecological communities are to be found in Sousa (1984) and Pickett and White (1985). A few examples of perturbations and their effects on succession are in order to give meaning to these comments.

Perturbations in Terrestrial Communities

Depending on their severity, both crown and ground fires can be significant perturbing agents in terrestrial communities as can clearcutting of forests. Likewise perturbing are devastating parasitic infestations such as occurred in the early part of the twentieth century when the Chinese sac fungus virtually wiped out the majestic American chestnut tree then predominant in temperate deciduous forests of the eastern United States.

Fire Ants.   During the 1940s, the fire ant *Solenopsis invicta* invaded the southeastern United States from South America, creating a wave of destruction of naturally occurring communities in the interim. The name derives from the severe burning sensation its bite creates. At a field station in central Texas, Porter and Savignano (1990) observed that an invasion of fire ants resulted in a 70 percent drop in the number of native ant species and a drop in the total population of native ants of 90 percent. Similarly, the number of species of non-ant arthropods (isopods, mites, and certain scarab beetles) dropped 30 percent and their population numbers 75 percent. The primary causal factor appears to have been competition, another result of which was that there was a ten- to thirtyfold increase in the number of ants at the infested sites, more than 99 percent of which were the fire ant. The likelihood of this arthropod community reestablishing itself is indeed remote.

Volcanic Intrusion.   The once pristine Spirit Lake, lying at the base of Mount St. Helens in the state of Washington and surrounded by steep and densely forested mountain slopes, was drastically perturbed on May 18, 1980, when the volcanic mountain exploded with the force of a 10-megaton nuclear explosion. The resulting pyroclastic lava flow carried immense quantities of debris, old and/or burnt trees, and mineral-containing rock into the lake, raising the temperature from about 10°C to 30°C and filling extensive portions of its basin. Extensive and intensive studies have been conducted on Spirit Lake since that perturbation, leading to the conclusion that it will never return to its preeruption condition (Larson 1993). Significant changes have and are occurring in its flora and fauna and in its chemical composition; in addition, its surrounding environs harbor pathogenic bacteria and prolific noxious plants. This is an instance where secondary succession is leading to a markedly different community than existed before as well as being a commentary on nature's power to dramatically alter the landscape.

SUCCESSION IN THE PAST

Succession in the present represents what occurs over a short period of time and can be studied by direct observation of existing communities, making certain assumptions and inferences in doing so. Succession in the past has occurred over long periods of time, namely thousands of years, and must be inferred from direct observations of relics of the past such as skeletal material, pollen, seeds, and tree rings. Whereas succession in the present focuses on changes in structure, as well as function in some cases, in more or less circumscribed locations, succession in the past tends to focus on large geographical regions and seeks an identification of particular communities with particular climates. Thus we describe the predominant composition and distribution of the major contemporary biomes (see Chapter 12), tying their characteristics to the major climatic patterns of the region in which they occur. Since there have been major climatic changes during Earth's history, major changes in the boundaries of biomes have also changed. This exciting dimension of ecology, generally referred to as **paleoecology,** deals with determining major ecological communities from their fossil record and thereby dating the climate in those particular regions. The assumption is that, with minor adjustments, particular kinds of communities observed today in particular climates existed in the past in similar climates.

Studying Paleoecological Succession

As a pond or lake undergoes succession, there is a progressive filling in by organic matter. Among the constituents of this organic matter are pollen grains released both from the community in the pond and the surrounding area. By removing a core of the sediment and tabulating the percentages of pollen grains of each species in successive levels of the deposit, deductions can be made of the community composition that prevailed at the time each level was deposited. The climate corresponding to each level is then inferred from the particular community composition, on the assumption that the genetically based climatic requirements of the species have not significantly changed in the interim.

PERIODIC CHANGES IN ECOLOGICAL COMMUNITIES

Earlier in this chapter, we discussed the phenomenon of phenology, the functional response of species and communities to annual periodicity of temperature, rainfall, and photoperiod. This periodicity and its accompanying phenological responses lead to changes in resource availability for given organisms on a seasonal basis. Seasonality may also be somewhat independent of climatic periodicity but be based on other cycles in the ecosystem, such as fruiting cycles of trees in tropical rainforests. Organisms in these types of ecosystems must therefore change their location (migrate), their resource sources, or their mode of obtaining resources on a seasonal basis.

Migration

The **migration** of animals has been observed and marveled at for millennia. Formally defined as behavior that has evolved for the movement of the individual organism in space (Dingle 1980), migration may involve movement across entire continents or oceans on an annual basis, or it may involve much smaller migrations, such as movement from one elevation level to another in a mountain environment (Escobar and Beall 1982). The relatively short migrations may still represent major changes in environment for an organism, leading to changes in basic behavioral adaptations for obtaining resources or coping with stressors. Not all migrations are seasonal in nature; some may involve daily or other periodic changes in position, while others are less obviously periodic in nature.

One of the smallest migratory movements studied by ecologists is the daily vertical migration of plankton. Much research has been undertaken to understand the adaptive basis of this movement, to decide whether it is undertaken to optimize resource intake (e.g., sunlight for photosynthetic plankton), to avoid predation, or for other reasons. As might be expected, data suggest that there are probably multiple reasons for the movement (Dingle 1980).

On the other end of the scale, prodigious migrations have been documented in birds, mammals, and some insects. The humpback whale *(Megaptera novaeangliae)* travels up to 7,000 km between summer feeding grounds in the Arctic and winter tropical breeding areas. The arctic tern, with seasonal migrations of 13,000 to 18,000 km between Arctic and Antarctic habitats, represents the extreme in long-distance migration. For its size, the monarch butterfly also ranks as a long-distance marvel, with individuals migrating from as far as southeastern Canada and New England to winter grounds in central Mexico. Some of the butterflies, those born in the summer, are short-lived and therefore do not complete a migratory cycle as individuals; however, their offspring complete the cycle (Baker 1978).

Seasonal Changes in Resources

Many organisms, whether they migrate or not, show seasonal patterns of change in use of resources. In fact, community structure may significantly change during the course of a year. In the extreme, organisms will forego or greatly reduce resource acquisition during parts of the year, living off stored resources. This can be seen in animals that live off their biological stores—such as adipose tissue—in conjunction with torpidity or hibernation to reduce their resource needs. Japanese "snow monkeys" *(Macaca fuscata)* have no adaptations for seasonal torpidity, and in winter the monkeys are often forced to rely on food resources for which they are poorly adapted, such as buds and bark from trees, or, at best, leaves from evergreen trees and grasses (Richard 1985). As a result the monkeys lose weight during the winter as they draw on their stored fat.

In general, resource seasonality increases with increasing latitude. In high latitudes, temperature variability represents the greatest seasonal change, but seasonal changes in rainfall, solar radiation, and other factors may contribute to temporal patterns.

One of the major seasonal changes in many biological communities is reflected in the timing of plant reproductive cycles, as we noted earlier. These show annual periods in high latitudes, but less of a seasonal pattern in tropical areas. Fruits or seeds produced by given plant species often represent important sources of food for animals in the community, and thus the periodicity in plant cycles may drive a more general periodicity in the community as a whole. Even in tropical rainforests annual cycles of fruiting may be present for some species. Even for those species that do not show seasonal patterns of fruiting in tropical regions, the timing of when individual trees produce fruit will affect animals confined to small areas of the forest. The temporal variability in fruiting increases the patchiness of resources of frugivorous (fruit-eating) animals. This may cause behavioral changes in animals, such as an increase in the spatial range in which animals habitually move in order to assure the availability of at least one patch of fruit at any given time, or a change in an animal's social group size to match up with resource availability in patches.

Seasonal Changes in the Mode of Obtaining Resources

It is obvious that when an organism's source for a given resource changes according to the season, the organism will often have to change the manner by which it obtains the resource. However, even when the source does not change seasonally, characteristics of the source or of the habitat may change, and thus animals must change their behavior to obtain needed resources. For instance, anoles (a type of lizard found widely in the Western Hemisphere) of the species *Anolis nebulosus* Weigman feed on insects year-round but change the manner in which they prey on these animals seasonally. In the dry season they hunt for insects on the ground and generally only attack from close range. Conversely, in the wet season they shift to arboreal hunting and attack from a greater average distance (Lister and Aguayo 1992).

These aspects of the structure and function of ecological communities affect the distribution and accessibility of resources needed to sustain life for all organisms, including humans, who may adversely affect natural communities as we will see. At this point, however, we are ready to explore further the relationships of humans to their resources in the context of ecological communities.

HUMAN POPULATIONS AND RESOURCE DISTRIBUTION

As noted in Chapter 5, human population size and growth rate can be limited by the amount of resources available. Group size is also affected by the spatial distribution of resources. A general rule of thumb is that if a population's resources are clumped, the population should be clumped, while if the resources are spread out, the population should be dispersed. In fact, things are much more complex than this simplistic rule. Factors related to human group size include relative amounts of resources, techniques of resource acquisition, and innumerable social considerations from kinship rules to military defense (Smith 1981). Also, group size can mean different things: procurement group size refers to the number of individuals in "work groups" involved in obtaining or processing resources, while there are many other types of social groups of varying sizes, from foraging bands to larger groups of people found in villages, towns, and cities among agriculturalists. As noted by Steward (1955), there has been a tendency for the number of different "levels of sociocultural integration" to increase in human groups, and this has increased the number of different-sized social groups to which a given person simultaneously belongs. We will focus on procurement group size in the following discussion, although other forms of group size will be noted where they are directly affected by ecological considerations. It is common to use the term *foraging group size* when discussing both human foragers—in this case used as a specific kind of procurement group size—and nonhuman foragers.

Group Size and Patchiness

Where resources are both sparse and regularly distributed in the environment, one would expect to find low population densities and small procurement group size of human populations that exploit those resources. This can, in fact, be seen among foraging peoples in many regions of the world. A classic example is based on accounts of the Shoshonean-speaking Indians of the Great Basin region of the United States before the extensive acculturative changes prompted by European-derived populations. These people lived in an environment that was very arid and had sparse resources that were not clumped into large patches. Resources were also unpredictable in location over time, as they largely depended on where rainfall might happen to be greater or less than average in a given year. The Shoshonean Indians had a low population density and spent most of the year in small family groups (Steward 1938, 1955). This permitted efficient foraging for the limited food resources.

Quite a different distribution of resources was available to native Americans to the east of the Shoshonean speakers, namely the Plains Indians. These populations had a major food resource that was mobile and highly clumped, the American bison. There is archaeological evidence for bison hunting on the Great Plains over 10,000 years BP, including the Casper site (Frison 1992). The Olsen-Chubbock site, located in Colorado and dated to about 8,000 years BP, is a place where people stampeded about 200 bison into a dry gully, where they slaughtered them (Frison 1992). Because of the need for large numbers of people to drive the animals and the rich patch of food that resulted, the communal hunts involved temporary large aggregations of people that, in turn, had sociopolitical ramifications for Plains Indians cultures: people who helped control these hunts obtained political power (Bamforth 1988).

A formal model of the relationship between resources and forager distribution has been formulated (Horn 1968) that predicts foraging group size will increase where resources are mobile, unpredictable, and clumped, while foraging group size will be small where resources are stable and evenly distributed. When the model was applied to the various groups of northern Athapascans of subarctic Canada and the United States, it was able to explain differences in settlement size among the Athapascan groups. Specifically, those Athapascan groups that relied heavily on large, mobile herds of caribou as a food resource had larger settlement sizes, while those that relied on more stable, evenly distributed resources had more distributed populations (Heffley 1981). All groups showed flexibility in their settlement sizes, however, to allow for seasonal and other temporal changes in the distribution of resources.

Settlement size is affected by resources other than food. In the Kalahari Desert of southern Africa, for example, the population size of foraging bands of San people is largely influenced by the distribution of water resources. In the (relatively) wet season, water is widely distributed in the environment in seasonal streams, permanent waterholes, and temporary ponds. The San people live in small, scattered groups during this time. During the dry season, surface water is available only in permanent water holes that are located in the bottoms of seasonal streams where bedrock is exposed (Lee 1993). These water holes represent a clumped resource, and people form relatively large settlements around them. This eventually leads to an ecological problem for the San: their groups are too clumped for their food resource base, which is fairly evenly distributed in the landscape, and they therefore become less efficient at food gathering as the dry season lasts. A major factor in their adaption to the environment is the distance from water to food resources at this time of year (Lee 1969). When the rains return, increased distribution of water resources allows them again to split up into smaller groups that can more efficiently forage for food.

The development of agriculture has brought with it a major change both in resource density and distribution: food resources are richer and more clumped. Thus, agricultural communities tend to have higher population densities and larger settlement sizes than are found among foraging peoples. Increasing intensification of agriculture has led to further increases in group size. The development of urban centers of population has occurred only in groups where intensive agriculture is practiced.

Group Size and Technique of Resource Acquisition

The manner in which people obtain resources also affects optimal procurement group size. Again, foraging peoples present good examples of this. Among the Shoshonean-speaking groups noted earlier, there were temporary concentrations of populations associated with collective hunting strategies, the most common of which were "rabbit drives," where people "beat the brush" to scare rabbits into large nets (Steward 1955).

Another example of how foraging technique leads to differences in foraging group size can be seen in two different types of seal hunting found among Canadian Inuit foragers. One form of seal hunting involves searching for seals at the edges of ice floes and is often stated to be best done individually or in pairs (Smith 1991). The other form of seal hunting involves catching them at their breathing holes and is stated to require several hunters to monitor as many of the breathing holes as possible (Smith 1981, 1991). Thus, foraging group size is larger on average for breathing-hole hunting than for ice-edge hunting.

A third example of hunting techniques and group size can be found among the Mbuti and other pygmy groups of central Africa, where there are two major hunting techniques—bow-and-arrow and net hunting, respectively. Bow-and-arrow hunting is best done individually, while net hunting requires large groups of people both as "beaters" and as net minders (Turnbull 1968; Bailey and Peacock 1988), although observations suggest there is some overlap in foraging group size using the two techniques (Bailey and Aunger 1989; Wilkie and Curran 1993). In areas where net hunting is the norm, Mbuti live in relatively larger groups than in areas where bow-and-arrow hunting is the usual technique (Turnbull 1968; Abruzzi 1979).

Social Considerations and Group Size

There are numerous other considerations involved with group size in non-human animals, including reproductive considerations, predator defense, and information sharing, among others. When we turn to humans, we can become overwhelmed by the number of other factors that must be considered. Suffice it to say that resource considerations may determine group size only when populations approach the carrying capacity of the environment, with the latter determined by a group's subsistence type and technology as well as by characteristics of the macroenvironment. In many circumstances group size is determined by sociocultural factors that appear to have little direct relationship to ecology.

Verticality of Resources and Human Ecology

Human populations must deal with the vertical as well as horizontal distribution of resources in the macroenvironment. This is a major consideration for populations living in rainforest ecosystems. Except in recently disturbed areas, much of the edible resources of the rainforest, including leaves, fruit, and the animals that eat them, are high above the ground in the canopy.

Seasonality in Human Ecology

The diversity of habitats in which human populations are found as well as differences in technology lead to great differences in the relative importance of seasonal changes in resource availability. Like other organisms, human populations may migrate, change the quality and type of dietary items, or change the manner in which they obtain resources to deal with seasonal fluctuations in the macroenvironment, or they may not need to make many changes at all.

Human Migration. Many human groups must move to follow their resources. This movement is found commonly among foragers and pastoralists, while people with crops to tend are less likely to migrate. However, individual migration occurs in many agricultural groups, as seen in migrant farm workers in the United States and among people who engage in seasonal wage employment. **Nomadism** is a term reserved for movement involving entire social groups due to resource needs. **Transhumance** is another form of human migration, found in some pastoralist groups, where only a portion of the social group moves to follow the herds while other group members remain in permanent settlements (Kottak 1994).

Archaeologists have discerned seasonal patterns in human populations from thousands of years ago. One of the best-documented examples is from ancient Mesoamerica, in the Tehuacàn Valley of Mexico. Based on the unusually well-preserved sites in this dry area, Richard MacNeish (1971) was able to establish a time sequence of change beginning about 10,000 years BP when small foraging groups with a nomadic lifestyle were present. By about 6,700 years BP a different pattern was evident: groups had seasonal migrations, with movements involving changes from small social groups (termed *microbands*) in winter to larger groups (termed *macrobands*) in the summer when food was more plentiful. Agricultural foods entered the diets of people in this valley beginning about 6,700 years BP but only slowly became a major element in their diet. In fact, even in the Formative Period (1500 B.C.–200 A.D.) part-time nomadism was still common in much of Mesoamerica (Coe and Flannery 1964), although seasonal migrations became less common as agricultural foods became more important.

Humans and their hominid ancestors have probably dealt with seasonal changes in resources for millions of years. The African savanna and open woodlands, generally regarded as the birthplace of hominids, have an annual cycle based chiefly on rainfall patterns, creating alternating dry and wet seasons. The savanna of East Africa is now occupied by peoples who experience similar seasonal patterns of wet and dry seasons but deal with it in a very different way. Modern East Africans are pastoralists, with cattle as their major resource. There are differences among the various populations of pastoralists in the region; however, we will focus on only one group—the Karimojong.

The Karimojong live in a region that permits some seasonal gardening activity to supplement their pastoral activities (Little and Morren 1976). However, rainfall is very unpredictable in both its timing and location. Their annual cycle is greatly influenced by seasonality, as shown in Figure 11–13. This figure shows a typical representation of a human population's annual cycle, with changes both in physical characteristics of the macroenvironment and in the population's activities listed around a circle that represents one full year.

Field clearing and cultivation by the Karimojong is done in February and March before the rainy season begins in April. Harvest takes place in the later part of the rainy season, and crops are dried for storage during the dry season (Dyson-Hudson and Dyson-Hudson 1969). Herds are moved about in search of good pasturage. In the dry season that normally begins in October the herds must usually move farther from the permanent settlement, so men must live in nomadic camps while women and children stay at the settlement and tend crops. Thus, the Karimojong practice transhumance during the dry season. Because food resources are scarce and susceptible to uncertain climatic factors, including frequent droughts, the Karimojong also do a small amount of foraging (both hunting and gathering) to supplement their food supply.

Figure 11–13   Annual cycle of the Karimojong cattle herders of East Africa. (Reproduced by permission from M. A. Little and G. E. B. Morren, Jr. 1976. *Ecology, energetics, and human variability.* Dubuque, IA: Wm. C. Brown Company.)

Seasonal Change in Resources Among Human Populations. Many human groups that are nonmigratory still must make adjustments to seasonal changes in resource availability. The changes must deal with temporal variability in both the amount and kind of resources. For foragers this involves adjusting to seasonal changes in dietary plant and animal resources. Many of these changes are related to reproductive cycles of plants and animals, including insects. For agriculturalists, seasonal cycles revolve around planting and harvest seasons. In developing countries many people in rural areas face food shortages in the months immediately before harvest, this sometimes leading to seasonal loss of body weight due to the use of biological reserves (Ferro-Luzzi and Branca 1993). Human populations have many strategies to deal with dietary seasonality, including food storage, trading relationships with other groups (Messer 1989), and scheduling of planting to yield staggered timing of harvests (Huss-Ashmore 1993). Seasonality in food resources also leads to seasonal changes in other economic activities (Harrison 1988), this leading to different physical activity patterns. The seasonal changes in activity may lead to changes in food needs during the year.

An example of the annual cycle of a group with a mixed subsistence strategy that combines pastoralism with crop agriculture is found among the Quechua Indians of the Peruvian altiplano (Figure 11–14). Like the Karimojong, the Quechua

Figure 11–14 Annual cycle of Quechua Indians of the Peruvian altiplano. (Reproduced by permission from M. A. Little and G. E. B. Morren, Jr. 1976. *Ecology, energetics, and human variability.* Dubuque, IA: Wm. C. Brown Company.)

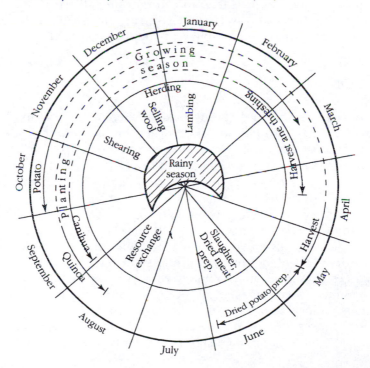

must adjust to seasonal dry and wet seasons. They differ from the Karimojong in their greater reliance on crops. Their cycle shows a concern for scheduling of activities and of harvest times, so as to spread these out in time (Thomas 1973, 1976). The wet season, from September through April, is a time for planting, tending, and harvesting crops, while the dry season is a time for drying potatoes and meat, slaughtering animals, and engaging in resource exchange with people from lower altitudes. Herding activities are carried out year-round, although there is seasonality to associated activities such as shearing and lambing. Storage techniques, involving freeze-drying of foods, allow for fairly stable diets throughout the year despite the seasonality of both harvests and slaughtering of domesticated animals.

Seasonal Change in Mode of Obtaining Resources Among Human Populations.   Some human groups do not need to change their types of resources but do have to change their strategy for obtaining them on a seasonal basis. For instance, Cree Indians of subarctic Canada use the same species of fish for food in both summer and winter (including lake whitefish, walleye, and northern pike), but the way in which they do their fishing changes (Winterhalder 1977, 1983). They use nets to catch fish in both winter and summer, but in winter the nets are set under the ice and checked fairly infrequently since the cold temperatures keep the trapped fish alive and fresh for long periods. In the summer, nets must be checked on a daily basis because fish will quickly die or otherwise become inedible if left in the nets.

There may also be seasonal changes in resource acquisition strategies among tropical populations. For instance, many foraging groups that reside in rainforest environments tend to concentrate gathering activities in the dry season, partly because travel is easier during this season (Moran 1982), although the resources may be available year-round.

CONCLUSION

Humans must balance effectiveness, efficiency, and risk in obtaining resources, but they must also balance short-term and long-term considerations. The large populations and complex technology of modern people have led to an enormous increase in resource use, with the rate of use often exceeding the rate of renewal of the resources in the environment. Through much of human history and prehistory the challenge has been to obtain a sufficient amount of various essential resources. We may be changing the ecological challenge to one of preventing overconsumption.

Clearly, calls for resource use strategies that maximize **sustained yields** are in order. This shift from optimizing short-term to long-term gains necessitates changes that go beyond human ecology; it will require creation of sustainable economic systems (Owen and Chiras 1995). Shifting to sustainable systems entails political and sociocultural changes (Bennett 1976) as well as a change in values concerning the relationship between humans and nature (Owen and Chiras 1995), at least for the majority of people now living on Earth. The question is whether humans can make these changes before long-term degradation of extensive areas of the biosphere takes place.

While observations that even human forager groups tend to opt for short-term gains are discouraging, public opinion polls in the 1990s showed that the majority of people support environmental efforts in general. Evidence for the success of environmental programs in developed countries is beginning to accumulate, with cleaner air and water as well as slowed rates of increase in per capita use of some resources having occurred between the 1960s and 1990s (Easterbrook 1995). Thus, contemporary human resource use presents us with a combination of optimism and concern. Modern humans are beginning to shift to a long-term view of resource use, but we must wonder whether the shift can occur quickly enough to counter our burgeoning population and expanding technological capacity to exploit the environment to our own detriment.

KEY TERMS

bands
community ecology
dispersion
ecological community
economics
foraging
growth forms
horticulture
intensive agriculture
labor-intensive agriculture
life form

migration
nomadism
nonrenewable resources
paleoecology
pastoralism
patch dynamics
phenology
photoperiod
phylogeny
physiognomy
primary succession

renewable resources
secondary succession
subsidized agriculture
succession
sustained yields
swidden agriculture
transhumance
vertical stratification
zonation

KEY POINTS

☐   Essential resources are those without which an organism cannot function; key resources are those that are difficult to obtain, are rare, or are costly.

☐   Resources in the human context involve consideration of the allocation of scarce resources, economics, political control of other people, and technology, among other factors.

☐   Renewable resources are those that are replaceable whereas nonrenewable resources are not.

☐   Cultural ecology posits that a group's means of subsistence is strongly related to other parts of the group's culture, the major means being foraging, pastoralism, horticulture, and agriculture.

☐   An ecological community is an interactive assemblage of species occurring together within a particular geographic area whose ecological functions and dynamics are in some way interdependent.

☐   The form and structure, or physiognomy, of an ecological community can be described on the basis of growth forms, life forms, stratification, zonation, horizontal dispersion, trophic levels, and phylogenetic composition.

☐   Functional aspects of an ecological community are affected by such abiotic factors as photoperiod and other periodic environmental changes (e.g., seasonal, temperature).

☐   Human group size is affected by relative amounts and distribution (patchiness) of resources (e.g., food, water), techniques of resource acquisition, and innumerable social considerations from kinship rules to military defense.

☐   Ecological communities tend to follow a fairly predictable pattern of changes in structure and function termed *succession,* that occurring in newly created environments termed *primary succession* and that occurring in environments that have been disturbed termed *secondary succession.*

☐   Paleoecology is the study of ecological communities based on their fossil record under the assumption that particular kinds of communities observed today in particular climates existed in the past in similar climates.

☐   Migration is the movement of individuals or their propagules (e.g., seeds) from one area to another.

☐   Nomadism is the migration of an entire social group to meet resource needs, whereas transhumance is a type of migration in which only a portion of the social groups moves, the other members remaining in permanent settlements.

☐   Nonmigratory human groups adapt to seasonal changes in resources through food storage, trading relationships, scheduling planting to yield staggered timing of harvests, and changing strategies for food acquisition.

12

Biomes and Human Populations

INTRODUCTION

There are two common ways by which human ecologists classify human populations. The first method, based on cultural ecology and discussed in the previous chapter, is by subsistence type. The notion is that there are commonalities among all human groups that rely on foraging, pastoralism, horticulture, or various forms of intensive agriculture, respectively. A difficulty with this classification scheme is the great diversity found within a given subsistence type. The Inuit and Mbuti are both examples of foragers, but it would be difficult to argue for similarities in their ecological adaptations.

A second means of classifying human populations is by the biomes in which they reside. **Biomes** are the large terrestrial ecosystems of the world that occur on major regional or subcontinental areas. Deserts, rainforests, and grasslands are examples of biomes, as are evergreen forests and deciduous forests. In classifying human populations according to their biomes, the idea is that human groups in a given biome must deal with similar ecological problems. They are faced with similar stresses and, perhaps to a lesser degree, similar resources. Again, the problem with classifying human populations based on biomes is the great diversity within a taxonomic category. Mbuti foragers and Hanunóo horticulturalists may both inhabit rainforests, but the specific characteristics of the Ituri rainforest of central Africa and that of Mindoro, the Philippines, are quite different, and the manner in which the two groups exploit their resources is markedly different.

Similar criticisms could be made of any classificatory scheme for human population ecology, but we must bear with a flawed classification if we are to attempt any generalizations. Therefore we must accept a biome classification as a heuristic tool for simplifying discussion of human ecology and not as a "real" taxonomy of human populations. This tool must be used with caution, however.

Before we undertake a brief discussion of the general ecological resource problems confronting human groups in different biomes, a general discussion of biomes is in order.

CHARACTERISTICS AND ORGANIZATION OF BIOMES

Although some ecologists recognize ten or more biomes, we will focus on six: tundra, boreal or coniferous forest, deciduous forest, grassland or savanna, desert, and tropical rainforest. This sequence more or less follows a southward direction from the North Pole to the equator (Figure 12–1). Further, some of the biomes tend to parallel lines of latitude, and in some instances, the same type of biome tends to be found within the same general latitudes around the Earth. The distribution of tundra and coniferous forest in the Old and New Worlds are particularly fine examples of this phenomenon.

In tall mountains, such as the Rockies, Andes, and Himalayas, the division lines between biomes are altitudinal rather than latitudinal (Figure 12–2). The particular biomes to be found at a given altitude also vary with latitude, a given zone occurring at progressively lower altitudes at progressively more northern latitudes. For example, the zone of Douglas fir–ponderosa pine lies from 675 to 2,000 m in the Cascade Mountains of the state of Washington, 1,350 to 2,300 m in the central Sierra Nevada, and 1,650 to 2,700 m in the southern Sierra Nevada of California.

The Role of Climate and Soil in Biome Distribution

Climate, the interaction of temperature and rainfall prevailing over relatively long periods of time, plays the most significant role in determining the location of biomes. As you well know, temperature is directly associated with latitude, it being colder to the north and warmer to the south in the northern hemisphere and the reverse in the southern hemisphere. Major wind patterns, which are associated with latitude, account in substantial measure for the distribution of precipitation. The type of soil also plays an important but less critical role in the distribution of biomes primarily because of the interaction with plants in the cycling of nutrients.

As we saw in Chapter 11 in the discussion of paleoecological studies on succession, the prevalent vegetational pattern of the past is not necessarily what exists today in a given place. One example, specifically in the context of biome distribution, seems appropriate.

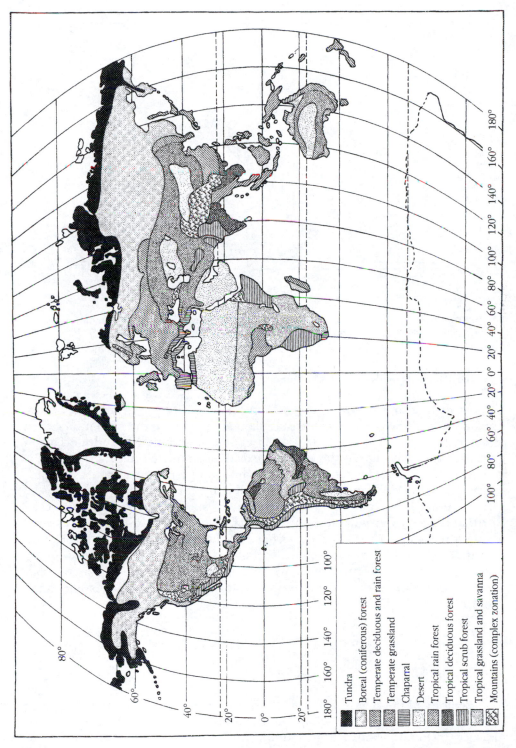

Figure 12–1 The major biome types of the world. (Figure from *Basic ecology* by Eugene P. Odum, Copyright © 1983 by Saunders College Publishing, reproduced by permission of the publisher.)

Legend:
- Tundra
- Boreal (coniferous) forest
- Temperate deciduous and rain forest
- Temperate grassland
- Chaparral
- Desert
- Tropical rain forest
- Tropical deciduous forest
- Tropical scrub forest
- Tropical grassland and savanna
- Mountains (complex zonation)

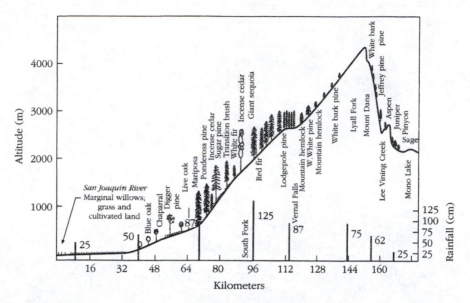

Figure 12–2   Profile of central Sierra Nevada showing altitudinal distribution of principal forest types. (Redrawn from B. O. Hughes and D. Dunning. 1949. *Pine forests of California*. Washington, DC: U.S. Department of Agriculture Yearbook.)

Biome Distribution in the Past

According to a major study by Watts (1979) on the vegetation of central Appalachia and the New Jersey coastal plain at the time of the maximum extent of the Wisconsin glacier (c. 15,000 years BP), grass-dominated tundra occurred in central Pennsylvania. At the same time, sedge-dominated tundra covered the higher mountains of central Appalachia, while southern Pennsylvania, New Jersey, and northern Virginia were dominated by forest tundra, consisting of spruce, dwarf birch, and tall herbs. Forests of spruce and jack pine covered North and South Carolina and northwestern Georgia. Broad-leaved trees were not the predominant vegetation anywhere on the coastal plain or in the Florida peninsula. These Pleistocene biome distributions are in striking contrast with the situation today (see Figure 12–1) wherein tundra is confined to arctic (and alpine) regions and broad-leaved deciduous forest is the prevailing biome in the eastern half of the United States.

THE MAJOR BIOMES OF THE WORLD

Tundra

Ecology of the Arctic Tundra.   **Tundra,** which means "marshy plain," lies largely north of latitude 60° North and constitutes about 20 percent of North America, including about 2.5 million km² in Canada, 2.0 million km² in Greenland, and 0.3 million km^2 in Alaska (Bliss 1988). It sits like the topping on an ice cream sundae over northern Europe and Asia (see Figure 12–1). Although there are considerable variations in climate, ice cover, soils, size of the flora, and composition of plant communities, arctic tundra can be characterized by the absence of trees, the predominance of dwarfed plants (5–20 cm high), and an upper ground surface that is spongy and uneven, or hummocky, as a result of freezing and thawing of this poorly drained land (Figure 12–3).

Also characteristic of the tundra is the presence of a permanently frozen soil **(permafrost)** at a depth of a few centimeters to several meters. The permafrost may be relatively dry in the case of coarse gravel or largely filled with ice in less porous soils. According to Bliss (1988), the thickness of the permafrost is about 400 m at Barrow, Alaska, 500–600 m in the Mackenzie River delta region, and 400–650+ m throughout the High Arctic. The permafrost line is the ultimate limit of plant root growth, but the immediate control is the depth to which soil is thawed in summer.

Tundra soils, above and within the permafrost, are quite poor in nutrients because of the slow rate of decomposition, the result of low temperatures. In addition to low temperatures, the warmest months averaging below 10°C, the coldest well below 0°C, precipitation is also low, the yearly average being about 12 cm and the wettest month being about 2.5 cm. During the winter months it is completely dark day and night (see Figure 11–10).

The vegetation consists of relatively few species of grass and sedge, the latter being characteristic of marshes and poorly drained areas, as well as substantial

Figure 12–3   Tundra biome: patterned ground near Point Barrow, Alaska. The polygons, 5 to 8 meters across, result from winter freezing; the cracks are filled with ice, which thaws at the surface in summer. Note where a tracked vehicle, a "weasel," has passed, lower left; the tracks of a "weasel" are nearly 2 meters at the outer edges and hence make an excellent scale in the photograph. (Photo courtesy of W. C. Steere)

areas of heath plants such as bilberries and dwarf huckleberries, low flowering herbs, and lichens. One of the most characteristic of the arctic plants is "reindeer moss," a lichen which is a symbiotic association of a fungus and an alga.

The principal herbivorous mammals are caribou (reindeer in Eurasia), musk ox, arctic hare, voles, and lemmings. Carnivores include the arctic fox and wolves. Characteristic birds are longspurs, plovers (which undergo tremendously lengthy migrations), snowy owls, and horned larks. Reptiles and amphibians are few or absent, and insects are rare, with the exception of blackflies and mosquitoes during the summer when they can be extremely abundant. For a comprehensive review of the North American arctic tundra, see Bliss (1988).

Ecology of Alpine Tundra. High mountainous areas, even in the tropics, resemble tundra in their general physiognomy and thus are referred to as **alpine tundra.** The latter differs, however, in the absence of a permafrost and in the presence of better drainage and generally a longer growing season. Mosses and lichens are less prominent, flowering plants more so (Figure 12–4). Lichens tend to be less abundant; sedges, dwarf willows, and grass more common. Elk, deer, and big horn sheep are found grazing in the summer; mountain goats, pikas, and marmots are also common herbivores. Birds and insects tend to be more common and diverse than in arctic tundra.

For comparison of arctic and alpine environments, see Ives and Barry (1974).

Figure 12–4   Alpine tundra in Yellowstone National Park. (Photo by E. J. Kormondy)

Humans in the Tundra.   The arctic tundra biome has been occupied by human groups for thousands of years. It presents formidable stresses in the form of extreme cold, blizzards, and long periods of light or dark on a seasonal basis. These stresses have also led to sparse amounts of plants, and thus a poor food resource base on land for human use. They have also made agriculture impossible. The absence of trees has also made fuel and building materials scarce resources. Arctic populations, such as most Inuit groups, have relied heavily on marine resources for food, clothing, and fuel. Traditionally, Inuit had diets that contained all needed nutrients (Draper 1977), although some have speculated that calcium and vitamin C levels may have been low (Moran 1982). Hunting and fishing are the major subsistence activities. Industrialized nations are now exploiting nonrenewable resources such as petroleum in arctic environments, and thus international economics has become an important consideration for residents.

Humans in High Mountains.   People living in high-altitude environments are faced with the stresses of diurnal cold and hypoxia as well as high levels of ultraviolet radiation and dustiness (Figure 12–5). They must also deal with severe resource problems: poor plant growth due to the physical stressors, soil erosion, aridity, and physical isolation from other peoples with whom trade could occur (Thomas 1979).

Figure 12–5   Alpine tundra near the summit of Mauna Kea, Hawaii. (Photo by D. E. Brown)

Most human populations in this biome utilize pastoralism as their major means of subsistence. People herd llamas, alpacas, and sheep in the Andes, while cattle and yaks are the mainstay of the herds of Himalayan and Tibetan populations. These populations generally have sufficient protein in their diets but may be limited by energy needs; this will be explored further in Chapter 14.

Many mountain ecosystems are characterized by vertical zonation. In fact, the transition between alpine tundra and boreal forest, to be described next, is characteristically rather abrupt, whereas in the arctic it is gradual and of wide dimension, up to 170 kilometers or so. By moving up or down the mountain, people can rapidly change the nature of their environment and therefore the available resources. Where people can utilize this diversity of resources, either through access to different vertical zones or through trade, mountains can provide a rich environment. This use of vertical zones characterized many of the ancient Andean urban cultures, including the Inca, allowing them to support fairly dense populations (Murra 1980).

Boreal Forest Biome

Ecology of the Boreal Forest Biome.   The **boreal,** or coniferous, **forest** biome is also referred to as **taiga** and as the "great north woods." It lies largely between 45° north latitude and 57° north latitude but extends south at higher elevations in the eastern United States and elsewhere. It occupies a substantial portion of northern Europe and nearly 80 percent of what was once the Union of Soviet Socialist Republics in Asia (see Figure 12–1).

The climate is cool to cold, with long winters and short summers, the average monthly temperature ranging from –10°C in winter to 15°C in summer, with more precipitation than in the tundra and occurring mostly in the summer, the yearly average being about 60 cm.

Although the soils are somewhat richer in nutrients than those of tundra, they are generally poor, the result of the movement of a large amount of water through the soil without a compensating upward movement by evaporation. Because the minerals move out of the reach of roots, only organic acids remain and thus the soil tends to be acidic. Because of the low rate of decomposition of the needle-shaped leaves of the predominant vegetation a deep layer of **litter,** the accumulation of dead plant and animal matter, is found throughout much of the biome.

The predominant vegetation is needle-leaved evergreen trees (Figure 12–6), the particular kinds varying regionally. For example, the predominant evergreens east of the Rocky Mountains are white spruce and balsam fir with red and white pine and hemlock dominant in the Great Lakes region. Black spruce is predominant west of Hudson Bay as are white and black spruce in Yukon and Alaska. Red spruce and balsam fir extend south to northern Georgia, where the latter is replaced by Fraser fir in the Appalachian Mountains. While the predominant vegetation is evergreen, deciduous trees do occur, especially quaking aspen, balsam poplar, and paper birch in burned areas in the eastern North American portion of the biome and on more moist soils. Understory plants include orchids, blueberry, and cranberry, among others.

Figure 12–6   Boreal forest biome: western red cedar and Alaska cedar on Skowl Arm, near Old Kasaan, Prince of Wales Island, South Tongass National Forest, Alaska. (U.S. Forest Service)

Mammals include moose, bear, deer, wolverine, marten, lynx, wolf, snowshoe hare, chipmunks, shrews, and bats, and there is a considerable variety of birds such as nuthatches, juncos, and warblers. Amphibians are relatively common in the southern parts, reptiles relatively rare. A wide variety of insects is found, among them pests of trees such as bark beetles and defoliating insects such as sawflies and budworms.

For further information on the coniferous biome, see Elliott-Fisk (1988) and Bonan and Shugart (1989).

Humans in the Boreal Forest Biome.   Human groups that reside in the boreal forest biome, like arctic dwellers, cannot successfully use agriculture and must deal with extreme cold and marked seasonal changes in light-dark cycles along with large accumulations of snow in the winter that can hinder mobility. Land resources generally tend to be much richer than in the arctic biome, with many plant and animal food sources and wood available for fuel and building material. Ecosystems in this biome tend to be quite patchy, with a mix of various woodland communities, muskeg, lakes and rivers, peat bogs, lichen areas, and so forth (Winterhalder 1977). Humans must adjust to this patchiness, as different resources are found in the different patches.

The temporal variability in boreal forests leads to ecological challenges for human populations. Besides dealing with temperature changes that are associated with seasonality of resource availability, people must cope with two seasons where travel is difficult and hazardous: breakup and freeze-up (Winterhalder 1983). These are the times of the year when surface water such as lakes and rivers begins to freeze or thaw, respectively, so ice is too thin to carry a person's weight. Since much of the area in this biome is some form of surface water, people may have difficulty obtaining resources during these seasons.

While many human populations in the boreal forest are foragers, some derive the majority of their subsistence from pastoralism. The Skolt Lapps of subarctic and arctic Scandinavia were, and some still are, traditional herders of reindeer. Historically the Lapps were hunters of reindeer, and even today their herds run free much of the time (Ingold 1980). In fact, the introduction of effective transportation devices such as snowmobiles has led to a decrease in the control people exert over their herds: owners of reindeer may see their animals only during periodic "roundups" (Ingold 1976). The Lapps engage in trade with other peoples, exchanging meat and skins for other needed resources. They are beginning to take on the characteristics of ranchers, as opposed to traditional pastoralists, since they are increasingly linked into national and international economic systems (Ingold 1980).

Temperate Deciduous Forest Biome

Ecology of the Deciduous Forest Biome. It is the **deciduous forest** biome that has been most affected by human habitation, primarily because within its confines the vast majority of the world's population exists and has existed for millennia, the consequence of its more favorable climate. As Figure 12–1 shows, this biome occupies most of the eastern half of the United States and Asia and nearly all of Europe.

Although the climate in the deciduous forest biome varies considerably from north to south and east to west, it is generally moderate with warm to hot summers, a definite winter period often characterized by snow and freezing in the north and coolness and rain in the southern portions. Annual average rainfall is between 80 and 150 cm. The warmer summer temperatures result in more rapid decomposition, so little litter accumulates on the forest floor and the soil is richer in nutrients than either the boreal forest or tundra biome.

Vegetation within this biome varies considerably, with maple, beech, oak, and hickory along with cottonwood, elm, and willow being dominant in different locations. Evergreens such as pine, hemlock, and cedar are also common in parts of this biome. Unlike the boreal forest biome, there is an abundance of shrubs and herbs growing under the tall trees, largely the result of the abundant solar radiation that strikes the forest floor in early spring before the canopy trees leaf out (Figure 12–7).

Displaced by humans over the years and now confined in restricted portions of the biome are large mammals such as black bear, moose, elk, mountain

Figure 12–7   Deciduous forest biome: 120-year-old stand of sugar maple, beech, and hemlock in Pennsylvania. (U.S. Forest Service)

lion, and wolf. Other more common mammals include deer, red and gray fox, opossum, raccoons, mice, squirrels, and chipmunks. There is a rich variety of birds as is also the case for amphibians, reptiles, and insects.

For further information on the deciduous forest biome, see Greller (1988).

Humans in the Deciduous Forest Biome.   In present times, human populations in this biome utilize intensive agricultural techniques for obtaining subsistence, usually in conjunction with an industrialized economy. This is certainly true for the eastern United States and Europe, and industrialization is increasing in eastern Asia as well. The use of intensive agriculture in the deciduous forest biome has a long history, making it difficult to identify examples of human populations that used other means of subsistence in this biome.

One of the last regions of the deciduous forest biome to utilize agriculture was the northeastern region of the United States. In fact, at the time of European contact agriculture was still primarily a supplement to foraging activities (Caldwell 1962). Archaeological studies have shown that agriculture was first used about 1,000 years BP. Before this, native Americans who resided in the U.S. Northeast foraged for deer, wild turkeys, turtles, fish, various nuts, and, for coastal groups, seafood (Kehoe 1981). In fact, hickory nuts were a favored food, and the decline of hickory in the northern area of the biome during a cool climatic phase beginning about 3,000 years BP may be associated with a human population decline. Nuts may have been of special importance because they could be stored for use in the winter.

The arrival of agriculture from the south as well as from the midwest, particularly of maize but also including squashes, beans, and sunflowers, led to human population increases. Some of the cultures at this time, such as the Owasco of New York and Pennsylvania, had fairly large populations. Large urban centers were not found in the region before European contact, and archaeologists continue to debate whether the region would have developed them as a consequence of increasing reliance on intensive agriculture (Caldwell 1962).

The conditions of the deciduous forest biome make agriculture possible where long enough growing seasons prevail. Water and soil resources allow intensification of agriculture to take place without perforce causing long-term environmental degradation. This does not necessarily mean that environmental factors in the biome have *caused* the development of intensive agriculture. We must look to complex factors of history, diffusion, and specific attributes of local cultures as well as to environmental elements to understand the association between this biome and intensive agriculture.

The environmental effects of the agricultural intensification and subsequent industrialization of this biome are more clear. Many of the native plants and animals have been displaced by human habitations with their attendant domesticated plants and animals, concrete, and pollution. It appears that all the news is not bad, however, as the eastern United States and Europe have seen increases in land area of forests at the end of the twentieth century. It is unlikely, however, that these new forests retain the characteristic structure of native forests before human disturbance.

Grassland Biome

Ecology of the Grassland Biome. **Grasslands** occupy a significant portion of the Earth's land surface (see Figure 12–1). The short-grass prairies or plains of western North America (Figure 12–8) and the tall-grass prairies farther east find their counterpart in the steppes of Europe and Asia, the llanos or pampas of South America (Figure 12–9), and the veldt or savannas of southern and eastern Africa. Whatever term is applied, this biome is characterized by the predominance of short or tall grass, the former where the climate is drier, coupled with flowering herbs and trees, particularly in stream valleys.

This biome is drier than both boreal and deciduous forests and wetter than deserts. Most of the precipitation occurs in late spring, summer, and early fall; temperatures vary, although below freezing in winter to very hot during the summer is very common throughout the biome.

Grassland soils are the richest in nutrients of all the biomes and hence the most fertile. Rapid decomposition of litter is a major factor in this richness; but the high rate of evaporation brings these nutrients closer to the surface and within reach of plant roots. These nutrients also counteract the organic acids in the soil, another factor in their high degree of fertility.

The dominant native mammals of grasslands are small burrowing herbivores such as prairie dogs, jack rabbits, and gophers. Among the larger herbivores

Figure 12–8 Grassland biome: short grass on the sand hills of north central Nebraska, near Valentine; note the presence of trees only in the valley. (Photo by E. Kormondy)

Figure 12–9 Tropical savanna in eastern Venezuela between Anaco and Maturin; the dominant grass is *Trachypogon*. (Photo by E. Kormondy)

are bison, pronghorn antelope, and elk in North America; yak and antelope in Asia; zebra, wildebeest, antelope, and gazelle in Africa; and giant anteater, armadillo, and capybara in South America. Carnivores include coyotes, wolves, and cougars in North America, and leopards and lions in Africa. The general absence of vertical stratification of the vegetation has the consequence of fewer kinds of birds, although there are rodent-eating hawks and various songbirds. Insects generally are more limited, but sometimes grasshoppers or locusts occur in great numbers and destroy tremendous areas.

For further information on grasslands on a global basis, see Coupland (1979) and Yang (1990).

Humans in Savannas and Temperate Grasslands.   **Savannas** generally refer to tropical and subtropical grassland ecosystems. Savanna ecosystems may be quite different from each other, but they all share a dry season that limits plant growth (Harris 1980), with this season lasting between 2.5 and 7.5 months. Savannas usually include some trees in locations where there is sufficient water to support them, but as just noted, grasses are the dominant plants. As we discussed in Chapter 1, savannas may have been of particular importance to humans because many scientists believe that much of our evolution (at least at the genus level) took place in such environments. Some paleoanthropologists suggest that open woodlands, as opposed to "pure" savannas, may have been more common habitats for early hominids (Potts 1996). Savannas of today are mostly exploited by pastoralist peoples or by ranchers.

Human adaptation to savanna ecosystems is usually dependent on the availability of water. Crucial considerations are the length of the dry season, the annual amount of rainfall, and predictability in time as well as location of rainfall. Where rainfall is sufficient in both amount and reliability people can raise crops as well as herds. Where rainfall is scarce and unreliable, people may be hard pressed to find pasturage for their herds. In general, people must adjust to seasonal variation in resources and to unpredictability in resources from year to year. Bad dry seasons may be balanced by particularly good wet seasons or vice versa (Little 1980). Perhaps the greatest adaptive challenge to human populations is uncertainty about future conditions.

Temperate grasslands today are the location of the world's breadbaskets, where the major cereal crops are grown. These crops are all forms of grasses such as wheat, maize, barley, rice, and oats.

Desert Biome

Ecology of the Desert Biome.   **Desert** is typically characterized by bush-covered land in which the plants are quite dispersed with much bare ground between them. Creosote bush, the dominant plant of the deserts of the southwestern United States, can be quite regularly spaced at intervals of 5 to 10 m (Figure 12–10). Deserts occupy about one-fifth of the Earth's land surface and are found on every continent (Figure 12–1). For size comparison, the vast

Figure 12-10   Desert biome: saguaro cactus and creosote bush in the Sonoran Desert in Saguaro National Monument, near Tucson, Arizona. (U.S. Forest Service)

Sahara Desert is about the size of the continental United States, and the great Gobi Desert of Asia is even larger.

Aridity rather than temperature best describes the climate of deserts. Precipitation is low and erratic, generally less than 25 cm a year, with most occurring in the winter months. At more extreme levels, the Sahara gets less than 15 cm of rain a year, and the central part of it and the desert of northern Chile receive little or none. From a temperature perspective, there are hot and cold deserts: hot ones include the Sahara, the Negev, and Arabian in the Middle East; the "outback" of Australia; and the Mojave and Sonoran of North America. The Great Basin Desert of North America and northern parts of the Gobi Desert are examples of cold deserts. In both hot and cold deserts, the temperatures of the air and soil show dramatic differences between night and day. Air temperature in a hot desert can be 15°C at midnight and 40°C at midday while the soil surface over that same time period can vary from 0°C to 65°C (see Figure 11–12)!

Soils are generally sandy and dry, and although decomposition can be very rapid, there is little litter because of the sparseness of vegetation. As a result there is little organic matter in the soil, and nutrients released by decomposition are often blown away. Nonetheless, the soils are relatively rich in nutrients although sometimes they are salty.

Plants survive in desert situations through a variety of adaptations including, among others, reduced leaf size and leaf dropping, both of which reduce water loss by evaporation; root systems that are close to the surface allowing access to any rainfall; life cycles in annuals that are attuned to accommodate to the short, moist period; and, in warm southern deserts, water storage in plants such as cacti, a property of their protoplasmic colloids. Plants such as algae and lichens actually dry out and reduce metabolic activity to a minimum but are able to restore quickly when water becomes available.

Animals, of course, are likewise faced with the stresses of temperature and aridity and have evolved a number of adaptations. These adaptations include drought avoidance through an impervious integument (e.g., snakes, tortoises, and lizards), water conservation through excreting a low-water-containing uric acid instead of high-water-containing urea, and reduction in direct water intake by conserving water produced metabolically. Most mammals tend to be nocturnal, and many burrow during the heat of the day. Some large desert animals have thick fur that insulates the body from the sun's heat; some like camels, which have no water storage places in their bodies, can lose 27 percent of their body water without damage, restoring this in a matter of minutes when water is available. Likewise, donkeys can lose up to 30 percent of their body water and restore it quickly when water is available. Because of their higher body temperature, birds are more tolerant of heat than mammals; nonetheless, they are most active early and late in the day, and even at rest are found in shady spots with their wings held away from their body. Insects are largely nocturnal, the most notorious among them being the desert locust which is prone to large outbreaks or "plagues" such as those recounted in biblical accounts of Egypt during the period of Jewish captivity and that which occurred in the Great Salt Lake Basin during the early Mormon settlements.

For further, general discussions of deserts, see Allen and Warren (1993).

Humans in Deserts. As just noted, in general, deserts are characterized by hot daytime temperatures and cool to cold nights. But it is the relative lack of water that constitutes the major limiting factor for biological populations, and therefore communities tend to be low in both density and diversity. Where water is present, either through rainfall or transport from other areas by surface or underground sources, plant growth may be extensive, and this may support dense animal populations as well.

Human adaptation to deserts is based upon the ability to locate and use water. This may entail learning where springs or other natural surface water sites are located. Adaptation may also involve learning where underground sources of water can be obtained, for instance through digging wells. With complex technology, humans can build aqueducts or pipes that bring water to desert areas. If large supplies of water can be utilized, deserts can support dense populations of humans quite comfortably. Where water is hard to find, as we will discuss in Chapter 16, human populations experience severe adaptive challenges.

Tropical Rainforest Biome

Ecology of the Tropical Rainforest Biome.   **Tropical rainforests** occur 10° or more north and south of the equator in Central and South America, central and western Africa, Southeast Asia, the East Indies, and northeastern Australia in addition to the oceanic islands generally within these same latitudes (see Figure 12–1). About 40 percent of the Earth's tropical and subtropical landmass is dominated by open or closed forest: of this, 42 percent is dry forest, 33 percent is moist forest, and only 25 percent is wet and rainforest (Murphy and Lugo 1986).

Tropical rainforests are among the most ancient of ecosystems. Fossil evidence in Malaysia and elsewhere suggests that tropical rainforests have existed continuously for more than 60 million years (Richards 1973). They hold considerable ecological significance because of their influence on climate, the global balances of carbon and atmospheric pollutants, and their highly diverse pools of species with considerable potential for new sources of food, fiber, and medicinal and industrial products (Jordan 1985).

In tropical rainforests, the annual rainfall exceeds 200 to 225 cm and is generally evenly distributed throughout the year. Temperature and humidity are relatively high and vary little throughout the year, the temperature averaging about 25°C.

Decomposition is very rapid, and the soils are subject to heavy leaching and thus tend to be acidic and nutrient poor. The potential nutrient loss is offset by the extremely rapid uptake by the plants with most of the nutrients being tied up in them. The high degree of leaching of the soils coupled with their peculiar chemistry often promotes a rocklike quality (laterite) when exposed to air, a quality that has prevented Western-style agriculture from being applied to the tropical forests.

Although tropical rainforests occupy only about 7 percent of Earth's land surface, they contain more than half the species of the entire biota of the world. The flora is highly diversified; for example, 300 different species of trees have been found in an area of 2.5 kilometers, a diversity unparalleled in any other biome. They are also typically well stratified vertically into a continuous canopy of trees 25 to 35 m tall, with an interrupted emergent layer of very tall trees with buttressed bases (see Figure 11–8). There is a well-developed understory of trees and shrubs especially near open areas. Epiphytic orchids and bromeliads, as well as vines, are very characteristic, as are ferns and palm. Most plants are evergreen, with large, dark green, leathery leaves.

As in the case of plants, there is a large variety of animals in tropical rainforests; for example, 20,000 different kinds of insects were found in a six-square-mile area in the Panama Canal Zone as compared with only a few hundred in all of France! Most of the animals, such as monkeys, flying squirrels,

iguana, geckos, snakes, and, of course, birds, live in the upper layers of the vegetation rather than on the ground. Ants, butterflies, moths, and grasshopper relatives are also common in the trees. Among ground dwellers are the akapi (a
primitive giraffe), anteaters, antelope, sloth, elephants, and rhinoceros.

There are numerous excellent references on the ecology of tropical rainforests, among the better ones being Collins (1990), Leith and Werger (1989),
and Whitmore (1990).

Humans in Tropical Rainforests.   Tropical rainforests present very different environmental challenges for human populations than other biomes do.
Rainforest communities are characterized by great diversity and are highly
structured with much verticality. People are exposed to humid heat and to parasites and other biological stressors. Plant growth is lush, and water is plentiful.
Food resources appear superficially to be abundant, but they may be unavailable
for humans or difficult to obtain. For instance, many of the edible resources are
high above the ground, making them difficult to reach for nonarboreal animals
such as humans. Later chapters will include discussions of generalizations made
by some human ecologists that it is difficult for human foraging groups in rainforests to obtain sufficient food energy or for forest horticulturalists to obtain
sufficient high quality protein. In many rainforest areas, foragers and horticulturalists have developed exchange relationships where protein and high energy
foods are traded (Peterson 1978; Hart and Hart 1986).

Soil nutrients are key resources for rainforest communities. Soils tend to be
poor in this biome because organic debris is quickly decomposed and taken up
by the extensive vegetation, and, as noted above, the rain leaches nutrients from
the soil, tending to create lateritic ("bricklike") soils that are hard and reddish
brown in color. The climax tropical rainforest has many vertical layers of plants
that help protect the fragile soil from the leaching effects of rain, but soils can
rapidly degrade when the forest is cleared. Swidden gardens often mimic the
tropical rainforest by containing several vertical layers of cultigens. Attempts at
clearcutting large areas of rainforest for intensive agricultural fields have frequently led to disaster, with soils suffering long-term degradation.

As in most other biomes, human activities have left their imprint on vast
areas of tropical rainforests that are currently considered mature. For example,
studies in Venezuela and Panama document that maize was cultivated in places
where a forest now stands (Roosevelt 1980; Bush and Colinvaux 1994).

CONCLUSION

The use of biomes as a classificatory device for community ecology has proved
useful. There are generalities within biomes as to climate and fundamental community structure. Biomes also serve a useful function for classifying ecological
challenges facing human populations. However, one must take care not to reify a
heuristic tool (or, in plain English, not to assume that a classificatory device that

we have created to simplify a complex world has somehow *become* the real world). While we believe that "the devil is in the details" and accordingly use many specific examples, we also believe that understanding requires generalization.

KEY TERMS

alpine tundra	desert	savanna
biome	grassland	taiga
boreal forest	litter	tropical rainforest
deciduous forest	permafrost	tundra

KEY POINTS

☐ Biomes are the large terrestrial ecosystems of the world that occur on major regional or subcontinental areas.

☐ The same type of biome tends to be found within the same general latitudes around the Earth; in tall mountains, the division lines between biomes are altitudinal rather than latitudinal.

☐ Climate plays the most significant role in the location of biomes, with soil playing a less critical role.

☐ Over time, biome distribution has changed as climate changed (e.g., tundra occurred where deciduous forest is now present).

☐ The major biomes are tundra, boreal forest (also known as taiga), deciduous forest, grassland, desert, and tropical rainforest, this sequence more or less following a southward direction from the North Pole to the equator.

☐ Tundra is characterized by the absence of trees, predominance of dwarfed plants, and an upper spongy ground surface below which is permafrost, or permanently frozen soil.

☐ Human populations in the arctic tundra biome face extreme cold, blizzards, and long periods of light or dark on a seasonal basis; they have relied heavily on marine resources for food, clothing, and fuel, with hunting and fishing being the major subsistence activities.

☐ Human populations in high mountains are faced with the stresses of diurnal cold and hypoxia as well as high levels of ultraviolet radiation and dustiness in addition to severe resource limitations; most of these populations utilize pastoralism as the major means of subsistence.

☐ The boreal forest biome, characterized by needle-leaved evergreen trees, is also known as taiga and the "great north woods" and occupies a substantial portion of northern North America, Europe, and the former USSR.

☐ Human populations in the boreal forest biome must deal with extreme cold, marked seasonal changes in light-dark cycles, large accumulations of snow, and alternately frozen and thawed rivers and lakes; many populations are foragers but some derive the majority of their subsistence from pastoralism.

☐ The deciduous forest biome is characterized by deciduous trees, with evergreens also present, and an abundance of shrubs and herbs under the tall trees.

☐ The vast majority of the world's population exists in the deciduous forest biome primarily because of its generally moderate climate; intensive agriculture, usually in conjunction with an industrialized economy, is the basis of subsistence.

☐ The grassland biome occupies a significant portion of the Earth's land surface and is characterized by the predominance of short or tall grass, the former where the climate is drier.

☐ Human adaptation to grassland ecosystems, particularly savannas, is usually dependent on the availability of water for pasturage; temperate grasslands house the world's breadbaskets.

☐ Deserts, which occur on every continent, are characterized by an arid climate and bush-covered land in which plants are quite dispersed with much bare ground between them.

☐ Lack of water is the major limiting factor for human and other biological populations, requiring an ability to locate and use sources of water on the surface or underground.

☐ Tropical rainforests are characterized by a heavy rainfall distributed generally equally throughout the year; a highly diversified, largely evergreen flora that is vertically stratified with a well-developed understory of trees and shrubs near open areas; and the most biologically diverse fauna of any biome.

☐ Human populations in tropical rainforests are exposed to humid heat, parasites, and other biological stressors; food may be abundant but difficult to obtain; foraging and horticulture are the main means of subsistence.

13

Ecological Energetics

INTRODUCTION

As we begin the discussion of resource acquisition we need to revisit some basic concepts concerning the flow of energy in ecosystems that were developed in Chapter 2 and then expand on them in sufficient depth to provide a foundation for their human implications.

The unidirectional flow of energy through ecosystems is one of the most fundamental of ecological principles. Energy from the sun is captured by chlorophyll (and certain other pigments) in green algae and plants in the process of photosynthesis. These solar energy capturers are collectively referred to as producers. Some of the captured energy is used for the producers' metabolism, development, and reproduction, and some is passed on to consumers, directly to herbivores and indirectly from herbivores to carnivores. Consumers also utilize some of their captured energy in metabolism, development, and reproduction; some of their energy, along with some from producers, is passed on to decomposers (bacteria and fungi). This unidirectional flow of energy is reflected in a food chain or food web. Concurrent with the flow of energy, nutrients are moved about in ecosystems but in cyclic rather than unidirectional fashion. Nutrients such as carbon and nitrogen are characterized by gaseous cycles, whereas others such as phosphorus and sulfur have sedimentary phases of long or short duration.

With this concise review of the two most fundamental ecosystem concepts and some basic terminology in hand we can now proceed to explore energy flow in ecosystems in more depth. In Chapter 15 we will explore nutrient cycling in more detail.

SOLAR RADIATION

Insolation, or **solar radiation,** produces direct heating of Earth as well as serving as the starting point of energy flow in ecosystems through the process of photosynthesis. The quality (i.e., wavelength, or color), intensity, and duration of insolation are all critical to biological activity.

Solar Energy

The sun is essentially a thermonuclear reactor that converts hydrogen into helium, a process that releases a tremendous amount of radiant energy in the form of electromagnetic waves. These emissions range from high-frequency, short-wave x-rays and gamma rays to low-frequency, long-wave radio waves. Although the energy is spread over this broad spectrum, 99 percent of it is in the ultraviolet to infrared range (wavelengths of 0.136 to 4.0 microns), and about half is in the region that encompasses the visible spectrum (0.38 to 0.77 microns), the portion most critical to life activities. This is an excellent example of adaptation of the latter to the former.

Of the sun's total output, only about one-fifty-millionth reaches the Earth's outer atmosphere, the rest being dissipated in space. And that which does reach the outer atmosphere falls differentially on the Earth's surface due to several factors. First, the Earth's rotation results in the diurnal variation we call day and night; second, because of the Earth's inclination of its equatorial plane to its orbital plane (see Figure 11–10), the flux of energy varies seasonally with latitude (see Figure 11–11); and, third, half or more of the solar energy is depleted as it passes through the Earth's atmosphere largely because of reflection from clouds and dust (amounting to about 42 percent) and absorption by gases such as ozone, oxygen, and water vapor or through diffuse scattering (a total of about 10 percent) (Figure 13–1). Quite obviously, cloudy days and the presence of smog also cut down the amount of solar radiation reaching the Earth's surface, and bright surfaces such as white sand reflect a considerable amount of energy back to the atmosphere.

Changes in Intensity and Quality

Intensity.   Temperature is directly related to the degree, or intensity, of solar radiation. The higher the degree of radiation, the higher the temperature; thus, changes in intensity of sunlight directly affect both temperature and biological activity. Likewise; since different portions of the electromagnetic spectrum have different energy levels, changes in the quality of sunlight also affect both temperature and biological activity.

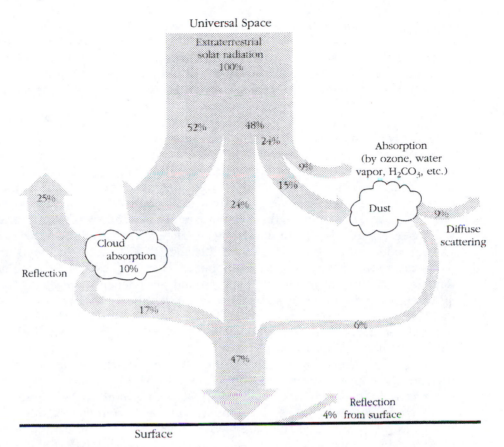

Figure 13–1   Energy intake at the Earth's surface at midday.

As shown in Figures 11–10 and 11–11, there are annual changes in solar intensity caused by the changes in the inclination of the Earth with respect to the sun. The key factor here is the angle of incidence. The lower the altitude of the sun, the smaller the angle of incidence and the longer the path of light through the atmosphere; this results in reduced intensity and consequently reduced temperature.

Quality.   The most dramatic changes in quality of sunlight occur as light penetrates water, during which it is reduced in intensity by absorption and by scattering. In pure water, the intensity of the red portion of the visible spectrum is reduced to about 1 percent at 4 meters, whereas blue light is reduced only to about 70 percent at a depth of 70 meters. Extinction is more rapid at the two ends of the spectrum (violet and red) than in the middle (blue). It is for this reason that deep, clear lakes such as Crater Lake in Oregon and the open ocean appear blue, since that is the color least absorbed and most reflected. Since natural waters often have suspended material, the spectral composition is modified, with the blue component being absorbed or scattered and the green remaining as the most penetrating, resulting in a greenish color to the water. Because photosynthesis is most active in the red-green section, and these wavelengths penetrate water less than blue does, it is in the upper portions of deep lakes and the ocean that most photosynthesis occurs and where most aquatic organisms are found.

Diurnal Changes.   Because it requires a great amount of heat to warm water (the amount of heat required to raise a substance's temperature by a given amount is technically known as specific heat), diurnal changes in temperature are minimal in aquatic environments, typically in the order of 1°C to 2°C. By contrast, temperature changes from night to day on land can be very considerable. The extensive range of diurnal temperature on the desert floor is a case in point (see Figure 11–12). In this case, the range at the ground surface is from 18°C at 3:30 AM to 65°C at 1:30 PM, or a change of 47°C. And, although the air temperature at 120 cm ranges from about 15°C to 38°C over the course of the day, the temperature at 40 cm below ground level remains constant at about 30°C. In such situations, desert shrubs are differentially adapted to withstand daily changes of considerable magnitude at the ground surface while simultaneously experiencing a less marked change a meter above ground and little or no change in their deeper roots.

Although the temperature extremes in this desert situation are quite marked, the temperature pattern at the ground surface interface is quite typical of terrestrial ecosystems. At the time of the warmest ground surface temperature (1:30 PM in Figure 11–12), the temperature above and below the ground decreases; by contrast, at the time of the coolest ground surface temperature (3:30 AM in Figure 11–12), the temperature above and below the ground increases.

Animals show a number of behavioral adaptations to living in these ambient temperature conditions (Figure 13–2).

Annual Changes in Temperature in Water.   Although daily changes in water temperature are minimal, considerable changes do take place over the course of a year, particularly in the upper waters of temperate aquatic ecosystems. During the summer months, the upper several meters of water are fairly uniform in temperature, averaging about 20°C; below this region, the temperature drops rapidly to about 10°C, followed by the lowest region, where the drop is less rapid, finally reaching a bottom temperature of about 4–5°C. During the fall (and again in the spring), the water "overturns," resulting in a quite uniform temperature from top to bottom of 4°C followed by an icing over of the lake during the winter. The winter season thus has an upper iced region at 0°C below which is a 4°C profile extending to the bottom. This property of water is the reason organisms don't freeze to death but can overwinter in lakes.

This temperature cycle in temperate aquatic ecosystems has profound effects on biological activities. Among the consequences are an altering of the

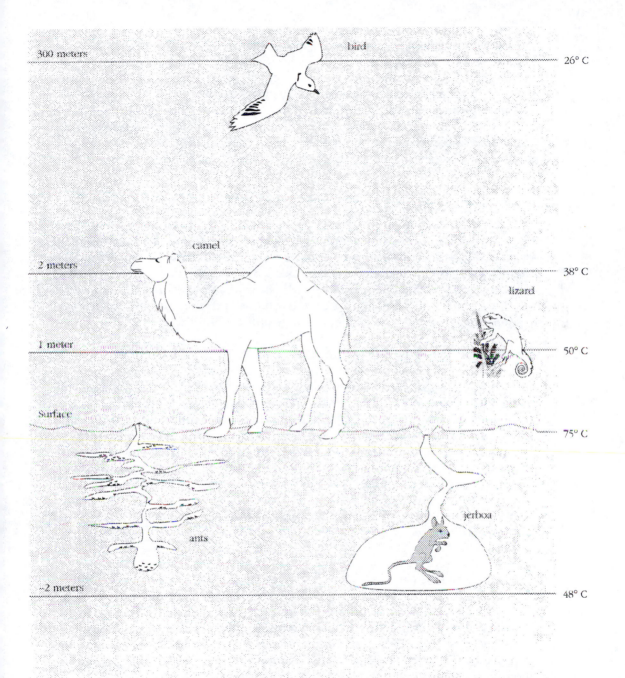

Figure 13–2 Temperature and animal distribution in the Negev Desert, Israel.

activity of organisms, especially those that are temperature-dependent; the absence of photosynthesis under the ice cover; and depletion of oxygen in the bottom region during the summer. Conversely, the spring and fall overturn results in the mixing and redistribution of nutrients that settled to the bottom during the winter and summer period.

In the deep ocean, temperature-induced mixing is largely limited to the upper several hundred meters, a phenomenon that largely accounts for the sedimentary stagnation of nutrient cycles that is characteristic of ocean water.

SOLAR ENERGY AND PRODUCERS

Since solar radiation is the primary agent in photosynthesis, the starting point for energy flow in ecosystems, it must be evident that diurnal, seasonal, and latitudinal changes in insolation must have concomitant effects on energy capture by producers. It is this radiant energy, whatever its intensity and quality, that is transformed to chemical energy in photosynthesis and then into mechanical and heat energy as it moves through consumers and decomposers.

Measuring Solar Energy Capture

In energy flow studies, the ecologist is interested in both the rate and amount of photosynthesis that occurs over a given period of time in an ecosystem. The total mass of organic matter that is manufactured in such situations is termed **production,** and the rate is **productivity.** (Obviously these terms have their counterpart in the field of economics.) Production and productivity at the producer level are known as **primary production** and **primary productivity,** respectively; at consumer levels the prefix *secondary* or *tertiary, herbivore* or *carnivore,* and the like are applied.

Measurement of primary production and primary productivity is founded on the photosynthetic equation:

$$6\ CO_2 + 12\ H_2O \xrightarrow[\text{chlorophyll}]{673\ \text{kilocalories}} C_6H_{12}O_6 + 6\ O_2 + 6\ H_2O$$

In words, 6 molecules of carbon dioxide plus 12 molecules of water are converted to 1 molecule of glucose (a carbohydrate) plus 6 molecules of oxygen and 6 molecules of water. This requires the presence of chlorophyll (or certain other photosynthetic pigments) and 673 kilocalories of energy (from the sun). A **kilocalorie** is 1,000 calories and is abbreviated kcal or C.

The photosynthetic equation provides the basis for calculating different components from the measurement of others. For instance, if the amount of carbon dioxide used over a given time period has been determined, the amount of carbohydrate (glucose) produced (usually the product of greatest interest) can be readily calculated. For example, if six units of carbon dioxide are used (or produced), one unit of carbohydrate has been produced. Likewise if six units of oxygen are generated, one unit of carbohydrate has also been produced.

One example, based on some of the earliest research on primary production, should make the basic point of the efficacy of the formula. In this case Edgar Transeau (1926) based his calculations on the harvest of 10,000 corn plants in which, based on the then known chemical composition of plants, he estimated the total amount of carbon to be 2,675 kilograms (kg). Since the carbon entered the plants only through photosynthesis, the amount of carbohydrate (glucose) was calculated to be 6,687 kg:

Molecular Composition		Molecular Weight		Metric Weight
$\dfrac{C_6}{C_6H_{12}O_6}$	$=$	$\dfrac{72}{180}$	$=$	$\dfrac{2{,}675 \text{ kg}}{X \text{ kg}}$

$$72X = 180 \times 2{,}675$$
$$X = 6{,}687 \text{ kg glucose}$$

To this value of net primary production Transeau added an estimate of the amount of glucose metabolized by the plants during the growing season and the amount of energy consumed in evaporation of the water produced in photosynthesis.

All this, however, goes beyond the basic point, namely that by assessing components of the fundamental photosynthetic equation, it is possible to develop estimates, some more refined than others, of production and productivity. Rather precise methodologies have been developed to determine the amount of carbon dioxide and oxygen involved over given time periods; discussion of these techniques is beyond the scope of this text and can be found elsewhere (e.g., Kormondy 1996). Very extensive application of these various techniques, particularly from about 1945 to 1980, have provided a substantial baseline for comparisons among ecosystems, natural and anthropogenic. Considerable refinements of these techniques over that time period have enabled ecologists to distinguish between **gross production/gross productivity** (the total over a given time period) and **net production/net productivity** (the total, or gross, minus that used for metabolism, growth, reproduction, and other life processes).

In addition, direct measurements of the amount of carbohydrate material produced can be made by such strategies as harvesting and weighing the vegetation at periodic intervals. This is the traditional agricultural method as reflected in such quantities as bushels of wheat or tons of sugar. Besides other limitations, the harvest method, however, fails to account for the amount of material/energy that may have been consumed metabolically by the plants themselves or by herbivores (e.g., insects, mice, birds) or decomposers. Nonetheless, the harvest method does render some approximations useful for comparing production from different ecosystems if the same harvesting and weighing techniques have been used.

Satellite remote sensing of production/productivity occurring in marine situations shows promise for ocean-scale studies (Platt and Sathyendranath 1988), and simulation models also show considerable potential (Reich et al. 1991, among others). Long-term production has been estimated in old, deep, isolated ocean basins (e.g., the Canadian Basin of the Arctic Ocean by MacDonald and Carmack 1991). In such an environment, the carbon compounds produced in the surface waters sink and accumulate in the bottom waters. Measurements of the current rates of photosynthesis, the rate of sinking of carbon-based compounds, and their total accumulation at various depths are then utilized to estimate the long-term production within the basin.

Efficiency of Energy Capture

By comparing the amount (or rate) of insolation to the amount of net or gross primary production an estimate of the efficiency of energy capture can be derived. According to a great many studies, it appears that the efficiency of energy capture in gross production under natural conditions is seldom more than 3 percent, although efficiencies of 6 to 8 percent have been recorded under intensive agriculture. Gross production efficiencies in fertile regions are approximately 1 to 2 percent but only 0.1 percent in infertile regions; the average for the biosphere as a whole is about 0.2 to 0.5 percent.

The validity of these numbers is subject to question for a variety of reasons, among them the use of yearly solar radiation values in temperate regions, wherein photosynthetic activity is largely concentrated in the April to October period; and the failure to adjust for the fact that only about half the wavelengths of visible light are captured in photosynthesis. In most cases this would tend to double the efficiencies.

In addition to these factors, the unit of measurement itself can greatly distort actual production efficiencies. For example, based on data collected from 30 sites (15 forests, 11 grasslands, and 4 deserts) in the continental United States, photosynthetic efficiency was highest for forests, being more than 100 times greater than for deserts (Webb et al. 1983). However, when this efficiency was evaluated per unit of foliage, the differences were much less, with a hot-desert site having the highest efficiency.

Finally, photosynthetic efficiency is typically based on the organs responsible for photosynthesis, and in the case of terrestrial ecosystems, on aboveground parts. Stanton (1988), however, has shown that 60 to 90 percent of the net primary productivity in grasslands occurs in the soil as roots. In tall-grass prairie, below-ground production is 48 to 64 percent of the total net primary production, in mixed-grass prairie 61 to 80 percent, and in short-grass prairie 70 to 78 percent. In some other environments, such as high mountains, most of the biomass is also below ground.

Gross and Net Productivity

The difference between gross and net productivity is, as already noted, a reflection of the amount of energy expended in self-maintenance, growth, transpiration (i.e., the evaporation of water), and reproduction. In temperate forests this expenditure reaches 50 to 60 percent, and in tropical forests, 70 to 75 percent. Based on a large number of studies, it appears that, in general, autotroph respiration accounts for 30 to 40 percent of gross production. Thus, only about 60 to 70 percent, and often less, of the initial solar energy captured generally results in net production. As a rough rule of thumb, it can be stated that net primary production is about half of gross production. Remember, however, that any "rule of thumb" does not necessarily apply in any specific situation.

Factors Influencing Production and Productivity

As you might expect, various factors influence the rate and amount of photosynthesis in any given ecosystem. In addition to the availability of basic chemical components of photosynthesis (carbon dioxide and water), changes in physical and biological factors exert an influence as do diurnal and seasonal changes in such factors as light, temperature, and moisture. An in-depth discussion of these many factors would take us too far astray, but a brief mention of a few will make the point.

Moisture and Soil.   When precipitation is more than 370 mm/yr in central U.S. grasslands, sandy soils with low water-holding capacity are more productive than loamy soils with high water-holding capacity; the opposite pattern occurs when precipitation is less than 370 mm/yr (Sala et al. 1988).

Nutrients.   Given the operation of the laws of the minimum and tolerance (see Chapter 6), it is not surprising that nutrients exert considerable influence on the rate and amount of productivity in ecosystems. For example aboveground net primary production was measured in a lodgepole pine (*Pinus contorta latifolia*) forest, a meadow dominated by western wheatgrass (*Agrophron smithii*) in southwestern Wyoming, and in short-grass (*Bouteloua gracilis*) prairie in northeastern Colorado (Hunt et al. 1988). In response to the addition of nitrogen in the form of ammonium nitrate (NH_4NO_3), production increased in the forest by 52 percent, in the meadow by 102 percent, and in the prairie by 81 percent over control plots in which no nitrogen was added.

Density.   Productivity in individual trees as well as forests, as might be expected, varies with density. For example, low, intermediate, and high density plots of red alder trees (*Alnus rubra*) (respectively 1,240, 4,068 and 10,091 trees/hectare) showed a total above-ground net production respectively of 8.83, 13.30, and 12.48 mg/ha (Bormann and Gordon 1984). When measured on an individual tree basis, a reverse trend was found, namely 7.07, 3.27, and 1.25

mg/tree. In other words, numbers of trees compensate for the reduced net production per tree in high density plots.

Maturity. The influence of age was evidenced in a plantation of Scots pine (*Pinus sylvestris*) in England where net production increased to a maximum of about 52×10^6 kcal/ha at about 30 years of age and leveled off thereafter (Ovington 1962). The seminal American ecologist Eugene Odum (1960) found that production in an old field in Georgia was highest in the first year after the field was allowed to go fallow and reached a plateau in the third year.

WORLD PRIMARY PRODUCTION

Perhaps the earliest estimate of world primary productivity was that by Justus von Liebig (1862), whose Law of the Minimum was discussed in Chapter 6. His estimate of world productivity at 500 g (dry matter)/m^2/yr was based on the assumption of the world's surface being covered by a moderately productive meadow. Whittaker and Likens (1973a) noted that this estimate was not too far from current estimates of the weighted mean production of the world, namely 320 g/m^2/yr.

Major summaries of estimates of world primary productivity in terrestrial and aquatic ecosystems have been made by a number of investigators. Among them, those by Whittaker and Likens (1973b) and Leith and Whittaker (1975) are the most comprehensive and detailed. Figure 13–3 depicts the average annual rate of production in kilocalories per square meter in the world's major ecosystems. The original data were expressed in grams of dry matter but have been converted here to energy units (calories).

Examination of Figures 13–3 and 13–4 and Table 13–1 shows that the terrestrial ecosystems with the highest productivity rates are in the tropics: tropical forest are nearly twice more productive than temperate forests and nearly three times more productive than coniferous ones. Data examined by Westlake (1963) extended this generalization to annual and perennial agricultural plants as well as to submerged and emergent aquatic plants in tropical and temperate conditions. In both instances, the tropical counterparts are about twice as productive. Annual production (rate of production per area of production) shows corresponding patterns: tropical forests—20×10^3 kcal/m^2; temperate forests—11.2×10^3 kcal/m^2; coniferous forests—4.8×10^3 kcal/m^2.

Although net annual productivity is higher in tropical ecosystems, the efficiency of conversion of gross to net productivity is lower. Box (1978) has shown that the percentage of gross primary productivity that results in net production is in the range of 40 to 50 percent in tropical ecosystems, whereas in temperate regions the percentage is in the range of 60 to 70 percent and reaches 80 percent in the Antarctic. The high temperatures of tropical environments result in plants expending more of their energy of gross production in respiration and transpiration (evaporation), thus reducing the amount of energy converted to net production.

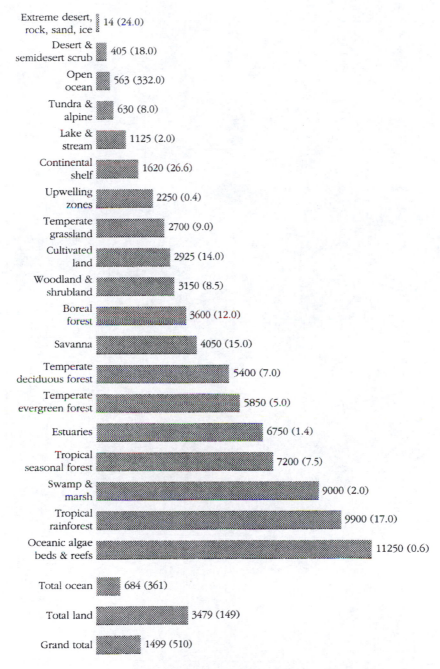

Figure 13–3 Annual average rate of net plant production. The number after the bar is kcal/m²/yr; the number within the parentheses is area in 10^6 km². (Derived from data in R. J. Whittaker. 1975. *Communities and ecosystems.* 2d ed. New York: Macmillan Inc.)

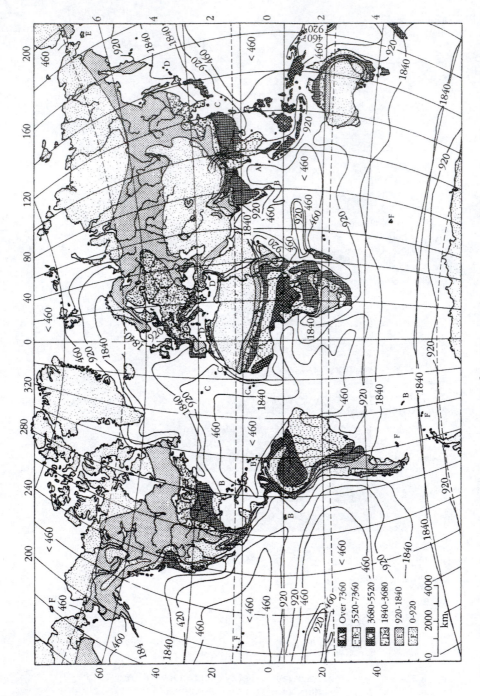

Figure 13–4 Annual net primary production in kcal/m²/yr. Mapped values are approximate and are incompletely adjusted for losses to consumers, decomposers, and substrate. (Redrawn by permission from a map in H. Leith and D. E. Reichle, eds. 1970. *Analysis of temperate forest ecosystems. Ecological Studies 1.* New York: Springer-Verlag.)

TABLE 13–1 Ranges of Net Primary Productivity (kcal/m^2/yr).

	Ranges		
Ecosystem	Low	Medium	High
Forest	1.0–1.3×10^3 Boreal forest (China) woodland (Kenya); chaparral (Mexico)	4.0–6.0×10^3 Mangroves (Burma); temperate deciduous forest (Mexico); broadleaf forest (China)	7.9–9.0×10^3 Tropical seasonal forest (Brazil); tropical rainforest (Brazil, Zaire, Indonesia)
Grassland	0.5–1.5×10^3 Stressed subtropical and montane formations (China, Sahel, Andes)	1.5–2.5×10^3 Temperate grassland (China, Turkey, Argentina)	2.5–3.5×10^3 Tropical grassland (Brazil, Sudan, India)
Cereals	0.15–0.3×10^3 Upper Volta (now called Burkina Faso), Nigeria, Zaire	0.45–0.6×10^3 Pakistan, Brazil, Mexico	0.75–0.9×10^3 Vietnam, China, Indonesia

Source: Data from V. Smil. 1979. Energy flows in the developing world. *American Scientist* 67:522–31.

Figures 13–3 and 13–4 also show that the open oceans and deserts are much less productive when compared with the ocean-land surface regions, such as the continental shelf, coral reefs, upwelling areas, and estuaries. Because the oceans constitute 70 percent of the Earth's surface and deserts about 28 percent of the land area, about 80 percent of the Earth's surface consists of the least productive ecosystems. Generally, low production in the sea is a function of nutrient limitation. The ocean-land interface, however, is rich in nutrients derived through runoff from the land or from upwellings of nutrient-rich sediments. In the desert, lack of moisture is the primary factor accounting for low productivity. Periodically, the availability of nutrients in the ocean or rain in the desert results in daily rates of production comparable to those of the higher producing regions. These are transitory situations, however; hence, as a result, the daily rate based on annual data is much lower.

Finally, although the large surface area of the sea compensates considerably for the low rate of production on a unit area basis (Figure 13–3), the total production of the sea (rate × area) of 2.5×10^{17} kcal/yr is but half that of the land, 5.2×10^{17}.

ENERGY FLOW THROUGH CONSUMERS AND DECOMPOSERS

Autotrophic Ecosystems

The classic study that laid the foundation for subsequent work in the energetics of ecosystems, or "trophodynamics" as he termed it, was conducted by a then graduate student at the University of Minnesota, Raymond L. Lindeman (1942). A detailed discussion of this seminal investigation would take us too far afield, but highlights will elucidate the principles of energy flow at the producer level and beyond.

Energy Flow in Cedar Bog Lake.   Figure 13–5 summarizes the fate of energy incorporated into the producers in Cedar Bog Lake, Wisconsin, the site of Lindeman's intensive study. The gross production of 111 kcal/cm²/yr is partitioned as follows: 20.7 percent is utilized in respiration (a combination of growth, development, maintenance, and reproduction); 13.5 percent is passed on to herbivores; 2.7 percent to decomposition; and 63.1 percent is not utilized and becomes part of the sediments. The accumulation of sediments eventually results in a bog being filled in from the bottom and being transformed gradually into a terrestrial ecosystem.

Ecosystem Energy and Thermodynamics

Similar fates of energy are demonstrated by herbivores and carnivores, that is, a portion is lost as respiration, some through decomposition and some not utilized accumulating as sediments. Figure 13–6 summarizes the energy flow in Cedar Bog Lake. What is presented is an energy budget in which all the incoming energy is accounted for at each step of the trophic transfer. Thus, Cedar Bog Lake (as well as other ecosystems) are in conformity with the **first law of thermodynamics,** namely, that the sum total of energy in a system is a constant, or perhaps more familiarly, that energy can neither be created nor destroyed.

Also, the amount of energy utilized by the ecosystem as a whole in respiration (26.4 percent) and not utilized at all (70.5 percent) can be ascertained. You can also see that more energy is expended progressively in respiration by herbivores and carnivores because of their locomotor activity, which results in the considerable expenditure of energy in activities used to get or produce their energy. Finally, the progressive decline in energy from producers through her-

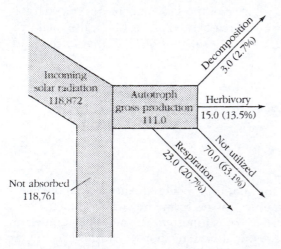

Figure 13–5   Fate of energy incorporated by autotrophs in Cedar Bog Lake, Minnesota, in gcal/cm²/yr. (Data of R. Lindeman. 1942. *Ecology* 23:399–418.)

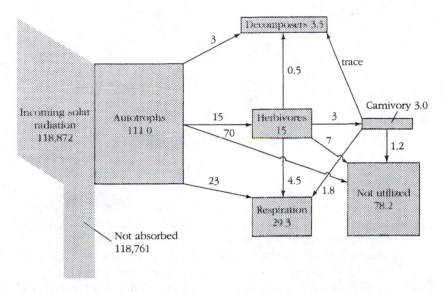

Figure 13–6   The energy budget of Cedar Bog Lake, Minnesota, in gcal/cm^2/yr. (Data of R. Lindeman. 1942. *Ecology* 23:399–418.)

bivores to consumers is evident with considerable loss as heat, the energy end product of respiration. This means that an ecosystem will "run down" if not supplied with a continuous influx of energy without which the dissipation of energy as heat leads to a loss of organized structure. This is the nature of the **second law of thermodynamics,** the tendency toward entropy or maximum disorganization of structure and maximum dissipation of utilizable energy.

Detritus Ecosystems

Autotrophic ecosystems such as Cedar Bog Lake depend directly on the influx of solar radiation. They are characterized by a dependence on energy capture by photosynthetic autotrophs and secondarily by movement of that captured energy through the system through herbivory and carnivory. A large number of ecosystems function in this way, and numerous herbivores, carnivores, and omnivores, including humans, are more or less completely dependent on such autotrophic ecosystems.

Other ecosystems depend less on direct solar energy incorporation and more on the influx of dead organic material, or **detritus,** produced in another ecosystem. Indeed, some are completely independent of direct solar energy and are instead completely dependent on the influx of detritus. These entities can be regarded as detritus-based ecosystems. In other instances, subcomponents of an ecosystem derive their energy entirely from that system's detritus through decomposition, as was noted in the foregoing discussion of autotroph-based ecosystems.

Decomposition.   Decomposition of organic material occurs in a variety of ways, among them leaching (i.e., water percolating through organic material and dissolving some of its mineral content) and fragmentation (i.e., the pulverizing of material into small particles). However, it occurs primarily through the activity of organisms that may, in turn, facilitate both leaching and fragmentation. The primary agents of the final stages of decomposition are microbes (bacteria largely on animal tissues and fungi on plant tissues) through the process of their own metabolism. To meet their metabolic needs, decomposers release digestive enzymes to their immediate environment; these enzymes break down complex foodstuffs into simple compounds that can be readily absorbed by the fungus or bacterium.

Numerous studies of energy flow in decomposition and detritus-based ecosystems have demonstrated that the detritus chain cannot be disregarded. The considerable amount of evidence that has been accumulating strongly indicates that the detritus chain is of greater importance in energy flow in many ecosystems than are herbivorous/carnivorous/omnivorous grazing chains with as much as 90 percent of the energy flow in various communities being through detritus feeders. In addition and importantly, the decomposition of detritus liberates stored nutrients, thereby making them available for the feeding of autotrophic productivity and, in turn, initiating the cyclic turnover of these nutrients.

Hubbard Brook Experimental Forest.   One of the most refined ecosystem studies is the work of Gene Likens and F. Herbert Bormann, who have carried out extensive and long-term studies on the Hubbard Brook Experimental Forest, a sugar maple, beech, and yellow birch forest in New Hampshire (Likens et al. 1977). Although the major focus of their studies was nutrient flow, the flow of energy through detritus also received emphasis (Gosz et al., 1978).

As Figure 13–7 shows, annual net primary production in the Hubbard Brook Forest is 45 percent of gross production, 55 percent being lost in the forest's metabolism. Of the annual net production (4,680 kcal/m^2/yr), 75 percent (3,481 kcal/m^2/yr) enters the grazing and detritus pathways; grazing, however, is insignificant, amounting to only about 1 percent a year. The remaining 25 per-

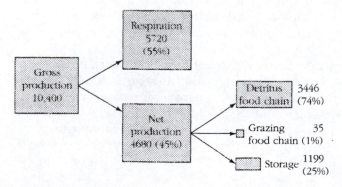

Figure 13–7   Fate of energy in the Hubbard Brook Experimental Forest. (Data of Gosz et al. 1978. *Scientific American* 238:93–102.)

cent of net annual production (1,199 kcal/m^2/yr) is stored above and below ground as accumulated litter and unused detritus.

An Energy Flow Model

The flow of energy in an ecosystem can be generalized in the form of a model (Figure 13–8). In this model an equal flow of energy is assumed to come from the two primary sources, photosynthesis and the import of living and dead organic matter. To apply the model to any given ecosystem, the amount of shading would be expanded or contracted to correspond to the energy recruitment by organic matter or by photosynthesis, the width of the energy channels, and the dimensions of the trophic-level boxes. For example, in a largely autotrophic ecosystem, the shading representing the import of organic matter would be considerably contracted, whereas in the instance of Cedar Bog Lake the storage box would be very large.

One of several alternative methods of graphically illustrating energy flow in ecosystems, most notably human ecosystems, is discussed in Chapter 14. This method simplifies some aspects of energy flow, permitting a sharper focus on energy production and expenditure of populations. As you will see, this focus has utility for studying energy flow in human populations.

Because of the complexities involved in garnering the information needed to construct an energy flow model for any given ecosystem, few ecosystems have been studied in detail. Instead, ecologists have turned increasingly to computer simulations and laboratory analyses that have allowed the development of several significant generalizations about energy flow that agree fairly well with available field data.

From studies based on laboratory populations, American ecologist Lawrence Slobodkin (1960) suggested that the **gross ecological efficiency,** that is, the percent of energy transferred from one trophic level to the next, was in the order of 10 percent. Thus, if there are 100 calories of net plant production, only about 10 calories of net production would be expected at the herbivore level and only 1 calorie at the carnivore level. Various studies to date show a range in gross ecological efficiency from 5 to about 30 percent, averaging about 10 percent from producer to herbivore and 15 percent from herbivore to carnivore. Any generalization about efficiency, however, is still uncertain largely because of the paucity of comprehensive studies of energy flow in a variety of ecosystems.

FOOD CHAINS AND FOOD WEBS

Implicit in the diagrams and discussions of energy flow either through herbivory/carnivory or through detrital decomposition is a connectedness or linkage of organisms dependent for their very existence on other organisms in the next lower trophic level. Such linkages are usually referred to as *food chains,* a

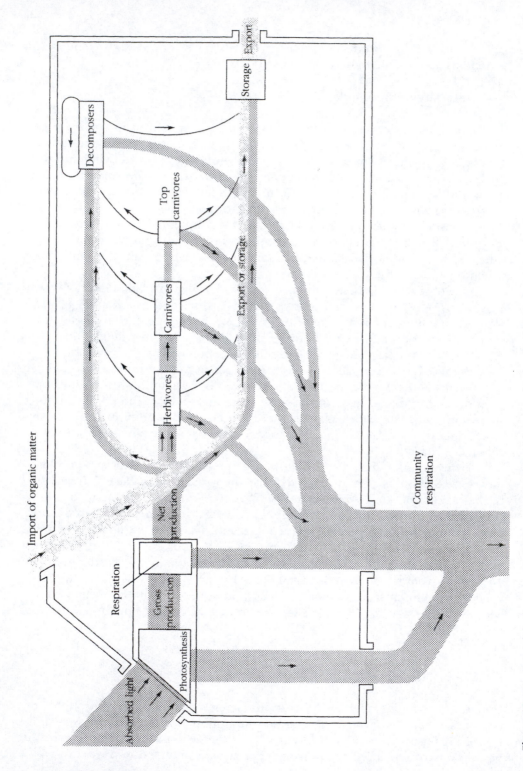

Figure 13-8   A model of energy flow. (Figure adapted from *Fundamentals of ecology, Second Edition* by Eugene P. Odum, copyright © 1959 by Saunders College Publishing and renewed 1987 by Eugene P. Odum and Howard T. Odum, reprinted by permission of the publisher.)

simple version of which is the model of energy flow from reindeer moss to reindeer to humans (Figure 2–1). A food chain is a sequence of energy links or trophic levels that starts with a species that eats no other species and ends with a species that is eaten by no other species.

More often than not, such simple food chains are oversimplified versions of the reality of feeding relationships. Instead, there are often multiple and interconnecting pathways as well as numbers of different species involved at each trophic level. These complex pathways resemble a web rather than a simple chain and are referred to as *food webs* (Figure 13–9). Since several species may occur in each of the trophic levels, the collection of organisms that feed on

Figure 13–9   The food web from the island of St. Martin in the northern Lesser Antilles consisting of 44 species, eight trophic levels, and a multitude of linkages with detritus (M) and fruit and seeds (Q) at the bottom and kestrels (b), nematodes (B, f, and o) a, and thrashers (l) at the top. (Reproduced by permission from L. Goldwasser and J. Roughgarden. 1993. *Ecology* 74:1216–33.)

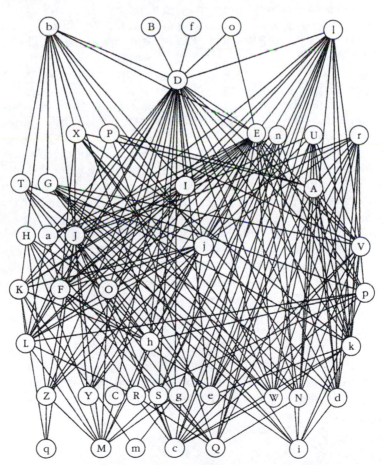

a common set of organisms and are fed on by another common set of organisms are referred to as a **trophic species** (Briand and Cohen 1984).

Length of Food Chains and Webs

Also implicit in the flow of energy through an ecosystem is that the number of trophic levels is limited because of the decreasing availability of energy resulting from the inefficiencies in energy transfer from one trophic level to the next. If this be the case, then one seemingly intuitive hypothesis concerning food chain length that has been advanced is that chains should be longer in ecosystems with higher primary productivity. This hypothesis is referred to as the "energetic hypothesis" (Hutchinson 1959). Based on a review of studies on impoverished to highly productive systems, however, Pimm (1982) concluded that there is no evidence to support the energetic hypothesis.

A second hypothesis concerning food chain length is known as the dynamical stability hypothesis and was advanced from theoretical or mathematical models by Pimm and Lawton (1978). Although the technical aspects of this hypothesis are beyond our consideration, the gist is that food chains should be longer in ecosystems that are not subjected to disturbances by catastrophic events such as fire, flooding, widespread disease, etc. The idea is developed from some mathematical models in which, once disturbed, ecosystems with longer chains take longer to return to equilibrium so that webs with longer chains may be less likely to persist in nature.

In their review of 113 community food webs from natural communities, Briand and Cohen (1987) found no evidence to support either the energetic or the dynamic stability hypotheses. They did conclude, however, that the spatial dimensions of an ecosystem are related to food chain length, with three-dimensional environments having longer food chains than two-dimensional ones. Two-dimensional environments were regarded as essentially flat, like a grassland, the tundra, a sea or lake bottom, a stream bed or the rocky intertidal zone; three-dimensional environments were regarded as solid, like a forest canopy or the water column of the open ocean.

Of the 113 natural food webs reviewed by Briand and Cohen (1987), the smallest food chain length was 2 and the maximum 10, the more general trend being 3 to 5. With respect to the number of trophic species, the numbers ranged from 3 to 48, the more general being about 15 to 20. The actual number of links of all the chains in the webs ranged from 2 to 138, with the general range being 20 to 30.

Although there is considerably more that could be discussed about the basic principles of energy flow in ecosystems, it is now timely to turn to the application and implications of these principles in human ecosystems, the subject of the next chapter.

KEY TERMS

autotrophic ecosystem
detritus
first law of thermodynamics
gross ecological efficiency
gross production
gross productivity

insolation
kilocalorie
net production
net productivity
primary production
primary productivity

production
productivity
second law of
  thermodynamics
solar radiation
trophic species

KEY POINTS

- ☐ Only a small portion of insolation, or solar radiation, reaches the Earth's outer atmosphere, and half of that is depleted by the time it reaches the Earth's surface.

- ☐ Changes in the intensity (degree) and quality (wavelength) of solar radiation directly affect temperature and biological activity.

- ☐ Diurnal changes in temperature are minimal in aquatic environments but can be considerable in terrestrial environments; annual and seasonal temperature changes in both environments can be considerable depending on latitude and altitude.

- ☐ Measurement of primary production and primary productivity is based on the photosynthetic equation, a reaction involving carbon dioxide and water in the presence of chlorophyll or other photosynthetic pigments that produces glucose, oxygen, and water.

- ☐ The efficiency of gross primary production under natural conditions is seldom more than 3 percent and is about 0.2 to 0.5 percent globally.

- ☐ Net primary production is about half of gross primary production, respiration accounting for the difference.

- ☐ The rate of photosynthesis is influenced by both physical (e.g., moisture, light, nutrients) and biological (e.g., density, maturity) factors.

- ☐ Tropical forests are nearly twice more productive than temperate forests and nearly three times more productive than coniferous forests; total production of the sea is about half that of land.

- ☐ Conforming to the first law of thermodynamics, the sum total of energy in an ecosystem is a constant, the energy neither being created nor destroyed, and all of it being accounted for.

- ☐ Ecosystems must be supplied with a continuous influx of energy to counter the tendency toward entropy embodied in the second law of thermodynamics.

- ☐ Autotrophic ecosystems depend directly on the influx of solar radiation, whereas detritus ecosystems depend on the influx of dead organic material (detritus). As much as 90 percent of the energy flow in ecosystems is through detritus feeders.

☐   A food chain is a sequence of energy links that starts with a species that eats no other species and ends with a species that is eaten by no other species. Food chains have interconnecting pathways with other food chains, resulting in a web of feeding relationships.

14

Human Adaptation and Energy Flow

In order to survive, human populations must "tap into" natural systems of energy flow in the ecosystems in which they reside. Energy is a major component of the diet, but human energy needs go far beyond dietary concerns. In fact, most human activities are related to energy in some manner (Harrison 1982). Many anthropologists, led by Leslie White (1959, 1969), have suggested that our species' increasing ability to capture and utilize energy has been the major factor in causing the changes between modernized societies and hunter-gatherer groups.

As shown in Chapter 13, energy can be measured in standardized units (frequently in terms of calories or joules), which allows the calculation of energy production and expenditure quantitatively. Because of the pervasive nature of energy concerns in human life (Odum and Odum 1976), ecologists employ it as a "currency" of resource use by which inputs and outputs of resource use can be measured (Ulijaszek 1992). Anthropologists and other social scientists have attempted to measure the value of human resources and the value of the labor required to obtain them by using monetary measures. However, the use of energy as a currency has the advantage of being a stable unit rather than one that varies depending on human values of relative worth (Baker 1979). Also, the use of energy allows comparisons with the ecology of nonhuman organisms.

Energy flow studies in human groups examine how the population gets all the energy it needs—including food and fuel—from the environment. In this regard, humans are much like any other living population, except for the fuel component. Measures of energy in human populations are of three types (Thomas 1974), namely, its production, expenditure, and consumption. **Energy production** measures how much energy can be obtained by the group and is equivalent to secondary production as measured for other consumers in food chains. **Energy expenditure** measures how much energy the group uses, or expends, in its various activities. This is usually quantified by physiological measurements of oxygen consumption, which is closely correlated with energy expenditure because, in the long term, human energy expenditure is based on aerobic metabolism (see Chapter 8). **Energy consumption** refers to how much energy the group uses, whether through their dietary intake or fuel consumption. This is based in part on nutritional intake studies, as well as by measuring fuel use.

MEASURING ENERGY USE IN HUMAN POPULATIONS

Since human energetics is a currency of resource use, human ecologists have devoted much time to measuring how humans obtain and use energy. They use different techniques to measure energy production, expenditure, and consumption, respectively.

Measurement of Human Energy Production

Energy production is usually measured for a group as opposed to an individual, as most people cooperate in obtaining energy resources. The group may refer to a household, a procurement group, or to some other social unit. Per capita energy production can be obtained by averaging group production values, but the use of multiple groups by an individual and instances of unequal sharing make these calculations difficult. Group values of production are determined by weighing all food and fuel obtained in a given amount of time. Reasonably accurate tables have been constructed listing energy values of food and many fuel sources by weight. The energy per weight values are obtained by measuring the amount of heat released when a known amount of the substance is completely burned and the total amount of energy released is measured. Many of these tables are computerized, allowing relatively easy conversion of resource weights into energy units such as kilocalories. In general, 1 gram of protein releases 4 kcal, 1 gram of carbohydrate also produces about 4 kcal, and 1 gram of fat contains 9.1 kcal of energy (Edholm 1967).

Human ecologists must account for seasonal variability in energy production in their measurements. Observations on a population in one season cannot be extrapolated to a full year. Thus, studies on human energetics conventionally follow a full year of activity. One must also account for changes over longer periods because populations experience variability in energy production from year to year.

Since our focus is always on environmental problems facing human populations, in this case the focus of interest is on whether energy production is too low to sustain a population's needs. In some cases populations have chronic, sustained problems with energy production, although it is more common for problems to occur in a particular season or an unusually bad year.

Measurement of Human Energy Expenditure

To assess human energetics we need to understand the output side of energy use as well as measuring input through energy production. The energy used by human populations is measured by the actual energy released through physical activities. This involves measuring the amount of energy required for each type of physical activity in which members of the population engage. Once energy expenditure per time is known for an individual—or, more commonly, for "typical" individuals in a given population—energy expenditure can be calculated based upon time-motion studies in which the amount of time spent at a task is multiplied by the average energy use per time for that task.

In practice it is very difficult to determine the amount of energy expended for a specific type of activity. In most studies the amount of molecular oxygen (O_2) consumed (i.e., the amount chemically combined with carbon and hydrogen) by people in doing a task has been used to measure expenditure. People engage in a timed activity while exhaling into a specially constructed bag or a similar container for the air. The air is then analyzed for its total volume and its oxygen content, the difference in oxygen content between inspired air (normally about 20.93 percent) and expired air then being computed. The product of total volume of air expired times the computed difference in oxygen content of inspired versus expired air equals the oxygen expenditure of the person over the time period of the activity. Since in the long run all human energy expenditure involves oxidation of food, oxygen expenditure can be converted into energy expenditure using appropriate formulas. The precise relationship between oxygen and energy expenditure is dependent on the proportion of fat, carbohydrates, and protein in the diet (Ulijaszek 1992).

Other methods for measuring energy expenditure include monitoring heart rate and the use of nonradioactive isotopes. For moderate physical activity levels, there is a close, linear relation between heart rate and energy expenditure as measured by oxygen consumption. One can therefore estimate expenditure by using lightweight pulse monitors on people while they do their normal activities. The monitors either store heart rate values at timed intervals or broadcast readings to a receiving unit that stores the values. The relation between heart rate and oxygen consumption must be determined for each individual under study, however, because of the great interindividual variability in this relationship (Åstrand and Rodahl 1986).

Another method of measuring energy expenditure is to have people drink water containing known amounts of nonradioactive isotopes of helium (deuterium) and oxygen (oxygen-18). The deuterium rapidly mixes into body water, while the oxygen-18 is mixed into the body's water and bicarbonate pools (Schoeller 1983; Ulijaszek 1992). The isotopes are excreted by the body at different rates, with the deuterium leaving as water and the oxygen-18 leaving combined in both water and carbon dioxide. The difference in the rate of loss of the two isotopes is related to the amount of carbon dioxide produced by the individual. This, in turn, is related to energy expenditure, since aerobic metabolism breaks down food into carbon dioxide and water.

Once people have been measured for energy expenditure in given activities, the human ecologist is faced with the daunting task of performing time motion studies on individuals to note how much time they spend at each task. In essence, this consists of following people around during their normal activities with a stopwatch and notepad, attempting to cause as little disruption as possible. It also requires that individuals be followed several times to allow for seasonal, weekly, or other differences in their daily patterns of activity. Many different people need to be measured because of interindividual differences in activity patterns, with special care taken to include people from different sex and age groups as well as from varying occupational or other social groups in the population. Admittedly, this is a very cumbersome procedure.

Measurement of Human Energy Consumption

Measurement of the energy consumed by individuals in the population generally refers to the caloric value of the diet for all members of the population in a given time period and hence amounts to a dietary survey of the population. To get precise values, all foods eaten by an individual in a given time period must be separately weighed before consumption. The caloric value of each food is then derived from nutritional tables, as discussed for energy production measurements. In practice, this is a harrowing task for both the human ecologist and the individual under study. People often like to mix up their foods before eating them and rarely like to be constantly interrupted for serial weighings of their plates as they attempt to eat. This method is often so disruptive that people change their eating habits to accommodate the measurements, thus making the measurements invalid.

Estimates of food consumption can be made at the household level by means of the "larder method," which involves weighing all foods in the household separately by type at any given point of time and then lurking outside the household to measure any incoming or outgoing food (including scraps in garbage), then weighing all food left in the household at the end of the measurement period. One then computes the difference between "incoming" food and original food stores on the one hand and "outgoing" and remaining food on the other hand to derive household consumption of food. Of course, one must still account for food eaten by household members outside the household area and for food eaten by nonmembers who visit the household.

More indirect methods of estimated energy consumption use self-reports by people of what they have consumed. People estimate portion sizes they have eaten of specific foods. These self-reports may be done prospectively, using so-called "diary" methods, or retrospectively by use of recall methods. There are difficulties with both types of self-reporting, including accidental—and some-times purposeful—lapses of memory, and difficulties with estimates of portion size and of proportions of ingredients in mixed dishes. One strategy has been to use "food frequency" recall surveys in which people estimate how frequently they eat each type of food over a long period of time (Medlin and Skinner 1988). For instance, people may be asked: "Over the past year, about how frequently have you eaten [some specific food]?" Possible answers span from never to monthly to several times per day, with many in-between choices. People from the same population will also be surveyed to ascertain average serving size of the specific foods, so total intake can be estimated.

Another method for assessing energy consumption is to simply weigh peo-ple at two points in time. A weight difference signifies a difference between energy consumption and energy expenditure over the time period between measurements, and thus one can be computed if the other is known (Himes 1991). This method is not very precise, but it is useful in identifying significant negative or positive energy balances in human populations.

To make matters more difficult, dietary studies should cover several days to assure the representativeness of the period under study, and in many popula-tions it is necessary to sample periods throughout the year to allow for seasonal changes in diet (Ulijaszek and Strickland 1993). Energy consumed by nonhumans, such as domesticated animals and machines, must also be considered. Energy consumption by domesticated animals is based on assessment of the energy con-tent of dietary items, much as this assessment is done for humans. Energy use by machines or fires is computed by measuring fuel use and converting to energy units based on the energy content per weight or volume of the specific type of fuel. Where energy is derived from nonfuel sources such as wind and water power, appropriate measurements must be made; while these are specific to the type of energy source, all can be converted into the same units of measurement (Grathwohl 1982).

Energy Efficiency

There are various means by which **energy efficiency** is calculated. In the previous chapter gross ecological efficiency was defined as the percentage of energy transferred from one trophic level to another. For human populations, energy efficiency is more commonly computed from the energy produced divided by energy expended in a given time period or for a given activity. Effi-ciency is a measure of *net* energy gain for a given activity; that is, it measures how much energy one has to expend in order to get some resource that contains energy. One can also calculate energy efficiency for the population as a whole by dividing total energy production by total expenditure over a given time period. This is usually computed for a year to allow for seasonal differences in energy production and use.

There is enormous variability in the energy efficiencies of various human subsistence systems. One must be careful to include all sources of energy expenditure in deriving efficiencies, however, For instance, for corn (maize) raised in some regions of the United States, there is a return of nearly 1,700 kcal for every single kcal of human energy expenditure; this may represent the highest efficiency in yield for human subsistence activities (Baker 1988a). The figure is misleading, however, because it does not include the energy expenditure from fossil fuels that are used in farm machinery as well as in fertilizers and pesticides. For instance, tractors in the United States consumed 21 gallons of gasoline and 20 gallons of diesel fuel per capita in 1975 (Dorf 1978). Odum (1971) estimated that about 60 kcal of energy from fossil fuels is applied each day to a square meter of intensively worked cropland, and about 100 kcal of energy per day is produced from that land area. Intensive, mechanized agriculture is therefore frequently less efficient than more extensive forms of agriculture, although yields per amount of human physical effort are much higher in the former (Pimentel et al. 1973; Smith 1991).

There is some difficulty in including energy costs of fossil fuels in human energy flow systems. Fossil fuel energy is valued, for the most part, for its ability to save physical labor costs as opposed to its actual energy value (Winterhalder 1977; Smith 1991). The human ecologist must decide what focus the energy flow study should have. If the interest is in yield per "effort" of the people, the energy content of fossil fuels becomes less important than its actual cost to them. For instance, if a farmer buys fossil fuel at a cost that is equivalent to a given amount of the harvested crop, the cost of the fossil fuel energy may be better represented by the energy content of the crop used to get it. Thus, if the cost of a pound of flour equals that of a gallon of gasoline, the farmer may perceive the energy expenditure of the gasoline at the converted rate of energy per pound of flour.

It is important to note that not all human subsistence activities are carried out in order to obtain energy; humans acquire other resources such as protein and vitamins from food. There are cases where people may actually expend more energy than they produce in a given subsistence activity. Energy efficiency takes on special importance for human ecology when human populations are deficient in energy or when energy is expensive. We return to the focus of this textbook: energy is important for us when it represents an ecological problem for a human population. If there is an excess of energy, interest turns to how the energy may be "invested" to aid with other ecological problems—for example, burning fuel for heat to deal with cold stress—or to sustain social phenomena that are not related to basic adaptive concerns. This latter topic moves well beyond the confines of this text.

A Shorthand Method for Tracing Energy Flow

Energy flow diagrams that were presented in the previous chapter traced energy from the sun through producer and consumer levels of food chains. These types of diagrams are often used to illustrate energy flow in human populations and include measures of energy production, expenditure, and consumption. Such diagrams commonly use special symbols as a shorthand for representing energy flow. Figure 14–1 shows some of the commonly used symbols, including energy sources, green plants, consumers, storage units, and so forth (Odum 1971).

These symbols are combined to illustrate energy flow in ecological communities, as shown in Figure 14–2. Figure 14–2a represents a simplified food chain, while Figure 14-2b shows the same food chain with more detail and added symbols to show identification of energy expended by consumers in order to obtain food. When this type of diagram is used to display systems that include human populations, quite complex illustrations can result.

We will now present some examples of energy flow systems involving human groups with a focus on how the energy flow helps illuminate basic adaptive strategies used by the groups to handle ecological problems.

Figure 14–1 Symbols commonly used in energy flow diagrams. (Modified and redrawn by permission from H. T. Odum. *Environment, power, and society.* Copyright © 1971 by John Wiley & Sons. Reprinted by permission of John Wiley & Sons, Inc.)

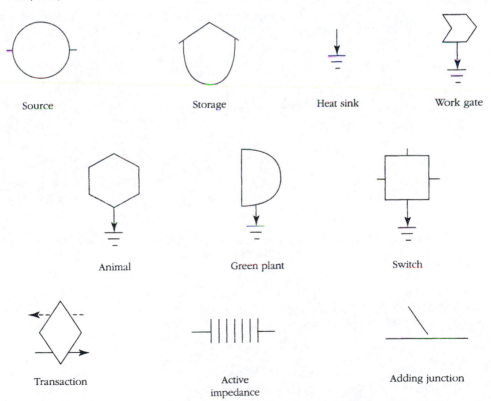

Source	Storage	Heat sink	Work gate
Animal	Green plant	Switch
Transaction	Active impedance	Adding junction

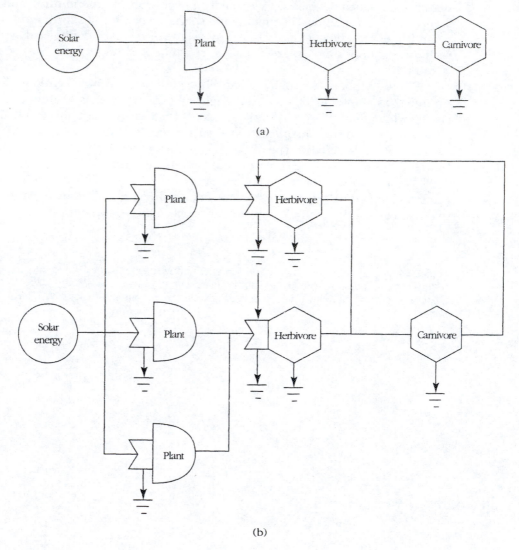

Figure 14–2   Food chains represented by energy flow symbols. (a) Simplified food chain. (b) More complex food chain showing work gates.

EXAMPLES OF ENERGY FLOW
IN HUMAN POPULATIONS

We have chosen examples that span different subsistence types and different biomes so at least some of the diversity in human energetics can be seen. Examples are chosen in which energetics is important for the population's adaptive activity.

The Dobe San of the Kalahari, Southern Africa

The San people from the Dobe region of the Kalahari live in a hot desert biome. They have a four- to six-month rainy season that coincides with their late spring and summer, a time in which temperatures average between 30 and 40°C and thus present a heat stress problem. Annual rainfall is quite variable, from 239 to 597 mm between 1963 and 1968 (Lee 1993), with consecutive drought years or excessive rainy years leading to problems in energy production for the human population.

The Dobe San relied on a balance of gathering and hunting for their subsistence needs at the time they were studied by Lee in the 1960s, but since then have relied more on wages, farming, and, especially, herding (Lee 1993). The following discussion is based on observations from the 1960s, when foraging represented almost all of their subsistence efforts.

Lee's study focused on a single 28-day period when he measured production and expenditure of energy in a small population at one camp, averaging 31 people on any given day. He noted that the San worked only about 20 hours per week on subsistence, that is, time spent gathering wild plants and hunting animals, although a number of other hours were spent in related activities, such as making tools and doing housework. Their major food source at the time of his study was mongongo nuts, and they averaged about an hour a day simply cracking the nuts as part of food preparation (Lee 1993).

Figure 14–3 presents a simplified energy flow diagram based upon Lee's data. He has lumped all animal sources together and listed only two sources of food from plant sources: mongongo nuts and all other vegetable foods, despite noting that the San list 85 plant species and 54 animal species as being edible (Lee 1969). It can be seen from the figure that mongongo nuts rate special consideration because of their importance to the San diet during the time of Lee's observations.

There are some problems with Lee's study, including the neglect of energy expenditure values beyond simply timing activities spent in subsistence in a single measure and lumping so many different food sources together. More serious for our understanding of San ecology is the limited time frame of Lee's study. The month in which Lee did his measurements was chosen as a time when subsistence was neither easiest nor most difficult for the San. His figures suggest that sufficient energy can be obtained by the population with little effort. However, a few months later in the year the picture is quite different. At the end of the dry season people have used up resources near their camps, which are situated near permanent water holes. At this time of year people must travel great distances and thus expend a great deal of energy to obtain resources. They may even expend more energy than they can obtain, thus losing biological stores of energy in the form of body fat.

San children engage in foraging activities mostly during the rainy season, since the long travel between camps and food sources during the dry season is difficult and dangerous for them (Blurton Jones et al. 1994). The San still reap

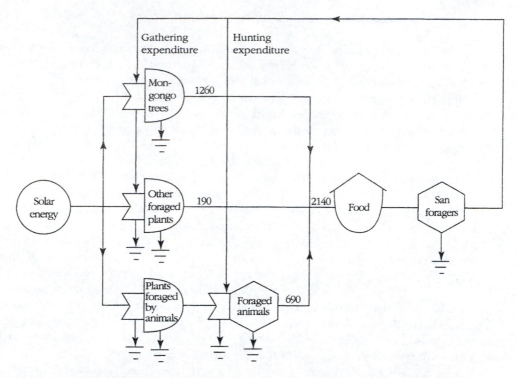

Figure 14–3   The flow of energy through the Dobe San foraging system. Numbers represent kcal/person/day. (Data from R. B. Lee. 1969. !Kung bushman subsistence: An input-output analysis. In *Contributions to anthropology: Ecological essays,* D. Damas, ed. Bulletin 230, Anthropological Series, no. 86. Ottawa: Natonal Museums of Canada.)

benefits from their children, as the latter are given the task of cracking nuts in the camps during the dry season while adults forage for the distant food resources. Calculations suggest that the time the child saves his or her mother by cracking nuts allows greater energy production for the family than if the child were to forage with the adults and then all were to share in nut-cracking duties (Blurton Jones et al. 1994).

Despite the drawbacks of the study, Lee's work gave human ecologists important information about foraging people, convincing most that foragers did not necessarily live constantly on the brink of starvation, as had been widely believed previously. On the other hand, overly romantic visions of the "original affluent society" (Sahlins 1972) probably also do not fit Lee's data.

The Inuit of Arctic Canada

We will now describe the energetics of another group of foragers who live in a very different biome: the Inuit of the Canadian Arctic. Contemporary Canadian Inuit frequently utilize a mixed economy, blending traditional subsistence activities with participation in the national and international monetary economy. Smith (1991) studied the community of Inujjuaq in the late 1970s at about the same time as an independent study of the community by the National Harvesting Research Committee (NHRC 1982, cited in Smith 1991). From these studies, estimates of energy flow through the community can be made.

Inujjuaq contained about 600 people, with 112 "potential" foragers identified who represented the healthy adult males in the community. The community is located on the eastern coast of Hudson Bay just above 58° north latitude and therefore has access both to terrestrial and marine resources. The area is in the tundra biome, with virtually no trees and a general lack of diversity in biological communities (Smith 1991). Temperatures are below freezing for much of the year, with mean daily temperatures reaching above freezing only during the summer, and there is a mean annual snowfall of 123 mm.

Figure 14–4 presents a simplified energy flow diagram for the community. The figure is based upon Smith's work and on data collected by the Native Harvest Research Committee (NHRC) as reported in Smith (1991). The NHRC data are based on long-term monitoring of the community for energy production, while Smith's research involved more intensive study of a sample of hunting activities done by community members and includes data on energy expenditure and consumption as well as production. Numbers in the figure are rough estimates based on extrapolations from Smith's sample to the larger sample in the NHRC study. Smith noted that imported food accounted for approximately half of the caloric consumption in the community during his time of study, and thus the figure presents a caloric value of imported food as equal to that of the carefully measured value of food from traditional subsistence activities.

There are many decisions about subsistence to be made by the Inujjuaq people. For instance, people must decide whether to hunt for marine or terrestrial food sources, and once deciding that, they decide which specific techniques to use and whether to attempt to obtain a given species once they have detected its presence. We will explore further how people make such decisions in a later chapter but will consider one decision here: whether to go hunting at all.

People can engage in wage labor and carving of soapstone for sale from which they can earn sufficient money to buy whatever food they require. In fact, some men do not hunt or do so rarely. Smith argues that those who hunt do so for economic reasons. While people earn more money from wage labor and carving than they do from export of furs and meat from hunting, the food obtained by hunting that is consumed by the Inuit has monetary value equal to what imported food would cost. Also, there may be more uncertainty in employment opportunities and in the prices of imported food than there is for traditional subsistence. Smith argues that these considerations make hunting a reasonable choice for the Inuit, even when factoring in the cost of fuel and ammunition.

This example shows that even when the comparatively simple ecology of foraging peoples is studied, complications exist. Nevertheless, Smith's study makes ecological sense of the persistence of traditional hunting activities in this community.

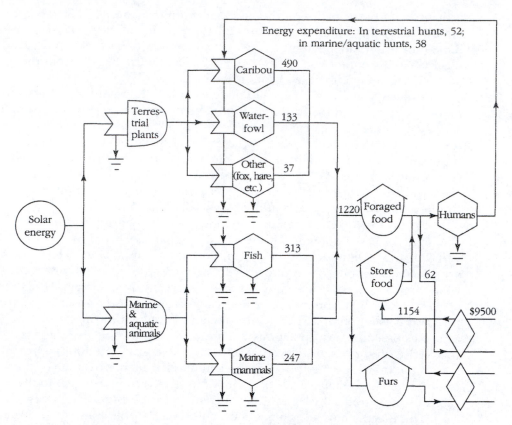

Figure 14–4   The flow of energy through the Inujjuaq foraging system. Numbers represent kcal/person/day. (Data from E. A. Smith. 1991. *Inujjuamiut foraging strategies: Evolutionary ecology of an arctic hunting economy.* New York: Aldine de Gruyter.)

Foragers in the Amazon: The Hiwi of Venezuela

The Hiwi consist of foraging groups located in Venezuela and Colombia that are related to other human populations in the region that are horticulturalists (Hurtado and Hill 1987). The Hiwi, however, rely almost entirely on foraging, with agricultural and imported foods constituting only about 5 percent of their diet (Hurtado and Hill 1990).

The tropical rainforest biome of the Amazon presents different ecological challenges to the Hiwi than those faced by the San or Inuit. One similarity is that seasonality is present, with distinct wet and dry seasons. In fact, about 90 percent of yearly rainfall occurs in the seven months between May and November. The late wet season appears to be a time when the highest amounts of energy production and consumption occur, with plants being more seasonal than animal food sources (Hurtado and Hill 1990). Since females are responsible for most of the plant gathering, women's productivity is much more variable between seasons than men's is, with women's productivity peaking in the late wet season, when root collection becomes an important subsistence activity.

Data have been collected over a 4-year period in which investigators were present in the months from November to May as well as in July. Time spent foraging was recorded each day, and all foods brought back to the homestead were identified and weighed. Also, all of the people in the population were weighed on a monthly basis. Figure 14–5 presents a summary of daily per capita energy consumption in the Hiwi population averaged over the time period that was observed (based upon data reported in Hurtado and Hill 1990). As can be seen, animal products account for 68 percent, roots for 19 percent, other plant foods for about 6 percent, honey for 2 percent, agricultural foods for 1 percent, and imported foods for 4 percent of the average daily caloric intake of the Hiwi. Foraging effort, although not measured directly as energy expenditure, is apparently fairly low. In no season did people average more than three hours per day in foraging activities, and they usually averaged under two hours of daily foraging outside the homestead.

Figure 14–5 The flow of energy through the Venezuelan Hiwi foraging system. Numbers represent kcal/person/day. (Data from A. M. Hurtado and K. R. Hill. 1990. *Journal of Anthropological Research* 46:293–346.)

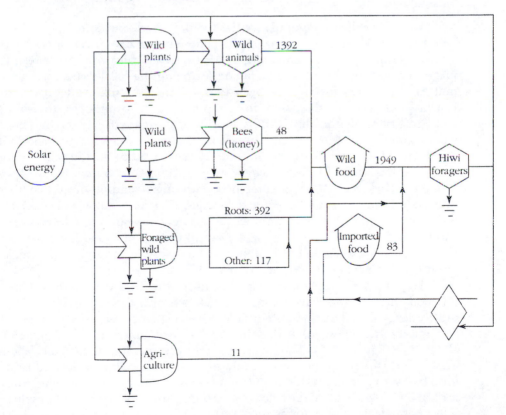

Seasonal differences in productivity are reflected in a seasonal fluctuation in average body weight. Men are heaviest during the late wet season when roots are available and lightest in the late dry season, with about a 1.9 kilogram fluctuation in average weight. Nonpregnant and nonnursing women show a somewhat different annual fluctuation in weight, in part because the root collection (late wet) season is not only the time of greatest consumption, but also of greatest caloric expenditure in foraging activities. They tend to be heaviest in the early wet season and, like the men, are lightest in the early dry season, with about a 1.8 kilogram fluctuation between lightest and heaviest time of the year (Hurtado and Hill 1990). The seasonality in women's energy consumption and body weight is also reflected in seasonality of fertility. By computing the date of conception by subtracting nine months from birth dates, it was noted that significantly fewer conceptions occurred during the early dry season than during other times of the year (Hurtado and Hill 1990). Analysis of the data, based upon 122 births reported by 24 women, suggests that conceptions were more closely related to variation in caloric intake than to body weight fluctuation. Our next example will illustrate an even greater seasonality in food intake, and also in fertility.

Pastoralists of East Africa: The Turkana

We now shift to a population that differs both in biome and subsistence type from the three previous examples. The Ngisonyoka Turkana are a pastoral people who live in the savanna of East Africa, specifically in northwestern Kenya just to the west of Lake Turkana, famed for being the locale where many important early hominid fossils have been found. The Turkana are located near the Karimojong people, discussed in Chapter 11, who practice transhumance between dry season herding camps and more permanent wet season residences where some crops are grown. The Turkana differ somewhat ecologically from the Karimojong, principally because the climate is more arid in their location.

The low annual rainfall, which varies from 10 to 60 cm per year, in the southern Turkana region is combined with high temperatures that increase evaporation and exacerbate water deficiency. A critical factor is the lack of predictability in rainfall. What rain does fall in a given year is usually concentrated within a few months—the "wet" season—and the amount that falls varies greatly from year to year (Little et al. 1990). In fact, serious droughts that negatively affect the Turkana occur on the order of once in ten years.

The greater aridity of the region requires the Turkana to rely less on crops for food than do the Karimojong. In fact, pastoral foods provide seven times more energy to the Turkana than do cultivated plants such as sorghum. This is illustrated in the energy flow diagram that is based on data from Coughenour et al. (1985). (Figure 14–6). The diagram points out much of importance about the Turkana. It shows that over 76 percent of their food energy is derived from pastoral foods, that less than 8 percent comes from foraging activities, and that even less, about 3 percent, comes from sorghum, an important food resource for other East African populations such as the Karimojong. The diagram also shows that imported foods such as sugar and maize account for about 13 percent of the calories in the Turkana diet (Coughenour et al. 1985; Little et al. 1990). Thus, the Turkana are a more "pure" example of a pastoral people than the Karimojong. Finally, it can be noted that the diagram shows an average daily intake of 1,275 kcal per person in the population. This daily intake is barely adequate for survival, indicating that energy intake can be an important ecological problem for the Turkana. In fact, data indicate that Turkana children are chronically undernourished and accordingly suffer from weak immunity to infectious diseases (Shell-Duncan 1995). What Figure 14–6 does not show is that the frequent droughts afflicting the region can lower the energy intake that is shown in the diagram. Also, the figure does not show the normal annual variation in energy intake—it simply sums the energy production and consumption for a full year.

The Turkana get food from their livestock principally by milking them (accounting for over 80 percent of food calories from pastoral activities) or bleeding them, the latter accounting for about 10 percent of calories obtained from livestock. They occasionally kill livestock for meat, but this accounts for less

Figure 14–6 The flow of energy through the Ngisonyoka Turkana pastoral system. Numbers represent kcal/person/day. (Adapted by permission from M. B. Coughenour et al. 1985. *Science* 230:619–25. Copyright 1985 American Association for the Advancement of Science.)

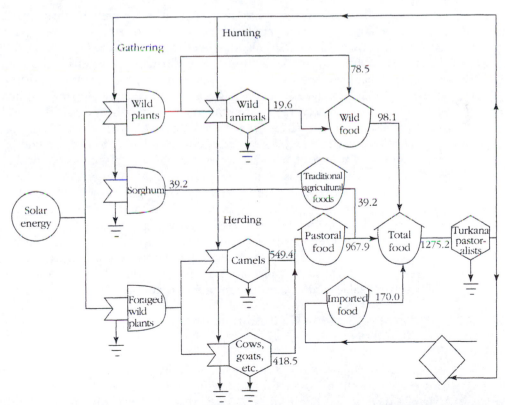

than 10 percent of energy gained from their animals. Camels are the chief producers of milk and blood, while goats and sheep are more commonly used for meat (Little et al. 1990).

The animals that are relied on by the Turkana suffer from seasonal changes in water availability due to the latter's effect on plants used for forage. The animals lose weight during the dry season, up to 20 percent of rainy season averages, and they also have reduced milk production during this time. Thus, milk provides a greater percentage of energy needs during the wet season than it does in the dry season. The people also lose body weight during the dry season, although their percentage of weight loss is less than that of their animals, with humans usually losing up to 5 or 6 kg—a little less than 12 percent of body weight—although population averages are about half that (Little 1989).

The seasonality of food supply has another important effect on the Turkana: it affects the pattern of births during the year, similar to Hiwi foragers. By subtracting nine months from the date of births in the population, it was noted that conceptions peaked during July and August, the end of the wet season and beginning of the dry season, when milk yield and human body weights are at their highest (Leslie and Fry 1989). The degree of seasonality in Turkana births is one of the highest known for all human populations. The completed fertility of the Turkana is fairly high, however, averaging about seven live births for each postmenopausal woman (Little et al. 1990).

While the seasonal variability in a "typical" year creates hardship for the Turkana, ecological problems are much more severe during a drought, which can last several years. Livestock populations can drop as much as 50 percent (McCabe 1988); this can force the Turkana to alter their normal way of getting food, migrate over large areas seeking forage for their herds, or emigrate to cities or other areas where they are no longer part of the pastoral system (Little et al. 1990). When such a drought ends, plants tend to recover much faster than the animals do, and hence the year following a long drought can be a difficult one for the Turkana.

The Turkana thus represent a human population for which energy flow studies have great importance. Energy is a problem for their ecology that they must solve in order to persist as a population. Relative energy scarcity is reflected in the growth patterns of their children: some slowing in growth in height at early ages, but a pronounced deficiency in weight for their height throughout the growth period (Little and Johnson 1987). Their high intake of protein prevents stunting, but the low energy intake prevents development of substantial stores of adipose tissue. There are no symptoms of marasmus or kwashiorkor among the children, but a high infant mortality rate suggests that their adaptation to the arid, unpredictable environment surrounding them is not a perfect one.

Pastoralists of the High-Altitude Andes: The Quechua of Nuñoa

The Quechua of Peru, descendants of the Inca, also rely on pastoralism for a major part of their subsistence but live in a very different biome from the East African savanna (see Figure 14–7). They reside on the high-altitude altiplano

Figure 14–7   Andean pastoralists. (Photo courtesy of Norris M. Durham)

(high plains) of the Andes mountains, where they face quite different environmental challenges than those faced by the Turkana. As outlined in Chapters 7
and 8, the Quechua must cope with high-altitude hypoxia and with extreme
swings in daily temperature, including cold nights. They also confront a similar
problem to that of the Turkana: poor primary productivity due to the physical
stressors in the environment (Thomas and Winterhalder 1976). This poor productivity is due to the stressors just mentioned as well as aridity, erosion of soil,
frequent frosts, and high levels of ultraviolet radiation.

The low primary productivity of the Andes highlands translates into
energy shortages for the Quechua, as clearly shown by Thomas's classic study in
the town and surroundings of Nuñoa, Peru (Thomas 1973, 1976). Thomas studied energy production, expenditure, and consumption in the Quechua population over an entire year and analyzed "strategic decisions" about subsistence
made by the people. Figure 14–8 summarizes much of the information in an
energy flow diagram that is somewhat more detailed than the others presented
thus far.

Energetic efficiency of the various subsistence tasks can be calculated from
Thomas's data. For instance, using energy produced divided by energy
expended as the measure of efficiency, cultivated crops have an efficiency of 11.5
(that is, the Quechua produce 11.5 kcal from their fields for every kcal of energy
they invest in them). For herding, the efficiency is only 2.0. So why do herding?
The answer is, in part, that the latter efficiency was based only on the caloric
value of the food they obtained from the herds. The Quechua also traded

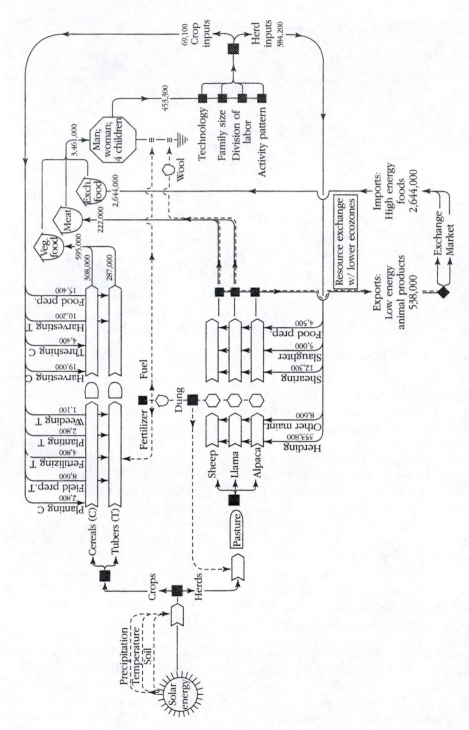

Figure 14–8 The flow of energy through a high-altitude Andean (Quechua) pastoral system. Numbers represent kcal/year. (Redrawn by permission from R. B. Thomas. 1974. Human adaptation to energy flow in the high Andes: Some conceptual and methodological considerations. In *Energy flow in human communities*, P. L. Jamison and S. M. Friedman, eds., 41–47. University Park, PA: Human Adaptability Coordinating Office, U.S. International Biological Program.)

products from their herds (wool, skins, meat) for "imported" goods, including such foods as sugar and flour. When the caloric value of these imported goods is added to the energy production from the herds, the energetic efficiency is calculated as 7.5 (Little and Morren 1976). Hence, to understand the subsistence activities of the Quechua we must look beyond their local area and consider trading relationships among human populations more broadly in the Andean region.

Perhaps the major finding of Thomas's study is that the Quechua do not produce enough food energy to meet their minimal caloric needs. Instead, they must rely on imported high-energy foods to make up the energy deficit (see Figure 14–9). As noted earlier and in Figure 14–8, they must exchange products from their pastoral activities for the imported foods. Even with these imported calories, energy intake is fairly low, averaging about 2,125 daily kcal in young men (ages 20 to 40) and 1,677 kcal in young women (Thomas 1976).

The diagram in Figure 14–8 also contains several "decision boxes," denoting places in the energy flow system at which people must make strategic choices. For instance, people must decide how much to rely on herds versus crops, which animals and how many of each to include in their herds (at least to the degree that they have control over these numbers), what crops to grow and where, and what resources to trade for exported resources. Because energy is in

Figure 14–9   Market in Pisac, Peru. Exchange of pastoral products for high-energy foods takes place in these kinds of markets. (Photo courtesy of H. J. Jacobi)

such short supply, energy concerns are of primary importance in these decisions. As an example, Thomas (1973) has suggested that the division of labor among people in the community is geared to minimize caloric expenditure. Since bigger people expend more energy on a given task than smaller individuals do, but are also stronger and more capable of performing strenuous activities, work is best apportioned such that the smallest people who can handle the work are the ones who usually perform it. Thus, the common reliance on young children to do the relatively light intensity daily herding activities is a choice based upon the lower energy expenditure required for the children than for adults. Older children, older adults, and young women do tasks of moderate intensity, while young men do the most intense physical activities such as foot plowing (Thomas 1973).

Figure 14–8 also shows the chief value of energy flow studies for human ecology: the decision boxes denote areas that may be critical for a group's adaptation to an area's resource base. The energy flow system thus points to processes or behaviors that need special study for understanding how a population copes with ecological problems. We will look at another of these decision boxes in Chapter 16 when we examine the importance of dung as a major source of both fuel and fertilizer.

Horticulturalists of Highland New Guinea: The Tsembaga Maring

The Tsembaga Maring also live in a mountain region, but reside at much lower altitude than the Quechua, from 700 to 2,500 m in the Simbai and Jimi valleys of Papua New Guinea (Rappaport 1968). The majority of this region is characterized as a lower montane rainforest zone (Little and Morren 1976). The Maring subsist primarily through swidden agriculture but also forage for some wild animals (chiefly pigs) and plants. They raise domesticated pigs as well. Most of their gardens are situated below 1,500 m altitude (Rappaport 1971).

Figure 14–10 shows an energy flow diagram for the Maring based on data from Rappaport (1971). Taro is their most important crop for human consumption, but sweet potato actually is produced in greater amounts; the majority of the latter is fed to pigs. It is clear from the diagram that the Maring are not energy deficient: they average about 2,600 kcal per day for men and 2,200 kcal per day for women, more than adequate amounts for these small-bodied people. Adult males average less than five feet tall and 103 pounds, while women average under four feet 7 inches and 85 pounds. Since energy does not appear to be a problem for the Maring, you may wonder why anyone would bother focusing on their energy flow.

Inspection of Figure 14–10 shows that a great deal of the caloric content of Maring crops goes to feed pigs. In fact, 37 percent of energy production from their gardens was used to feed pigs. Things appear even more curious when we look at energy efficiency: total efficiency from human crops is about 18.0 (the Maring obtain 18 kcal for every kcal expended in raising crops for human con-

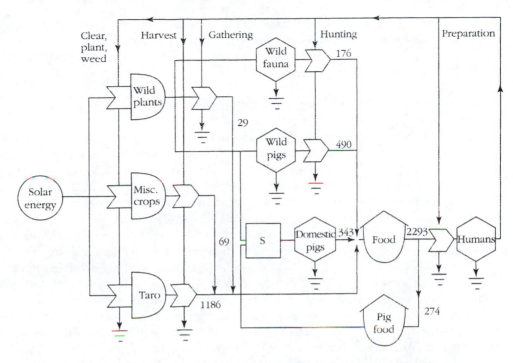

Figure 14–10 The flow of energy through the Tsembaga Maring horticultural system. Numbers represent kcal/person/day. (Redrawn by permission from M. A. Little and G. E. B. Morren, Jr. 1976. *Ecology, energetics, and human variability*. Dubuque, IA: Wm. C. Brown Company.)

sumption), while the efficiency of pig herding is about 1.5 (Little and Morren 1976). The latter efficiency figure is obtained by dividing the calories consumed from eating pigs by the calories consumed in raising crops for the pigs and doing other subsistence activities related to herding. So why raise pigs?

Again, to understand choices in energy production we must look more broadly at ecological problems. The Maring, while producing sufficient amounts of food energy, tend to have marginal amounts of protein in their diet, in part because their major crops are high-carbohydrate, low-protein foods. Rappaport (1967) estimates the daily consumption of protein from vegetable foods at between 43 to 55 grams for males and between 36 to 48 grams for females, which is slightly above daily requirements. However, the small body size and observation of soft, discolored hair (a sign of protein deficiency) in some children suggests that protein is in short supply. High-quality protein comes from eating their pigs. The pigs are eaten only during ritual occasions, such as occur during funerals, warfare, illness, or injuries. This is believed to be a means of allocating the low-protein supplies to people who are under stress and therefore in greater need of protein (Rappaport 1967).

Study of the Tsembaga Maring energy flow system suggests that energy per se is not an ecological problem, but energy helps solve a different problem. They utilize excess energy to increase their supply of high-quality protein, which is a key resource for this population.

Energy Flow in Rice Growing Populations

Rice is a fascinating crop for many reasons, not the least of which is that it is the staple food for a large percentage of humankind (see Chapter 5). It is also interesting for the human ecologist because it is consumed by people with varying subsistence modes. Wild rice is utilized by people who forage to supplement agricultural activities, while domesticated rice is grown in swidden gardens or by various types of intensive agricultural techniques (Hanks 1972). Intensive rice cultivation tends to involve increased manual labor, i.e., energy expenditure for subsistence rises, but at a lower rate than the resulting increase in energy production (Bray 1986). Thus, while intensive rice cultivation involves more work, it has a greater energy efficiency than is found with foraging or horticultural techniques for obtaining rice. In the last quarter of the twentieth century, there has been an increase in mechanized approaches to rice cultivation, involving the use of fossil-fuel-driven pumps and mills and, less commonly, power tillers, transplanters, and reaper-bonders (Bray 1986), as well as the use of fossil-fuel-derived fertilizers and pesticides.

Wild rice gathering was an important seasonal component of the subsistence for Southeast Asian peoples for thousands of years, adding to hunting, fishing, and the gathering of other plant foods (Hanks 1972). As agriculture became more important for subsistence, wild rice remained as a significant supplement to the diet of some populations. There are no available quantitative data on productivity and energy expenditure of rice gathering activities, but in contemporary populations both measures are likely to be low: little production for little effort.

In a comparative study of rice farmers in various locales in Southeast Asia, Hanks (1972) compared the energetics of shifting (swidden), broadcasting, and transplanting techniques of rice cultivation. The latter two techniques are forms of labor-intensive agriculture, with transplanting involving a greater degree of labor than broadcasting does. The broadcasting technique of rice cultivation involves the use of fields that are plowed and seeded and then flooded, usually through natural means such as seasonal river flooding caused by monsoons or other seasonal weather patterns. The transplanting technique involves intensive use of irrigation techniques to flood fields. Here, rice is densely planted in specially prepared nursery plots that have been fertilized and have a well-controlled water supply. The rice is pulled from the nursery field after a few weeks, trimmed, and replanted in larger fields where the plants are spaced out. For both nursery and large fields, a great deal of preparation, including plowing, precedes planting, and carefully controlled irrigation permits flooding of fields to optimal levels.

Table 14–1 presents data on labor costs of the three rice growing techniques. The table contains a surprise: shifting agriculture has a higher labor cost

TABLE 14–1 Labor Costs of Rice Cultivation Techniques

Mode of Cultivation	Avg. Labor Cost (person-days/acre)	Labor Cost per Season (person-days)	Capital Cost (dollars)	Capital Cost (person-days equivalent)	Total Labor Cost per Season (person-days equivalent)
Shifting	67	255	2	4	259
Broadcasting	17	179	61	122	301
Transplanting	53	292	69	138	430

Source: Reproduced with permission from L. M. Hanks. 1992. *Rice and man: Agricultural ecology in Southeast Asia.* Honolulu: University of Hawaii Press.

than broadcasting as measured by "person-days" per acre and "person-days" per season for a household, although shifting is usually considered a non-labor-intensive form of agriculture. This is partly explained by the use of draft animals and various types of equipment for the broadcasting technique. Converting these capital inputs into labor costs by assuming a rate of $0.05 per day for labor, the final column of the table shows that shifting agriculture has a lower total cost when these other investments are taken into consideration. The data in the table do not include long-term costs of irrigation systems, thus making the figures for the intensive techniques lower than they actually are.

Table 14–2 presents the productivity of the three cultivation techniques. Intensive techniques are more productive and also more efficient than shifting cultivation, although the data suggest that transplanting, which is the most intensive technique, is less efficient than broadcasting, although the gross production (both per hectare and per season for a household) is highest for households using the transplantation technique. Hanks (1972) suggests that the gross production rates are related to population density. In populations that use the shifting mode of rice production, average population density is 12 people per square kilometer. Populations that utilize the broadcasting technique average 98 people per square kilometer. Populations that employ the transplantation technique average 381 people per square kilometer. The difference in population density supported by the two intensive techniques is due to the fact that households that use broadcasting require on average 4.2 hectares (about 10.5 acres) for rice cultivation, while those that use transplanting require only 2.2 hectares. Thus, the most labor-intensive technique of cultivating rice is less efficient in terms of labor cost to a

TABLE 14–2 Production and Efficiency of Rice Cultivation Techniques

Mode of Cultivation	Output (short tons of rice per season)	Efficiency (short tons of rice per person day of labor)
Shifting	2.45	0.0095
Broadcasting	6.24	0.0207
Transplanting	5.36	0.0125

Source: Reproduced with permission from L. M. Hanks. 1992. *Rice and man: Agricultural ecology in Southeast Asia.* Honolulu: University of Hawaii Press.

household per amount of food produced, but the ability to raise more rice per unit of land allows support of a greater human population density.

Energy Flow in the United States: Complexity in an Industrial Society

Analysis of energy flow in a society as complex as that of the United States is no easy matter. For instance, in 1970, the U.S. gross energy consumption was over 16×10^{15} kcal, much of which is not directly related to subsistence. If we single out food energy, U.S. agriculture supplies each individual with about 10,000 kcal per day (Cook 1971). The 10,000 kcal can be subdivided into about 1,500 kcal that is wasted at various steps in the processing and marketing of foods, 2,200 kcal that is consumed as plant foods by humans, and 6,300 kcal that is used as animal feed, with 900 kcal of that energy returned in the form of human meat consumption. Thus, Americans consume on average 3,100 kcal of food energy per day, representing 31 percent of the agricultural production.

Food represents only a small part of the energy expenditure in the United States. Per capita energy consumption is about 230,000 kcal per day (Cook 1971), over five times the average per capita for the world (Grathwohl 1982), and therefore food consumption represents less than 1.4 percent of an individual's energy consumption. The other energy is used for transportation, lighting and heating, running industrial processes, recreation, and a host of other uses.

Figure 14–11 illustrates energy consumption in societies that use different subsistence strategies, divided into food versus other energy uses. The chart shows the increase in per capita energy consumption that accompanies intensification and industrialization. Since these processes also increase the population density of humans, intensification and industrialization lead to enormous increases in the total amount of energy consumption by humanity.

There is a fairly close relationship between energy use per capita and relative wealth of different nations as measured, for instance, by the Gross National Product (in dollars) per person (Cook 1971). The implication of this is that any constraints placed on energy consumption may lead to a decline in wealth, although there is quite a bit of room for increased efficiency of energy use. A long-term problem for the Earth's ecology is the increase in atmospheric carbon dioxide that results from the burning of fossil fuels and the clearing of forests (Woodwell et al. 1983; Houghton and Woodwell 1989). The increased carbon dioxide concentration acts as a "greenhouse gas," trapping solar energy as heat and thus leading to global warming. Global warming is believed to pose a threat to many human populations, as some areas will become drier, others will face more common hazards due to floods or storms, while still others will confront rising sea levels that threaten their land (Owen and Chiras 1995). Hence, reliance on fossil fuels is doubly chancy in the long term, both because these fuels are nonrenewable and because their use may create climatic change that will cause great problems for humans, and all living organisms, in the coming decades.

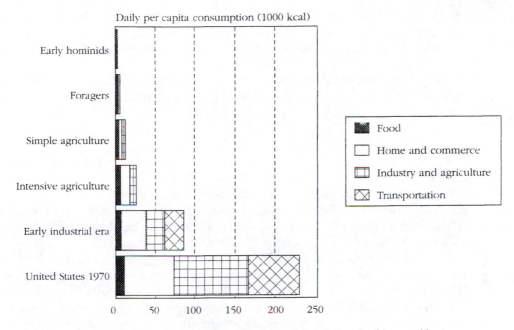

Figure 14–11   Daily energy consumption in different societies (kcal/person/day). (Redrawn by permission from E. Cook. 1971. The flow of energy in an industrial society. *Scientific American* 225:135–43.)

CONCLUSION: THE UTILITY OF ENERGY FLOW STUDIES FOR HUMAN ECOLOGY

Energy flow studies enjoyed great popularity in human ecology for a period in the late 1960s and 1970s but were undertaken less often afterward. There are several possible reasons for this. For one, these studies are difficult and time-intensive (and thus also expensive) to conduct. Simultaneous measurement of energy production, expenditure, and consumption requires great effort on the part of the investigator. The measurements should properly be done over a full year's activities because energy resources are usually quite seasonal, and greater validity of results would come from even longer-term studies to allow for year-to-year variability. More problematical is the possible inaccuracy of measurements from all human energy flow studies due to the great difficulty in carrying them out. On the other hand, one can argue that an understanding of human ecology is bound to be difficult. Taking the easier route may not be the better way to learn how human populations adapt to their environment.

A second reason for the decline in popularity of energy flow studies is criticism of them for assuming greater stability in a population's energetics than is actually the case. This is due in part to the time and expense required to obtain quantitative data over long periods. In fact, when examining energy flow studies of the major biomes, one finds that many assumptions are used due to the absence of adequate quantitative data (Moran 1982). Some human ecologists limit energy flow studies to periods of time when energy is likely to be a limiting resource for the population under study rather than averaging over long periods of time.

A third reason for the decline in use of human energy flow studies is due to the level of analysis of these studies: energy flow studies are carried out at the population level. Many investigators are more interested in the individual level. For instance, while a population may average sufficient energy production per capita, if there is very uneven distribution of the energy within the population many individuals may obtain an insufficient amount of energy, leading to serious difficulties. While energy production is often based on shared activities, it is usually possible to determine individual productivity. Energy consumption and expenditure tend to be measured in individuals and summed for populations. Therefore, it is possible to derive energy balance at the individual level where this is important for understanding of adaptive processes.

A fourth reason for declining interest in energy flow studies is the notion that energetics is often not a critical area for study in human ecology. This is certainly true for societies in which all necessary resources are plentiful. These societies have probably been rare in human history. Energy flow studies are most useful when carried out in societies where energy is in short supply. In these populations, study of energy flow allows one to understand how the people cope with a major ecological problem. There are also many populations in which energy is available in required amounts, but other resources are more problematical, such as water in the desert biome. Energy flow is also of value for the study of those populations that must utilize some of their energy to obtain other resources, such as using fossil fuel to convert salt water to fresh water in arid Saudi Arabia. When energy flow studies are carried out in other circumstances, the amount of effort that goes into the study seems to outweigh the results. We must think about the energy efficiency of human ecologists as well as of human populations!

Human ecology studies of energetics in the 1980s and 1990s have tended to take a more focused approach to energy flow. While some have compiled full energy flow calculations for societies, often the energy studies are used to answer specific questions. For instance, some studies have focused on seasonal or other temporal variation, particularly emphasizing periods of scarcity when energy becomes a major concern for people. Other investigators have used energy as a measuring device to evaluate theories of optimal resource use or other ecological theories (e.g., Leonard 1989), and thus energetics becomes a means rather than an ends in the investigation.

Energy flow studies have utility beyond aiding our understanding of resource use. They can give information needed to understand fertility, physical growth patterns, variability in adult body size and composition, work capacity of individuals, and morbidity and mortality patterns of different populations (Baker 1974). More broadly, energy is fundamental to structure, including social structure, and to information exchange (Odum 1971; Adams 1974). Thus, energy flow studies may be extrapolated to "information flow" considerations, allowing understanding of cultural processes that occur within populations (Odum 1971). Human energy flow studies go beyond simply describing paths of energy flow—they are tools for understanding the adaptive dynamics of human populations.

This brings us back to the recurring theme of this textbook: human ecology is best studied through a problem-oriented approach. Where energy is a problem, or where it is part of the solution to a problem, energy flow studies have great value in helping to understand the ecology of human populations. Otherwise the human ecologist is advised to focus on other concerns, whether they be other resources or environmental stressors, to understand the specific circumstances faced by a specific group of people.

KEY TERMS

energy consumption
energy efficiency
energy expenditure
energy production

KEY POINTS

☐ Measures of energy in human populations consist of its production, expenditure, and consumption based on a group rather than an individual; measurements generally cover a full year of activity to account for seasonal variability and multiple years to account for variability from year to year.

☐ Energy expenditure can be measured by the amount of molecular oxygen consumed, monitoring heart rate, and drinking nonradioactive isotopes of helium and oxygen.

☐ Measurements of energy consumption are beset by methodological problems involved in dietary surveys, the "larder method," self-reporting of dietary intake, weighing at different times, and the variability that can occur day to day and season to season.

☐ Measurements of energy efficiency encompass computation of all sources of energy production, including the amount of fossil fuels involved in the manufacture and use of tractors and fertilizers, and energy consumption. It is of special significance where energy is deficient or expensive.

☐ Human populations adapt to their environment to meet their energy needs: the desert-dwelling pastoralist Dobe San modify their activities to seasonal food source availability; the Inuit of the Canadaian Arctic combine hunting with the purchase of food from the sale of soapstone carving; the Hiwi of Venezuela and

Colombia accommodate their foraging to the wet and dry seasons, reflected in part by an annual fluctuation in body weight; the pastoral Turkana of East Africa derive food from livestock by milking or bleeding them; the pastoral Quechua of the high-altitude Andes rely on exchanging products of their pastoral activities for imported foods; the Tsembaga Maring of Highland New Guinea practice swidden agriculture, taro being the most important food crop, and derive protein from pigs fed on horticultural products.

☐   Rice is produced in shifting (swidden) and intensive (broadcasting and transplanting) agriculture, the latter being more productive and efficient but requiring greater energy expenditure by the farmer.

☐   Food consumption in the United States amounts to about 1.4 percent of individual energy consumption, the remainder being used for transportation, lighting and heating, industrial processes, and recreation, among other activities.

☐   A fairly close relationship exists between energy use per capita and relative wealth of nations as measured by the Gross National Product per person.

☐   The decline in popularity of energy flow studies in human populations is the result of several factors: the difficulty and time-intensive nature of such studies, the assumption of greater stability in a population's energetics than is actually the case, the level of the analysis being the population whereas more interest is at the level of the individual, and the notion that energetics is often not a critical area for study in human ecology except where energy is in short supply.

15

Nutrient Cycling
in Ecosystems

INTRODUCTION

The importance of nutrients and their cycling through ecosystems has been touched upon a number of times thus far. It is now appropriate to recognize more fully the cyclical patterns of these nutrients, to seek out the general patterns that may exist among them, and subsequently to consider the effects resulting from inadvertent or purposeful human interaction with them. But, at first, a brief introduction to the nature and importance of nutrients will be helpful in setting the stage for understanding the importance of the cycling processes.

NUTRIENTS

Life is dependent not only on energy but also on the availability of some 20 chemical elements required in the life processes of most organisms and an additional 10 or so required by different species, usually in trace amounts. Although carbohydrates can be photosynthesized from the hydrogen, carbon, and oxygen contained in water and carbon dioxide, the more complex organic substances require additional elements either in considerable amounts, as in the case of nitrogen and phosphorus, or in trace amounts, as in the case of zinc and molybdenum. Furthermore, photosynthesis and other metabolic reactions in both plants and animals occur in the presence of enzymes that themselves contain a variety of elements in trace amounts.

Those elements needed in relatively large amounts are generally referred to as **macronutrients,** each constituting 0.2 percent or more of dry organic weight. **Micronutrients** are those elements needed in trace amounts, each constituting less than 0.2 percent of dry organic weight. It is noteworthy that all of the 32 elements that have been identified as nutrients are among the lightest in the periodic table of elements.

Macronutrients

Macronutrients may be considered in two groups: (1) those that constitute more than 1 percent each of dry organic weight—carbon, oxygen, hydrogen, nitrogen, and phosphorus; and (2) those that constitute 0.2 to 1 percent of dry organic weight—sulfur, chlorine, potassium, sodium, calcium, magnesium, iron, and copper. In humans, there are only four macronutrients: hydrogen—63 percent; oxygen—25.5 percent; carbon—9.5 percent; and nitrogen—1.4 percent (Frieden 1972).

Role of Macronutrients.   The role of the first group of macronutrients is well known: oxygen as a building block of protoplasm and the primary agent in biological oxidation; carbon as the building block of all organic compounds; hydrogen as an acceptor of oxygen; nitrogen as the building block of protein and nucleoprotein as well as a component of enzymes; and phosphorus as a constituent in photosynthetic biochemicals, proteins, and nucleoproteins.

The second group of macronutrients plays a variety of roles: sulfur is a basic constituent of protein; chlorine, required in minute amounts by plants but in greater quantities in animals, is a key factor in maintaining the acid-base balance in the latter; potassium is involved in the formation of sugars in plants and of proteins in animals; sodium also aids in maintaining the acid-base balance in animals; calcium is needed for normal root tip development in plants and for a variety of functions in animals including maintaining acid-base balance, contraction of muscles, and in vertebrates, arthropods, and mollusks it is the key element in providing structural support (bones, exoskeletons, and shells); magnesium is critical to the structure of chlorophyll and energy transfer reactions; iron is required in electron transfer in photosynthesis and is the key element in hemoglobin; and copper, present in chloroplasts, influences the rate of photosynthesis.

Micronutrients

The known micronutrients include aluminum, arsenic, boron, bromine, chromium, cobalt, fluorine, gallium, iodine, manganese, molybdenum, nickel, selenium, silicon, strontium, tin, titanium, vanadium, and zinc. Actually some of these micronutrients may be macronutrients for some species, whereas some of the second group of macronutrients, for example, sodium and chlorine in plants, may be micronutrients for other species. The list of micronutrients continues to expand, with four new essential trace elements (arsenic, nickel, silicon, and vanadium) identified in animals in the 1970s (Mertz 1981) and at least one, nickel, being the first identified in plants in nearly thirty years when its presence was determined to be essential for development and functioning of root nodules in soybeans (Eskew et al. 1983). As research continues, there is considerable likelihood that additional elements will be identified as essential.

Role of Micronutrients.   Discussion of all the trace elements would require more space than seems appropriate. In general, however, it can be stated that many of the micronutrients play key roles in enzymatic activity. Some, however, are involved in a wide variety of roles; boron, for example, is involved in cell division, translocation of water in plants, and carbohydrate metabolism, among a number of other functions. Aluminum is necessary for normal development of some ferns, silicon is the structural element of the outer glasslike covering (i.e., tests) of diatoms, and cobalt is required in root nodules for proper functioning of nitrogen-fixing bacteria.

Nutrient Interaction

The presence or absence of an essential nutrient may adversely affect the availability or activity of another nutrient. Howarth and Cole (1985) showed that sulfate inhibits the assimilation of molybdenum by phytoplankton, thus making it less available in sea water than it is in fresh water. Molybdenum is required in the conversion of elemental nitrogen to nitrate, the form in which it can be utilized by plants, as well as in the assimilation of nitrate. Thus, a reduced amount of molybdenum requires a greater expenditure of energy for these nitrogen processes in sea water than in fresh water and may explain the relatively low levels of nitrogen in coastal marine ecosystems.

THE HYDROLOGIC CYCLE

Although water technically is not a nutrient since it is a chemical compound rather than an element, it is crucial to many biological processes as well as being the medium in which a substantial portion of the world's organisms live. Its cycle also plays a significant role in the cycling of many if not virtually all nutrients because of its solvent properties. There is no other chemically inert solvent that can compare with water in the number and variety of things it can dissolve or in the amount of them it can hold in solution.

The major pathway of the **hydrologic cycle** is an interchange between the Earth's surface and the atmosphere by way of precipitation and evaporation, the energy for which is derived from the sun (Figure 15–1). The cycle is a steady-state one, the total precipitation being balanced by total evaporation. Although

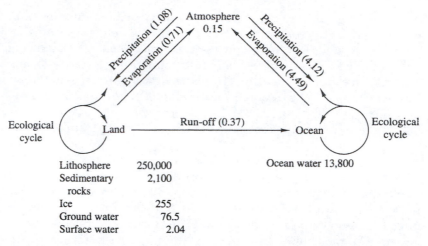

Figure 15–1 The general pattern of the hydrologic cycle and the distribution of water in 10^{17} kg; amounts in parentheses are annual rates. The ecological cycle involves uptake by photosynthesis and imbibition and loss by respiration and transpiration. (Data from Hutchinson 1951, Nace 1967, Kalinin and Bykov 1969, and *International Hydrological Decade* 1970.)

there is a disbalance in favor of the precipitation that occurs over land, there is greater evaporation from the ocean; the compensating factor is the runoff from land to the ocean. Ecosystems with their biota constitute an accessory whose presence or absence has no significant effect on this major movement, although transpiration does reduce runoff in local environments. However, significant amounts of water are incorporated by ecosystems in protoplasmic synthesis, and a substantial return to the atmosphere occurs by way of transpiration from living plants.

As Figure 15–1 shows, of the total estimated water on the Earth and in its atmosphere, only a little more than 5 percent is actually or potentially free and in circulation, and nearly 99 percent of that is in the ocean. In contrast, nearly 95 percent of the Earth's water is bound in the **lithosphere** and in **sedimentary rocks.** Fresh water amounts to a little more than 0.1 percent of the total supply of water, and three-quarters of it is bound up in polar ice caps and glaciers. It has been estimated that were this ice-bound water to melt completely, it would equal a water layer 50 m deep over the entire surface of the Earth.

Although total precipitation (5.2×10^{17} kg or 5.2×10^8 km³) is an impressive quantity, it is even more significant to note that its source—namely, atmospheric water vapor—constitutes an infinitesimal amount relative to the distribution of water on the Earth. It has been estimated that this amount of water vapor is the equivalent of 2.5 cm of rain over the entire surface of the Earth. By dividing the total annual precipitation by the amount in the atmosphere, the implication is a turnover about 35 times a year, or approximately every 11 days.

BIOGEOCHEMICAL CYCLES

*Bio*logical organisms and their *geo*logical (atmosphere or lithosphere) environment are involved in the movement of *chemical* elements. Collectively, these movements are referred to as **biogeochemical cycles.**

In one group of biogeochemical cycles, the atmosphere constitutes a major reservoir, or supply storage compartment, of the element that exists there in a gaseous phase. Such **gaseous nutrient cycles** show little or no permanent change in the distribution and abundance of the element, though over shorter periods of geological time there may be greater accumulations in a given compartment of the cycle. Carbon and nitrogen are prime representatives of biogeochemical cycles with a prominent gaseous phase.

In a **sedimentary nutrient cycle,** the major reservoir is the lithosphere, from which the elements are released largely by weathering. The sedimentary cycles, exemplified by phosphorus, sulfur, iodine, and most of the other biologically important elements, have a tendency to stagnate. In such cycles, a portion of the supply may accumulate in large quantities, as in the deep-ocean sediments, and thereby become inaccessible to organisms and to continual cycling. Some of the elements that are characterized by sedimentary cycles do have a gaseous phase, sulfur and iodine being among them, but these phases are insignificant in that there is no large gaseous reservoir.

As these biogeochemical cycles are discussed, you should become alert to their common, fundamental characteristic: large available pools are often coupled with small available pools that are extremely labile and highly dependent on continual input. Further, it will become evident that although there is interaction among biological, chemical, and geological components of the cycles, there is significant biological control of the chemical factors in the environment (Redfield 1958; Lovelock and Margulis 1974).

GASEOUS NUTRIENT CYCLES

Carbon Cycle

Perhaps the simplest of the nutrient cycles is one whose general components are quite well recognized—the carbon cycle (Figure 15–2). Carbon is the most significant element in organisms, constituting 49 percent of their dry weight. The carbon cycle is essentially a perfect one in that carbon is returned to the environment about as fast as it is removed. Also, it is one that involves a gaseous phase, atmospheric carbon dioxide (CO_2). The basic movement of carbon is from the atmospheric reservoir to producers to consumers, and from both these groups to decomposers, and then back to the reservoir. In this cycle, the gaseous reservoir is the atmosphere, which has an average concentration of about 0.032 percent (or 320 parts per million [ppm]) of carbon dioxide.

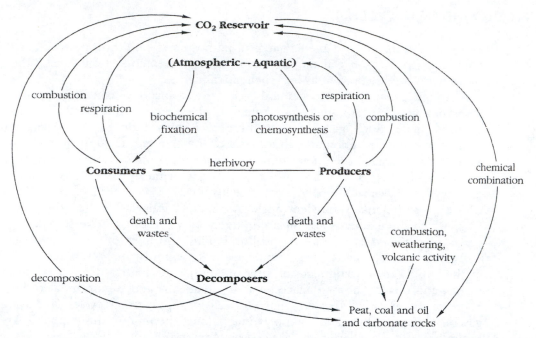

Figure 15–2   The carbon cycle.

Daily and Seasonal Variation.   There is considerable daily as well as seasonal variation in the amount of atmospheric carbon dioxide (CO_2) because of geographical and other factors that influence removal through photosynthesis and return by respiration. As a result of respiration, for instance, CO_2 levels near the ground may rise to 0.05 percent at night and drop to well below the average concentration of 0.032 percent during the day as it is taken up in photosynthesis. Seasonally, photosynthetic uptake of carbon dioxide exceeds return to the atmosphere by respiration and decomposition during the summer; the reverse is true during the winter. In northern latitudes, carbon dioxide content just above the ground is at a minimum in late winter and late fall (about 330 ppm) and at a maximum in June and July (about 355 ppm).

Biological Cycling of Carbon.   Carbon dioxide is the major state in which carbon is involved in biological or trophic-level cycling. Between 4×10^{13} and 9×10^{13} kg of carbon are used annually in autotrophic photosynthesis. For some organisms, notably mussels, clams, and tube worms in the vicinity of hydrocarbon seeps on the ocean floor, methane is the carbon source (Brooks et al. 1987; Cary et al. 1988) and is assimilated by the collaboration of symbiotic methane bacteria.

Respiratory activity in producers and consumers accounts for the return of a considerable amount of the biologically fixed carbon as gaseous carbon dioxide to the atmosphere. The most substantial return, however, is accomplished through the respiratory activity of decomposers in their processing of the waste materials and dead remains of other trophic levels. Additional return from the biota occurs through the nonbiological process of combustion, both through the purposive use of wood for fuel and accidental fires in a forest or building. Such combustion can and does involve consumers and decomposers as well as producers.

The Geochemical Cycling of Carbon.   The distribution of carbon on Earth is shown in Table 15–1. Earlier estimates by Bolin (1970) placed the amount of carbon in fossil fuels and in the sediments at twice the amounts shown in the table. Estimates by Berner and Lasaga (1989) give the amount in the sediments as seven times larger and that in dead organisms as five times larger than those shown in Table 15–1. Whichever of these estimates is taken, the amount of carbon in organic form is but a fraction (less than 0.1 percent) of that occurring in the geological component of the environment; further, the major reservoir of carbon is inorganic, with some 99 percent being in sedimentary form. This means that the major supply of carbon to the Earth's surface, where it becomes biologically involved, is by erosion and metamorphism of sediments. Another way of conceptualizing the distribution of carbon is to note that at any given time, one part in one thousand is in the ocean-atmosphere system, and the rest is in sedimentary rocks (Broecker 1973) and such animal remains as protozoan tests, coral, mollusk shells, and echinoderm and vertebrate skeletal material.

The Global Cycling of Carbon

Carbon Regulation in the Ocean and Atmosphere.   According to Broecker (1973), the **residence time** (the length of time spent in a given compartment of the cycle) of carbon in the sediments is in the order of 100 million years, whereas residence time in the ocean-atmosphere system is 100 thousand years. Because of both the greater content of carbon in the ocean than in the atmosphere (Table 15–1) and the chemistry of the aquatic-atmosphere interchange of carbon, the ocean, in effect, dictates to the atmosphere what its CO_2 content will be. The ocean and its sediments thus take on a singular importance in the global cycling of carbon. Given the proportionately large size of the Pacific Ocean, it is not surprising that portions of it (the central and eastern equatorial regions) are the largest natural ocean source of carbon dioxide (Murray et al. 1994).

Broecker (1973) has further noted that organisms produce about five times as much calcium carbonate ($CaCO_3$) as that brought into the oceans from land drainage. If all this carbon remained preserved in the sediments, ocean water would run a very large carbon deficit and that, in turn, would pull carbon from

TABLE 15–1   Distribution of Carbon on Earth in 10^9 Metric Tons (1 metric ton = 2204.6 pounds)

Atmosphere	692	Organisms	3,432
Ocean water	35,000	Living	592
Sediments	>10,000,000	Dead	2,840
		Fossil fuels	>5,000
	Total organic	8,432	
	Total inorganic	10,035,692	

Source: Data derived from B. Bolin et al. 1979. *The global carbon cycle.* New York: John Wiley and Sons.

the atmosphere, creating a deficit there. Such a turn of events is avoided by a chemical feedback mechanism involved with the carbonate ion, a topic too technical to delve into here. For our purposes, however, this feedback controls the carbon balance in the ocean, and this balancing, in turn, keeps the atmospheric carbon content under regulation.

Long-Term Implications of Global Carbon Cycling.   Although the introductory explanation of the carbon cycle conveyed a rather simple situation, it should be obvious that the cycle is, in fact, relatively complex in the number of ways, as well as duration of time, in which carbon is utilized, stored, and restored as it circulates. It is also obvious that there are many unknowns and uncertainties as to quantities and rates involved in the many transfers involved. In a very general way, the various pathways do, however, constitute self-regulating feedback mechanisms resulting in a relatively homeostatic system (Garrels et al. 1976). Over time, additions and deletions can be eliminated or compensated for. However, the degree to which the Earth as a total ecosystem can withstand or adapt to a long-term disturbance of the existing equilibrium is at this time both uncertain and a matter of contention among ecologists and other scientists (Bazzaz 1990; Post et al. 1990).

Nonetheless, most authorities agree that the past more than 100 years of increased use of fossil fuels, deforestation, and various agricultural practices has resulted in increases of atmospheric carbon, the precise amount of which is, as just noted, debated (Solomon et al. 1985; Trabalka et al. 1985). Assuming a concentration of about 260 to 275 ppm of CO_2 in the mid-nineteenth century, there had been about a 20 percent increase by the 1990s (Figure 15–3). Based on measurements made in the period 1959–1969, when a 3 percent increase (9 ppm) in atmospheric CO_2 was recorded, coupled with the accelerated rate in the use of fossil fuels; increased deforestation, especially of tropical rainforests; and increasingly intensive and expanding agricultural practices, the predictions were for an increase in atmospheric CO_2 to between 375 and 400 ppm (an increase of 14 to 21 percent) by the end of the century. An unknown factor, however, is the extent to which the ocean can continue to act as a sink for the extra carbon inserted into the atmosphere. Present combustion rates of 5×10^9 to 6×10^9 metric tons per year, for example, should be increasing atmospheric CO_2 by about 2 ppm per year. The actual increase, however, is only about one-third that amount. The other two-thirds is absorbed largely by the ocean and, to some extent, perhaps by increased plant production. The long-term effects of such increases, particularly on global climate, is a matter of considerable concern. This legitimate concern about global climate has resulted in an outpouring of publications (*Annual Review of Ecology and Systematics* 1992 among many others).

The Greenhouse Effect.   Carbon dioxide plays a critical role in controlling the Earth's climate because as an aerosol it absorbs and reflects or scatters incoming radiation on the one hand and absorbs and reradiates outgoing infrared radiation on the other. This latter phenomenon results in what is popularly called the **Greenhouse Effect,** an analogy to what happens in a greenhouse.

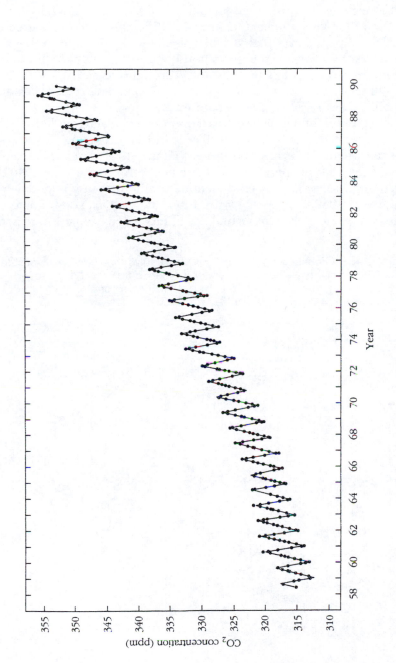

Figure 15–3 Monthly variations in the concentration of atmospheric CO_2 content at Mauna Loa Observatory, Hawaii, observed with a continuously recording nondispersive infrared gas analyzer. The yearly oscillations reflect seasonal variations in the amount of photosynthesis; the dots indicate monthly average concentration. (Data courtesy of C. D. Keeling)

The greenhouse analogy, however, is not perfect. Greenhouse glass and greenhouse gases like carbon dioxide allow the passage of sunlight to the Earth's surface and then keep the heat within. The difference is that in a greenhouse all the heat is trapped, except that which is allowed to escape by regulating the glass louvers; by contrast, the greenhouse gases trap only the heat of infrared radiation. However, as less heat escapes through the glass louvers of a greenhouse, the temperature within the greenhouse rises, and similarly as the level of greenhouse gases rises, Earth's climate warms up.

Direct observations as well as computer modeling indicate that global warming due to the Greenhouse Effect is indeed occurring. A warming trend that began about 1880 has continued (Figure 15–4), and Jones and Wigley (1990) suggest that temperatures will rise between 1 and 4°C by 2040 to 2065.

Although there have been dissenters on the warming phenomenon (Kerr 1989; Roberts 1989b), a report by the International Panel on Climate Exchange in midsummer 1990 brought virtual unanimity among some 170 scientists from

Figure 15–4   Global warming from 1880 to 1990 as shown by deviations from the 1950–1980 mean temperature. Except for the period from 1940 to 1975, when the trend inexplicably reversed itself, the increase has been consistently upward. (Redrawn from M. La Brecque. 1989. *Mosaic* 20(4):1–17.)

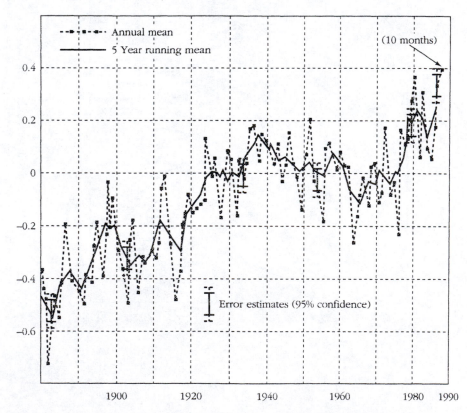

25 different countries that a warming is on the way, and in fact that the average global temperature has increased between 0.3 and 0.6°C since the late nineteenth century (Kerr 1990a). According to the panel's estimate, anthropogenic enhancement of carbon dioxide since 1765 will be doubled during the next 35 years if no significant steps are taken to reduce the yearly increases of carbon dioxide and other greenhouse gases.

Based on an extensive review of vast quantities of evidence, the United Nations Intergovernmental Panel on Climate Change (IPCC 1990) used a five-star rating system to describe the probability of various scenarios for global warming (Table 15–2). Among other projections: global warming by 2.5°C (or as high as 4°C) with a consequent rise in sea level between 8 and 29 cm by 2030 and continental interiors, the breadbaskets of North America and Eurasia, might be dry during the summer (Karl et al. 1991).

The severity of the impact would depend on the level of atmospheric carbon dioxide, the amount and kind of particulates, solar activity (which in fact varies) (Friss-Christensen and Lassen 1991), the Earth's wobble, and still other factors that interact to produce the complex environmental component known

TABLE 15–2 The Probable Major Environmental Changes Resulting from a Doubling of CO_2 as Deduced from Models

Degree of Confidence[a]	Predicted Change
Temperature	
*****	The lower atmosphere and Earth's surface warm
*****	The stratosphere cools
***	Near the Earth's surface, the global average warming lies between +1.5°C and +4.5°C, with a "best guess" of 2.5°C
***	The surface warming at high latitudes is greater than the global average in winter but smaller than in summer (in time-dependent simulations with a deep ocean, there is little warming over the high-latitude ocean)
***	The surface warming and its seasonal variation are least in the tropics
Precipitation	
****	The global average increases (as does that of evaporation); the larger the warming, the larger the increase
***	Increases at high latitudes throughout the year
***	Increases globally by 3 to 15 percent (as does evaporation)
**	Increases at midlatitudes in winter
**	The zonal mean value increases in the tropics, although there are areas of decrease; shifts in the main tropical rain bands differ from model to model, so there is little consistency between models in simulated regional changes
**	Changes little in subtropical arid areas
Soil Moisture	
***	Increases in high latitudes in winter
**	Decreases over northern midlatitude continents in summer
Snow and Sea Ice	
****	The area of sea ice and seasonal snow cover diminish

[a] The number of stars indicates the degree of confidence, five stars indicating virtual certainty and one star low confidence in the prediction.

Source: Reprinted by permission from IPCC. 1990. *Climate change: The IPCC scientific assessment.* J. T. Houghton, G. J. Jenkins, and J. J. Ephraums, eds. Cambridge: Cambridge University Press.

as climate. Already, however, there is evidence of widespread warming of the permafrost by 2 to 4°C in northernmost Alaska (Lachenbruch and Marshall 1986); an increase of 2°C in air and lake temperature and a three-week increase in the ice-free season on lakes of the central boreal forest (Schindler et al. 1990); large-scale changes in precipitation over the Northern Hemisphere over the last 30 to 40 years (Bradley et al. 1987); and an increase in coastal upwelling (Bakun 1990) but only a slight rise in sea level, on the order of 1 millimeter per year (Peltier and Tushingham 1989). Others have suggested a world with an abundance of male alligators, migrating tree species, and a plethora of parasites (Roberts 1988).

Some scientists have projected a positive side of the Greenhouse Effect by way of growth enhancement of natural vegetation in the presence of abundant carbon dioxide (Esser 1992, among others). In contrast, others are less sanguine, largely because of our lack of sufficient knowledge of the many factors impacting global climate (Paine 1993, among others).

Whether the uncertainties about these estimates and projections are large enough to suggest delaying the development of new policies and regulations on greenhouse gases becomes not a scientific question but a value judgment (Schneider 1989; Kerr 1997).

A Geological Perspective on the Greenhouse Effect.   Quite naturally, we of the latter part of the twentieth century are increasingly concerned about the consequences of the Greenhouse Effect on our lives and livelihood. Geologically, however, it appears the Earth has experienced a number of "greenhouse" episodes followed by "icehouse" episodes (Berner 1990; COHOP Members 1988, among others). During the Mesozoic period, 100 million years BP, dinosaurs roamed in a climate that was warm and maritime with narrow temperature gradients across latitudes and within the oceans; polar icecaps were small or even nonexistent, and global sea level was high. During the succeeding Eocene "icehouse" period, temperature gradients were steeper, climate was continental, that is, temperate with stronger seasonal variation, and ocean circulation was more vigorous (McGowran 1990). Speculation is that natural geochemical processes resulted in the slow buildup of atmospheric carbon dioxide causing a Greenhouse Effect during the Mesozoic (Raynaud et al. 1993).

But, as recently as 10,000 years BP during the most recent ice age, sea level was nearly 120 m lower than today. This expanded the land occupied by the present state of Florida to nearly twice its width and extending all the way to New Orleans (Schneider 1997).

Carbon Dioxide: A Lethal Gas

Although generally regarded as beneficial with respect to human health, too much carbon dioxide can cause asphyxiation and death preceded by an anesthetic effect that can produce sensory hallucinations. On August 21, 1986, a sudden release of carbon dioxide from Lake Nyos, a crater lake, in the north-western area of Cameroon, West Africa caused the deaths of at least 1,700 peo-ple and 3,000 cattle within a 10 km area (Kling et al. 1987). Birds, insects, and small mammals were not seen for 48 hours after the event, but plant life was essentially unaffected. A water surge had washed up the southern shore to a height of about 25 m, and a fountain of water and froth had splashed over an 80-m-high promontory on the southwestern shore. Two days after the disaster, the lake surface was calm but littered with floating mats of vegetation and had turned from its normal clear blue color to a rusty red. The gas was presumably derived from magma beneath the lake in this basaltic volcano country and was stored in its deep waters. Its release was triggered not by volcanic activity but presumably because of the volume reaching limits of containment.

An earlier release of lethal gas, probably also carbon dioxide, from Lake Monoun, also a crater lake, caused the deaths of 37 people. These two instances are the only recorded events in which gas released from lakes has caused the loss of human life. Kling et al. (1987) note that the nature of the gas released sug-gests that hazardous lakes may be identified and monitored to reduce the dan-ger of such incidents in the future.

Nitrogen Cycle

Because of its role in the construction of proteins and nucleic acids and its importance as a potential limiting factor in many biological phenomena, nitro-gen is a significant element biochemically and thereby akin to oxygen, carbon, and hydrogen. Since nitrogen makes up a large portion of the Earth's atmo-sphere (about 78 percent), the problem with its availability is not an absolute but a relative shortage, that is, scarcity of usable or metabolizable nitrogen during critical growth periods. It is thus one of the major limiting factors controlling the dynamics and functionings of ecosystems. For example, plants encounter short-ages of inorganic nitrogen, such as nitrate or ammonium ions, and animals experience shortages of organic nitrogen, largely as the amine group (NH_2) for specific proteins or amino acids (Mattson 1980).

The biogeochemical cycle of nitrogen, which is quite complex but essen-tially a complete or perfect one (Figure 15–5), bears general similarities to the carbon cycle (compare with Figure 15–2), but there are a number of marked dif-ferences. First, although it is abundant, the gaseous form of nitrogen cannot be used by most organisms; second, nitrogen is not released in the gaseous form as a waste product; and third, biological involvement in its cycle is far more exten-sive, complicated, ordered, and specific in that certain organisms are able to act only in certain phases of the cycle.

With an atmospheric concentration of 78 percent, it would seem that the nitrogen reservoir ought to be the atmosphere. But, as noted above, because few organisms are able to use elemental nitrogen, the crucial reservoir is the store occurring in both inorganic (ammonia, nitrite, and nitrate) and organic (urea, protein, nucleic acid) form. Unlike carbon, which is readily available in reservoir

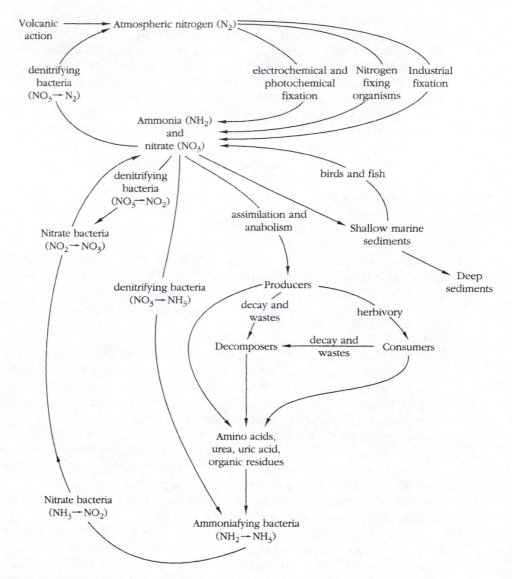

Figure 15–5   The nitrogen cycle.

quantities both in the air and water, atmospheric nitrogen must be fixed into an inorganic form, largely nitrate and ammonia, before it can be tapped for general biological processes in the majority of organisms.

Although the nitrogen cycle is technically and chemically complex, a brief description of each of its four major steps (fixation, ammoniafication, nitrification, and denitrification) will demonstrate its environmental importance. For those so inclined, there is a comprehensive review of the nitrogen cycle by Sprent (1987).

Nitrogen Fixation. **Nitrogen fixation** involves the conversion of nitrogen gas (N_2) from the atmosphere to ammonia (NH_3) and nitrate (NO_3) by two major groups of organisms: symbiotic nitrogen fixers (largely bacteria but also including fungi and algae) and free-living nitrogen fixers (both bacteria and algae and perhaps other microorganisms). Symbiotic nitrogen fixation occurs largely in terrestrial situations, whereas fixation by free-living forms occurs in both terrestrial and aquatic situations, the former being quantitatively a hundredfold more significant.

The most studied instances of symbiotic nitrogen fixation are the *Rhizobium* bacteria that are associated with leguminous plants (peas, beans, clover, etc.). These bacteria, which are highly host-specific (that is, particular strains are associated only with particular species of legumes) penetrate the plants' root hairs; in response to this invasion, the root hair undergoes differential growth resulting in an enlargement, the nodule, in which nitrogen fixation occurs. Crop rotation, which includes planting of legumes, results in natural fertilization of the soil with these vital nitrates. Another type of natural nitrate fertilization occurs by alder (*Alnus*), the first trees to reforest coniferous areas of the Northwest; alder, a nonleguminous plant, also has symbiotic nitrogen-fixing bacteria. Curiously, symbiotic intestinal bacterial fixation of nitrogen also occurs in certain termites (Benemann 1973).

Commercial nitrogen fixation, initially for weapons and today for agricultural fertilizers, is much more energy-expensive than biological fixation is and accounts for about 40 percent of the 2×10^8 metric tons produced annually by both means (Leschine et al. 1988). Industrially produced fertilizer is now the largest source of new nitrogen entering ecosystems (Vitousek et al. 1997).

Ammoniafication. The nitrates produced through nitrogen fixation undergo conversion into an organic form (again, largely amines) in the synthesis of proteins and nucleic acids, the latter being the stuff of heredity. As proteins and nucleic acids are metabolized, the organic nitrogen is eliminated as urea (in humans and many other organisms), uric acid (birds, some insects), or in some other form. Heterotrophic bacteria and fungi in soil and water utilize this organic, nitrogen-rich substrate for their own sustenance, converting and releasing it as a waste product in an inorganic form, ammonia (NH_3)—hence the term **ammoniafication** for this process. Some of the ammoniafying microorganisms are substrate-specific, using only a given protein but not others or even simple amino acids, or using urea but not uric acid; other species appear to be able to use a wide variety of organic nitrogen sources.

Nitrification. Although some autotrophic and many heterotrophic marine bacteria can use ammonia or ammonium salts to synthesize their own protoplasm, ammonia is not generally accessible in this form and must be converted to nitrate (NO_3) in a process termed **nitrification.** Occurring slowly, if at all, in acid conditions but more rapidly in other situations, nitrification takes place by bacteria in two steps: first, the conversion of ammonia or ammonium salts to nitrite (NO_2), a toxic form even in small concentrations; and second, the conversion of nitrite to nitrate.

Nitrate (as well as nitrite) is easily leached out of soil, especially in acidic conditions, and may become "lost" to the ecosystem in which it was produced. But through groundwater circulation, it may become available in another ecosystem elsewhere. The deserts of Chile, for example, are rich in nitrates leached from the Andes Mountains. They are so rich, in fact, that they provided a sufficient supply of nitrates to meet the needs for explosives by Western powers during World War I.

Denitrification. Ammoniafication followed by nitrification allows for recycling without starting the whole process again with atmospheric nitrogen. Alternatively, **denitrification** of nitrate to the gaseous form (N_2) returns the element to the atmosphere for recycling via the nitrogen fixation process, thus completing the cycle. Denitrifying bacteria in anaerobic situations, such as poorly aerated soils, use the nitrate as an oxygen source.

Within some ecosystems, however, the major processes of nitrification and denitrification are well attuned to the productivity demands of the ecosystems. These processes in the nitrogen cycle, for example, are most rapid in winter in temperate zones, resulting in maximum amounts of nitrate in the spring and early summer, the time when nitrate demand for plant growth and reproduction is highest. In many ecosystems, however, no denitrification occurs. Although nitrogen fixation generally enables ecosystems to stay ahead of nitrogen deficiency, denitrification, where it occurs, ensures that the margin is always slim.

Global Nitrogen Budget

The global distribution of nitrogen is shown in Table 15–3, wherein it can be seen that the amount of organic nitrogen is infinitesimally small compared with inorganic nitrogen. Although cyclic overall, the movement of nitrogen is multidirectional, regulated, and energy dependent. Numerous routes are avail-

TABLE 15–3 Nitrogen in the Biosphere (in 10^6 metric tons)

Atmosphere	3,800,000	Ocean water (dissolved)	20,000
Land organisms	772	Ocean organisms	901
Living	12	Living	1
Dead	760	Dead	900
Inorganic N (land)	140	Inorganic N (ocean)	100
Earth's crust	14,000,000	Sediments	4,000,000
	Total organic	1,673	
	Total inorganic	21,820,240	

Source: Data derived from C. C. Delwiche. September 1970. *Scientific American.*

able at virtually every major way station, each route is biologically or nonbiolog-
ically regulated, and energy is consumed or released in each process. These
numerous self-regulating, energy-dependent feedback mechanisms lead to the
assumption that the global nitrogen cycle is balanced, nitrogen fixation being
balanced by denitrification. This assumption is in question, however. Whatever
possible balance may exist is increasingly stressed by the accelerating rate of
industrial nitrogen fixation (largely for fertilizers) without being compensated
for by an increased rate of denitrification. A further disturbance of the nitrogen
system is created by the burning of fossil fuels in automobiles and trucks. This
source of nitrite release to the atmosphere constitutes a major source of air pollution, the nitrite also being a pollutant especially detrimental to the respiratory
system and to the maintenance of the ozone layer in the atmosphere.

The excess nitrogen from fertilizers and the burning of fossil fuels results
in plants utilizing more carbon dioxide, thereby putting some brake on the
Greenhouse Effect; however, there is evidence that, at least in grasslands, the
spurred growth favors weed plants at the expense of native species (Wedin and
Tilman 1996).

Numerous studies have indicated that large amounts of nitrogen (and
other nutrients) are lost by runoff to adjacent ecosystems from surface soils after
clearcutting, especially if followed by burning (Matson et al. 1987). The amount
lost in this manner is equivalent to more than half of the industrial nitrogen
fixed globally and is greater than the total amount of nitrogen delivered by
rivers to the ocean. If this nitrogen is lost to the atmosphere or to aquatic systems, there would be a detrimental effect particularly on tropical ecosystems,
which must recycle minerals very rapidly to remain productive.

These various anthropogenic activities have at least doubled the transfer of
nitrogen from the atmosphere into the land-based nitrogen cycle, with all
regions of the globe being affected, most notably the northern hemisphere
(Vitousek et al. 1997). There are no positive signs that such activity is lessening,
the consequences of which are not fully known but are not likely to be beneficial.

SEDIMENTARY NUTRIENT CYCLES

Although some essential nutrients like sulfur may have a gaseous phase (e.g.,
sulfur dioxide), such phases are relatively insignificant, for there is no large
gaseous reservoir. Furthermore, none of these nutrients cycle so readily as carbon and nitrogen. In their pathways there are fewer self-correcting, homeostatic mechanisms, and more stages in which short- or long-term stagnation can
occur. Most significant of the stagnation stages is sedimentation in the oceans
and deep continental lakes. We will briefly examine the sedimentary cycle of sulfur, a nutrient of critical significance in growth and metabolism because of its
role in the bonding of proteins. Also, it is a relatively well understood biogeochemical cycle.

Sulfur Cycle

Sulfur is not only a critical component of essential biological compounds such as the amino acids cysteine and methionine, its cycle, like that of nitrogen, plays a substantial role in the regulation of other nutrients, including oxygen and phosphorus. The heart of the sulfur cycle involves the uptake of sulfate (SO_4) by producers, largely through their roots, and the release and transformation of the sulfur in a number of different steps and variety of forms including sulfhydryl (SH), hydrogen sulfide (H_2S), sulfites (SO_3), and molecular sulfur (S). Like the nitrogen cycle, the sulfur cycle is complex (Figure 15–6); unlike the nitrogen cycle, it doesn't fall into discretely packaged steps such as nitrogen fixation, ammoniafication, etc. Hence, where we begin to describe the cycle is somewhat arbitrary, but we shall start with the assimilation of sulfur into plants (more or less at the center of Figure 15–6).

Assimilation and Release of Sulfur by Plants. Sulfur enters the trophic cycle in terrestrial plants via root adsorption in the form of inorganic sulfates (e.g., calcium sulfate, sodium sulfate) or by direct assimilation of amino acids released in the decomposition of dead or excreted organic matter. Bacterial and fungal breakdown of the organic sulfhydryl in amino acids followed by oxidation results in sulfate; this adds to the sulfate pool for root adsorption.

Under anaerobic conditions, sulfuric acid may be reduced directly to sulfides, including hydrogen sulfide, by certain bacteria. Sulfate is also reduced under anaerobic conditions to elemental sulfur or to sulfides, including hydrogen sulfide, by specific heterotrophic bacteria. These sulfate-reducing, anaerobic bacteria use the sulfate as a hydrogen acceptor in metabolic oxidation in a manner comparable to the use of nitrite and nitrate by denitrifying bacteria.

Until recently, sulfate reduction had been thought to occur only under anaerobic conditions since in the presence of even traces of oxygen, nitrates, or other electron acceptors sulfate reduction was inhibited. However, Canfield and Des Marais (1991) found that sulfate reduction occurs in the upper, well-oxygenated, photosynthetic zone of hypersaline microbial mats from Baja California, Mexico. Thus, sulfate reduction is not strictly an anaerobic process, but the degree to which aerobic reduction contributes on a broad scale is yet to be determined.

It is important to note that although photosynthesis accounts for the bulk of oxygen in the atmosphere, without denitrifying and sulfate-reducing bacteria, the oxygen cycle would be out of balance. There are no other mechanisms for releasing the considerable amount of oxygen bound up in nitrates and sulfates than the reduction processes that occur in the nitrogen and sulfur cycles.

The presence of large quantities of hydrogen sulfide in the anaerobic, and usually deeper, portions of aquatic ecosystems is inimical to most life. For example, hydrogen sulfide inhibits oxygen release from and nutrient uptake by rice plants; but, when present, a filamentous bacterium significantly reduces hydrogen sulfide levels and increases oxygen release from the rice plants (Joshi and Hollis 1977). The presence of hydrogen sulfide probably accounts for the

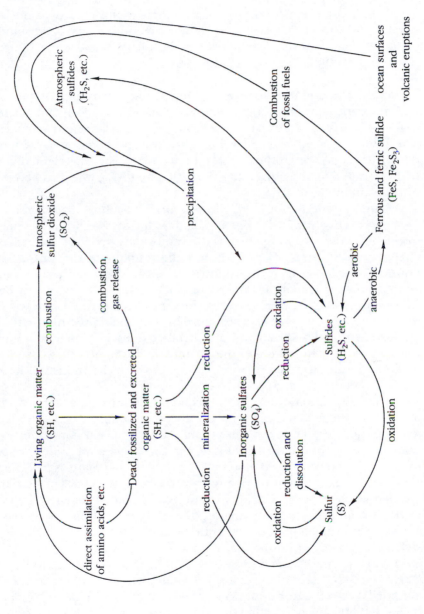

Figure 15–6 The sulfur cycle.

absence of fish and other more complex animals below 200 m in the Black Sea and has been considered responsible for kills of fish in valley impoundments polluted by pulp mill effluents, which are rich in sulfates.

The existence of archaebacterial sulfate reducers at extremely high temperatures (70 to 110°C) can explain the formation of hydrogen sulfide observed in submarine hydrothermal systems, deep oil wells and fumerols (steam vents) (Stetter et al. 1987; Jorgensen et al. 1992).

Sulfur in the Atmosphere.   Sulfur in the atmosphere is the result of several different sources: decomposition or combustion of organic matter, combustion of fossil fuels, and dispersion from ocean surfaces and volcanic eruptions. The most prevalent form of sulfur entering the atmosphere is sulfur dioxide (SO_2); it, along with other atmospheric forms such as elemental sulfur and hydrogen sulfide, is oxidized to sulfur trioxide (SO_3), which combines with water to form sulfuric acid (H_2SO_4).

Atmospheric sulfur, largely in the form of sulfuric acid, is removed by two general processes: rainout, which includes all processes within clouds that result in removal; and washout, which is the removal by precipitation below the clouds (Kellogg et al. 1972). Depending on the amount of the various sulfur compounds available to form the sulfuric acid, the degree of acidity can be strong enough to approximate that of battery acid, one of the strongest known acids. Atmospheric sulfuric acid accounts for approximately 70 percent of the phenomenon known as **acid rain** (or more broadly, **acid precipitation**); the remaining acids are derived from various nitrous oxides and other compounds. These acids are attributed largely to the burning of fossil fuels that has increased dramatically in the last 150 or so years, the period of the Industrial Revolution.

Acid Precipitation.   Acid precipitation is a prime example of the interaction of ecosystems, since the acids produced in one area tend to have their major detrimental effect on ecosystems at some considerable distance. For example, the acids resulting from industries located in the Ohio River Valley are precipitated in the northeastern United States in upper New York State, New Hampshire, and Vermont. These acids have an adverse impact on the cycles of nutrients that are affected by the degree of acidity (most notably the nitrogen cycle) and on lakes with poor buffering capacity (that is, the ability to neutralize additions of acids or alkalis). Unfortunately, many lakes in the northeastern part of North America as well as large areas of Minnesota, Wisconsin, and upper Michigan (and comparable regions in Europe and elsewhere) fall in this category. Acidification of such lakes adversely affects their biota. For example, in 1975 40 percent of the high-altitude lakes in the Adirondacks were devoid of fish (Ember 1981); in Sweden in the mid-1980s, all bodies of freshwater were acidified, with 15,000 too acidified to support sensitive aquatic life and an additional 1,800 nearly lifeless (Starke 1988).

In terrestrial ecosystems, acid precipitation results in the loss of large quantities of minerals (e.g., calcium and magnesium) from the soil. These minerals are exported from the ecosystem by drainage water (Likens et al. 1996).

Acid precipitation has caused considerable damage to architectural structures by corroding such famous monuments as the six caryatids that support the porch of the Acropolis in Athens, the Parthenon, the Taj Mahal, Rome's Colosseum, the Lincoln Memorial, and the Washington Monument. The U.S. Council on Environmental Quality estimated in 1979 that the annual cost in the United States alone in architectural damage due to acid precipitation was nearly $2 billion. And the National Academy of Sciences put the total damage to materials, forests, agriculture, aquatic ecosystems, and health and water systems at $5 billion in 1978.

In response to the adverse effect of acid precipitation, many industrialized nations in Europe and North America enacted legislation or regulations (e.g., the Clean Air Act) to reduce the release of sulfur dioxide (and nitrogen oxides) with the expectation that such reductions would rejuvenate forests, lakes, and streams. However, although the release of these compounds has been reduced dramatically as a result of tighter controls, rain falling in Europe and North America is still demonstrably acidic. The explanation appears to be twofold: first, the phenomenon of acid rain is much more complex than previously thought; and second, there has been a significant reduction in atmospheric dust-borne particles, whose base properties counteract (i.e., neutralize) the acids (Hedin and Likens 1996). These atmospheric dust particles originate anthropogenically from fossil fuel combustion, industrial activities (e.g., cement manufacture and mining), construction, farming (e.g., plowing), and traffic on unpaved roads, among other sources. Forest fires and wind erosion on arid soils with limited plant cover are natural sources of such particles. All of the anthropogenic sources have been reduced or curtailed (e.g., by scrubbing particles from smokestacks) more or less simultaneously with the reductions in sulfur and nitrogen emissions. It would appear the two are canceling out each other; the consequence is that acid precipitation remains a serious environmental problem.

Global Cycle of Sulfur.   Unlike the situations for carbon and nitrogen, the total amount of sulfur in various compartments of the biosphere and the rate at which the various forms of sulfur turn over is not as well understood. Although the annual turnover of sulfur has been estimated, the amount of the more or less long-term losses to the sediments is not easily assessed. Given the holding action of the sediments (discussion of which would take us too far afield), this part of the cycle suggests that the overall sulfur cycle is not balanced, although the ebb and flow from ocean and land to atmosphere and back would make it appear to be so. For example, the annual total output of sulfur to the atmosphere of 550×10^6 tons is balanced by the return to the Earth's surface of the same amount (Kellogg et al. 1972). Although the total amount of sulfur in the biosphere is a constant, the ever-increasing release of sulfur by the combustion of fossil fuels will continue to increase the amount annually cycled. The resulting increase in the amount of sulfuric acid (and other acids) in precipitation carries the consequence of correlative increases in the damage to ecosystems in particular parts of the world, as we have just briefly discussed.

POLLUTION

In this and other chapters, particularly Chapter 10, there has been frequent notice given to anthropogenic impact on biogeochemical cycles on water, land, and air. In large measure, this interaction has resulted in contamination of these environmental media by agricultural and industrial activities compounding the wastes created in the business of just living. Before discussing a few additional examples, it is important to understand what pollution is and why this is the most pertinent place to expand on the topic.

Pollution: A Definition

"To make or render unclean; to defile; desecrate; profane"—this is the meaning of the verb pollute according to *Webster's New Collegiate Dictionary*. These are strong words but less informative than the following definition of pollution adopted by the Environmental Pollution Panel, of the President's Science Advisory Committee, in its report, *Restoring the Quality of Our Environment,* in November 1965, a definition that is still operative:

> Environmental pollution is the unfavorable alteration of our surroundings, wholly or largely as a by-product of man's actions, through direct or indirect effects of changes in energy patterns, radiation levels, chemical and physical constitution, and abundances of organisms. These changes may affect man directly, or through his supplies of water and of agricultural and other biological products, his physical objects or possessions, or his opportunities for recreation and appreciation of nature.

The key phrases here are "unfavorable alteration" and "by-products of man's actions"—the residues of things humans make, use, and throw away. These are the concomitants of society that are exacerbated by those societies with a high standard of living and are increasing both because of population increase and increasing expectations for higher living standards. Pollution can be regarded as primarily a result of human behavior that largely disregards consequences, one that unwisely uses and discards resources. But pollutants also include the natural byproducts of human metabolic activity and that of the organisms on which humans depend for food, biological waste products, and farm animal excreta.

Seen in this perspective, a pollutant is not something apart from humans but is inherent in their very biology and culture; it is a result of their peculiar adaptations and attributes. In this framework, why should a "natural" byproduct be considered "unnatural," that is, polluting? *Pollutants,* a value- and emotion-laden word today, are, in fact, normal byproducts of people as purely biological organisms and as creative social beings. They are the inorganic and organic wastes of metabolic and digestive processes and of creativity in protecting and augmenting the production of crops, of warming homes, clothing the body, and harnessing the atom. The problem is not in the natural elaboration of byproducts. It is in the disposition of them. As the foregoing definition aptly states, the problem is a case of a "resource out of place," too much in one system and not enough in another. The problem is a resource being present in a system that is not adapted to it and thus constituting an unaccustomed stimulus, stress, or "insult" to that system. These are the stimulants that may terminate some or initiate other biological processes, alter efficiency, affect species composition and community structure, and, in general, alter the dynamics and development of an ecosystem.

The hydrologic and biogeochemical cycles are the vehicles by which pollutants are moved around, from atmosphere to land or water and vice versa. It is this cyclical movement that results in a byproduct from one locale becoming a pollutant in another, even one far removed as we discussed in the case of acid precipitation. And, portions of these cyclical movements can result in the accumulation of byproducts for longer or shorter periods of time in different components of ecosystems where their impact may be salutary (e.g., natural nitrate as a fertilizer) or polluting (e.g., excess carbon dioxide in the atmosphere).

Byproducts, like the adage about the poor, will always be with us. They will increase as technology and living standards increase; they will become exacerbated as urbanization proceeds and more people live in smaller areas. Solutions do not and cannot lie solely in removing the cause because as long as humanity exists, it will have byproducts. Rather, answers lie in intelligent management of that production through regulating the "unfavorable alteration of our surroundings." Further, given that there are ultimate limits to the amount of these resources, it becomes an expression of wisdom to plan ahead to a steady-state system, not to an ever-expanding one.

Although a full exploration of pollution is well beyond the limits of this textbook, an example of pollution in two of the three major environmental media, water and land, will provide some further concrete examples of this aspect of human interaction with the environment. Earlier in this chapter, other examples of pollution in the atmosphere (i.e., the Greenhouse Effect and acid precipitation) were described.

Mercury and Aquatic Ecosystems

The element mercury in its methylated form, known as methyl mercury, is a highly toxic substance that causes neurological damage, produces chromosomal aberrations, and results in congenital birth defects (Hammond 1971). Substantial mercury pollution in the Great Lakes became apparent in March 1970, when it was detected in pickerel shipped from Canada. Its source was identified as industrial waste in the form of inorganic mercury or phenyl mercury, from which it is converted by anaerobic bacteria in the sediments into a methylated form.

Methyl mercury accumulated in fish in two ways: through the food chain/web and by direct absorption into body tissues. The reason for concern about the mercury in the Great Lakes was the episodes of mercury contamination in Sweden and Iraq (Bakir et al. 1973), as well as near Minamata, Japan, where 111 persons died or suffered serious neurological damage between 1953 and 1960 as a result of eating fish and shellfish from mercury-contaminated waters. Among the 111 were 19 congenitally defective babies born of mothers who had eaten mercury-contaminated fish and shellfish (Madati and Kormondy 1989; Totsuka 1989). Fortunately, typical mercury concentrations in Lake Erie fish were considerably below that in Minamata fish; furthermore, fish then formed a much less significant part of the American diet as compared with that of the Japanese. Nonetheless, the "mercury scare" was significant in curtailing commercial fishing and in increasing regulation of mercury discharge in industrial waters.

Although there has been control of point source mercury pollution (industrial discharges) in the Great Lakes, including Lake Erie, its airborne input has not been brought under control. Mercury is an unusual pollutant because natural sources emit more than do anthropogenic sources. According to the National Academy of Sciences, natural sources emit more than 1,000 metric tons (1 metric ton = 2,204.6 pounds) annually, whereas anthropogenic sources account for about 650 metric tons, the major sources of the latter being coal combustion followed by municipal waste incineration (Hileman 1988).

Pesticides and Terrestrial Ecosystems

Pesticides encompass a broad array of chemicals that are used to control plant growth (herbicides), insects (insecticides), worms (vermicides), bacteria (bactericides), fungi (fungicides), and other organisms. Almost without exception, pesticides are used to benefit humans by the control of unwanted species of plants (e.g., weeds in a lawn), disease-causing bacteria (e.g., *Pneumococcus*, the causative agent of pneumonia), disease-carrying insects (e.g., malarial or yellow-fever mosquitoes), or in controlling destruction of agricultural products by disease-causing organisms (e.g., corn borers and the virus of anthurium blight). Although they are by and large mostly beneficial, pesticides used both properly and improperly are also "resources out of place," that is pollutants, that are subject to normal ecological processes.

Some pesticides are subject to normal biological degradation by soil and water bacteria and are thus rendered harmless; the commonly used weedkiller 2, 4-D, is one of them. This particular compound is a synthesized growth regulator and simulates many of the naturally occurring ones. It is not surprising then that such natural, or quasi-natural, products are ecologically accommodated in normal ecosystem dynamics. On the other hand, other plant growth regulators and insecticides are quite resistant to biological decomposition. If such nonbiodegradable compounds should become "fixed" in the soil by being bound to the clay or humus fractions, they are of less consequence to an ecosystem; the insecticides dieldrin and DDT fall in this category.

It is significant to note, however, that a substantial proportion of insecticides is not permanently fixed by the soil. Also, they collect on plant surfaces and can thus be passed directly along a food chain. And, importantly, because of differential metabolic and retention capacities of organisms, residue levels tend to increase with higher trophic levels, popularly referred to as **biological magnification.** For example, in a study of DDT concentrations in organisms along the southern shore of Long Island, where this insecticide was used to control mosquitoes for some 20 years, the DDT level was 0.00005 ppm in water. In the process of biological magnification, the level in cormorants, a bird that eats large fish, was 26.4 ppm, a 500,000-fold increase!

Dioxin. Dioxin is a highly toxic compound found as a contaminant in certain herbicides (e.g., 2,4,5-T), chlorophenols, and other related chemicals. It is very persistent in soil except when exposed to light (McConnell et al. 1984). This pesticide has been shown to cause death, spontaneous abortion, and cancer in guinea pigs and rats, and is suspected of doing so in humans as well (Roberts 1991). It has also been indicted in the die-off of seals in northern Europe (Kerr 1994). The Environmental Protection Agency retained its classification of dioxin as a "probable human carcinogen" as well as asserting that in levels found in food supplies, it may trigger such problems as endometriosis in women and decreased sperm counts in men (Stone 1994). Other scientists, however, question such links as well as the dioxin levels in food supplies used by the agency in its estimates.

Regardless of the continuing controversy about its toxicity and carcinogenicity in humans, dioxin is a known contaminant in "Agent Orange," an herbicide widely used in the 1960s by the U.S. military to defoliate Viet Cong sanctuaries during the Viet Nam War. Although a number of Viet Nam veterans have developed various cancers and fathered seriously handicapped children, direct linkage to Agent Orange (actually to dioxin) has been a matter of continual contention among Viet Nam veterans, Dow Chemical Company (the major manufacturer of Agent Orange), and the political establishment (Magnuson 1990). Nonetheless, discovery of dioxin in the soil of Times Beach, Missouri, led to the evacuation of the town and a $33 million government offer to buy out all property owners; and a modern state office building in Binghamton, New York was abandoned and sealed after a transformer fire in 1981 spewed dioxin-tainted soot throughout the eighteen-story structure (Rempel and Randolph 1983).

An incident that occurred in Seveso, Italy, in July 1976 has considerable direct bearing on the dioxin problem. An explosion at the ICMESA chemical plant, which was manufacturing the herbicide TCP, released a cloud of dioxin that resulted in the death of pets and other animals within a few days (Madati and Kormondy 1989). Humans developed skin rashes, itching, vomiting, and diarrhea; long-term effects are still being studied. Unfortunately, a mass evacuation of the 700 inhabitants did not occur for several days while company and political officials argued, unnecessarily exposing the population to chronic dosages longer than should have been the case (Walsh 1977). The full details and effects of this disaster are as yet not clear; nor are the linkages to dioxin as uncontrovertible as scientists would like.

CONCLUDING COMMENT

Based on the foregoing discussion, it is relatively easy to be caught up in the emotion elicited by the term *pollution*. What is important, however, is to realize again that what we are dealing with are byproducts, the wastes of a natural ecological agent—*Homo sapiens*. We are, and our wastes are, as much a part of the living world as the microbe and its wastes. But humans have a peculiar and potential dominance over ecosystems even though they are in no way independent of them; when they insult an ecosystem, they can expect to be slapped back. As they put resources out of place, they can expect changes—undesirable concentrations of toxic substances, consequent reductions in the number and abundance of species, and a resultant and consequential community instability. Humans cannot, nor can any organism, exist without producing wastes. The problem thus concerns intelligent and resourceful management. The quality of our environment will be a reflection of our capacity to manage it. It will require much more understanding of ecological ramifications than are presently known and much more interplay of the myriad facets of a complex society in their resolution.

Resolution, however, does not lie solely as a province of ecology—it along with sociology, economics, political science, anthropology, geography, law, psychology, and, in the final analysis, ethics are inextricably intertwined in addressing these global matters. There will be no return to a bygone Arcadia or Camelot or a maintenance of the status quo. That is contrary to perhaps the most basic tenet of ecological and evolutionary principles, that of dynamic and adaptive change. Change is the essence of nature, both the gradual change that transforms a pond to a forest, and the devastating kind by which a tornadic wind denudes a landscape. Humanity's hopes and future lie in the regulation of the changes that they, as a natural and integral part of the landscape, induce. Human activities are partners with other natural processes in the stewardship of resources and the management of cultural and biological wastes. The future depends on our intelligence and ability to develop a body of knowledge about such management and on the wisdom that few now possess to apply that knowledge.

KEY TERMS

acid precipitation	denitrification	micronutrients
acid rain	gaseous nutrient	nitrification
ammoniafication	cycle	nitrogen fixation
biogeochemical	Greenhouse Effect	residence time
cycle	hydrologic cycle	sedimentary
biological	lithosphere	nutrient cycle
magnification	macronutrients	sedimentary rock

KEY POINTS

☐ Essential elements are the some twenty required in the life processes of most organisms and an additional ten or so required by different species, usually in trace amounts.

☐ Macronutrients such as carbon, hydrogen, oxygen, nitrogen, and phosphorus are the building blocks of protoplasm, whereas other macronutrients play a variety of structural or physiological roles.

☐ Many micronutrients play key roles in enzymatic activity, whereas others play a variety of structural and physiological roles.

☐ The presence or absence of an essential nutrient may adversely impact the availability or activity of another nutrient.

☐ The hydrologic cycle is a steady-state one in which total precipitation is balanced by total evaporation. Nearly 95 percent of Earth's water is in the lithosphere and in sedimentary rocks, and 99 percent of the water in circulation is in the oceans.

☐ In gaseous biogeochemical cycles, such as carbon and nitrogen, the atmosphere is a major reservoir of the element in a gaseous phase; in sedimentary cycles, such as phosphorus, the major reservoir is the lithosphere.

☐ The carbon cycle is essentially a complete or perfect one, carbon being returned to the environment about as fast as it is removed because of a number of self-regulating feedback mechanisms.

☐ In spite of self-regulating feedback mechanisms, the amount of carbon dioxide in the atmosphere has increased, resulting in the increased trapping of heat (the Greenhouse Effect) with consequent global warming, which Earth has experienced a number of times geologically.

☐ Although generally beneficial, carbon dioxide in large amounts can cause asphyxiation and death.

☐ The nitrogen cycle is essentially a perfect or complete one consisting of four major steps (fixation, ammoniafication, nitrification, and denitrification), each governed by specific organisms as well as physical factors, and in which energy is consumed or released.

☐ In sedimentary biogeochemical cycles, such as sulfur, there are fewer self-correcting, homeostatic mechanisms and more stages in which short- or long-term storage can occur.

☐ Atmospheric sulfuric acid accounts for approximately 70 percent of acid precipitation; it and the other acids involved are attributed largely to the burning of fossil fuels.

☐ Pollutants, byproducts of human activity, are moved around by the hydrologic and biogeochemical cycles and generally are inimical to life.

☐   Biological magnification, the tendency of the level of a residue (e.g., a toxin) to increase with higher trophic levels in a food chain, occurs because of differential metabolic and retention capacities of organisms.

☐   The quality of our environment rests with intelligent and resourceful management of the byproducts of our physiological and cultural activities.

16

Human Populations and Nutrient Cycles

INTRODUCTION

Humans, like other organisms, utilize materials in natural nutrient cycles and, in so doing, become parts of the cycles themselves. People require most of the same nutrients as other organisms, although in some cases need them in slightly different proportions than other species. For most animals the majority of nutrients are obtained from food, although other sources are sometimes used, such as water directly from surface water sources and salt from sea water or salt licks. With humans, nutrients are frequently found in nonfood (or at least not what is traditionally considered food) sources, from the chemical laboratories of "processed-food" corporations to the petroleum fields that yield fertilizer for cultigens. We will primarily focus on food sources of nutrients here.

There are several nutrients that must be considered in dealing with human ecology. We will lump some together in this discussion to make things manageable. Human energy needs can be filled, in our food, by carbohydrates and fats, molecules that are composed of three different elements: carbon, hydrogen, and oxygen. In fulfilling energy needs, humans also fulfill their requirements for those elements. Humans require other nutrients as well. In fact, humans require non-food sources of water, even though water is composed of only the two elements hydrogen and oxygen that are found in food energy sources. Other elements required by humans include nitrogen and sulfur, which are found in proteins, along with the elements that make up carbohydrates and fat; calcium, sodium, chlorine, and potassium, commonly termed *electrolytes*, that are found in salt; and various other micronutrients discussed in Chapter 9.

In addition to these nutrients, human populations that practice agriculture must ensure that their cultivated plants receive the nutrients they require, either through natural nutrient cycles or more commonly through the application of some type of fertilizer. Hence, in discussing human nutrient cycles, we will focus on the following materials: water, salt, protein, and fertilizer. Human populations must face the problem of obtaining sufficient amounts of each (but not too much—tolerance limits have maxima as well as minima!) without disrupting long-term nutrient cycles in so doing. In some instances, this has proved to be a daunting task.

HUMAN POPULATIONS AND THE HYDROLOGIC CYCLE

As noted in the previous chapter, the hydrologic cycle involves global considerations of precipitation, evaporation, drainage of surface water from the land to the ocean, and long-term addition of water to the biosphere from deep geologic sources through volcanic eruptions as well as from extraterrestrial sources, namely comets. Today's oceans are in large part the result of the latter two sources acting over billions of years, and thus life on Earth depends for its existence on volcanic spew and comet juice.

Humans influence the global hydrologic cycle chiefly through their effects on drainage patterns. Water flow toward the oceans has accelerated where people have built concrete cities and roadways over large land areas. This has effectively increased the turnover rate of water on land, thus reducing the amount of water available for use. People have also used wells and pumps to bring water from underground sources to the surface. While this has increased water availability to surface ecosystems, in some cases it has led to long-term depletion of the underground reservoirs, as has happened with the huge Ogallala aquifer of the U.S. Midwest. On the other hand, people have also constructed dams, reservoirs, and other water storage devices that have increased the residence time of water on land, thus effectively increasing water availability. It is therefore difficult to assign generalities to the effects of humans on the water cycle; they are complex and often locally specific. One generality is warranted: over time human populations have strived to direct larger proportions of the local water supply to their own needs. In many cases they have succeeded.

Water as a Limiting Factor for Human Populations

There are many locations where water serves as a major limiting factor for human populations, particularly in hot deserts where water sources are limited and requirements are high (see Chapter 7 for a discussion of the special requirements that humans have for water and Chapter 12 on the desert biome). In these locations, understanding the ecology of human groups requires a focus on water resources and their use.

The G/wi San of the Central Kalahari.   Perhaps the most starkly compelling description of a people's struggle for survival with water scarcity was made by George Silberbauer (1981) in his study of the G/wi San people of the Central Kalahari Reserve in Botswana, southern Africa. These people are related to the San people discussed in previous chapters but live in a more challenging environment. Unlike the earlier described San people, the G/wi San live in an area with no permanent water holes. Silberbauer's studies covered a period of extended drought (the late 1950s and first half of the 1960s), a period of unusual conditions. Perhaps this is fitting, as our understanding of human adaptability is enhanced by noting how people deal with extreme conditions: if the G/wi San cannot adapt to drought conditions, they cannot persist as a group over the long term in the central Kalahari.

Over the five-year period that Silberbauer (1981) studied the G/wi San, annual rainfall averaged approximately 450 mm but varied considerably in its temporal and geographic distribution. During the rainy season, water accumulates in pans and other places where it can be used as a source of drinking water for people; unfortunately, this usually occurs for only six to eight weeks each year. For the rest of the year, plant foods represent the major source of water for the G/wi San, with individuals obtaining approximately 4.5 liters of fluid per day in the hot dry season. Tanaka (1976) has estimated that over 90 percent of the water requirement for central Kalahari San comes from plant sources. The plants gathered include berries, roots and tubers, beans, and melons. When available, the favored plant for obtaining water is the tsama melon, which can be stored for short periods and contains about 90 percent water. Unfortunately, it is during the hottest, driest period of the year that plant resources are at their minimum, although tsama melon is available during this time. If we focus on the plants as sources of water, we must use the calculus of water expenditure from perspiration in the effort of finding and gathering the plants (often requiring digging out tubers in very hot conditions) versus the amount of water obtained from the plant.

Other water sources include the body fluids of animal prey, particularly large antelope, and rainwater that has collected in the hollow trunks of certain trees. These sources are much less important than plants. The G/wi San thus have a daily intake of fluids of about 4.5 liters during the hot-dry season, which is barely sufficient to balance fluids lost to sweat and exhalation during the day. To alleviate this water shortage, the G/wi attempt to minimize physical activity where possible during midday, when sweat loss would be greatest. They rest in shade where this is available and cool themselves by lying in sand moistened with urine. Silberbauer (1981) suggested that the G/wi San showed preliminary symptoms of heatstroke "which . . . indicate how slender the margin of survival sometimes becomes under these conditions" (p. 277).

While the drought conditions faced by the G/wi San represented a major adaptive challenge for them, the water shortage may actually have shielded them from social challenges. In fact, when the drought conditions ended in the late 1960s, pastoralists from other ethnic groups migrated into the central Kalahari and in many cases took over G/wi San lands for their herds. The G/wi San have largely lost their identity as foraging, independent people, becoming part (the lower part) of larger economic units. They apparently coped better with the physical challenge of low water availability than with the social challenge posed by the incursion of pastoral peoples.

Prehistoric Hawaiians on Nihoa Island. Northwest of the main Hawaiian Islands, the Hawaiian archipelago stretches for thousands of miles. It includes atolls and the eroded remains of ancient volcanoes. One of the latter makes up Nihoa Island, a small island with a land area of about 63 hectares (Figure 16–1). Nihoa has steep cliffs on three sides of the island, no good landing area for boats, and a steeply sloped terrain for much of its land area (Cleghorn 1987). The island is covered with grass and shrubs and is the home for thousands of seabirds. This landscape led to a surprise for Kenneth Emory and Bruce Cartwright, Jr., archaeologists who were members of the Tanager Expedition in 1923 to the northwestern Hawaiian archipelago: they found extensive archaeological remains on Nihoa (Emory 1928).

Figure 16–1 Nihoa Island, Hawaii. (Photograph by Palmer Sekora, used by permission of U.S. Fish and Wildlife Service)

As of 1984, 88 archaeological sites had been recorded on Nihoa, all believed to be due to a Polynesian occupation from pre-European contact times. The sites have features similar to precontact sites on the main Hawaiian Islands, including terracing, with agricultural systems like those common in Hawaiian leeward (drier sides of the islands) regions (Cleghorn 1987). The evidence suggests that a small population, variously estimated between 100 and 174 people, of Hawaiians established a residence on the island, managing to grow sweet potatoes, with their diet probably supplemented with seabirds, eggs, and some marine resources. The lack of adequate landing sites for canoes or of a protective reef would have made gathering of marine resources hazardous.

It appears that the major problem the population would have confronted was water scarcity. Rainfall on the island is estimated at between 500 and 750 mm per year, with most occurring during unpredictable, sudden rain squalls. Three freshwater seeps have been recorded on the island, but these are acrid, possibly due to dissolved bird guano, and thus not palatable. The presence of a human resident population may have reduced the bird population, thus making these water sources more acceptable in the past. The water would have been necessary not only for human consumption but also for crop irrigation (Cleghorn 1987).

It is unclear how long the Hawaiians maintained a permanent or semipermanent population on Nihoa, but we do know that the island had been abandoned before the first European sighting of Nihoa in 1789. We can only guess at why the Hawaiians left Nihoa, but water was surely a major factor. Cleghorn (1987) has also suggested that wood for fuel or building materials would have been a major limiting factor, as few trees are available. Fuel would have been necessary because no people are known who habitually eat uncooked sweet potatoes. Wood would also have been needed to build canoes to allow foraging for marine resources as well as for contacting people on the main Hawaiian Islands. If Cleghorn is correct, water is still ultimately the limiting factor for people, as water scarcity is a major factor in the paucity of trees on the island.

The Pastoralists of North Africa and West Asia.   The deserts of North Africa and West Asia have provided difficult challenges for human adaptability once populations have ventured outside riverine areas. In these great deserts, the major source of water is underground aquifers that result either from the trapping of rainfall above limestone formations or from water that has flowed underground from nondesert regions. Oases form where the underground water sources reach the surface.

In addition to using oases, human coping strategies focus on finding and exploiting the underground sources of water, along with strict conservation. The pastoralists of North Africa and West Asia, often termed Bedouins, frequently utilize shallow wells of under six meters depth that are characterized by narrow necks plugged with a rock to reduce evaporation. The use of wells is sometimes elaborated on sloping topography with underground tunnels constructed and then a chain of wells excavated into the tunnels (Moran 1982). A special adaptation for obtaining water is found among the Harasiis Bedouin of Oman on the Arabian Peninsula. These pastoralists lay blankets over shrubs to collect the heavy dew that is common during the winter in the desert of the Jiddat-il-Harasiis. They then squeeze the moisture out of the blankets, providing water for their animals (primarily camels and goats). The Harasiis themselves obtain their fluids from milk (Reader 1988).

The camel is a major factor in the ability of the pastoralists to cope with the exceedingly arid regions of North Africa and West Asia. Besides allowing transport of goods across the desert, which permits the pastoralists to supplement their subsistence economy with profits from trading activities, the camels convert meager water and plant resources into milk, which is a major source of fluid as well as food for the people (Sweet 1965).

The pastoralists also use adaptations to conserve water. Much conservation occurs by using tents and voluminous robes to provide shade and a somewhat cooler microenvironment than their surroundings, thus slowing perspiration and subsequent evaporation. The Tuaregs of the Sahara have obtained the name "blue men" because the dyes from their indigo-stained robes sometimes stain their skin.

The Economics of Water Scarcity

Water as Currency.   As with energy, when water is scarce it is a major factor in a population's economy. In Chapter 14 it was noted that energy is often used as a substitute for money as a "currency" for quantifying human ecological activities. In regions where water is scarce, water can be used as such a currency. In fact, as a general rule whatever resource is most limiting to a population usually serves as the most useful form of currency for ecological accounting purposes. Similar to energy, water units can be converted into other units of interest in ecology. For instance, it takes a given amount of water to produce a specific amount of agricultural produce since plants require water, whether through natural sources or irrigation, to grow. Specifically, it requires about 500 liters of water to produce a kilogram of dry wheat, 1,650 to 2,100 liters to produce a kilogram of rice, about 7,900 liters to produce a liter of milk, and from 21,000 to 50,000 liters to produce a kilogram of meat (Ehrlich and Ehrlich 1970). Technological advances such as drip irrigation techniques bring these water costs down somewhat (Shoji 1977).

For arid countries, water can be as abundant as desired if one is willing to pay the price for it. The price can be through outright purchase of fresh water from other nations and then transporting it, or through desalination of sea water followed by transport, or even by towing icebergs from polar regions. Unfortunately, the cost of the water—in energy, monetary units, or whatever other currency one wishes to use—is often far too high to pay.

The Political Economy of Water Resources.   In arid regions, water becomes a major political, as well as economic, concern. Water rights, access, and large construction schemes for transport of water become major political issues.

The U.S. Southwest serves as an instructive case study, where competition for water between agricultural and urban interest groups has been a major political issue. There are actually many competitors for water in this region, including farmers, mining companies, cities, the federal government, Native American tribes, manufacturers, and so forth, with farmers having the greatest amount of water rights (Smith 1989). The political process is quite diverse, in large part depending upon whether major decisions about water access are made in state legislatures, in local courtrooms, by an appointed water rights board, or in negotiations involving several states (Mann 1982; Smith 1985). These processes are taking on greater importance as water resources in the Southwest become more scarce (Miller 1989).

Irrigation

Intensive agriculture requires large amounts of water per unit of land used for growing crops. This requirement inevitably leads the farmer to provide water to his crops beyond natural rainfall. The resulting irrigation practices vary considerably around the world, taking the form of diversion of surface waters, such as from streams or rivers, or provision of subsurface water from wells onto fields. The variability comes in the relative complexity of irrigation works. In some places, such as in Egypt through much of its long history, people largely relied on natural flood cycles of rivers to provide necessary water to their fields. This water had to be retained, drained, or otherwise controlled so that crops were neither parched nor drowned, with this control sometimes requiring elaborate artificial waterways. The natural flooding of the Nile is utilized by surrounding fields with earthen walls to retain the water. Water is also applied to fields through the shadoof system, in which a counterbalanced pole with a bucket on one end is filled with river water and then raised, with the water poured into an irrigation ditch (Wild 1994).

Water control is a major factor in rice production. While some rice growing techniques simply utilize natural flooding, most regions require artificial water control. This can entail use of dikes to retain rainwater, with the height of the dike limiting the water level in the field. More elaborate systems utilize sluices to provide running water for fields. Irrigation of paddies in some regions involves careful control of water level through a complex network of canals, ditches, sluices, levees, and diverse other devices for water transport such as paddles, pumps, or water wheels (Hanks 1972).

Irrigation sometimes entails large-scale management of water resources, with water transported through aqueducts, pipes, or canals for long distances. There are many examples of enormous construction projects used for water transport. One example is found along the northern coast of Peru, where remains of water canals built by the pre-Inca Chimu state have been studied by archaeologists. These canals extended as far as 70 kilometers from rivers to agricultural fields (Ortloff 1988). The Roman aqueduct system was truly remarkable. Some of it is still usable 2,000 years after its construction, and vestiges of the system are still found on three continents. The aqueducts represent the largest architectural works of the Romans, including the tallest structures that they built (Hauck 1989; Smith 1978).

Long-term irrigation carries with it a cost: increasing salinity (salt content) of soils. This is due to the evaporation of irrigation waters from the soil, with the salts that had been dissolved in the water left behind. The increasing salinity of soils due to irrigation is believed to have been a major factor in the collapse of many ancient civilizations (Pillsbury 1981). The chief method for dealing with the salt problem is to apply extra water to dissolve some of the salt and carry it away. This requires the expense of the extra water and also leads to problems of disposal of drainage waters. The problem of excess salt caused by irrigation is a major one in arid and semiarid regions. For instance, by the 1970s in the 17 western U.S. states, about one-fourth of irrigated farm land was believed to have an excess salinity problem (Thorne 1979).

Another long-term problem posed by extensive irrigation is the depletion of groundwater resources. The vast Ogallala aquifer, which lies underneath much of the central United States, has been tapped for irrigation water at a rate much faster than it is recharged by rainfall and flows from riverine sources. By the 1990s, groundwater levels had dropped by over 30 meters in some states, requiring deeper wells to be constructed and causing further depletion of the aquifer (Owen and Chiras 1995). Subsidence, or sinking of land, over the aquifer as it is depleted has occurred in many areas. A major concern is where water will come from for this major agricultural region once the aquifer is further depleted.

The historian Karl Wittfogel (1957) has presented a theory that the rise of state political systems, in which political power became centralized and a bureaucracy developed, was due to intensification of agriculture caused by increasing population density. The intensification necessitated development and maintenance of large-scale irrigation schemes, which required an elite class of managers. In Wittfogel's so-called hydraulic theory, it is this managerial class that develops into a despotic ruling class. The hydraulic theory of irrigation causing the rise of centralized states is now seen as being less general than originally formulated, with irrigation believed to be only an indirect cause, or only one factor among others, in the origin of these political entities (Webster et al. 1993). Nevertheless, the theory points to the importance of irrigation in human history, as well as to our subsistence.

Control of Water Abundance

Too much water, as well as water scarcity, can be a bad thing, drowning people or their food sources, or destroying possessions. Snow melt, seasonal rainy seasons, or unusual weather patterns can lead to flooding, particularly in riverine areas. While these annual floods have been used by people to help irrigate and fertilize fields, flooding all too frequently exceeds people's control, resulting in destruction and death.

To mitigate flooding hazards, people have had to invest resources in flood control measures, including dams, levees, drainage canals, and intricate sewer systems. A major concern is protection of crops, and the same system used for irrigation may provide for drainage of fields to prevent drowning of crops. Among the Maya, for example, canals and raised fields were used to protect plants (Hammond 1986).

It is clear from the foregoing that water has served as a key resource for many human populations. In some cases, such as among the G/wi San and in northern Africa, water needs have limited population size. In other cases it serves as an important force in a population's economy. Humans influence the global water cycle by changing runoff rates and tapping underground aquifers, but water in turn has a major influence on human populations.

SALT REQUIREMENTS AND HUMAN ADAPTABILITY

Salt is another nutrient required by humans, as well as other organisms. While common table salt is composed of sodium and chloride, salt as used here refers to all the elements that are electrolytes (substances that dissociate into ions when in solution). These include the anions (negatively charged ions) chloride and fluoride and the cations (positively charged ions) sodium, potassium, magnesium, and calcium. For most human populations, these nutrients are present in abundance. For instance, populations with access to oceans or to ocean resources have adequate sources of salt. Salt is obtained directly from dry salt, from saline in drinking water, and from food sources. As noted above, excess salinity problems can be a major challenge to agriculturalists who utilize irrigation. In groups that are far from the ocean, salt may be a scarce resource that limits human populations. It appears, however, that humans in populations with low salt resources have adjusted to survive with only a scant dietary intake of salt (McArthur 1977).

The Tuareg pastoralists of the Sahara have engaged in salt trading for centuries, providing them with a major source of income to obtain resources for which they are not self-sufficient, such as tea and sugar. For instance, the Tuareg will purchase salt from mines in Niger and carry them for hundreds of miles over the desert to Nigeria, where they sell it at a profit (Arritt 1993).

The New Guinea highlands contain regions where salt is scarce. Sodium is particularly deficient in the eroded soils found among many agricultural groups in the highlands, and thus crops used as foods by people are low in sodium. Some people from the highlands travel down to the lowlands to trade for salt; as a side effect, the people engaging in this trade become exposed to diseases, such as malaria, that are more common in the lowlands (Cattani 1992). It has been hypothesized that the low sodium levels have led to the observed lower sweat rate in highlanders as compared with coastal people in New Guinea as a physiological adaptation for lowering sodium loss (Lourie et al. 1992).

The salt found naturally in New Guinea also contains iodine, another needed nutrient. A switch to trade salt with little or no iodine after European contact led people in the Jimi Valley of the Western Highlands Province to suffer from iodine deficiency, leading to goiter and high levels of cretinism (Heywood 1992).

Salt has also been an important factor in Chinese history. For over 2,000 years Chinese rulers have attempted to maintain a monopoly over salt production and trade throughout the country. The majority of the salt was derived from marine sources, but areas far from the ocean relied upon wells. The Chinese of Sichuan Province were noted for the deep wells they excavated to reach brine (salty water). By 900 BP, over 1,100 brine wells were officially registered in the province. By the sixteenth century, these wells reached depths of 300 meters, and, remarkably, a well over a kilometer deep was dug at Xinhai in the early nineteenth century (Vogel 1993). The effort that went into obtaining salt is a measure of its value. This was not only true for China: salt was used as a unit of currency by many human populations, including the ancient Romans.

The word *salt* is derived from *salary*. For example, in ancient Rome, a soldier received a part of his pay in the form of a *salarium*, or salary, that was an allowance for the purchase of salt *(sal)*. Salt, which was not readily available then, was known to be essential to health. A soldier who was not worthy didn't earn this allowance. This is the source of the saying "Not worth his weight in salt."

Salt deficiency may have led to a biological adaptation, particularly in West African and African American populations, for very efficient salt retention by the kidneys in a high proportion of people. When people from these groups live in modernized societies with high-salt diets, this adaptation for efficient salt use might make them more vulnerable to salt-sensitive hypertension (Diamond 1991; Grim et al. 1995).

Salt requirements have not had as great an influence on human ecology as other nutrients have, but in selected regions where salt is scarce it has been an important influence on human economies.

HUMANS AND PROTEIN REQUIREMENTS

Protein contains several nutrients required by people, particularly nitrogen and sulfur, that are not found in other components of our diet. Thus, protein is a major resource requirement for human populations. Since protein is a basic constituent of all living organisms, virtually all foods contain some protein. Some foods, however, have only small amounts of or poor-quality protein (see Chapter 9). Human populations that rely on these poor protein foods as a major component of their diet may suffer from protein deficiency, the resulting malnutrition representing a major adaptive challenge to these populations.

Virtually all human foragers rely on diverse food sources in their diet. Populations with diverse diets are likely to have sufficient protein if their diets provide sufficient energy (Bailey and Headland 1991). Thus protein malnutrition, separate from food scarcity as a whole, probably arose with the development of agriculture, specifically with agricultural systems in which the population's diet became narrowed to just a few species of cultivated plants.

Human populations that suffer from protein malnutrition independent of total food shortages are found today chiefly in tropical regions. The populations at risk are those that rely on one or just a few starchy root crops for the vast majority of their diet. Human ecologists have examined the effects of protein scarcity in several tropical regions.

Protein Scarcity as a Possible Ecological Problem for Human Populations in the Amazon Basin

The Amazon Basin has a low population density, approximately one person per square kilometer, and this may have been the case in prehistoric times as well. Several anthropologists have proposed explanations for the low density, including poor soils that precluded intensive agriculture (Meggers 1954) and protein scarcity (Gross 1975). Protein scarcity is believed to be found among horticultural groups that live away from rivers, where fish can supply high-quality protein; these groups rely chiefly on manioc, sweet potatoes, and plantains, starchy but protein-poor foods. Gross believes that supplementation of the diet with meat is difficult in the Amazon because most of the potential prey is high in the forest canopy and thus difficult for a human hunter to obtain. Also, prey abundance appears to be very patchy, with many large areas of the Amazon having a scarcity of potential prey. Large populations in the Amazon region are therefore found only near water, fresh or marine, that contains animal protein resources (Dornstreich 1977).

Gross (1975) suggests that Amazon peoples have adapted to protein scarcity in several ways, including maintenance of small, dispersed settlements; frequent movement of the settlements; and long fallow periods in their swidden gardens. These adaptations prevent overhunting and, since the secondary regrowth on fallow gardens provides a good habitat for terrestrial prey species, aid in growth of prey populations. People also maintain "no-man's land" between settlements that act as game preserves, these areas being too dangerous in which to hunt. Finally, Gross suggests that people have maintained low rates of population growth as a result of the low protein availability.

There have been strong disagreements with Gross's hypothesis. A main objection has been Gross's emphasis on meat as the source of high-quality protein. In fact, many populations in the region utilize wild vegetable foods, such as palm nuts, that are relatively good protein sources. When populations such as the Yanomamo have been studied intensively by ecological anthropologists, the data suggest that protein is adequate (Chagnon and Hames 1979). Game depletion appears to be only a minor determinant in settlement movement among Amazonian peoples (Vickers 1988). Archaeological work in the 1980s and 1990s has suggested that some regions of the Amazon had fairly large population densities before European contact (Roosevelt 1991). The low population densities and small, scattered settlements may be a result of introduced diseases, historical slaving activities in the region, and an attempt to avoid the foreign, modernized peoples who have entered the region in the past few centuries. The Amazon Basin is quite heterogeneous in its soils, flora, and fauna (Moran 1990; Sponsel 1986); hence, it may be that any generalization for such a broad region is likely to be either only partially applicable or completely wrong.

Protein Scarcity as an Ecological Problem in the Highlands of Papua New Guinea

Human ecologists have also suggested that protein scarcity is a major ecological concern among horticulturalists in the highlands of New Guinea. Low levels of protein intake have been documented in several populations in Papua New Guinea, and in detailed studies people have been observed to be in negative nitrogen balance while on their usual diet (Heywood and Jenkins 1992). The Enga, for instance, who derive most of their diet from sweet potatoes, ingest an average of 2,300 kcal per day, with 94.6 percent of the energy derived from carbohydrates; protein makes up only 3 percent of their dietary calories (Sinnett 1977). New Guinea highlanders often budget a large amount of time and energy to maintaining their pig populations since these animals represent a major source of high-quality protein (Rappaport 1968, 1971).

Studies on the growth rates of children in the highlands have documented some of the slowest growth rates observed worldwide in human populations (Eveleth and Tanner 1976). Children more commonly suffer from **stunting** (defined as a deficit in body length for a given age) in these populations than from **wasting** (defined as a deficit in body weight for a given body length) (Heywood and Norgan 1992). Stunting is usually considered to be due to long-term malnutrition, while wasting occurs during a short-term, acute period of food shortage (McElroy and Townsend 1989). These conditions are reversible if the children receive improved diets; therefore, dietary deficits are responsible for the slowed growth. Furthermore, slowed growth is generally associated with high infant and child mortality (Heywood 1982). Measures of body size, such as body length or height, that are associated with stunting are more highly associated with high childhood mortality than are measures related to wasting, such as weight for height (Gage and Zansky 1996). Thus, growth patterns of highland children are of the kind particularly associated with high mortality rates. Fairly unacculturated populations in the Central Highlands have infant and child mortality rates of 20 to 30 percent (Dennett and Connell 1988), suggesting that poor diets, slowed growth, and high childhood mortality are indeed common in New Guinea.

The evidence for protein scarcity as an important ecological problem in the New Guinea highlands appears to be much stronger than that for the Amazon Basin already discussed. Perhaps the best evidence for a protein problem in the Amazon is evidence of slow growth, particularly stunting, of children in the region, although this is not as extreme as that found in the New Guinea highlands. In the Amazon, stunting may be due as much to the effects of infectious diseases as to malnutrition (Dufour 1992). As with other forms of malnutrition, protein scarcity appears to have its greatest effects upon children. These effects can affect population growth rates, particularly when childhood mortality rates reach the level that is all too common in the highlands.

Population Density and Protein Resources

While protein and other needed nutrients may be found in a reasonably balanced vegetarian diet, availability of high-quality, often animal-based, protein foods has been associated with human population density in many regions of the world. For instance, the highest population densities of native Americans along the Atlantic coast at the time of first European contact were found in rich fishing (including shellfish) areas such as the Narragansett and Chesapeake Bays (Baker 1988a).

The Huron. An example of a population whose density was influenced by protein sources is the Huron (also termed the Wyandot). These Native Americans, located in what is now southern Ontario, Canada, are related to the Iroquois, although at the time of European contact these two groups were rivals (Kehoe 1981). The earliest Huron were foragers, but by about 1500 BP maize had been introduced to them from the south, and within 500 years it had become an important staple, with settled villages surrounded by palisades becoming common (Trigger 1990). The increasing reliance on maize created a problem: protein and certain vitamin deficiencies may have been common, as indicated by low bone cortical indices in skeletal samples (Pfeiffer and King 1983). Maize is an excellent source of calories, but is deficient in certain amino acids as we noted earlier.

Game such as moose and deer may have been key resources for human populations in the region (Campbell 1983). The introduction of beans to the Huron about 700 BP led to a marked improvement in protein quality in their diet (see the section in Chapter 9 on protein complementarity). This was accompanied by an increased settlement size and a general increase in population density (Trigger 1990). Thus, protein quality may have been an important factor limiting population density of the Huron.

Pacific Islanders and Population Density. Human population size on Pacific islands is usually thought to be closely related to food yields from agricultural activities. For instance, Kirch (1984) has noted a strong relation between population size and the amount of arable land on Polynesian islands. However, population size is more closely related to total land area of islands than it is to arable land area, suggesting that agricultural yields do not tell the whole story of population density. Baker (1988a) suggests that human population size is closely connected to the length of coastlines on Polynesian islands, and therefore marine resources may be a more important factor for determining population size than agricultural production is. Since the marine resources of fish and shell-fish are high-quality protein sources, there may be a connection between protein and population density in Polynesia.

In Micronesia, where islands are usually quite a bit smaller than those found in Polynesia (see Figure 16–2), many factors are related to population size, including rainfall, soil quality, frequency of typhoons, and degree of isolation from other islands (Alkire 1978). Marine resources that are rich in protein are another important factor in the size of a human population that can be supported on an island. Islands with extensive coral reefs and lagoons can support enormous population densities, in some cases exceeding 500 people/km. These densities are based on the number of people per land area, but actual population density should account for the area from which marine resources are obtained. Contemporary Micronesians extract marine resources with great efficiency and have instituted conservation strategies such as temporary closures of sections of reef from fishing activities to allow fish populations to rebound (Severance 1976). The need for such strategies suggests that these populations are approaching the limits of marine resource availability. Pacific islands that have scant reefs or no lagoons, such as Niue in Polynesia, support much lower population densities than islands with richer marine resources (Knudson 1970; Alkire 1978). It is unclear to what degree, if any, this is based on the protein content of the resources or if population size is constrained by the total amount of available food.

Protein requirements have affected human ecology in important ways. In some instances, protein scarcity has probably limited population size. Scarcity

Figure 16–2   A Pacific atoll. (Photo courtesy of Craig Severance)

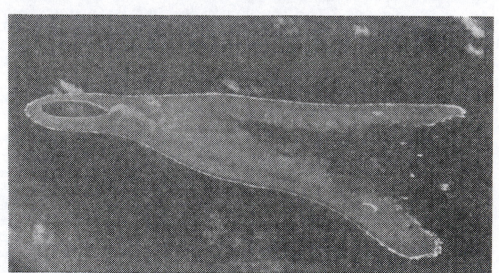

has also affected physical growth rates and people's ability to defend themselves against disease. In many regions, however, people's preoccupation with protein may be more of a "want" than a "need."

RETURNING NUTRIENTS TO PLANTS: HUMAN POPULATIONS AND FERTILIZER USE

Human interaction with nutrient cycles goes beyond ingestion of nutrients. The vast majority of human populations rely on agriculture as a major source of food and thus must enable their cultivated plants to obtain needed nutrients from their environment. In fact, natural nutrient cycles are often disrupted by agricultural activities, and humans often, therefore, apply nutrients in the form of fertilizers to their crops to attain adequate yields. There is a great deal of diversity in both the manner and degree to which human populations utilize fertilizer for their crops.

Swidden Agriculture

One of the most common forms of horticulture is swidden, or slash-and-burn, agriculture (see Chapter 11). In its simplest form, the only form of fertilizer used by swidden farmers is the ashes of the burned natural vegetation previously found where a new garden is prepared. One of the disadvantages of reliance on the ash as fertilizer is that some nitrogen and sulfur are lost as gases during the burn. However, heating the soil increases nitrification, which increases the availability of nitrogen for the plants (Moran 1982). The nutrients are also short-lived, with most lost from the soil within a year or two due to erosion, leaching, or assimilation by plants. Perhaps the greatest single benefit from the ash is the large amount of phosphorus it provides for the plants. Hence, swidden gardens are frequently found on soils that are otherwise deficient in phosphorus.

The success of swiddens depends on the specifics of soil types. There are diverse types of soil found in tropical rainforests where swiddens are common (Moran 1990), but two are particularly common: oxisols and ultisols. Both are forms of laterites (from the Latin word for "brick"), so named because they form a bricklike, impermeable surface when the upper soil layer is washed away (Park 1992). Oxisols are usually well drained and deep but are also quite acidic and frequently have high iron and aluminum levels that may inhibit plant growth. As their name implies, these soils are characterized by the presence of oxides, particularly of iron and aluminum. Ultisols are usually directly derived from the weathering of rocks and are less leached than oxisols (Moran 1981). Specific swidden practices must allow for the differences in soil types; there is evidence that horticulturalists in fact make these distinctions in their swiddening techniques (Conklin 1954; Hecht and Posey 1989; Behrens 1989).

Clearing by bulldozers has replaced traditional swidden practices in some cases. Where this has occurred, crop yields have been significantly lower on the bulldozed plots than on neighboring plots that maintained traditional slash-and-burn practices. This is true for cases where no additional fertilization is used, and for cases where comparisons have been made between bulldozed and traditionally cleared plots with equal amounts of additional fertilizer application (Nicholaides 1979).

In a study of human populations in the Brazilian rainforest, comparisons were made of population carrying capacity based on different subsistence strategies, including swiddening, use of annual cropping with fertilization of soil, and cattle raising in forests converted to pastureland. Fearnside (1986) concluded that the highest carrying capacity was associated with traditional swiddening techniques. This was partly due to a high rate of "failures" by populations utilizing annual cropping and ranching, with the failures being measured by such criteria as land degradation.

Legumes and Crop Rotation

People sometimes plant crops that enhance soil fertility in swiddens. For example, legumes are frequently planted. These plants, through their association with nitrogen-fixing bacteria, add nitrogen to the soil (see Chapter 15). Archaeological evidence suggests that between 800 BP and 1300 BP swidden farmers in the New Guinea highlands planted *Casuarina oligodon* trees in fallow gardens. These trees supplied wood building material and fuel as well as fixing nitrogen in the garden soil (Brookfield and Padoch 1994). A contemporary example occurs in some northern provinces of Thailand, where peanuts, a legume, have become the second most important swidden crop, after rice (Chapman 1978).

The use of legumes in crop rotation allows intensification of agriculture without the need for added fertilizer, or with a reduction in fertilizer requirements. Where Amazonian communities have attempted to produce annual crops on given plots of land, peanuts or soybeans are usually planted alternately with maize (Fearnside 1987). In another example the Kofyar, who practice intensive agriculture in northern Nigeria, plant leguminous groundnuts alternately in fields with other crops, such as rice (Netting 1968). In the United States, farmers have frequently rotated crops to include a legume such as alfalfa in their fields on a regular basis.

Irrigation as a Carrier of Nutrients

Irrigation water often carries with it silt containing nutrients that can be assimilated by cultivated plants. In some places this process occurs without much in the way of human intervention. For instance, many people have utilized natural seasonal flooding cycles of rivers to both irrigate and fertilize their fields.

The classic example is Egypt, where the annual flooding of the Nile permitted very intensive agricultural practices that supported high population densities in a narrow strip along the banks of the river.

Irrigation through artificial means also carries nutrients to crops. For example, irrigation water for rice paddies carries many nutrients for the rice plants. Also, blue-green algae that grow in the warm irrigation water fix nitrogen, thus adding to the nutrient content of the water (Geertz 1963).

Human Use of Organic Fertilizers

"Natural" organic fertilizers such as animal, as well as human, dung have been used by human agriculturalists for millennia. Composting practices utilizing such organic fertilizers have been very important in sustaining intensive agricultural systems in many places throughout the world.

Fertilizer Use in China.   China provides an excellent case study in fertilizer use as a function of the degree of intensification of agriculture. For fertilizers, traditional Chinese agriculture relied chiefly on silt from seasonal flooding of rivers, such as the Yangtse and Huangho, or from irrigation systems that carried water to fields. By 900 BP, Chinese farmers were supplementing their fields with organic fertilizers derived from a host of sources, including "night soil" (human wastes), animal dung, mud from river and lake bottoms, agricultural wastes such as grasses, and lime, with most benefit coming from the first two sources (Hsu 1982; Anderson 1988). Later, fertilizer became supplemented with bean cakes, although this was costly due to the need for growing bean plants to be used for making the fertilizer. There are differences in the make-up of organic fertilizers in different regions of China, as well as differences in methods of composting, that yield varying quality of the fertilizer (Grist 1965). A general characteristic of these methods is an emphasis on conservation and recycling that has led to their emulation in the establishment of the organic farming movement in the West (Anderson 1988).

There have been increasing pressures to increase agricultural yields in China since 1949 that have led to increased use of organic fertilizer. In fact, in the ten-year period between 1947 and 1957 fertilizer use per hectare more than doubled on prime cultivated land (Hsu 1982). Since 1960, emphasis has been placed on use of chemical fertilizers to further increase crop yields.

Fertilizer Use in the Andes.   In the high-altitude Andes region, soils are very poor due to erosion and the consequent loss of soil down mountain slopes. In general, soils are deficient in organic matter, nitrogen, and phosphorus. As noted in Chapter 14, the human populations in this region are limited by food energy. While they rely on their herds directly for a large portion of their food and indirectly as a means of exchange for imported foods, they also rely on crops such as potatoes and Andean cereals. Fields must be fertilized to obtain adequate yields. Among the Quechua in Nuñoa, fields to be used for potatoes are fertilized, then the field is reused for cereals the following season (Thomas 1976). The only affordable source of fertilizer is animal dung.

In the Peruvian highlands, even dung is a precious commodity. Dogs devour human wastes; chickens utilize dog wastes. Since humans eat chickens and eggs, nutrients are cycled back to them.

Dung is a key resource for the Nuñoans because it is the main source of fuel as well as of fertilizer. They chiefly rely on llamas, alpaca, and sheep as domesticated animals, since such other animals as cattle and horses do not handle high-altitude hypoxia as well. Sheep dung is principally used as a fertilizer, while llama dung is mainly used for fuel. Analyses of herd structure suggest that the Nuñoans keep more animals than they require for wool and meat: herd size is determined by requirements for dung (Winterhalder et al. 1974). In fact, gathering of dung is a major work task, usually assigned to children, although virtually all people are involved. Hence, fertilizer may be an important limiting factor for food production in the high Andes.

Human Use of Chemical Fertilizers

Chemical fertilizers, largely derived from fossil fuels, have become the major form of fertilization in the intensive agricultural systems of developed countries. Use of chemical fertilizers has increased dramatically since World War II. For instance, in the United States between 1950 and 1964, nitrogen content in fertilizers increased by 300 percent, while phosphate use increased 150 percent, and potash increased 172 percent (National Academy of Sciences 1969). By the 1990s, U.S. fertilizer use increased 500 percent over 1950 values (Owen and Chiras 1995).

Chemical Fertilizer Use in the United States. Figure 16–3 shows values for use of fertilizers in the United States between 1943 and 1985, when the U.S. Department of Agriculture stopped collecting such statistics. These fertilizers, combined with pesticide and other fossil fuel use, have contributed to huge increases in the productivity of U.S. farms during the same time period. Between 1950 and 1964, wheat productivity increased 12.2 times, rice production increased 4 times, and maize production increased 7.8 times (National Academy of Sciences 1969). Some of the increase was due to increased yield (amount produced per area farmed), while some was due to increased acreage used to grow these cereals. Figure 16–4 shows data on average rice, maize, and wheat yields per hectare in the United States from 1950 to 1990.

Global Use of Chemical Fertilizers. The United States leads the world in use of chemical fertilizers, but the upward trend in its use has become a global characteristic. Use of some forms of fertilizer has leveled off in some developed countries. In the United Kingdom, for instance, most growth in fertilizer use has been in nitrogenous forms, with use of phosphorus and potassium fertilizers leveling off (Simpson 1986). In fact, questions have been raised about the efficiency

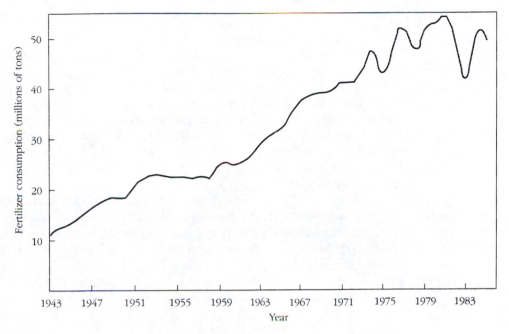

Figure 16–3 U.S. consumption of fertilizer from 1943 to 1985 (in millions of tons).

Figure 16–4 U.S. crop yields for the major cereal crops rice, maize, and wheat from 1950 to 1990 (in kg/hectare).

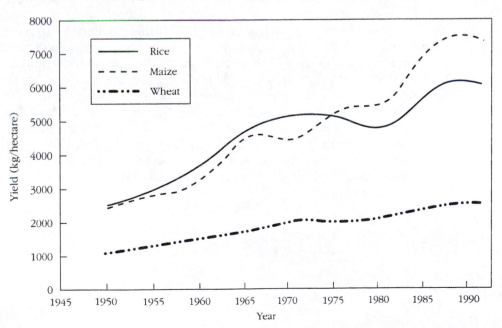

of fertilizer use in increasing crop yields beyond a certain point; we may have reached a level of diminishing returns.

Subsidies to agriculture from fossil-fuel-based fertilizers have created a revolution in our ability to produce food: a green revolution. The revolution is dependent upon the continued availability of fossil fuels, however, and as noted in Chapter 10 has caused serious pollution problems for human societies and the ecosystems in which they reside. A main concern at the local level is the degree to which the green revolution has made farmers dependent upon global distribution systems of fertilizer and pesticides. The loss of self-sufficiency at the local level makes these farmers vulnerable to oil prices and other concerns far removed from their control.

Thus, fertilizer use may be viewed as a technological innovation that has enabled humans to greatly increase their agricultural production per unit land area. This in turn has enabled human population density to increase dramatically in areas where fertilization of crops occurs. On the other hand, fertilization does not come without a "down side," including pollution of water supplies from field runoff and overuse of non- or slowly renewable resources that serve as sources of fertilizers, from guano deposits to fossil fuels.

CONCLUSION

Humans have always been part of natural nutrient cycles, but they have added to the complexity of these cycles. Besides foods, humans have utilized materials for clothing, shelter, tools, and fuel. These include organic and inorganic materials. In recent times a new type of material has become important: synthetic (usually derived from fossil fuel sources). Most of these materials are renewable, and prudent use allows their replenishment. Some materials are not renewable and therefore must be reused if humans wish to continue their use in the future (Brown 1970). Of those materials to be reused, some are part of natural nutrient cycles, while others are part of unique human recycling systems.

Human use of nonrenewable resources has increased dramatically since the Industrial Revolution. Mining for metals and fossil fuels has become more expensive as more easily obtained sources have become depleted. We must make serious choices between recycling and exploration of new sources. Clearly, long-term human adaptation depends on our ability to make these choices wisely in the use of our materials.

KEY TERMS

stunting
wasting

KEY POINTS

☐ Humans utilize materials from natural nutrient cycles in their metabolism and cultural practices, thereby becoming integral parts of the cycles.

☐ By modifying drainage patterns and bringing water from underground sources, human populations have directed larger proportions of the local water supply to their own needs.

☐ Water is a major limiting factor for human (and other) populations in many locations such as deserts (e.g., the G/wi San of the Central Kalahari and pastoralists of North and West Africa) and volcanic islands (e.g., Polynesians on Nihoa in Hawaii). In such situations, water can serve as a substitute for money as a currency for quantifying human ecological activities, and water rights become a major political concern.

☐ Irrigation, a necessity for intensive agriculture, requires the development of water control (e.g., dams, levees) and distribution (e.g., sluices, aqueducts) mechanisms; long-term irrigation can increase soil salinity and decrease groundwater resources.

☐ Where salt, a vital nutrient, is a scarce resource, populations have adapted physiologically through efficient salt retention by the kidneys and culturally through trading and digging very deep wells.

☐ Human populations that suffer from protein malnutrition independent of total food shortages are found chiefly in tropical and some highland regions (e.g., Papua New Guinea), where the diet consisting of one or few starchy root crops results in some of the slowest growth rates worldwide.

☐ The availability of high-quality, often animal-based, protein foods has been associated with high human population density (e.g., the Huron of southern Ontario, Pacific Islanders).

☐ Human interaction with nutrient cycles includes the ingestion of nutrients and the use of naturally occurring fertilizers (e.g., ash in swidden agriculture, planting of legumes, animal and human dung, composting of vegetation) as well as of chemical ones (e.g., those derived largely from fossil fuels containing nitrogen, phosphate, and potash).

17

Optimization Models in Human Ecology

The outline of human ecology presented in previous chapters has emphasized description of human behaviors or biological responses to the environment based upon general concepts of evolution and ecology. Human ecologists in the 1980s and 1990s have attempted to carry ecological analyses further. A major strategy uses what has been termed *middle-level theories*, with generation of testable, specific hypotheses about human responses under carefully stated conditions (Smith 1991; Winterhalder 1981c).

The middle-level theories of human ecology stem in large part from models used in general ecology that in turn derive from economics. These models are mathematical in nature and deal with interactions between individuals. We will provide a simple, largely non-mathematical introduction to such models in this chapter, touching briefly on models of social behaviors related to reproductive success but chiefly focusing on models of resource acquisition. Of special interest is that some of the models are useful in generating hypotheses that may begin to explain aspects of human cultural diversity, a topic that has long captivated anthropologists and other social scientists.

SOCIOBIOLOGY AND MODELS OF REPRODUCTIVE SUCCESS

Sociobiology (sometimes also termed socioecology) deals with the natural selection of social behavioral traits (Wilson 1975). It is based on the notion that behavior is, for the most part, genetically determined (or at least it deals specifically with behaviors that have a strong genetic component) and that such behavior is subject to evolutionary selection (Trivers 1985). The effects of social behavior are measured in terms of relative reproductive success—computations are made of benefits versus costs for both actor (the individual doing the behavior) and recipient (the individual of the same species as the actor to whom the behavior is directed). There are four possibilities (not counting zero effects): both gain (defined as **cooperative behavior**), the actor gains but the recipient incurs cost (defined as **selfish behavior**), the actor confers a benefit on the recipient but itself incurs a loss (termed **altruistic behavior**), and both suffer a net cost (defined as **spiteful behavior**).

Much of the interest in sociobiology lies in the notion that organisms do not have identical interests in their interactions. If evolutionary selection has determined their behavior, they should each behave in a manner that will tend to maximize their reproductive success, thus passing on the genetic background for those behaviors to their offspring who, in turn, will behave in a similar manner. Thus, one can conceive of an "evolutionary arms race" in which individuals will interact socially in ways that enhance their own reproductive output, even if at the expense of other individuals.

Social Behaviors Studied in Sociobiology

Cooperation.   In instances of cooperative behavior, evolutionary selection favors both individuals or species. However, sociobiologists sometimes consider the *relative* advantages of cooperative traits over the long term, that is, they recognize that one individual may benefit relatively more than the other. For example, in observing the sexual division of labor in lions, the males seem to get more advantages than the females from hunting, although females take more risks. Sociobiologists attempt to explain these observations of inequalities in cooperative behavior.

Selfish Behavior.   In selfish behavior the actor benefits while the recipient incurs a cost. Natural selection operating on the actor may favor selfish acts, but the potential recipient is expected to be selected to avoid receiving costs. One can conceive of a coevolutionary struggle between the tendency to perform selfish acts and the tendency to avoid the selfish acts of others. The degree of costs versus benefits is the major consideration here.

A clear example of selfish behavior occurs among langur monkeys (*Presbytis entellus*) who live in groups with only one reproductively active adult male and one or more adult females (Hrdy 1977). When a male takes over a group of females, he often kills the infants who are under the age of six months. This occurs in some localities but is not universal within the species. Sociobiologists suggest that this is to the male's advantage because the infants are not his own, and the death of an infant causes the mother to come into **estrus** (the time in the female's reproductive cycle when she is fertile) more quickly, thus allowing the male greater reproductive success. This is particularly important because males lead groups for only a limited time period before being usurped by another male. When infants are about eight months old, they are weaned and no longer inhibit the mother's reproduction, so the male rarely kills infants this old. In fact, the males usually kill the youngest infants first. Males have been known to kill infants up to six months after a takeover, since gestation is about seven months.

Female langur monkeys have their reproductive success harmed by the males, so they resist them in several ways. First, females will often support their current male to prevent a takeover in the first place. Second, after a takeover, females sometimes act cooperatively to save the infants. Third, some females will temporarily leave the group (sometimes with the old male) or travel on the outskirts of the group until the infant is past the vulnerable age. In this case, however, they trade more risk of predation due to the loss of group security for a lower risk of infanticide. Finally, the female might try to fool the male into accepting the infant as "his." For instance, a pregnant female was seen to have a "pseudoestrus" and to copulate with the male who had recently taken over the group; when her infant was born, the male accepted it as his.

Infanticide may be an important factor in explaining the cooperation between male and female lions just noted. Males defend the cubs they have fathered from the depredations of other males, and thus their mates cooperate with them in this defense, as well as in other activities including the sharing of food (Packer and Pusey 1997).

Sociobiologists deal with conflicts between the actor and recipient of behavior through computation of **inclusive fitness** (Hamilton 1964). This involves conceptualizing the outcome of behavior from the gene's point of view. A major consideration is to what degree an individual shares the same genes as another individual. If selection works on individual genes, a benefit to the first individual with many of the same genes as the second individual is a benefit to the latter. Thus, sociobiologists consider the degree of relatedness of individuals in social contact, as close relatives have similar genes (e.g., parents and children share half of the genes, as do siblings; grandparents, aunts, and uncles share a quarter of the genes; etc.). Thus, selfish behavior is less likely to be found toward close relatives. Mathematically (in simple terms), if the cost to the recipient (C) times the degree of relatedness (R) is greater than the benefit (B) to the actor ($C \times R > B$), then one would expect no selfish behavior. There is another complication, however: selfish individuals may incur *later* acts of selfishness toward them (a form of revenge) and are less likely to be recipients of cooperation and altruism.

Altruism. In altruistic behavior, the actor takes on some cost, while the recipient gains from the interaction. This makes little sense in evolutionary terms unless one invokes the concept of inclusive fitness. Actually, there are three ways in which natural selection might favor altruism: kinship (inclusive fitness), reciprocity, and parasitism.

In considering inclusive fitness, altruism is favored when the benefit to the recipient (B) times the degree of relatedness (R) is greater than the cost to the actor (C) (B × R > C). For example, if a mother saves her own child from certain death (benefit = 1) but takes a 25 percent risk of losing her own life: $1 \times 0.5 > 0.25$, she is behaving in an adaptive manner. If the mother faces certain death, the calculations suggest she must save at least two children (or eight first cousins, etc.) to balance the cost-benefit equation.

Altruism becomes a kind of cooperation in considerations of reciprocity. This can take the form of individuals trading altruistic acts. The prediction is that animals are more likely to act altruistically to a nonrelative if the nonrelative had in the past acted altruistically to the first animal. In baboons, if one male helps a second in a fight, he is likely to be helped by that second male in a future fight. The key problem is how to distinguish cheaters—individuals who receive altruistic behaviors but don't return them. If interactions are frequent, the cheater can be discerned, and altruistic acts in favor of the cheater cease. The loss of future altruism may well be more costly than the short-term benefit of cheating.

For parasitism, the actor "induces altruism" by the recipient. A classic example is brood parasitism in birds, in which one individual deposits its eggs in the nest of another to be raised by the other individual (which has led to counterselection for the ability to detect "foreign" eggs). This is actually a form of selfish behavior, since the actor is the benefactor of the behavior. However, it points out the whole problem of individuals pretending to have a degree of relatedness or a degree of reciprocity that they really don't possess.

Spiteful Behavior.   With spiteful behavior both actor and recipient suffer. Natural selection would seem to work against this type of behavior. It does occur sometimes and may be related to *relative fitness*. That is, you may harm a competitor (sexual or otherwise) more than you are harmed. Spiteful behavior is sometimes seen, for example, among males who are competing for reproductive access to females (such as among mountain sheep). In several macaque species, adult females harass the infant and juvenile daughters of other monkeys and therefore interfere with the ability of the young females to acquire resources. This leads to lowered female survival relative to males in these groups (referred to as "troops"). This type of behavior has been explained based on the fact that only females remain in their birth troop once reaching adulthood in these species. Males move to other troops when they mature. Since group size is limited by resources, attacking the daughters of others may increase the space available for one's own offspring.

Sociobiology Applied to Human Behavior

A major question about sociobiology involves attempts to apply it to humans. While some of these concerns stem from the simple-minded use of sociobiology to suggest that all human behaviors are innate (biologically determined) and therefore unchangeable (e.g., Ardrey 1961; Lorenz 1963), there are also concerns with the human sociobiological works of serious scientists such as E. O. Wilson (Lumsden and Wilson 1981). Controversies and disagreements have occurred among anthropologists, geneticists, and other scientists and social scientists (e.g., Sahlins 1976; Alexander 1977). One question concerns the relative genetic versus environmental (learning) aspects of behaviors. Sociobiology assumes that behaviors are determined (at least mostly) by genetics and thus are amenable to natural selection. Is this likely when we consider the very complex social interactions found in humans (or other primates, for that matter)? In a sense, sociobiology presupposes a precise one-to-one relationship between specific actions and specific genomes. A full comprehension requires consideration of the complex field of behavioral genetics. Complicating the issue is the recognized observation that the social behaviors of interest may be passed down from parents to offspring by nongenetic means. As yet, however, this is a relatively new scientific field in which there is little certainty.

Wealth and Reproduction.   Irons (1979) sums up his conception of the connection between human sociobiology and anthropology clearly: "Human beings track their environments and behave in ways which, given the specific environment in which they find themselves, maximize inclusive fitness; what is observed as culture and social structure is the outcome of this process" (p. 258). This suggests that the behaviors considered successful from a cultural perspective should, when analyzed, be just those behaviors that maximize reproductive success. In his study of the Turkmen population in Persia, Irons (1979) showed a strong relationship between wealth (as defined by the Turkmen) and a measure of reproductive success that accounts for inclusive fitness.

Similarly, Cronk (1991) has found a relationship between wealth, measured by amount of livestock, and reproductive success among Mukogodo men. The Mukogodo are pastoralists in northern Kenya and practice **polygyny,** a marriage pattern in which men have more than one wife, at least when they can economically support them. The greater reproductive success of the wealthy Mukogodo men is related to their ability to practice polygyny.

Bridewealth and Reproduction.   In another study of the relation between wealth and reproductive concerns, Borgerhoff Mulder (1995) observed variability in the amount of **bridewealth** paid by the Kipisigis, who are East African pastoralists. Bridewealth is the practice found in many cultures in which the groom's family is expected to pay (in money or goods) the bride's family to recompense them for her loss. The Kipisigis are a patrilineal, patrilocal social group, meaning that after marriage a wife generally moves in with her husband's kin group. Among the many factors affecting the amount of bridewealth paid are age at menarche and marital distance. These two factors were not as important in the 1990s as previously, but observations done in the 1980s suggested that bridewealth payments were higher when the prospective bride had reached menarche earlier, suggesting a longer period of fertility (Borgerhoff Mulder 1989). These payments were also higher when the bride resided a greater distance from the groom's home, because then she could not socialize much with, or do chores for, her natal family, and this would often lead to greater economic productivity on her part for the husband's family.

Bridewealth payments among the Kipisigis were not as clearly related to productive and reproductive concerns in the 1990s as the population became more modernized. For instance, a woman's family may lower requested bridewealth payments in order to entice a higher-ranking groom and thus assure a secure economic status for the woman (Borgerhoff Mulder 1995).

It is clear that the relationship between wealth and reproductive success is not a simple one for all human populations. One complication, for instance, is that wealth may be inherited through bequests from parents and thus may be passed down for several generations, affecting the reproductive success of descendants (Rogers 1992). Furthermore, in developed countries there is a general trend toward decreasing fertility in higher socioeconomic classes. Irons suggests that this may be explained by the rapid changes that have occurred in modernized societies, including the development of effective technologies of contraception. Thus, humans may not have "tracked" these environmental changes fast enough to be reflected in their fertility. Also, Irons suggests that lower fertility may have higher fitness in modernized societies when such considerations as lowered mortality of wealthy people are considered. At any rate, connections between culturally based (emic) perceptions of success and reproductive success are neither simple nor clear from observations of modernized societies.

How Many Offspring Should One Have?   Complexity in understanding what constitutes reproductive success stems from the notion of inclusive fitness. The bottom line for an individual is to maximize the number of surviving offspring who in turn are capable of maximizing the number of their offspring, although notions of inclusive fitness also necessitate computing the reproductive success of all close relatives. Simply having large numbers of offspring may not maximize reproductive success because of two major considerations. First, in general, each offspring's risk of mortality increases as the number of its siblings increases, since large "litter sizes" lead to a need to share a finite amount of resources with many others. Second, individuals generally increase their risk of mortality when they reproduce—this represents the "cost of reproduction" (Charnov and Krebs 1974). This increased risk is due both to a need for greater amounts of resources and to a greater risk of predation during the reproductive period (and, for many organisms, the period of nurturance after the birth of the offspring). These considerations are illustrated in Figure 17–1, where it can be seen that maximal success for a given parent is reached at some number of offspring (this number would differ depending on species-specific and environment-specific factors), while a given offspring's survival chances decline with increasing litter size. This leads us to the quality/quantity tradeoff problem (Borgerhoff Mulder 1992): does one maximize the number of one's offspring (quantity) or the chances for each one's survival (quality)?

There is no single answer to the quantity/quality tradeoff problem; the optimum strategy depends upon species-specific characteristics including the

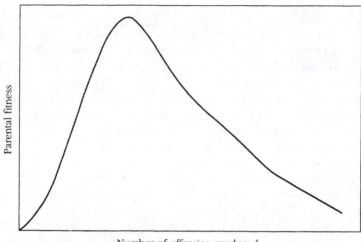

Figure 17–1   Model of parental fitness as a function of litter size.
(Redrawn by permission from E. L. Charnov and J. R. Krebs. 1974.
On clutch size and fitness. *Ibis* 116:733–38.)

intrinsic rate of reproduction as well as specific conditions in the environment—
such as resource availability—that affect mortality rate of parents and offspring
as related to litter size. For humans, a consideration of great importance may be
the time interval between births. Long interbirth periods yield a "quality" strategy of birth number, while short interbirth intervals yield a "quantity" strategy.

Birth Spacing Among the San.   A specific example of research on birth
spacing in human populations was done among the Kalahari San people (Blurton
Jones and Sibly 1978) who have been discussed several times previously in this
text. The San traditionally practiced fairly long interbirth periods, averaging
about four years, despite the lack of modern contraception practices (Lee 1972).

An important consideration for the San people is the necessity for long
walks to gathering sites for food resources—often mongongo nuts—during the
dry season. Women, who do the majority of gathering, bring young children
(under four years of age) when they go on long gathering excursions, often
physically carrying them. If a woman has two young children, she will have to
exert more effort in carrying the children and as a result will not be able to carry
back as much food—and this occurs when the food requirements are higher
because of the larger number of children. As children get older their food
requirements increase, but the work required in transporting them decreases
since they no longer need to be carried. Blurton Jones and Sibly (1978) computed a model of the weight of mongongo nuts required for each adult and
child, with children of different ages assigned appropriate values based on the
notion that they would require 76 percent of Western standards for caloric
requirements at a given age. If a woman is to attempt to carry back enough food

for two or three days, her load will be quite heavy—for instance, each adult requires 3.08 kg of nuts per day. Expected weight loads for the mother were calculated based on different interbirth intervals, allowing for caloric needs of the family and for the work effort of carrying small children. Computer simulations suggest that a mother's expected average carrying weight is considerably lower when her interbirth interval is four years than if it is any shorter. The calculations suggest average loads for women that are higher than those actually observed by Lee (1972), but if infant and child mortality are considered, predicted loads approach those observed, namely between 15 and 20 kg. This weight approaches the limits of safety for women of the average body size of the San before risk for back and joint injuries increases and thus suggests that the San women approach an optimum in balancing child spacing and workloads.

If we return to considerations of optimal birth spacing to yield the highest number of *surviving* children (as shown in Figure 17–1), Blurton Jones (1986) showed that the four-year average interbirth interval yields the highest survival rate for children beyond age ten (after which mortality rates tend to drop considerably). Specifically, the optimal interbirth interval computed from his model was 50 months, while the actual data from the San population shows a median interbirth interval of 48 months (Borgerhoff Mulder 1992). This is illustrated in Figure 17–2.

Figure 17–2   Number of surviving offspring versus interbirth interval among the San. The line graph shows the predicted relationship between surviving offspring and interbirth interval, with a maximum at 50 months. The bar graph presents the observed data from the San, showing a median value of 48 months. (Redrawn by permission from N. Blurton Jones. 1986. *Ethology and Sociobiology* 7:91–105. Elsevier Science Inc.)

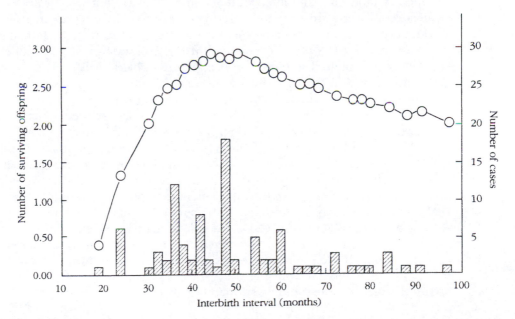

The relation between birth spacing and reproductive success among the San is very specific for their population. Among the Hadza foragers of Tanzania, for instance, children begin foraging activities at a considerably younger age than among the San, and this leads to important changes in the foraging strategy decisions of mothers, who may choose to shorten foraging trips to allow her children to more easily forage with her, thus maximizing the family food production (Hawkes et al. 1995). The mothers are therefore not as constrained by the requirement of carrying offspring on long foraging trips; thus this is not as significant a factor in determining birth intervals among the Hadza.

OPTIMAL FORAGING STRATEGIES

The basic notion of the models used in these middle-level theories, based on evolutionary theory, is that organisms will be selected over generations to reach an *optimum* level of resource acquisition and to utilize those resources for ensuring their own survival, including avoidance of predators, and reproductive success (Pianka 1974; Stephens and Krebs 1986). In the real world organisms are not likely actually to achieve an optimum state, but natural selection should result in an approximation of this. The models are used to attempt to predict the optimum state given certain environmental conditions. It is then the job of the ecologist to observe the behavior and biology of organisms and to determine to what degree their actual characteristics approach those predicted by the models.

A difficulty of this enterprise arises when the models deal with animal behavior, as many species rely to some degree on learned, as opposed to genetically determined, behaviors that are therefore not subject to the usual processes outlined in modern evolutionary theory since they are not genetically inherited from successful ancestors. Thus we return to some of the uncertainties noted for sociobiological theories and models when they are applied to humans. The resource models presented here, derived from evolutionary ecology, differ from traditional sociobiological theory in the great emphasis placed on details of the environment and in their predictions of flexible, complex behaviors that are the hallmark of human culture (Winterhalder and Smith 1992).

Some anthropologists have suggested that human learned adaptive behaviors, as organized in culture, may be passed down in a manner similar to biological evolution, with innovation, from individuals within the population and from diffusion of ideas from external sources, combined with selective retention of adaptive cultural elements (Campbell 1965). The transmission of cultural traits is analogous to reproduction in biological evolution, and the changes (innovations) that occur in the learning process are analogous to mutational changes in biology (Cavalli-Sforza and Feldman 1981). The role of natural selection in this analogy is ascribed to selective retention of behaviors, whether due to conscious decision making or not. If the selective retention of behavioral/cultural traits is due primarily to the adaptiveness of the traits, then models from evolutionary ecology are applicable to understanding human behavior.

Optimum foraging models that have been applied to human populations include those used to explain dietary choice, selection of places to hunt, decisions about how long to spend foraging in a given place, relation of human settlement patterns to patterns of prey distribution, and explanations of food sharing patterns. The following presents basic concepts used in the models and illustrative examples.

Model of Diet Breadth in Foragers: What Should Be Hunted?

This model attempts to predict how many different prey species a given predator will include in its diet. The model is computed by ranking prey by how much net gain a predator gets from attempting to hunt for it. Here one must consider the yield from a successful hunt, the average cost of engaging in the hunt (in terms of time or energy), and the risk that the hunt will be unsuccessful. The model assumes that predators will always hunt the highest-ranked prey species. Next, one must consider whether it is worthwhile for the predator to add the second-ranked prey species to its diet: will it obtain a net gain? If the second prey species is worthwhile, should the predator add the third-ranked species to its diet? The predator should keep adding prey to its diet choices until it reaches a potential prey species that costs more than it is worth (MacArthur and Pianka 1966).

Another way of presenting the model is in balancing two kinds of cost for the predator: the cost of searching for prey versus the cost of pursuing the prey once it (or its traces—such as odor or footprints) has been found. As more prey species are added to the diet, the cost of finding any one of those prey species is lowered for the predator; searching is more difficult if the predator is choosy about its prey. On the other hand, as more prey are added to the diet lower-ranked species are included, meaning that the average cost of pursuing prey (once they have been discovered) goes up (Winterhalder 1981b). This is illustrated in Figure 17–3. The "search cost" curve can be seen to decline as number of prey in the diet increases, while the "pursuit cost" curve increases; the optimal diet breadth occurs where the two curves intersect.

Diet Breadth Among the Cree of Northern Ontario. Winterhalder tested the diet breadth model's applicability to human foragers in fieldwork done among the Cree Indian community of Muskrat Dam Lake (Winterhalder 1977, 1981c). He discovered that precise, quantitative testing of the model was very difficult because of the great seasonality in hunting faced by the Cree. Ranking of preferred prey species changed over short time intervals during the year because of several factors: seasonal changes in mobility of both prey and Cree due to such factors as icing over of lakes, snowfall, and periods of hazardous travel during ice breakup or freeze-up. The prey also change their distribution in the landscape seasonally, for instance, preferring different patch types in the winter than summer. A specific example is found with moose, which prefer wet

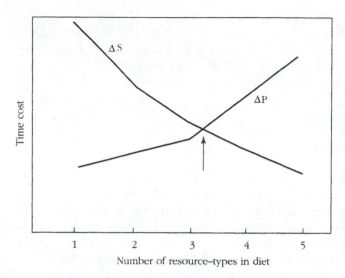

Figure 17–3 Diet breadth model of MacArthur and Pianka. The ΔS curve represents the search costs of a predator as less favored prey species are added to its diet, while the ΔP curve represents changing pursuit costs as prey species are added to the diet. (Redrawn by permission from *American Naturalist* 100:603–9, by R. H. MacArthur and E. R. Pianka. Copyright © 1966 University of Chicago.)

bog patch types in the summer but in winter are more apt to stay in shrub and deciduous tree habitats where at least some woody browse can be obtained (Winterhalder 1977).

Winterhalder was able to qualitatively test the model by looking at the historical record of the Cree as well as by interviewing elders about differences in the recent past. Two major changes have occurred in the history of Cree hunting: the introduction of firearms several centuries ago (and in the early part of the twentieth century when more efficient firearms and better fish nets were introduced), which greatly reduced pursuit time, and the more recent introduction of motorized transport, including snowmobiles and motorized boats, which greatly reduced search time. Thus, the Cree historically have had three distinct patterns of search and pursuit in their hunting, as illustrated by Figure 17–4: in the distant past, they had both high search and high pursuit costs, which would lead to an early intersection of the two cost curves in the model, thus predicting a small number of prey in their diet (Figure 17–4c). After guns were obtained, they had a hunting pattern of high search costs but low pursuit costs, yielding a predicted high number of prey species in their diet (Figure 17–4b). More recently, motorized transport has led to a hunting pattern of low search and pursuit costs, yielding an early intersection of cost curves and a prediction of a lower number of prey species in their current diet, as shown in Figure 17–4a (Winterhalder 1981a).

Winterhalder has not tested the first prediction of the model: that before the introduction of firearms the Cree were very selective in the type of prey pursued at any given time of year, but suggests that ethnohistorical sources could be used to test the prediction. The second prediction, that diet breadth was much broader in the recent past before motorized transport was available, appears to be accurate. Winterhalder interviewed older hunters who stated that they had

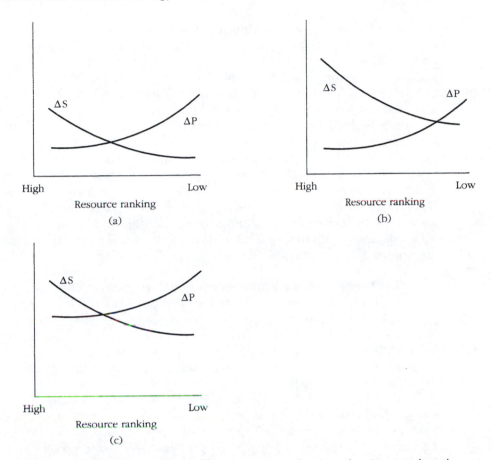

Figure 17–4   Historic pattern of hunting among the Cree showing search and pursuit costs. (a) Contemporary times with motor-assisted search and efficient fire-arms-assisted pursuit technology. (b) Recent past with no motor-assisted search but firearms-assisted pursuit technology. (c) More distant past with neither motor-assisted search nor efficient firearms-assisted pursuit technology. (Redrawn by per-mission from B. Winterhalder. 1977. Foraging strategy adaptations of the boreal forest Cree: An evaluation of theory and models from evolutionary ecology. Ann Arbor, MI: University microfilms.)

changed their hunting habits during their own lifetimes as a result of trans-portation changes, now traveling to favored locations far from home to hunt for specific prey. An ethnographic account by Rogers, who accompanied Cree hunters in the 1950s—before motorized transport was used in hunting activities in the area—states that many species of game were pursued at the time on any given hunt (Winterhalder 1977). Finally, Winterhalder notes that older Cree judge a good hunter by the ability to hunt many different animal species, often disparaging younger men as being adept at hunting only a few species. Thus, it appears that the Cree have narrowed their diet breadth in recent years, as pre-dicted by the model.

Diet Breadth Among the Inujjuamiut Inuit of Canada. Smith (1991) has taken another approach to analyzing diet breadth of human foragers in a seasonal environment. He has identified seven different "hunt types" among the Inuit population he studied (see Chapter 14 for more details on the Inujjuamiut and their energy flow), including summer canoe hunts, in which a few hunters in a shared canoe search near-shore areas for prey; winter caribou hunts, in which hunters specifically intend to hunt caribou but sometimes hunt other animals; spring goose hunts, where hunters either wait at blinds or travel while searching for geese; and lake ice jig hunts, where Inuit, often in mixed-sex and -age groups, jig (fish with a line through holes in the ice) for trout and may also hunt ptarmigan. Smith analyzes diet breadth models for each hunt type and also analyzes why the Inuit choose to use a given one. He concludes that the models predict diet breadth for four of the seven hunt types, and of all but four of the 23 prey types utilized by the Inujjuamiut, with special circumstances explaining the cases where the models are not predictive (see Smith 1991 for a detailed discussion).

Diet Breadth Among Piro Hunters of the Amazon. The Piro are a group of horticulturalists/foragers who live in southeastern Peru. While they receive 71 percent of dietary calories from their horticultural activities, raising plantains and manioc, they get most of their dietary protein and fat from hunting and fishing (Alvard 1995). Contemporary Piro hunters utilize shotguns, which has reduced their "pursuit" costs, although these costs are not negligible given the expense of shotgun shells.

Alvard's study indicated that the major factor in deciding on prey types was the body size of the animal to be hunted. The Piro never used shotguns to hunt prey that were under 1.5 kg, occasionally hunted prey that were between 1.5 and 4 kg, and consistently hunted prey that were over 4 kg (Alvard 1993b, 1995). Here, the cost of pursuing is essentially the same for all prey: the cost of a shotgun shell. The benefit from the hunt is related to the prey's body weight. Therefore, the cost-benefit ratio for Piro hunting is primarily based on prey body weight, which is how the Piro in fact decide what animals to fire upon. For the Piro, choice of prey type is not based upon species designations.

Model of Patch Use in Foragers: Where Should They Hunt?

This model is somewhat similar to the diet breadth model just described, but here the model predicts the optimal places, based on patch type, to forage for resources. The model assumes that the landscape can be divided into different, large patch types with varying kinds and amounts of resources. The forager can then enter a patch and forage within it for some period of time. The model predicts how many different patch types will be used by a forager. Patch types are ranked based upon net production per cost, much as prey types were ranked in the diet breadth model. The cost of foraging is again divided into two types, here specified as hunting time within a patch and travel time between patches

(MacArthur and Pianka 1966). If people are very picky about what type of patch they will use, within-patch hunting effort will on average be very low, since they are using only the very best patches. However, if people use few patch types, on average they will have to travel great distances to get from one of these patches to another and therefore their travel costs will be high. As more patch types are added to their foraging repertoire, within-patch hunting costs will rise on average since less highly ranked patches will be included in their hunting, but the average travel time to get to a patch that they utilize will decrease since they are less picky. The patch use model is shown in Figure 17–5.

Winterhalder attempted to test the patch use model among the Canadian Cree but was unable to do so because they did not fit the assumptions of the model. The model, as noted above, requires large patches in the environment, or what is termed a **coarse-grained environment.** The Cree, however, live in a fine grained environment where patches are relatively small. In fact, a Cree hunter's bullet can traverse more than one patch, allowing hunting in several patches at once. For the Cree case, a model that focuses on strategies for hunting in regions *between* favored patches as opposed to within patches is more useful (Winterhalder 1981a).

Patch Use Among the Alyawara of Australia.   The Alyawara are an Australian aboriginal group located in an arid region in central Australia. There are two major patch types in which they forage: sandhill and mulga woodland patches (O'Connell and Hawkes 1981). The sandhill patches are generally more productive than mulga woodlands, although both patch types are used due to the great distances between patches. However, when motorized transport is available, the Alyawara tend to focus more on sandhill patches alone, unless they had already depleted the resources in these patches. Thus, the Alyawara behave in a manner the model suggests is optimal: when travel costs are low, they

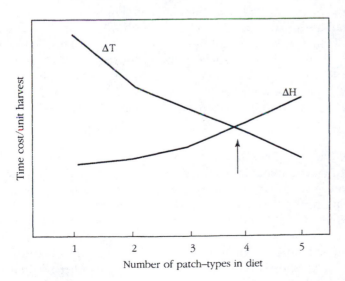

Figure 17–5   Patch use model of MacArthur and Pianka. The ΔH curve represents the average within-patch foraging costs of a predator as less favored patch types are added to its hunting repertoire, while the ΔT curve represents the between-patch travel costs as these patches are added. (Redrawn by permission from *American Naturalist* 100:603–9 by R. H. MacArthur and E. R. Pianka. Copyright © 1966. University of Chicago.)

reduce patch types to lower within-patch foraging costs, but when their travel costs are high (when motorized transport is unavailable) they increase patch types to minimize between patch travel costs.

Model of Group Size and Distribution in Foragers

As noted in Chapter 11, a standard rule of thumb in ecological studies of predator-prey relations is that if a predator's prey is clumped, the predator population should clump. Conversely, if the prey is widely dispersed, the predator population should be dispersed. In fact, this simple dictum masks a fairly complex question about optimal group size and distribution based upon resource distribution.

Clumping and dispersion are relative terms—a dispersed resource for an elephant may represent a highly clumped resource for a grasshopper; crumbs from a human's meal represent a feast for a small rodent. Group size is also a complex measure, particularly when humans are the species of interest (Smith 1981). Human group size includes various politically, socially, and economically defined units. Here, as in Chapter 11, we will confine our analyses to procurement group size.

The Horn model for optimal forager group size and dispersion attempts to predict the distribution pattern that requires individual predators to travel the shortest distance in order to succeed in finding food (Horn 1968; Winterhalder 1981c). The model operates by computing the distance from a forager to its resource, with allowance made for the probability of finding the resource at any given point in the landscape.

The model is based on the idea that as the forager population increases, the cost-benefit equation for individual group members will change, with a maximal net benefit at an intermediate group size (Smith 1981; Wilson 1975). The results of application of the model are illustrated in Figure 17–6, where resources are divided into those that are stable and evenly distributed versus those that are mobile and clumped. The symbol $\bar{d}$ stands for the mean distance to a resource weighted by the probability of successfully locating that resource. As shown in (a) and (b) in Figure 17–6, foragers have a lower $\bar{d}$ when they are dispersed in cases where their resource is evenly dispersed. As shown in (c) and (d) in Figure 17–6, aggregated foragers have a lower $\bar{d}$ when hunting mobile, clumped resources.

Settlement Size Among the Cree.   Winterhalder tested this model in a qualitative fashion among Canadian Cree by contrasting groups that relied heavily on caribou as prey—which represent mobile, clumped resources—with groups that rely on other prey species such as beaver—which represent stable, evenly distributed resources. Cree residing in northern Quebec have caribou as a major food resource. Lichen patches, a favored habitat for caribou, take up a large part of the total land area in northern Quebec, and thus caribou are common. The Cree in northern Ontario reside in a region where lichen patches are less common, and thus caribou are more rare. The Ontario Cree

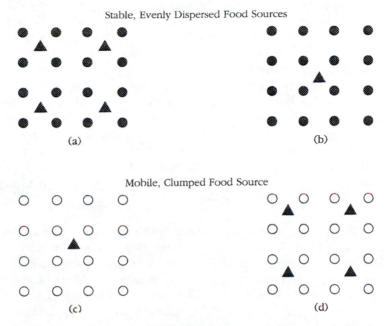

Figure 17–6 Model of forager group size and dispersion for food resources that are either evenly dispersed and stable or mobile and clumped. Triangles represent locations of foraging groups; circles represent locations of food resources. (a) Foragers dispersed, resources dispersed ($\underline{d}$ = 1.42). (b) Foragers aggregated, food resources dispersed ($\underline{d}$ = 2.94). (c) Foragers aggregated, food resources clumped ($\underline{d}$ = 2.94). (d) Foragers dispersed, food resources dispersed ($\underline{d}$ = 3.86). (Redrawn by permission from H. S. Horn. 1968. The adaptive significance of colonial nesting in the Brewers blackbird *(Euphagus cyanocephalus)*. *Ecology* 49:682–94.)

rely more on beaver and other types of prey that represent evenly distributed resources.

The settlement pattern in northern Ontario is one of small villages of 100–500 people, separated by over 30 miles. These communities represent a year-round aggregation of people, but in the recent past people would have dispersed for most of the year over the region in small family foraging groups. The move to aggregated settlements was due to the influence of modernization. For example, increased dependence on traders for goods and foods, missionization, political moves (the government wants them aggregated for administrative purposes), construction of permanent housing, localized distribution of welfare, and so forth all represent, in a sense, clumped resources. This has occurred mainly since World War II. In terms of the model, the aggregation reduces foraging efficiency but has compensatory advantages in nonforaging processes. Quebec Cree, although with similar group sizes today, have more foraging area per group. This represents a more aggregated settlement pattern, as the model predicts (Winterhalder 1977).

Settlement Size Changes Among the Chipewyan.   The Chipewyan are, like the Cree, Algonkian speakers who reside in the boreal forest biome of Canada to the west of Hudson Bay. Caribou are a major food resource for the Chipewyan. In the terms of the Horn model, about 90 percent of their food resources are mobile and clumped (Heffley 1981). The caribou undergo seasonal changes in group size, however, aggregating into large migrating herds in spring and fall but dispersing into smaller groups during summer and winter. As predicted by the Horn model, the Chipewyan group size changes accordingly, with larger group sizes during spring and fall than during other times of the year. The larger Chipewyan settlements were usually near caribou migration paths. Thus the Chipewyan settlement pattern appears to have been related to the relative aggregation of their major prey type, thus providing further support for the Horn model.

Settlement Size Changes Among the Ingalik.   The Ingalik are also northern Algonkians but live in the Yukon and Kuskokwim River basins of Alaska. Unlike their eastern kin, the Ingalik have long maintained fairly large, permanent villages that were occupied for about nine months out of the year. In the summer, the population dispersed into small fishing camps (Heffley 1981). A major resource for the Ingalik was salmon. This resource helps explain their difference from the Cree and Chipewyan in residence patterns. The salmon could be caught in such quantities and stored so effectively that the large villages could be sustained for much of the year. The stored salmon represented a rich, aggregated resource. Also, the Ingalik hunted caribou in the fall, and their use of this clumped resource occurred at the time they moved from the dispersed fishing camps to the aggregated settlement pattern represented by the villages. Thus, Ingalik population distribution mirrored that of their resources: dispersed in the summer along rivers and aggregated in the winter in villages.

The Ingalik example points out an important consideration in studies of human optimal foraging: food storage. Food stores represent aggregated resources and have a great influence on human behavior. Studies that deal with the relationship between humans and their resources must allow for our species' ability to manipulate and store resources in a very flexible manner.

Models of Food Sharing

Ecological models have also been used to attempt to explain patterns of food sharing among people within a group. Sharing of food represents an altruistic act and, if adaptive, needs to be explained in terms of kinship (inclusive fitness), reciprocity, or parasitism. Sharing of food with close relatives is easily explained by sociobiological principles; it is when sharing occurs beyond the family that explanations become more difficult. One explanation focuses on the use of trade, by which an individual trades a resource that is of low value for one that has higher value (Kaplan and Hill 1985). Value here depends on the perceptions and circumstances of an individual. A person with more than sufficient food energy but poor protein resources would trade energy for protein with an individual in the opposite situation. This would then represent cooperative, rather than altruistic, behavior.

Another possibility is that food sharing reduces risk when foraging success for individuals is unpredictable or variable (Bliege Bird and Bird 1977). Thus, the individual gains stability in resource acquisition through reciprocity.

A third possibility involves the assessment of the costs of defending food resources from other members of the group versus the benefit of such defense. If an individual has consumed some of the resource, what is left has reduced value if the individual does not need more of it; in formal terms, the resource has diminishing marginal value to the individual (the acquirer) who acquired it as the amount of resource acquired increases. The relative value of the resource is higher for an individual who does not have any of it, and thus "scrounging" or "tolerated theft" by the latter individual may be permitted by the acquirer (Winterhalder 1996).

An important point about food sharing is that expectations of sharing can affect an individual's daily foraging decisions (Minnegal 1997). If certain food items are expected to be shared and others are not, the latter items may be preferentially foraged when the number of individuals who will potentially share food is high. Thus, decisions about resource utilization are not based solely on production, as assumed in the models discussed throughout this section, but also on complex notions of sharing in the consumption of the resources.

CONCLUSION

The use of "middle-level theory" and mathematically based modeling has great promise for human ecology studies. These theories are based upon the overarching premise that human behavior is adaptive. More specifically, they are based on the assumption that the selective retention of behaviors throughout the cultural history of a population is based on the relative adaptiveness of the behaviors. The primary benefit of such studies is the ability to make specific predictions about human behavior that can be empirically tested. The move from descriptive studies to those involving hypothesis testing is a major development in the history of any science and is an important step in our ability to understand the ecology of our species.

Much of the work done with these models has been applied to human foraging groups under the assumption that human foragers will better fit models developed to understand foraging animals. Clearly these models can be modified to fit other human subsistence strategies. There have been some preliminary studies carried out among nonforaging humans (e.g., De Boer and Prins 1989) and are likely to be others in the near future. It will be interesting to see if these models will help our understanding of the strategies used by humans in making subsistence decisions across a wide range of biomes and subsistence types.

There are criticisms that can be made of these early attempts at specific, quantitative hypothesis testing in human ecology. The main one is the obvious disparity between the precise quantitative nature of predictions and much more qualitative nature of the empirical results. This disparity can be seen in the brief case studies noted in this chapter, particularly those related to foraging practices. The models often include assumptions about the nature of the environment in relation to foragers which are not met in the human examples that have been studied. For instance, in one of the most extensive case studies, Winterhalder's work among the Cree, assumptions about prey ranking are confounded by the great seasonality of such rankings, making accurate analyses impossible (Winterhalder 1977). When empirical tests are qualitative, the models may simply degenerate into commonsensical notions such as the fact that people don't usually walk five miles for a resource that they can obtain with only a two-mile walk.

Another problem is that many of the foraging models were initially developed to analyze the behavior of solitary hunters, but humans clearly often collaborate in their foraging. The models also often assume that foragers move randomly through their environment, or through specific patches in the environment, but humans usually have information about their surroundings that allows them to use planned, nonrandom movements in their search for prey (Durham 1981). In fact, information itself is a resource for humans that carries value (Moore 1981).

Still another problem lies in what measure should be used in cost-benefit equations. The most commonly used measure of productivity is energy–both production and consumption. Measures of cost include both energy expenditure and time. Obviously, money has been used by economists as a measure of both cost and benefit. As we have seen in Chapter 16, however, people often must allocate time, money, or energy to obtain resources other than energy, such as water and protein. Potential modelers must understand what the key resources are for a human population if they are to understand the people's behavior related to resource acquisition (Hill 1988).

A final problem to be considered here is the question of just what is to be optimized. These models usually are based on the assumption that humans will maximize for net gain or efficiency. Humans must also be concerned with risk. If resources are hazardous to obtain they may be avoided even if they represent a great net gain in productivity. Beyond this is the question of whether humans optimize at all. As noted in Chapter 9, human societies vary a great deal in their definition of "food," with some potential nutrients excluded from the diet. For instance, although optimal foraging models predict that the Valley Bisa of Zambia should hunt zebras with some regularity, they were not observed to ever hunt them (Marks 1976; Mithen 1989). Eating of zebra meat is not considered to be socially appropriate.

While the problems with these quantitative models are formidable, human ecologists should neither despair nor retire. Humans are complex creatures, and we should not expect understanding to come easily or quickly. The approaches described here are still fairly new but remain promising. While models must be refined to be appropriate for our unique species, the real work comes in the "shoe leather" expenditure of detailed, quantitative fieldwork in human communities. The scarcity of such studies is due to difficulty, not impossibility.

KEY TERMS

altruistic behavior	estrus	selfish behavior
bridewealth	inclusive fitness	sociobiology
coarse-grained environment	polygyny	spiteful behavior
cooperative behavior		

KEY POINTS

☐ Middle-level theories of human ecology derive in large part from models used in general ecology that in turn derive from economics, models that are mathematical and deal with interactions between individuals.

☐ Sociobiology deals with behavior (e.g., cooperative, selfish, altruistic, spiteful) that has a strong genetic component, is subject to evolutionary selection, and is measured in terms of relative reproductive success.

☐ The application of sociobiology to humans remains controversial, largely because of differing interpretations of the relative genetic and learned aspects of behavior (such as the relationship between wealth and reproduction, the number of offspring desired, and birth spacing) and thereby whether these aspects are amenable to natural selection.

☐ Optimum resource models (e.g., diet breadth, patch use, group size and distribution of foragers, and settlement size) based on evolutionary theory are beset by controversy over the degree to which the acquisition behavior is genetically determined or culturally learned.

☐ Middle-level theory, based on the premise that human behavior is adaptive, holds great promise for human ecology studies in spite of the disparity between the precise quantitative nature of predictions and the more qualitative nature of the empirical results, the measure(s) that should be used in cost-benefit equations, and what is to be optimized (e.g., net gain, efficiency, risk).

18

Human Ecology
and the
Ecology of Humans

In this concluding chapter, we will briefly assess the status of the scientific field of human ecology. We will also give an overview of the prospects for the future of *Homo sapiens* given the state of its ecology.

HUMAN ECOLOGY: THE STATE OF THE SCIENCE

The take-home lesson about the ecology of *Homo sapiens* is that it is very complex. We have attempted to simplify things by looking at many examples of human populations that are relatively small and not modernized. What you have discovered by now is that even in these circumstances, human ecology is too complex to comprehend readily. This is not a circumstance unique to our own species. The science of ecology as a whole and in fact all population biology disciplines face a daunting complexity in the understanding of biological interactions.

Problems with Complexity for Evolutionary Theory

Population biologists face problems with their ability to make predictions, a problem that is faced by evolutionary biologists as well. For instance, selection acts on individuals, but it is the species population that evolves. Evolutionary theorists must balance selective and mutational (or generating) forces in attempting to foresee future evolution. Selective forces act on the organism's phenotype, which itself is the complex product of genetic, developmental, and environmental processes; but mutational forces act directly on the genome and thus are only indirectly expressed in the phenotype. These fundamental problems are compounded by the indeterminate nature of these processes such that at best one can make only statistical arguments for the likelihood of given outcomes. An organism with superior genetics and optimal development in a congenial environment may be an evolutionary failure after being hit by a random bolt of lightning!

Optimality Models in Evolutionary Theory. Some theorists have made more modest goals for predictability of evolutionary theories. For instance, Slobodkin and Rapoport (1974) stated: "Our goal is to be able, in some sense, to assess the evolutionary health of an organism and to be able to answer a hypothetical organism that requests expert opinion on how it best ought to evolve." To meet this goal, they utilize a model based upon game theory, where species are seen as contestants in a game, and optimal strategies for playing the game are derived.

It turns out that evolution is a strange game: one cannot "win"—one can only hope to remain in the game (that is, not become extinct). Thus, evolution becomes an "existential game." Given such a game, an optimal model predicts that the best strategy for a species to use is a very conservative one. If one can lose but cannot win, it is best not to take risks. It also pays to be flexible. The model predicts that species that are generalists as opposed to specialists in their evolutionary adaptations have the best chance for persistence. Species, however, are often confronted with the short-term benefits of specialization, such as the ability to gather resources efficiently in specific environmental conditions. Selection occurs based on the short-term benefits, not based on some theoretical long-term strategy for species preservation. This model has ramifications for understanding human evolutionary prospects that will be discussed later in the chapter.

The Challenges Facing the Science of Ecology

Scientists who study biological ecology alternate between exhilaration from the progress of the field and depression from the seemingly insurmountable barriers to understanding. Because the interactions faced by living organisms in the real world are highly complex and ever-changing, ecologists do what most scientists do: simplify reality. They have simplified by two means: performing experiments and developing simulations.

Simplification of reality is one of the hallmarks of science. In general, we learn about our world by making simplifying assumptions, seeing if these assumptions "work" under the special conditions they call for, and then adding complexity to the conditions as understanding of the simple conditions is gained. Even Newtonian physics, one of the best understood of all areas of science, meets with difficulty when attempting to predict motions of three bodies under mutual gravitational forces. The difficulty is compounded enormously when a population biologist attempts to predict characteristics of real-world populations given the abiotic and biotic forces that interact in any ecosystem.

A Classic Example of the Use of Experimentation to Simplify Ecology. Gause's experiments that were described in Chapter 4 provide a clear example of simplification of feeding relationships (see Figure 4–6). In this instance, interaction was permitted between only two species, the one, *Didinium,* a predator on the other, *Paramecium.* The results were unambiguous: the predator decimated the prey. However, in a natural setting, feeding relationships are typically much more complex, with more than one predator feeding on the same prey or having other interactions with other species (e.g., competition). These complex interactions are evident in the feeding relationships demonstrated in the somewhat simplified interspecific studies on *Paramecium* as shown in Figure 4–7 and decidedly in those of a food web (see Figure 13–9). While simplification can lead to clarification and therefore greater understanding of a process, it most often is exactly what simplification means—to render less complex—and not necessarily to reflect the reality of truly complex situations.

Fluctuation in Insect Numbers: An Example of a Computer Simulation in Ecology. Robert May (1974) constructed a mathematical model to simulate changes in population numbers of insects from year to year. He simplified things by stipulating that the population would change due to only two factors: birthrate and the effect of overcrowding on population size. Many simplifying assumptions were used, including nonoverlapping generations, no interaction from other populations, no environmental stressors, and so forth. What was surprising was the result: despite the simplifications, if the birthrate and overcrowding effects were given fairly high values, the model produced a chaotic result (Pool 1989a). As in other chaotic systems, the predictions of the model are very sensitive to initial conditions, so sensitive that predictions are nearly impossible.

Whither Ecology? Ecology as a science has suffered from the confounding of different approaches to the field. One serious restraint on the development of the science of ecology has been the confusion between environmentalism and ecology. Environmentalism is essentially a political position that stresses the need for conservation and other human activities that will protect Earth's ecosystems. While environmentalism may grow out of the scientific study of ecology, much as multiculturalism and antiracism have in part developed from anthropological studies, it is important to separate the subjective nature of the former from the objective study of the latter.

Another schism within ecology has been between the empirically based fieldworkers and the mathematically based theorists. A major advance in ecology since the 1970s has been an increase in the amount of work done in integrating theory with field data. Robert MacArthur (1972), in his last publication as sole author before his untimely death, stated: "Ecology is now in position where the facts are confirmed by theory and the theories at least roughly confirmable by facts. But both the facts and the theories have serious inadequacies providing stumbling blocks to present progress." This statement remains accurate in the 1990s. Ecology as a whole, like human ecology, may have initially erred in attempting to derive theories of too great a generality. The science may require more circumspect theories geared to the details of specific situations (Hutchinson 1975). As our knowledge increases, particularly as our data sets become richer, ecologists may need to move from the linear models and equilibrium approaches employed by most ecologists to the more complex models derived from nonlinear dynamics, including the study of chaos in ecology (Hastings et al. 1993).

Although the basic aim of ecology is to assemble myriad tiny details into a coherent picture of how nature works, most of the fieldwork to build such concepts has been narrowly based and not focused on the big picture. David Tilman found that 70 percent of all field studies lasted only one or two seasons, and Peter Kareiva determined that half of population dynamics studies were done on plots a meter or less in diameter (Baskin 1997). Such simplifications may reflect attunement to the time spent in graduate training or the "publish-or-perish" threat to academic success. Whatever, this narrow focus obviates composing the big picture questions in ecology and seeking solutions to such major environmental problems as global climatic change and sustainable development.

The Challenges Facing the Science of Human Ecology

The problems that confront ecologists must be multiplied several times to understand the challenges facing the human ecologist. Here, an understanding of all the uncertainties of human behavior must be added to the complexities of environmental interactions among species before a full comprehension of human ecology is possible. This full comprehension may well be impossible to achieve.

Like the evolutionary theorists discussed above, we must be more modest in our goals for a science of human ecology. The specificity of predictions that we can expect to achieve in a mature science of human ecology may depend on the nature of what we attempt to predict. We may achieve fairly specific predictions about behaviors directly involved with subsistence, as noted in our discussion of optimal foraging models in Chapter 17. For other sorts of behaviors, however, predictions based on ecological models may be much more general. For instance, ecological models may have little to offer us in understanding details of religious observances found in a given human cultural group. On the other hand, human ecologists have offered explanations for some religious practices as a means of ensuring that individuals practice adaptive behavior. Examples include the use of scapulomancy ("readings" of what appear to be [to Western observers] random cracks in the shoulder blades of animals) by Canadian Naskapi Indians to ensure a randomized hunting strategy (Moore 1965); consumption of pigs in religious rituals by the Tsembaga Maring of New Guinea as part of a complex cycle that regulates protein intake, human population density, and frequency of warfare (Rappaport 1968); and religious proscriptions on the eating of beef in India as a means of avoiding the premature killing of oxen that are needed for agricultural practices (Harris 1978).

Environmentalism and Human Ecology.   Just as a confounding of environmentalism with the science of ecology has been common, environmentalism has even more often been a replacement for an objective science of human ecology. In many textbooks of ecology, one will find discussions of population growth, interspecies interactions, energy flow, and so forth, but when discussion turns to the human species (usually in a concluding chapter), all of these discussions disappear and are replaced by a lamentation of the human ecological tragedy. While such a discussion is of the greatest importance (and we will turn to such matters in the next section of this chapter) it should not replace a discussion of the science of human ecology. The omission of such discussions has, we believe, served to slow the development of a science of human ecology based on the principles of biological ecology as a whole. This has left the study of human ecology predominately to social scientists, which in turn has led to an emphasis on human ecological uniqueness. It may be that if biological ecologists had been the major force in the study of human ecology, there would have been an emphasis on how humans are fundamentally like other species in their interactions with the environment. As people trained in biological ecology increasingly turn to objective study of human ecology, perhaps a balance can be reached in our understanding of the degree to which human ecology can be understood in the dichotomous terms of general ecology versus the special framework for human ecology derived from the social sciences.

THE ECOLOGY OF HUMANS:
THE STATE OF THE SPECIES

The former mayor of New York City, Ed Koch, used to ask many of his constituents "How'm I doing?" to get feedback on his job performance during his term of office. Now it is time for us to ask the same question of our species in an ecological context: "How're we doing?" The answer, as might be expected, depends on who is asked. Here, we will simplify things by narrowing our discussion to four major topics: resources and population, ecosystem degradation, threats to biodiversity, and potential disruptions to global ecology.

Resources and Population

The topic of human population size and its relationship to resources has been covered to some extent in previous chapters, but a brief summary is warranted. The potential problem was arrestingly summarized by Harrison Brown (1954), who calculated that the increase in human population size from a population of 10 million in about 7000 BP until today would have reached a level where our biomass would now outweigh "the combined weights of all the stars in our physical universe" had growth rates not been limited by such factors as resource availability and disease.

Limitations caused by resources ensure that there will not be a future universe composed mainly of human biomass. In fact, there have been predictions of global famines caused by the rapid increase in numbers of people (e.g., Ehrlich 1968). Several of the "doomsday" predictions have not materialized, such as Ehrlich's statement that hundreds of millions of people would starve to death in the 1970s. Does this mean that concerns of possible devastating effects of human population increase are simply "myth" as argued by Bailey (1995)?

The answer, for us as for Malthus, is based on how the population growth rate will be moderated. More than other species, humans have the ability to change "the rules of the game" in an ecosystem. We have the ability to find new sources for needed resources, whether imported from other ecosystems or derived from previously inaccessible sources within the ecosystem, such as energy from fossil fuels. Thus, we can cause the carrying capacity to increase over time. However, limits must still exist in any ecosystem, as our capacity to increase is of galactic proportions and thus can outstrip any rise in carrying capacity. Our choices mirror those described by Malthus: natural inhibitions on growth, due to famine or pestilence, or artificial controls on growth, primarily through birth control (Keyfitz 1989). Thus, we can hope that the prophesied devastating effects of population will not come to pass, but we cannot count on this without addressing the related problems of overpopulation and resource depletion.

The consumption of nonrenewable resources is of major ecological and economic concern. As of 1997, 750 million people of developing areas in Eastern Europe, the former Soviet Union, China, India, Southeast Asia, and Latin America had entered the consumption classes (a number equal to the long-established consumers in rich countries); as more enter in the future, the problem will become even more critical (Myers 1997). To a considerable extent, the answer, at least in part, rests on increasing the emphasis on **sustainable development,** that is, meeting the needs of the present generation without compromising the ability of future generations to meet their own needs.

Ecosystem Degradation

Humans tend to optimize for the short term, rather than for the long term, in adapting to the environment. This was demonstrated clearly in the previous chapter in which it was shown that ecological models of human behavior appear to be most accurate when short-term gains are the focus of the models. This implies that behaviors that maximize resource output at the expense of ecosystem degradation will be adopted by human populations.

Unfortunately, there is abundant evidence for anthropogenic changes to ecosystems that have long-term, even permanent, negative effects. Many have reserved this characteristic to people in modernized societies, but a careful look at the evidence suggests that this is not so—the detrimental effects occur more quickly or to a greater extent as a result of modernization but are not different in kind.

Conversion of Forest to Grassland. One of the clearest examples of anthropogenic degradation is the existence of the "green deserts" of Southeast Asia. These vast areas feature *imperata* savanna grass where rainforest once flourished, the result of poorly managed swidden agriculture in the past (Geertz 1963). Similarly, *puna* grasslands of the Andes expanded at the expense of forests due to agricultural activities along with cutting of trees for fuel and construction purposes, with these processes begun long before the Spanish Conquest (Thomas and Winterhalder 1976). Conversion of forests into grasslands has accelerated with intensification of agricultural practices. For instance, the spread of cattle ranching has been a major contributor to deforestation in the Amazon and Central America, with much of this beef being used to support the U.S. appetite for fast-food hamburgers.

Erosion. Erosion is another serious outcome of anthropogenic degradation of ecosystems. Some of the clearest examples come from islands in the Pacific, such as eastern Polynesia and Hawaii (Kirch 1983; Nunn 1994), where erosion has not only led to the loss of land from island highlands but often also has led to the covering of some lowland areas with deposited soil. Erosion has become a serious problem in many other areas of the world, much of it as a result of people cutting down trees for use as firewood (Owen and Chiras 1995). Desertification, discussed more fully in Chapter 5, often results from the erosion and deforestation that accompanies flawed agricultural or animal husbandry practices.

Intensification of agricultural practices leads to more extensive erosional problems. There is an estimated annual loss of 24 billion metric tons of topsoil on agricultural lands worldwide due to erosion (Owen and Chiras 1995). This soil loss decreases agricultural productivity and can make some areas unusable (Brown 1981).

Pollution and Immune Systems. In the earlier discussions of pollution, a number of more or less easily observed effects were noted such as acid precipitation and mercury poisoning. Here it is pertinent to describe a much more subtle impact, namely the effects on immune systems. Although studies on this subject by toxicologists and others are yet at early stages, the finger of guilt points in the direction of the buildup of chronic pollutants negatively affecting the resistance capacity of immune systems in a wide variety of animals, including humans. For example, within a six-month period in 1988, some 20,000 harbor seals in northern Europe died. The direct cause of death was attributed to a newly discovered distemper virus that ordinarily would have been kept under control by the seal's immune system, the so-called T and B cells and others in the blood (Cone 1996a). PCBs, the now-banned but still widespread industrial lubricant, along with mercury, lead, dioxins, and various pesticides including DDT (whose use was long ago banished), have been indicted as probable culprits in the phenomenon known as **immunosuppression,** that is, suppression of the immune system. PCBs have so far been shown to be the most potent of these immunosuppressors.

Marine animals such as harbor seals as well as sea lions, sea otters, caspian terns, oysters, common and striped dolphins, beluga whales, and many others appear to be susceptible to immunosuppression, with consequent sometimes devastating effects on their populations. But humans are not in the free zone, and especially those who depend on the sea for their sustenance such as the Inuit of Arctic Canada (Cone 1996b). The milk fat in Inuit women has been measured at 1,052 ppb (parts per billion) of PCBs as compared with 1,002 ppb in whale blubber and 527 ppb in seal blubber. As a result, Inuit infants appear to build up dangerously high levels of this industrial pollutant after relatively short periods of breast-feeding. It is highly suspected that the immunosuppressing effects of the PCBs are responsible for the increased susceptibility of Inuit infants to life-threatening meningitis, of which there has been a twentyfold increase, as well as pneumonia, bronchitis, and ear infections.

Pollution and Environmental Estrogens.   Beginning in the 1930s, DDT, a synthetic chemical, was widely used as an agricultural pesticide, a malaria control agent, and a means of delousing military personnel during World War II. During the 1960s there was increasing evidence that DDT had adverse health effects, and by the early 1970s it was banned in the United States and many European countries; it is, however, still used in some developing countries. Unlike some other synthetic chemicals, DDT does not degrade quickly and persists in soils and sediments for long periods of time. As a result, this once lauded chemical has now been indicted as an **environmental estrogen,** that is an environmental chemical that mimics the female hormone estrogen. DDT, and a number of other synthetic chemicals, is believed to be responsible for the feminizing of wildlife (e.g., Florida alligators with smaller penises than those of normal males) and in humans as a possible cause of reduced sperm counts in males and increased breast cancer in females (MacLachlan and Arnold 1996). Curiously, these environmental estrogens, or ecoestrogens, in no way resemble the chemical structure of the natural hormones or growth factors.

Although these pollution impacts are sad indeed, they are yet strikingly stark examples of the well-established ecological principle that the entire global ecosystem is just that, a huge, complex, interacting unit in which an insult (in this case a pollutant) introduced in one part of the system can have impacts elsewhere, and sometimes far removed. As was noted in Chapter 15, acid components released into the atmosphere in the midwestern United States end up as acid precipitation in northeastern regions of the United States.

We may not be one world in a political sense, but we are certainly one gigantic ecosystem in which everything is related to everything else. A prime example is seen in the aftermath of a nuclear meltdown.

Chernobyl and Its Impacts.   Since the dawn of the nuclear age in 1945 with the bombing of Nagasaki and Hiroshima in Japan, scientists, engineers, and technicians have sought valiantly to contain the potential hazards of nuclear bomb testing, nuclear plant meltdowns, and environmental contamination from disposal of nuclear wastes (Madati and Kormondy 1989). Unfortunately, however, accidents involving radiation and radioactive elements do occur, most often as a result of human negligence, events that are followed by heightened public concern for health and safety.

On April 26, 1986, there was a serious **meltdown,** the melting of the core of a nuclear reactor, of the nuclear power plant at Chernobyl, in the northeastern Ukraine (then part of the USSR), resulting in both loss of life and serious extensive radiation damage to people (Anspaugh et al. 1988; Goldman 1987; Read 1993; Scherbak 1996; Stone 1996). The fallout from Chernobyl was the equivalent of 10 Hiroshima bombs, producing Geiger counter readings millions of times above normal. Similar to the movement of atmospheric acids, radioactive debris spread over much of eastern Europe and, by normal circular atmospheric movements, a few days later over Greenland, three-quarters of the way around the Earth (Figure 18–1).

The official death toll at Chernobyl remains at 31, which was the number of Chernobyl workers and firefighters who died as a result of the explosion or from radiation sickness; unofficial estimates, however, run between 5,000 and 10,000 deaths. More than 40,000 people were evacuated from areas of the Ukraine and Belarus. However, in the mid-1990s, some 270,000 people continued to live in areas with levels of radioactivity high enough to require expensive and disruptive measures to monitor and control foodstuffs (Williams and Balter 1996).

Children became the first victims of the immediate fallout of the radioactive form of iodine, known as iodine-131, which the body selectively takes up in the thyroid gland (Balter 1996). As a result, there has been a dramatic increase in childhood thyroid cancer cases in the three republics most affected by Chernobyl between 1986 and 1994: in the Russian Federation, the increase has been from 0 to about 10 in 1994; in Ukraine, from 1 or 2 to about 35; and in Belarus from about 9 to about 80 (Balter 1995).

The adverse and time-delayed impacts of the Chernobyl meltdown are still being reckoned. In 1996, there was evidence that children who were in utero in Greece during the time of the Chernobyl nuclear meltdown were demonstrating increased radioactivity-induced illnesses.

Indeed we live in an interactive, interrelated, interdependent, complex ecosystem.

Threats to Biodiversity

One of the gravest impacts of recent human activities has been on **biodiversity,** the number and abundance of species, by way of global mass extinctions. Geological history has recorded several of these events, with the best known being the Permian event, in which 96 percent of the world's then existing

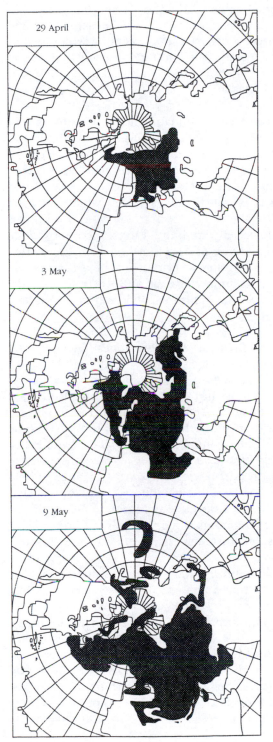

Figure 18–1 The spread of cesium-137 emitted from Chernobyl. (Reprinted with permission from C. I. Davidson et al. 1987. *Science* 237:633–34. Copyright 1987 American Association for the Advancement of Science.)

species are estimated to have become extinct, and the Cretaceous event, in which 76 percent of then existing species, including all the dinosaurs, became extinct (Price 1996). In fact, these two events are the markers by which geologists divide up the major spans of multicellular life into the Paleozoic (before the Permian event), Mesozoic (between the Permian and Cretaceous events), and Cenozoic (after the Cretaceous event) Eras.

Anthropogenic Extinctions in the Past.   Human contributions to extinctions are believed to have a long history. For instance, the mass extinction at the end of the Pleistocene Epoch, which unlike previous events was restricted primarily to land organisms, particularly large mammals, is hypothesized to have been largely caused by human hunting activities (Martin 1984). In fact, evidence for numerous extinctions of species is present in many places where humans have migrated during our spread over the globe. Again, clear cases are known from Pacific islands where many bird species were hunted to extinction by early human colonists, including the disappearance of the largest birds in the world, the moas of New Zealand (Anderson 1990). Similar evidence for extinctions following human colonization can be found on Madagascar and Australia (Wilson 1992) as well as the classic case of the dodo on Mauritius, an island in the Indian Ocean (Quammen 1996).

Anthropogenic Extinctions in the Present.   Modern times have brought with them an increased ability by humans to affect their environment. The current anthropogenic mass extinctions are caused by several factors, including overharvesting (like the prehistoric examples just cited related to overhunting), destruction or alteration of physical habitat, displacement by introduced (i.e., alien) species, pollution, and hybridization with other species or subspecies due to human activities (Wilson 1992). Critics have argued that the data are not accurate enough to state that human activities have caused a marked increase in extinction rates (Mann 1991). This is in part due to our own ignorance of just how much biodiversity exists on the Earth. Although some 1.4 million species are recorded, estimates of the total number of species range from 3 million to 70 million (Groombridge 1992). Whatever the number, a great deal of evidence has been gathered in specific local ecosystems that suggests a general trend toward decreased biodiversity.

What is the consequence of this extinction and its diminishment of the world's biodiversity? The best answer is that no one really knows (Reaka-Kudla et al 1997). Many biologists are very concerned, in part because of our own inability to make accurate predictions about ecology as noted earlier in the chapter. Our studies of ecology have shown that the loss of a single species (a so-called keystone species) from an ecosystem can have widespread repercussions, leading to major, permanent changes in the ecological community (Paine 1969; Roughgarden 1983). What impact these changes will have on humanity probably will depend on specifics of the local habitat. Globally, the loss of biodiversity will impoverish the biosphere and its genetic reservoir and may both take away potential sources of medicines or foods and enhance the amount of parasitism directed toward what biomass is left, that of the human species. As we have seen, many organisms function in nutrient cycles, some of which have global effects; others are important in the maintenance and development of soils; still others prey upon organisms that would otherwise become pests for humans (Ehrlich and Wilson 1991). What is striking is our ignorance, but probably warranted fear, of just what the specific consequences of these continued extinctions will be.

Humans and the Game Theory of Evolution.   Besides the loss of species diversity caused by human activities, in modern times humans are also facing a loss of their own diversity. As noted earlier in the chapter, Slobodkin and Rapoport (1974) have used a game theory model to predict that conservative, flexible strategies are conducive to long-term evolutionary success for a species. The human "evolutionary strategy" has, in large part, been to maintain a conservative, generalized biological status, while utilizing behavioral and cultural means to deal with specialized environments. Our species has therefore maintained flexibility to deal with environmental changes and thus appears to have an excellent evolutionary strategy based on the game theory model. Changes in recent times suggest that this strategy may have altered. Cultural diversity is rapidly declining as modernization takes place, giving our species fewer available options in case of major environmental change. We increasingly rely on the modern industrial social system that grew out of the Industrial Revolution within the past two centuries or so. On an evolutionary time scale, this is a new, relatively untested system that may not have bright long-term prospects. Perhaps our increasing behavioral specialization will lead us into an evolutionary dead-end.

Global Ecological Disruptions

Human activities may be leading to environmental changes on a global scale that will have major effects on all of Earth's ecosystems; we have already discussed the Greenhouse Effect on global warming. As we have declared, the limitations on our knowledge of ecology are very evident, as there is little consistency in quantitative predictions by different ecologists and even contradictions in some cases. We will briefly explore here predictions of stratospheric ozone levels on a global level.

Ozone Depletion in the Atmosphere.   Although we have noted that data on some environmental problems such as global warming are sometimes ambiguous and even contradictory, the data are much clearer about another global problem: the depletion of stratospheric ozone, particularly in polar regions. **Ozone,** a form of oxygen in which three oxygen atoms are bound together, is a serious form of air pollution when found in the troposphere, or lower atmosphere, where it is a major component of smog. In the presence of sunlight, tropospheric ozone is formed by the oxidation of nitrogen oxides and hydrocarbons both of which are byproducts of industrial as well as domestic fossil fuel combustion, primarily by automobiles. Tropospheric ozone causes irritation of the mucous membranes in humans and has been indicted as a significant factor in the dieback of vegetation downwind of heavily polluted cities. It also has negative effects on the production of such crops as corn, wheat, soybeans, and peanuts, being responsible for some 90 percent of crop loss in the United States (MacKenzie and El-Ashry 1988; Tinghey et al. 1994). On the positive side, because of its effectiveness in killing microorganisms, ozone has the potential for being used as a disinfectant in sewage treatment and improving the water quality of purified sewage.

Unlike its role in the troposphere, ozone in the stratosphere (9 to 18 miles above the Earth) serves an important function for the organisms living below: it partially shields them from solar ultraviolet radiation. An increase in incident ultraviolet radiation has many effects: limiting the growth of phytoplankton and destroying larval forms of some marine life; reducing the productivity of agricultural crops; increasing prevalence of skin cancer in humans, both non-melanoma and the more severe melanoma that is fatal nearly one-third of the time; also in humans, decreasing the viability of circulating lymphocytes, thereby negatively affecting the immune system; and producing a slight warming of the Earth's atmosphere (Maugh 1979, 1980, 1982; MacKenzie and El-Ashry 1988; Roberts 1989a; and Toon and Turco 1991).

Between 1977 and 1984, the springtime amounts of ozone over Halley Bay, Antarctica, decreased by more than 40 percent, and later research showed that the region of ozone depletion spanned over several million square miles, wider than the continent itself (Figure 18–2) (Farman et al. 1985; Stolarski 1988). Within the "ozone hole," the abundance of ozone is about half that of what it was a decade before. In 1992, a record low of global ozone was reached, 2 to 3 percent lower than any earlier year (Gleason et al. 1993). The eruption of Mount Pinatubo in the Philippines contributed to this depletion through the release of ozone-destroying chlorine gases (Tabazadeh and Turco 1993).

Depletion of atmospheric ozone has also been seen in the northern polar region and more recently over temperate regions in North and South America as well. The Arctic losses, so far, are not as severe as those in the Antarctic, the hardest-hit layers having lost only 15 to 20 percent of their ozone (Kerr 1990b). In 1997, two ozone holes were detected over Russia exposing an area twice the size of Texas east of the Ural Mountains and a smaller gap over the densely populated northwestern region spanning Moscow, St. Petersburg, and the now independent Baltic States (Williams 1997).

In contrast to the tropospheric production of ozone by the oxidation of hydrocarbons and nitrogen oxides, stratospheric destruction of ozone is largely due to the effects of an anthropogenic pollutant: the chlorofluorocarbons (CFCs) (Graedel and Crutzen 1989). CFCs have been used widely in refrigerants and also in solvents and for other industrial uses. The internationally agreed to 1987 Montreal Protocol on Substances That Deplete the Ozone Layer has placed limits on CFCs, with their use to be eventually phased out. Unfortunately, due to their chemical stability in the atmosphere the destructive effects of CFCs on stratospheric ozone will continue for many years after their production by

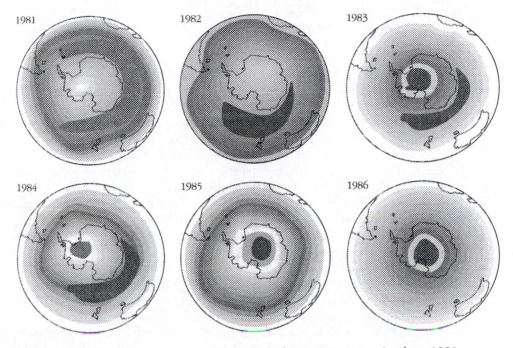

Figure 18–2   The degree and extent of ozone depletion over Antarctica from 1981 to 1986. The clear central area shows the least amount of ozone, the progressively grayer areas show increasing amounts of ozone, and the darkest crescent-shaped band shows an ozone-rich region. (Based on data from the U.S. National Aeronautics and Space Administration.)

humans ceases. Nonetheless, the use of CFCs, particularly in developed countries, has decreased quite markedly, giving some optimists the hope that ozone should be recovering by 2000 and return to the 1979 levels—the year the Antarctic ozone hole became obvious—by around 2050 (Kerr 1996).

CHANGE AS A CONSTANT IN ECOSYSTEMS

Earth's environment is not constant; rather, the constant is that it is always changing. The dynamics of interaction of organisms with their environment and with each other has been amply demonstrated throughout the text. In fact, our major stress has been on the impact of organisms, particularly humans, on their environment—enhancing, destroying, polluting, conserving, preserving—and, conversely, the impact of the environment on organisms—drought, flooding, freezing, warming. For the most part, the interactions that have occupied our attention to this point have been of relative recency—ozone depletion by chlorofluorocarbons, neurological damage by mercury in fish, desertification, and acid rain, among many others.

Since the universe was created in the "Big Bang," and since planet Earth condensed out of nebulous gases, change has been the nature of Nature. When the Earth cooled sufficiently and circumstance led to the primordial goo that enabled protolife, the latter began to affect the former and vice versa. As life as well as Earth evolved over eons of time, Earth and organisms changed. What we now know as the major continents were at one time a single large continent; over time, they separated due to what we now recognize as plate tectonics. Imperceptible to our sensitivity day to day but measurable by sophisticated instrumentation, the plates continue to move, sliding over and under each other and thereby creating tensions that are relieved in earthquakes. Volcanic eruptions, which geologists believe have been part of Earth's dynamics virtually since Earth's origin, continue to change the landscape as well as the atmosphere. The tilting of the Earth appears to be one factor in the major cooling and warming of the Earth in its history, resulting in falling and rising sea levels over eons of time. These historical changes in the composition, temperature, and circulation of the Earth's atmosphere and ocean, as well as in its geology, biology, and sea level, are chronicled in sediments, rocks, and ice caps; today they continue, sometimes subtly, sometimes overtly, but they occur inexorably now and will in the future, recognized and recorded today in a myriad of contemporary measuring instruments and by more sophisticated ones in the future. An excellent review of these global environmental changes in the past, present, and future is found in Turekian (1996).

The informing lesson of this principle that change is in the nature of Nature is that changes are natural, they occurred prior to humankind—and, depending on how humankind responds to these changes, will occur in the future even if there is no humankind.

What should be clear from this brief discussion of change and from preceding chapters is that the scale of disharmony and resulting environmental degradation has been changed radically as human population burgeoned and required more and different uses of the environment, placing tremendous pressure on Earth's life support capacity. It thus behooves us collectively to develop and apply the knowledge required to conserve and wisely manage Earth's resources in sustainable fashion.

VALUING NATURE

The Economic Value of Nature

Nature is fundamentally a life support system for all organisms, one we tend to take for granted until there is a disruption such as an earthquake, tornado, or drought. The natural products and processes that occur in ecosystems are the components of that support system; they are critical to survival and therefore have value in economic as well as other terms.

The natural products of ecosystems on which humans depend include grains, vegetables, seafood, game and other animals, fodder, fuel wood, timber, and pharmaceutical products, among many other goods. As goods they have economic value. For example, the annual world fish catch of about 100 million metric tons has a value of between $50 billion and $100 billion and serves as the leading source of animal protein, with over 20 percent of the population in Africa and Asia dependent on fish as their primary source of protein (UNFAO 1993). Add to this the commercial harvest of other seafood (e.g., lobsters, shrimp, scallops as well as kelp) and of freshwater fish worldwide and the employment generated by sport-fishing activities, it is evident there is tremendous economic value in Earth's aquatic ecosystems.

The services provided by ecosystems are multiple, including the purification of air and water, detoxification and decomposition of wastes, regulation of climate, mitigation of floods and droughts, pollination and seed dispersal, natural pest control, regeneration of soil fertility, and production and maintenance of biodiversity, from which key ingredients of our agricultural, pharmaceutical, and industrial enterprises are derived (Daily et al. 1997). These services, provided *pro bono* daily, also have economic value. As but one example, New York City determined that the natural water purification services of the Catskill Mountain ecosystem (the source of its water) was over $3 billion—more economical than using a water treatment plant.

Although some price tags can be placed on some ecosystem goods and services, as just noted, valuing any natural ecosystem or the entire global ecosystem is fraught with difficulties. Nonetheless, it has been attempted by focusing on what economists term *environmental externalities*, the benefits from resources that belong to no one in particular and so are enjoyed for free. A group of conservation-minded ecologists and economists have put a $33 trillion price tag on the economic services provided by Mother Nature (Roush 1997). Whether this is a realistic number or not, and that has been questioned, is not so much the point as is the fact that the natural products and services of ecosystems in particular and the global ecosystem in general have an inherent value.

Values and Choices: A Basis for Environmental Ethics

In his play *Professional Foul*, American playwright Tom Stoppard (1978) has one of his characters state, "There would be no moral dilemmas if moral principles worked in straight lines and never crossed each other." It is only when two or more ethical values or principles come into conflict that choice is involved and a dilemma arises as to which to choose.

The ethical values in the human-nature relationship devolve from the traditions of imperialism and Arcadianism. **Imperialism** is based on the premise that humans are not an integral part of nature and instead have dominion over nature, deriving from a very literal interpretation of the Old Testament, namely Genesis 1:26: "let them have dominion over the fish of the sea . . . and over every creeping thing that creepeeth upon the earth" and 1:28: "Be fruitful and multiply, and replenish the earth and subdue it; and have dominion . . . over every living thing that moveth upon the earth" (White 1967). **Arcadianism** derives from Arcadia, that region of ancient Greece in the mid-Peloponnesus inhabited by pastoral people of idyllic satisfaction. Its premise is that humans are an integral part of nature and have an innate reverence for nature because of its beneficence.

It should be patent that these two diametrically opposed traditions do not run in straight, parallel lines and thus often lead to choices between humans and nonhumans, between rights and entitlements of individuals and of society, and even between present and future generations. The ethics of manipulating nature derive from a consideration of whether the knowledge of how to control nature at any cost is prized or whether humankind is regarded as one of many species, but of no higher rank in the biosphere.

In practice, there is not usually an easy solution. For example, in the late 1970s, the Tellico Dam project in the eastern United States, presumably of benefit to humans, was interrupted for an endangered species, a tiny fish known as the snail darter. In the 1990s, logging in old-growth forests of the northwestern United States was sharply curtailed for another endangered species, the spotted owl. Who has more right—humans or fish? Humans or owls?

Likewise, the choice between yielding to individual rights by compromising societal rights, or more usually vice versa, necessitates careful assessment of the issues of beneficence, justice, and fair play. For example, are the individual's rights to an off-road vehicle ride to be compromised by society's right to conserve a fragile ecosystem? Is the individual's right of procreation to be compromised by the right of society to control its population to assure that it is justly fed, clothed, and housed? Do those living now have rights to consume natural resources to destruction or exhaustion without concern for what some regard as the identical rights of our descendants?

The choices we make are ultimately based on a value system. Such a system derives from the ethical principles we espouse, principles such as autonomy (personal liberty, independence, self-reliance), nonmaleficence (doing no harm or injury), beneficence (contributing to the health and welfare of others), and justice (receiving what one deserves and can legitimately claim). These principles become manifest as we judge whether the outcome or ends of an action justifies the means of getting there (a utilitarian ethic) or whether under no circumstance can any set of means justify even a desirable end (a deontological ethic) (Hardin 1993; Kormondy 1990; Hargrove 1989; Rolston 1988; Westra 1994; among others. Also consult the journal *Environmental Ethics*, 1 [1979], et seq.).

What is demanded is a rethinking of our place in nature, a rethinking of attitudes about the total environment—in the words of Leopold (1949), the development of a new ethic for the land, and of Potter (1971), the development of an ethic of survival. The Westerner's view is that land is an adversary to be conquered, a servant to be exploited for human ends, a possession of rightful and eminent domain, and an entity of unlimited capacity. This view must give way to an ecological conscience, to a love, respect, admiration, and understanding for the total ecosystem of which we are a part; to an ethic that ensures the survival of the human species with quality, dignity, and integrity.

CONCLUSION

One cannot help but be impressed by our species' adaptive success. From humble hominid beginnings in the mosaic environment of Africa's woodlands and savannas three million to four million years ago, humans have inhabited virtually all land biomes on Earth. We have truly been fruitful and multiplied. Humans have increasingly directed more and more of the Earth's resources to their own ends, including using the resources to avoid or at least buffer themselves from many of the environmental stressors with which they were once afflicted.

The question is: are we now the victims of our own success? In this and other chapters we have seen that many ecologists believe that we are facing very serious environmental problems caused by our own activities. The problem is that in virtually all cases the limitations in our knowledge of ecology, and specifically human ecology, do not permit us much certainty in our assessments of our predicament, still less the knowledge of how to "fix" it. Our assessments of the science of human ecology and of the ecology of humans, therefore, are connected. Improvements in the former are required for improvements in the latter. It is our greatest hope that one of the readers of this text will develop an increased interest in the study of human ecology and advance the field in a manner that allows us to better see our way in these perplexing times.

We humans are best viewed as an incredibly adaptable species; part of this adaptation must be to changes caused by our own behavior. We have seen that our adaptation consists of balancing gains in effectiveness and efficiency with reductions in risk. The potential risks delineated here are so great that it behooves us to take steps to reduce them, even if we are uncertain of their magnitude. It remains to be seen if we can continue adapting to the changes we make in our own evolutionary "game."

KEY TERMS

Arcadianism
biodiversity
environmental
  estrogen

immunosuppression
imperialism
meltdown
ozone

sustainable
  development

KEY POINTS

- [ ] Evolution may be regarded as an "existential game" in which the best strategy for a species to use is a very conservative one of being flexible and a generalist.

- [ ] Faced with the complexity of ecosystems, ecologists have simplified reality by performing experiments and developing simulations.

☐   Scientific development of ecology has been constrained by the confusion between environmentalism and ecology and the schism between empirically based fieldworkers and mathematically based theorists.

☐   Scientific development of human ecology has been largely in the hands of social scientists, leading to an emphasis on human ecological uniqueness, rather than in the hands of biological ecologists, who note that humans are like other species in their interactions with the environment even though they have the ability to change the rules of the game.

☐   Among others, the human species faces four major ecological problems: provision of sufficient resources; degradation of ecosystems; diminished biodiversity; and disruption of global ecology.

☐   Although change has been a constant, natural factor in the evolution of Earth and life on it, the scale of disharmony and resulting environmental degradation has changed radically as the human population burgeoned and spread.

☐   As a life support system, nature has economic value for its products and services. Its ethical values devolve from the traditions of imperialism and Arcadianism.

Glossary

Abiotic environment The nonliving components of an ecosystem (e.g., chemical elements, water, air).

Acclimatization A form of nonhereditary adaptation through which an individual compensates for a complex of environmental factors.

Acid precipitation Precipitation that is acidic (technically, having a pH lower than 5.0) resulting from the presence of sulfuric acid and other compounds dissolved in atmospheric water.

Acid rain See *Acid precipitation*.

Active metabolism The metabolic activity that generates additional heat as a byproduct of the additional energy requirements of muscular work.

Acute mountain sickness A common ailment upon first arriving at high altitude characterized by headache, dizziness, lightheadedness, and nausea due to lowered oxygen intake or respiratory alkalosis.

Adaptation The process of developing or enhancing structural, physiological, or behavioral characteristics that improve chances for survival and reproduction in a given environment. As a noun, the term is the characteristic itself.

Adaptive radiation The divergence from a single ancestral form that results from the exploitation of different habitats.

Adiposity The amount of body fat.

Aerobic The production of energy by metabolism in the presence of oxygen.

Aerobic capacity The highest rate at which oxygen can be consumed in metabolism.

Aerobic power The aerobic capacity per body weight.

Age structure The relative proportions of young, middle-aged, and older individuals in a population.

AIDS An acronym for Acquired Immune Deficiency Syndrome, a disease caused by the human immunodeficiency virus (HIV) that is transmitted through semen and blood and is often fatal.

Allen's rule A tenet that, in widely distributed homeothermic species, populations in cold climates will tend to have shorter extremities than those in mild climates.

Alpine tundra A region in mountainous areas above tree line that is characterized by dwarf plants; unlike arctic tundra, there is no permafrost.

Altruistic behavior Social interaction in which the actor confers a benefit on the recipient but itself incurs a loss.

Alveoli The tiny air sacs in the lungs across the surface of which oxygen and carbon dioxide are exchanged with blood.

Ammoniafication The conversion of nitrates ultimately to ammonia.

Anabolism The metabolic process in which food is changed into tissue.

Anemia A condition in which there is defective red blood cell production, often owing to a severe iron deficiency.

Anthropogenic Activities that are generated by humans.

Anthropology The study of human behavioral and biological diversity, both geographical and temporal.

Antigenic drift A genetic mutation causing a minor change in the outer protein coat of a virus.

Antigenic shift A genetic mutation resulting in a major change in the outer protein coat of a virus.

Apocrine sweat glands Glands in mammals that are associated with hair follicles and secrete a fluid rich in lipids and proteins.

Arcadianism A premise that humans are an integral part of nature and have an innate reverence for it because of its beneficence.

Arteriosclerosis The hardening of arteries, in which the blood vessel wall becomes fragile and susceptible to aneurysm or rupture.

Atherosclerosis The existence of hard, lipid-containing deposits (plaques) on the interior walls of arteries.

Autotroph An organism that meets its own nutritional requirements by capturing energy and using it to synthesize molecules that serve its nutritional requirements; also known as a producer.

Autotrophic ecosystem An ecosystem that depends directly on the influx of solar energy.

Balanced polymorphism A genetic trait that exists in multiple forms, with heterozygotes having greater selective advantage than either of the homozygotes.

Bands People within small groups, often of the same kinship.

Barometric pressure The pressure of the atmosphere as measured by a barometer.

Basal metabolism The metabolic activity that is generated by animals during complete rest.

Bergmann's rule A tenet that, in a widely distributed, homeothermic species, populations in colder environments will tend to be bigger than those in mild climates.

Beriberi The thiamine deficiency disease leading to cardiovascular and neurological disorders and a swelling of the body.

Biodiversity A term describing species richness, ecosystem complexity, and genetic variation.

Biogeochemical cycle The movement of chemical elements from organisms to the physical environment and back to organisms in more or less circular pathways.

Biological magnification   The increase in concentration of a residue (e.g., a toxin) along a food chain.

Biome   A large terrestrial ecosystem that occurs on major regional or subcontinental areas.

Biosphere   See *Ecosphere*.

Biotic environment   The living components of an ecosystem (e.g., plants and animals).

Biotic potential   The maximum reproductive capacity of a species, expressed as a rate.

Boreal forest   The circumpolar, subarctic coniferous forest of high northern latitudes; also known as taiga.

BP   "Before the present," a usage that avoids the need for the abbreviations B.C. and A.D. and is particularly applicable in reference to geological time.

Bridewealth   The amount a groom's family is expected to pay (in money or goods) to the bride's family to recompense them for her loss.

Cancer   A condition in which there is uncontrolled growth of the cells.

Carnivore   A meat eater or secondary consumer that obtains its food by eating primary consumers (herbivores).

Carrying capacity   The maximum population of a species that a particular environment can support.

Cerebral edema   The accumulation of fluid in brain tissues.

Character displacement   The principle that closely related species living together become recognizably different even though virtually indistinguishable when each occurs alone.

Cholera   An intestinal disease characterized by cramps, diarrhea, vomiting, and severe dehydration and that can result in shock and subsequent death.

Chronic mountain sickness   A condition of natives or long-term residents of high altitude characterized by a loss of acclimatization, lowered ventilation rate, and a great increase in polycythemia.

Coarse-grained environment   An environment in which resources are distributed in relatively large patches.

Cold-induced vasodilation   Dilation of peripheral blood vessels during exposure to cold.

Commensalism   A symbiotic association in which one species (the commensal) is benefited while the other (the host) is not affected.

Community ecology   The study of the structure and function of biological communities.

Competition   A symbiotic association in which the growth or survival of one of the species populations is adversely affected in instances in which a common resource is in short supply.

Competitive exclusion principle   The principle that two or more resource-limited species, having identical patterns of resource use, cannot coexist in a stable environment, one outcompeting and eventually eliminating the other.

Componential analysis   An ethnological approach used to derive meaningful components or characteristics that make up terms.

Conduction   The transfer of heat between two solid objects in physical contact.

Consumers   Organisms that obtain their food directly from producers; also known as heterotrophs.

Convection   The heat exchange between an object and a gas or liquid.

Cooperative behavior   Social interaction in which both the actor and recipient gain.

Cori cycle An adaptive process for conserving glucose, involving a switch to anaerobic metabolism in muscle with glucose broken down to lactose instead of to carbon dioxide and water.

Countercurrent heat exchange A heat exchange between arteries and veins that warms venous blood that has cooled in peripheral areas.

Cretinism A condition in which there is severe neurological damage and resultant mental retardation that results from depressed thyroid function during infancy or early childhood.

Cultural ecology A field of study in which a group's means of subsistence is held to be strongly related to other parts of the group's culture.

Culture The set of understandings and learned behavior patterns that are shared by the people in a society.

Culture areas Regions of the world within which both the basic environmental conditions and the cultures of human populations are similar.

Culture core A group's subsistence, including its basic economy and technology.

Cybernetics The study of communications systems and of system control in organisms and machines.

Deciduous forest The broad-leaved forest of the middle latitudes in which leaves are shed seasonally.

Decomposers Organisms that derive their nutrition from both producers and consumers, usually by utilizing their wastes or remains.

Demographic transition The decline in mortality followed by a decline in natality that occurs as countries become industrialized.

Denitrification The conversion of nitrate to nitrogen, the gaseous form.

Density-dependent Processes that are regulated by the number of individuals present in a given space, e.g., those that either increase mortality or decrease natality as the number of individuals in the population increases.

Density-independent Processes that are not regulated by the number of individuals present in a given space.

Desert Bush-covered land of arid regions in which the plants are quite dispersed with much bare ground between them.

Desertification The process of desert formation and expansion.

Detritus Dead organic material.

Detritus ecosystem An ecosystem that is directly dependent on the influx of detritus.

Diabetes mellitus A disorder involving the incapacity of the body to metabolize carbohydrates in a normal manner.

Directional selection Natural selection in which there is a progressive shift toward the extreme of a particular characteristic, usually occurring in response to a steady change in environmental conditions. Also known as diversifying selection.

Disease reservoir All the hosts of a given pathogen in a given area; also all of the organisms from which a vector derives its infection.

Dispersion The horizontal spacing of plants or animals that may be random, uniform or regular, or clumped or contagious.

Diversifying selection See *Directional selection*.

Doubling time The number of years in which a population would double in size if the then present growth rates were to remain constant.

Eccrine sweat glands Glands, particularly numerous in humans, that produce a liquid consisting of water with a salt concentration about equal to that of body water in general.

Ecological amplitude   The range of tolerance to environmental conditions and/or factors.

Ecological anthropology   The study of the ecology of human populations throughout the world, in the past as well as present.

Ecological community   An assemblage of species populations occurring together within a particular geographic area whose ecological functions and dynamics are in some way interdependent.

Ecological psychology   A field of study that attempts to predict behavior based on observations of the environment in which the behavior occurs.

Ecological system   See *Ecosystem.*

Ecology   The scientific study of the environment, including its living and nonliving components.

Economics   The study of how people allocate scarce resources for various uses.

Ecosphere   The thin layer of Earth comprising a gigantic network of ecosystems; also referred to as the biosphere.

Ecosystem   An organizational unit consisting of both living and nonliving things that occur in a particular place.

Ecotone   The transition zone between two or more different communities that is typically richer in resources and species than each community alone.

Edema   An abnormal accumulation of fluid resulting in swelling.

Emic   A perspective in which the investigator attempts subjectively to see an individual's worldview through the eyes of that other person.

Energy   The capacity to do work.

Energy consumption   The amount of energy that a group uses through dietary intake or fuel consumption.

Energy efficiency   The percentage of energy computed from the energy produced divided by the energy expended; a measure of the net energy gain for a given activity.

Energy expenditure   The amount of energy that a group uses or expends in physical activity.

Energy production   The amount of energy that can be obtained by a group; the equivalent of secondary production as measured for other consumers in food chains.

Environmental determinism   The idea that specific features of the environment have a causal effect on the presence of specific cultural features.

Environmental estrogen   An environmental chemical that mimics the female hormone estrogen.

Environmental possibilism   The principle that emphasizes the primacy of specific historical events in the creation of cultures through continuous change over time, with environmental features serving to limit what events are possible.

Environmental psychology   A field of study that focuses on the perception individuals have of their environment, particularly resources, threats, and problems.

Environmental resistance   The totality of abiotic and biotic environmental forces that prevent the biotic potential of a species from being realized.

Environmental stress   An external condition that causes a potentially injurious change in biological systems.

Essential resources   Materials that are required to support a group.

Estrus   The time in the female reproductive cycle when she is fertile.

Ethnocentrism   The notion that one's own cultural conventions are superior, or more natural, than those of other cultures.

Ethnoecology   A field of study derived from linguistics that attempts to determine people's viewpoint from their language.

Etic   A perspective in which an objective outsider's viewpoint is employed to understand a group's culture.

Evaporation   The conversion of a liquid to a gas, a process that requires energy and thus a loss of heat from the surrounding area.

Fecundity   The reproductive capacity of an organism.

Fertility   The actual (or realized) reproductive rate of an organism.

Fertility rate   The number of live births per 1,000 women between the ages of 15 and 49.

First law of thermodynamics   The principle that the sum total of energy in a system is a constant, or that energy can neither be created nor destroyed but may be converted from one form to another.

Food chain   The chain of energy movement from producer to consumer.

Food web   The interlinking of food chains.

Foraging   Subsistence activities that rely on wild food resources for the major portion of the food supply.

Founder effect   The derivation of a new population from a single or few individuals in which the founding population's genetic composition represents a very small sample of the genetic pool of the original population; subsequently, natural selection yields gene combinations different from the original population.

Gaseous nutrient cycle   A biogeochemical cycle in which the atmosphere is a major reservoir, the element being in a gaseous state.

Gause's principle   See *Competitive exclusion principle*.

Generation time   The length of time between generations of a population.

Genetic drift   Random fluctuations in the genetic composition of one or both groups of a separated population such that the genes among the offspring do not perfectly represent the parental population's genetic composition.

Gloger's rule   The general tendency for skin color in species with broad geographic ranges to vary from dark to light as latitude increases.

Glycogenesis   The synthesis of glycogen from the simple sugar glucose.

Glycogenolysis   The breakdown of glycogen into glucose.

Glycosylation   A process in which glucose combines with protein; it is believed to accelerate cellular aging.

Goiter   An enlargement of the thyroid gland often as a result of iodine deficiency.

Gradualism   A theory holding that the origin and evolution of species and higher orders occur more or less continuously over relatively long periods of time.

Grassland   Areas covered by vegetation dominated by grasses; referred to as steppes in Europe and Asia, llanos or pampas in South America, and veldt or savanna in southern and eastern Africa.

Greenhouse Effect   The warming that results from heat retention in the lower atmosphere due to the absorption and reradiation of long-wave (infrared) radiation by carbon dioxide and other gases.

Gross ecological efficiency   The percent of energy transferred from one trophic level to the next.

Gross production   See *Production*.

Gross productivity   See *Productivity*.

Growth form   The morphology of a plant (e.g., needle-leaved).

Growth rate   The change in the number of individuals in a population over a given time period.

Habitat   The place in which a species lives.

Habituation   The process of becoming less reactive to any particular stimulus or stress.

Hemoglobin   The protein that gives red blood cells their color and their capacity to transport oxygen and carbon dioxide.

Herbivore   A primary consumer, that is, an animal that obtains its food from plants.

Heterotroph   An organism whose nutritional needs are met by feeding on other organisms; also known as a consumer.

Heuristic   Something used to help understanding without necessarily being accurate; devices used to reduce complexity and facilitate understanding.

Homeostasis   The relative constancy of internal body conditions.

Hominids   The group of primates comprising modern and ancestral humans.

Hookworm   An infection with parasitic worms with a hooklike shape (notably *Necator americanus* and *Ancyclostoma duodenale*).

Horticulture   Subsistence agriculture using simple tools and without complex irrigation and fertilization techniques.

Hydrologic cycle   The circular flow of water between the Earth's surface and the atmosphere through precipitation and evaporation.

Hypertension   Persistently high arterial blood pressure.

Hypoxia   Low oxygen levels.

Immunosuppression   Suppression of the immune system.

Imperialism   The premise that humans are not an integral part of nature and instead have dominion over it.

Incidence rate   The number of new cases of a disease per population size that appear during a given period of time.

Inclusive fitness   A measure of the adaptive value of an individual based not only on that individual's own success but also on the success of all its kin.

Infant mortality   The number of deaths per 1,000 individuals between birth and one year of age.

Influenza   An acute, infectious disease caused by any of a specific group of viruses and characterized by inflammation of the respiratory tract, fever, and muscular pain; probably the most significant infectious disease in developed countries.

Inheritance of acquired characteristics   A theory of evolution proposed by Jean Baptiste de Lamarck in the early nineteenth century which states that characteristics acquired by an organism during its lifetime are transmitted to the reproductive cells and inherited by the next generation.

Insolation   The amount of solar radiation that is received over a unit area of the Earth's surface.

Insulative adaptation   An adaptation to cold or heat stress involving body size, form, and composition as well as regulation of blood flow.

Insulin   A hormone produced by beta cells in the pancreas that regulates the metabolism of blood sugar.

Insulin-dependent diabetes mellitus   A condition in which an individual's immune system recognizes insulin-producing beta cells as a foreign antigen and attacks them.

Intensive agriculture   A subsistence activity in which technology and labor are used to create artificial ecosystems, with domesticated plants and animals supplanting the native community and human use of fertilizers and irrigation systems supplanting natural nutrient cycles.

Intrinsic rate of natural increase The biotic potential of a species measured under optimal conditions.

J-shaped growth curve The shape of a growth curve in which there is a rapid exponential growth up to the limits imposed by the environment, at which point the population undergoes a rapid die-off.

Key resources Essential resources that are expensive, rare, or simply difficult to acquire.

Keys The evaluation of terms based on a number of "yes/no" attributes that divide the world into a series of alternate categories.

Kilocalorie One thousand calories, abbreviated as kcal or C; a calorie is a measure of the amount of heat required to raise the temperature of water 1°C.

Kwashiorkor A deficiency disease in childhood caused by severe protein malnutrition and characterized by muscle atrophy, growth failure, skin rash, edema, and in some cases depigmentation of skin or hair.

Labor-intensive agriculture A subsistence activity in which most of the energy used to transform the natural world into an artificial landscape is from human muscular effort.

Law of the Minimum The principle that, under steady-state conditions, growth and development of an organism are dependent on all requisite needs being present in at least minimal amounts.

Law of Tolerance The principle that both a deficiency or an excess of a factor may limit an organism or population.

Life expectancy The estimated life span at the time of birth or the number of years that an individual of any given age may expect, on the average, to live.

Life form The morphology of a plant based on the relation of the ground surface to the plant's embryonic or regenerating tissue.

Limiting factor That environmental component whose presence is beyond the limits of tolerance required for growth and development of an organism.

Lithosphere The upper solid, rocky layer of the Earth; the Earth's crust.

Litter The accumulation of dead plant and animal matter on the soil surface.

Macroenvironment See *Macrohabitat*.

Macrohabitat The general habitat in which a species exists (e.g., hot desert, freshwater pond); also referred to as macroenvironment.

Macronutrients Elements needed in relatively large amounts, each constituting 0.2 percent or more of dry organic weight.

Macroparasites Parasites that are typically large, have longer generation times than microparasites do, and have no direct reproduction within the host.

Maintenance selection See *Stabilizing selection*.

Malaria A debilitating and sometimes fatal infectious disease, generally intermittent and recurrent, caused by species of the mosquito genus *Plasmodium* that are parasitic in red blood cells and that are transmitted to humans by the bite of mosquitoes of the genus *Anopheles*.

Malnutrition A condition resulting from lack of food, a deficiency of one or more essential nutrients, or genetic or environmental illness in which there is interference with digestion, absorption, or metabolism. Too much food or too much of one type of nutrient is also regarded as a form of malnutrition.

Marasmus A protein deficiency disease in children characterized by muscle atrophy, loss of most body fat, slowing or cessation of growth, a wizened appearance of the head, and dehydration caused by vomiting and diarrhea.

Mean life expectancy The age at which one-half of an initial population is still alive; technically, the median life expectancy.

Measles An acute, infectious, communicable viral disease characterized by small red spots on the skin, high fever, and nasal discharge that occurs most frequently in childhood; also known as rubeola.

Median age The age at which exactly half the population is younger and half is older.

Meltdown The melting of the core of a nuclear reactor.

Metabolic adaptation An adaptation to cold or stress involving basal metabolism as well as metabolic heat generation from muscular activity.

Microenvironment See *Microhabitat*.

Microhabitat The specific habitat in which a species exists (e.g., under rocks in a hot desert); also referred to as microenvironment. An organism's behavior may significantly modify the conditions in its microhabitat.

Micronutrients Elements needed in trace amounts, each constituting less than 0.2 percent of dry organic weight.

Microparasites Parasites that are generally small, have short generation times, and have direct reproduction, usually at high rates, within the host.

Migration The movement of individuals or their propagules (e.g., seeds, spores, larvae) from one area to another.

Model A simplification of an object, an organization, or a process in the real world.

Morbidity rate A measure of the number of people suffering from a disease in relation to population size.

Mortality Death rate, the number of deaths in a cohort in a given time frame.

Mortality rate A measure of the number of fatalities due to a disease per population size.

Muscle strength The amount of force a muscle can provide based on the cross-sectional area of muscle.

Mutagen A physical or chemical agent that increases the rate of mutation.

Mutualism A symbiotic relationship in which both species benefit and neither can survive without the other.

Myxedema A widespread edema in the body owing to a severe loss of thyroid function.

Natality Birth rate, the number of births in a cohort in a given time frame.

Natural hazards Naturally occurring perils such as storms, earthquakes, tsunamis, and volcanic eruptions.

Natural selection A theory of evolution proposed by Charles Darwin, and independently by Alfred Russel Wallace, in which variations in an organism's structure, physiology, or behavior that improve survival are preferentially transmitted to future generations.

Neo-Darwinism The theory of evolution incorporating Darwin's theory of evolution by natural selection and the science of genetics (Mendelism) that provides the explanation for the source of variation.

Net production The total, or gross, production minus that used for metabolism, growth, reproduction, and other life processes.

Net productivity The rate at which net production takes place.

Net reproductive rate The number of female offspring that replace each female of the previous generation.

Neutralism A symbiotic association in which the species populations have no effect on each other.

Niche   The functional position of a species in ecological processes—what it does, where it is, and what is done to it.

Niche divergence   A phenomenon in which similar species change their ecological role, thereby reducing competition for commonly sought resources.

Nitrification   The conversion of ammonia or ammonium salts to nitrate.

Nitrogen fixation   The conversion of nitrogen gas from the atmosphere to ammonia and nitrate.

Nomadism   The movement of an entire social group to meet resource needs.

Non-insulin-dependent diabetes mellitus   A condition in which body cells have fewer insulin receptors in their membranes and thus do not respond well to insulin.

Nonrenewable resources   A resource that is not replaceable (e.g., fossil fuel).

Nonshivering thermogenesis   An adaptation occurring in some mammals, and possibly humans, in which the hormone norepinephrine causes a general increase in the basal metabolism rate due to changes in lipid metabolism.

Nonvenereal syphilis   A disease found typically in semiarid regions of the Old World caused by the spirochete bacteria *Treponema pallidum* (which also causes venereal syphilis) that is spread by skin contact and oral routes (kissing, sharing drinking vessels) and characterized by lesions around the mouth.

Nutrients   The stuff of life, including chemical elements and inorganic and organic compounds.

Omnivore   A consumer that derives its nutrition from producers as well as from primary or other secondary consumers.

Onchocerciasis   A disease caused by filarial worms of the genus *Onchocerca* transmitted by the fly vector *Simulium damnosum*.

Optimal foraging strategies   Foraging techniques that are most effective or efficient.

Osteomalacia   The adult vitamin D deficiency disease; adult rickets (see *Rickets*).

Osteoporosis   The reduction in bone mass owing to calcium deficiency and particularly prevalent in postmenopausal women.

Overnutrition   A type of malnutrition that results in increased adiposity.

Ozone   A form of oxygen in which three atoms are bound together.

Paleoecology   The study of ecological communities based on their fossil record.

Pandemic   A disease that is epidemic over a large region.

Paradigm   A pattern, example, or model.

Parasitism   A symbiotic association in which one organism, typically small (the parasite), lives in or on another (the host), from which it obtains food, shelter, or other requirements.

Pastoralism   The reliance on herding of domesticated animals as the major food resource for a society.

Patch dynamics   The conditions created by a disturbance in a given area (a patch) and the responses of organisms to the disturbance.

Pellagra   A disease caused by a deficiency of niacin (vitamin B_3) characterized by skin problems (including dermatitis), diarrhea, and neurological symptoms.

Permafrost   Permanently frozen soil at a depth of a few centimeters to several meters and characteristic of tundra.

Phenology   The periodic phenomena in organisms that are tied to periodic environmental change.

Phenotypic plasticity   Observable biological changes that are induced by the environment.

Photoperiod   The relative periods of light and dark associated with day and night.

Photosynthesis   The chemical process in which the energy of sunlight is employed to convert inorganic to organic compounds.

Phylogeny   The origin and evolution of a group of animals or plants.

Physical fitness   The ability to maintain homeostatic conditions during strenuous activity or to rapidly restore those conditions after exercise.

Physiognomy   The form and structure of an ecological community.

Pinta   A treponemal disease caused by the spirochete bacteria *Treponema carateum,* characterized initially by scaly skin lesions of blue coloration and occurring in hilly areas of Mexico, Central America, and parts of South America.

Plaques   Hard, lipid-containing deposits on the interior wall of arteries.

Pollution   The defilement of the natural environment by a byproduct of human activity.

Polycythemia   A condition in which the percent of blood occupied by red blood cells increases from about 43-47 percent to well over 50 percent on the average.

Polygyny   A marriage pattern in which it is preferred that a man has more than one wife.

Pongids   The group of primates comprising modern gorillas, chimpanzees, orangutans, and their ancestors.

Predation   A symbiotic association in which one organism, typically larger (the predator), obtains energy by consuming, usually killing, another (the prey).

Prevalence rate   The number of cases of a disease per population size at any given point in time.

Primary consumer   An organism that obtains its food directly from producers; also known as a herbivore.

Primary production   See *Production.*

Primary productivity   See *Productivity.*

Primary succession   The sequential changes that occur in ecological communities that develop in newly created environments.

Producers   Organisms that capture the energy of the sun in the process of photosynthesis.

Production   The total mass of organic matter that is manufactured in an ecosystem in a given period of time; also termed gross production and primary production.

Productivity   The rate at which organic matter is manufactured in an ecosystem; also termed gross productivity and primary productivity.

Protein quality   The degree to which a given type of dietary protein matches the ratio of essential amino acids required by humans.

Protocooperation   A symbiotic association in which both species benefit but the relationship is not obligatory.

Pulmonary edema   The accumulation of fluid in the lungs, blocking oxygen transport.

Punctuated equilibrium   The theory that evolution is characterized by geologically long periods of stability (equilibrium) interrupted by short periods of rapid change (punctuation).

Radiation   The exchange of electromagnetic energy between objects in range of each other.

Reaction norms   Observable changes in organisms that vary as a function of environmental variation.

Reductionism   The breaking down of complexity into constituent parts for closer examination; the use of simple models to reduce details or circumstances.

Renewable resource   A resource that is replaceable (e.g., oxygen).

Reproductive isolation   The failure of one population to breed with other populations, the most important cause being geographic isolation.

Reproductive potential   The capacity of an individual to produce offspring, expressed as a rate.

Residence time   The length of time an element spends in a given compartment of its biogeochemical cycle.

Retrovirus   A virus in which the genetic information is carried in an RNA molecule instead of a DNA molecule.

Rickets   The vitamin D deficiency childhood disease characterized by bowing of bones, delayed tooth eruption, and defective development of tooth enamel.

Savanna   A tropical or subtropical grassland ecosystem.

Scurvy   The vitamin C deficiency disease characterized by poor wound healing, breakdown of old scars, and widespread hemorrhage leading to sore joints and gums.

Second law of thermodynamics   The principle that there is a tendency toward entropy or maximum disorganization of structure and maximum dissipation of utilizable energy in a system.

Secondary consumer   An organism that obtains its food by eating primary consumers; also known as a heterotroph and as a carnivore.

Secondary succession   The sequential changes that occur in ecological communities that have been disturbed.

Sedimentary nutrient cycle   A biogeochemical cycle in which the major reservoir of the element is the lithosphere.

Sedimentary rock   Rocks formed by the deposit of matter by water or wind.

Selfish behavior   Social interaction in which the actor gains but the recipient incurs a cost.

Sexual selection   Natural selection in which characteristics of either sex enhance success in mating and are perpetuated.

Shivering   Involuntary muscular activity that is induced by skin receptors that are activated by a lowering of skin temperature.

Sickle-cell trait   A heterozygous genetic condition in which the presence of sickle-shaped red blood cells confer some resistance to malaria.

Sigmoid growth curve   See *S-shaped growth curve.*

Slash-and-burn agriculture   See *Swidden agriculture.*

Smog   A form of air pollution resulting from the combination of smoke and fog.

Sociobiology   The study that deals with the natural selection of social behavioral traits based on the premise that they are genetically determined.

Sociological ecology   A field of study based in part upon the use of analogy between natural and human-made environments, with competition regarded as being the most important force.

Solar radiation   See *Insolation.*

Species   A population of organisms in which the individuals interbreed, produce fertile offspring, and do not breed successfully with other populations.

Spiteful behavior   Social interaction in which both actor and recipient suffer a net cost.

S-shaped growth curve   The more or less smooth curvilinear shape representing the rate of growth of a population in which density initially increases slowly, then rapidly, and subsequently declines to zero.

Stabilizing selection   Natural selection in which innovation is inhibited, extremes tend to be eliminated, and usually occurring in an environment that changes little in space and time. Also known as maintenance selection.

Stunting   A deficit in body length for a given age, usually due to long-term malnutrition.

Subacute infantile mountain sickness   A condition found in some infants born or brought to high altitude, characterized by low oxygen levels in blood, elevated levels of polycythemia, and a high risk of mortality.

Subsidized agriculture   A subsistence activity in which fossil fuels or other external energy sources power the transformation of natural to artificial landscapes.

Subsistence   The major means by which a population obtains food.

Succession   The tendency of ecological communities to follow fairly predictable patterns of change.

Survivorship curve   A graph representing the survival of individuals in a population from birth to the maximum age attained by any one member, usually plotted logarithmically.

Sustainable development   Meeting the needs of the present generation without compromising the ability of future generations to meet their own needs.

Sustained yields   The maintenance of resources that can be replaced or renewed and therefore are not depleted.

Swidden agriculture   A horticultural practice in which vegetation is slashed and burned to clear a plot for planting crops.

Symbiosis   A term describing the interaction of two species that live together in close association.

Syphilis   See *Venereal syphilis* and *Nonvenereal syphilis*.

System   A unit consisting of two or more components that interact and that is surrounded by an environment with which it may or may not interact.

Taiga   See *Boreal forest*.

Thermoregulation   The maintenance of a balance between heat gain and loss.

Thrifty genotype hypothesis   A postulation of the relationship among fatness, genetics, and non-insulin-dependent diabetes mellitus that allows adaptation to food availability cycles through storage of food during "feast" periods and subsequent utilization of the stored foods during "famine" periods.

Transhumance   The movement of only a portion of a social group to meet resource needs, the other portion of the group remaining in a permanent settlement.

Treponematosis   A disease caused by spirochete bacteria of the genus *Treponema* and including venereal syphilis, yaws, pinta, and nonvenereal syphilis.

Trophic species   The collection of organisms that feed on a common set of organisms and are fed on by another common set of organisms.

Tropical rainforest   The evergreen forests of the permanently wet tropics.

Tsunami   A seismic sea wave.

Tundra   A plain characterized by the absence of trees, the predominance of dwarfed plants, and an upper ground surface that is spongy and uneven.

Undernutrition   A condition resulting from a diet in which the amount of food in general or specific required nutrients are inadequate.

Vasoconstriction   The narrowing of superficial blood vessels, which reduces the rate of heat loss from the body to the air.

Vasodilation   The expansion of superficial blood vessels, which increases the rate of heat loss from the body to the air.

Vector   The organism by which parasites are transferred from an infected individual to a susceptible host.

Venereal syphilis   A disease caused by the spirochete bacteria *Treponema pallidum* that is transmitted sexually or congenitally and is characterized initially by lesions (chancres) and enlargement of the lymph nodes in the genital area.

Ventilation rate   The total amount of air moving in and out of the lungs in a given amount of time.

Ventilatory drive   The sensitivity of ventilation rate to hypoxic exposure.

Vertical stratification   The differences in height distribution of different organisms in an ecological community.

Virgin soil epidemic   The high morbidity caused by a contagious disease owing to the absence of previous immunity of all individuals in the population.

Wasting   A deficit in body weight for a given body length, usually occurring during a short-term, acute period of food shortage.

Work capacity   The ability to use oxygen at a fast rate.

Yaws   A disease occurring usually among poor children in tropical regions that is caused by the spirochete bacteria *Treponema pertenue*, which is transmitted by direct contact with an open lesion and is characterized initially by yellow to red lesions.

Zonation   A vertical or horizontal belt characterized by a particular assemblage of plants or animals.

References

ABRAHAM, S., M. D. CARROLL, M. F. NAJJAR, and R. FULWOOD. 1983. *Obese and overweight adults in the United States*. Vital and Health Statistics, series 11, no. 230. Hyattsville, MD: U.S. Department of Health and Human Services.

ABRUZZI, W. S. 1979. Population pressure and subsistence strategies among the Mbuti pygmies. *Human Ecology* 7:183–89.

ADAIR, L. S. 1987. Nutrition in the reproductive years. In *Nutritional anthropology*, F. E. Johnston, ed., 119–54. New York: Alan R. Liss, Inc.

ADAMS, R. N. 1974. The implications of energy flow studies on human populations for the social sciences. In *Energy flow in human communities*, P. L. Jamison and S. M. Friedman, eds., 21–31. University Park, PA: Human Adaptability Coordinating Office, U.S. International Biological Program.

ADOLPH, E. F. 1949. Desert. In *The physiology of heat regulation and the science of clothing*, L. W. Newburg, ed., 330–38. Philadelphia: W. B. Saunders Company.

ALBRECHT, H. P., and K. J. LITTELL. 1972. Plasma erythropoietin in men and mice during acclimatization to different altitudes. *Journal of Applied Physiology* 32:54–58.

ALDHOUS, P. 1993. Malaria: Focus on mosquito genes. *Science* 261:546–48.

ALEXANDER, R. D. 1977. Review of *The use and abuse of biology: An anthropological critique of sociobiology* by Marshall Sahlins. *American Anthropologist* 79:917–20.

ALKIRE, W. H. 1978. *Coral Islanders*. Arlington Heights, IL: AHM Publishing Corporation.

ALLEN, G. E. 1995. Review of *Science as a way of knowing. The foundations of modern biology*. J. A. Moore. Harvard University Press. *American Scientist* 83:97–98.

ALLEN, T., and A. WARREN. 1993. *Deserts. The encroaching wilderness*. Oxford: Oxford University Press.

ALVARD, M. S. 1993a. Testing the "ecologically nobel savage" hypothesis: Interspecific prey choice by Piro hunters of Amazonian Peru. *Human Ecology* 21:355–87.

ALVARD, M. S. 1993b. A test of the ecologically noble savage hypothesis: Interspecific prey choice by neotropical hunters. *Human Ecology* 21:355–87.

ALVARD, M. S. 1995. Intraspecific prey choice by Amazonian hunters. *Current Anthropology* 36:789–818.

AMUNDSON, R. 1990. Doctor Dennett and Doctor Pangloss: Perfection and selection in biology and psychology. *Behavior and Brain Sciences* 13:577–84.

461

ANAGNOSTAKIS, S. L. 1982. Biological control of chestnut blight. *Science* 215:466–71.

ANDERSON, A. 1990. *Prodigious birds: Moas and moa-hunting in prehistoric New Zealand*. New York: Cambridge University Press.

ANDERSON, E. N. 1988. *The food of China*. New Haven: Yale University Press.

ANDERSON, H. R. 1978. Respiratory abnormalities in Papua New Guinea children: The effects of locality and domestic wood smoke pollution. *International Journal of Epidemiology* 7:63–72.

ANGELA, P. and A. ANGELA. 1993. *The extraordinary story of human origins*. Buffalo, NY: Prometheus Books.

Annual Review of Ecology and Systematics. 1992. Special section on global environmental change. 23:1–235.

ANSPAUGH, L. R., R. J. CATLIN, and M. GOLDMAN. 1988. The global impact of the Chernobyl reactor accident. *Science* 242:1513–19.

ARDREY, R. 1961. *African genesis*. London: Collins.

ARMSTRONG. J. R. M., and H. CAMPBELL. 1991. Indoor air pollution exposure and lower respiratory infections in young Gambian children. *International Journal of Epidemiology* 20:424–29.

ARRITT, S. 1993. *The living earth book of deserts*. Pleasantville, NY: Reader's Digest Association.

ÅSTRAND, P.-O. 1956. Human physical fitness with special reference to sex and age. *Physiological Reviews* 36:307–35.

ÅSTRAND, P.-O., and K. RODAHL. 1986. *Textbook of work physiology*. 3d ed. New York: McGraw-Hill Inc.

AUMANN, G. D., and J. T. EMLEN. 1965. Relation of population density to sodium availability and sodium selection by Microtine rodents. *Nature* 208:198–9.

BAHADORI, M. N. 1978. Passive cooling systems in Iranian architecture. *Scientific American* 238:144–54.

BAILEY, K. V. 1975. Malnutrition in the African region. *WHO chronicle* 29:354–464.

BAILEY, N. T. J. 1975. *The mathematical theory of infectious diseases and its applications*. New York: Hafner Press.

BAILEY, R. 1995. Seven doomsday myths about the environment. *The Futurist* 29:14–18.

BAILEY, R. C., and R. AUNGER, JR. 1989. Net hunters vs. archers: Variation in women's subsistence strategies in the Ituri forest. *Human Ecology* 17:273–79.

BAILEY, R. C., and T. N. HEADLAND. 1991. The tropical rain forest: Is it a productive environment for human foragers? *Human Ecology* 19:261–85.

BAILEY, R. C., and N. R. PEACOCK. 1988. Efe pygmies of northeast Zaire: Subsistence strategies in the Ituri forest. In *Coping with uncertainty in food supply*, I. De Gardine and G. A. Harrison, eds., 88–117. Oxford: Clarendon Press.

BAKER, B. J., and G. J. ARMELAGOS. 1988. The origin and antiquity of syphilis: Paleopathological diagnosis and interpretation. *Current Anthropology* 29:703–37.

BAKER, P. T. 1958. The biological adaptation of man to hot deserts. *American Naturalist* 92:337–57.

BAKER, P. T. 1966a. Ecological and physiological adaptations in indigenous South Americans with special reference to the physical environment. In *The biology of human adaptability*, P. T. Baker and J. S. Weiner, eds., 275–301. Oxford: Clarendon University Press.

BAKER, P. T. 1966b. Human biological variation as an adaptive response to the environment. *Eugenics Quarterly* 13:81–91.

BAKER, P. T. 1974. The implications of energy flow studies on human populations for human biology. In *Energy flow in human communities*, P. L. Jamison and S. M. Friedman, eds., 15–20. University Park, PA: Human Adaptability Coordinating Office, U.S. International Biological Program.

BAKER, P. T. 1979. The use of human ecological models in biological anthropology—Examples from the Andes. *Collegium Anthropologicum* 3:157–71.

BAKER, P. T. 1982. Human population biology. A viable transdisciplinary science. *Human Biology* 54:203–20.

BAKER, P. T. 1984a. The adaptive limits of human populations. *Man* 19:1–14.

BAKER, P. T. 1984b. Migrations, genetics, and the degenerative diseases of South Pacific islanders. In *Migration and mobility*, A. J. Boyce, ed., 209–39. London: Taylor and Francis.

BAKER, P. T. 1986. Modernization, migration and health: A methodological puzzle with examples from the Samoans. *Journal of the Indian Anthropological Society* 21:1–22.

BAKER, P. T. 1988a. Human adaptability. In *Human biology: An introduction to human evolution, variation, growth, and adaptability*. 3d ed., G. A. Harrison, J. M. Tanner, D. R. Pilbeam, and P. T. Baker, eds., 439–547. Oxford: Oxford University Press.

BAKER, P. T. 1988b. Human population biology: A developing paradigm for biological anthropology. *International Social Science Journal* 116:255–63.

BAKER, P. T., and F. DANIELS. 1956. Relationship between skinfold thickness and body cooling for two hours at 15°C. *Journal of Applied Physiology* 8:409–16.

BAKER, P. T., and J. S. WEINER. 1966. *The biology of human adaptability.* Oxford: Oxford University Press.

BAKER, R. R. 1978. *The evolutionary ecology of animal migration.* New York: Holmes & Meier Publishers, Inc.

BAKIR, F., S. F. DAMLUJI, L. AMIN-ZAKI, M. MURTADHA, A. KHALIDI, N. Y. AL-RAWI, S. TIKRITI, H. I. DHAHIR, T. W. CLARKSON, J. C. SMITH, and R. A. DOHERTY. 1973. Methylmercury poisoning in Iraq. *Science* 181:230–41.

BAKUN, A. 1990. Global climate change and intensification of coastal ocean upwelling. *Science* 247:198–201.

BALLEW, C., R. M. GARRUTO, and J. D. HAAS. 1989. High-altitude hematology: Paradigm or enigma? In *Human population biology,* M. A. Little and J. D. Haas, eds., 239–62. New York: Oxford University Press.

BALLEW, C., and J. D. HAAS. 1986. Hematologic evidence of fetal hypoxia among newborn infants at high altitude in Bolivia. *American Journal of Obstetrics and Gynecology* 155:166–69.

BALTER, M. 1995. Chernobyl's thyroid cancer toll. *Science* 270:1758–59.

BALTER, M. 1996. Children become the first victims of fallout. *Science* 272:357–60.

BAMFORTH, D. B. 1988. *Ecology and human organization on the Great Plains.* New York: Plenum Press.

BARKER, R. G. 1968. *Ecological psychology: Concepts and methods for studying the environment of human behavior.* Stanford, CA: Stanford University Press.

BAR-OR, O. 1983. *Pediatric sports medicine for the practitioner.* New York: Springer-Verlag.

BASKIN, Y. 1997. Center seeks synthesis to make ecology more useful. *Science* 275:310–11.

BATES, D. G., and F. PLOG. 1991. *Human adaptive strategies.* New York: McGraw-Hill Inc.

BAZZAZ, F. A. 1990. The response of natural ecosystems to the rising global CO_2 levels. *Annual Review of Ecology and Systematics* 21:167–96.

BEALL, C. M. 1984. Aging and growth at high altitudes in the Himalayas. In *The people of South Asia,* J. R. Lukacs, ed., 365–85. New York: Plenum Publishing Corp.

BEALL, C. M., G. M. BRITTENHAM, K. P. STROHL, M. J. DECKER, M. C. GOLDSTEIN, J. BLANGERO, S. WILLIAMS-BLANGERO, L. ALMASY, and C. WORTHMAN. 1997. Ventilation and hypoxic ventilatory response of Tibetan and Aymara high altitude natives. *American Journal of Physical Anthropology* Supplement 24:73. (Abstract).

BEARD, K. D., Y. TONG, M. R. DAWSON, J. WANG, and X. HUANG. 1996. Earliest complete dentition of an anthropoid primate from the late middle Eocene of Shanxi Province, China. *Science* 272:82–85.

BEGON, M., J. L. HARPER, and C. R. TOWNSEND. 1986. *Ecology. Individuals, populations, and communities.* Sunderland, MA: Sinauer Associates Inc.

BEHRENS, C. 1989. The scientific basis for Shipibo soil classification and land use: Changes in soil-plant associations with cash-cropping. *American Anthropologist* 91:83–100.

BELDING, D. L. 1965. *Textbook of parasitology.* 3d ed. New York: Appleton-Century-Crofts.

BENEMANN, J. R. 1973. Nitrogen fixation in termites. *Science* 181:164–65.

BENNETT, J. W. 1976. *The ecological transition: Cultural anthropology and human adaptation.* New York: Pergamon Press Inc.

BERENSON, G. S. 1980. *Cardiovascular risk factors in children: The early natural history of atherosclerosis and essential hypertension.* New York: Oxford University Press.

BERKES, F. 1977. Fishery resource use in a subarctic Indian community. *Human Ecology* 5:289–307.

BERLIN, B., D. E. BREEDLOVE, and P. H. RAVEN. 1974. *Principles of Tzeltal plant classification: An introduction to the botanical ethnography of a Mayan-speaking people of highland Chiapas.* New York: Academic Press.

BERNER, R. A. 1990. Atmospheric carbon dioxide levels over phanerozoic time. *Science* 249:1382–86.

BERNER, R. A., and A. C. LASAGA. 1989. Modeling the geochemical carbon cycle. *Scientific American* 260(3):74–81.

BERRYMAN, A. 1992. The origins and evolution of predator-prey theory. *Ecology* 73:1530–35.

BESHIR, M. E. H., and M. O. MUBAREK. 1989. Sudan. In *International handbook of pollution control,* E. J. Kormondy, ed., 297–307. Westport, CT: Greenwood Press.

BINDON, J. R., and S. ZANSKY. 1986. Growth and body composition. In *The changing Samoans: Behavior and health in transition,* P. T. Baker, J. M. Hanna, and T. S. Baker, eds., 222–53. New York: Oxford University Press.

BIRD-DAVID, N. 1992. Beyond "the original affluent society." *Current Anthropology* 33:25–47.

BIRDSELL, J. B. 1953. Some environmental and cultural factors influencing the structuring of Australian aboriginal populations. *American Naturalist* 87:171–207.

BIRDSELL, J. B. 1993. *Microevolutionary patterns in aboriginal Australia: Gradient analysis of clines.* New York: Oxford University Press.

BLACK, F. L. 1992. Why did they die? *Science* 258:1739–40.

BLIEGE BIRD, R. L., and D. W. BIRD. 1997. Delayed reciprocity and tolerated theft: The behavorial ecology of food-sharing strategies. *Current Anthropology* 38:49–78.

BLISS, L. C. 1988. Alpine vegetation. In *North American terrestrial vegetation.* M. C. Barbour and W. D. Billings, eds., 391–420. Cambridge: Cambridge University Press.

BLOOM, B. L. 1988. *Health psychology: A psychosocial perspective.* Englewood Cliffs, NJ: Prentice-Hall.

BLOT, W. J., J.-Y. LI, P. R. TAYLOR, W. GUO, S. DAWSEY, G.-Q. WANG, C. S. YANG, S.-F. ZHENG, M. GAIL, G.-Y. LI, Y. YU, B. LIU, J. TANGREA, Y. SUN, F. LIU, J. F. FRAUMENI, JR., Y.-H. ZHANG, and B. LI. 1993. Nutrition intervention trials in Linxian, China: Supplementation with specific vitamin/mineral combinations, cancer incidence, and disease-specific mortality in the general population. *Journal of the National Cancer Institute* 85:1483–92.

BLUMENBERG, B., and N. B. TODD. 1974. On the association between *Homo* and *Australopithecus. Current Anthropology* 15:386–88.

BLURTON JONES, N. 1986. Bushman birth spacing: A test for optimal interbirth intervals. *Ethology and Sociobiology* 7:91–105.

BLURTON JONES, N., K. HAWKES, and P. DRAPER. 1994. Foraging returns of !Kung adults and children: Why didn't !Kung children forage? *Journal of Anthropological Research* 50:217–48.

BLURTON JONES, N., and R. M. SIBLY. 1978. Testing adaptiveness of culturally determined behaviour: Do Bushmen women maximize their reproductive success by spacing births widely and foraging seldom? In *Human behaviour and adaptation,* N. Blurton Jones and V. Reynolds, eds., 135–57. London: Taylor and Francis Ltd.

BOAS, F. 1964 (originally published in 1888). *The central Eskimo.* Lincoln: University of Nebraska Press.

BOAS, F. 1896. The limitations of the comparative method of anthropology. *Science* 4. Reprinted in *High points in anthropology,* 2d ed., P. Bohannan and M. Glazer, eds., 85–93. New York: Alfred A. Knopf.

BOAZ, N. T. 1977. Paleoecology of early *Hominidae* in Africa. *Kroeber Anthropological Society Papers* 50:37–62.

BOAZ, N. T. 1993. *Quarry. Closing in on the missing link.* New York: The Free Press.

BODENHEIMER, F. S. 1958. Animal ecology today. *Monographiae Biologicae* 6:1–276.

BOLEN, E. G., and W. L. ROBINSON. 1995. *Wildlife ecology and management.* 3d ed., Englewood Cliffs, NJ: Prentice-Hall.

BOLIN, B. 1970. The carbon cycle. *Scientific American* 223(3):124–32.

BONAN, G. B., and H. H. SHUGART. 1989. Environmental factors and ecological processes in boreal forests. *Annual Review of Ecology and Systematics* 20:1–28.

BONGAARTS, J. 1980. Does malnutrition affect fecundity? A summary of evidence. *Science* 208:564–69.

BONGAARTS, J. 1994a. Can the growing human population feed itself? *Scientific American* 270(3):36–42.

BONGAARTS, J. 1994b. Population policy options in the developing world. *Science* 263:771–76.

BORGERHOFF MULDER, M. 1989. Early maturing Kipsigis women have higher reproductive success than later maturing women, and cost more to marry. *Behavioral Ecology and Sociobiology* 24:145–53.

BORGERHOFF MULDER, M. 1992. Reproductive decisions. In *Evolutionary ecology and human behavior,* E. A. Smith and B. Winterhalder, eds., 339–74. New York: Aldine De Gruyter.

BORGERHOFF MULDER, M. 1995. Bridewealth and its correlates: Quantifying changes over time. *Current Anthropology* 36:573–603.

BORMANN, B. T., and J. C. GORDON. 1984. Stand density effects in young red alder plantations: Productivity, photosynthate partitioning, and nitrogen fixation. *Ecology* 654:394–402.

BOSERUP, E. 1965. *The conditions of agricultural growth.* Chicago: Aldine Publishing Company.

BOUCHARD, C., L. PERUSSE, C. LEBLANC, A. TREMBLAY, and G. THERIAULT. 1988. Inheritance of the amount and distribution of human body fat. *International Journal of Obesity* 12:205–15.

BOUCHARD, C., M.-C. THIBAULT, and J. JOBIN. 1981. Advances in selected areas of work physiology. *Yearbook of Physical Anthropology* 24:1–36.

BOUVEROT, P. 1985. *Adaptation to altitude-hypoxia in vertebrates.* Berlin: Springer-Verlag.

BOUVIER, L. F., and C. J. DeVITA. 1991. The baby boom—entering middle life. *Population Bulletin* 46(3):1–35.

BOX, E. 1978. Geographical dimensions of terrestrial net and gross productivity. *Radiation and Environmental Biophysics* 15:305–22.

BRADLEY, E. S., H. F. DIAZ, J. K. EICHEID, P. D. JONES, P. M. KELLY, and C. M. GOODESS. 1987. Precipitation fluctuations over northern hemisphere land area since the mid-19th century. *Science* 237:171–75.

BRADY, N. S. 1982. Chemistry and world food supplies. *Science* 218:847–53.

BRAY, F. 1986. *The rice economies: Technology and development in Asian societies.* Oxford: Basil Blackwell Ltd.

BRAY, F. 1994. Agriculture for developing nations. *Scientific American* 271(1):30–37.

BRIAND, F., and J. E. COHEN. 1984. Community food webs have scale-invariant structure. *Nature* 307:264–67.

BRIAND, F., and J. E. COHEN. 1987. Environmental correlates of food chain length. *Science* 238:956–60.

BRIGGS, L. C. 1975. Environment and human adaptation in the Sahara. In *Physiological anthropology,* A. Damon, ed., 93–129. New York: Oxford University Press.

BROAD, W., and N. WADE. 1982. *Betrayer of the truth. Fraud and deceit in the halls of science.* New York: Simon & Schuster.

BROECKER, W. S. 1973. Factors controlling CO_2 content in the oceans and atmosphere. In *Carbon and the biosphere,* G. M. Woodwell and E. V. Pecan, eds., 32–50. Washington, DC: U.S. Atomic Energy Commission.

BROOKFIELD, H., and C. PADOCH. 1994. Appreciating agrodiversity: A look at the dynamism and diversity of indigenous farming practices. *Environment* 36(5):6–20.

BROOKS, J. M., M. C. KENNICUTT II, C. R. FISHER, S. A. MACKO, K. COLE, J. J. CHILDRESS, R. R. BIDIGARE, and R. D. VETTER. 1987. Deep-sea hydrocarbon seep communities: Evidence for energy and nutritional carbon sources. *Science* 238:1138–42.

BROWN, D. E. 1981. General stress in anthropological fieldwork. *American Anthropologist* 83:74–92.

BROWN, D. E. 1982. Physiological stress and culture change in a group of Filipino-Americans: A preliminary investigation. *Annals of Human Biology* 9:553–63.

BROWN, H. 1954. *The challenge of man's future.* New York: The Viking Press.

BROWN, H. 1970. Human materials production as a process in the biosphere. *Scientific American* 223:115–24.

BROWN, J. L., and E. POLLITT. 1996. Malnutrition, poverty and intellectual development. *Scientific American* 274(2):38–43.

BROWN, K. H., R. H. GILMAN, A. GAFFAR, S. M. ALAMGIR, J. L. STRIFE, A. Z. KAPIKIAN, and R. B. SACK. 1981. Infection associated with severe protein-calorie malnutrition in hospitalized infants and children. *Nutrition Research* 1:33.

BROWN, L. R. 1981. World population growth, soil erosion, and food security. *Science* 214:995–1002.

BROWN, L. R. 1994. Facing food insecurity. In *State of the world 1994. A Worldwatch Institute report on progress toward a sustainable society,* L. Starke, ed., 177–97. New York: W. W. Norton & Company, Inc.

BROWN, L. R., and C. FLAVIN, 1988. The Earth's vital signs. In *State of the world 1988. A Worldwatch Institute report on progress toward a sustainable society,* L. Starke, ed., pp. 3–21. New York: W. W. Norton & Company, Inc.

BROWN, W. J., J. F. DONOHUE, N. W. AXNICK, J. H. BLOUNT, N. H. EWEN, and O. G. JONES. 1970. *Syphilis and other venereal diseases.* Cambridge, MA: Harvard University Press.

BRUSH, S. R. 1975. The concept of carrying capacity for systems of shifting cultivation. *American Anthropologist* 77:799–811.

BRYANT, C. A., A. COURTNEY, B. A. MARKESBERY, and K. M. DeWALT. 1985. *The cultural feast: An introduction to food and society.* St. Paul, MN: West Publishing Company.

BULLARD, F. M. 1979. Volcanoes and their activity. In *Volcanic activity and human ecology,* P. D. Sheets and D. K. Grayson, eds., 9–48. New York: Academic Press.

BULMER, R. 1967. Why is the cassowary not a bird? A problem of zoological taxonomy among the Karam of the New Guinea highlands. *Man* 2:5–25.

BURNET, M., and D. O. WHITE. 1972. *Natural history of infectious disease.* 4th ed. Cambridge: Cambridge University Press.

BURTON, I., R. W. KATES, and G. F. WHITE. 1978. *The environment as hazard.* New York: Oxford University Press.

Bush, M. P., and P. A. Colinvaux. 1994. Tropical forest disturbance: Paleoecological records from Darien, Panama. *Ecology* 75:1761–68.

Butler, M. 1996. Children become the first victims of fallout. *Science* 272:357–60.

Byun, J., L. S. Lieberman, and N. Rowland. 1994. The psychophysiological reaction of Korean-American victims to life-change events from the 1992 Los Angeles riots. *American Journal of Human Biology* 6:118. (Abstract)

Cahill, G. F., Jr. 1970. Starvation in man. *New England Journal of Medicine* 282:668–75.

Caldwell, J. R. 1962. Eastern North America. In *Courses toward urban life*, R. J. Braidwood and G. R. Willey, eds., 288–308. Chicago: Aldine Publishing Company.

Caldwell, J. C., and P. Caldwell. 1996. The African AIDS epidemic. *Scientific American* 274(3):62–68.

Calhoun, J. 1962. Population density and social pathology. *Scientific American* 206:139–47.

Campbell, B. 1983. *Human ecology*. New York: Aldine Publishing Company.

Campbell, D. T. 1965. Variation and selective retention in socio-cultural evolution. In *Social change in developing areas*, H. R. Barringer, G. I. Blanksten, and R. W. Mack, eds., 19–49. Cambridge: Schenkman.

Canfield, D. E., and D. J. Des Marais. 1991. Aerobic sulfate reduction in microbial mats. *Science* 251:1471–73.

Cannon, W. B. [1915] 1959. *Bodily changes in pain, hunger, fear and rage*. Boston: Bradford Press.

Cannon, W. B. 1932. *The wisdom of the body*. London: Kegan, Paul.

Carbonelli, E., J. M. Bermudez de Castro, J. L. Asuaja, J. C. Diez, A. Rosas, G. Cuenca-Bescos, R. Sala, M. Mosquera, and X. P. Rodriguez. 1995. Lower pleistocene hominids and artifacts from Atapuerca-TD6 (Spain). *Science* 269:826–32.

Carey, G. W. 1972. Density, crowding, stress, and the ghetto. *American Behavioral Scientist* 15:495–509.

Carson, R. P., W. O. Evans, J. L. Shields, and J. P. Hannon. 1969. Symptomatology, pathophysiology, and treatment of acute mountain sickness. *Federation Proceedings* 28:1085–91.

Cartwright, F. F. 1972. *Disease and history*. New York: Thomas Y. Crowell.

Cary, S. C., C. R. Fisher, and H. Felbeck. 1988. Mussel growth supported by methane as sole carbon and energy source. *Science* 240:78–80.

Cates, W., Jr. 1982. Legal abortion: The public health record. *Science* 215:1586–90.

Cattani, J. A. 1992. The epidemiology of malaria in Papua New Guinea. In *Human biology in Papua New Guinea: The small cosmos*, R. D. Attenborough and M. P. Alpers, eds., 302–12. Oxford: Clarendon Press.

Catton, W. R., Jr., and R. E. Dunlap. 1978. Environmental sociology: A new paradigm. *American Sociologist* 13:41–49.

Cavalli-Sforza, L. L. 1981. Human evolution and nutrition. In *Food, nutrition and evolution*, D. N. Walcher and N. Kretchmer, eds., 1–7. New York: Masson Publishing USA, Inc.

Cavalli-Sforza, L. L., and M. W. Feldman. 1981. *Cultural transmission and evolution: A quantitative approach*. Princeton, NJ: Princeton University Press.

Chagnon, N. A., and R. B. Hames. 1979. Protein deficiency and tribal warfare in Amazonia: New data. *Science* 203:910–13.

Chapman, E. C. 1978. Shifting cultivation and economic development in the lowlands of northern Thailand. In *Farmers in the forest: Economic development and marginal agriculture in Northern Thailand*, P. Kunstadter, E. C. Chapman, and S. Sabhasri, eds., 222–35. Honolulu: East-West Center.

Chapman, R. 1928. The quantitative analysis of environmental factors. *Ecology* 9:111–22.

Charlson, R. J., and T. M. L. Wigley. 1994. Sulfate aerosol and climatic change. *Scientific American* 270(2):48–57.

Charnov, E. L., and J. R. Krebs. 1974. On clutch size and fitness. *Ibis* 116:733–38.

Choi, G. H., and D. L. Nuss. 1992. Hypovirulence of chestnut blight fungus conferred by an infectious viral cDNA. *Science* 257:800–803.

Clark, J. D. 1980. Early human occupation of African savanna environments. In *Human ecology in savanna environments*, D. R. Harris, ed., 41–71. London: Academic Press.

Clark, W. C. 1989. Managing planet Earth. *Scientific American* 261(3):46–54.

Clarke, R. J., and P. V. Tobias. 1995. Sterkfontein Member 2 footbones of the oldest South African hominid. *Science* 269:521–24.

Cleghorn, P. L. 1987. *Prehistoric cultural resources and management plan for Nihoa and Necker Islands, Hawaii*. Honolulu: Bishop Museum.

Clements, F. E. 1905. *Research methods in ecology*. Lincoln, NE: University Publishing Co.

CLIFF, A., and P. HAGGETT. 1984. Island epidemics. *Scientific American* 250(5):138–47.

COCKBURN, A. 1963. *The evolution and eradification of infectious diseases.* Baltimore: Johns Hopkins University Press.

COE, M. D., and K. V. FLANNERY. 1964. Microenvironments and Mesoamerican prehistory. *Science* 143:650–54.

COHEN, M. L. 1992. Epidemiology of drug resistance: Implications for a post-antimicrobial era. *Science* 257:1050–55.

COHOP MEMBERS (COOPERATIVE HOLOCENE MAPPING PROJECT). 1988. Climatic changes of the last 18,000 years: Observations and model simulations. *Science* 241:1043–52.

COLE, M. M. 1986. *The savannas: Biogeography and geobotany.* London: Academic Press.

COLEMAN, J. C. 1972. *Abnormal psychology and modern life.* 4th ed. Glenview, IL: Scott, Foresman & Company.

COLLINGS, D. A., S. D. SITHOLE, and K. S. MARTIN. 1990. Indoor woodsmoke pollution causing lower respiratory disease in children. *Trop. Doctor* 20:151–55.

COLLINS, M., ed. 1990. *The last rainforests. A world conservation atlas.* Oxford: Oxford University Press.

CONE, M. 1996a. Destroying the balance of nature. *Los Angeles Times* (May 12):1, 15.

CONE, M. 1996b. Human immune systems may be pollution victims. *Los Angeles Times* (May 13):1, 14–15.

CONKLIN, H. C. 1954. An ethnoecological approach to shifting agriculture. *Transactions of the New York Academy of Sciences* 17:133–42.

COOK, E. 1971. The flow of energy in an industrial society. *Scientific American* 224:135–44.

COON, C. S., S. M. GARN, and J. B. BIRDSELL. 1950. *Races: A study of the problems of race formation in man.* Springfield, IL: Charles C Thomas, Publisher.

COPPENS, Y. 1994. East side story: The origin of humankind. *Scientific American* 270(5):88–95.

COUGHENOUR, M. B., J. E. ELLIS, D. M. SWIFT, D. L. COPPOCK, K. GALVIN, J. T. McCABE, and T. C. HART. 1985. Energy extraction and use in a nomadic pastoral ecosystem. *Science* 230:619–25.

COUPLAND, R. T., ed. 1979. *Grassland ecosystems of the world: Analysis of grasslands and their uses.* London/ New York: Cambridge University Press.

COWLES, H. C. 1899. The ecological relations of the vegetation of the sand dunes of Lake Michigan. *Botanical Gazette* 27:95–117, 167–202, 281–308, 361–91.

CREWS, D. E., and G. D. JAMES. 1991. Human evolution and the genetic epidemiology of chronic degenerative diseases. In *Applications of biological anthropology to human affairs*, C. G. N. Mascie-Taylor and G. W. Lasker, eds., 185–206. Cambridge: Cambridge University Press.

CRONK, L. 1991. Wealth, status, and reproductive success among the Mukogodo of Kenya. *American Anthropologist* 93:345–60.

CROSSON, P. R., and N. J. ROSENBERG. 1989. Strategies for agriculture. *Scientific American* 261(3):128–35.

CULOTTA, E. 1995a. Asian anthropoids strike back. *Science* 270:918.

CULOTTA, E. 1995b. Asian hominids grow older. *Science* 270:1116–17.

DAILY, G. C., S. ALEXANDER, P. R. EHRLICH, L. GOULDER, J. LUBCHENCO, P. A. MATSON, H. A. MOONEY, S. POSTEL, S. H. SCHNEIDER, D. TILMAN, and G. M. WOODWELL. 1997. Ecosystem services: Benefits supplied to human societies by natural ecosystems. *Issues in Ecology, No. 2.* Washington, DC: Ecological Society of America.

DARLING, F. F., and R. F. DASMANN. 1969. The ecosystem view of human society. *Impact of Science on Society* 19:109–21.

DARWIN, C. R. [1859] 1959. *The origin of species by means of natural selection.* London: John Murray. (This classic has been reprinted by a number of different publishers.)

DAVIS, K. 1967. Population policy: Will current programs succeed? *Science* 158:730–39.

DEANGELIS, D. L., W. M. POST, and C. C. TRAVIS. 1986. *Positive feedback in natural systems.* New York: Springer-Verlag.

DE BOER, W. F., and H. H. T. PRINS. 1989. Decisions of cattle herdsmen in Burkina Faso and optimal foraging models. *Human Ecology* 17:445–64.

DEEVEY, E. S., JR. 1947. Life tables for natural populations of animals. *Quarterly Review of Biology* 22:79–94.

DE GARINE, I., and S. KOPPERT. 1990. Social adaptation to season and uncertainty in food supply. In *Diet and disease in traditional and developing societies*, G. A. Harrison and J. C. Waterlow, eds., 240–89. Cambridge: Cambridge University Press.

DEMENOCAL, P. B. 1995. Plio-pleistocene African climate. *Science* 270:53–59.

DENNETT, G., and J. CONNELL. 1988. Acculturation and health in the highlands of New Guinea. *Current Anthropology* 29:273–99.

DENTAN, R. K. 1979. *The Semai: A nonviolent people of Malaya*. New York: Holt, Rinehart and Winston, Inc.

DES JARLAIS, D. C., and S. R. FRIEDMAN. 1994. AIDS and the use of injected drugs. *Scientific American* 270(2):82–88.

DESOWITZ, R. S. 1981. *New Guinea tapeworms and Jewish grandmothers: Tales of parasites and people*. New York: W. W. Norton & Company, Inc.

DIAMOND, J. 1991. The saltshaker's curse. *Natural History* (October):20, 22–26.

DICKEMAN, M. 1975. Demographic consequences of infanticide in man. *Annual Review of Ecology and Systematics* 6:107–37.

DICKMAN, C. R. 1986. An experimental study of competition between two species of dasyurid marsupials. *Ecological Monographs* 56:221–41.

DICKMAN, S. 1991. AIDS threatens Asia. *Nature* 351:682.

DINGLE, H. 1980. Ecology and evolution of migration. In *Animal migration, orientation and navigation*, S. A. Gauthreaux, Jr., ed., 1–101. New York: Academic Press.

DOBYNS, H. F. 1983. *Their number become thinned*. Knoxville: University of Tennessee Press.

DOLL, R., and R. PETO. 1981. *The causes of cancer*. New York: Oxford University Press.

DORF, R. C. 1978. *Energy, resources, and policy*. Menlo Park, CA: Addison-Wesley Publishing Company Inc.

DORNSTREICH, M. D. 1977. The ecological description and analysis of tropical subsistence patterns: An example from New Guinea. In *Subsistence and survival: Rural ecology in the Pacific*, T. P. Bayliss-Smith and R. G. Feachem, eds., 245–71. London: Academic Press.

DOYLE, R. 1996. World birth-control use. *Scientific American* 275(3):34.

DRAPER, H. H. 1977. The aboriginal Eskimo diet. *American Anthropologist* 79:309–16.

DREYFUS, P. M. 1979. Nutritional disorders of the nervous system. In *Nutrition: Metabolic and clinical applications*, R. E. Hodges, ed., 53–81. New York: Plenum Press.

DUBOS, R. 1965. *Man adapting*. New Haven, CT: Yale University Press.

DUBOS, R. 1987. *Mirage of health*. New Brunswick, NJ: Rutgers University Press.

DUDLEY, W. C., and M. LEE. 1988. *Tsunami!* Honolulu: University of Hawaii Press.

DUFOUR, D. L. 1992. Nutritional ecology in the tropical rain forests of Amazonia. *American Journal of Human Biology* 4:197–207.

DUNN, F. L. 1968. Epidemiological factors: Health and disease in hunter gatherers. In *Man the hunter*, R. B. Lee and I. DeVore, eds., 221–28. Chicago: Aldine-Atherton.

DURHAM, W. H. 1981. Overview: Optimal foraging analysis in human ecology. In *Hunter-gatherer foraging strategies*, B. Winterhalder and E. A. Smith, eds., 218–31. Chicago: University of Chicago Press.

DYSON-HUDSON, R., and N. DYSON-HUDSON. 1969. Subsistence herding in Uganda. *Scientific American* 220(2):76–89.

EASTERBROOK, G. 1995. Here comes the sun. *New Yorker* (April 10):38–43.

EDELSTEIN, S. J. 1986. *The sickled cell: From myths to molecules*. Cambridge, MA: Harvard University Press.

EDHOLM, O. G. 1967. *The biology of work*. New York: McGraw-Hill Inc.

EDHOLM, O. G., and H. S. LEWIS. 1964. Terrestrial animals in cold: Man in polar regions. In *Handbook of physiology*, Section 4: *Adaptation to the environment*, D. B. Dill, E. F. Adolph, and C. G. Wilbur, eds., 435–46. Washington, DC: American Physiological Society.

EDHOLM, O. G., and J. S. WEINER. 1981. Thermal physiology. In *The principles and practice of human physiology*, O. G. Edholm and J. S. Weiner, eds., 111–90. London: Academic Press.

EHRLICH, P. 1968. *The population bomb*. New York: Ballantine Books.

EHRLICH, P. R., and A. H. EHRLICH. 1970. *Population resources environment: Issues in human ecology*. San Francisco: W. H. Freeman and Company.

EHRLICH, P. R., A. H. EHRLICH, and J. P. HOLDREN. 1973. *Human ecology: Problems and solutions*. San Francisco: W. H. Freeman and Company.

EHRLICH, P. R., D. D. MURPHY, M. C. SINGER, C. B. SHERWOOD, R. R. WHITE, and I. L. BROWN. 1980. Extinction, reduction, stability and increase: The responses of checkerspot butterfly (*Euphydryas*) populations to the California drought. *Oecologia* 46:101–5.

EHRLICH, P. R., and E. O. WILSON. 1991. Biodiversity studies: Science and policy. *Science* 253:758–62.

EKVALL, R. B. 1968. *Fields on the hoof: Nexus of Tibetan nomadic pastoralism*. Prospect Heights, IL: Waveland Press.

ELDREDGE, N., and S. J. GOULD. 1972. Punctuated equilibria: An alternative to phyletic gradualism. In *Models in paleobiology*, T. J. M. Schopf, ed., 85–115. Cambridge: Cambridge University Press.

ELLIOTT-FISK, D. L. 1988. The boreal forest. In *Northern American terrestrial vegetation*, M. G. Barbour and W. D. Billings, eds., 33–62. Cambridge: Cambridge University Press.

ELLIOTT, G. R., and C. EISDORFER. 1982. *Stress and human health: Analysis and implications of research*. New York: Springer.

ELLISON, P. T., N. PEACOCK, and C. LANGER. 1986. Salivary progesterone and luteal function in two low-fertility populations of northeast Zaire. *Human Biology* 58:472–83.

ELTON, C. 1927. *Animal ecology*. London: Sidgwick and Jackson.

EMBER, R. 1981. Acid pollutants: hitchhikers ride the wind. *Chemical & Engineering News* 59(37):20–31.

EMORY, K. P. 1928. Archaeology of Nihoa and Necker Islands. *Bernice P. Bishop Museum Bulletin* 53.

EPSTEIN, L. H. 1993. New developments in childhood obesity. In *Obesity: Theory and therapy*, 2d ed., A. J. Stunkard and T. A. Wadden, eds., 301–12. New York: Raven Press.

ERBSEN, C. E. 1979. Mauritania losing life-death struggle against the sands of the Sahara. *The Bulletin* (November 22):53.

ESCOBAR, M. G., and C. M. BEALL. 1982. Contemporary patterns of migration in the central Andes. *Mountain Research and Development* 2:63–80.

ESKEW, D. L., R. M. WELCH, and E. E. CARY. 1983. Nickel: an essential micronutrient for legumes and possibly all higher plants. *Science* 222:621–23.

ESSER, G. 1992. Implications of climate change for production and decomposition in grasslands and coniferous forests. *Ecological Applications* 2:47–54.

ETKIN, N. L., and P. J. ROSS. 1991. Recasting malaria, medicine, and meals: A perspective on disease adaptation. In *The anthropology of medicine: From culture to method*, L. Romanucci-Ross, D. E. Moerman, and L. R. Trancredi, eds., 230–58. New York: Bergin and Garvey.

EVANS, F., and F. SMITH. 1952. The intrinsic rate of natural increase for the human louse, *Pediculus humanus* L. *American Naturalist* 86:299–310.

EVELETH, P. B., and J. M. TANNER. 1976. *Worldwide variation in growth*. Cambridge: Cambridge University Press.

EWALD, P. W. 1993. The evolution of virulence. *Scientific American* 268(4):86–93.

EWALD, P. W. 1994. *Evolution of infectious disease*. Oxford: Oxford University Press.

FALK, D. T., B. GAGE, B. DUDEK, and T. R. OLSON. 1995. Did more than one species of hominid coexist before 3.0 Ma?: Evidence from blood and teeth. *Journal of Human Evolution* 29:591–600.

FARB, P., and G. ARMELAGOS. 1980. *Consuming passions: The anthropology of eating*. Boston: Houghton Mifflin Company.

FARMAN, J. C., B. G. GARDINER, and J. D. SHANKLIN. 1985. Large losses of total ozone in Antarctica reveal seasonal ClO_x/NO interaction. *Nature* 315:207–10.

FAVIER, R., H. SPIELVOGEL, D. DESPLANCHES, G. FERRETTI, B. KAYSER, and H. HOPPELER. 1995. Maximal exercise performance in chronic hypoxia and acute normoxia in high-altitude natives. *Journal of Applied Physiology* 78:1868–74.

FEARNSIDE, P. M. 1986. *Human carrying capacity of the Brazilian rainforest*. New York: Columbia University Press.

FEARNSIDE, P. M. 1987. Rethinking continuous cultivation in Amazonia. *BioScience* 37:209–14.

FEDUCCIA, A. 1995. Explosive evolution in tertiary birds and mammals. *Science* 267:637–38.

FEIST, D. D., and R. G. WHITE. 1989. Terrestrial animals in the cold. In *Advances in comparative and environmental physiology*, vol. 4: *Animal adaptation to cold*, L. C. H. Wang, ed., 327–60. Berlin: Springer-Verlag.

FENNER, F. 1970. The effects of changing social organisation on the infectious diseases of man. In *The impact of civilization on the biology of man*, S. W. Boyden, ed., 48–68. Toronto: University of Toronto Press.

FERRO-LUZZI, A., and F. BRANCA. 1993. Nutritional seasonality: The dimensions of the problem. In *Seasonality and human ecology*, S. J. Ulijaszek and S. S. Strickland, eds., 149–65. Cambridge: Cambridge University Press.

FISCHMAN, J. 1994. Putting our oldest ancestors in their proper place. *Science* 265:2011–12.

FISCHMAN, J. 1996. Evidence mounting for our African origins—and alternatives. *Science* 271:1364.

FITZPATRICK, E. A. 1979. Radiation. In *Arid-land ecosystems: Structure, functioning and management*, D. W. Goodall and R. A. Perry, eds., 347–72. Cambridge: Cambridge University Press.

FLINN, M. V., and B. G. ENGLAND. 1993. Glucocorticoid stress response, immune function, and disease among children in a rural Caribbean village. *American Journal of Physical Anthropology* Supplement 16:87. (Abstract)

FLINN, M. V., and B. G. ENGLAND. 1995. Childhood stress and family support. *Current Anthropology* 36:854–66.

FLINN, M. V., and B. G. ENGLAND. 1997. Social economics of childhood glucocorticoid stress response and health. *American Journal of Physical Anthropology* 102:33–53.

FLINN, M. V., M. QUINLAN, R. QUINLAN, M. TURNER, and B. G. ENGLAND. 1995. Glucocorticoid stress response, immune function, and illness among children in a rural Caribbean village. *American Journal of Human Biology* 7:122. (Abstract)

FOLK, G. E. 1974. *Textbook of environmental physiology*, 2d ed. Philadelphia: Lea & Febiger.

FOULKS, E. F. 1972. *The arctic hysterias of the north Alaskan Eskimo*. Anthropological Studies no. 10. Washington, DC: American Anthropological Association.

FOWLER, C. S. 1977. Ethnoecology. In *Ecological anthropology*, D. L. Hardesty, ed., 215–43. New York: John Wiley & Sons.

FOWLER, C. S., and J. LELAND. 1967. Some northern Paiute native categories. *Ethnology* 6:381–404.

FRANKE, R. G., and D. N. FRANKE. 1975. *Man and the changing environment*. New York: Holt, Rinehart and Winston, Inc.

FRANKENHAEUSER, M. 1973. Experimental approaches to the study of human behavior as related to neuroendocrine functions. In *Society, stress and disease*, vol. I: *The psychosocial environment and psychosomatic diseases*, L. Levi, ed., 22–35. London: Oxford University Press.

FRANKENHAEUSER, M., and B. GARDELL. 1976. Underload and overload in working life. A multidisciplinary approach. *Journal of Human Stress* 2:35–46.

FREDERICKSON, A. G., and G. STEPHANOPOULOS. 1981. Microbial competition. *Science* 213:972–79.

FRIEDEN, E. 1972. The chemical elements of life. *Scientific American* 227(1):52–60.

FRIEDERICHS, K. 1958. A definition of ecology and some thoughts about basic concepts. *Ecology* 39:154–59.

FRIEDMAN, M., and R. H. ROSENMAN. 1974. *Type A behavior and your heart*. Greenwich, CT: Fawcett Publications.

FRIEDMAN, M. J., and W. TRAGER. 1981. The biochemistry of resistance to malaria. *Scientific American* 244(3):154–64.

FRISANCHO, A. R. 1988. Origins of differences in hemoglobin concentration between Himalayan and Andean populations. *Respiration Physiology* 72:13–18.

FRISANCHO, A. R. 1993. *Human adaptation and accommodation*. Ann Arbor: University of Michigan Press.

FRISANCHO, A. R., H. G. FRISANCHO, M. MILOTICH, T. BRUTSAERT, H. SPIELVOGEL, M. VILLENA, E. VARGAS, and R. SORIA. 1994. Influence of developmental acclimatization and activity level on bioenergetic adaptation to high altitude hypoxia. *American Journal of Physical Anthropology* Supplement 18:89–90. (Abstract)

FRISANCHO, A. R., and L. P. GREKSA. 1989. Developmental responses in the acquisition of functional adaptation to high altitude. In *Human population biology*, M. A. Little and J. D. Haas, eds., 203–221. New York: Oxford University Press.

FRISCH, R. 1987. Body fat, menarche, fitness and fertility. *Human Reproduction* 2:521–33.

FRISON, G. C. 1992. *Prehistoric hunters of the high plains*. 2d ed. New York: Academic Press.

FRISS-CHRISTENSEN, E., and K. LASSEN. 1991. Length of the solar cycle: An indicator of solar activity closely associated with climate. *Science* 254:698–700.

FULCO, C. S., and A. CYMERMAN. 1988. Human performance and acute hypoxia. In *Human performance physiology and environmental medicine at terrestrial extremes*, K. B. Pandolf, M. N. Sawka, and R. R. Gonzalez, eds., 467–95. Indianapolis: Benchmark Press.

GABRIEL, S. E., K. N. BRIGMAN, B. H. KOLLER, R. C. BOUCHER, and M. J. STUTTS. 1994. Cystic fibrosis heterozygote resistance to cholera toxin in the cystic fibrosis mouse model. *Science* 266:107–9.

GAGE, T. B., J. M. McCULLOUGH, C. A. WEITZ, J. S. DUTT, and A. ABELSON. 1989. Demographic studies and human population biology. In *Human population biology*, M. A. Little and J. D. Haas, eds., 45–65. New York: Oxford University Press.

GAGE, T. B., and S. M. ZANSKY. 1996. Anthropometric indicators of nutritional status and level of mortality. *American Journal of Human Biology* 7:679–91.

GARN, S. M., and D. C. CLARK. 1976. Trends in fatness and the origins of obesity. *Pediatrics* 57:443–56.

GARN, S. M., and M. LAVELLE. 1985. Two-decade follow-up of fatness in early childhood. *American Journal of Diseases in Children* 139:181–85.

GARRELS, R. M., A. LERMAN, and F. R. MACKENZIE. 1976. Controls of atmospheric O_2 and CO_2 past, present, and future. *American Scientist* 64:306–15.

GASCON, C. 1991. Population- and community-level analyses of species occurrences of central Amazonian rainforest tadpoles. *Ecology* 72:1731–46.

GATES, D. M. 1980. *Biophysical ecology.* New York: Springer.

GAUSE, G. F. 1934. *The struggle for existence.* Baltimore, MD: Williams and Wilkins Company.

GEERTZ, C. 1963. *Agricultural involution: The process of ecological change in Indonesia.* Berkeley: University of California Press.

GIBBONS, A. 1994. Rewriting—and redating—prehistory. *Science* 263:1087–88.

GIBBONS, A. 1996a. Did Neandertals lose an evolutionary "arms" race? *Science* 272:1586–87.

GIBBONS, A. 1996b. On the many origins of species. *Science* 273:1496–99.

GIBBS, W. W. 1996. Gaining on fat. *Scientific American* 275(2):88–94.

GLANTZ, M. H. 1987. Drought in Africa. *Scientific American* 256(6):34–40.

GLASS, D. C., and J. E. SINGER. 1972. *Urban stress.* New York: Academic Press.

GLEASON, J. F., P. K. BHARTIA, J. R. HERMAN, R. MCPETERS, P. NEWMAN, R. S. STOLARSKI, L. FLYNN, G. LABOW, D. LARKO, C. SEFTOR, C. WELLEMEYER, W. D. KOMHYR, A. J. MILLER, and W. PLANET. 1993. Record low global ozone in 1992. *Science* 260:523–26.

GODSON, G. N. 1985. Molecular approaches to malaria vaccines. *Scientific American* 252(5):52–59.

GOLDMAN, M. 1987. Chernobyl: A radiobiological perspective. *Science* 246:201–2.

GOLLEY, F. B. 1993. *A history of the ecosystem concept in ecology. More than the sum of the parts.* New Haven, CT: Yale University Press.

GONZALEZ, R. R. 1988. Biophysics of heat transfer and clothing considerations. In *Human performance physiology and environmental medicine at terrestrial extremes,* K. B. Pandolf, M. N. Sawka, and R. R. Gonzalez, eds., 45–95. Indianapolis: Benchmark Press.

GOODNER, K. 1965. The vibrios—Cholera. In *Bacterial and mycotic infections of man,* R. J. Dubos and J. G. Hirsch, eds., 649–58. Philadelphia: J. B. Lippincott Company.

GOPALAN, C. 1992. The contribution of nutrition research to the control of undernutrition: The Indian experience. *Annual Review of Nutrition* 12:1–17.

GORE, R. 1996. The dawn of humans: Neandertals. *National Geographic* 189(1):2–35.

GORTMAKER, S. L., W. H. DIETZ, A. M. SOBOL, and C. A. WEHLER. 1987. Increasing pediatric obesity in the United States. *American Journal of Diseases in Children* 141:535–40.

GOSZ, J. R., R. T. HOLMES, G. E. LIKENS, and F. H. BORMANN. 1978. The flow of energy in a forest ecosystem. *Scientific American* 238(3):92–102.

GOULD, S. J., and N. ELDREDGE. 1977. Punctuated equilibria: The tempo and mode of evolution reconsidered. *Paleobiology* 3:115–51.

GOULD, S. J., and R. C. LEWONTIN. 1979. The spandrels of San Marco and the Panglossian paradigm: A critique of the adaptationist programme. *Proceedings of the Royal Society of London* B205:581–98.

GRAEDEL, T. E., and P. J. CRUTZEN. 1989. The changing atmosphere. *Scientific American* 261(3):58–68.

GRANT, P. R. 1994. Ecological character displacement. *Science* 266:645–47.

GRATHWOHL, M. 1982. *World energy supply: Resources technologies perspectives.* Berlin: Walter de Gruyter & Company.

GREENE, L. S. 1977. Hyperendemic goiter, cretinism and social organization in highland Equador. In *Malnutrition, behavior, and social organization,* L. S. Greene, ed., 54–94. New York: Academic Press.

GREENE, L. S. 1993. G6PD deficiency as protection against falciparum malaria: An epidemiologic critique of population and experimental studies. *Yearbook of Physical Anthropology* 36:153–78.

GREENWOOD, N. H., and J. M. B. EDWARDS. 1973. *Human environments and natural systems: A conflict of dominion.* North Scituate, MA: Duxbury Press.

GREKSA, L. P. 1988. Effect of altitude on the stature, chest depth and forced vital capacity of low-to-high altitude migrant children of European ancestry. *Human Biology* 60:23–32.

GREKSA, L. P., and C. M. BEALL. 1989. Development of chest size and lung function at high altitude. In *Human population biology,* M. A. Little and J. D. Haas, eds., 222–38. New York: Oxford University Press.

GREKSA, L. P., H. SPIELVOGEL, and L. PAREDES-FERNANDEZ. 1985. Maximal exercise capacity in adolescent European and Amerindian high altitude natives. *American Journal of Physical Anthropology* 67:209–16.

GRELLER, A. M. 1988. Deciduous forest. In *North American terrestrial vegetation,* M. G. Barbour and W. D. Billings, eds., 287–316. Cambridge: Cambridge University Press.

GRIFFIN, W. V., J. H. MAURITZEN, and J. V. KASMAR. 1969. The psychological aspects of the architectural environment: A review. *American Journal of Psychiatry* 125:1057–62.

GRIM, C. E., J. P. HENRY, and H. MYERS. 1995. High blood pressure in blacks: Salt, slavery, survival, stress, and racism. In *Hypertension: Pathophysiology, diagnosis, and management*, 2d ed., J. H. Laragh and B. M. Brenner, eds., 171–207. New York: Raven Press.

GRIST, D. H. 1965. *Rice*. 4th ed. London: Longman Group Ltd.

GRMEK, M. D. 1990. *History of AIDS: Emergence and origin of a modern pandemic*. Princeton, NJ: Princeton University Press.

GROOMBRIDGE, B., ed. 1992. *Global diversity: Status of the Earth's living resources*. London: Routledge.

GROSS, D. R. 1975. Protein capture and cultural development in the Amazon Basin. *American Anthropologist* 77:526–49.

GROVES, B. M., T. DROMA, J. R. SUTTON, R. G. McCULLOUGH, R. E. McCULLOUGH, J. ZHUANG, G. RAPMUND, S. SUN, C. JANES, and L. G. MOORE. 1993. Minimal hypoxic pulmonary hypertension in normal Tibetans at 3,658 m. *Journal of Applied Physiology* 74:312–18.

GUPTA, A. 1988. *Ecology and development in the third world*. London: Routledge.

GUYTON, A. C. 1971. *Textbook of medical physiology*. 4th ed. Philadelphia: W. B. Saunders Company.

HAAS, J. D., and G. G. HARRISON. 1977. Nutritional anthropology and biological adaptation. *Annual Review of Anthropology* 6:69–101.

HAAS, J. D., and D. L. PELLETIER. 1989. Nutrition and human population biology. In *Human population biology: A transdisciplinary science*, M. A. Little and J. D. Haas, eds., 152–67. New York: Oxford University Press.

HAAS, J. D., D. A. TUFTS, J. L. BEARD, R. C. ROACH, and H. SPIELVOGEL. 1988. Defining anemia and its effect on physical work capacity at high altitudes in the Bolivian Andes. In *Capacity for work in the tropics*, K. J. Collins and D. F. Roberts, eds., 85–106. Cambridge: Cambridge University Press.

HAECKEL, E. 1870. *Generelle Morphologie der Organismen: Allgemeine Grundzuge der organischen Formenwissenschaft, mechanisch begrundt durch die von Charles Darwin reformirte Descendenz-Theorie*. Berlin: Vorlag von George Reiner.

HAENSZEL, W., M. KURIHARA, M. SEGI, and R. C. K. LEE. 1972. Stomach cancer among Japanese in Hawaii. *Journal of the National Cancer Institute* 49:969–88.

HALDANE, J. B. S. 1932. *The causes of evolution*. Ithaca, NY: Cornell University Press.

HALL, T. S. 1969. *Ideas of life and matter: Studies in the history of general physiology 600 B.C.–1900 A.D.*, vol. 1. Chicago: University of Chicago Press.

HAMILTON, W. D. 1964. The genetical evolution of social behaviour, Parts I and II. *Journal of Theoretical Biology* 12:1–52.

HAMLET, M. P. 1988. Human cold injuries. In *Human performance physiology and environmental medicine at terrestrial extremes*, K. B. Pandolf, M. N. Sawka, and R. R. Gonzalez, eds., 435–66. Indianapolis: Benchmark Press.

HAMMOND, A. L. 1971. Mercury in the environment: Natural and human factors. *Science* 171:788–89.

HAMMOND, N. 1986. The emergence of Maya civilization. *Scientific American* 255(2):106–15.

HANKS, L. M. 1992. *Rice and man: Agricultural ecology in southeast Asia*. Honolulu: University of Hawaii Press.

HANNA, J. M. 1968. Cold stress and microclimate in the Quechua Indians of southern Peru. In *High altitude adaptation in a Peruvian community*, P. T. Baker, et al., eds., 196–326. Occasional Papers in Anthropology, no. 1. University Park: Department of Anthropology, Pennsylvania State University.

HANNA, J. M. 1970. A comparison of laboratory and field studies of cold response. *American Journal of Physical Anthropology* 32:227–32.

HANNA, J. M. 1971. Responses of Quechua Indians to coca ingestion during cold exposure. *American Journal of Physical Anthropology* 34:273–77.

HANNA, J. M., and D. E. BROWN. 1979. Human heat tolerance: Biological and cultural adaptations. *Yearbook of Physical Anthropology* 22:163–86.

HANNA, J. M., and D. E. BROWN. 1983. Human heat tolerance: An anthropological perspective. *Annual Review of Anthropology* 12:259–84.

HANNA, J. M., G. D. JAMES, and J. M. MARTZ. 1986. Hormonal measures of stress. In *The changing Samoans: Behavior and health in transition*, P. T. Baker, J. M. Hanna, and T. S. Baker, eds., 203–21. New York: Oxford University Press.

HANNA, J. M., M. A. LITTLE, and D. M. AUSTIN. 1989. Climatic physiology. In *Human population biology: A transdisciplinary science*, M. A. Little and J. D. Haas, eds., 132–51. New York: Oxford University Press.

HARBISON, S. F. 1986. The demography of Samoan populations. In *The changing Samoans: Behavior and health in transition*, P. T. Baker, J. M. Hanna, and T. S. Baker, eds., 63–92. New York: Oxford University Press.

HARDESTY, D. L. 1977. *Ecological anthropology.* New York: John Wiley & Sons.

HARDIN, G. 1960. The competitive exclusion principle. *Science* 131:1292–97.

HARDIN, G. 1993. *Living within limits: Ecology, economics, and population taboos.* New York/Oxford: Oxford University Press.

HARGROVE, E. C. 1989. *Foundations of environmental ethics.* Englewood Cliffs, NJ: Prentice-Hall.

HARRINGTON, G. S. 1991. Effects of soil moisture on shrub seedling survival in a semi-arid grassland. *Science* 72:1138–49.

HARRIS, D. R. 1980. Tropical savanna environments: Definition, distribution, diversity, and development. In *Human ecology in savanna environments,* D. R. Harris, ed., 3–27. London: Academic Press.

HARRIS, M. 1978. *Cows, pigs, wars and witches: The riddles of culture.* New York: Vintage Books.

HARRIS, M. 1988. *Culture, people, nature: An introduction to general anthropology.* New York: Harper-Collins Publishers.

HARRISON, G. A. 1966. Human adaptation with reference to the IBP proposals for high altitude research. In *The biology of human adaptability,* P. T. Baker and J. S. Weiner, eds., 509–19. Oxford: Oxford University Press.

HARRISON, G. A. 1982. Preface. In *Energy and effort,* G. A. Harrison, ed., vii–ix. London: Taylor and Francis.

HARRISON, G. A. 1988. Seasonality and human population biology. In *Coping with uncertainty in food supply,* I. De Gardine and G. A. Harrison, eds., 26–31. Oxford: Clarendon Press.

HARRISON, G. A. 1995. *The human biology of the English village.* Oxford: Oxford University Press.

HARRISON, G. A., C. F. KUCHERMAN, M. A. S. MOORE, A. J. BOYCE, T. BAJU, A. E. MOURANT, M. J. GODBER, B. G. GLASGOW, A. C. KOPEC, D. TILLS, and E. J. CLEGG. 1969. The effects of altitudinal variation in Ethiopian populations. *Philosophical Transactions of the Royal Society of London, series B* 256:147–82.

HARRISON, G. A., C. D. PALMER, D. JENNER, and V. REYNOLDS. 1981. Associations between rates of urinary catecholamine excretion and aspects of lifestyle among adult women in some Oxfordshire villages. *Human Biology* 53:617–33.

HART, T. B., and J. A. HART. 1986. The ecological basis of hunter-gatherer subsistence in African rain forests: The Mbuti of eastern Zaire. *Human Ecology* 14:29–55.

HASTINGS, A., C. L. HOM, S. ELLNER, P. TURCHIN, and H. C. J. GODFRAY. 1993. Chaos in ecology: Is Mother Nature a strange attractor? *Annual Review of Ecology and Systematics* 24:1–33.

HAUB, C. 1997. New UN projections depict a variety of demographic futures. *Population Today* 25(4):1–3.

HAUCK, G. F. W. 1989. The Roman aqueduct of Nîmes. *Scientific American* 260(3):98–104.

HAVILAND, W. A. 1990. *Cultural anthropology.* 6th ed. Fort Worth: Holt, Rinehart and Winston.

HAWKES, K., J. F. O'CONNELL, and N. G. BLURTON JONES. 1995. Hadza children's foraging: Juvenile dependency, social arrangements, and mobility among hunter-gatherers. *Current Anthropology* 36:688–700.

HEATH, D., and D. R. WILLIAMS. 1977. *Man at high altitude.* Edinburgh: Churchill Livingstone.

HECHT, S., and D. POSEY. 1989. Preliminary results on soil management techniques of the Kayapo Indians. *Advances in Economic Botany* 7:174–88.

HEDIN, L. O., and G. E. LIKENS. 1996. Atmospheric dust and acid rain. *Scientific American* 275(6):88–92.

HEFFLEY, S. 1981. The relationship between northern Athapascan settlement patterns and resource distribution: An application of Horn's model. In *Hunter-gatherer foraging strategies: Ethnographic and archaeological analyses,* B. Winterhalder and E. A. Smith, eds., 126–47. Chicago: University of Chicago Press.

HEIMSTRA, N. W., and L. H. McFARLING. 1974. *Environmental psychology.* Monterey, CA: Brooks/Cole Publishing Company.

HENDRY, P. 1988. Food and population: Beyond five billion. *Population Bulletin* 43(2):1–40.

HENSHAW, S. K., and J. VAN VORT. 1992. *Abortion Factbook, 1992 Edition.* New York: Alan Guttmacher Institute.

HERBERT, T. B., and S. COHEN. 1993. Stress and immunity in humans: A meta-analytic review. *Psychosomatic Medicine* 55:364–79.

HEY, E., and G. KATZ. 1969. Evaporative water loss in the newborn baby. *Journal of Physiology* 210:1–4.

HEYWOOD, P. F. 1982. The functional significance of malnutrition: Growth and prospective risk of death in the highlands of Papua New Guinea. *Journal of Food and Nutrition* 39:13–19.

HEYWOOD, P. F. 1992. Iodine-deficiency disorders in Papua New Guinea. In *Human biology in Papua New Guinea: The small cosmos,* R. D. Attenborough and M. P. Alpers, eds., 355–62. Oxford: Clarendon Press.

HEYWOOD, P. F., and C. JENKINS. 1992. Nutrition in Papua New Guinea. In *Human biology in Papua New Guinea: The small cosmos*, R. D. Attenborough and M. P. Alpers, eds., 249–67. Oxford: Clarendon Press.

HEYWOOD, P. F., and N. G. NORGAN. 1992. Human growth in Papua New Guinea. In *Human biology in Papua New Guinea: The small cosmos*, R. D. Attenborough and M. P. Alpers, eds., 234–48. Oxford: Clarendon Press.

HILEMAN, B. 1988. The Great Lakes cleanup effort. *Chemical and Engineering News* 66:22–39.

HILL, K. 1988. Macronutrient modifications of optimal foraging theory: An approach using indifference curves applied to some modern foragers. *Human Ecology* 16:157–97.

HIMES, J. H. 1991. Introduction. In *Anthropometric assessment of nutritional status*, J. H. Himes, ed., 1–3. New York: John Wiley & Sons.

HINMAN, C. W. 1984. New crops for arid lands. *Science* 225:1445–48.

HOFFMAN, A. A., and P. A. PARSONS. 1991. *Evolutionary genetics and environmental stress*. Oxford: Oxford University Press.

HOFLER, W. 1968. Changes in the regional distribution of sweating during acclimatization to heat. *Journal of Applied Physiology* 25:503–6.

HOLDEN, C. 1996. New populations of old add to poor nations' burdens. *Science* 273:46–48.

HOLDEN, J. E., C. K. STONE, C. M. CLARK, W. D. BROWN, R. J. NICKLES, C. STANLEY, and P. W. HOCHACHKA. 1995. Enhanced cardiac metabolism of plasma glucose in high-altitude natives: Adaptation against chronic hypoxia. *Journal of Applied Physiology* 79:222–28.

HOLMES, B. 1993. A new study finds there's life left in the Green Revolution. *Science* 261:1517.

HONG, S. K. 1973. Pattern of cold adaptation in women divers of Korea. *Federation Proceedings* 32:1614–22.

HONIGMANN, J. J. 1976. *The development of anthropological ideas*. Homewood, IL: The Dorsey Press.

HORIUCHI, S. 1992. Stagnation in the decline of the world population growth rate during the 1980s. *Science* 257:761–65.

HORN, H. S. 1968. The adaptive significance of colonial nesting in the Brewers blackbird *(Euphagus cyanocephalus)*. *Ecology* 49:682–94.

HOTEZ, P. J., and D. I. PRITCHARD. 1995. Hookworm infection. *Scientific American* 272(6):68–74.

HOUGHTON, R. A., and G. M. WOODWELL. 1989. Global climatic change. *Scientific American* 260:36–47.

HOUSTON, C. S. 1992. Mountain sickness. *Scientific American* 267(4):58–66.

HOWARTH, R. W., and J. COLE. 1985. Molybdenum availability, nitrogen limitation, and phytoplankton growth in natural waters. *Science* 229:653–55.

HRDY, S. B. 1977. *The langurs of Abu: Female and male strategies of reproduction*. Cambridge, MA: Harvard University Press.

HSU, R. C. 1982. *Food for one billion: China's agriculture since 1949*. Boulder: Westview.

HUBBARD, R. W., and L. E. ARMSTRONG. 1988. The heat illnesses: Biochemical, ultrastructural, and fluid-electrolyte considerations. In *Human performance physiology and environmental medicine at terrestrial extremes*, K. B. Pandolf, M. N. Sawka, and R. R. Gonzalez, eds., 305–59. Indianapolis: Benchmark Press.

HUDSON, E. H. 1965. Treponematosis and man's social evolution. *American Anthropologist* 67:885–901.

HULL, T. 1983. Decision making process in the demography of the family. *Proceedings of the international population conference, 1981* 4:IUSSP 117–26.

HULTGREN, H. N. 1979. High altitude medical problems. *Western Journal of Medicine* 131:8–23.

HUNT, H. W., E. R. INGHAM, D. C. COLEMAN, E. T. ELLIOTT, and C. P. P. REID. 1988. Nitrogen limitation of production and decomposition in prairie, mountain meadow, and pine forest. *Ecology* 69:1009–16.

HUNTINGTON, E. 1945. *Mainsprings of civilization*. New York: The New American Library.

HURTADO, A. 1964. Animals in high altitudes: Resident man. In *Handbook of physiology*, Section 4: *Adaptation to the environment*, D. B. Dill, E. F. Adolph, and C. G. Wilbur, eds., 843–60. Washington, DC: American Physiological Society.

HURTADO, A. M., and K. R. HILL. 1987. Early dry season subsistence ecology of Cuiva (Hiwi) foragers of Venezuela. *Human Ecology* 15:163–87.

HURTADO, A. M., and K. R. HILL. 1990. Seasonality in a foraging society: Variation in diet, work effort, fertility, and sexual division of labor among the Hiwi of Venezuela. *Journal of Anthropological Research* 46:293–346.

HUSS-ASHMORE, R. A. 1993. Agriculture, modernisation and seasonality. In *Seasonality and human ecology*, S. J. Ulijaszek and S. S. Strickland, eds., 202–19. Cambridge: Cambridge University Press.

HUTCHINSON, G. E. 1959. Homage to Santa Rosalia, or why are there so many kinds of animals? *American Naturalist* 93:145–59.

HUTCHINSON, G. E. 1975. Variations on a theme by Robert MacArthur. In *Ecology and evolution of communities*, M. L. Cody and J. M. Diamond, eds., 492–521. Cambridge, MA: Belknap Press.

HUTT, M. S. R., and D. P. BURKITT. 1986. *The geography of non-infectious disease*. Oxford: Oxford University Press.

INGOLD, T. 1976. *The Skolt Lapps today*. Cambridge: Cambridge University Press.

INGOLD, T. 1980. *Hunters, pastoralists and ranchers: Reindeer economies and their transformations*. Cambridge: Cambridge University Press.

IPCC (Intergovernmental Panel on Climate Change). 1990. *Climate change: The IPCC scientific assessment*, J. T. Houghton, G. J. Jenkins, and J. J. Ephraums, eds. Cambridge: Cambridge University Press.

IRONS, W. 1979. Cultural and biological success. In *Evolutionary biology and human social behavior*, N. A. Chagnon and W. Irons, eds., 257–72. North Scituate, MA: Duxbury Press.

IVES, J. D., and R. G. BARRY, eds. 1974. *Arctic and alpine environments*. London: Methuen and Co., Ltd.

JACKSON, S. T., R. P. FUTYMA, and D. A. WILCOX. 1988. A paleoecological test of a classical hydrosere in the Lake Michigan dunes. *Ecology* 69:928–36.

JAMES, G. D. 1984. *Stress response and lifestyle differences among Western Samoan men*. Ph.D. dissertation, The Pennsylvania State University, University Park.

JAMES, G. D. 1991. Blood pressure response to the daily stressors of urban environments: Methodology, basic concepts, and significance. *Yearbook of Physical Anthropology* 34:189–210.

JAMES, G. D., and P. T. BAKER. 1990. Human population biology and hypertension: Evolutionary and ecological aspects of blood pressure. In *Hypertension: Pathophysiology, diagnosis, and management*, J. H. Laragh and B. M. Brenner, eds., 137–45. New York: Raven Press.

JAMES, G. D., P. T. BAKER, D. A. JENNER, and G. A. HARRISON. 1987. Variation in lifestyle characteristics and catecholamine excretion rates among young Western Samoan men. *Social Science and Medicine* 25:981–86.

JAMES, G. D., and D. E. BROWN. 1997. The biological stress response and lifestyle: Catecholamines and blood pressure. *Annual Review of Anthropology* 26:313–35.

JAMES, G. D., D. E. CREWS, and J. PEARSON. 1989. Catecholamines and stress. In *Human population biology*, M. A. Little and J. D. Haas, eds., 280–95. New York: Oxford University Press.

JAMES, G. D., L. S. YEE, G. A. HARSHFIELD, S. BLANK, and T. G. PICKERING. 1986. The influence of happiness, anger and anxiety on the blood pressure of borderline hypertensives. *Psychosomatic Medicine* 48:502–8.

JELLIFFE, D. B. 1968. *Child nutrition in developing countries*. Washington, DC: Agency for International Development, U.S. Department of State.

JENNER, D. A., V. REYNOLDS, and G. A. HARRISON. 1979. Population field studies of catecholamines. In *Response to stress: Occupational aspects*, C. MacKay and T. Cox, eds., 112–19. London: IPC Science and Technology Press.

JIN, R. L., and Z. K. CHENG. 1989. People's Republic of China. In *International handbook of pollution control*, E. J. Kormondy, ed., 357–76. Westport, CT: Greenwood Press.

JITSUKAWA, M., and C. DJERASSI. 1994. Birth control in Japan: Realities and prognosis. *Science* 265:1048–51.

JOCHIM, M. A. 1981. *Strategies for survival: Cultural behavior in an ecological context*. New York: Academic Press.

JONES, P. D., and T. M. L. WIGLEY. 1990. Global warming trends. *Scientific American* 263(2):84–91.

JORDAN, C. F. 1985. *Nutrient cycling in tropical forest ecosystems*. New York: John Wiley & Sons.

JORGENSEN, B. B., M. F. ISAKESEN, and H. W. JANNASCH. 1992. Bacterial sulfate reduction above 100°C in deep-sea hydrothermal vent sediments. *Science* 258:1756–57.

JOSHI, M. M., and J. P. HOLLIS. 1977. Interaction of *Beggiatoa* and rice plants: Detoxification of hydrogen sulfide in the rice rhizosphere. *Science* 195:178–79.

KANG, B. S., S. H. SONG, C. S. SUH, and S. K. HONG. 1963. Energy metabolism and body temperature of the Ama. *Journal of Applied Physiology* 18:483–88.

KAPLAN, H., and K. HILL. 1985. Food sharing among the Ache foragers: Tests of explanatory hypotheses. *Current Anthropology* 26:223–46.

KARL, T. R., R. R. HEIM, JR., and R. G. QUAYLE. 1991. The Greenhouse Effect in central North America: If not now, when? *Science* 251:1058–61.

KATZ, S. L., and J. F. ENDERS. 1965. Measles virus. In *Viral and rickettsial infections of man*, 4th ed., F. L. Horsfall and I. Tamm, eds., 784–801. Philadelphia: J. B. Lippincott Company.

KAY, R. F., C. ROSS, and B. A. WILLIAMS. 1997. Anthropoid origins. *Science* 275:797–804.

KAYSER, B., H. HOPPELER, H. CLAASSEN, and P. CERRETELLI. 1991. Muscle structure and performance capacity of Himalayan Sherpas. *Journal of Applied Physiology* 70:1938–42.

KEATINGE, W. R. 1960. The effects of subcutaneous fat and of previous exposure to cold on the body temperature, peripheral blood flow and metabolic rate of men in cold water. *Journal of Physiology* 153:166–78.

KEGELES, S. M., et al. 1988. Sexually active adolescents and condoms: Changes over one year in knowledge, attitudes and use. *American Journal of Public Health* 78:460–61.

KEHOE, A. B. 1981. *North American Indians: A comprehensive account.* Englewood Cliffs, NJ: Prentice-Hall.

KELLOGG, W. W., R. D. CADLE, E. R. ALLEN, A. L. LAZRUS, and E. A. MARTELL. 1972. The sulfur cycle. *Science* 175:587–96.

KENNEDY, G. E. 1980. *Paleoanthropology.* New York: McGraw-Hill Inc.

KERR, R. A. 1989. Greenhouse skeptic out in the cold. *Science* 246:1118–19.

KERR, R. A. 1990a. New greenhouse report puts down dissenters. *Science* 249:481–82.

KERR, R. A. 1990b. Ozone destruction closer to home. *Science* 247:1297.

KERR, R. A. 1994. Dioxins dominate Denver gathering of toxicologists. *Science* 266:1162–63.

KERR, R. A. 1995. Did Darwin get it all right? *Science* 267:1421–22.

KERR, R. A. 1996. Ozone-destroying chlorine tops out. *Science* 271:32.

KERR, R. A. 1997. Greenhouse forecasting still cloudy. *Science* 276:1040–42.

KERSLAKE, D. M. 1972. *The stress of hot environments.* Cambridge: Cambridge University Press.

KERSON, T. S. 1985. *Understanding chronic illness.* New York: The Free Press.

KEYFITZ, N. 1989. The growing human population. *Scientific American* 261(3):119–26.

KEYS, A., J. BROZEK, A. HENSCHEL, O. MICKELSEN, and H. L. TAYLOR. 1950. *The biology of human starvation.* Minneapolis: University of Minnesota Press.

KIMBEL, W. H., D. C. JOHANSON, and Y. RAK. 1994. The first skull and other new discoveries of *Australopithecus afarensis* at Hadar, Ethiopia. *Nature* 368:449–51.

KIMBEL, W. H., R. C. WALTER, D. C. JOHANSON, K. E. REED, J. L. ARONSON, Z. ASSEFA, C. W. MAREAN, G. G. ECK, R. BOBE, E. HOVERS, Y. RAK, C. VONDRA, T. YEMANE, D. YORK, Y. CHEN, N. M. EVENSON, and P. E. SMITH. 1996. Late Pliocene *Homo* and Oldowan tools from the Hadar Formation (Kada Hadar member), Ethiopia. *Journal of Human Evolution* 31:549–61.

KIRCH, P. V. 1983. Man's role in modifying tropical and subtropical Polynesian ecosystems. *Archaeology in Oceania* 18:26–31.

KIRCH, P. V. 1984. *The evolution of the Polynesian chiefdoms.* Cambridge: Cambridge University Press.

KIRKENDALL, M. A. 1994. Differential responses to infectious disease in the Pacific at European contact. Paper presented at the 59th Annual Meetings, Society for American Archaeology, Anaheim, CA, March 22–24.

KIRSCHBAUM, C., T. KLAUER, and D. H. HELLHAMMER. 1995. Sex-specific effects of social support on cortisol and subjective responses to acute psychological stress. *Psychosomatic Medicine* 57:23–31.

KLIKS, M. M. 1983. Paleoparasitology: On the origins and impact of human-helminth relationships. In *Human ecology and infectious diseases*, N. A. Croll and J. H. Cross, eds., 291–313. New York: Academic Press.

KLING, G. W., M. A. CLARK, H. R. COMPTON, J. D. DEVINE, W. C. EVANS, A. M. HUMPHREY, E. D. KOENIGSBERG, J. P. LOCKWOOD, M. I. TUTTLE, and G. N. WAGNER. 1987. The 1986 Lake Nyos gas disaster in Cameroon, West Africa. *Science* 236:169–75.

KNUDSON, K. E. 1970. *Resource fluctuation, productivity, and social organization on Micronesian coral islands.* Ph.D. dissertation, University of Oregon. Ann Arbor, MI: University Microfilms.

KOEHN, R. K., and B. L. BAYNE. 1989. Towards a physiological and genetical understanding of the genetics of the stress response. *Biological Journal of the Linnean Society* 37:157–71.

KORMONDY, E. J. 1959. The systematics of *Tetragoneuria*, based on ecological, life history, and morphological evidence (Odonata: Corduliidae). *Miscellaneous Publications of the Museum of Zoology, University of Michigan* 107:1–79.

KORMONDY, E. J. 1969. Comparative ecology of sandspit ponds. *American Midland Naturalist* 82:28–61.

KORMONDY, E. J. 1990. Ethics and values in the biology classroom. *American Biology Teacher* 52:403–7.

KORMONDY, E. J. 1996. *Concepts of ecology.* 4th ed. Englewood Cliffs, NJ: Prentice-Hall.

KORMONDY E. J., and J. F. McCORMICK. 1981. *Handbook of contemporary developments in world ecology.* Westport, CT: Greenwood Press.

KOTTAK, C. P. 1994. *Anthropology.* 6th ed. New York: McGraw-Hill Inc.

KROEBER, A. I. 1939. *Cultural and natural areas of native North America.* Berkeley: University of California Press.

KROG, J., B. FOLKOW, R. H. FOX, and K. L. ANDERSEN. 1960. Hand circulation in the cold of Lapps and north Norwegian fishermen. *Journal of Applied Physiology* 15:654–58.

KUNO, E. 1987. Principles of predator-prey interaction in theoretical, experimental, and natural population systems. *Advances in Ecological Research* 16:249–337.

KUPCHELLA, C. E. 1987. *Dimensions of cancer.* Belmont, CA: Wadsworth Publishing Company.

LACHENBRUCH, A. H., and B. V. MARSHALL. 1986. Changing climate: Geothermal evidence from permafrost in the Alaskan Arctic. *Science* 234:689–96.

LACK, D. 1961. *Darwin's finches.* New York: Harper & Row.

LAHIRI, S. 1977. Physiological responses and adaptations to high altitude. In *Environmental physiology II*, vol. 15, D. Robertshaw, ed., 217–51. Baltimore: University Park Press.

LANGER, W. L. 1972. Checks on population growth: 1750–1850. *Scientific American* 226(2):92–99.

LARRICK, R., and R. L. CIOCHON. 1996. The African emergence and early Asian dispersal of the genus *Homo. American Scientist* 84:538–51.

LARSON, D. 1993. The recovery of Spirit Lake. *American Scientist* 81:166–77.

LASKER, G. W. 1969. Human biological adaptability. *Science* 166:1480–86.

LAUGHLIN, W. S. 1980. *Aleuts: Survivors of the Bering land bridge.* New York: Holt, Rinehart and Winston, Inc.

LAZARUS, R. S. 1966. *Psychological stress and the coping process.* New York: McGraw-Hill Inc.

LAZARUS, R. S. 1993. Coping theory and research: Past, present, and future. *Psychosomatic Medicine* 55:234–47.

LEATHERMAN, T. L., and R. B. THOMAS. 1987. Patterns of illness and work disruption in a rural Andean population. *American Journal of Physical Anthropology* 72:223. (Abstract)

LeBLANC, J. 1975. *Man in the Cold.* Springfield, IL: Charles C Thomas, Publisher.

LeBLANC, J. 1978. Adaptation of man to cold. In *Strategies in cold, natural torpidity and thermogenesis*, L. C. H. Wang and J. W. Hudson, eds., 695–715. London: Academic Press.

LEE, R. B. 1969. !Kung bushman subsistence: An input-output analysis. In *Contributions to anthropology: Ecological essays*, D. Damas, ed., Bulletin 230, Anthropological Series, No. 86. Ottawa: National Museums of Canada.

LEE, R. B. 1972. The !Kung bushmen of Botswana. In *Hunters and gatherers today*, M. G. Bicchieri, ed., 327–67. New York: Holt, Rinehart and Winston, Inc.

LEE, R. B. 1993. *The Dobe Ju/'hoansi.* 2d ed. Fort Worth, TX: Harcourt Brace College Publishers.

LEITH, H., and M. J. A. WERGER, eds., 1989. *Tropical rain forest ecosystems: Biogeographical and ecological studies. Ecosystems of the world*, vol. 14B. Amsterdam: Elsevier Science Publishers.

LEITH, H., and R. H. WITTAKER, eds. 1975. *The primary productivity of the biosphere.* New York: Springer-Verlag.

LENFANT, C., and K. SULLIVAN. 1971. Adaptation to high altitude. *New England Journal of Medicine* 284:1298–1309.

LEONARD, W. R. 1989. On the adaptive significance of energetic efficiency. *Human Ecology* 17:465–70.

LEONARD, W. R., P. T. KATZMARZYK, A. G. COMUZZIE, M. H. CRAWFORD, and R. I. SUKERNIK. 1994. Growth and nutritional status of the Evenki reindeer herders of Siberia. *American Journal of Human Biology* 6:339–50.

LEONARD, W. R., and R. B. THOMAS. 1988. Changing dietary patterns in the Peruvian Andes. *Ecology of Food and Nutrition* 21:245–63.

LEOPOLD, A. 1949. The land ethic. In *A Sand County almanac.* New York: Oxford University Press.

LESCHINE, S. B., K. HOLWELL, and E. CANALE-PAROLE. 1988. Nitrogen fixation by anaerobic cellulolytic bacteria. *Science* 242:1157–59.

LESLIE, P. W., and P. H. FRY. 1989. Extreme seasonality of births among nomadic Turkana pastoralists. *American Journal of Physical Anthropology* 79:103–15.

LEVIN, S. A., B. GRENFELL, A. HASTINGS, and A. S. PERELSON. 1997. Mathematical and computational challenges in population biology and ecosystems science. *Science* 275:334–43.

LIGHTFOOT, D. C., and W. B. G. WHITFORD. 1987. Variation in insect densities on desert creosote-bush: Is nitrogen a factor? *Ecology* 68:547–57.

LIKENS, G. E., F. H. BORMAN, R. S. PIERCE, J. S. EATON, and N. M. JOHNSON. 1977. *Biogeochemistry of a forested ecosystem.* New York: Springer-Verlag.

LIKENS, G. E., C. T. DRISCOLL, and D. C. BUSO. 1996. Long-term effects of acid rain: Response and recovery of a forest ecosystem. *Science* 272:244–46.

LINDEMAN, R. L. 1942. The trophic-dynamic aspect of ecology. *Ecology* 23:399–418.

LINDEN, E. 1994. More power to women, fewer mouths to feed. *Time* (September 26).

LIPPMANN, M., and R. B. SCHLESINGER. 1979. *Chemical contamination in the human environment.* New York: Oxford University Press.

LISTER, B. C., and A. G. AGUAYO. 1992. Seasonality, predation, and the behaviour of a tropical mainland anole. *Journal of Animal Ecology* 61:717–33.

LITTLE, M. A. 1970. Effects of alcohol and coca on foot temperature responses of highland Peruvians during a localized cold exposure. *American Journal of Physical Anthropology* 32:233–42.

LITTLE, M. A. 1980. Designs for human-biological research among savanna pastoralists. In *Human ecology in savanna environments*, D. R. Harris, ed., 479–503. London: Academic Press.

LITTLE, M. A. 1989. Human biology of African pastoralists. *Yearbook of Physical Anthropology* 32:215–47.

LITTLE, M. A., N. DYSON-HUDSON, R. Dyson-Hudson, J. E. ELLIS, K. A. GALVIN, P. W. LESLIE, and D. M. SWIFT. 1990. Ecosystem approaches in human biology: Their history and a case study of the South Turkana Ecosystem Project. In *The ecosystem approach in anthropology: From concept to practice*, E. F. Moran, ed., 389–434. Ann Arbor: University of Michigan Press.

LITTLE, M. A., and J. D. HAAS. 1989. Introduction: Human population biology and the concept of transdisciplinarity. In *Human population biology*, M. A. Little and J. D. Haas, eds., 113–31. New York: Oxford University Press.

LITTLE, M. A., and J. M. HANNA. 1978. The response of high-altitude populations to cold and other stresses. In *The biology of high-altitude peoples*. P. T. Baker, ed., 251–98. London: Cambridge University Press.

LITTLE, M. A., and D. H. HOCHNER. 1973. *Human thermoregulation, growth, and mortality*. Addison-Wesley Module in Anthropology, no. 36. Reading, MA: Addison-Wesley Publishing Company Inc.

LITTLE, M. A., and B. R. JOHNSON, JR. 1987. Mixed longitudinal growth of Turkana pastoralists. *Human Biology* 59:695–707.

LITTLE, M. A., and G. E. B. MORREN, JR. 1976. *Ecology, energetics, and human variability*. Dubuque, IA: Wm. C. Brown Company Publishers.

LIVELY, C. M. 1986. Canalization versus developmental conversion in a spatially variable environment. *American Naturalist* 128:561–72.

LIVI-BACCI, M. 1992. *A concise history of world population*, C. Ipsen, trans. Cambridge, MA: Blackwell Publishers.

LOOK, M. A. 1982. A mortality study of the Hawaiian people. Research and Statistics Report no. 38. Honolulu: Hawaii State Department of Health.

LOOMIS, W. F. 1967. Skin pigment regulation of Vitamin-D biosynthesis in man. *Science* 157:501–6.

LORENZ, K. 1963. *On aggression*. New York: Harcourt Brace Jovanovich.

LOTKA, A. J. 1925. *Elements of physical biology*. Baltimore: Williams & Wilkins.

LOURIE, J., G. BUDD, and H. R. ANDERSON. 1992. Physiological adaptability in Papua New Guinea. In *Human biology in Papua New Guinea: The small cosmos*, R. D. Attenborough and M. P. Alpers, eds., 268–80. Oxford: Clarendon Press.

LOVELOCK, J. E., and L. MARGULIS. 1974. Atmospheric homeostasis, by and for the biosphere: The Gaia hypothesis. *Tellus* 26:1–10.

LUMSDEN, C. J., and E. O. WILSON. 1981. *Genes, mind and culture*. Cambridge, MA: Harvard University Press.

LUNDBERG, U. 1976. Urban commuting, crowdedness and catecholamine excretion. *Journal of Human Stress* 2:26–34.

LYNCH, T. F. 1978. The South American Paleo-Indians. In *Ancient native Americans*, J. D. Jennings, ed., 455–89. San Francisco: W. H. Freeman and Company.

MACARTHUR, R. H. 1972. Coexistence of species. In *Challenging biological problems*, J. A. Behnke, ed., 253–59. New York: Oxford University Press.

MACARTHUR, R. H., and E. R. PIANKA. 1966. On optimal use of a patchy environment. *American Naturalist* 100:603–9.

MACDONALD, R. W., and E. C. CARMACK. 1991. Age of Canada Basin deep waters: A way to estimate primary production for the Arctic Ocean. *Science* 254:1348–50.

MACKENZIE, J. J., and M. T. EL-ASHRY. 1988. *Ill winds: Airborne pollution's toll on trees and crops*. Washington, DC: World Resources Institute.

MACLACHLAN, J. A., and S. F. ARNOLD. 1996. Environmental estrogens. *American Scientist* 84:452–61.

MACNEISH, R. S. 1971. Speculations about how and why food production and village life developed in the Tehuacàn Valley, Mexico. *Archaeology* 24:307–15.

MADATI, P. J., and E. J. KORMONDY. 1989. Introduction. In *International handbook of pollution control*, E. J. Kormondy, ed., 1–17. Westport, CT: Greenwood Press.

MAGNUSON, E. 1990. A cover-up on Agent Orange? *Time* (July 23):27–28.

MALATT, A. E., and H. R. TAYLOR. 1992. Onchocerciasis. *Infectious Disease Clinics of North America* 6:963.

MALCONIAN, M. K., and P. B. ROCK. 1988. Medical problems related to altitude. In *Human performance physiology and environmental medicine at terrestrial extremes*, K. B. Pandolf, M. N. Sawka, and R. R. Gonzalez, eds., 545–63. Indianapolis: Benchmark Press.

MALTHUS, T. R. [1798] 1959. *An essay on the principle of population as it affects the future improvement of society.* Ann Arbor: University of Michigan Press.

MANN, C. C. 1991. Extinction: Are ecologists crying wolf? *Science* 253:736–38.

MANN, D. 1982. Institutional framework for agricultural water conservation and reallocation in the west: A policy analysis. In *Water and agriculture in the western U.S.: Conservation, reallocation, and markets,* G. D. Weatherford, ed., 9–52. Boulder, CO: Westview Press.

MARANO, L. 1983. Boreal forest hazards and adaptations: The present. In *Boreal forest adaptations: The northern Algonkians,* A. T. Steegmann, Jr., ed., 269–88. New York: Plenum Press.

MARCHAND, P. J. 1987. *Life in the cold: An introduction to winter ecology.* Hanover, NH: University Press of New England.

MARKS, S. A. 1976. *Large mammals and a brave people: Subsistence hunters in Zambia.* Seattle: University of Washington Press.

MARMOT, M. G., S. L. SYME, A. KAGAN, H. KATO, J. B. COHEN, and J. BELSKY. 1975. Epidemiologic studies of coronary heart disease and stroke in Japanese men living in Japan, Hawaii and California: Prevalence of coronary and hypertensive heart disease and associated risk factors. *American Journal of Epidemiology* 102:514–25.

MARTIN, L. G. 1991. Population aging policies in East Asia and the United States. *Science* 251:527–31.

MARTIN, P. S. 1984. Prehistoric overkill: The global model. In *Quaternary extinctions,* P. S. Martin and R. G. Klein, eds., 354–403. Tucson: University of Arizona Press.

MASCIE-TAYLOR, C. G. N. 1991. Nutritional status: Its measurement and relation to health. In *Applications of biological anthropology to human affairs,* C. G. N. Mascie-Taylor and G. W. Lasker, eds., 55–82. Cambridge: Cambridge University Press.

MATSON, P., and A. BERRYMAN, eds. 1992. Ratio-dependent predator-prey theory. *Ecology* (Special Feature) 73:1529–66.

MATSON, P. A., P. M. VITOUSEK, J. J. EWEL, M. J. MAZZARINO, and G. P. ROBERTSON. 1987. Nitrogen transformations following tropical forest felling and burning on a volcanic soil. *Ecology* 68:491–502.

MATTSON, W. J. 1980. Herbivory in relation to plant nitrogen content. *Annual Review of Ecology and Systematics* 11:119–61.

MAUGH, T. H., II. 1979. Restoring damaged lakes. *Science* 203:425–27.

MAUGH, T. H., II. 1980. Ozone depletion would have dire effects. *Science* 207:394–95.

MAUGH, T. H., II. 1982. New link between ozone and cancer. *Science* 216:396–97.

MAY, R. M. 1974. Biological populations with nonoverlapping generations: Stable points, stable cycles, and chaos. *Science* 186:645–47.

MAY, R. M. 1983. Parasitic infections as regulators of animal populations. *American Scientist* 71:36–45.

MAYER, W. V. 1987. Wallace and Darwin. *American Biology Teacher* 49:406–10.

MAYR, E. 1988. Is biology an autonomous science? In *Toward a new philosophy of biology,* E. Mayr, ed., 8–23. Cambridge, MA: Harvard University Press.

MAZESS, R. B. 1970. Cardiorespiratory characteristics and adaptation to high altitudes. *American Journal of Physical Anthropology* 32:267–78.

MAZESS, R. B. 1975. Biological adaptation: Aptitudes and acclimatization. In *Biosocial interrelations in population adaptation,* E. S. Watts, F. E. Johnston, and G. W. Lasker, eds., 9–18. The Hague: Mouton Publishers.

McAFEE, K. 1990. Why the third world goes hungry. *Commonweal* (June 15):380–85.

McARTHUR, M. 1977. Nutritional research in Melanesia: A second look at the Tsembaga. In *Subsistence and survival: Rural ecology in the Pacific,* T. P. Bayliss-Smith and R. G. Feachem, eds., 91–128. London: Academic Press.

McCABE, J. T. 1988. Drought and recovery: Livestock dynamics among the Ngisonyoka Turkana of Kenya. *Human Ecology* 15:371–89.

McCANCE, R. A., and E. M. WIDDOWSON. 1965. Nutritional changes. In *The physiology of human survival,* O. G. Edholm and A. L. Bacharach, eds., 207–33. London: Academic Press.

McCONNELL, E. E., G. W. LUCIER, R. C. RUMBAUGH, P. W. ALBRO, D. J. HARVIN, J. R. HASS, and M. W. HARRIS. 1984. Dioxin in soil: Bioavailability after ingestion by rats and guinea pigs. *Science* 223:1077–79.

McELROY, A., and P. K. TOWNSEND. 1989. *Medical anthropology in ecological perspective.* 2d ed. Boulder, CO: Westview Press.

McFALLS, J. A., Jr. 1991. Population: A lively introduction. *Population Bulletin* 46(2):1–41.

McGARVEY, S. T., J. R. BINDON, D. E. CREWS, and D. E. SCHENDEL. 1989. Modernization and adiposity: Causes and consequences. In *Human population biology,* M. A. Little and J. D. Haas, eds., 263–79. New York: Oxford University Press.

McGarvey, S. T., and D. E. Schendel. 1986. Blood pressure of Samoans. In *The changing Samoans: Behavior and health in transition,* P. T. Baker, J. M. Hanna, and T. S. Baker, eds., 350–93. New York: Oxford University Press.

McGowran, B. 1990. Fifty million years ago. *American Scientist* 78:30–39.

McIntyre, D. A. 1981. Design requirements for a comfortable environment. In *Bioengineering, thermal physiology and comfort,* K. Cena and J. A. Clark, eds., 195–220. Amsterdam: Elsevier Science Publishers.

McKeown, T. 1988. *The origins of human disease.* Oxford: Basil Blackwell Ltd.

McMillan, D. 1993. Diversification and successful settlement in the river blindness control zone of West Africa. *Human Organization* 52:269–82.

McNeill, W. H. 1976. *Plagues and peoples.* New York: Doubleday.

Medlin, C., and J. D. Skinner. 1988. Individual dietary intake methodology: A 50-year review of progress. *Journal of the American Dietetic Association* 88:1250–57.

Meffe, G. K. 1984. Effects of abiotic disturbance on coexistence of predator-prey fish species. *Ecology* 65:1525–34.

Meggers, B. J. 1954. Environmental limitation on the development of culture. *American Anthropologist* 56:801–24.

Mertz, W. 1981. The essential trace elements. *Science* 213:1332–38.

Mervis, J. 1995. China's unique environment favors large intervention trials. *Science* 270:1149–51.

Messer, E. 1989. Seasonal hunger and coping strategies: An anthropological discussion. In *Coping with seasonal constraints,* R. Huss-Ashmore, ed., 131–41. Philadelphia: MASCA, University Museum, University of Pennsylvania.

Miller, T. R. 1989. The pending water crisis. In *Water and the future of the Southwest,* Z. A. Smith, ed., 47–67. Albuquerque: University of New Mexico Press.

Minnegal, M. 1997. Consumption and production: Sharing and social construction of use-value. *Current Anthropology* 38:25–48.

Mithen, S. J. 1989. Modeling hunter-gatherer decision making: Complementing optimal foraging theory. *Human Ecology* 17:59–83.

Moffat, A. 1996. Ecologists look at the big picture. *Science* 273:1490.

Moore, J. A. 1981. The effects of information networks in hunter-gatherer societies. In *Hunter-gatherer foraging strategies,* B. Winterhalder and E. A. Smith, eds., 194–217. Chicago: University of Chicago Press.

Moore, L. G., P. W. Van Arsdale, J. E. Glittenberg, and R. A. Aldrich. 1980. *The biocultural basis of health.* St. Louis: The C. V. Mosby Company.

Moore, O. K. 1965. Divination—A new perspective. *American Anthropologist* 59:69–74.

Moos, R. H. 1974. Systems for the assessment and classification of human environments: An overview. In *Issues in social ecology: Human milieus,* R. H. Moos and P. M. Insel, eds., 5–28. Palo Alto, CA: National Press Books.

Moran, E. F. 1981. *Developing the Amazon.* Bloomington: Indiana University Press.

Moran, E. F. 1982. *Human adaptability: An introduction to ecological anthropology.* Boulder, CO: Westview Press.

Moran, E. F. 1990. Levels of analysis and analytical level shifting: Examples from Amazonian ecosystem research. In *The ecosystem approach in anthropology: From concept to practice,* E. F. Moran, ed., 279–308. Ann Arbor: University of Michigan Press.

Moran, E. F. 1991. Human adaptive strategies in Amazonian blackwater ecosystems. *American Anthropologist* 93:361–82.

Morehouse, L. E., and A. T. Miller, Jr. 1967. *Physiology of exercise.* 5th ed. St. Louis: The C. V. Mosby Company.

Morgan, M. G. 1993. Risk analysis and management. *Scientific American* 269(1):32–41.

Morris, D. 1967. *The naked ape.* New York: Dell Publishing Company.

Morris, K., M. Morganlander, J. L. Coulehan, S. Gahagen, and V. C. Arena. 1990. Wood-burning stoves and lower respiratory tract infection in American Indian children. *American Journal of Diseases of Children* 144:105–8.

Mueller, W. H. 1988. Ethnic differences in fat distribution during growth. In *Fat distribution during growth and later health outcomes,* C. Bouchard and F. E. Johnston, eds., 127–45. New York: Alan R. Liss, Inc.

Muir, C. S. 1976. The evidence from epidemiology. In *Health and the environment,* J. Lenihan and W. W. Fletcher, eds., 88–115. New York: Academic Press.

Murphy, P. E., and A. E. Lugo. 1986. Ecology of tropical dry forest. *Annual Review of Ecology and Systematics* 17:67–88.

MURRA, J. V. 1980. *The economic organization of the Inka state.* Greenwich, CT: JAI Press.

MURRAY, J. W., R. T. BARBER, M. R. ROMAN, M. P. BACON, and R. A. FEELY. 1994. Physical and biological controls on carbon cycling in the equatorial Pacific. *Science* 266:58–65.

MYERS, N. 1997. Consumption: Challenge to sustainable development. *Science* 276:53–55.

MYLES, D. 1985. *The great waves.* New York: McGraw-Hill Inc.

NASH, J. M. 1995. When life exploded. *Time* (December 4).

National Academy of Sciences. 1969. *Resources and man.* San Francisco: W. H. Freeman and Company.

National Academy of Sciences. 1974. *Recommended daily allowances.* 8th ed. Washington, DC: National Academy of Sciences.

National Research Council. 1989. *Diet and health: Implications for reducing chronic disease risk.* Washington, DC: National Academy Press.

NEEL, J. V. 1982. The thrifty genotype revisited. In *The genetics of diabetes mellitus,* J. Kobberling and J. Tattersall, eds., 283–93. New York: Academic Press.

NELMS, J. D., and D. J. G. SOPER. 1962. Cold vasodilation and cold acclimatization in the hands of British fish filleters. *Journal of Applied Physiology* 17:444–48.

NETTING, R. McC. 1968. *Hill farmers of Nigeria: Cultural ecology of the Kofyar of the Jos Plateau.* Seattle: University of Washington Press.

NEWMAN, M. T. 1962. Ecology and nutritional stress in man. *American Anthropologist* 64:22–34.

NEWMAN, R. W. 1970. Why man is such a sweaty and thirsty naked animal: A speculative review. *Human Biology* 42:12–27.

NEWMAN, R. W. 1975. Human adaptation to heat. In *Physiological anthropology,* A. Damon, ed., 80–92. New York: Oxford University Press.

NICHOLAIDES, J., III. 1979. Crop production systems on acid soils in humid tropical America. In *Soil, water and crop production,* D. W. Thorne and M. D. Thorne, eds., 243–77. Westport, CT: Avi Publishing Company.

NICHOLAISEN, J. 1963. *Ecology and culture of the pastoral Tuareg.* Copenhagen: National Museum of Copenhagen.

NICHOLSON, A. J. 1957. The self-adjustment of populations to change. *Cold Spring Harbor Symposium of Quantitative Biology* 22:153–72.

NICHTER, M., and M. NICHTER. 1987. Cultural notions of fertility in South Asia and their impact on Sri Lankan family planning practices. *Human Organization* 46:18–28.

NIERMEYER, S., P. YANG, SHANMINA, DROLKAR, J. ZHUANG, and L. G. MOORE. 1994. Adequate arterial O_2 saturation in Tibetan but not Han newborns at high altitude. *American Journal of Physical Anthropology* Supplement 18:153. (abstract)

NIERMEYER, S., P. YANG, SHANMINA, DROLKAR, J. ZHUANG, and L. G. MOORE. 1995. Arterial oxygen saturation in Tibetan and Han infants born in Lhasa, Tibet. *New England Journal of Medicine* 333:1248–52.

NOTKINS, A. L. 1979. The causes of diabetes. *Scientific American* 241(5):62–73.

NUNN, P. D. 1994. *Oceanic islands.* Oxford: Blackwell Publishers.

NUSSENZWEIG, R. S., and C. A. Long. 1994. Malaria vaccines: Multiple targets. *Science* 265:1381–83.

O'BRIEN, W. J. 1979. The predator-prey interaction of planktivorous fish and zooplankton. *American Scientist* 67:572–81.

O'CONNELL, J. F., and K. HAWKES. 1981. Alyawara plant use and optimal foraging theory. In *Hunter-gatherer foraging strategies,* B. Winterhalder and E. A. Smith, eds., 99–125. Chicago: University of Chicago Press.

O'NEILL, R. V., D. L. DeANGELIS, J. B. WADE, and T. F. H. ALLEN. 1986. *A hierarchical concept of ecosystems.* Princeton, NJ: Princeton University Press.

ODUM, E. P. 1959. *Fundamentals of Ecology.* 2d ed. Philadelphia: Saunders.

ODUM, E. P. 1960. Organic production and turnover in old field succession. *Ecology* 41:34–49.

ODUM, E. P. 1962. Relationships between structure and function in ecosystems. *Japanese Journal of Ecology* 12:108–12.

ODUM, H. T. 1971. *Environment, power, and society.* New York: John Wiley & Sons.

ODUM, H. T., and E. C. ODUM. 1976. *Energy basis for man and nature.* New York: McGraw-Hill Inc.

OLSHANSKY, S. J., B. A. CARNES, and C. CASSEL. 1990. In search of Methuselah: Estimating the upper limits to human longevity. *Science* 250:634–40.

ORTLOFF, C. R. 1988. Canal builders of pre-Inca Peru. *Scientific American* 259(6):100–107.

OSHIMA, S. 1996. Japan: Feeling the strains of an aging population. *Science* 273:44–45.

OSMOND, C. B., M. P. AUSTIN, J. A. BERRY, W. D. BILLINGS, J. S. BOYER, J. W. H. DACEY, P. S. NOBEL, S. D. SMITH, and W. E. WINNER. 1987. Stress physiology and the distribution of plants. *BioScience* 37:38–48.

OSPOVAT, D. 1981. *The development of Darwin's theory. Natural history, natural theology, and natural selection, 1838–1859.* New York: Cambridge University Press.

OVINGTON, J. D. 1962. Quantitative ecology and the woodland ecosystem concept. In *Advances in Ecological Research,* vol. 1, J. B. Cragg, ed., 103–92. New York: Academic Press.

OWEN, O. S., and D. D. CHIRAS. 1995. *Natural resource conservation: Management for a sustainable future.* 6th ed. Englewood Cliffs, NJ: Prentice-Hall.

PACKER, C., and A. E. PUSEY. 1997. Divided we fall: Cooperation among lions. *Scientific American* 276(5):52–59.

PAGE, L. B., A. DARRON, and R. C. MOELBERG. 1974. Antecedents of cardiovascular disease in six Solomon Island societies. *Circulation* 49:1132–46.

PAINE, R. T. 1969. A note on trophic complexity and community stability. *American Naturalist* 103:91–93.

PAINE, R. T. 1993. A salty and salutary perspective on global change. In *Biotic interactions and global change,* P. M. Kareiva, J. G. Kingsolver, and R. B. Huey, eds., 347–55. Sunderland, MA: Sinauer Associates Inc.

PALM, R. I. 1990. *Natural hazards.* Baltimore: The Johns Hopkins University Press.

PALMORE, E. 1975. *The honourable elders.* Durham, NC: Duke University Press.

PALUMBO, P. J., and L. J. MELTON III. 1985. Peripheral vascular disease and diabetes. In *Diabetes in America,* National Diabetes Data Group, XV, 1–21. Bethesda, MD: National Institutes of Health.

PANDEY, M. R., R. P. NEUPANE, A. GAUTAM, and I. B. SHRESTHA. 1989. Domestic smoke pollution and acute respiratory infections in a rural community of the hill region of Nepal. *Environment International* 15:337–40.

PARK, C. C. 1992. *Tropical rainforests.* London: Routledge.

PARK, R. E. 1936. Human ecology. *American Journal of Sociology* 42:1–15.

PARK, R. E., E. W. BURGESS, and R. D. MCKENZIE. 1925. *The city.* Chicago: University of Chicago Press.

PASTORAK, R. A. 1981. The effects of predator hunger and food abundance on prey selection by *Chaoborus* larvae. *Limnology and Oceanography* 25:910–25.

PATTERSON, K. D. 1978. River blindness in northern Ghana, 1900–50. In *Disease in African history,* G. W. Hartwig and K. D. Patterson, eds., 88–117. Durham, NC: Duke University Press.

PAUL, B. D. 1958. The role of beliefs and customs in sanitation programs. *American Journal of Public Health* 48:1502–6.

PAWSON, I. G. 1986. The morphological characteristics of Samoan adults. In *The changing Samoans: Behavior and health in transition,* P. T. Baker, J. M. Hanna, and T. S. Baker, eds., 254–74. New York: Oxford University Press.

PAWSON, I. G., and C. R. JANES. 1981. Massive obesity in a migrant Samoan population. *American Journal of Public Health* 71:508–13.

PEARL, R. 1928. *The rate of living.* New York: Alfred A. Knopf.

PEARSON, J. D., J. M. HANNA, M. H. FITZGERALD, and P. T. BAKER. 1990. Modernization and catecholamine excretion of young Samoan adults. *Social Science and Medicine* 31:729–36.

PEARSON, J. D., G. D. JAMES, and D. E. BROWN. 1993. Stress and changing lifestyles in the Pacific: Physiological stress responses of Samoans in rural and urban settings. *American Journal of Human Biology* 5:49–60.

PELTIER, W. R., and A. M. TUSHINGHAM. 1989. Global sea level rise and the Greenhouse Effect: Might they be connected? *Science* 244:806–10.

PETERSON, J. T. 1978. Hunter-gatherer/farmer exchange. *American Anthropologist* 80:335–51.

PFEIFFER, S., and P. KING. 1983. Cortical bone formation and diet among protohistoric Iroquoians. *American Journal of Physical Anthropology.* 60:23–28.

PIANKA, E. R. 1974. *Evolutionary ecology.* New York: Harper & Row.

PICKETT, S. T. A., and P. S. WHITE, eds. 1985. *The ecology of natural disturbance and patch dynamics.* New York: Academic Press.

PIGGOTT, C. D., and K. TAYLOR. 1964. The distribution of some woodland herbs in relation to the supply of N and P in the soil. *Journal of Ecology* (Supplement) 52:175–85.

PILLSBURY, A. F. 1981. The salinity of rivers. *Scientific American* 245(1):55–65.

PIMENTEL, D., L. E. HURD, A. C. BELLOTTI, M. J. FORSTER, I. N. OKA, O. D. SHOLES, and R. J. WHITMAN. 1973. Food production and the energy crisis. *Science* 182:443–49.

PIMENTEL, D., and F. A. STONE. 1968. Evolution and population ecology of parasite-host systems. *Canadian Entomologist* 100:655–62.

PIMENTEL, D., E. C. TERHUNE, R. DYSON-HUDSON, S. ROCHEREAU, R. SIMES, E. A. SMITH, D. DENMAN, D. REIFSCHNEIDER, and M. SHEPARD. 1976. Land degradation: Effects on food and energy resources. *Science* 194:149–55.

PIMM, S. L. 1982. *Food webs*. London: Chapman and Hall.

PIMM, S. L., and J. H. LAWTON. 1978. On feeding on more than one trophic level. *Nature* 275:542–44.

PIMM, S. L., J. H. LAWTON, and J. E. COHEN. 1991. Food web patterns and their consequences. *Nature* 350:669–74.

PLANALP, J. M. 1971. *Heat stress and culture in north India*. Special Technical Report, U.S. Army Institute of Environmental Medicine, Natick, MA.

PLATT, T., and S. SATHYENDRANATH. 1988. Oceanic primary production: Estimation by remote sensing at local and regional scales. *Science* 241:1613–20.

PLUCKNETT, D. L., N. J. H. SMITH, J. T. WILLIAMS, and N. M. ANISHETTY. 1987. *Gene banks and the world's food supply*. Princeton, NJ: Princeton University Press.

PLUCKNETT, D. L., and D. L. WINKELMANN. 1995. Technology for sustainable agriculture. *Scientific American* 273(3):182–86.

POOL, R. 1989a. Ecologists flirt with chaos. *Science* 243:310–13.

POOL, R. 1989b. Is it chaos, or is it just noise? *Science* 243:25–28.

PORTER, S. D., and D. A. SAVIGNANO. 1990. Invasion of polygyne fire ants decimates native ants and disrupts arthropod community. *Ecology* 71:2095–106.

POST, W. M., T. H. PENG, W. R. EMANUEL, A. W. KING, V. H. DALE, and D. L. DeANGELIS. 1990. The global carbon cycle. *American Scientist* 78:310–26.

POTTER, V. 1971. *Bioethics: Bridge to the future*. Englewood Cliffs, NJ: Prentice-Hall.

POTTS, R. 1996. Evolution and climate variability. *Science* 273:922–23.

POWERS, P. S. 1980. *Obesity: The regulation of weight*. Baltimore: Williams & Wilkins.

PRICE, P. W. 1996. *Biological evolution*. Fort Worth, TX: Saunders.

PRICE, P. W., M. WESTOBY, B. RICE, P. R. ATSATT, R. S. FRITZ, J. N. THOMPSON, and K. MOBLEY. 1986. Parasite mediation in ecological interactions. *Annual Review of Ecology and Systematics* 17:487–505.

PRIOR, I. A. M. 1974. Cardiovascular epidemiology in New Zealand and the Pacific. *New Zealand Medical Journal* 80:245–52.

PRIOR, I. A. M., and F. DAVIDSON. 1966. The epidemiology of diabetes in Polynesians and Europeans in New Zealand and the Pacific. *New Zealand Medical Journal* 65:375–83.

PULLIAM, H. R., and N. M. HADDAD. 1994. Human population growth and the carrying capacity concept. *Bulletin of the Ecological Society of America* 75(3):141–57.

PURVIS, A. 1991. TB takes a deadly turn. *Time* 138:85.

PUTMAN, R. J. 1994. *Community ecology*. London: Chapman & Hall.

PYKE, M. 1970. *Man and food*. New York: McGraw-Hill Inc.

QUAMMEN, D. 1996. *The song of the dodo. Island biogeography in an age of extinctions*. New York: Charles Scribner's Sons.

QUILICI, J. C., and H. VERGNES. 1978. The haematological characteristics of high-altitude populations. In *The biology of high-altitude peoples*, P. T. Baker, ed., 189–218. London: Cambridge University Press.

RAPOPORT, A. 1969. *House form and culture*. Englewood Cliffs, NJ: Prentice-Hall.

RAPPAPORT, R. A. 1967. Ritual regulation of environmental relations among a New Guinea people. *Ethnology* 6:17–30.

RAPPAPORT, R. A. 1968. *Pigs for the ancestors: Ritual in the ecology of a New Guinea people*. New Haven, CT: Yale University Press.

RAPPAPORT, R. A. 1971. The flow of energy in an agricultural society. *Scientific American* 224:104–15.

RAUNKIAER, C. 1934. *The life-form of plants and statistical plant geography*. Oxford: Clarendon Press.

RAYNAUD, D., J. JOUZEL, J. M. BARNOLA, J. CHAPPELLAZ, R. J. DELMAS, and C. LORIUS. 1993. The ice record of greenhouse gases. *Science* 259:926–41.

READ, P. P. 1993. *Ablaze. The history of the heroes and victims of Chernobyl*. New York: Random House.

READER, J. 1988. *Man on earth*. Austin: University of Texas Press.

REAKA-KUDLA, M. L., D. E. WILSON, and E. O. WILSON. 1997. *Biodiversity II: Understanding and protecting our biological resources*. Washington, DC: Joseph Henry Press.

REDFIELD, A. C. 1958. The biological control of chemical factors in the environment. *American Scientist* 46:205–21.

REES, J. D. 1979. Effects of the eruption of Paricutín Volcano on landforms, vegetation, and human occupancy. In *Volcanic activity and human ecology*, P. D. Sheets and D. K. Grayson, eds., 249–92. New York: Academic Press.

REGANOLD, J. P., R. I. PAPENDICK, and J. E. PARR, 1990. Sustainable agriculture. *Scientific American* 262(6):112–20.

REICH, J. W., E. B. RASTETTER, J. M. MELILLO, D. W. KICKLIGHTER, P. A. STEUDLER, B. J. PETERSON, A. L. GRACE, B. MOORE III, and C. J. VOROSMARTY. 1991. Potential net primary production in South America: Application of a global model. *Ecological Applications* 1:399–429.

RELETHFORD, J. H. 1994. *The human species: An introduction to biological anthropology.* 2d ed. Mountain View, CA: Mayfield Publishing Company.

REMPEL, W. C., and E. RANDOLPH. 1983. Lethal dioxin: Monster guest in chemical lab. *Los Angeles Times* (May 9):1, 8.

REPETTO, R. 1987. Population, resources, environment: An uncertain future. *Population Bulletin* 42(2):1–44.

REPETTO, R. 1990. Accounting for environmental assets. *Scientific American* 266(6):94–100.

REYNAFARJE, B. 1962. Myoglobin content and enzymatic activity of muscle and altitude adaptation. *Journal of Applied Physiology* 17:301–5.

RICE, E. L. 1974. *Allelopathy.* New York: Academic Press.

RICHARD, A. F. 1985. *Primates in nature.* New York: W. H. Freeman and Company.

RICHARDS, P. W. 1973. The tropical rain forest. *Scientific American* 229(6):59–67.

RINK, T. J. 1994. In search of a satiety factor. *Nature* 372:406–7.

ROBERTS, D. F. 1978. *Climate and human variability.* 2d ed. Menlo Park, CA: The Benjamin-Cummings Publishing Co.

ROBERTS, L. 1988. Is there life after climate change? *Science* 242:1010–12.

ROBERTS, L. 1989a. Does the ozone hole threaten Antarctic life? *Science* 244:288–89.

ROBERTS, L. 1989b. Global warming: Blaming the sun. *Science* 246:992–93.

ROBERTS, L. 1991. Dioxin risks revisited. *Science* 251:624–25.

ROBEY, B., S. O. RUTSTEIN, and L. MORRIS. 1993. The fertility decline in developing countries. *Scientific American* 269(6):60–67.

ROBINSON, S., H. S. BELDING, F. C. CONSOLAZIO, S. M. HORVATH, and E. S. TURRELL. 1965. Acclimatization of older men to work in heat. *Journal of Applied Physiology* 20:583–86.

RODE, A., and R. J. SHEPHARD. 1971. Cardiorespiratory fitness of an Arctic community. *Journal of Applied Physiology* 31:519–26.

ROGERS, A. R. 1992. Resources and population dynamics. In *Evolutionary ecology and human behavior,* E. A. Smith and B. Winterhalder, eds., 375–402. New York: Aldine de Gruyter.

ROLSTON, H. III. 1988. *Environmental ethics. Duties to and values in the natural world.* Philadelphia: Temple University Press.

ROMENOFSKY, A. F. 1987. *Vectors of death: The archaeology of European contact.* Albuquerque: University of New Mexico Press.

ROOSEVELT, A. C. 1980. *Parmana: Prehistoric maize and manioc subsistence along the Amazon and Orinoco.* New York: Academic Press.

ROOSEVELT, A. C. 1991. *Moundbuilders of the Amazon: Geophysical archaeology on Marajo Island, Brazil.* San Diego: Academic Press.

ROSENBERG, A. A., M. J. FOGARTY, M. P. SISSENWINE, J. R. BEDDINGTON, and J. G. SHEPHERD. 1993. Achieving sustainable use of renewable resources. *Science* 262:828–29.

ROUGHGARDEN, J. 1983. The theory of coevolution. In *Coevolution,* D. J. Futuyma and M. Slatkin, eds., 33–64. Sunderland, MA: Sinauer Associates Inc.

ROUSH, W. 1997. Putting a price tag on nature's bounty. *Science* 276:1029.

ROYAMA, T. 1984. Population dynamics of the spruce budworm *Choristoneura fumiferana. Ecological Monographs* 54:429–62.

RYDEN, H., and S.-O. BORGEGARD. 1991. Plant characteristics over a century of primary succession on islands: Lakek Hjalmaren. *Ecology* 72:1089–1101.

SAHLINS, M. D. 1960. Evolution: Specific and general. In *Evolution and culture,* M. D. Sahlins and E. R. Service, eds., 12–44. Ann Arbor: University of Michigan Press.

SAHLINS, M. D. 1972. *Stone age economics: Production, exchange, and politics in small tribal societies.* Chicago: Aldine Publishing Company.

SAHLINS, M. D. 1976. *The use and abuse of biology: An anthropological critique of sociobiology.* Ann Arbor: University of Michigan Press.

SALA, O. E., W. J. PARTON, L. A. JOYCE, and W. K. LAUENROTH. 1988. Primary production of the central grassland region of the United States. *Ecology* 69:40–45.

SALT, G. W. 1979. A comment on the use of the term *emergent properties. American Naturalist* 113:145–48.

SANTOLAYA, S., S. LAHIRI, R. T. ALFARO, and R. B. SCHOENE. 1989. Respiratory adaptation in the highest inhabitants and highest Sherpa mountaineers. *Respiratory Physiology* 77:253–62.

SATTENSPIEL, L. 1990. Modeling the spread of infectious disease in human populations. *Yearbook of Physical Anthropology* 33:245–76.

SAWKA, M. N., and C. B. WENGER. 1988. Physiological responses to acute exercise-heat stress. In *Human performance physiology and environmental medicine at terrestrial extremes,* K. B. Pandolf, M. N. Sawka, and R. R. Gonzalez, eds., 97–151. Indianapolis: Benchmark Press.

SCHAD, G. A., T. A. NAWALINSKI, and V. KOCHAR. 1983. Human ecology and the distribution and abundance of hookworm populations. In *Human ecology and infectious diseases*, N. A. Croll and J. H. Cross, eds., 187–223. New York: Academic Press.

SCHALL, J. I. 1991. *Blood pressure and lifestyle change among the Manus of Papua New Guinea: A migrant study*. Ph.D. dissertation, University of Pennsylvania, Philadelphia.

SCHELL, L. M. 1991. Pollution and human growth: Lead, noise, polychlorobiphenyl compounds and toxic wastes. In *Applications of biological anthropology to human affairs*, C. G. N. Mascie-Taylor and G. W. Lasker, eds., 83–116. Cambridge: Cambridge University Press.

SCHERBAK, Y. M. 1996. Ten years of the Chernobyl era. *Scientific American* 274(4):44–49.

SCHINDLER, D. W., K. G. BEATY, E. J. FEE, D. R. CRUIKSHANK, E. R. DEBRUYN, D. L. FINDLAY, G. A. LINSEY, J. A. SHEARER, M. P. STAINTON, and M. A. TURNER. 1990. Effects of climatic warming on lakes of the central boreal forest. *Science* 250:967–70.

SCHLESINGER, W. J., J. F. REYNOLDS, G. L. CUNNINGHAM, L. F. HUENNEKE, W. M. JARRELL, R. A. VIRGINIA, and W. G. WHITFORD. 1990. Biological feedbacks in global desertification. *Science* 213:1220–27.

SCHLUTER, D. 1994. Experimental evidence that competition promotes divergence in adaptive radiation. *Science* 266:798–801.

SCHNEIDER, D. 1997. The rising seas. *Scientific American* 276(3):112–17.

SCHNEIDER, H. K. 1974. *Economic man*. New York: The Free Press.

SCHNEIDER, S. H. 1989. The Greenhouse Effect: Science and policy. *Science* 243:771–81.

SCHOELLER, D. A. 1983. Energy expenditure from doubly labelled water: Some fundamental considerations in humans. *American Journal of Clinical Nutrition* 38:999–1005.

SCHOLANDER, P. F., H. T. HAMMEL, J. S. HART, D. H. LEMESSURIER, and J. STEEN. 1958. Cold adaptation in Australian aborigines. *Journal of Applied Physiology* 13:211–18.

SCRIMSHAW, N. S. 1991. Iron deficiency. *Scientific American* 265(4):46–52.

SCRIMSHAW, N. S., C. E. TAYLOR, and J. E. GORDON. 1968. *Interactions of nutrition and infection*. Geneva: World Health Organization.

SELYE, H. 1956. *The stress of life*. New York: McGraw-Hill Inc.

SELYE, H. 1973. The evolution of the stress concept. *American Scientist* 61:692–99.

SEVERANCE, C. 1979. The tsunami story. *Hawaii Tribune-Herald* (April 1):11–20.

SEVERANCE, C. J. 1976. *Land, food and fish: Strategy and transaction on a Micronesian atoll*. Ph.D. dissertation, University of Oregon. Ann Arbor, MI: University Microfilms.

SEVERINGHAUS, J. W. 1995. Hypothetical roles of angiogenesis, osmotic swelling, and ischemia in high-altitude cerebral edema. *Journal of Applied Physiology* 79:375–79.

SHELL-DUNCAN, B. 1995. Impact of seasonal variation in food availability and disease stress on the health status of nomadic Turkana children: A longitudinal analysis of morbidity, immunity, and nutritional status. *American Journal of Human Biology* 7:339–55.

SHEPHARD, R. J. 1987. *Physical activity and aging*. 2d ed. London: Croom Helm.

SHOJI, K. 1977. Drip irrigation. *Scientific American* 237(5):62–68.

SHREEVE, J. 1995. Sexing fossils: A boy named Lucy? *Science* 270:1297–98.

SHREEVE, J. 1996a. New skeleton gives path from trees to ground an odd turn. *Science* 272:654.

SHREEVE, J. 1996b. Sunset on the savanna. *Discover* 17:116–25.

SHU, X. O., W. ZHENG, N. POTISCHMAN, L. A. BRINTON, M. C. HATCH, Y.-T. GAO, and J. F. FRAUMENI, JR. 1993. A population-based case-control study of dietary factors and endometrial cancer in Shanghai, People's Republic of China. *American Journal of Epidemiology* 137:155–65.

SIBLY, R. M., and P. CALOW. 1986. *Physiological ecology of mammals: An evolutionary approach*. Oxford: Blackwell Scientific Publications.

SILBERBAUER, G. B. 1981. *Hunter and habitat in the central Kalahari Desert*. Cambridge: Cambridge University Press.

SIMKIN, T. 1994. Distant effects of volcanism—How big and how often? *Science* 264:913–14.

SIMMONS, L. 1970. *The role of the aged in primitive society*. Hamdon, CT: Archon Books.

SIMON, J. L. 1990. Population growth is not bad for humanity. *National Forum* 70:12–16.

SIMONDON, K. B., E. BÉNÉFICE, F. SIMONDON, V. DELAUNAY, and A. CHAHNAZARIAN. 1993. Seasonal variation in nutritional status of adults and children in rural Senegal. In *Seasonality and human ecology*, S. J. Ulijaszek and S. S. Strickland, eds., 166–83. Cambridge: Cambridge University Press.

SIMONS, E. 1972. *Primate evolution*. New York: Macmillan Inc.

SIMPSON, K. 1986. *Fertilizers and manures*. Harlow, Essex: Longman Scientific and Technical.

SINNETT, P. F. 1977. Nutritional adaptation among the Enga. In *Subsistence and survival: Rural ecology in the Pacific*, T. P. Bayliss-Smith and R. G. Feachem, eds., 63–90. London: Academic Press.

SIRI, W. E., D. C. VAN DYKE, H. S. WINCHELL, M. POLLYCOVE, H. G. PARKER, and A. S. CLEVELAND. 1966. Early erythropoietin, blood, and physiological responses to severe hypoxia in man. *Journal of Applied Physiology* 21:73–80.

SJÖSTRÖM, L. 1993. Impacts of body weight, body composition, and adipose tissue distribution on morbidity and mortality. In *Obesity: Theory and therapy*, 2d ed., A. J. Stunkard and T. A. Wadden, eds., 13–41. New York: Raven Press.

SKLAR, J., and B. BERKOV. 1975. The American birth rate: Evidence of a coming rise. *Science* 189:693–700.

SLOBODKIN, L. 1960. Ecological energy relationships at the population level. *American Naturalist* 95:213–36.

SLOBODKIN, L. B., and A. RAPOPORT. 1974. An optimal strategy of evolution. *Quarterly Review of Biology* 49:181–200.

SMITH, E. A. 1981. The application of optimal foraging theory to the analysis of hunter-gatherer group size. In *Hunter-gatherer foraging strategies: Ethnographic and archaeological analyses*, B. Winterhalder and E. A. Smith, eds., 36–65. Chicago: University of Chicago Press.

SMITH, E. A. 1991. *Inujjuamiut foraging strategies: Evolutionary ecology of an arctic hunting economy*. New York: Aldine de Gruyter.

SMITH, N. 1978. Roman hydraulic technology. *Scientific American* 238(5):154–61.

SMITH, R. M., and J. M. HANNA. 1975. Skinfolds and resting heat loss in cold air and water: Temperature equivalence. *Journal of Applied Physiology* 39:93–102.

SMITH, Z. A. 1985. *Groundwater policy in the Southwest*. El Paso: Texas Western Press.

SMITH, Z. A. 1989. The policy environment. In *Water and the future of the Southwest*, Z. A. Smith, ed., 9–18. Albuquerque: University of New Mexico Press.

SOLOMON, A. M., J. R. TRABALKA, D. E. REICHLE, and L. D. VOORHEES. 1985. The global cycle of carbon. In *Atmospheric carbon dioxide and the global carbon cycle*, J. R. Trabalka, ed., 1–13. (DOE/ER-0239). Washington, DC: U.S. Department of Energy.

SOLOMON, E. P., and P. W. DAVIS. 1983. *Human anatomy and physiology*. Philadelphia: Saunders.

SOUSA, W. P. 1984. The role of disturbance in natural communities. *Annual Review of Ecology and Systematics* 15:353–91.

SOUTHWICK, E. E., and G. HELDMAIER. 1987. Temperature control in honey bee colonies. *BioScience* 37:395–99.

SPINK, W. W. 1978. *Infectious diseases*. Minneapolis: University of Minnesota Press.

SPITZ, M. R., and G. R. NEWELL. 1992. *Recommendations for cancer prevention*. St. Louis: Mosby-Year Book, Inc.

SPONSEL, L. E., 1986. Amazon ecology and adaptation. *Annual Review of Anthropology* 15:67–97.

SPRENT, J. I. 1987. *The ecology of the nitrogen cycle*. Cambridge: Cambridge University Press.

SPURR, G. B. 1983. Nutritional status and physical work capacity. *Yearbook of Physical Anthropology* 26:1–35.

STAMLER, J. 1993. Epidemic obesity in the United States. *Archives of Internal Medicine* 153:1040–44.

STANTON, N. L. 1988. The underground in grasslands. *Annual Review of Ecology and Systematics* 19:573–89.

STARKE, L., ed. 1988. *State of the World 1988. Worldwatch Institute report on progress toward a sustainable society*. New York: W. W. Norton & Company, Inc.

STASKI, E., and J. MARKS. 1992. *Evolutionary anthropology*. Fort Worth, TX: Harcourt Brace Jovanovich.

STEARNS, S. C. 1989. The evolutionary significance of phenotypic plasticity. *BioScience* 39:436–45.

STEEGMANN, A. T., JR. 1972. Cold response, body form, and craniofacial shape in two racial groups of Hawaii. *American Journal of Physical Anthropology* 37:193–221.

STEEGMANN, A. T., JR. 1975. Human adaptation to cold. In *Physiological anthropology*, A. Damon, ed., 80–92. New York: Oxford University Press.

STEEGMANN, A. T., JR., M. G. HURLICH, and B. WINTERHALDER. 1983. Coping with cold and other challenges of the boreal forest: An overview. In *Boreal forest adaptations: The northern Algonkians*, A. T. Steegmann, Jr., ed., 317–51. New York: Plenum Press.

STEFÁNSSON, V. 1913. *My life with the Eskimo*. New York: The Macmillan Company.

STEIN, Z., and M. SUSSER. 1975. Fertility, fecundity and famine: Food relations in the Dutch famine 1944/45 have a causal relation to fertility and probably to fecundity. *Human Biology* 47:131–54.

STEMBERGER, R. S., and J. J. GILBERT. 1985. Body size, food concentration, and population growth in planktonic rotifers. *Ecology* 66:1151–59.

STEPHENS, D. W., and J. R. KREBS. 1986. *Foraging theory*. Princeton, NJ: Princeton University Press.

STETTER, K. O., G. LAUERER, M. THOMM, and A. NEUNER. 1987. Isolation of extremely thermophilic sulfate reducers: Evidence for a novel branch of Archebacteria. *Science* 236:822–24.

STEWARD, J. H. 1938. *Basin-plateau aboriginal sociopolitical groups*. Bureau of American Ethnology, Bulletin 120. Washington, DC: Smithsonian Institution.

STEWARD, J. H. 1955. *Theory of culture change.* Urbana: University of Illinois Press.

STILES, F. G. 1992. Effects of a severe drought on the population biology of a tropical hummingbird. *Ecology* 73:1375–90.

STINE, G. J. 1993. *Acquired immune deficiency syndrome: Biological, medical, social, and legal issues.* Englewood Cliffs, NJ: Prentice-Hall.

STINI, W. A. 1972. Reduced sexual dimorphism in upper arm muscle circumference associated with protein-deficient diet in a South American population. *American Journal of Physical Anthropology* 36:341–52.

STINI, W. A. 1975. *Ecology and human adaptation.* Dubuque, IA: Wm. C. Brown Company Publishers.

STINI, W. A. 1981. Body composition and nutrient reserves in evolutionary perspective. In *Food, nutrition and evolution,* D. N. Walcher and N. Kretchmer, eds., 107–20. New York: Masson Publishing USA, Inc.

STINNETT, J. D. 1983. *Nutrition and the immune response.* Boca Raton, FL: CRC Press.

STINSON, S., and A. R. FRISANCHO. 1978. Body proportions of highland and lowland Peruvian Quechua Indians. *Human Biology* 50:57–68.

STOKOLS, D. 1972. On the distinction between density and crowding: Some implications for future research. *Journal of the American Institute of Planners* 38:72–83.

STOLARSKI, R. S. 1988. The Antarctic ozone hole. *Scientific American* 258(1):30–36.

STOMMEL, H., and E. STOMMEL. 1979. The year without a summer. *Scientific American* 240(6):176–84.

STONE, R. 1994. Dioxin report faces scientific gauntlet. *Science* 265:1650.

STONE, R. 1996. The explosions that shook the world. *Science* 272:353–54.

STOPPARD, T. 1978. *Every good boy deserves favor* and *Professional foul. Two plays.* New York: Grove Press.

STOUTE, J. A., M. SLAOUI, D. G. HEPPNER, P. MOMIN, K. E. KESTER, P. DESMONS, B. T. WELLDE, N. GARÇON, U. KRZYCH, M. MARCHAND, W. R. BALLOU, and J. D. COHEN, for the RTS, S Malaria Vaccine Evaluation Group. 1997. A preliminary evaluation of a recombinant circumsporozoite protein vaccine against *Plasmodium falciparum* malaria. *New England Journal of Medicine* 336:86–91.

STRINGER, C., and C. GAMBLE. 1993. *In search of the Neanderthals: Solving the puzzle of human origins.* New York: Thames & Hudson Press.

STRYER, L. 1988. *Biochemistry.* 3rd ed. New York: W. H. Freeman and Company.

STUNKARD, A. J., T. I. A. SORENSEN, C. HANIS, T. W. TEASDALE, R. CHAKRABORTY, W. J. SCHULL, and F. SCHULSINGER. 1986. An adoption study of human obesity. *New England Journal of Medicine* 314:193–98.

SULLIVAN, J. H., A. H. TERAMURA, and L. H. ZISKA. 1992. Variation in UV-B sensitivity in plants from a 3,000-m elevational gradient in Hawaii. *American Journal of Botany* 79:737–43.

SWANSON, D. A., and R. L. CHRISTIANSEN. 1973. Tragic base surge in 1790 at Kilauea Volcano. *Geology* 1:83–86.

SWEDLUND, A. C. 1974. The use of ecological hypotheses in australopithecine taxonomy. *American Anthropologist* 76:515–29.

SWEET, L. E. 1965. Camel pastoralism in north Arabia and the minimal camping unit. In *Man, culture, and animals: The role of animals in human ecological adjustments,* A. Leeds and A. P. Vayda, eds., 129–52. Washington, DC: American Association for the Advancement of Science.

SWISHER, C. C., III, G. H. CURTIS, T. JACOB, A. G. GETTY, A. SUPRIJO, and WIDIASMORO. 1994. Age of the earliest known hominids in Java, Indonesia. *Science* 263:1118–21.

SWISHER, C. C., III, W. J. RINK, S. C. ANTON, H. P. SCHWARCZ, G. H. CURTIS, A. SUPRIJO, and WIDIASMORO. 1996. Latest *Homo erectus* of Java: Potential contemporaneity with *Homo sapiens* in Southeast Asia. *Science* 274:1870–74.

SZATHMÁRY, E. J. E. 1994. Non-insulin dependent diabetes mellitus among aboriginal North Americans. *Annual Review of Anthropology* 23:457–82.

TABAZADEH, A., and R. P. TURCO. 1993. Stratospheric chlorine injection by volcanic eruptions. HCl scavenging and implications for ozone. *Science* 260:1082–86.

TANAKA, J. 1976. Subsistence ecology of the central Kalahari San. In *Kalahari hunter-gatherers: Studies of the !Kung San and their neighbors,* R. B. Lee and I. De Vore, eds., 98–119. Cambridge, MA: Harvard University Press.

TANSLEY, A. G. 1935. The use and abuse of vegetational concepts and terms. *Ecology* 16:284–307.

TAYLOR, H. R., M. PACQUÉ, B. MUÑOZ, and B. M. GREENE. 1990. Impact of mass treatment of onchocerciasis with ivermectin on the transmission of infection. *Science* 250:116–18.

TAYLOR, R., N. D. LEWIS, and T. SLADDEN. 1991. Mortality in Pacific island countries around 1980: Geopolitical, socioeconomic, demographic and health service factors. *Australian Journal of Public Health* 15:207–21.

TEMPEST, R. 1996. The rapid graying of China. *Los Angeles Times* (July 11):1, 6.

THOMAS, R. B. 1973. *Human adaptation to a high Andean energy flow system*. Occasional Papers in Anthropology, no. 7. University Park, PA: The Pennsylvania State University.

THOMAS, R. B. 1974. Human adaptation to energy flow in the high Andes: Some conceptual and methodological considerations. In *Energy flow in human communities*, P. L. Jamison and S. M. Friedman, eds., 41–47. University Park, PA: Human Adaptability Coordinating Office, U.S. International Biological Program.

THOMAS, R. B. 1975. The ecology of work. In *Physiological anthropology*, A. Damon, ed., 59–79. New York: Oxford University Press.

THOMAS, R. B. 1976. Energy flow at high altitude. In *Man in the Andes: A multidisciplinary study of high-altitude Quechua*, P. T. Baker and M. A. Little, eds., 379–404. Stroudsburg, PA: Dowden, Hutchinson and Ross.

THOMAS, R. B. 1979. Effects of change on high mountain human adaptive patterns. In *High altitude geoecology*, P. Webber, ed., 139–88. Boulder, CO: Westview Press.

THOMAS, R. B., T. B. GAGE, and M. A. LITTLE. 1989. Reflections on adaptive and ecological models. In *Human population biology*, M. A. Little and J. D. Haas, eds., 296–319. New York: Oxford University Press.

THOMAS, R. B., T. L. LEATHERMAN, J. W. CAREY, and J. D. HAAS. 1988. Biosocial consequences of illness among small scale farmers: A research design. In *Capacity for work in the tropics*, K. J. Collins and D. F. Roberts, eds., 249–76. Cambridge: Cambridge University Press.

THOMAS, R. B., and B. WINTERHALDER. 1976. Physical and biotic environment of southern highland Peru. In *Man in the Andes: A multidisciplinary study of high-altitude Quechua*, P. T. Baker and M. A. Little, eds., 21–59. Stroudsburg, PA: Dowden, Hutchinson and Ross.

THOMAS, R. B., B. WINTERHALDER, and S. D. McRAE. 1979. An anthropological approach to human ecology and adaptive dynamics. *Yearbook of Physical Anthropology* 22:1–46.

THOMPSON, J. N. 1978. Within-patch structure and dynamics in *Pastinaca sativa* and resource availability to a specialized herbivore. *Ecology* 59:443–48.

THORNE, D. W. 1979. Irrigated farming in arid and semi-arid temperate zones. In *Soil, water and crop production*, D. W. Thorne and M. D. Thorne, eds., 229–42. Westport, CT: Avi Publishing Company.

TIEMAL, C., Y. QUAN, and W. EN. 1994. Antiquity of *Homo sapiens* in China. *Nature* 368:55–56.

TIEN, H. Y., WITH Z. TIANLU, P. YU, L. JINGNENG, and L. ZOHNGTANG. 1992. China's demographic dilemmas. *Population Bulletin* 47(1):1–43.

TILMAN, D. 1982. *Resource competition and community structure*. Princeton, NJ: Princeton University Press.

TINGHEY, D. R., D. M. OSZYK, A. A. HERSTROM, and E. H. LEE. 1994. Effects of ozone on crops. In *Tropospheric ozone: Human health and agricultural impacts*, D. J. McKee, ed., 175–206. Boca Raton, FL: Lewis Publishers.

TOON, O. B., and R. P. TURCO. 1991. Polar stratospheric clouds and ozone depletion. *Scientific American* 264(6):68–74.

TOTSUKA, T. 1989. Japan. In *International handbook of pollution control*, E. J. Kormondy, ed., 323–25. Westport, CT: Greenwood Press.

TRABALKA, J. R., J. A. EDMONDS, J. REILLY, R. H. GARDNER, and L. D. VOORHEES. 1985. Human alterations of the global carbon cycle and the projected future. In *Atmospheric carbon dioxide and the global carbon cycle*, J. R. Trabalka, ed., 247–87. (DOE/ER-0239). Washington, DC: U.S. Department of Energy.

TRANSEAU, E. 1926. The accumulation of energy by plants. *Ohio Journal of Science* 26:1–10.

TRIGGER, B. G. 1990. *The Huron: Farmers of the north*. 2d ed. Fort Worth, TX: Harcourt Brace Jovanovich.

TRIVERS, R. 1985. *Social evolution*. Menlo Park, CA: The Benjamin/Cummings Publishing Co.

TUREKIAN, K. K. 1996. *Global environmental change. Past, present, and future*. Upper Saddle River, NJ: Prentice-Hall.

TURNBULL, C. M. 1968. The importance of flux in two hunting societies. In *Man the hunter*, R. B. Lee and I. DeVore, eds., 132–37. Chicago: Aldine Publishing Company.

TURNER, T. B. 1965. The spirochetes. In *Bacterial and mycotic infections of man*. R. J. Dubos and J. G. Hirsch, eds., 573–609. Philadelphia: J. B. Lippincott Company.

ULIJASZEK, S. J. 1992. Human energetics methods in biological anthropology. *Yearbook of Physical Anthropology* 35:215–42.

ULIJASZEK, S. J., and S. S. STRICKLAND. 1993. Nutritional studies in biological anthropology. In *Research strategies in human biology: Field and survey studies*, G. W. Lasker and C. G. N. Mascie-Taylor, eds., 108–39. Cambridge: Cambridge University Press.

UNFAO (United Nations Food and Agriculture Organization). 1993. *Marine fisheries and the law of the sea: A decade of change.* Fisheries Circular no. 853. UNFAO: Rome.

UNICEF. 1990. *The state of the world's children 1990.* Oxford: Oxford University Press.

U.S. Bureau of the Census. 1987. *An aging world.* International Population Reports Series P-95, no. 78. Washington, DC: U.S. Department of Commerce.

USDHEW (U.S. Department of Health, Education, and Welfare). 1971. *The health consequences of smoking. A report of the surgeon general: 1971.* DHEW Publication no. (HSM) 71–7513.

USDHHS (U.S. Department of Health and Human Services). 1986. *The health consequences of involuntary smoking. A report of the surgeon general.* DHHS Publication no. (CDC) 87–8398.

VALLERAND, A. L., J. ZAMECNIK, and I. JACOBS. 1995. Plasma glucose turnover during cold stress in humans. *Journal of Applied Physiology* 78:1296–302.

VAN SLYKE, L. 1988. *Yangtze. Nature, history and the river.* Reading, MA: Addison-Wesley Publishing Company Inc.

VAYDA, A. P., and B. J. McCAY. 1975. New directions in ecology and ecological anthropology. *Annual Review of Anthropology* 4:293–306.

VAYDA, A. P., and R. RAPPAPORT. 1968. Ecology, cultural and noncultural. In *Introduction to cultural anthropology,* J. Clifton, ed., 477–97. Boston: Houghton Mifflin Company.

VERANO, J. W., and D. H. UBELAKER, eds. 1992. *Disease and demography in the Americas.* Washington, DC: Smithsonian Institution Press.

VICKERS, W. T. 1988. Game depletion hypothesis of Amazonian adaptation: Data from a native community. *Science* 239:1521–22.

VITOUSEK, P., J. ABER, R. W. HOWARTH, G. E. LIKENS, P. A. MATSON, D. W. SCHINDLER, W. H. SCHLESINGER, and G. D. TILMAN. 1997. Human alteration of the global nitrogen cycle: Causes and consequences. *Issues in Ecology* 1:1–15.

VOGEL, H. U. 1993. The great wall of China. *Scientific American* 268(6):116–21.

VOLTERRA, V. 1928. Variations and fluctuations of the number of individuals in animal species living together. In *Animal ecology,* R. N. Chapman, trans. New York: Arno.

VON LIEBIG, J. 1862. *Die Naturgesetze des Feldbaues.* Braunschweig: Vieweg & Sohn.

WALKER, A. S. 1982. Deserts of China. *American Scientist* 70:366–76.

WALLACE, A. R. 1859. On the tendency of varieties to depart indefinitely from the original type. *Proceedings of the Linnaean Society of London* 3:45–62.

WALSH, J. 1977. Seveso: The questions persist where dioxin created a watershed. *Science* 197:1064–67.

WALSH, J. 1988. Sahel will suffer even if rains come. *Science* 224:467–71.

WATTS, W. A. 1979. Late-Quaternary history of Central Appalachia and the New Jersey coastal plain. *Ecological Monographs* 49:427–69.

WEBB, W. L., W. K. LAUENROTH, S. R. SZAREK, and R. S. KINERSON. 1983. Primary production and abiotic controls in forests, grasslands, and desert ecosystems in the United States. *Ecology* 64:134–51.

WEBSTER, D. L., S. T. EVANS, and W. T. SANDERS. 1993. *Out of the past: An introduction to archaeology.* Mountain View, CA: Mayfield Publishing Company.

WEDIN, D. A., and D. TILMAN. 1996. Influence of nitrogen loading and species composition on the carbon balance of grasslands. *Science* 274:1720–23.

WEINER, J. 1985. Size hierarchies in experimental plant populations of annual plants. *Ecology* 66:743–52.

WEINER, J. S. 1980. Work and wellbeing in savanna environments: Physiological considerations. In *Human ecology in savanna environments,* D. R. Harris, ed., 421–37. London: Academic Press.

WEISS, M. L., and A. E. MANN. 1990. *Human biology and behavior.* 5th ed. Glenview, IL: Scott, Foresman & Company.

WEITZ, C. A. 1984. Biocultural adaptations of the high altitude sherpas of Nepal. In *The people of South Asia,* J. R. Lukacs, ed., 387–420. New York: Plenum Press.

WEITZ, C. A., L. P. GREKSA, R. B. THOMAS, and C. M. BEALL. 1989. An anthropological perspective on the study of work capacity. In *Human population biology,* M. A. Little and J. D. Haas, eds., 113–31. New York: Oxford University Press.

WELLIN, E. 1955. Water boiling in a Peruvian town. In *Health, culture and community,* B. D. Paul, ed., 71–103. New York: Russell Sage Foundation.

WENDORF, M. 1989. Diabetes, the ice free corridor, and the Paleoindian settlement of North America. *American Journal of Physical Anthropology* 79:503–20.

WENGER, C. B. 1988. Human heat acclimatization. In *Human performance physiology and environmental medicine at terrestrial extremes,* K. B. Pandolf, M. N. Sawka, and R. R. Gonzalez, eds., 153–97. Indianapolis: Benchmark Press.

WESSEN, A. F., A. HOOPER, J. HUNTSMAN, I. A. M. PRIOR, and C. E. SALMOND. 1992. *Migration and health in a small society: The case of Tokelau.* Oxford: Clarendon Press.

WEST, J. B. 1979. *Respiratory physiology.* 2d ed. Baltimore: Williams & Wilkins.

WESTLAKE, D. F. 1963. Comparisons of plant productivity. *Biological Reviews* 38:385–425.

WESTOFF, C. F. 1986. Fertility in the United States. *Science* 234:554–59.

WESTRA, L. 1994. *An environmental proposal for ethics: The principal of integrity.* Lanham, MD: Rowman and Littlefield Publishers.

WHELAN, E. M. 1993. *Toxic terror: The truth behind the cancer scares.* Buffalo, NY: Prometheus Books.

WHITE, L. 1967. The historical roots of our ecological crisis. *Science* 155:103–7.

WHITE, L. A. 1959. *The evolution of culture.* New York: McGraw-Hill Inc.

WHITE, L. A. 1969. *The science of culture: A study of man and civilization.* New York: Farrar, Straus and Giroux.

WHITE, R. M. 1990. The great climate debate. *Scientific American* 263(1):36–43.

WHITE, T. D., G. SUWA, and B. ASFAW. 1994. *Australopithecus ramidus,* a new species of early hominid from Aramis, Ethiopia. *Nature* 371:306–12.

WHITMORE, T. C. 1990. *An introduction to tropical rainforests.* Oxford: Oxford University Press.

WHITTAKER, R. H., and G. E. LIKENS. 1973a. Carbon in the biota. In *Carbon and the biosphere,* G. M. Woodwell and E. V. Pecan, eds., 281–302. Washington, DC: U.S. Atomic Energy Commission.

WHITTAKER, R. H., and G. E. LIKENS. 1973b. The primary production of the biosphere. *Human Ecology* 1:299–369.

WHYTE, W. H. 1988. *City: Rediscovering the center.* New York: Doubleday.

WIJKMAN, A., and L. TIMBERLAKE. 1988. *Natural disasters: Acts of God or acts of man?* Philadelphia: New Society Publishers.

WILD, A. 1994. *Soils and the environment: An introduction.* New York: Cambridge University Press.

WILKIE, D. S., and B. CURRAN. 1993. Why do Mbuti hunters use nets? Ungulate hunting efficiency of archers and net-hunters in the Ituri rain forest. *American Anthropologist* 95:680–89.

WILLIAMS, C. 1997. Russia faces new threat from above. *Los Angeles Times* (May 31): A2.

WILLAMS, N., and M. BALTER. 1996. Chernobyl research becomes international growth industry. *Science* 272:355–56.

WILLIAMS, R. R., N. L. STEGENS, and J. R. GOLDSMITH. 1977. Associations of cancer site and type with occupation and industry from the Third National Cancer Survey interview. *Journal of the National Cancer Institute* 59:1147–86.

WILLIAMSON, P. G. 1981. Palaeontological documentation of speciation in Cenozoic molluscs from Turkana basin. *Nature* 293:437–43.

WILSON, E. O. 1975. *Sociobiology: The new synthesis.* Cambridge, MA: Belknap Press.

WILSON, E. O. 1992. *The diversity of life.* New York: W. W. Norton & Company, Inc.

WINSLOW, R. M. 1984. High-altitude polycythemia. In *High altitude and man,* J. B. West and S. Lahiri, eds., 163–73. Bethesda, MD: American Physiological Society.

WINSLOW, R. M., K. W. CHAPMAN, C. C. GIBSON, M. SAMAJA, C. C. MONGE, E. GOLDWASSER, M. SHERPA, F. D. BLUME, and R. SANTOLAYA. 1989. Different hematologic responses to hypoxia in Sherpas and Quechua Indians. *Journal of Applied Physiology* 66:1561–69.

WINTERHALDER, B. 1977. *Foraging strategy adaptations of the boreal forest Cree: An evaluation of the theory and models from evolutionary ecology.* Ph.D. dissertation, Cornell University. Ann Arbor, MI: University Microfilms International.

WINTERHALDER, B. 1980. Hominoid paleoecology: The competitive exclusion principle and determinants of niche relationships. *Yearbook of Physical Anthropology* 23:43–63.

WINTERHALDER, B. 1981a. Foraging strategies in the boreal forest: An analysis of Cree hunting and gathering. In *Hunter-gatherer foraging strategies,* B. Winterhalder and E. A. Smith, eds., 66–98. Chicago: University of Chicago Press.

WINTERHALDER, B. 1981b. Hominid paleoecology and competitive exclusion: Limits to similarity, niche differentiation, and the effects of cultural behavior. *Yearbook of Physical Anthropology* 24:101–21.

WINTERHALDER, B. 1981c. Optimal foraging strategies and hunter-gatherer research in anthropology: Theory and models. In *Humter-gatherer foraging strategies,* B. Winterhalder and E. A. Smith, eds., 13–35. Chicago: University of Chicago Press.

WINTERHALDER, B. 1983. History and ecology of the boreal zone in Ontario. In *Boreal forest adaptations: The northern Algonkians,* A. T. Steegmann, Jr., ed., 9–54. New York: Plenum Press.

WINTERHALDER, B. 1996. A marginal model of tolerated theft. *Ethology and Sociobiology* 17:37–53.

WINTERHALDER, B., R. LARSEN, and R. B. THOMAS. 1974. Dung as an essential resource in a highland Peruvian community. *Human Ecology* 2:89–104.

WINTERHALDER, B., and E. A. SMITH. 1992. Evolutionary ecology and the social sciences. In *Evolutionary ecology and human behavior.* E. A. Smith and B. Winterhalder, eds., 3–23. New York: Aldine de Gruyter.

WITTFOGEL, K. A. 1957. *Oriental despotism: A comparative study of total power.* New Haven, CT: Yale University Press.

WOLDA, H. 1988. Insect seasonality: Why? *Annual Review of Ecology and Systematics* 19:1–18.

WOOD, B. 1994. The oldest hominid yet. *Nature* 371:280–81.

WOOD, C. S. 1979. *Human sickness and health.* Palo Alto, CA: Mayfield Publishing Company.

WOODWELL, G. M., J. E. HOBBIE, R. A. HOUGHTON, J. M. MELILLO, B. MOORE, B. J. PETERSON, and G. R. SHAVER. 1983. Global deforestation: Contribution to atmospheric carbon dioxide. *Science* 222:1081–6.

World Bank. 1986. *Poverty and hunger: Issues and options for food security in developing countries.* Washington, DC: World Bank.

World Food Council. 1989. *The Cyprus initiative against hunger in the world. Introduction and part one. World hunger fifteen years after the World Food Conference: The challenges ahead.* Cairo, Egypt: Fifteenth Ministerial Session. New York: United Nations.

World Health Organization. 1963. *Malnutrition and disease.* Geneva: World Health Organization.

World Health Organization. 1972. *Vector ecology.* WHO Technical Report Series, no. 501. Geneva: World Health Organization.

World Health Organization. 1993a. Cholera in 1992. *Bulletin of the World Health Organization* 71:641–42.

World Health Organization. 1993b. *World health statistics annual.* Geneva: World Health Organization.

WORTMAN, S. 1980. World food and nutrition: The scientific and technological base. *Science* 209:157–64.

WRAY, G. A. 1995. Punctuated evolution of embryos. *Science* 267:1115–16.

WYNDHAM, C. H., A. J. S. BENADE, C. G. WILLIAMS, N. B. STRYDOM, A. GOLDIN, and A. J. HEYNES. 1968. Changes in central circulation and body fluid spaces during acclimatization to heat. *Journal of Applied Physiology* 25:586–93.

WYNDHAM, C. H., and J. F. MORRISON. 1958. Adjustment to cold of bushman in the Kalahari Desert. *Journal of Applied Physiology* 13:219–25.

XU, Z.-Y., W. J. BLOT, H.-P. XIAO, A. WU, Y.-P. FENG, B. J. STONE, J. SUN, A. G. ERSHOW, B. E. HENDERSON, and J. F. FRAUMENI, JR. 1989. Smoking, air pollution, and the high rates of lung cancer in Shenyang, China. *Journal of the National Cancer Institute* 81:1800–1806.

YANG, H. 1990. *Grassland vegetation, August 15–20, 1987, Hohhut, The People's Republic of China.* Beijing: Science Press.

YOUNG, A. J. 1988. Human adaptation to cold. In *Human performance physiology and environmental medicine at terrestrial extremes,* K. B. Pandolf, M. N. Sawka, and R. R. Gonzalez, eds., 401–34. Indianapolis: Benchmark Press.

YOUNG, G. L. 1974. Human ecology as an interdisciplinary concept: A critical inquiry. *Advances in Ecological Research* 8:4–40.

YOUNG, V. R., and N. S. SCRIMSHAW, 1971. The physiology of starvation. *Scientific American* 225(4):14–21.

ZHAI, S., P. D. LEVINSON, and S. T. MCGARVEY. 1993. Cardiovascular risk factors in Samoans. *American Journal of Physical Anthropology* (Supplement) 16:215. (Abstract)

ZHANG, J., T. DROMA, S. SUN, C. JANES, R. E. MCCULLOUGH, R. G. MCCULLOUGH, A. CYMERMAN, S. Y. HUANG, J. T. REEVES, and L. G. MOORE. 1993. Hypoxic ventilatory responsiveness in Tibetan compared with Han residents of 3,658 m. *Journal of Applied Physiology* 74:303–11.

ZHANG, Y., R. PROENCA, M. MAFFEI, M. BARONE, L. LEOPOLD, and J. M. FRIEDMAN. 1994. Positional cloning of the mouse *obese* gene and its human homologue. *Nature* 372:425–32.

ZHIMIN, A. 1982. Palaeoliths and microliths from Shenia and Shuanghu, Northern Tibet. *Current Anthropology* 23:493–99.

ZIELINSKI, G. A., P. A. MAYEWSKI, L. D. MEEKER, S. WHITLOW, M. S. TWICKLER, M. MORRISON, D. A. MEESE, A. J. GOW, and R. B. ALLEY. 1994. Record of volcanism since 7000 B.C. from the GISP2 Greenland ice core and implications for the volcano-climate system. *Science* 264:948–52.

ZIMMET, P., R. KIRK, S. SERJEANTSON, S. WHITEHOUSE, and R. TAYLOR. 1982. Diabetes in Pacific populations—Genetic and environmental interactions. In *Genetic environmental interaction in diabetes mellitus,* J. S. Melish, J. M. Hanna, and S. Baba, eds., 9–17. Amsterdam: Excerpta Medica.

Index